WILLS, PROBATE AND ESTATES

WILLS, PROBATE AND ESTATES

Editor and Co-author

Padraic Courtney

Authors

Nuala Casey
John Glennon
Anne Stephenson

OXFORD
UNIVERSITY PRESS

Great Clarendon Street, Oxford, OX2 6DP,
United Kingdom

Oxford University Press is a department of the University of Oxford.
It furthers the University's objective of excellence in research, scholarship,
and education by publishing worldwide. Oxford is a registered trade mark of
Oxford University Press in the UK and in certain other countries

© Law Society of Ireland 2022

The moral rights of the authors have been asserted

Fourth edition 2014
Fifth edition 2016
Sixth edition 2018
Impression: 2

All rights reserved. No part of this publication may be reproduced, stored in
a retrieval system, or transmitted, in any form or by any means, without the
prior permission in writing of Oxford University Press, or as expressly permitted
by law, by licence or under terms agreed with the appropriate reprographics
rights organization. Enquiries concerning reproduction outside the scope of the
above should be sent to the Rights Department, Oxford University Press, at the
address above

You must not circulate this work in any other form
and you must impose this same condition on any acquirer

Public sector information reproduced under Open Government Licence v3.0
(http://www.nationalarchives.gov.uk/doc/open-government-licence/open-government-licence.htm)

Published in the United States of America by Oxford University Press
198 Madison Avenue, New York, NY 10016, United States of America

British Library Cataloguing in Publication Data

Data available

Library of Congress Control Number: 2021948592

ISBN 978–0–19–884688–8

Printed and bound in the UK by
TJ Books Limited

Links to third party websites are provided by Oxford in good faith and
for information only. Oxford disclaims any responsibility for the materials
contained in any third party website referenced in this work.

PREFACE TO THE SEVENTH EDITION

This text has been prepared as a practice guideline for students at the Law Society of Ireland's Law School. It is not intended as a comprehensive statement of the law or practice and is designed to be read in conjunction with the Professional Practice Course Probate and Taxation module material from lectures and tutorials, and in particular with the Trusts and the Capital Taxation lecture and tutorial materials provided. As such, this book contains a number of references to Trusts Lecture Notes and CAT Lecture Notes: these are available to students and can be purchased by non-students from the Law Society's website, http://www.lawsociety.ie.

Members of the profession who consult these materials will appreciate that solicitors' practice in the conduct of cases varies and should note that it is not the intention of this material to cover all varying practices in the areas concerned. Likewise, as is the case for all legal materials, they may be superseded by legislation and/or case law. If advice on the law or on any particular set of circumstances is required, professional advice should be sought and lawyers should do their own legal research.

While every care has been taken in the production of these materials, no responsibility is accepted by the Law School or the Law Society or by any author of these materials for any errors or omissions.

This book could not have been written without the valued contribution of many practitioners who have lectured, tutored, and written on this subject for the Law Society's Law School down the years. In addition, the authors have received advice and assistance from colleagues, members of the legal and other professions, and public servants during the preparation of the text. In particular, the current and past staff of the Probate Office have been immeasurably generous in their provision of advice, assistance, and precedent materials.

It is not possible to name them all, but certain people deserve special mention and credit: Paula Fallon, Christopher Lehane, Keyna McEvoy, Anne McKenna, the late Eamonn Mongey, Annette O'Connell, Brian Spierin, and Nora Sweeney, in particular, have written and/or lectured for the Law Society in the past on these topics, and this book would be much poorer indeed if not for their generosity in sharing their talents.

Padraic Courtney

ACKNOWLEDGEMENTS

Copyright material from the Houses of the Oireachtas is reproduced under the Oireachtas (Open Data) PSI Licence.

AUTHORS

Nuala Casey (BCL) was admitted as a solicitor in 1977 and is a consultant solicitor with Shiel Solicitors LLP. She has extensive experience in the area of Probate Practice. She is a consultant, tutor, and internal examiner for the Professional Practice Courses in the Law School, Parts I and II, and lectures in Probate and Applied Land Law for the Law Society's Continuing Professional Development (CPD) programme. She is a registered Trust and Estate practitioner and a former member of the Committee of the Society of Trust and Estate Practitioners (STEP) Ireland, and has lectured and tutored on the Law Society/STEP Diploma in Trust and Estate Practice. She is a member of the founding Committee of Solicitors for the Elderly (SFE) Ireland. She is editor and co-author of the Oxford University Press *Conveyancing* manual.

Padraic Courtney qualified as a solicitor in 1994 and has worked for the Law Society's Law School as a course manager, specialising in Probate and Taxation, for more than twenty years. He holds the Law Society Diploma in Property Tax. A registered Trust and Estate Practitioner and former Committee member of STEP Ireland, he is also a founding Committee member and former Chair of SFE Ireland and secretary to the Law Society of Ireland Probate, Administration and Trusts Committee. He has lectured and tutored on Probate and Tax at PPC I and II levels, and has delivered seminars for CPD, Skillnets, the DSBA, STEP Ireland, and regional Bar Associations. He runs the Wills, Probate and Estates Masterclasses offered by Law Society Professional Training.

John Glennon (BL MBA) is the High Court Probate Officer. He was appointed to that post in July 2018. Other than a period of time spent working as Head of Administration in the Law Reform Commission, he has spent his entire career working in various offices of the Supreme and High Court. He has worked on two occasions in the Central office of the High Court and has also worked in the Wards of Court Office, the Taxing Masters Office, and the Probate Office. He has also worked as a full-time Registrar in the High Court. Following the establishment of the Courts Service, John was appointed as the first Personnel Officer and subsequently became the Director of Human Resources. In recent years he was appointed as Examiner of the High Court and more recently appointed Probate Officer. John also served as a member of the Courts Service Board in recent years. He was called to the Bar in 1988 and lectures for the Law Society on the PPC I and CPD Skillnets.

Anne Stephenson qualified as a solicitor in 1985. She is the principal of Stephenson Solicitors, a specialist practice providing an advisory service for solicitors and financial institutions in the areas of Wills, Trusts, Probate, Administration of Estates, and Tax Planning. She is a member of STEP, the DSBA Probate and Taxation Committee, and the Probate Liaison Committee of the Law Society, and of the Probate, Administration and Trust Committee of the Law Society. She is also a member of the founding Committee of SFE Ireland. A co-author of the Oxford University Press *Conveyancing* manual, Anne lectures, examines, and tutors on the Law Society's Professional Courses on the Wills, Trusts, Probate, Tax Planning, and Conveyancing modules and on the Law Society/STEP Diploma in Wills, Trust and Estate Planning. She also lectures on the Law Society's CPD/Skillnets courses, and to the DSBA and numerous other professional bodies, including the Stephenson series of Probate Practice Seminars. She regularly contributes articles to various other publications, including the *Law Society Gazette*, *The Parchment*, and the *Tax Review*.

OUTLINE CONTENTS

1	Introduction to Will Drafting	*1*
2	Basic Elements of a Will and Mutual Wills	*8*
3	The Legal Personal Representative	*47*
4	Will Drafting—The Rights of Spouses/Civil Partners, Cohabitants, and Children	*67*
5	Instructions, Attendance, and Execution	*120*
6	Administration of Estates: Probate Practice and Procedure	*157*
7	Extracting a Grant of Probate	*216*
8	Extracting a Grant of Administration Intestate	*264*
9	Extracting a Grant of Administration with Will Annexed	*312*
10	Second and Subsequent Grants (*De Bonis Non* Grants)	*341*
11	Non-Contentious Applications (Either to the Probate Officer or to the Court)	*365*
12	Administration after the Grant has Issued	*407*
13	Beneficiaries Including: Spouses/Civil Partners, Cohabitants, and Children of the Deceased	*436*
14	Obligations, Duties, and Claims on the Estate	*452*
15	Distributing the Estate, Vesting of Property, and Finalising Matters	*467*

Bibliography *497*

Index *503*

DETAILED CONTENTS

Preface to the Seventh Edition   v

Acknowledgements   vi

Authors   vii

Table of Cases   xxi

Table of Legislation   xxiv

Table of Statutory Instruments   xxix

Introduction   xxxi

1 Introduction to Will Drafting 1

1.1 The Constituent Elements of a Will, Including the Statutory Formalities............. 1
- What is a Will?
- Of What Can a Will Dispose?
- When Does a Will Take Effect?
- Why Make a Will?
- The Role of the Solicitor in Making a Will
- Statutory Formalities for the Making of a Will

1.2 The Basic Elements of a Will 7

2 Basic Elements of a Will and Mutual Wills 8

2.1 Introduction: The Constituent Elements of a Will 8

2.2 Name and Address of the Testator 8

2.3 Revocation of Previous Wills 8
- Applicable Legislation
- Best Practice and Common Errors
- Precedent Clauses

2.4 The Appointment of Executors 12
- Applicable Legislation
- Best Practice and Common Errors
- Precedent Clauses

2.5 Appointment of Trustees 16

2.6 Appointment of Guardians 17
- Applicable Legislation
- Best Practice and Common Errors
- Precedent Clause

2.7 Provision for Specific or Pecuniary Bequests in the Form of Legacies/Devises ... 19
- Applicable Legislation
- Best Practice and Common Errors
- The Doctrine of Lapse
- Ademption
- Abatement
- Section 47: Property Subject to a Charge
- Identify the Beneficiary
- Identify the Property that is the Subject of the Bequest
- Joint Accounts
- Lists
- Distinction between Freehold and Leasehold Interests in Land
- Summary of the Distinction between Different Types of Legacies

2.8	The Establishment of a Trust (If Required)	32
2.9	Residue	33
	Applicable Legislation	Best Practice and Common Errors
2.10	Enabling Clauses: Advancement, Appropriation, Apportionment, Charging Clause for Executors/Trustees	35
	Advancement	Apportionment
	Appropriation	Charging Clause
2.11	Powers of Trustees	39
2.12	Date of Will	39
2.13	Signature of Testator	39
	Applicable Legislation	Best Practice and Common Errors
2.14	Attestation Clause	40
	Applicable Legislation	
2.15	Signature of Witnesses	40
	Applicable Legislation	Precedent Clauses
2.16	Conclusion of Basic Elements	41
	Physical Condition of Will/Will Printed on Single Sheets with Writing on One Side Only	
2.17	Precedent Will Illustrating Basic Components of a Will	42
2.18	Mutual Wills	44
	Application of Mutual Wills	Precedent Clause in Respect of Mutual Will

3	**The Legal Personal Representative**	**47**
3.1	The Role of a Legal Personal Representative	47
3.2	Who Can be Appointed an Executor?	47
	Can a Family Member be an Executor?	Can a Professional be an Executor?
	Can a Trust Corporation be Appointed as an Executor?	Can a Person under a Disability be an Executor?
	Can a Minor be an Executor?	Can an Unnamed Person be Appointed as an Executor?
	Can a Charitable Body be an Executor?	
3.3	How is an Executor Appointed?	51
	What is an Executor According to Tenor?	
3.4	How Many Executors Can be Appointed?	51
3.5	Does an Executor Have to Act?	51
	Acceptance	Renunciation
	Reservation	Can an Executor be Removed?
3.6	The Role and Duties of an Executor	55
	The Role of an Executor	The Duties of an Executor
3.7	How to Advise an Executor of a Ward of Court	59
3.8	The Powers of an Executor	60
	Powers of Executor Conferred by Statute	What is the Difference between the Roles of an Executor, a Trustee, and a Guardian?
	Powers Conferred on an Executor by Will	

4 Will Drafting—The Rights of Spouses/Civil Partners, Cohabitants, and Children 67

4.1 Introduction 67
Civil Partnership Act
Taking Instructions re Spouses, Civil Partners, and Cohabitants

4.2 Who is a Civil Partner in Ireland? 69
Is a Foreign Civil Partnership Recognised?
How Can a Civil Partner Cease to be a Civil Partner for Succession Act Purposes?

4.3 Spouses'/Civil Partners' Rights 71

4.4 Death 'wholly or partly testate' 71

4.5 The Surviving Spouse's/Civil Partner's Legal Right Share 71
What Exactly is the Legal Right Share?
Calculating the Legal Right Share and the Residue—Two Different Things and thus Two Different Calculations
The Priority of the Legal Right Share
Section 114 (Bequest in Addition to Legal Right Share)
What Choices Are Open to the Surviving Spouse/Civil Partner?
Limitation Periods—Enforceability of Legal Right Share
Section 56—Appropriation in Favour of a Surviving Spouse/Civil Partner of the Family Home
How Can a Surviving Spouse/Civil Partner Cease to be a Surviving Spouse/Civil Partner for the Purposes of the Succession Act, 1965?
What is the Effect on the Will/Administration of the Estate of the Surviving Spouse/Civil Partner Taking their Legal Right Share?
What Property Will the Court Consider in Relation to a Surviving Spouse's/Civil Partner's Legal Right Share or a Successful Application by a Child under Section 117 Or 117(3A)?
Section 121 of the Succession Act, 1965—Dispositions with a View to Diminishing the Estate

4.6 Children's Rights 94
Steps to be Taken
To What is a Child Entitled?
'Types' of Children
What Actions can a Child Take Against an Estate?
Underage Children
The Tax Status of a Child
Other Legislation Relating to Children which may Affect a Will

4.7 Cohabitants 116
To Whom Does it Apply?
What is a 'Qualified Cohabitant'?
What Provision can be Made for a Qualified Cohabitant on the Death of the Other?
Time Limits
What Will the Court Consider?
Which Parties Must the Cohabitant Notify?
What Can a Cohabitant Receive?
Cohabitant versus Surviving Spouse
Cohabitant versus Civil Partner
The Cohabitant and the Legal Personal Representative
Can a Cohabitant Contract Out of the Redress Scheme under the Act?
Can a Cohabitant 'Renounce'?
What is the Status of Cohabitant Agreements Signed before the Civil Partnership Act Commenced?

5 Instructions, Attendance, and Execution 120

5.1 The Difference between Taking Instructions and Drafting an Attendance 120
The Distinction between Instructions and Attendance

5.2 Precedent Instruction Sheet for a Will 123

5.3 Taking the Instruction Sheet Section by Section 131

DETAILED CONTENTS xiii

5.4 Taking Instructions in Special Cases 136
- Mental Capacity
- Capacity to Make a Will
- Taking Instructions where the Client Is Ill/In Imminent Danger of Death/In Hospital or Nursing Home or Psychiatric Institution/is a Ward of Court

5.5 What is the Absolute Best Practice when Taking Instructions for a Will in Relation to Mental Capacity? 145

5.6 Outside Influences 145
- Presumed Undue Influence

5.7 Taking Instructions Regarding an Elderly Beneficiary 147

5.8 Attendances 147
- Attendances Regarding Instructions
- Attendance Regarding Execution

5.9 The Solicitor's Duty of Care 148
- Risk Management

6 Administration of Estates: Probate Practice and Procedure 157

6.1 Introduction and Overview 157
- Steps in Administering an Estate (Pre-Grant)
- Overview of Chapters 7 to 11
- Further Steps in Administering an Estate (Post-Grant)
- General Notes on Administration of Estates
- Stages of the Administration of an Estate

6.2 Immediate Tasks of the Practitioner on Notification 161
- Keep Accurate Records
- Check the Purported Will
- Where Apparently There is No Will
- Burial Directions or Other Urgent Matters

6.3 Is it Necessary for the Solicitor to Extract a Grant? 163
- Joint Tenancies
- Nominated Gratuities
- Small Estates
- Personal Application
- Summary

6.4 Where a Grant is Always Necessary 165
- Realty (Freehold Land)
- Where a Grant may be Necessary Even Though there are no Assets
- The Estate of a Ward of Court
- Distinction between Personal Representatives and Trustees

6.5 Preparing for the Initial Interview with the Personal Representative 166
- Introduction and Issues That may Arise

6.6 Instruction and Progress Sheet Combining Questions Raised in the Form SA.2 167
- Sample Sheet
- General Notes on Completing the Instruction Sheet
- Page One of the Instruction Sheet and the Form SA.2: Deceased Details
- Executors/Administrators
- (Irish Assets) Cover Screen
- Foreign Assets and Debts of the Estate
- Joint Property
- Beneficiaries Details
- Trusts
- Miscellaneous Details
- Tax Clearances
- If the Deceased was Separated/Divorced

6.7 The First Meeting with the Personal Representative 191
- Potential Beneficiaries
- Protection of Assets

6.8 Initial Steps to be Taken after the First Meeting with the Personal Representative 193
- Precedent Letter (Section 150)
- Precedent Letter Giving Authority to Act (to Comply with Solicitors' Regulations)
- Opening an Executor's/Administrator's Account
- Letters to Establish Value of Estate

xiv DETAILED CONTENTS

6.9 Statement Of Affairs (Probate) Form SA.2 203
General Information Re the Form SA.2
Details of the Applicants
Declaration
Property in the State Forming Part of the Estate: The Asset Cover Screen
Property outside the State
Asset Detail Screen
Individual Beneficiary Screen and Summary of Benefits
Notice of Acknowledgement (Probate)

7 Extracting a Grant of Probate 216

7.1 Probate Practice Background 216
Use of Precedent Forms
Contentious and Non-Contentious Probate Applications
Issue of Grants
Grants of Representation Generally
Personal Representatives
Types of Grants of Representation

7.2 Extracting a Grant of Probate 219
When does a Grant of Probate Arise?
Renunciations Generally

7.3 Who May Apply for a Grant of Probate? 223
Number of Proving Executors

7.4 Documents/Proofs Required for Grant of Probate 223
Death Certificate
Original Will (and Codicil if Applicable)
Certified Copy Will/Engrossment of Will (and Codicil if Any)
Oath of Executor
Notice of Application
Renunciation of Executor
Statement of Affairs (Probate) Form SA.2
Probate Tax Clearance Certificate
Notice of Application
Affidavit of Attesting Witness or Witnesses
Affidavit of Due Execution
Affidavit of Plight and Condition
Affidavit of Mental or Testamentary Capacity
Charitable Bequest Form
Fees

7.5 The Grant Itself 245
Revocation of Grant

7.6 Office of Executor 245
Executor according to Tenor
Executor under Disability: Grant to a Committee of a Ward of Court

7.7 Other Problems with Wills and Possible Solutions 246
Will in Pre-Printed Standard Will Form
Original Will is Missing
Application to Prove a Will in Terms of a Copy
Document Referred to in a Will/Incorporation by Reference

7.8 Precedent Probate Application—John Smyth Deceased—*Obiter* 8 March 2021 248
Will Dated 10 August 1998
Notice of Application
Notice of Acknowledgement (Probate)
Oath of Executor
Grant of Probate Incorporating Probate Engrossment

7.9 Where a Trust Corporation Acts as Executor 260
Oath for Executor when Executor is a Trust Corporation (in this Case AIB)
Resolution of Bank Board Referred to in Affidavit

7.10 Seat Office Checklist 261

8 Extracting a Grant of Administration Intestate 264

8.1 Introduction 264

8.2 Notes on Establishing Entitlements to Grants 265
The Interest is Determined at Date of Death
The Grant Follows the Interest
Number of Applicants

DETAILED CONTENTS xv

8.3 Documents Required when Applying for a Grant of Letters of Administration Intestate 267
   Notice of Application
   Oath of Administrator Intestate with the Bond
   Part C Administration Bond
   Justification of Surety
   Auctioneer's Letter of Current Market Value
   Renunciation on Intestacy
   Specimen Renunciation on Intestacy Titles

8.4 Order of Entitlement on Intestacy after 1 January 1967 275
   Revocation of Grant of Administration Intestate

8.5 *Per Stirpes* Rule (i.e. By the Roots) 278
   Issue of a Deceased are Inheriting (Sections 67(2) and 67B(2))
   Where Siblings of a Deceased are Inheriting (Section 69(1))

8.6 Relatives of Half-Blood and Step-Relatives (No Blood Relationship) 283
   Relatives of Half-Blood
   Step-Relatives

8.7 Ascertainment of Next of Kin 284
   Examples
   Chart of Intestate Succession for Deaths on or after 1 January 1967
   Chart of Degrees of Blood Relationship

8.8 Precedent Administration Intestate Application Documents 288
   Attendance
   Form SA.2 Summary and Notice of Acknowledgement (Probate)
   Notice of Application
   Oath for Administatrix Incorporating Administration Bond
   Letters of Administration

8.9 Seat Office Checklist—Grant of Administration Intestate 301

8.10 Disclaiming on Intestacy 302
   Deeds of Disclaimer in General
   Effect of Disclaimers on Intestacy prior to 5 May 1997
   Effect of Disclaimers on Intestacy after 5 May 1997
   Spouse Disclaiming on Intestacy
   Direct Lineal Ancestor (e.g. Father, Grandfather) Disclaiming on Intestacy
   General Operation of Section 72A (Everyone Else)
   Sample Deed of Disclaimer on Intestacy
   Specimen Titles when Disclaiming on Intestacy

8.11 Status of Children Born Outside Marriage and Their Property Rights 307
   Historical and Legal Background
   Status of Children Act, 1987: Commencement Date and Effects
   Deaths Intestate before 14 June 1988
   Deaths Intestate after 14 June 1988
   Remoter Relationships than Parent–Child where the Applicant is Claiming through a Person Whose Parents have not Married Each Other, e.g. 'Non-Marital Nephew' to Uncle
   Prudent Guidelines

9 Extracting a Grant of Administration with Will Annexed 312

9.1 Notes on Grant of Administration with Will Annexed 312

9.2 Entitlement to Extract the Grant 312
   Who is Entitled to Extract the Grant?

9.3 What Proofs (Documents) are Required to Apply for the Grant? 314
   Oath for Administrator with the Will Annexed Incorporating Administration Bond
   Justification of Surety
   Auctioneer's Letter of Current Market Value

9.4 Letters of Administration with Will Annexed Grants Compared with Other Grants of Representation 320
   Grant of Probate
   Grant of Letters of Administration Intestate

9.5	Conclusion	321
9.6	Precedent Application for a Grant of Letters of Administration with Will Annexed	321

Statement of Facts
Will of William Ferry
Notice of Acknowledgement (Probate)
Notice of Application

Oath for Administrator with the Will Annexed Incorporating Administration Bond
Form to be Completed Online for the Charities Regulatory Authority

9.7	Simultaneous Deaths (*Commorientes*)—Section 5 of the Succession Act	334

Example 1
Example 2

9.8	Exception to Doctrine of Lapse—Section 98 of the Succession Act	336

Three Conditions must be Satisfied for Section 98 to Apply
Issue may not Necessarily Benefit under Section 98
Distinction between Section 98 and Section 67 (*Per Stirpes*)

Does not Apply to Benefits Ceasing on the Death of the Predeceased Beneficiary
Example of Operation of Section 98

9.9	Seat Office Checklist—Grant of Administration with Will Annexed	338
10	**Second and Subsequent Grants (*De Bonis Non* Grants)**	**341**
10.1	Background and Introduction to *De Bonis Non* Grants	341

Distinction between *De Bonis Non* Grants and Revocation of Grant

De Bonis Non Grants and Deeds of Assent
Probate Fees

10.2	How to Determine What Type of *De Bonis Non* Grant to Apply For	342

Who is Entitled to Apply for the *De Bonis Non* Grant?

Where to Apply for a *De Bonis Non* Grant

10.3	Documents/Proofs Required to Extract a *De Bonis Non* Grant in Either Case	344

Original or Primary Grant

Inland Revenue Form A3(E) or A3(C) for Deaths on or Before 5 December 2001

10.4	Proofs Required for Grant of Letters of Administration with Will Annexed *De Bonis Non*	346

Oath for Administrator with the Will Annexed *De Bonis Non* Incorporating Administration Bond

Probate Engrossment or Certified Copy Will
Evidence of Current Market Value

10.5	The Administration Bond *De Bonis Non*	349

Administration with Will Annexed Bond *De Bonis Non* (for Deaths Pre-1 June 1959)
Administration with Will Annexed Bond *De Bonis Non* (for Deaths

between 1 June 1959 and 31 December 1966)
Administration Bond *De Bonis Non* (for Deaths Post-1 January 1967)
Renunciation if Appropriate

10.6	Documents Never Required for a Will Annexed *De Bonis Non* Grant	350
10.7	Proofs Required for a Grant of Letters of Administration Intestate *De Bonis Non*	350

Sample Titles Administration Intestate *De Bonis Non* (Deaths on or after 1 January 1967)

10.8	When is a *De Bonis Non* Grant Not Required?	351

Applications under the Registration of Title Act, 1964

Relying on the Decision in *Mohan v Roche*

10.9	Chain of Executorship	353

10.10	Other Second or Subsequent Grants	353

Unadministered Probate
Double Probate
Supplemental Probate

10.11	Deeds of Assent	354

Property Registration Authority Titles
Registry of Deeds Titles
Personal Property
Problems Regarding Assents

10.12	Precedent Application Documents for Grant of Letters of Administration Intestate *De Bonis Non*	355

Statement of Facts
Instruction Sheet
Revenue Form A3(C) and CA6
Primary Grant of Administration Intestate
Oath of Administrator Incorporating Administration Bond *De Bonis Non*
Letter of Current Market Value
Precedent *De Bonis Non* Grant

11 Non-Contentious Applications (Either to the Probate Officer or to the Court) 365

11.1	Practice and Procedure in Respect of Non-Contentious Matters Coming before the Probate Officer	365

Introduction
Powers of the Probate Officer
Orders of the Probate Officer Pursuant to Order 79 of the Rules of the Superior Courts
Requirements of Probate Office in Respect of Applications under Order 79 of the Rules of the Superior Courts

11.2	Revocation and Amendment of Grants	376

Revoking and Cancelling a Grant
Amending a Grant
Revoking a Grant
Precedent Application to Lead to Revocation of a Grant

11.3	Practice and Procedure in Respect of Non-Contentious Probate Matters Coming before the High Court	378

Introduction
Where Such Applications are Necessary
Practice and Procedure
Section 27(4) of the Succession Act, 1965
Application to Prove a Will in Terms of a Copy
Rival Applications for a Grant of Administration
Leave to Presume Death on Information and Belief for the Purpose of Extracting a Grant
To Admit a Will to Proof by Presumption as to Due Execution
Simultaneous Deaths—Section 5 of the Succession Act, 1965
Applications for a Grant Limited for a Particular Purpose or to a Particular Part of the Estate

11.4	Caveats	385

What is a Caveat?
Who may Lodge a Caveat and What is its Effect?
Why Lodge a Caveat?
How may a Caveat be Lodged?
How Long does a Caveat Last?

11.5	Warnings	386

What is a Warning and When is it Appropriate to use it?
What is the Effect of the Warning?
Appearance to Warning

11.6	Citations	388

What is a Citation?
What is the Value of a Citation?
Why Issue a Citation?
Procedural Steps
Example of a Citation in Operation

11.7	Rival Applications	390

Procedure for Obtaining Twenty-One-Day Order from Probate Officer—Order 79, Rule 5(3)

xviii DETAILED CONTENTS

11.8 Precedent Testamentary Pleadings 391
Caveat
Warning to Caveat
Appearance to a Warning
Citation to Introduce and Deposit a Will, and to Accept or Refuse Probate Thereof
Plenary Summons
Statement of Claim
Defence
Reply
Notice of Motion

11.9 Appendices 397
Appendix A: Preparation of Wills on Word Processors
Appendix B: Time Limits
Appendix C: Probate Office Fees
Appendix D: Structure of the Probate Office

12 Administration after the Grant has Issued 407

12.1 Introduction and Overview 407
Re-Read the File (Especially the Will)
Read the Residuary Clause Carefully—Partial Intestacy
Dealing with a Partial Intestacy
Executor's Account

12.2 Further Meeting with the Personal Representative 409
Collection of Assets of the Estate Including Noting of the Grant
Surviving Spouse/Civil Partner/Qualifying Cohabitee—Part IX of the Succession Act, 1965

12.3 Collection of Assets of the Estate 411
Cash in House
Bank Accounts
Building Society/Credit Union
Post Office Savings Account, Savings Certificates, and Bonds
Stocks and Shares (Transfer and/or Sale)
Insurance Policies
Prize Bonds
Social Welfare Old-Age Pensions
Civil Service Gratuities
Miscellaneous

12.4 Payment of Liabilities (First Schedule, Parts I and II, Succession Act, 1965) 419
Insolvent Estates
Solvent Estates

12.5 Steps to Take Prior to Distribution of Assets 424
Protection of Representatives
Section 49 Notice to Creditors
Executor's Year
Protection of Purchasers And Creditors
Partial Distribution

12.6 Joint Property 427
Presumption of Advancement/Resulting Trust
Distinction between Real/Leasehold Property and Joint Deposits
Best Practice
Taxation Consequences of Joint Property

12.7 Nominations 431
Statutory Nominations
Non-Statutory Nominations
Nominations and the Legal Right Share

12.8 Section 72 Policies (Formerly Known as 'Section 60 Policies') 433

12.9 Appropriation 433
Valuation for Appropriation Purposes
Appropriation *In Specie*

13 Beneficiaries Including: Spouses/Civil Partners, Cohabitants, and Children of the Deceased 436

13.1 Introduction 436

13.2 Dealing with Beneficiaries in General 436
A Beneficiary under Age
Beneficiary under Disability
Missing Beneficiary
Contentious Beneficiary
Elderly Beneficiary
Deceased Beneficiary
Charitable Beneficiary

13.3	Communication with Beneficiaries 441
13.4	Summary of Guidelines for Dealing with Beneficiaries in Any Estate 441
13.5	Spouses, Civil partners, Cohabitants, and Children 442

Intestacy

13.6 Testate Estates and the Spouse/Civil Partner's Legal Right Share 443

Priority of Legal Right of Spouse/Civil Partner
Right to Elect between Legal Right Share and Bequest under Will Where the Testator Died Wholly Testate
Right to Elect between Legal Right Share and Bequest under Will Where the Testator Died Partially Intestate
Distinction between the Legal Right Share and the Right to Elect

13.7 Right of Spouse/Civil Partner to Appropriate Dwellinghouse and Contents 448

Effect Of Section 56 On Beneficiary Of Family Home

13.8 Children 449

Introduction
Section 63: Advancements to Children to be Brought into Account
Non-Marital Children and the Status of Children Act, 1987
Section 117 Applications

14 Obligations, Duties, and Claims on the Estate 452

14.1 Undertakings 452

'Conditional' Undertakings or Letters on which a Third Party Might Rely
Discharge from Undertaking

14.2 Interest and 'Negative Interest'/Bank Charges 454

The 'Executor's Year'
Exceptions to the 'Executor's Year'

14.3 Section 339 of the Social Welfare (Consolidation) Act, 2005 (Liability of Personal Representative) 455

Outline and History
Obligation on Personal Representative to Inform Minister
Personal Liability of Personal Representative
Notification
Best Practice

14.4 Nursing Home Support Scheme 'Fair Deal' 457

14.5 Statutory Notice to Creditors (Section 49 Notice) 458

Precedent Statutory Notice to Creditors

14.6 Payment of Legacies 459

Precedent Letter to Residuary Legatee/ Intestate Successor
Precedent Receipt and Indemnity

14.7 Taxation Obligations 460

Introduction
Capital Acquisitions Tax
Income Tax Clearance
Capital Gains Tax
Stamp Duty
Local Property Tax
Household Charge
The Non Principal Private Residence (NPPR) Charge

15 Distributing the Estate, Vesting of Property, and Finalising Matters ... 467

15.1 Introduction 467

15.2 Assents 467

Definition of 'Assent'
Where the Personal Representative is Also the Beneficiary
Assent Subject to a Charge
Execution
Stamp Duty on Assents
Precedent Deed of Assent
Memorials of Assent/Application Form 1

15.3 Deeds of Family Arrangement 473
Introduction and Overview
A Deed of Family Arrangement
Precedent Deed of Family Arrangement
Tax Implications
Transactions between Spouses/Civil Partners
All Voluntary Dispositions

15.4 Disclaimers 478
What is the Effect of a Disclaimer?
What is the Effect of Disclaimers on the Right to Extract a Grant?
Capital Acquisitions Tax and Disclaimers

15.5 Finalising Matters 480
Section 47 (Charges on Property)

15.6 Doctrine of Lapse 481
Exceptions to the Doctrine of Lapse

15.7 Costs 481
Section 150 Notice
Basis of Charging Costs
Bill of Costs

15.8 Administration Accounts 483
Necessity for Accounts
Purpose and Type of Accounts
Estate Account
Cash Account
Distribution Account
Precedent Set of Administration Accounts

15.9 Limitation Periods 490
Introduction
Claims by Beneficiaries against the Estate
Actions by the Estate to Recover Land Belonging to the Deceased

15.10 Time Limits and Periods of Notice 494

Bibliography *497*

Index *503*

TABLE OF CASES

ABC (ded'd); XC, YC and ZC v RT, KU and JL [2003] 2 IR 250 . . . 103
Adams v Barry (1845) 2 Coll 285 . . . 401
Alkin v Redmond and Whelan [2010] WTLR 1117 . . . 54
Allhusen v Whittle (1867) LR 4 Eq 295 . . . 37, 486
Angus v Emmott [2010] EWHC 154 (Ch) . . . 54
Application by Denise Brewster for Judicial Review (Northern Ireland), Re [2017] UKSC 8 . . . 117
Aroso v Coutts & Co [2002] 1 All ER (Comm) 241 . . . 429

B, K v D, Re unreported (8 December 2000) (High Court) . . . 106
Baker, Re the goods of [1985] IR 101 . . . 9
Banks v Goodfellow (1870) LR 5 QB 549 . . . 124, 140, 142, 144
Barker, Re the goods of (1886) 40 Ch D 1 . . . 38
Barrett v Kasprzyk unreported (3 July 2000) . . . 143
Beatty, Re (1888) 29 LRIR 290 . . . 310
Benjamin, Re [1902] 1 Ch 723 . . . 382, 438
Bird v Luckie (1850) 8 Hare 301 . . . 140
Blackhall (Helena) (dec'd) Re unreported (1 April 1998) (Supreme Court) . . . 140
Blake, Re [1955] IR 89 . . . 22
Bolan, Re [1942] IR Jur Rep 2 . . . 6
Bourke v O'Donnell and the Bank of Ireland [2010] IEHC 348 . . . 4, 121
Bourne (Inspector of Taxes) v Norwich Crematorium Limited [1967] 2 All ER 576 . . . 56
Boylan, Re [1942] Ir Jur Rep 2 . . . 6
Boyle (dec'd); O'Rourke v Gallagher unreported (February 2000) (Letterkenny Circuit Court) . . . 99
Brennan v O'Donnell [2015] IEHC 460 . . . 10
Burke v O'Donnell and Bank of Ireland [2010] IEHC 348 . . . 149

C v C [1989] 1 ILRM 815 . . . 102
Cancer Research Campaign v Ernest Brown & Co (a firm) (1997) STC 1425 . . . 4, 153
Carr-Glynn v Frearsons [1998] 4 All ER 225 . . . 31, 131, 149–50
Carroll v Carroll [1999] 4 IR 241 . . . 120–1, 146
Cavey v Cavey [2012] IEHC 537, [2014] IESC 16 . . . 31, 113, 121, 495
Cawley v Lillis (No 2) [2012] IEHC 70 . . . 90–1
Cawley v Lillis [2011] IEHC 515 . . . 90
Chaine Nickson v Bank of Ireland [1976] IR 393 . . . 484
Clarke v Earley [1980] IR 223 . . . 6, 384
Cleaver, Re [1981] 1 WLR 939 . . . 46
Coleman v Coleman (1975) 1 All ER 675 . . . 9
Coleman v Mullen [2011] IEHC 179 . . . 130
Collins (Mary Francis) (dec'd), Estate of; Collins v Bank of Ireland unreported (27 March 1996) (High Court) . . . 144, 152
Condon v Law Society [2010] IEHC 52 . . . 193
Corbett v Bond Pearce [2001] EWCA 559 . . . 151
Corbett v Newey [1996] 3 WLR 729 . . . 153
Corboy, Re [1969] IR 148 . . . 147
Corby, Re [2012] IEHC 408 . . . 146
Coster, Re unreported (19 January 1978) . . . 381
Coster, Re unreported (19 January 1979) . . . 11
Courtney, In the estate of [2016] IEHC 318 . . . 10
Coyle v Finnegan and Finnegan [2013] IEHC 463 . . . 31
Crowley v Flynn [1983] ILRM 513 . . . 61
Cummins; O'Dwyer v Keegan, Re [1997] 2 IR 585; [1997] 2 ILRM 401 . . . 75, 78–9, 447
Curtin Deceased [2015] IEHC 623 . . . 10–11

Dale, Re [1993] 4 All ER 129 . . . 45
Darby v Shanley [2009] IEHC 459 . . . 124, 150–1, 153
Darling, Re the goods of [1983] IR 150 . . . 6
DC v DR (unreported) 5 May 2015, High Court . . . 117
De Souza Wearen v Gannon (unreported) 20 February 2004, High Court . . . 140
Dodd v Jones [1999] SASC 458 . . . 57
Donoghue v Stephenson [1932] AC 562 . . . 149
Doran v Delaney [1998] 2 IR 61 (SC) . . . 120–1
Drohan v Drohan [1981] ILRM 473 . . . 401
Drohan v Drohan [1984] IR 311 . . . 491, 496
Dufour v Pereira (1769) 1 Dick 419; 21 ER 332 . . . 45
Dunne v Heffernan [1997] 3 IR 431 . . . 53

EB v SS and G McC [1998] 4 IR 527 . . . 102, 106
Elliott v Stamp [2008] IESC 10 . . . 106, 146

Elliott, Re [1952] Ch 217 . . . 21
Estate of Bulloch, In the [1968] NI 96 . . . 5
Estate of K. Deceased, Re [2013] No.
　7394 . . . 31
Esterhuizen v Allied Dunbar [1998] 2 FLR
　668 . . . 154
Ewing v Bennett [2001] WTLR 249 . . . 143

F (dec'd), Re; S1 v PR1 and PR2 [2013] IEHC
　407 . . . 101, 494
Finlay v Murtagh [1979] IR 249 . . . 148
Flannery v Flannery [2009] IEHC 317 . . . 140,
　142
Fleming, In the estate of [1987] ILRM 638 . . . 10
Flood, Flood v Flood, Re [1999] 2 IR 234 . . . 53

Gartside v Sheffield [1983] NZLR 37 . . . 144, 152
Gill v RSPCA [2009] EWHC B34 (Ch) . . . 146
Gleeson v Feehan (No 2) [1997] 1 ILRM
　522 . . . 492–3
Gleeson v Feehan and O'Meara [1991] ILRM
　738 . . . 401
Gleeson v Feehan and Purcell (No 1) [1991]
　ILRM 783; [1993] 2 IR 113 . . . 491, 492
Glynn (dec'd), Re [1990] 2 IR 326 . . . 139, 143
GM, Re: FM v TAM [1972] 106 ILTR 82 . . . 77,
　93, 101
Goodchild, Re [1996] 1 All ER 670 . . . 46
Gray v Richards Butler (a firm) [2002] WTLR
　143 . . . 155
Green, Re [1951] Ch 148 . . . 44
Gregg v Kidd [1956] IR 183 . . . 146
Grey v Buss Murton [1999] PNLR 882 . . . 121
Griffith v Burke [1887] 21 LRIR 92 . . . 26

H v H [1978] IR 138 . . . 82, 433
H v H unreported (February 2001) (High
　Court) . . . 105
H v O [1978] IR 194 . . . 62–3, 92, 433–4, 444
Hagger, Re [1930] 2 Ch 190 . . . 44
Hamilton; Hamilton v Armstrong, Re [1984]
　ILRM 306 . . . 83
Hargraves v Wood (1862) 2 Sw & Tr 602 . . . 51
Harris (dec'd), Re the goods of [1952] P 319 . . . 6
Haughty v J and E Davy TA Davies 2014 12 HC
　206 . . . 4, 121
Hedley Byrne & Co v Heller [1964] AC
　465 . . . 149
Hogan, In the goods of [1990] ILRM 24 . . . 10
Hooper v Fynmores (Times of London, 19 July
　2001) . . . 153
Howe v Dartmouth . . . 37
Hudson v Barnes (1926) 43 TLR 71 . . . 6
Hurlingham Estates Ltd v Wilde & Partners (A
　Firm) Ch D 627; [1997] STC 627 . . . 122

JH (dec'd), Re the goods of [1984] IR 599 . . . 103
JH v WJH unreported (20 December 1979)
　(High Court) . . . 84, 401
John Mc Partlan (dec'd), In the estate of [2020]
　IEHC 447 . . . 9
Johnson, Re [1986] NYIB 16 . . . 22
Junior (James Mullen) v James Mullen [2014]
　IEHC 407 . . . 7, 29

K v K (2018) IEHC 615 . . . 113
K v K and O'R unreported (25 January 2007)
　(High Court) . . . 79–80
Kavanagh; Healy v MacGillicuddy & Lyons
　[1978] ILRM 175 . . . 147
Kennedy, Re unreported (31 January 2000)
　(High Court) . . . 384
Kershaw v Micklethwaite [2010] EWHC 506
　(Ch) . . . 54
Key v Key [2010] EWHC 408 (Ch) . . . 5, 124, 142
King, Re 200 NY 189 . . . 25
Kotke v Saffarini [2005] EWCA Civ 221 . . . 116

Lambert v Lyons [2010] IEHC 29 . . . 146
LC (a minor) v HSE (2014) IEHC 32 . . . 91
Leeburn v Derndorfer (2004) WLTR 867 . . . 56
Letterstedt v Broers (1884) 9 App Cas 371 . . . 54
Lewis v Warner [2016] EWHC 1786 (QB) . . . 117
Lynch v Burke and Allied Irish Banks Plc
　[1991] IR 1 (HC); [1996] 1 ILRM 114
　(SC) . . . 187–8, 428–9
Lynch v Butterly unreported (26 July 1996)
　(High Court) . . . 186

Marsh v Marsh (1860) 1 Sw & Tr 528 . . . 10
Martin, In the goods of (1955–56) Ir Jur Rep
　52 . . . 47
MC (A Ward of Court) v FC [2013] IEHC
　272 . . . 121
McA v McA [2000] 1 IR 457 . . . 116
McC(M) and N(B) v M(DH) and H(E) [2001]
　10 JIC 3104 . . . 103
McCann (Esther), Re unreported (8 October
　1998) (Dublin Circuit Court) . . . 91
McCarran v McCarran unreported (13 February
　1997) . . . 112, 130
McCausland v O'Callaghan [1904] 1 IR
　376 . . . 420
McDermott, In the estate of [2015] IEHC
　622 . . . 10–11
McDonnell v Norris [1999] ILRM 270 . . . 103
McEntee, Re [1960] IR Jur Rep 55 . . . 420
McEvoy v Belfast Banking Corporation [1934]
　NI 67 . . . 188
McLaverty, Re, unreported (27 January 2003)
　(High Court) . . . 5
Mehjoo v Harben Barker (A Firm) [2014]
　EWCA Civ 358 . . . 122
Messitt v Henry [2001] 3 IR 313 . . . 62–3, 434
MK (dec'd), Re the estate of [2010] IEHC
　530 . . . 65
MO'S v EC Circuit Court (unreported) 12
　January 2015 . . . 117
Mohan v Roche [1991] 1 IR 560 . . . 352, 355,
　468
Molyneux v White (1894) 13 LR IR . . . 61
Morelli, In bonis; Vella v Morelli [1968]
　IR 11 . . . 106
Morris, Re [2001] WTLR 1137 . . . 141
Moyles v Mahon [2000] IEHC 197 . . . 123,
　139, 142
MPD v MD [1981] ILRM 179 . . . 101, 107,
　400, 493
Myles, Re [1993] ILRM 34 . . . 6

Naylor v Maher [2012] IEHC 408 . . . 30
Nevin v Nevin [2013] IEHC 80 . . . 90
Nevin, Re unreported (13 March 1997) (High Court) . . . 90–1, 387

O'B v S [1984] IR 316 . . . 308
O'Brien (Noel) (dec'd), Re the estate of [2011] IEHC 327 . . . 9–10, 125
O'Connell v Bank of Ireland [1998] 2 ILRM 465 . . . 28
O'Donnell, Andrew Deceased (unreported) 24 March 1999, High Court . . . 140
O'Donohue v O'Donohue [2011] IEHC 511 . . . 4, 129
Otway v Sadlier (1850) 4 IR Jur (ns) 97 . . . 9

Parker v Felgate (1883) 8 PD 171 . . . 143–4
Parris v Trinity College Dublin Case C-443/15 [2017] 2 CMLR 17 . . . 117
Pascoe v Turner [1979] 2 All ER 945 . . . 112
Perrins v Holland [2010] EWCA Civ 840 . . . 143
Philip Davies and Joan Davies v Marian Hutchinson [2017] IEHC 693 . . . 55
Pooley, Re (1888) 4 Ch D 1 . . . 38
Porter, Re [1975] NI 157 . . . 22
Prendergast v McLaughlin [2009] IEHC 250 . . . 495
Public Trustee v Till [2002] WTLR 1169 . . . 141

R v Fox (1841) 2 QB 246 . . . 56
RG v PSG and JRG unreported (20 November 1980) (High Court) . . . 408
Reeves v Reeves (No 1) (1909) 2 IR 521 . . . 10
Regan, Re [1964] IR Jur Rep 56 . . . 247
Revenue Commissioners v Matthews, Exham and Clarke (1954) 92 ILTR 44 . . . 177
Richards v Alan [2001] WLTR 1031 . . . 140, 143
Richmond v Richmond (1914) 111 LT 273 . . . 143
Robinson v Fleming (1861) 4 Macq 167 . . . 149
Roche v Peilow [1986] ILRM 189 . . . 150
Rojack v Taylor and Buchalter [2005] IEHC 28 . . . 449
Ross v Caunters [1980] Ch 297 . . . 149, 154–5
Rudd v Rudd [1895] 1 IR 15 . . . 401
Russell v Scott (1936) 55 CLR 440 . . . 188
Ryan v Public Trustee [2000] 1 NZLR 700 . . . 141

S v H unreported (12 March 2010) (High Court) . . . 80
Samson v Devereaux [1996] 1 ICLMD 75; [1996] 3 ICLMD 75 . . . 423

Sandys v Law Society of Ireland [2015] IEHC 363; [2016] IECA 395 . . . 193
Scally v Rhatigan [2010] IEHC 475; [2012] IEHC 389; [2012] IEHC 140 . . . 5, 54, 124, 139–40, 142, 144
Shannon v Shannon [2019] IEHC 400 . . . 29
Shaughnessy v Shaughnessy [2016] IEHC 303 . . . 53
Sherrington v Sherrington [2005] EWCA Civ 326 . . . 153
Shiels v Flynn [1975] IR 296 . . . 61
Simpson, Re (1977) 121 Sol Jo 224 . . . 141, 143
Smith v Claremont Haynes & Co (Times of London, 3 September 1991) . . . 153
Smith v Halpin (1997) 2 ILRM 38 . . . 30, 112
Solicitor, Re A [1975] QB 475 . . . 151
Stevens, Re [1897] 1 Ch 422 . . . 388
Strong v Holmes [2010] IEHC 70 . . . 433–4

Tankard, Re [1942] Ch 69 . . . 426
Tassone v Pearson 2012 BCSC 1262 . . . 2
Thorpe v Bestwick (1881) 6 QBD 311 . . . 41
Tiernan, Re the goods of [1942] IR 572 . . . 6
Townson v Tickell, 106 Eng Rep. 575 (KB 1819) . . . 478
Trentdale Ltd v O'Shea [2018] IEHC 47 . . . 352, 468

Urquhart, Re [1974] IR 197 . . . 75, 77–9, 447–8

Vaughan v Vaughan [2002] EWHC 699 . . . 140
Vynior's case (1609) 8 Co Rep 816 . . . 2

Wall v Hegarty and Callanan [1980] ILRM 124 . . . 149, 154
Wester Wemyss, Re [1940] Ch 1 . . . 420
White v Jones [1995] 2 AC 207; [1995] 1 All ER 691 . . . 144, 149, 152
Williams v Williams [1882] 20 Ch D 659 . . . 56
Worby v Rosser [1998] EWCA Civ 1438 . . . 141, 149

X v Wollcombe Young [2001] WTLR 308 . . . 144, 150, 153

Yelland, Re [1975] 119 SJ 562 . . . 247
Yu, Re [2013] QSC 322 . . . 6

TABLE OF LEGISLATION

Table of Statutes

Administration of Estates Act, 1959 . . . 218–19,
    271, 354, 365
  s 10 . . . 218
  s 25 . . . 365
Adoption Act, 1952 . . . 265
  s 26 . . . 95
Age of Majority Act, 1985 . . . 49, 115
  s 2 . . . 115
  s 2(1) . . . 115
  s 3 . . . 116
Assisted Decision Making (Capacity) Act,
    2015 . . . 137–40, 437, 439
  s 3 . . . 145
  s 140. . . . 137–8
Bankruptcy Act, 1988 . . . 420
  Pt VI . . . 420
  s 59 . . . 478
  s 81 . . . 420
  ss 115–122 . . . 420
  s 115 . . . 420
  s 116(1) . . . 420
  s 116(2) . . . 420
  s 117 . . . 420
  s 119 . . . 420
Capital Acquisitions Tax Act, 1976 . . . 98
  s 54 . . . 24
Capital Acquisitions Tax Consolidation Act,
    2003 . . . 98, 194, 494
  s 2(1) . . . 284
  s 7 . . . 430
  s 12 . . . 480
  s 13 . . . 187
  s 13(1) . . . 430
  s 13(2) . . . 430
  s 26 . . . 207
  s 27 . . . 207
  s 27(4) . . . 207
  s 36 . . . 213
  s 39 . . . 212
  s 40 . . . 212
  s 45AA . . . 461
  s 45AA(1)(a) . . . 14
  s 48(10) . . . 14, 453, 461
  s 48A . . . 203, 231, 262, 302, 340
  s 48A(2) . . . 256, 295, 329
  s 48A(3) . . . 203

  s 71 . . . 477
  s 72 . . . 129, 170, 183, 294, 433, 477
  s 73 . . . 170, 183, 294
  s 76 . . . 24, 441
  s 76(2) . . . 24
  s 80 . . . 432
  s 84 . . . 129
  s 86 . . . 187
  s 89(3) . . . 29–30, 128
  s 109 . . . 430
  Sch 2, Pt 1, para 1 . . . 98
  Sch 2, Pt 10 . . . 308
Capital Taxes Acts . . . 160
Central Bank Act, 1942 . . . 48, 228, 230, 261
Charities Act, 1961 . . . 114
  s 47 . . . 24, 135
  s 52 . . . 244, 333, 440
  s 58 . . . 243–4, 333, 440
Charities Act, 1973
  s 4 . . . 24
  s 16 . . . 244, 333, 440
  s 21 . . . 24
Charities Act, 2009 . . . 160, 243
  s 81 . . . 243
  s 82 . . . 243–4, 333, 440
Children and Family Relationships Act,
    2015 . . . 73, 95–6, 100, 115, 120, 124,
    126, 445
  Pt 11 . . . 443, 451
  s 50 . . . 17–18, 66
  s 51 . . . 18
  s 67 . . . 101, 107
  s 69 . . . 101, 107
Civil Law (Miscellaneous Provisions) Act, 2008
    . . . 61, 334
  s 67 . . . 61, 426
  s 68 . . . 334
Civil Law (Presumption of Death) Act,
    2019 . . . 438
Civil Liability Act, 1961 . . . 91
  s 9 . . . 495
  s 9(2) . . . 400
Civil Partnership and Certain Rights and
    Obligations of Cohabitants Act,
    2010 . . . 67–70, 85, 101, 108, 120,
    133, 151, 160, 210, 217, 411
  Pt 5 . . . 86
  Pt 8 . . . 67

TABLE OF LEGISLATION xxv

Pt 15 . . . 67, 116, 119
s 3 . . . 69
s 5 . . . 70, 89
s 5(1) . . . 70
s 5(4) . . . 70
s 26 . . . 70
s 28 . . . 477
ss 43–52 . . . 86
s 79 . . . 58, 70
s 87 . . . 125
s 107 . . . 70
s 110 . . . 70
s 120 . . . 126
s 127 . . . 71, 125, 127
s 127(11) . . . 71, 89
s 172 . . . 116
s 172(2) . . . 116, 126, 133
s 172(3) . . . 117
s 172(5) . . . 117, 126, 133
s 172(6) . . . 68, 117, 126, 133
s 173 . . . 119, 173
s 173(3) . . . 118
s 173(6) . . . 118
s 174 . . . 118, 126–7, 133, 173
s 175 . . . 118, 126–7, 133, 173
s 176 . . . 126–7, 133
s 187 . . . 118, 126–7, 133, 173
s 194 . . . 116–19, 126, 133, 411, 443, 494
s 194(2) . . . 118
s 194(6) . . . 118
s 196(4) . . . 117
s 198 . . . 119
s 202 . . . 119, 126, 133
s 202(2) . . . 119
s 202(3) . . . 119
s 202(4) . . . 119, 126, 133
s 202(5) . . . 119
Civil Registration Act, 2004 . . . 70
   Sch 3 . . . 70
   s 37 . . . 176
Competition Act, 1991 . . . 481
Conveyancing Acts . . . 166
Conveyancing Act (Ireland), 1634
   s 10 . . . 478
   s 14 . . . 478
Conveyancing Act, 1881
   s 42 . . . 114, 437
   s 43 . . . 39, 114, 437
Court Officers Act, 1926 . . . 365
Court of Probate (Ireland) Act, 1859 . . . 365
Courts Act, 1981
   s 20 . . . 455
Credit Union Act, 1977
   s 23 . . . 164
Credit Union Act, 1997 . . . 210, 431
   s 21 . . . 179
   s 21(3) . . . 210
   s 23 . . . 210
Debtors (Ireland) Act, 1840
   s 26 . . . 455
Family Home Protection Act, 1976 . . . 477
   s 3 . . . 477
Family Law Act, 1995 . . . 89
   s 9 . . . 127

s 11 . . . 85
s 11(1)(b) . . . 86
s 11(2)(b) . . . 85
s 11(2)(c) . . . 85
s 12 . . . 85
s 12(2) . . . 85
s 13 . . . 86
s 13(1) . . . 88
s 14 . . . 67, 86–7, 127, 174, 399–400
s 15A . . . 86–7, 174, 399
s 15A(1) . . . 86
s 15A(2) . . . 87
s 15A(5) . . . 87
s 15A(6) . . . 87
s 15A(10) . . . 87
s 18 . . . 71, 85
s 18(4) . . . 71
s 29 . . . 89
s 31 . . . 115
s 31(1) . . . 5
Family Law (Amendment) Act, 1996
   s 18(10) . . . 127
Family Law (Divorce) Act, 1996 . . . 87–8, 101
   s 18 . . . 67, 87, 399–400
   s 18(1) . . . 88
   s 18(2) . . . 88
   s 18(3) . . . 88
   s 18(5) . . . 88
   s 18(6) . . . 88
   s 18(7) . . . 88
   s 18(8) . . . 88
   s 18(10) . . . 88, 174
   s 46 . . . 400
   s 52(d) . . . 85
   s 52(g) . . . 86, 399
Family Law (Miscellaneous Provisions) Act, 1997
   s 6 . . . 302, 303, 307
Finance Act, 1985
   s 60 . . . 183
Finance Act, 1988
   s 74 . . . 98
Finance Act, 1993 . . . 232
Finance Act, 1999 . . . 211
Finance Act, 2000
   s 23 . . . 211
Finance Act, 2001 . . . 99
Finance Act, 2010 . . . 14, 48, 58, 194
   s 147(1)(l) . . . 453
Finance (No 3) Act, 2011 . . . 100, 186
   Sch 3 . . . 98
Finance Act, 2012
   s 98 . . . 136
   s 115 . . . 453
Finance (No 3) Act, 2012 . . . 477
Finance Act, 2015 . . . 29, 128, 156
Finance Act, 2016 . . . 156
Finance Act, 2017 . . . 156
   Finance Act, 2019 . . . 156
   s 63 . . . 203, 231
Finance Acts . . . 160
Finance (Local Property Tax) Act, 2012 . . . 462
   s 11 . . . 463–4
   s 11(3) . . . 463
   s 11(4) . . . 463

Finance (Local Property Tax) Amendment Act, 2013 . . . 462
   s 4 . . . 464
Friendly Societies Act, 1896
   s 58 . . . 425
Guardianship of Infants Act, 1964 . . . 95, 314
   s 7 . . . 17, 18, 66, 115
   s 8 . . . 18
Industrial and Provident Societies Act, 1893 . . . 431
Intestates' Estates Act, 1954 . . . 365
Judicial Separation and Family Law Reform Act, 1989 . . . 85
   Pt I . . . 85
   Pt II . . . 85
   s 17 . . . 87, 174, 399
   s 25 . . . 85
Land and Conveyancing Law Reform Act, 2009 . . . 24, 64, 114, 120, 147, 155, 160, 166, 190, 437, 439, 448
   Pt 4 . . . 130, 437
   Pt 5 . . . 3
   s 19 . . . 60, 114–15, 147, 162, 437
   s 20 . . . 114
   s 74 . . . 478
Legal Services Regulation Act, 2015 (LSRA, 2015)
   s 5 . . . 14
   s 150 . . . 38, 194–5, 197, 481–3
   s 150(4)(c) . . . 482
   s 152 . . . 482
   Sch 1, para 2 . . . 482
Legitimacy Act, 1931 . . . 307
   s 9 . . . 307
   s 9(1) . . . 367
   s 9(2) . . . 367
   s 29 . . . 309
Local Government (Charges) Act, 2009 . . . 160, 465
Local Government (Household Charge) Act, 2011 . . . 465–6
Marriage Act, 2015 . . . 10, 67, 69, 120, 132, 228, 265, 451
   s 11 . . . 70
   s 11(6) . . . 70
   s 11(7) . . . 70
   s 11(8) . . . 70
   s 11(9) . . . 70
   s 11(10) . . . 70
   s 12 . . . 70
   s 16 . . . 70
   s 17 . . . 10
   s 67 . . . 68
   s 69 . . . 68
Nursing Home Support Scheme Act, 2009 . . . 27, 211, 426, 457
   Pt 4 . . . 457
   s 27 . . . 458
Personal Insolvency Act, 2012 . . . 65, 420
Powers of Attorney Act, 1996 . . . 138
Registration of Title Act, 1964
   s 61 . . . 354
   s 61(7) . . . 351–2
Settled Land Acts, 1882–1890 . . . 147, 439

Social Welfare Act, 1991
   s 33 . . . 455
Social Welfare Act, 1998 . . . 175
Social Welfare (Consolidation) Act, 1981
   s 174 . . . 455
Social Welfare (Consolidation) Act, 2005 . . . 421
   s 139 . . . 455–6
   s 339 . . . 426, 455–7
   s 339(1)(b) . . . 457
   s 339(2) . . . 456
   s 339(3) . . . 456
Social Welfare (Miscellaneous Provisions) Act, 2002 . . . 24
   Pt 2 . . . 135
Solicitors (Amendment) Act, 1994 . . . 483
   s 66(1)(f) . . . 483
   s 68 . . . 37, 193–4, 194, 481, 483
Stamp Duties Consolidation Act, 1999 . . . 98
   s 29 . . . 475
   s 96 . . . 477
Status of Children Act, 1987 . . . 43, 97–8, 120, 134, 151, 265, 307–9, 374, 450
   Pt V . . . 98–9, 307–8
   Pt VI . . . 310
   Pt VIII . . . 310
   s 3 . . . 98, 308, 366
   s 3(1) . . . 97
   s 3(2) . . . 99
   s 10 . . . 309
   s 15 . . . 309
   s 27 . . . 308
   s 29 . . . 96, 98, 266, 308–10
   s 29(2) . . . 98, 308
   s 30 . . . 98, 310
   s 31 . . . 308
   s 35(8) . . . 309
   s 46 . . . 96
   s 46(3) . . . 309
   s 49 . . . 310–11, 342
Statute of Limitations, 1957 . . . 401–2
   s 13(2) . . . 401, 491
   s 14(2) . . . 401, 495
   s 24 . . . 491, 493
   s 45 . . . 77, 400–1, 491
   s 45(1) . . . 399–400, 490–1
   s 45(2) . . . 400
   s 46 . . . 400
   s 49 . . . 493, 495
   s 49(2)(d) . . . 493
   s 59(5) . . . 402, 496
   s 68(5) . . . 402, 496
Statutes of Limitations, 1957–91 . . . 490
Succession Act, 1965 . . . 3, 13, 46, 60, 65, 71, 74, 79, 98, 100, 108, 120, 160, 165, 217, 365, 382, 396–7, 480, 492
   Pt IV . . . 204
   Pt VI . . . 94, 159, 264, 266, 275, 303, 343
   Pt VII . . . 5Pt IX . . . 67, 69, 73, 77–8, 93–4, 206, 410
   Pt X . . . 78
   s 3 . . . 83, 426
   s 3(1) . . . 61
   s 3(2) . . . 96

TABLE OF LEGISLATION xxvii

s 4 . . . 308, 318
s 4A . . . 98
s 4A(2) . . . 266
s 5 . . . 34, 334–5, 379, 384
s 10 . . . 192, 206, 401, 496
s 10(4) . . . 135
s 10(5) . . . 72
s 14 . . . 32
ss 16–25 . . . 12
s 16 . . . 62
s 17 . . . 12, 52, 222, 496
s 18(1) . . . 52
s 19 . . . 166, 353
s 19(1) . . . 353
s 20 . . . 65
s 20(1) . . . 13, 60
s 22 . . . 425
s 24 . . . 192
s 25 . . . 61
s 26 . . . 376
s 26(2) . . . 53, 376
s 27 . . . 376, 380
s 27A . . . 98
s 27(1) . . . 264, 312, 385
s 27(2) . . . 53, 376
s 27(3) . . . 178, 220, 365
s 27(4) . . . 219, 312, 370, 378–9, 385
s 27(5) . . . 380, 385
s 27(7) . . . 99
s 28 . . . 218
s 29 . . . 165, 218
s 30 . . . 13, 48–9, 228, 260
s 30(1) . . . 48
s 30(2) . . . 48
s 30(4) . . . 48, 223
s 30(4)(b)(ii) . . . 230, 261
s 30(4)(c) . . . 49
s 31 . . . 398
s 31(1) . . . 219
s 32 . . . 49
s 34 . . . 271, 349
s 34(1) . . . 320
s 35(1) . . . 376
s 37 . . . 343
s 38 . . . 385–6
s 45(1) . . . 92, 135–6, 443–4, 449
s 46 . . . 27, 92, 421
s 46(2) . . . 421
s 46(2)(b) . . . 421
s 46(3) . . . 92
s 46(6) . . . 92, 421, 444–4
s 47 . . . 2, 19, 27–8, 72, 127, 181, 185, 457, 480
s 49 . . . 65, 72, 185, 352, 398, 419, 425–6, 457–8, 495
s 50 . . . 60
s 51 . . . 61, 426
s 52 . . . 467
s 52(2) . . . 165, 468
s 52(4) . . . 398, 468, 495
s 52(5) . . . 468
s 53 . . . 355
s 54 . . . 354
s 55 . . . 36–7, 42, 61–3, 81, 83, 398, 409, 414, 433–4, 495

s 55(3) . . . 61–2, 398, 434
s 55(4) . . . 62
s 55(5) . . . 62
s 55(6) . . . 62
s 55(11) . . . 62
s 55(12) . . . 62
s 55(14) . . . 62
s 55(17) . . . 64
s 56 . . . 36, 61, 64, 71, 81–3, 93, 127, 135, 206, 358, 398–400, 409, 411, 433–4, 448–9
s 56(1) . . . 82
s 56(2) . . . 82
s 56(3) . . . 82
s 56(4) . . . 82
s 56(5) . . . 81–2
s 56(6) . . . 82
s 56(5)(a) . . . 494
s 56(8)(a) . . . 82
s 56(9) . . . 64, 83, 93
s 56(10) . . . 93
s 56(10)(b) . . . 83, 448
s 56(10)(c) . . . 448
s 56(10)(d) . . . 82, 93
s 56(14) . . . 180
s 57 . . . 64, 82–3, 113–15, 162, 166, 411, 437–8
s 57(5) . . . 114
s 57(6) . . . 115
s 58 . . . 64, 114
s 58(2) . . . 64, 114, 437
s 58(3) . . . 166
s 59 . . . 425
s 60 . . . 64
s 60(3) . . . 64
s 60(4) . . . 64
s 60(8) . . . 64, 208
s 61 . . . 61, 426
s 62 . . . 53, 426, 454
s 62(1) . . . 399, 401, 495
s 62(2) . . . 399
s 63 . . . 2, 36, 43, 97, 108–11, 126, 134, 449–50
s 63(1) . . . 35, 109
s 63(2) . . . 36, 109
s 63(3) . . . 110
s 63(4) . . . 110
s 63(5) . . . 36, 110
s 63(6) . . . 36, 109
s 63(10) . . . 450
s 64 . . . 483
s 67 . . . 95, 99, 126, 303, 336–7
s 67(1) . . . 275
s 67(2) . . . 275–6, 278, 303, 389
s 67(4) . . . 450
s 67A . . . 107, 217, 449, 451, 496
s 67A(1) . . . 275
s 67A(2) . . . 275–6
s 67A(3) . . . 68, 73, 95, 100, 107–8, 111, 125, 275, 451
s 67A(5) . . . 494
s 67A(6) . . . 108
s 67A(7) . . . 108
s 67B(1) . . . 276

s 67B(2) . . . 107, 275–6, 278, 283, 439
s 68 . . . 276
s 69(1) . . . 276, 279, 282, 284
s 69(2) . . . 277
s 70 . . . 277
s 70(1) . . . 284
s 70(2) . . . 279, 282, 284
s 71 . . . 265, 277–8, 284, 303, 334
s 71(1) . . . 284
s 71(2) . . . 284, 286
s 72 . . . 121, 283
s 72A . . . 303–5, 307, 479
s 73 . . . 303
s 73(1) . . . 266
s 74 . . . 409
s 76 . . . 1
s 77 . . . 5, 139–40
s 77(1) . . . 240
s 77(b) . . . 5
s 78 . . . 5, 39, 40, 233, 383
s 78(1) . . . 234
s 78(2) . . . 40, 237
s 78(4) . . . 6, 234
s 78(5) . . . 234
s 81(1) . . . 88
s 82 . . . 14, 37–8, 41, 50, 149
s 84 . . . 121
s 85 . . . 8–10
s 85(1) . . . 9, 70, 228
s 85(1A) . . . 10
s 86 . . . 2, 237
s 87 . . . 9–10
s 90 . . . 29
s 91 . . . 19, 24–6, 33, 129, 318, 334, 336, 439, 481
s 92 . . . 20, 32, 318
s 93 . . . 135–6
s 98 . . . 2, 19, 25–6, 33–4, 96–7, 121–2, 126, 129, 134, 177, 318, 336–7, 408, 439, 441, 468, 481
s 102(a)–(d) . . . 370
s 109 . . . 71, 79
s 109(1) . . . 71
s 109(2) . . . 71, 72, 432
s 111 . . . 73–4, 77–8, 399–401, 443, 446–7, 490, 494
s 111A . . . 73–4
s 111(2) . . . 78
s 112 . . . 74, 92, 421, 443, 444
s 113 . . . 74, 78, 84
s 113A . . . 71, 74, 84
s 114 . . . 74, 82
s 114(2) . . . 74
s 115 . . . 69, 75, 81, 212, 401, 444–9, 494
s 115(2) . . . 76
s 115(2)(a) . . . 446
s 115(4) . . . 77, 399, 448
s 115(5) . . . 77
s 117 . . . 65, 68, 74, 91, 93, 95, 97–108, 111, 113, 127, 134, 151, 210, 217, 232, 308, 387, 400, 445, 449, 451, 493–4, 496
s 117(1) . . . 102
s 117(2) . . . 100
s 117(3) . . . 100
s 117(3A) . . . 68, 73–4, 77, 93, 95, 100, 125, 451
s 117(5) . . . 106
s 117(6) . . . 101, 400
s 117A . . . 217
s 120 . . . 71, 89–91, 125, 400, 495
s 120(2) . . . 400
s 120(2)(A) . . . 90
s 120(3) . . . 90, 400
s 120(5) . . . 90
s 121 . . . 94, 106–7, 177, 187, 400, 413, 430, 432–3, 495
s 121(2) . . . 94
s 121(6) . . . 94
s 121(9) . . . 94, 187, 429
s 123 . . . 401, 496
s 124 . . . 402, 496
s 125 . . . 402, 493, 494, 496
s 125(1) . . . 402, 493
s 125(2) . . . 402, 494
s 126 . . . 77, 399–401, 448, 490–1, 494–6
s 126(2) . . . 490
s 127 . . . 101, 402, 493, 496
s 128 . . . 365
Sch1 . . . 28
Sch1, Pt I . . . 92, 160, 419
Sch 1, Pt II . . . 27, 73, 76, 92–3, 160, 419, 422, 444
Sch 2, Pt II . . . 76
Succession Act (Scotland), 2016 . . . 10
Taxes Consolidation Act, 1997 . . . 98, 194, 211
Ch 1 . . . 210
s 108 . . . 207
s 960P . . . 421
s 982 . . . 421
Trustee Act, 1893 . . . 114, 437–8
s 10 . . . 52
s 11 . . . 52
s 25 . . . 114
Trustee Acts . . . 160, 166
Trustee (Authorised Investments) Act, 1958 . . . 114
Trustee Savings Bank Acts, . . . 431
Wills Act, 1837 . . . 41

TABLE OF STATUTORY INSTRUMENTS

Capital Acquisitions Tax (Electronic Probate)
    Regulations, 2020 (SI 341/2020) . . . 205
    reg 3(1) . . . 215
    reg 6 . . . 205
    reg 9 . . . 256, 295, 329
Civil Partnership (Recognition of Registered
    Foreign Relationships) Order, 2010 (SI
    649/2010) . . . 70, 126
Rules of the Superior Courts (Civil Partnership
    and Cohabitation), 2011 (SI 348/2011)
    . . . 265
Civil Partnership (Recognition of Registered
    Foreign Relationships) Order, 2012 (SI
    505/2012) . . . 70, 126
Civil Partnership (Recognition of Registered
    Foreign Relationships) Order, 2011 (SI
    642/2011) . . . 126
Solicitors (Professional Practice, Conduct and
    Discipline – Conveyancing Conflict of
    Interest) Regulation, 2012 (SI 375/2012)
    . . . 146
Civil Partnership (Recognition of Registered
    Foreign Relationships) Order, 2013 (SI
    490/2013) . . . 70, 126
Civil Partnership (Recognition of Registered
    Foreign Relationships) Order, 2014 (SI
    2012/2014) . . . 70, 126
Circuit Court Rules
    O 50 . . . 106
Civil Partnership (Recognition of Registered
    Foreign Relationships) Order, 2010 (SI
    648/2010) . . . 70
Courts Act, 1981 (Interest on Judgment Debts)
    Order, 1989 (SI 12/1989) . . . 455
Credit Union Act 1997 (Alteration of Financial
    Limits) Regulations, 2006 (SI 546/2006)
    . . . 164, 179
European Union (Basic Payment Scheme
    Inheritance) Regulations, 2017 (SI
    639/2017) . . . 30, 155
Finance (Local Property Tax) Regulations, 2013
    (SI 91/2013) . . . 465
Land Registration Rules, 2012 (SI 483/2012)
    . . . 354, 469
Legal Services Regulations Act, 2015
    (Commencement of Certain Provisions)
    (No 2) Order, 2019 (SI 502/2019)
    Art 2(a) . . . 194

Marriage and Civil Partnership (Scotland) Act
    2014 (Commencement No. 2 and Saving
    Provisions) Order 2014 . . . 70
Registration of Deeds Rules, 2008 (SI 52/2008)
    . . . 470
Rules of the Superior Courts, 1986 (SI
    15/1986) . . . 312, 437, 481
    O 3 . . . 54, 105
    O 55, r 41 . . . 455
    O 55, r 42 . . . 455
    O 55, r 43 . . . 455
    O 67, r 87 . . . 59
    O 67, r 89 . . . 59
    O 67, r 92 . . . 60
    O 73 . . . 438
    O 77 . . . 438
    O 79 . . . 217, 365–6, 397
    O 79, r 2 . . . 13
    O 79, r 3 . . . 217, 390
    O 79, r 5 . . . 51, 220, 246, 264, 303, 479
    O 79, r 5(1)–(5) . . . 321
    O 79, r 5(1) . . . 159, 178, 220, 265, 273, 303,
        316–17, 343
    O 79, r 5(1)(c) . . . 366
    O 79, r 5(1)(e) . . . 366
    O 79, r 5(2) . . . 266
    O 79, r 5(3) . . . 266, 366, 367–9, 390
    O 79, r 5(4) . . . 266, 420
    O 79, r 5(6) . . . 159, 178, 220, 313, 316, 343,
        347
    O 79, r 5(6)(e) . . . 317, 366, 369
    O 79, r 5(8) . . . 366, 369
    O 79, r 5(8)(c) . . . 51, 246
    O 79, r 5(9)(b) . . . 220, 266, 280, 313
    O 79, r 5(10) . . . 366, 370
    O 79, r 5(12) . . . 222, 266
    O 79, r 5(13) . . . 222
    O 79, r 5(14) . . . 51, 223
    O 79, r 6 . . . 40, 237–8, 263, 340, 366, 372,
        382
    O 79, r 7 . . . 238, 366, 372
    O 79, r 8 . . . 237
    O 79, r 9 . . . 238
    O 79, r 13 . . . 226, 366, 372
    O 79, r 14 . . . 372
    O 79, r 19 . . . 49
    O 79, r 23 . . . 50, 366, 372
    O 79, r 25 . . . 366, 373, 375

O 79, r 26 . . . 50, 246
O 79, r 27 . . . 50, 246, 366, 376
O 79, r 28(1) . . . 220
O 79, r 29 . . . 272, 320
O 79, r 33 . . . 159, 218, 245
O 79, r 36 . . . 226
O 79, r 37 . . . 225, 262, 338, 347
O 79, r 38 . . . 52, 223
O 79, r 41 . . . 237
O 79, r 47 . . . 387
O 79, rr 52–57 . . . 389
O 79, r 63 . . . 236, 263, 340
O 79, r 65 . . . 266
O 79, r 66 . . . 266
O 79, r 73 . . . 302, 340
O 79, rr 87–88 . . . 403
O 80 . . . 365
O 80, r 6 . . . 382
App Q . . . 216, 220, 226, 233, 262–3, 301, 315, 339–40
Pt 1 . . . 349
Pt 5 . . . 349
Rules of the Superior Courts (Affidavits), 2009 (SI 95/2009) . . . 229, 262, 301
Rules of the Superior Courts (Funds in Court), 2012 (SI 488/2012) . . . 165
Rules of the Superior Courts (No 4) (Euro Changeover), 2001 (SI 585/2001) . . . 165
Rules of the Superior Courts (Probate and Administration Oaths and Bonds), 2020 (SI 590/2020) . . . 216, 226, 272, 301, 315, 339, 349

Savings Certificates Rules, 1926 . . . 179, 210
Savings Certificates (Seventeenth Issue) Rules, 2007 (SI 827/2007)
r 15 . . . 164
Solicitors Accounts Regulations 2001 . . . 483
Solicitors Accounts Regulations, 2014 (SI 516/2014) . . . 409
Solicitors Remuneration General Order, 1986 . . . 483
Supreme Court and High Court (Fees) Order, 2013 (SI 239/2013) . . . 403
Supreme Court and High Court (Fees) (Amendment) Order, 2021 (SI 80/2021) . . . 224, 245, 263, 342
Trustee (Authorised Investments) Order, 1998 (SI 28/1998) . . . 114, 437
Trustee (Authorised Investments) Order, 1998 (Amendment) Order, 2002 (SI 595/2002) . . . 437

Table of European Law
Regulation (EU) No 650/2012 of the European Parliament and of the Council . . . 123

Table of International Instruments
Hague Convention on the Conflict of Laws relating to the Form of Testamentary Dispositions 1961 . . . 94
Hague Convention on the Law Applicable to the Estates of Deceased Persons 1989 . . . 94

INTRODUCTION

This textbook deals with the following areas of wills, trusts, probate, and administration of estates:

The drafting and execution of wills in accordance with the testator's informed instructions. These informed instructions would include the legal obligations on the testator in certain circumstances. The drafting and execution of wills would include the legal background to trusts and the drafting and administration of will trusts in accordance with the testator's informed instructions.

The extraction of a grant of representation on behalf of the personal representative, whether the deceased died testate (leaving a will), intestate (leaving no will), or partially testate and partially intestate. Where there is no executor appointed by will, this would include identifying the person(s) entitled to administer the estate in these circumstances.

The administration of the estate of a deceased person on behalf of the personal representative of the estate, including advising the client of the legal and taxation obligations.

Tax issues arise constantly in this area of practice. Taxation issues are referred to but not dealt with in detail in this book and are taught as part of the Probate and Taxation module on the PPC I. Students, and indeed practitioners, consulting this book should always consider the tax consequences of any action.

In this book, all references to the male gender apply equally to the female unless specifically stated otherwise. For example, reference to a testator (male person making a will) shall apply equally to the testatrix (female person making a will).

Similarly, references to 'he', 'him', and 'his' shall apply equally to 'she', 'her', and 'hers'.

The primary legislation governing the area of wills, probate, and administration of estates is the Succession Act, 1965, which will be referred to throughout this book as 'the Act'.

A bibliography at the end of the manual provides full details of all books and articles referred to within the book.

CHAPTER 1

INTRODUCTION TO WILL DRAFTING

1.1 The Constituent Elements of a Will, Including the Statutory Formalities

1.1.1 WHAT IS A WILL?

If a person wishes his assets to be distributed in a certain way on his death this can normally only be achieved by leaving a testamentary instrument known as a will.

James C Brady in *Succession Law in Ireland*, 2nd edn (1995) defines the word 'will' as:

> 'used to describe the document or documents in which a person called the testator or testatrix according to gender sets out his or her wishes in relation to certain matters which are to take effect on his or her death.'

Thus, a will may consist of a number of documents read together. The original and more detailed document is referred to as a 'will' and subsequent additional written amendments or changes or additions to the will are sometimes known as 'codicils'.

1.1.2 OF WHAT CAN A WILL DISPOSE?

Section 76 of the Succession Act, 1965 (hereafter 'the Act') deals with what property can be disposed of by will and states that:

> '*A person may by his will, executed in accordance with this Act, dispose of all property which he is beneficially entitled to at the time of his death and which on his death devolves on his personal representative.*'

The word 'property' here includes both real and personal property. It does not, however, include joint property, held as joint tenants, which will usually pass by survivorship. In certain circumstances joint property will not pass by survivorship but will revert to the deceased's estate under a resulting trust. The matter of joint ownership of assets will be dealt with at paras **2.7.9** and **12.6**.

It is very important to ensure as far as possible that all assets to which a testator will be entitled on death are disposed of by the will. This does not mean it is necessary for each and every asset belonging to a testator to be specifically named in a will, and in fact this would be inappropriate in most circumstances.

However, it is absolutely vital to ensure that all assets to which a testator is entitled or may be entitled on death are caught within the terms of a will and the consequences considered. This will be dealt with in greater detail under the heading 'Residue' at para **2.9**.

2 INTRODUCTION TO WILL DRAFTING

In addition to disposing of his own property, the testator may, in his will, leave instructions in relation to the distribution of property over which he has power to dispose, i.e. he leaves instructions in relation not only to his own property but to the property of another. For example, it may be that the testator holds a power of appointment over property which is exercisable by will. This will be dealt with at para **5.3**. Students wishing to know more should see *Tassone v Pearson* (2012) BCSC 1262, which considered the status of such a power in a will in detail.

1.1.3 WHEN DOES A WILL TAKE EFFECT?

The will does not take effect until the death of the testator. Therefore, the testator remains free to deal with property which he has purported to dispose of by his will and he may in fact sell or give it away (dispose of it) in his lifetime so that references to same in his will shall become redundant.

It is a common misconception among clients that if they leave property to a person in their will, they cannot dispose of it in their lifetime.

Equally, the will, when it does take effect, can operate to dispose of property which was only acquired by the testator after the will was executed.

The will may be revoked at any time by the testator, even if the document is stated (and it usually is) to be irrevocable when executed: *Vynior's case* (1609) 8 Co Rep 816.

Thus, it may be stated that the salient characteristics of a will are that:

1. it does not take effect until the death of the testator; and
2. it is revocable by the testator at any time before his death (s 86 of the Succession Act, 1965) (see para **2.3.2**).

1.1.4 WHY MAKE A WILL?

This is a question frequently asked by clients.

One of the main reasons, and the best advantage of making a will, is that it allows a client to provide for the devolution of his property by means of a clear legal document. It is not left to the State (under the laws of intestacy) to decide on the client's behalf.

Further, it allows the client to provide for any special needs of family members, for example a child with special needs.

Also, the administration of a testate estate by an executor is quicker and less expensive, not least because an insurance bond should not have to be obtained from an insurance company.

It also acts as an opportunity to ensure that the absolute minimum amount of tax is paid on death. This is referred to as tax planning and is covered in detail in the CAT Lecture Notes (see Preface).

In addition, it allows a client, should he so wish, to vary provisions of the Succession Act, 1965 that he may not wish to apply, for example, ss 47, 63, and 98.

Solicitors often find in practice that a large number of people are extremely reluctant to make wills, either because they have a superstitious notion that death follows a will or because they do not wish to give the time to the consideration of organising their affairs on death.

All adults of sound disposing mind can make a will and solicitors should strongly advise all clients to do so, and indeed to execute an enduring power of attorney.

Making one's will is not something that should be done only at the last minute or only by elderly people. It is something that should be thought about and planned for, and should be considered by all age groups, but especially by couples with young children. While it is generally true that a person may leave only one effective will on death (see para **2.3.2**), this does not mean that he should only make one will in his lifetime.

It is a fallacy to think that because a person does not have significant asset wealth, somehow a will is less necessary. A will is relevant to every person who has responsibilities as well as assets.

While people can have wills dealing with property in different jurisdictions, this will not be dealt with in detail in this book. Clients should always be advised to seek appropriate advice regarding the succession regime and the taxation regime in any foreign jurisdiction in which they may have assets.

In fact, in addition to encouraging clients to make a will, solicitors should also encourage them to review their wills and, as their life circumstances change, to make a new will in accordance with their current circumstances (see para **2.3.2**).

For clients with particular tax planning needs, tax changes occur with virtually every Finance Act nowadays, meaning that their wills should be at least reviewed and probably updated on an annual basis.

Another very good reason for making a will is that the client can choose who is to handle his affairs on his death, i.e. he can appoint an executor or (if the appointee is female) an executrix (or indeed more than one: it is recommended that a testator should appoint at least two executors). In intestacy situations, where a person dies without leaving a valid will, there is no such choice, as the order of entitlement to extract a grant of administration intestate is governed by law.

The absence of a will is tantamount to losing control over the distribution of assets on death as the Succession Act, 1965 then determines who is to inherit and who is responsible for the administration. In many cases this can be contrary to what the deceased would have wished for, and quite often results in the most unsuitable person assuming the role of personal representative.

A situation may also arise where a person dies testate but leaving no executor surviving him. In that case, his real and personal estate, until the administration is granted, vests in the President of the High Court. This is not what most people want, and when the reasons noted here for making a will are explained to clients, the vast majority of them are more than happy to do so.

1.1.5 THE ROLE OF THE SOLICITOR IN MAKING A WILL

The skill involved in drafting a basic will for a client is one that is required of all practitioners. It is also a skill that may not be put to the test for many years after the will is drawn. In the absence of any legislation to allow for the variation of wills after death in this country (except the limited ability under Part 5 of the Land and Conveyancing Law Reform Act, 2009 to apply to court for a variation of a will trust), solicitors administering the estate of the testator are restricted to working within the basic framework of the will that has been created, and that can often be difficult. Difficulties may arise when a will drafted many years before the testator dies is not relevant to the current financial or family circumstances of the testator or a will drafted with a particular taxation element may not be applicable because the taxation laws changed in the interim.

The preparation of a will is probably the only legal service the solicitor will be in a position to offer to all clients. It can keep a link between the solicitor and the client that can be valuable at a time when a client's loyalty can shift in the marketplace. As stated, a will often needs to be reviewed on an ongoing basis, and the question of who is responsible for instigating any review can be problematic (see para **5.9.1.2**).

For some unknown reason, it is also one area of law where the layman may feel a sense of confidence in 'having a go': after all, any person can prepare a will. Such wills are often referred to as 'home-made wills' or 'holographic wills'. Any solicitor who has had to administer such a home-made will will be fully aware of the legal and practical difficulties of

4 INTRODUCTION TO WILL DRAFTING

unravelling the consequences. See the case of *O'Donohue v O'Donohue* [2011] IEHC 511 for the consequences of a home-made will.

In particular, if the statutory formalities for making a will, as outlined in **Chapter 2**, are not complied with, there is a risk that the will may be deemed invalid, and the testator's wishes as expressed on paper will not be complied with.

The role of the solicitor is to take a structured and considered approach to will drafting on behalf of the client and to draft a will that is relevant to the predictable circumstances at the time of death and, in particular, to predict the needs of beneficiaries, particularly providing a structure for beneficiaries with disabilities.

The skill of will drafting is not one that appears to be highly valued. Clients are reluctant to pay substantial fees for a will and it is often a service that is thrown in for free or where a solicitor does not expect to recover the cost of the time involved. In many cases it can be left to apprentices or to junior solicitors to take the initial instructions. The danger is that it is a highly charged area fraught with pitfalls and often it is only the 'nose' of experience which can detect a problem. In many cases it is the hunch that all is not as it seems that is so important. It is a fact that our clients do not always tell the full truth initially, and making a will can become akin to a confessional.

The duty of care required of a solicitor when drafting a will, is, quite rightly, a high one. Further, this duty of care is owed not only to the testator but to beneficiaries, potential beneficiaries, and indeed, sometimes, third parties. In addition, the fact of our ageing population is causing capacity to become an issue and while it is not correct to equate becoming older with lacking capacity, it is correct that the duty of care owed to the elderly or the otherwise vulnerable is of an even higher standard than that owed to testators in general.

There is an enhanced duty of care imposed on all professionals dealing with clients who are vulnerable (see the High Court cases of *Bourke v O'Donnell and the Bank of Ireland* [2010] IEHC 348 and *Haughty v J and E Davy TA Davies* (2014) 12 HC 206) and solicitors are no exception; thus steps need to be taken to both fulfil and manage that duty. See **Chapter 5**.

Over-reliance on precedents is another potential pitfall for the unwary practitioner. Too often, we blindly trust precedents as providing the magic formula. This 'cut and paste' approach can have drastic results. It is also one of the main 'danger areas' for practitioners. In particular, practitioners should beware of UK precedents!

There are two excellent Irish precedent books for wills, namely Spierin, *Wills—Irish Precedents and Drafting*, 3rd edn (2020) and *Bloomsbury Irish Conveyancing Precedents* online service (*Bloomsbury Irish Conveyancing Precedents* are sometimes referred to as *Laffoy's Conveyancing Precedents* by older practitioners as they were originally drafted by Ms Mary Laffoy SC before she became a judge of first the High Court and then the Supreme Court). However, as with all precedents, care should be taken, and the precedent should be correctly adapted to suit the individual testator's wishes.

The purpose of this part of the book is to break down into building blocks and explain the basic elements of a will in order to enable students to approach the drafting of a will in a coherent and safe way, using precedents (where appropriate) in an informed and logical manner.

However, it is not sufficient for the solicitor to take instructions from a client, and to draft a will exactly in accordance with those circumstances, without taking the taxation consequences into account. Should a beneficiary face a substantial charge to tax that could have been avoided had the solicitor given proper tax and estate planning advice, it is quite possible that such a beneficiary may have an action in negligence against that solicitor. See *Cancer Research Campaign v Ernest Brown & Co (a firm)* [1997] STC 1425 and Harman J's comment in particular re the responsibility for tax advice:

> '*I do not doubt the solicitor, in considering the will, must consider what inheritance tax implications that testator will cause by the bequests for which he is given instructions …*'

As stated, tax planning is not dealt with in detail in this book. See Chapter 11 of the CAT Lecture Notes (see Preface).

1.1.6 STATUTORY FORMALITIES FOR THE MAKING OF A WILL

Part VII of the Act deals with the statutory formalities for the making of wills.

1.1.6.1 Who can make a will?

Section 77 of the Act provides that a will may be made by a person who:

> 'a) has attained the age of eighteen years or is or has been married, and
>
> b) is of sound disposing mind.'

The exception for married persons has little relevance now, as the age of marriage has been amended by s 31 of the Family Law Act, 1995. Under subsection (1):

> 'Marriage solemnized after the commencement of this section between persons either of whom is under the age of eighteen years will not be valid in law.'

This section also contains an important provision in that a person who is entitled to appoint a guardian of an infant may make the appointment by will, notwithstanding that he or she has not attained eighteen years of age or been married.

Note, however, that the court may, on application, grant an exemption from the minimum age requirement.

It is beyond the scope of this chapter to deal with s 77(b) (i.e. capacity) in detail but, of course, this is a vital element of taking instructions for a will, especially in light of the changing test for capacity and the new capacity legislation. Suffice it to say at present that the test is a legal one, not a medical one, and detailed attendance notes should be made in all cases confirming the position. This issue is dealt with in more detail at para **5.4.2.1**. See also *Scally v Rhatigan* [2012] IEHC 389 and *Key v Key* [2010] EWHC 408 (Ch). In addition, see numerous Law Society Guidelines for Solicitors, in particular '*Drafting Wills for the Elderly Client*', Guidelines for Solicitors, *Law Society Gazette*, January/February 2009.

1.1.6.2 What are the requirements for a will to be validly executed?

While s 77 governs the capacity of an individual to make a will, s 78 then sets out in some detail the rules governing the formal validity of a will and generally also any subsequent alterations to the will, and it states as follows:

> '*To be valid the will shall be in writing and be executed in accordance with the following rules:*
>
> 1. *It should be signed at the foot or end thereof by the testator or by some person in his presence and by his direction. [Note that it is possible for a will to be signed by an individual at the direction of the testator and in the testator's presence. This may occur if the testator is physically incapable of executing the will, as for example, would occur where the testator is the victim of a stroke and cannot write.]*
>
> 2. *Such signature shall be made or acknowledged by the testator in the presence of each of two or more witnesses, present at the same time, and each witness shall attest by his signature the signature of the testator in the presence of the testator, but no form of attestation shall be necessary nor shall it be necessary for the witnesses to sign in the presence of each other.*'

There are two essential elements:

1. The testator must sign in the presence of each of two or more witnesses (a testator can also acknowledge his signature); and

2. Those witnesses must attest by their signatures the signature of the testator in the presence of the testator, but not necessarily in the presence of each other. To constitute 'in the presence of each other' it is enough that they are within visual sight (see *In the Estate of Bulloch* [1968] NI 96 and *Re McLaverty* (unreported) 27 January 2003, HC. In this case a will was held to be valid where the testator had signed in the presence of both but there was a time lag (more than two months) between the first witness signing and the second witness signing).

Although the section states that no form of attestation is necessary (i.e. an attestation clause; see *Clarke v Early* [1980] IR 223), it is considered good practice to insert a proper attestation clause in each and every will and this is dealt with at para **2.14**.

> *'(3). So far as concerns the position of the signature of the testator or of the person signing for him under Rule 1, it is sufficient if the signature is so placed at or after, or following or under, or beside, or opposite to the end of the will that is apparent on the face of the will that the testator intended to give effect by the signature to the writing signed as his will.'*

The basic rule is that the signature must be found at the foot or end of the will, which is well established. However, case law has given the words *'foot or end'* a broad interpretation and s 78(4) contains certain saving provisions regarding the signature. See *Re Boylan* [1942] Ir Jur Rep 2.

Section 78(4)

'No such will shall be affected by the circumstances—

(1)   that the signature does not follow or is not immediately after the foot or end of the will;

(2)   that a blank space intervenes between the concluding word of the will and the signature; or

(3)   that the signature is placed amongst the words of the testimonium clause or the clause of attestation or follows or is after or under the clause of attestation either with or without a blank space intervening or follows or is after or under or beside the names or one of the names of the attesting witnesses; or

(4)   that the signature is on a side or page or other portion of the paper or papers containing the will on which no clause or paragraph or disposing part of the will is written above the signature; or

(5)   that there appears to be sufficient space on or at the bottom of the preceding side or page or other portion of the same paper on which the will is written to contain the signature; and the enumeration of the above circumstances shall not restrict the generality of rule 1.'

However, note the following provision in subsection (5):

'A signature shall not be operative to give effect to any disposition or direction inserted after the signature is made.'

The seminal case in this area is *Re Myles* [1993] ILRM 34.

1.1.6.3   What is 'in writing'?

The definition of 'in writing' has been very liberally interpreted by the courts. For example, a will can be hand-written, typed, lithographed, or indeed, as in one famous case, chipped out in the form of a strip cartoon over 176 blocks of marble. See *Hudson v Barnes* (1926) 43 TLR 71, where a will written on an eggshell was upheld.

It is interesting to note that in the case of *Re Yu* [2013] QSC 322 the Supreme Court of Queensland Australia held that an electronic will saved to a smart phone should be admitted to probate, and while this is not law here it does point the way to the future. The material upon which a will may be written must satisfy the requirement of permanency but otherwise there is no reason in principle why any restriction should be placed on such material. Basically, 'writing' can be taken to mean some permanent evidence of the testator's intention or of the terms of the will. There are a number of decided cases on this matter, for example:

- *Re Bolan* [1942] IR Jur Rep 2;
- *Re the Goods of Tiernan* [1942] IR 572;
- *Re the Goods of Harris Deceased* [1952] P 319;
- *Re the Goods of Darling* [1983] IR 150.

1.2 The Basic Elements of a Will

Drafting a will is essentially building a structure by using a set of elements or building blocks. Certain wills may be very straightforward, but as long as they contain all of the necessary elements and have the appropriate clarity, very little should go wrong. In relation to clarity and the construction of wills see *James Mullen Junior v James Mullen* [2014] IEHC 407, where Cregan J gave a very good review of the Rules of Construction.

More complex wills can involve trusts, but still require the necessary elements or building blocks and the same basis of construction. Practitioners can go astray when an essential element of the will becomes lost in the drafting. It is possible to lose the substance in the detail and become blind to the overall effect. It is prudent to put the draft will before a colleague in the office to read it for sense and clarity prior to its execution. It is sobering, not to say humbling, to see what can be picked up immediately by another person.

While complex will trusts may run to many pages, the actual setting up of the trust may only require a short paragraph and the rest of the provisions may be the addition of powers for trustees etc (see Chapter 2 of the Trusts Lecture Notes (see Preface)). It is important that the solicitor be able to identify what exactly he wishes to accomplish by the will, rather than hoping that a precedent will somehow fit the bill. For this part of the book, the concentration will be on custom-made wills, with assistance from precedents.

Obviously, common sense indicates that a will is an individual document and should be drafted on the basis of the client's instructions. However, every will should contain at least nine basic elements and may also contain a further five elements if required:

1. Name and address of the testator.
2. Revocation of previous wills and testamentary dispositions (codicils).
3. Appointment of executors, giving their addresses and their relationships to the testator (if any).
4. Appointment of trustees (if required).
5. Appointment of guardians (if required).
6. Provision for specific bequests or pecuniary bequests in the form of legacies and/ or devises.
7. The establishment of a trust (if appropriate), whether it is of a specific item or sum, or a trust of the residue of the estate.
8. A clear residuary clause that deals with all eventualities.
9. Enabling clauses, such as a power of advancement, appropriation, apportionment, and miscellaneous (if required).
10. A schedule containing additional powers for executors and trustees (if required).
11. The date.
12. The signature of the testator.
13. An attestation clause.
14. The signature of the two witnesses with their addresses and their descriptions.

If it is ensured that each will drafted contains these elements, it gives the will a structure from which to operate, thus lessening the possibility of error. This is particularly true in the case of emergency wills, drafted at short notice without access to precedents. Such special cases will be dealt with at para **5.4**.

CHAPTER 2

BASIC ELEMENTS OF A WILL AND MUTUAL WILLS

2.1 Introduction: The Constituent Elements of a Will

The best teacher of will drafting is dealing with a difficult administration of an estate which could have been prevented, or at least the difficulties lessened, if the will had been drafted correctly. In the absence of this experience, one tried and tested method of drafting a will is to view it as building a structure, and using a set of elements or building blocks, as listed in **Chapter 1**.

Taking each element in turn, this chapter will examine the blocks in terms of the applicable legislation, best practice and common errors, and precedent clauses. There are two excellent Irish precedent books for wills: Spierin, *Wills—Irish Precedents and Drafting*, 3rd edn (2020) and *Bloomsbury Irish Conveyancing Precedents* online service. However, as with all precedents, care should be taken, and the precedent should be correctly adapted to suit the individual testator's wishes. See **Chapter 5**.

2.2 Name and Address of the Testator

While this may seem obvious, it is opportune to ascertain if the name by which the testator is commonly referred to is the name on that testator's birth certificate. All too often, practitioners deal with people whose 'name' is not that on their birth certificate. If any potential for confusion can arise, this should be dealt with in the will. The testator should be referred to as, for example, *'Cornelius (otherwise known as "Neil") O'Brien'*. Further, this will assist greatly post-death during the administration in general, but especially when gathering in assets, for example, shares or bank accounts in variants of the deceased's name.

2.3 Revocation of Previous Wills

2.3.1 APPLICABLE LEGISLATION

Section 85

'(1) A will shall be revoked by the subsequent marriage of the testator, except a will made in contemplation of that marriage, whether so expressed in the will or not.

(2) Subject to subsection (1), no will, or any part thereof shall be revoked except by another will or codicil duly executed, or by some writing declaring an intention to revoke it and executed in the manner in which a will is required to be executed, or by the burning, tearing, or destruction of it by the testator or by some person in his presence and by his direction, with the intention of revoking it.'

Section 87

'No will or any part thereof, which is in any manner revoked, shall be revived otherwise than by the re-execution thereof or by a codicil duly executed and showing an intention to revive it; and when any will or codicil which is partly revoked, and afterwards wholly revoked, is revived, such revival shall not extend to so much thereof as was revoked before the revocation of the whole thereof, unless an intention to the contrary is shown.'

The rule is that a will is revocable until the testator dies or loses capacity to revoke.

There are therefore generally five ways in which a will may be revoked:

1. By a subsequent marriage or civil partnership. In general, a will is revoked by a subsequent marriage. The exceptions to this are: if civil partners subsequently marry each other; where the will states otherwise or it is made in contemplation of that particular marriage or civil partnership and should a mutual will (not a mirror will) apply, see para **2.18.2**.

   There is an extremely obscure form of revocation called a 'dependent relative revocation'; however, it is exceptionally rare. A solicitor dealing with such circumstances should refer to Spierin, *Wills—Irish Precedents and Drafting*, 3rd edn (2020), para 4.12.

   Contemplation of marriage does not have to be expressed in the will, although it is the better practice to do so. See the case of *Re the Estate of O'Brien Deceased* [2011] IEHC 327, which particularly reviewed the meaning of s 85 and the words *'contemplation of that marriage'* and has clarified this section of the Succession Act, 1965. The subsequent case of *In the Estate of John Mc Partlan Deceased* [2020] IEHC 447 cites O'Brien approvingly and also sets out at para 59 ten principles of law to apply when applying s 85(1).

   As we have seen, s 85 of the Succession Act, 1965 (as amended) states that a will is automatically revoked by a subsequent marriage (or entry into civil partnership) of the testator. This was the position at common law: see *Otway v Sadlier* (1850) 4 IR Jur (ns) 97, *Re the Goods of Baker* [1985] IR 101, and *Coleman v Coleman* (1975) 1 All ER 675 (the latter being particularly helpful on the nature of the contemplation required).

   However, there always was and still is an exception to this rule, which is that a will made in contemplation of a particular marriage is not revoked by that marriage. Although it is clear that there is no strict necessity for the will to state that it was made in contemplation of a particular marriage (this now includes the registration of a particular civil partnership), of course it is always prudent to do so. Interestingly, in England the will has to state that it is in contemplation of a particular marriage.

   This is not the case in this jurisdiction and, as can be seen from *Re the Estate of O'Brien*, judicial recognition has been given to the fact that the will does not have to state 'in contemplation of' and that extrinsic evidence may be adduced to show if the terms of the exception are met.

   Failure to advise a client of this could well give rise to a negligence action in certain circumstances, such as where a subsequently married/civil partner client dies intestate following the revocation of his will by marriage/civil partnership.

2. By a subsequent will or codicil properly executed.

3. By some writing declaring an intention to revoke the will and executed in the manner in which the will is required to be executed.

4. By the burning, tearing, or destruction of the will by the testator, with the intention of revoking it.

5. By the burning, tearing, or destruction of the will by some person who is in the presence of the testator and by his or her direction, with the intention of revoking it.

10 BASIC ELEMENTS OF A WILL AND MUTUAL WILLS

2.3.2 BEST PRACTICE AND COMMON ERRORS

1. A will is revoked by marriage (except, as noted, where civil partners subsequently marry each other; see s 85(1A) of the Succession Act, 1965 as inserted by s 17 of the Marriage Act, 2015). The Marriage Act, 2015 provided that no new civil partnerships would be entered into after the six-month notice period after commencement of the Act had lapsed. The Marriage Act was commenced on 15 November 2015 and six months after that date (15 May 2016) was the last date on which a civil partnership could be entered into. However, we will be dealing with clients in civil partnerships for years to come as existing civil partnerships were unaffected by this and are dealt with in **Chapter 4**.

   To be effective, the marriage or civil partnership must be valid, but if it should be rendered void it will not revoke a will made in contemplation of that marriage or civil partnership: see *In the Estate of Fleming* [1987] ILRM 638.

   A will is not revoked by divorce or dissolution of a civil partnership in Ireland.

   However, on 1 November 2016 the Succession Act (Scotland), 2016 came into force and while obviously it is not Irish law, it does affect certain estates. Briefly, it excludes an ex-spouse from inheriting under a will that was made before a divorce unless the will explicitly states the contrary intention, which could happen but would be unlikely.

   Under Irish law a divorce does not invalidate a will and so such an ex-spouse could inherit here, or indeed, unless there is a blocking order, seek provision from the courts. See para **4.5.8.3**.

   Irish law also provides that old wills that have been revoked are not automatically revived if the new will is in turn revoked. See s 87 of the Succession Act, 1965.

   In the event of a client's divorce or dissolution of civil partnership, testamentary arrangements will need to be reviewed. It is very important to advise single or widowed clients that a subsequent marriage will revoke their wills unless such a will is made in contemplation of that particular marriage: see s 85 of the Succession Act, 1965, as amended. As noted, the case of *Re the Estate of O'Brien Deceased* [2011] IEHC 327 is instructive in this regard as it confirms that the fact that the will is made in contemplation of marriage does not have to be stated as such on the face of the will.

2. Failure to advise a client of this could well give rise to a negligence action in certain circumstances, for example where a subsequently married/civil partner client dies intestate following the revocation of his will by marriage or civil partnership.

3. A new will or codicil will only expressly revoke an earlier will and codicil if it contains a proper *revocation clause*. This can be overlooked. The consequence is that if a revocation clause is not inserted, it will only revoke a previous will or codicil in so far as the later will is inconsistent with the earlier will: see *Reeves v Reeves (No 1)* (1909) 2 IR 521. It would necessitate an application to the Probate Judge to have all documents admitted together as constituting the last will of the testator. This is very tedious and can, indeed should, be avoided.

   In relation to codicils, be careful, especially when dealing with the revival of a revoked will. Section 87 of the Succession Act, 1965 provides a statutory method for revival of wills. For this to occur, intention to revive must be shown: see *Marsh v Marsh* (1860) 1 Sw & Tr 528.

   It would be the better practice to make a new will. In the present era one might assume that codicils are redundant and no longer an issue, but they are still relevant. See *In the Goods of Hogan* [1990] ILRM 24, *In the Estate of McDermott* [2015] IEHC 622, *Curtin Deceased* [2015] IEHC 623, *Brennan v O'Donnell* [2015] IEHC 460, and *In the Estate of Courtney* [2016] IEHC 318. See also see Stephenson Solicitors' 31st Seminar, 12 May 2017, *The Probate Dance—In and Out and All About*.

4. The solicitor should always check if the testator has made any wills in any *other jurisdictions*. A full revocation clause could automatically revoke all testamentary

arrangements made by the testator. If it is the intention that the current will should deal with only the testator's property in this jurisdiction, this must be expressly declared in the will in order that it does not have the unintentional effect of revoking other wills. The revocation clause should clearly state that the current will is only to revoke any previous wills, dealing with a testator's property in Ireland or in accordance with the testator's instructions. It is vitally important that if the revocation clause is being amended to deal with a will in another jurisdiction, the residuary clause also reflects the position. Otherwise, there could be a contradiction on the face of the will. A testator will usually be relying on his solicitor for direction on this point, and the solicitor must ask questions in relation to foreign property.

5. If a client has property in other jurisdictions, the solicitor should warn him to be careful in relation to the execution of *foreign wills*, to ensure that such foreign wills do not inadvertently revoke any Irish will. It is vital that a will made in the Irish jurisdiction does not inadvertently revoke a will made in a foreign jurisdiction or vice versa. In order to revoke a will there must be *animus revocandi* (the intention to revoke); however, it is better practice to avoid having any doubts as to the testator's intention. The solicitor should obtain a certified copy and a certified translation in order to confirm this. Solicitors are increasingly faced with situations where testators own property in a number of jurisdictions. Where a person dies leaving wills in a number of jurisdictions, certified copies of these wills will need to be lodged in the Probate Office, as the Probate Officer needs to be sure that any such foreign will does not revoke the Irish will.

6. Problems will arise where a will is destroyed but, not by the testator or by some person *in his presence* and by his direction. Solicitors should never destroy a will on the instructions of the testator over the phone. Similarly, written instructions from the testator to destroy the will are not sufficient. The letter itself may be a sufficient revocation, but only if the letter has itself been executed in the manner in which a will is required to be executed. See para **1.1.6.2**. The testator will not be aware of this, but the solicitor should be.

7. An act of destruction must be done *animo revocandi*, and therefore the destruction of a will through inadvertence or mistake or accident will not affect its revocation. The solicitor may have difficulties in proving the will, but revocation will not be one of them.

   To reiterate, for revocation by destruction to occur, two elements must be present:

   (a) physical destruction by or in the presence of the testator; with
   (b) the intention of revoking the will.

8. There is a presumption, when a will which was last known to be in the possession of a testator cannot be found after death, that the testator destroyed it *animo revocandi* (see *Re Coster* (unreported) 19 January 1979, Supreme Court). Of course, as with all presumptions, this could be rebutted by showing that the destruction of the will may have happened by accident or, alternatively, by showing that while the testator had custody of the will he did not have the capacity to revoke it during the period when it was in his custody.

As is true of most presumptions, the presumption of revocation in such circumstances is difficult to rebut. This is because the circumstances surrounding the destruction are generally unknown or indeed the actual date of the destruction may not be known, therefore rendering it impossible to ascertain the capacity or intention of the testator at the material time unless there are exceptional circumstances. Two judgments of Baker J in this area (*Re McDermott Deceased* [2015] IEHC 622 and *Re Curtin Deceased* [2015] IEHC 623, intended to be read in conjunction with each other) are a very effective re-statement of the law in this area. In the *McDermott* case, on the facts, Baker J found that the evidence rebutted the presumption of revocation by destruction. The testatrix had moved to a new house on a number of occasions prior to being placed in a home and being made a Ward of Court. In the *Curtin* case, Baker J found that the evidence supported the presumption of revocation by destruction as the deceased had expressed disquiet about the contents in writing and to her solicitor and the will had last been in her possession. As is often the position, so much depends on the facts of each particular case. Solicitors dealing with a 'missing' will after the death of a testator should read both cases.

12 BASIC ELEMENTS OF A WILL AND MUTUAL WILLS

The same presumption of destruction *animo revocandi* does not apply to wills held in solicitors' offices. See para **11.3.5** for details on proving a will in terms of a copy and the presumptions which apply depending on who last had the will.

For this reason, it is best practice to keep wills in a fireproof, waterproof safe in the solicitor's office.

When giving the original will to a testator, after execution, for safekeeping, it should be recorded that the original will has been handed over to the testator and a copy should be carefully kept in the office in case an application to prove the will in terms of a copy is required and capable of being brought in the future.

It would be better practice in such cases to instruct the testator, in writing, to keep the will safe and to advise him to inform his executors where the will might be found. Further, advise the client that it would be wise to lodge it in a bank or some other place of safe custody. At the very least, some other person should know of the whereabouts of the will. From the point of view of reducing liability in the case of a dispute on the testator's death, it would be advisable also to add in the letter that in the event that the original will is lost or is not forthcoming after the testator's death it would be presumed to be revoked by destruction, and this may result in him dying intestate.

2.3.3 PRECEDENT CLAUSES

An example of a simple revocation clause would be as follows:

> '*I hereby revoke all former Wills and other Testamentary Dispositions made by me.*'

A simple revocation clause re codicils would be as follows:

> '*I hereby revoke my will dated the day of (and the codicil(s)) thereto dated the day of and the day of.*'

In relation to foreign assets, obviously the revocation clause and laterally the devise of the residuary clause will vary widely according to the individual circumstances of the testator.

Some choices are:

Restrict the revocation to Irish wills:

> '*I hereby revoke all former Wills and other Testamentary Dispositions made by me dealing with my estate in the Republic of Ireland [or define the property to which the will should apply]. This revocation does not affect any Will or other Testamentary Disposition which I may previously have executed in connection with property in any jurisdiction other than the Republic of Ireland.*'

Do not restrict the revocation to Irish wills but exclude foreign wills which are to remain in force:

> '*I hereby revoke all former Wills and other Testamentary Dispositions made by me in so far as they relate to my property of every kind wheresoever situate except in (name of foreign jurisdiction).*'

 Always use the phrase '*Wills and Testamentary Dispositions*' to include all codicils or other written documents that may be testamentary in nature.

2.4 The Appointment of Executors

2.4.1 APPLICABLE LEGISLATION

Sections 16–25 of the Succession Act, 1965

Section 17

'Where a person appointed executor by a will

(a) survives the testator but dies without having taken out probate, or

(b) is cited to take out probate and does not appear to the citation, or

BASIC ELEMENTS OF A WILL AND MUTUAL WILLS

(c) renounces probate, his rights in respect of the executorship shall wholly cease, and the representation to the testator and the administration of his estate shall devolve and be committed in like manner as if that person had not been appointed executor.'

Section 20

'(1) Where probate is granted to one or some of two or more persons named as executors, whether or not power is reserved to the other or others to prove, all the powers which are by this Act or otherwise by law conferred on the personal representative may be exercised by the proving executor or executors or the survivor or survivors of them and shall be effectual as if all the persons named as executors had concurred therein.'

Section 30

This section contains detailed provisions re the appointment of a trust corporation as an executor. Note here that not all charities are trust corporations and thus, making a charity the sole residuary beneficiary can create some problems in the administration. See para **2.4.2**, at point 6, para **3.2.2**, and the article in the *Parchment*, September 2012, entitled 'A Different Type of Legal Personal Representative?' by Una Burns, solicitor.

2.4.2 BEST PRACTICE AND COMMON ERRORS

Note the distinction between appointing a person as an executor and as a trustee. The two functions are quite distinct. The function of an executor/administrator is to extract a grant to administer the estate and they have all the powers in the Succession Act, 1965, including the power of sale of assets. See **Chapter 3**.

1. Executors should be chosen with extreme care. While one executor is sufficient, it is the wiser policy to appoint more than one. A situation can arise where a testator does not give sufficient attention to the suitability of the persons that they wish to be appointed as executors; perhaps the proposed executor is too elderly or may still be a minor. There are obvious reasons against appointing a minor as an executor. Although a minor can act, a grant will issue to the guardian of the minor until such time as the minor reaches the age of eighteen. Indeed, an executor can act who is suffering from a medical or physical disability but could do so via Power of Attorney. See Rules of the Superior Courts, 1986, O 79, r 2.

2. A testator can unwittingly impose too heavy a burden on an executor. Both the solicitor and the client should always be aware of the possibility of a conflict of interest should an executor also be a beneficiary in an estate, or where an executor is appointed 'wearing too many hats', such as an appointment as a trustee or guardian as well. The best executor to have is one who knows the deceased, whether in a personal or a professional capacity, who has an abundance of common sense, and with whom there is no possibility of a conflict of interest.

3. If an executor is not able to act, there is also the possibility of encouraging a testator to appoint a substitute executor. Do not appoint an alternative executor, i.e. 'A or B', as this wording may well fail for uncertainty.

4. Problems can arise if too many executors are appointed. Note that there is no limit on the number of executors that can be appointed, but, for practical purposes, administration can be delayed and made more expensive by having more than three persons acting in the administration of an estate, if all three have to attend to sign documents and be consulted and agree on every decision.

5. Problems can arise when the sufficiency of powers of an executor under the Succession Act, 1965 are not fully considered. In the appointment of executors, practitioners need to be absolutely clear on the powers conferred on executors, as quite often these powers are simply not sufficient for executors to deal with the administration. It may be necessary for additional powers to be conferred on executors (and trustees). From a drafting point of view, it is advisable that these powers should be contained in a schedule at the end of the will (but before execution) in

order that the content of the will itself and its dispositive provisions can be drafted in a tighter fashion.

6. If a client wishes to appoint a bank as an executor or trustee, the solicitor should ensure that the testator is aware of the fees involved, and in all cases obtain the consent of the bank to so act. Note that in the event of the appointment of a trust corporation, a charging clause will be required. A bank will normally require a draft of the will to be furnished to them prior to signature. As this is a confidential document, the solicitor should always get the testator's permission to do so in advance. The bank will also require a copy of the executed will to be sent to them for the purposes of their records.

It should be noted, however, that where a trust corporation is appointed, it is not unusual that a bank nevertheless declines to act post-death. Thus, at least appoint a second executor or a substitute. There is little point in appointing a trust corporation for a relatively small estate. The two sets of fees—one for the trust corporation and one for the solicitor administering the estate—can amount to a significant sum in circumstances where it is not absolutely required. See precedent clause at para **2.4.3**. In addition, care should be taken where there is any possibility, either through initial appointment or default, of a trust corporation becoming the legal representative, as this can cause problems when applying for the grant. For further information on this see the article in the *Parchment* by Úna Burns, cited earlier.

7. When appointing a solicitor as an executor, many solicitors forget to insert a charging clause; the result is that they are not entitled to charge a professional fee without the consent of those liable to pay same. This is an extremely important point, which is frequently forgotten by solicitors, with negative results. If a solicitor is appointed as an executor, the solicitor, the solicitor's spouse, or any partner of the solicitor should not witness the will, notwithstanding the existence of a charging clause. See s 82 of the Succession Act and para **2.10.4**. See also the Practice Note issued in the February 2011 edition of the *Law Society Gazette*.

If a partner in a firm of solicitors is being appointed as an executor, in the absence of any provision to the contrary, the partners, as at the date the will is made, are the relevant individuals. This is an exception to the rule that a will speaks from the date of death. If a testator wishes to appoint the partners as at the date of death of the testator, which would be advisable, or wishes to appoint named individuals, this needs to be specifically referred to. If only one or two partners intend to extract a grant, as would be the norm, a resolution of the partnership needs to be passed, indicating which partners will so act. Again, this resolution will need to be exhibited in the oath.

8. From a practical point of view, the solicitor should always encourage the testator to ask a person whether they are willing to act as an executor, rather than 'land' an executor with the role on the death of the testator, which may be renounced.

9. If an executor is appointed who is outside the jurisdiction, it can be difficult to administer the estate from a practical point of view. An attorney in this jurisdiction can be appointed, which usually gets around this problem.

Note also that since the Finance Act, 2010 (3 April 2010), there is an additional issue if the legal personal representative is outside the jurisdiction in that where there is no Irish resident legal personal representative, the legal personal representative must appoint a solicitor holding a practising certificate in the State (the solicitor referred to in s 48(10) of the Capital Acquisitions Tax (CAT) Consolidation Act, 2003 as inserted by the Finance Act, 2010) to act before seeking probate or letters of administration, and then that solicitor has a liability for the CAT. However, he shall be liable only to the extent that he has control of the property passing on the death (the assets referred to in s 45AA(1)(a) of the CAT Consolidation Act, 2003 as inserted by the Finance Act, 2010), or would have control but for his own neglect or default. See CAT Lecture Notes (see Preface). For further information on when and how to appoint different types of executors, see Stephenson Solicitors' 19th Seminar, *Legal Personal Representatives: The Good, the Bad and the Indifferent*, pp 16–33.

10. Where the testator has certain types of assets e.g. a solicitor's practice or literary assets, then the testator should be asked, should a special executor be appointed to deal specifically with those assets (see para **2.4.3** below)?

2.4.3 PRECEDENT CLAUSES

An example of a proper appointment clause would be as follows:

'I hereby appoint X [insert full name and any "other" name by which the person is known; for example, Denis otherwise known as "Dinny" Murphy] of [insert full current address] to be the sole executor of this my will.'

or

'I hereby appoint X and Y [see above] as executors of this my will and I appoint them as Trustees for the purposes of section 57 of the Succession Act, 1965, the Conveyancing Acts 1881–92 and the Land and Conveyancing Law Reform Act, 2009.'

An example of a clause appointing a substitutionary executor would be as follows:

'I appoint X [see above] as executor of this my will but if he does not survive me for a period of 30 days or dies without proving my will or renounces his rights to prove my will or is unable to act as my executor then in those events or any of them I appoint Y as my executor.'

An example of a clause for the appointment of a firm of solicitors would be as follows:

'The firm of solicitors practising under the style and title of Stephenson Solicitors as executors and trustees of my will, provided always that it shall be the partners of the said firm at the date of my death who shall be entitled to prove the said will and in the event that the said firm shall amalgamate with another firm under its own or a new name or the said firm shall be incorporated into another firm of solicitors the amalgamated firm of solicitors or the firm of solicitors into which the said firm shall be incorporated shall be deemed to be the executors and trustees of this my will.'

An example of a clause for the appointment of a literary executor would be as follows:

'I APPOINT X as the executors of this my will in respect only of my literary estate. They shall have the same powers in relation to my literary estate as my executors have in relation to my estate. My literary estate shall mean all of my published and unpublished literary works, manuscripts, letters, copyrights and other related rights and privileges and I declare that all cost and expenses in relation to the administration of my literary estate, shall be borne out of my literary estate.'

An example of a clause for the appointment of a digital executor would be as follows:

'I appoint X as the executor of this my will in respect only of my digital assets. He/she shall have the same powers in relation to my digital estate as my executors have in relation to my estate.

My digital estate shall include files stored on my digital devises, including but not limited to, desktops, laptops, tablets, peripherals, storage devises, mobile phones, smartphones and any other digital devise which currently exists or may exist as technology develops or as such comparable items as technology develops.

The term digital assets also includes, but is not limited to, cryptocurrencies, email accounts, emails received, digital music, photographs, videos, software licences, social network accounts, cloud storage accounts, file sharing accounts, financial accounts, domain registrations, web hosting accounts, online accounts or similar digital items which currently exist or may exist as technology develops or as such comparable items as technology develops regardless of the ownership of the physical device upon which the digital item is stored.'

An example of a clause for the appointment of a solicitor as special executor or 'practice trustee' in a solicitor's own will would be as follows:

'I appoint, solicitor, of as special executor of this my will in relation to my solicitor's practice currently carried on by me under the name of at (hereinafter called "my practice trustee") and I declare that this appointment as special executor shall be limited to my practice estate as defined below.

I give to my practice trustee all the assets and liabilities of my practice estate as defined below on trust to sell my practice as a going concern, if that be possible, upon such terms as my practice trustee shall in his/her absolute discretion think proper, whether by disposal of individual assets by sale or otherwise or the closure of the practice and the collecting in of outstanding fees and the realisation of work in progress and the payment of debts and liabilities of the practice with power to postpone the sale or closure without any liability for loss as if he/she were beneficially entitled to my practice. Until sale or closure, my practice trustee shall continue to carry on the practice either from the practice address or from his/her own offices for the benefit of my estate for so long as he/she considers it beneficial to do so.

If my practice trustee does not hold a current practising certificate from the Law Society of Ireland at the date of my death, he/she shall appoint another solicitor who does to be my practice trustee in his/her place and that solicitor's name and address shall be deemed to appear in this my will above in the place of the said as my special executor. My practice estate comprises the following: the goodwill, furniture and equipment of the practice all unpaid fees, book debts, undertakings, liens, work in progress, money standing to the credit of the practice at any bank or elsewhere and the benefit of all contracts relating to the practice, any interest in the practice premises, any property of mine used wholly and exclusively in the practice, all liabilities and debts in connection with the practice at the date of my death.

My practice trustee shall hold my practice estate and the annual profits of my practice after payment of all expenses and the net proceeds of any sale, collection of fees or realisation of assets and work in progress as part of my residuary estate and shall pay the same to my trustees.

My practice trustee shall have power to purchase my practice from my estate, provided that the purchase price shall not be less than the current market value at the date of the transfer and my practice trustee shall first obtain a valuation and report on the proposed transaction from a professional valuer (such valuation and report to be paid for by my practice trustee) and if the valuer does not advise against the transaction for any reason, my practice trustee may proceed, provided that the purchase price shall not be less than the amount of the valuation.

My practice trustee shall be entitled to charge and be paid all professional fees or other charges for any business or act done by him, including acts which an executor or trustee could have done personally.'

An example of a clause of appointment of a trust corporation would be as given here. Most trust corporations have a precedent of the wording that they would prefer to be used and obviously they should be contacted to establish what that wording is. However, a typical precedent of such a clause would be as follows:

'I hereby appoint   having its registered office at   executor of this my will. The conditions upon which acts as executor last published before the date of this will shall apply to its appointment and the said trust corporation shall be remunerated in accordance with the scale of such remuneration current at the date of my death and as may be varied from time to time in accordance with the aforesaid conditions during the course of the administration of my estate and any trust arising under this my will.'

See para **2.10.4** for an example of a charging clause.

The functions and powers of a trustee are detailed in Chapter 1 of the Trusts Lecture Notes (see Preface). An executor may be appointed by implication rather than expressly. An executor appointed by implication is usually called an executor according to 'tenor'. See para **3.3.1**. Where there is a will, but no executor is appointed or available to act, the grant to be extracted is a grant of letters of administration with will annexed. This type of grant, and the question of who is entitled to extract such a grant, will be dealt with in **Chapter 9**.

On the death of a client for whom a will is held, the solicitor should check the surviving spouse's/civil partner's will. If the deceased had been appointed executor in the surviving spouse's/civil partner's will, a replacement executor should be appointed immediately.

2.5 Appointment of Trustees

This is dealt with in Chapter 1 of the Trusts Lecture Notes (see Preface).

2.6 Appointment of Guardians

2.6.1 APPLICABLE LEGISLATION

Section 7 of the Guardianship of Infants Act, 1964 as repealed and replaced by s 50 of the Children and Family Relationships Act, 2015:

> '50. The Act of 1964 is amended by the substitution of the following section for section 7:
>
> **Power of parents to appoint testamentary guardians**
>
> (1) On the death of the guardian ('deceased guardian') of a child, a guardian ('surviving guardian') surviving the deceased guardian, if any, shall be guardian of the child jointly, where applicable, with—
>
>   (a) any other surviving guardian, and
>
>   (b) any person or persons appointed testamentary guardian by the deceased guardian in accordance with this section.
>
> (2) A guardian who is—
>
>   (a) the parent of a child, or
>
>   (b) not being the parent of the child, has custody of him or her to the exclusion of any living parent of the child,
>
> may by deed or will appoint a person or persons to be guardian ('testamentary guardian') of the child after his or her death.
>
> (3) On the death of a guardian referred to in subsection (2), the testamentary guardian appointed by the deceased guardian shall, subject to subsections (4) and (5), act jointly with a surviving guardian of the child so long as the surviving guardian remains alive.
>
> (4) Where subsection (3) applies and—
>
>   (a) a surviving guardian referred to in that subsection objects to a testamentary guardian acting jointly with him or her, or
>
>   (b) the testamentary guardian considers that a surviving guardian is unfit to have the custody of the child,
>
> the surviving guardian or the testamentary guardian, as the case may be, may apply to the court for an order under this section.
>
> (5) On an application under subsection (4), the court may make an order providing that—
>
>   (a) the appointment of the testamentary guardian is revoked and the surviving guardian shall remain guardian of the child concerned,
>
>   (b) the testamentary guardian shall act jointly with the surviving guardian, or
>
>   (c) the testamentary guardian shall act as guardian of the child to the exclusion, insofar as the court thinks proper, of the surviving guardian.
>
> (6) Where the court makes an order under subsection (5)(c), it may make all or any of the following orders:
>
>   (a) such order regarding the custody of the child and the right of access to the child of the surviving guardian as it thinks proper;
>
>   (b) an order that a parent of the child shall pay to the guardian or guardians, or any of them, towards the maintenance of the child such weekly or other periodical sum as, having regard to the means of the surviving parent, it considers reasonable.
>
> (7) An appointment of a testamentary guardian by deed may be revoked by a subsequent deed or by will.'

See Stephenson Solicitors' 28th Seminar, *Quis custodiet ipsos Custodes et al*? for a fuller review of this legislation and the practitioners' bible on the subject of the Children and Family

18 BASIC ELEMENTS OF A WILL AND MUTUAL WILLS

Relationships Act, 2015, Dr Geoffrey Shannon's book, *Children and Family Law in Ireland: Practice and Procedure* (2016).

2.6.2 BEST PRACTICE AND COMMON ERRORS

1. It should be made clear to the client that where a testator dies leaving the other parent surviving, such surviving parent is the legal guardian of the child in the majority of cases.

2. If there is a non-marital child involved, it is not always appreciated that it may be necessary for the father of the child to apply to court to be appointed as a guardian, whereas the mother of such child automatically has the right to guardianship.

3. In any other case, where a testator wishes for another person to be appointed as guardian (where the other parent has predeceased or both parents die in a common calamity), a guardian/s must be appointed under s 50 of the Children and Family Relationships Act, 2015, which allows for testamentary guardians.

    The old position was that only a mother or a father (provided she or he was also a guardian) could appoint a person as testamentary guardian of their child in the event of their death.

    However, ss 50 and 51 of the Family Relationships Act, 2015 amend ss 7 and 8 of the 1964 Act. Now, under the amended 1964 Act, all parents who are also guardians of the child can appoint a testamentary guardian of a child, and indeed it is possible for guardians to appoint a guardian in their own will.

    Thus, the testator must be asked whether he is a guardian of a child but not the parent. In addition, note that a guardian who is not a parent of a child but has custody of that child to the exclusion of any living parent of the child can also appoint a testamentary guardian of a child.

    Pursuant to s 7 of the 1964 Act (as inserted by s 50 of the 2015 Act) the appointment of a testamentary guardian must be done by deed or will. A non-parental guardian can have custody of the child to the exclusion of the surviving parent of the child. The non-parental guardian can appoint a testamentary guardian who may seek a court order seeking exclusive custody of the child and maintenance from the parent of that child.

4. It is possible for an executor or trustee of the will to be appointed as a testamentary guardian but both solicitor and testator should always be alert to the suitability of the proposed candidate. The guardian may act alone as a guardian without having any other role in the administration of the estate.

5. The will should never appoint '*X or Y*' as a guardian. Absolute certainty as to the identity of the guardian is essential. Further, an 'either/or' situation will be void for uncertainty. As stated earlier, this also applies to the appointment of executors and trustees.

2.6.3 PRECEDENT CLAUSE

An example of a proper appointment clause for guardians would be as follows:

'I hereby appoint [insert full name as outlined above for testators] of [insert full current address] as testamentary guardian of any of my children who are under the age of eighteen at the date of my death.'

Where a guardian is appointing a guardian, the clause would be as follows:

'I hereby appoint [insert full name as outlined above for testators] of [insert full current address] as testamentary guardian of [insert full name of minor(s)] of whom I am guardian who is/are under the age of eighteen at the date of my death.'

2.7 Provision for Specific or Pecuniary Bequests in the Form of Legacies/Devises

2.7.1 APPLICABLE LEGISLATION

Sections 91, 98, and 47 of the Succession Act, 1965—see **2.9.1** for s 91.

Section 91

'Unless a contrary intention appears from the will, any estate comprised or intended to be comprised in any devise or bequest contained in the will which fails or is void by reason of the fact that the devisee or legatee did not survive the testator, or by reason of the devise or bequest being contrary to law or otherwise incapable of taking effect, shall be included in any residuary devise or bequest, as the case may be, contained in the will.' *Residue*

Section 98

'Where a person, being a child or other issue of the testator to whom any property is given (whether by a devise or bequest or by the exercise by will of any power of appointment and whether as a gift to that person as an individual or as a member of a class) for any estate or interest not determinable at or before the death of that person, dies in the lifetime of the testator leaving issue, and any such issue of that person is living at the time of the death of the testator, the gift shall not lapse, but shall take effect as if the death of that person had happened immediately after the death of the testator, unless a contrary intention appears from the will.' *child of T leaving issue — won't lapse.*

Section 47

'(1) Where a person dies possessed of, or entitled to, or under a general power of appointment, by his Will disposes of, an interest in property, which at the time of his death is charged with the payment of money, whether by way of a legal or equitable mortgage or charge or otherwise (including a lien for unpaid purchase money), and the deceased person has not by will, deed or other document signified a contrary or other intention, the interest so charged shall as between the different persons claiming through the deceased person, be primarily liable for the payment of the charge and every part of the said interest, according to its value, shall bear a proportionate part of the charge on the whole thereof. *debts owing (mortgage)*

(2) Such contrary or other intention shall not be deemed to be signified

　a) by a general direction for the payment of debts or of all the debts of the testator out of his estate or any part thereof, or

　b) by a charge of debts upon any such estate,

unless such intention is further signified by words expressly or by necessary implication referring to all or some part of the charge.'

2.7.2 BEST PRACTICE AND COMMON ERRORS

The possibility for errors here is high and the topic so broad that 'best practice and common errors' in relation to legacies will be dealt with in some detail. No testator instructs his solicitor that he wants to leave a general legacy, pecuniary legacy, demonstrative legacy, or specific legacy to a particular beneficiary. Yet, without using these terms, a testator frequently instructs his solicitor to create different types of legacies. Therefore, a practitioner needs to be familiar with the differences between different types of legacies and their respective effects. Further, these effects must be explained to the testator and understood by him, so that what he instructs his solicitor to do will be 'informed instructions' and have the legal and tax effect that he actually intends.

2.7.2.1 The importance of understanding the different types of bequests

One reason why the distinction is so important is that if there are insufficient assets in the estate to pay all the bequests in full, the different types of legacies abate in a particular order. See paras **4.5.5.2** and **12.4.2.2**.

Any assets arising in a partial intestacy are looked to first and then the residue is looked to, followed by general legacies (pro rata) and then specific legacies (also pro rata). A demonstrative legacy is treated as a general legacy for the purpose of abatement.

The end result is that a legacy can be made more secure for a beneficiary if it is left by way of specific bequest rather than by way of the residue. However, even doing so may not secure the bequest or the full value of the bequest for a beneficiary: see further para **2.7.2.2**.

Practitioners should be very careful when drafting the attachment of conditions to legacies, and this should be avoided if at all possible. It is an area that is fraught with difficulty and doubt. The distinction between a condition precedent and a condition subsequent is not always clear and it just leads to problems. Always be aware that a condition attached to a gift may be void as against public policy, and if this is the case the beneficiary simply takes the gift without the condition attaching. Further, the courts lean against conditional bequests and attempts to 'control beyond the grave' in general.

2.7.2.2 Substantial and numerous general legacies

Another potential problem area for legacies is when the testator is fixated on providing for numerous benefits by way of general legacies under the terms of a will. Take the (usually) unmarried old lady who very generously wishes to leave numerous pecuniary legacies to various beneficiaries and institutions. This may be termed the 'A to Z list of pecuniary legacies' because there are often twenty-six or more of them. See para **2.7.3.1**. Similarly, where the testator wishes to leave a long list of personal effects to various beneficiaries this can lead to difficulties.

Why this could be a problem

The value of the estate may have substantially decreased by the time of the testator's death (consider nursing home fees) and in that instance, there may not be sufficient assets to meet these legacies. The question of abatement will then apply and this can be tricky in practice, and indeed disappointing for beneficiaries, particularly if a charity or charities are involved. It also means that the preparation of the accounts can be a nightmare and the solicitor is not able to tell beneficiaries at the outset exactly what they can expect to receive. Indeed, it is always very dangerous to give a specific figure to a beneficiary in any case. It also means that solicitors have to be very careful at the outset in the administration and management of the assets. This should be clearly pointed out to testators. In order to explain clearly to testators the different types of legacies and then to take their informed instructions, the terms referring to different types of legacies need to be clearly understood.

2.7.2.3 Legacy and devise

A *legacy* is a bequest of personal property. Personal property is all property except real property which is unregistered land held in fee simple. All other property, including long leasehold interests and registered land, is considered personal property. See para **2.7.11** and s 92 of the Succession Act. A beneficiary inheriting personal property is referred to as a *legatee*.

A *devise* is a bequest of real property. A beneficiary inheriting real property is known as a *devisee*. Thus, if one is unsure of the status of a bequest it is the wiser practice to say in a will '*I give, devise and bequeath*'. This would arise, for example, where the testator owns their house but is unsure of the nature of the title.

Both legacies and devises can be specific or general. A specific legacy or devise is a bequest of a particular item. The item should be described as clearly as possible. A specific devise would be '*My house at 47 Blackhall Place to*'. When making a bequest of a house, the solicitor should always ask if it is intended that the contents of that house are to be included and the clause will say:

'*I give, devise and bequeath my house at 47 Blackhall Place together with the contents thereof to.*'

If a particular item of jewellery is being bequeathed, *'my engagement ring'*, for example, would be sufficient to describe the item, assuming the testatrix was engaged only once. A further example of a specific legacy would be where the testator wishes to leave his car to a beneficiary. Most people own one car, which they replace on a regular basis. In their case the following clause is sufficient:

> *'I give and bequeath whatever motor car I die possessed of to my nephew, Paul Murphy, son of my brother, Michael.'*

If the testator is a collector of veteran/vintage cars, each car will have to be identified separately, usually by brand, model, year, and registration number. Specific bequests run the risk of ademption see para **2.7.4**.

A general legacy is the gift of an item of personal property which is not specifically described, e.g. *'a piece of jewellery from my collection'*. Most general legacies take the form of a pecuniary legacy. This is a gift of cash from the estate, for example, *'the sum of Ten Thousand Euro (€10,000) to my nephew John Murphy, the son of my brother James Murphy'*. General legacies run the risk of abatement (see paras **2.7.5** and **12.4.2.2**).

2.7.2.4 A demonstrative legacy

This is a mixture of a specific and a general legacy, for example:

> *'I give to my god-child, Amy Smyth, €2,000 (Two Thousand Euro) out of my bank account with Bank of Ireland in Blackrock.'*

The advantage of this type of legacy over a specific legacy is that it is not adeemed if the funds in the bank account in Bank of Ireland in Blackrock (as per this example) are insufficient to meet the legacy. Should this arise, the demonstrative legacy is then treated as a general legacy and assumes all the characteristics of a general legacy. The disadvantage of this is that the legacy is now liable to abatement alongside all the other general legacies.

It is important not to confuse a demonstrative legacy with the following:

> *'I give to my god-child, Amy Smyth, my bank account with Bank of Ireland in Blackrock.'*

This is a specific legacy of the bank account, regardless of the amount contained in that account. If the bank account is closed prior to death, Amy gets nothing.

2.7.2.5 A conditional legacy

It is relatively uncommon, but by no means unknown, for a testator to wish to impose a condition on a bequest in his will where it is intended that non-compliance will bring about forfeiture.

Example: *'I leave my property at 1 Anglesea Road, to my son, Joseph, provided he gives to his sister, Anne, €100,000.00 (One Hundred Thousand Euro).'*

Such a condition, as given in the example, would be called a condition precedent, and in that case compliance with it is a precondition to the vesting of the gift to the devisee, in this example, Joseph. It is also possible that it may be a condition subsequent, which would govern the retention of the gift by the donee.

A question then arises as to what happens if the condition precedent is something which is:

(a) void as offensive to public policy;

(b) void on the ground of uncertainty;

(c) a devise of realty, which fails altogether.

Does the beneficiary take the bequest free of the condition?

This was decided in the case of *Re Elliott* [1952] Ch 217, where it was held that if the condition is void as involving *malum prohibitum* and not *malum in se* the beneficiary will take the bequest of personalty free of the condition. However, this differentiation is very esoteric and was criticised heavily by Dixon J in *Re Blake* [1955] IR 89, 100, and there is some question as to whether this is correct. Ronan Keane in *Equity and Trusts in the Republic of Ireland* (1988) at p 193 comes to the conclusion that in a question as to whether a condition is *malum prohibitum* or *malum in se* the bequest should be void.

In relation to whether a condition is certain enough and as to whether the condition has been fully performed, the courts have, in line with their preference for early vesting, adopted a very lenient approach. In essence, the donee need satisfy only a test of reasonable compliance and the courts are, as Lowry LCJ puts it in *Re Porter* [1975] NI 157, 161:

> *'willing to facilitate the taking of a gift by a person who comes within any reasonable meaning of the condition but unwilling to divest a vested interest unless the circumstances which could lead to divesting are clear.'*

This position needs to be differentiated from failure to comply with a condition subsequent (which results in divestiture). The courts in this type of situation have required that such conditions satisfy a higher test of certainty.

The approach of the courts to this is particularly well illustrated in the Northern Ireland case of *Re Johnson* [1986] NYIB 16.

In this case, the testator had bequeathed his house to his sister for life with remainder to his grandnephew, on condition that the grandnephew resided with the testator's sister until her death. If he did not do so, there was a gift over to certain charitable institutions. However, the testator's sister refused to have the nephew reside with her and therefore the nephew's performance of the condition was rendered impossible.

The court had to determine the nephew's entitlement to the gift or not, in the light of the facts of the case. While the obligation was considered correctly to be in the nature of a condition subsequent, the judge in this case, Carswell J, decided that the sister's refusal to allow the nephew to reside with her made the performance of the condition impossible in law.

It followed, therefore, that however hard it might be on the beneficiary, his honest efforts to comply with the condition could be frustrated at the will or even by the whim of the life tenant. It did not make that condition invalid for impossibility. Carswell J went on further and said:

> *'nor was it possible to exercise the jurisdiction of the court to grant relief against the breach of a condition where it was equitable to do so since such jurisdiction is not available when there is a gift over and failure to perform the condition.'*

However, clearly wishing to favour the nephew and avoid the patently inequitable result (in his view) that the nephew's interest was forfeit, Carswell J found that the condition was invalid as:

1. offending public policy (at the time of the testator's death the grandnephew was fifteen and the condition clearly envisaged that he ceased to reside with his own parents and would reside with the testator's sister); and
2. lacking the degree of certainty required of such a condition.

This illustrates the different views which the courts take to a condition precedent and a condition subsequent. It would be wise, therefore, for any solicitor taking instructions from a testator in relation to either a condition precedent or indeed a subsequent condition to make sure that it is:

1. not against public policy;
2. certain.

Thus, in broad terms, it would appear that a testator is reasonably free to attach conditions to any inheritance and, provided that such conditions are not impairing the constitutional rights of others, against public policy, or in some way inconsistent with general legal equitable principles, they can and will be enforced.

Thus, be very careful of, or avoid if at all possible, the attachment of conditions to legacies. It is an area that is fraught with difficulty and doubt. The distinction between a condition precedent and a condition subsequent is not always clear and it just leads to problems.

As stated above, always be aware that a condition attached to a gift may be void as against public policy, and if this is the case, the beneficiary just takes the gift without the condition attaching.

2.7.2.6 Charitable legacy

Where a charity is involved, it is important at the will-drafting stage to ensure that such charity is sufficiently identified. Problems can arise where a charity is carelessly or incorrectly described or, for instance, where a particular charity has ceased to exist or its functions have been taken over by a similar charity. Its correct name and address should be obtained so that the property passes to the intended beneficiary.

The Charities Regulation Authority (CRA) maintains a register of charities (https://charitiesregister.ie/) which can be searched by name, CHY number, or Charities Registration number. A search should identify the charity in question, which will then give details of the full name of the charity, its registered address, details of its activities, and the officers of the charity. In order to avoid possible difficulties post-death, it is advisable at the will-drafting stage to determine the appropriate person from whom the personal representative or the solicitor acting on his behalf should obtain a receipt.

Then, when drafting the will, the solicitor should insert in the will that the appropriate person (who would normally be the 'Secretary' or 'Treasurer' in a lay organisation, or, in the case of a religious organisation the 'Superior', and in the case of a trust corporation the 'Secretary') is the person authorised to give a sufficient discharge for the executors. Otherwise, problems can arise where the charity is incorrectly named or where a charity has ceased to exist, or where its functions have been taken over by a similar charity.

Examples of charitable bequests

1. To a lay charity:

    '*I bequeath to the Irish Red Cross, 16 Merrion Square, Dublin 2, recognised as a charity by the Irish Charity Commission, Registered Charity Number 2005184, CHY 3950, the sum of €1,000 (One Thousand Euro) ... for its general charitable purposes. The receipt of the appropriate officer of the said Society shall be sufficient receipt to my executors for payment of the said sum.*'

2. To a religious charity:

    '*I give and bequeath the sum of €500 (Five Hundred Euro) to the Parish Priest for the time being of Kilternan Parish, in the County of Wicklow for the upkeep of the church in Kilternan, but in the event that it shall not be practicable or possible to expend the legacy in this way, then the legacy shall be applied for general charitable purposes in the parish of Kilternan, in such manner that the Parish Priest for the time being of Kilternan Parish may in his absolute discretion see fit. The receipt from the Parish Priest for the time being of Kilternan Parish shall be sufficient receipt to my executors for payment of the said sum.*'

3. For the saying of Masses, see the precedent will at para **2.17**. Strictly speaking this is not a charitable bequest but it is nevertheless treated as one and listed on the Charitable Bequest Form. See para **7.4.14.2**.

4. For preservation of the bequest other than by use of the *cy près* doctrine, a clause similar to the 'reconstruction and amalgamation clause' in relation to shares (see para **2.7.4.1**) may be used with the testator's consent:

    '*Any Institution, Society or Body of Persons (Incorporated or Unincorporated) which is intended to benefit by any Will made by me herein or in any Codicil hereto (and which is referred to hereby or by such Codicil as a Charity or Charitable) shall be found never to have existed or to have existed or exit or to have been amalgamated with another Institution, Society or Body of Persons or Changed his name or constitution before my death, the benefit intended to be given under such Will shall be paid, transferred or applied to such Charitable Institutions, Societies or Bodies of Persons established in Ireland for such Charitable purposes in Ireland and if more than one in such shares as my Trustees in their absolute discretion think fit and I express the wish without imposing any trust or obligation that in carrying out the foregoing trust, my trustees shall seek to benefit a Charity or Charities as close as possible in purpose to those of the Institution, Society or Body of Persons intended to be benefited by my said original gift.'*

Cy près doctrine

The general principle is that a charitable bequest will not fail for uncertainty. As far back as 1961, Section 47 of the Charities Act, 1961 provided a list of circumstances in which a *cy près* application of funds may be made without having to make an application to the High Court. These have been further extended by s 4 of the Charities Act, 1973 and by the Land and Conveyancing Law Reform Act, 2009. Initially, the maximum level of funds which could avail of *cy près* application was set at £25,000. This has been increased over the years and finally, since the coming into force of the Social Welfare (Miscellaneous Provisions) Act, 2002, there has been no monetary limit on a scheme to apply the inheritance property *cy près*. However, it is a necessary prerequisite that the gift be a charitable one before the *cy près* jurisdiction can be invoked. *Cy près* is dealt with in detail in the Trusts Lecture Notes (see Preface) at para **1.2.5**.

An example of the utility of the *cy près* doctrine is the will of Ms Elizabeth Burke, which left €500,000 to the Limerick Branch of the Royal Society for the Prevention of Cruelty to Animals (RSPCA), which no longer operates in Ireland. The solicitor acting in the administration of the estate referred the matter to the Commissioners for Charitable Donations and Bequests under s 21 of the Charities Act (as amended).

The Commissioners were advised that there were two animal welfare organisations in the Limerick area, Limerick Animal Welfare (LAW) and Limerick Society for the Prevention of Cruelty to Animals (LSPCA) and decided that the money should be divided equally between the two charities.

Tax and charities

A charity is exempt from *capital acquisitions tax* by virtue of s 76 of the Capital Acquisitions Tax Consolidation Act, 2003 (formerly s 54 of the Capital Acquisitions Tax Act, 1976, as amended), which provides in s 76(2) as follows:

'A gift or an inheritance which is taken for public or charitable purposes is exempt from tax and is not taken into account in computing tax, to the extent that the Commissioners are satisfied that it has been, or will be, applied to purposes which, in accordance with the Law of the State, are public or charitable.'

For further detail on charities, charitable bequests, and qualifying as a charity, see Chapter 1 of the Trusts Lecture Notes (see Preface) and para **7.4.14** of this book.

2.7.3 THE DOCTRINE OF LAPSE

It is established that, where a beneficiary predeceases a testator, the legacy left to him under the testator's will fails. This is known as the doctrine of *lapse* and its effect must be understood and explained to the testator to ensure his wishes are carried out.

Section 91 of the Succession Act, 1965 directs that if a legacy fails because the legatee did not survive the testator or the benefit was otherwise incapable of taking effect, the property which was the subject-matter of the gift will fall into the residuary estate.

If the residuary estate has not been disposed of by will, then the property will be distributed according to the rules of intestacy. This emphasises once again the absolute necessity of the solicitor inserting a residuary clause in each and every will drafted.

Essentially, a bequest lapses where a beneficiary predeceases the testator.

BASIC ELEMENTS OF A WILL AND MUTUAL WILLS 25

There are a number of exceptions to this doctrine:

1. Section 98, which can 'save' a bequest from lapsing, deals with bequests to issue and will be dealt with in detail later. See para **9.8**. Solicitors should take particular care when dealing with bequests to children or other issue as there have been a number of cases involving negligence actions against solicitors on the basis of their misinterpretation of s 98.

2. Where there is a bequest in discharge of a legal or moral obligation—if the beneficiary predeceases, such bequest will then be payable to the estate of such beneficiary. Always seek to identify any such bequest.

3. Where there is a bequest to an individual on trust for another—in that instance the real beneficiary is not the trustee so appointed and the bequest will not lapse. This would also apply to a secret trust. This would not be very common but remains an area of risk.

4. Where a will provides for what will happen in the event of a beneficiary predeceasing—this is often referred to as a 'gift over' clause and may be used to override the provisions of s 98. This is a matter that should be thought out and provided for at the will-drafting stage with the testator and there should be full discussion as to what would happen in the event of a beneficiary predeceasing. Solicitors should, where possible, provide for a gift over. This is vital in the case of a universal or residuary legatee or devisee. The failure to provide for a gift over of the residue can result in the estate being distributed on a partial intestacy.

2.7.3.1 Framing bequests to a number of people

Solicitors should take great care in the wording of bequests to a number of people. In this regard, care must be taken in the way a bequest is framed, and the use of a 'handy' precedent is to be discouraged. Unfortunately, precedents are often not fully understood and are incorrectly applied, with the result that what the testator intended does not actually occur. Precedents that can be of great assistance, and which we all use, are to be used with knowledge, remembering the comment from Werner J (*In the matter of King* 200 NY 189, 192 (1910)) that has been so often quoted, that 'no will has a twin brother'.

If a precedent is being used, then the precedent must be fully understood and correctly adapted to the needs of each individual case. For example, a bequest to a number of people jointly (i.e. the creation of a joint tenancy) will accrue to the survivor or survivors of the beneficiaries. If a bequest is drafted without defining the terms of the bequest, for example '*to my children*', a *joint tenancy* is created.

On the other hand, a gift to a number of beneficiaries, for example, 'in equal shares' or 'between' a number of individuals (or any other words which could be construed as words of division or severance which define the terms of the bequest), will confer a specified share to each individual beneficiary. This is known as a *tenancy in common*. This type of benefit may lapse in the event of the beneficiary predeceasing the testator. Where this type of bequest is given as part of the residue of the estate and a beneficiary predeceases the testator, a partial intestacy of the testator's estate comprising the specific share of the residue due to the predeceased beneficiary may occur unless s 98 of the Act applies: see para **2.9.2.1**.

The testator's specific instructions should be sought on the type of tenancy he wishes to create. Failure to obtain definitive informed instructions at the drafting stage can lead to the testator's intentions being frustrated.

2.7.3.2 The inter-effect of s 91 and s 98 and bequests to several beneficiaries

The operation of s 98 is overridden by:

1. the bequest being left to one or more beneficiaries as joint tenants; or

2. the testator inserting a substitutionary or 'gift over' clause which is to take effect in such circumstances; or

3. the testator leaving a life interest to the beneficiary as s 98 only arises where the benefit passing is not a benefit ceasing on death.

In short: Section 91 - V - Section 98 ....Section 98 prevails
Section 98 - V - Tenancy in Common ....Section 98 prevails
Section 98 - V - Life Interest Life .... Interest prevails
Section 98 - V - Joint Tenancy ....Joint Tenancy prevails

2.7.4 ADEMPTION

Ademption occurs where the subject-matter of a specific devise or bequest is disposed of by the testator during his lifetime or ceases to exist during the testator's lifetime and so the devise or the bequest cannot be fulfilled. For example, if a testator leaves his house at 47 Blackhall Place to his daughter in his will and subsequently sells 47 Blackhall Place and buys 24 Whitehall Avenue without changing the terms of his will, his daughter does not inherit 24 Whitehall Avenue. She gets nothing and 24 Whitehall Avenue forms part of the residue of his estate.

A further example would be, where for instance, a testator bequeaths a specific holding of shares to his son and disposes of such shares during his lifetime: then the legacy is adeemed.

2.7.4.1 Shares and the further possibility of ademption

As a general rule, a gift of shares in a limited company should be avoided, as ademption may take place. With shares, the ademption may be as simple as the company being taken over by or amalgamating with another company or the assets of the company being purchased by another company, payment to take the form of shares in that company. However, if a gift of shares must be provided for, then the following precedent as an example of a specific gift of shares with provision for substitution in the event of amalgamation can be useful:

> 'I give to   of   for his or her own benefit absolutely all my [define type of share if necessary—i.e. ordinary/preference/voting/non-voting, etc.] shares in   Ltd. having its registered office at   now standing in my name and declare that if at my death those shares shall by virtue of any amalgamation, reconstruction or rearrangement of the capital of the company or sale of the company's business be represented by a different capital holding whether in the same company or in any other company to which at my death I am entitled then this gift shall take effect as if it has been a gift of the capital holding or capital holdings resulting from such amalgamation, reconstruction or re-arrangement of capital or sale.'

2.7.4.2 Equitable doctrine of ademption

Note also that there is an equitable doctrine of ademption, which is not the same thing. This occurs where a bequest or devise is followed by a subsequent gift to the same person and then the bequest or devise provided for in the said will is said to be adeemed. For example, in the case of *Griffith v Burke* [1887] 21 LRIR 92 the legacy to a parish priest for the erection of a new church at Claremorris was held to be adeemed by a subsequent gift for the same purpose to the Archbishop of Tuam.

2.7.5 ABATEMENT

Abatement arises where there are insufficient funds to pay bequests (usually pecuniary legacies) in full.

Pecuniary legacies are paid out of the residue (unless a contrary instruction is given in the will). Where the residue is insufficient to pay the debts and liabilities, pecuniary legacies will be the first to abate. For example, pecuniary legacies amounting to €10,000 are bequeathed but the amount available after payment of debts and liabilities to pay pecuniary legacies is €8,000. Each pecuniary legatee will receive 80 per cent of his legacy, i.e. each bequest to each pecuniary legatee is proportionately reduced. See para **12.4.2.3**.

Where an estate is solvent, but there are insufficient assets in the residue to pay all the debts and funeral and testamentary expenses, then the general and pecuniary legacies and devises abate pro rata and then specific legacies and devises (also pro rata). A demonstrative legacy is treated as a general legacy for the purpose of abatement. See para **12.4.2.3**.

The end result is that a legacy can be made more secure for a beneficiary if it is left by way of specific bequest rather than by way of the residue. However, even doing so may not secure the bequest or the full value of the bequest for a beneficiary.

The rules for abatement are set out at para **12.4.2.3**.

2.7.5.1 Application of assets

There are strict rules governing the order of application of assets to discharge debts. These rules are set out at s 46 and Part II of the First Schedule to the Succession Act, 1965, which can be found at para **12.4.2.2**.

2.7.6 SECTION 47: PROPERTY SUBJECT TO A CHARGE

Another common issue that arises is where the subject-matter of a devise or bequest is charged with the payment of money, whether by way of legal or equitable mortgage or charge or otherwise. Normally, people think of this arising in the case of real or immovable property, but a car, for example, could be subject to a charge.

Unless a will otherwise directs, if a property is subject to a mortgage or charge and the property is specifically devised or bequeathed, the beneficiary takes it with and subject to the mortgage. This may be academic in certain instances where there is a mortgage protection policy in place covering the charge, but practitioners should be absolutely clear that any such mortgage or charge is not automatically paid out of the residue of the estate. There are also the practical difficulties that can arise where a mortgage and/or a mortgage protection policy was not being paid in the period immediately prior to death and the policy lapses.

This is increasingly not an academic point, due to the 'Fair Deal' legislation, i.e. the Nursing Homes Support Scheme Act, 2009, which brings its own issues. See para **6.9.6.6**.

Simplistically, the scheme looks at both the income and assets of an individual. Individuals are required to contribute 80 per cent of their assessable income and 7.5 per cent (5 per cent for applications prior to 25 July 2013) of the value of any assets per annum except for the first €36,000 of assets for an individual or €72,000 of assets for a couple. Where assets include land and property, in recognition of the fact that it may be difficult to raise 7.5 per cent of the value of them annually (other than in respect of the principal private residence or under certain limited circumstances the individual's farm or business where the contribution is capped at three years or 22.5 per cent in total), this 7.5 per cent annual contribution in respect of the property (provided the property is situate in the State) can be deferred and collected later by the State from the estate of the person needing care after they die.

It is this deferral which is termed ancillary state support and is the subject of the charge in favour of the State which could be caught under s 47 of the Succession Act. Depending on how long the person is in receipt of nursing home care, the amount charged may mount considerably.

In the ordinary course of making a will, solicitors would take instructions from the testator as to whether there are any loans secured on any part of his property and, if there are, then take further instructions from him as to whether s 47 should apply to that loan or not.

If the charge for ancillary state support is created by the testator himself, he may be aware of the consequences of it and be further aware that he should perhaps adapt his will accordingly.

To properly advise testators, therefore, of the implications of s 47 of the Succession Act, the provisions of the ancillary state support section of the Act should be gone through with

28 BASIC ELEMENTS OF A WILL AND MUTUAL WILLS

them in detail even if they are not at the time in receipt of nursing home care, and in circumstances where it may be important to them that certain properties are taken by certain beneficiaries free of any charge, then a specific direction will need to be included in the will to provide that any such charge on any one or other particular property should be repaid not out of the property against which the charge is registered but, for example, in accordance with the rules as to application of assets contained in the First Schedule to the Succession Act.

A general direction to the executors to pay *'all of my debts'* or even a direction to pay *'all of my debts from the residue of the estate'* is not enough. The will (or other written direction to the executors as per s 47) needs to be very specific and clear.

2.7.7 IDENTIFY THE BENEFICIARY

A common mistake, which can arise from carelessness or the lack of full instructions, arises where the will (as a result of bad drafting by the solicitor) fails adequately to identify the beneficiary. It is not usually the testator's fault: he is relying on his solicitor.

2.7.7.1 Identify the beneficiary

As stated earlier, the identity of the beneficiary must be absolutely clear. The first step in achieving this is to take full and precise instructions. The names and current addresses of the beneficiary and the relationship to the testator must be stated correctly. However, in some cases this will not be precise enough.

It is entirely plausible for a testator to have two relatives of the same name, living at the same address (e.g. a son and grandson of the same name living in the same house). When identifying a nephew or niece care must be taken; for example, *'my niece Mary Jones, daughter of my sister Lynne Jones, formerly Lynne Murphy'*.

O'Connell v Bank of Ireland [1998] 2 ILRM 465 (Circuit Court, which was appealed to the High Court) is a perfect example of this type of error; here the testatrix left her estate to her grandsons Michael O'Connell and John O'Connell, which was fine, except that she had two grandsons of each name.

Clearly and correctly stating the full name and present address and the relationship to the deceased will avoid, for example, the situation in a recent settled case where, due to bad drafting, it was not clear whether the deceased's sister or niece should inherit a large portion of the estate. In this case the bequest of *'all the rest residue of my estate to my niece A O'S'* of a certain address raised an issue in that there was no niece at that address. There was an A O'S, a niece, at a different address but unfortunately there was also a sister, A O'S, who did live at the address as stated in the will. The resulting litigation could have been avoided if the name and address of the beneficiary and the relationship to the deceased tallied.

2.7.8 IDENTIFY THE PROPERTY THAT IS THE SUBJECT OF THE BEQUEST

Another common mistake arises where the will (as a result of bad drafting by the solicitor) fails adequately to identify the property which is the subject-matter of the bequest.

2.7.8.1 Identify the property

When land is being bequeathed, it is prudent first to check the title deeds. It is not at all uncommon to discover that the property is not in the testator's name or not in his sole name. If the land is registered in the Land Registry it should be easily identifiable; however, the solicitor should check with the testator that the land in the folio is in fact the land intended to be bequeathed and that all the lands have been accounted for. The title and the map must be examined carefully, and if necessary updated.

The recent case of *Shannon v Shannon* [2019] IEHC 400 is instructive. The deceased testator owned two folios that were contiguous to each other and in his will left 'his farm of lands at [ ] with stock and contents and farm entitlements' to one beneficiary and 'All the rest, residue and remainder of my property, both real and personal, and wheresoever situate' to another. The question that arose was whether both folios were to go to the beneficiary inheriting the farm or whether one folio went to that beneficiary and the other folio formed part of the residue. The court decided that no ambiguity arose and that both folios were to go to the beneficiary inheriting the 'farm of lands' even though the evidence of the solicitor who drafted the will was that he did not believe that the deceased intended to devise and bequeath what he describes as both of his dwellinghouses and both of his farms to the beneficiary inheriting the farm.

If the testator owns registered land, and if there is any intention to give separate folios to separate beneficiaries, identify the folios, the land involved, and if necessary prepare maps to avoid any potential ambiguity. If the testator wishes to leave only part of the registered land to a particular beneficiary then that part must be delineated very carefully, preferably by an accurate map drawn up by a suitably qualified engineer or surveyor. Bear in mind, however, that reference to a map can create problems when extracting a grant. However, if reference to a map or, indeed a list, is the only way of precisely identifying the bequest then potential post-death issues should not prevent them being used. Be sure, however, that the map or list is not drawn up after the will is executed but is in existence prior to the execution of the will and attached to the will itself. Ideally, the list or map should be referred to in the attestation clause, as this will assist when extracting the grant. See para **2.14**, which deals with the attestation clause. In the case of a list, it would be the better practice, if somewhat tedious, not to attach a list to the will but to insert it in the body of the will itself.

If the land is registered in the Registry of Deeds and the entire holding of the testator is being bequeathed there should be little problem, but once again the title should be checked.

Whether or not the land being bequeathed is registered in the Land Registry or Registry of Deeds or includes the entirety of the testator's holding or part of it, it must be identified in a fool-proof manner. Practitioners are all familiar with the testator who wishes to leave his *'land at the right of the crossroads'* or the *'field behind Dr Stephenson's house'*. To use these terms is not precise enough.

There is a procedure post-death if the beneficiary or the bequest is not clearly identifiable and/or there are two or more beneficiaries claiming the same bequest. This confusion can be clarified by applying *'what the testator meant'*. Leaving aside, for a moment, the problem that each arguing beneficiary will be quite sure they know what the testator meant, extrinsic evidence may be brought to bear on the will under the terms of s 90 of the Succession Act where there is a contradiction on the face of the will itself via a s 90 application. See *James Mullen Junior v James Mullen* [2014] IEHC 407, where Cregan J gave a very good review of the Rules of Construction.

2.7.8.2 Bequests of farmland and ancillary assets

Despite the radical changes in Irish life in the past forty years, a large proportion of the population still owns farmland and there are few solicitors who never encounter a client who is a farmer or who owns farmland who wishes to make a will. Therefore, practitioners must be able to consider the appropriate clauses for the bequeathing of farm assets and a specific section on this type of bequest is appropriate.

Of course, any solicitor, when taking instructions from a testator farmer or a testator who is bequeathing farmland or utilising s 89(3) of the CAT Consolidation Act, 2003, should advise in detail on agricultural relief for CAT purposes and inform the testator what steps any prospective beneficiary should or should not take to put or keep himself in a position to obtain same, in particular following the changes made by the Finance Act, 2015 to Agricultural Relief. See Revenue eBrief No 68/15 for details. See Chapter 8 of the CAT Lecture Notes (see Preface).

30 BASIC ELEMENTS OF A WILL AND MUTUAL WILLS

In particular, when taking instructions relating to bequests of farmland the following should always be considered:

1. Bequeathing livestock, bloodstock, plant, and machinery.

2. Bequeathing cash as a conditional bequest under s 89(3) of the CAT Consolidation Act, 2003.

2.7.8.3 Direct Payment Scheme (formerly Single Farm Payment Scheme)

Note that there is an Inheritance Enquiry Unit to assist the legal personal representative/s of a deceased and it also assists solicitors. The unit acts as a single repository for all legal documentation submitted by the legal personal representative (and solicitors) of the deceased, which is very helpful as it removes the necessity of forwarding duplicate copies to several sections of the Department. It also assists by:

1. identifying those schemes (which change name/value and alienability every few years) in which the deceased person participated and establishing whether there are any outstanding payments of any type due to the estate of the deceased;

2. helping the legal personal representative contacting various sections of the Department and advising on which legal documents are required.

Further details in relation to the unit can be obtained either by post at the Department of Agriculture, Fisheries and Food, Eircom Building, Knockmay Road, Portlaoise or by phone at 1890 200 560, or by email at: inheritance@agriculture.gov.ie. See also, SI 639/2017, 'Drafting Wills and EU Entitlements' which confirms at s 4 of same that where the will is silent, entitlements transfer with the land.

2.7.8.4 Bequests of livestock, bloodstock, plant, and machinery

It is unfortunately very common to come across wills where the testator leaves the farm to a beneficiary intending that the livestock, bloodstock, plant, and machinery relating to same should pass to the same beneficiary. However, that is not what it says in the will, which in most cases simply bequeaths the land.

In many circumstances, where the family is reasonable (but the residue does not always go to family), the will is 'ignored' and the beneficiary receives the farmland together with livestock, bloodstock, plant, and machinery. However, one cannot depend on this happening and even when it does, it has unwelcome taxation considerations. It has arisen that the farm went to one beneficiary where it was intended that everything on it should also pass to that beneficiary and the farmland, bloodstock, plant, and machinery passed via the residue to another beneficiary.

This could be a costly mistake for the solicitor involved, especially if the residuary beneficiary declined to surrender same to the 'intended beneficiary' without a substantial payment. Therefore, make sure to take the client's instructions and, assuming he intends the same beneficiary to take both the land and the livestock, bloodstock, and farm machinery, word the bequest accordingly.

2.7.8.5 Proprietary estoppel and farmland

It is clear that proprietary estoppel applies not only to farmland but to any asset, but the principle is raised in relation to farmland in particular as while estoppel can occur in relation to businesses, property, or other types of assets, it most often occurs in relation to farms, and certainly most of the case law arising in this area concerns agricultural land.

It is important therefore to ask the testator, when taking instructions for the will, whether there is any possibility that he is or may be perceived to be bound to leave certain assets to certain beneficiaries. It would be prudent, if there is any possibility of this perception arising where the testator is not leaving the asset to the person who may raise such a claim, to take a full affidavit from the testator.

The leading Irish case on this subject is *Smith v Halpin* (1997) 2 ILRM 38 and there is also the High Court decision in *Naylor v Maher* [2012] IEHC 408, where the plaintiff, William

Naylor, succeeded in establishing a legal entitlement to a substantial farm. The more recent, in legal terms at least, case of *Coyle v Finnegan and Finnegan* [2013] IEHC 463 reaffirms that a detriment for the purposes of proprietary estoppel need not take the form of monetary expenditure on the land. See also *Cavey v Cavey* [2014] IESC 16, where the Supreme Court, as well as dealing with estoppel per se, dealt with the time limits within which proceedings must issue in such cases. The Supreme Court confirmed that a claim for proprietary estoppel must be brought within the relevant period or within two years of the date of death of the deceased, whichever expires first. This case also highlighted the need for solicitors to consider and discuss with the client all issues of the matter, not just the ones raised by the client, and indeed the absolute need for contemporaneous notes of instructions taken and advices given. See para **5.8**. See also, *In the Matter of the Estate of K. Deceased* [2013] No. 7394.

2.7.9 JOINT ACCOUNTS

It is very important at this stage to identify any joint accounts held by the testator with any other person or persons. Where there is a joint current account between spouses/civil partners and both parties contribute to this account and household bills are paid out of it, ownership of this joint current account should not be controversial. In every other case, full enquiries should be made as to the testator's intention when opening such a joint account, particularly a joint deposit account where the sums were provided by the testator.

Having done this, the solicitor, with the client's written authority, should write to the bank looking for copies of all mandate forms to ensure that the record held by the bank is in accordance with the stated intention of the testator.

In the absence of any written record being available from the financial institution, it is imperative to ensure that the client's intention is recorded in the attendance and, if necessary, in the will. Practitioners are aware of the English case of *Carr-Glynn v Frearsons* [1998] 4 All ER 225. In that case, the solicitor did not ascertain whether a property held with the testatrix's nephew was held in common or on a joint tenancy. The solicitor's failure to do so was held to result in a cash loss to a beneficiary.

Such a record and/or clause should confirm whether the joint deposit account is to go to the survivor or the estate. A clause to this effect could be as follows:

> *'I confirm that the proceeds of my Joint Bank Account with my nephew AB (son of my brother BB) held in XYZ Bank, Account No: 1234567 are*
>
> *[either] to pass to my nephew AB by survivorship for his own use and benefit absolutely*
>
> *[or] to form part of the residue of my estate [or otherwise as per the testator's instructions] as a joint account created and administered for my sole convenience of which I have been at all times the sole beneficial owner.'*

Particular care should be taken where the client's instructions are that he set up a joint account for his convenience (lodging pension, paying bills, buying groceries, etc) with a person in relation to whom there would be a presumption of advancement (apart from a spouse or civil partner, as outlined earlier). In this case, a written authority from the client confirming his instructions should be forwarded to the bank at the time of making the will. This should contain a specific instruction to the bank not to pay out to the surviving joint account holder on the death of the client. It should be pointed out to the client that if he fails to instruct the solicitor to do so, the account may be dissipated in the period after the death and prior to the will being read.

2.7.10 LISTS

As discussed earlier, the general rule is that any item not specifically disposed of by will falls into the residue of the estate. If a testator provides for a specific bequest of items by way of reference to a list, the list must be in existence at the date that the will is executed, and further, that list must be admitted to the Probate Office and will form part of the will.

32 BASIC ELEMENTS OF A WILL AND MUTUAL WILLS

It is not possible for such a list to be drawn up after the will is executed. This type of practice is not to be recommended and, although it may seem tedious, if a testator wishes specific items to be disposed of, these should be set out under the terms of the will.

The attestation clause should be amended accordingly, for example:

'SIGNED and acknowledged by the above-named Testatrix as and for her last Will and Testament in the presence of us both present at the same time who in her presence at her request and in the presence of each other have hereunto subscribed our names as witnesses this Will having been printed on the front side only of the foregoing x sheets of A4 paper incorporating 3 maps attached thereto marked as referred to above and the incorporated maps were signed by the above-named Testatrix prior to the execution of the will in the presence of us both present at the same time who in her presence at her request and in the presence of each other have hereunto subscribed our names as witnesses.'

2.7.11 DISTINCTION BETWEEN FREEHOLD AND LEASEHOLD INTERESTS IN LAND

Problems can be encountered when the distinction between freehold and leasehold interests is not fully appreciated. Section 14 provides that, for the purpose of the Succession Act, 1965, the estate of the deceased person shall, unless a contrary intention appears, include references to both his real and personal estate. Since the Succession Act, the gift of a testator's whole estate includes both his real and personal property unless a contrary intention appears.

By s 92 a general devise of land will be construed to include leasehold interests, again unless a contrary intention appears in the will. In the event, therefore, of a testator wishing to make a gift of his personal estate and wishing to include his leasehold interest in this (not very usual, but possible), this should be specified in the will. Otherwise, any gift of real estate will be taken to include a leasehold interest.

2.7.12 SUMMARY OF THE DISTINCTION BETWEEN DIFFERENT TYPES OF LEGACIES

It is clear, therefore, that great care must be taken to be fully au fait with the differences between different types of legacies and their effects. This must be explained to the testator and understood by him.

A *general* legacy normally takes the form of a pecuniary legacy payable out of the general estate or the gift of an item of personal property which is not further specified.

A *specific* legacy is a legacy of a specific item. The subject-matter of the specific legacy should be described as clearly as possible.

A *demonstrative* legacy is where there is a fund designated for the payment of the legacy concerned, for example '*€5,000 (Five Thousand Euro) from my savings account with TSB*'. This type of legacy is a hybrid of a general and a specific legacy.

The reason why the distinction is so important is that if there are insufficient assets in the estate to pay the debts, the different types of legacies abate in a particular order. The residue is looked to firstly, then general legacies (pro rata), and then specific legacies (also pro rata). A demonstrative legacy is treated as a general legacy for the purpose of abatement. The end result is that a legacy can be made more secure for a beneficiary if it is left by way of specific bequest rather than by way of residue. What are the testator's instructions on this?

2.8 The Establishment of a Trust (If Required)

The creation of a will trust is dealt with in Chapters 1 and 2 of the Trusts Lecture Notes (see Preface). At this stage, suffice to say that it is just one further element in the drafting of the will.

2.9 Residue

2.9.1 APPLICABLE LEGISLATION

Section 91 of the Succession Act, 1965

> *'Unless a contrary intention appears from the will any estate comprised or intended to be comprised in any devise or bequest contained in the will which fails or is void by reason of the fact that the devisee or legatee did not survive the testator or by reason of the devise or bequest being contrary to law or otherwise incapable of taking effect, shall be included in any residuary devise or bequest, as the case may be, contained in the Will.'*

2.9.2 BEST PRACTICE AND COMMON ERRORS

Understanding the distinction between 'universal' and 'residuary' legatee and devisee and indeed 'legatee' and 'devisee' is important before drafting any residue clause.

Residuary beneficiaries are dealt with at para **2.9**. Briefly, a residuary beneficiary (usually referred to in the will as a 'residuary legatee and devisee') inherits the residue of the estate after other bequests as outlined earlier have been made.

A universal beneficiary (usually referred to in the will as a 'universal legatee and devisee') inherits the entirety of the estate. An example of a clause appointing a spouse as a universal legatee and devisee can be found in the precedent will at para **2.17**. In that example, it is a conditional appointment, subject to the spouse surviving for thirty days. When dealing with grants of administration with will annexed (see **Chapter 9**), all references to a residuary legatee and devisee also apply to a universal legatee and devisee.

A residuary legatee receives the personal estate and a residuary devisee the real estate.

If either are not appointed then the personal or real estate, as the case may be, passes on intestacy (see paras **9.3.1**, **9.3.1.2**, and **9.3.1.3**); this may also affect the Title in the Oath: see para **9.3.1**. Given the effect of s 91 (note that this is overridden by s 98 if applicable or a joint tenancy) it is alarming how often a residuary clause is omitted through inadvertence.

It is important to appreciate that the residue will catch all the estate not otherwise specifically disposed of by will or codicil and is a vital part of every will. The law always presumes a residue, and even if the testator has given away every cent in a will, the will speaks from the date of death and will catch all assets in the deceased's estate not specifically bequeathed.

2.9.2.1 Lapse, residue, and section 98

If a residuary benefit lapses it will go on intestacy unless it has otherwise been specifically provided for under the terms of the will. See para **2.7.3** on the doctrine of lapse under the heading of legacies, which equally applies to the residue. This should always be caught at the will-drafting stage.

The residuary clause should be kept simple and straightforward. There is no need for complicated residuary provisions where a simple solution will suffice. If it is a straightforward situation where, for example, a number of children who are of full age are expected to benefit under the terms of the residue, there is no need to go into a complicated trust scenario unless the taxation position otherwise directs.

Do not forget the application of s 98. Remember that if s 98 is not to apply, then this must be dealt with and proper trust arrangements for children of any predeceased child made, particularly where they may be minors. This is a case where a simple trust is commonly used, i.e. where there is a chance that any children of a child of a testator may benefit. It is unwise to leave open the possibility that minors may benefit without having simple trust provisions and powers.

34 BASIC ELEMENTS OF A WILL AND MUTUAL WILLS

2.9.2.2 Section 5 of the Succession Act, 1965 and 'simultaneous' deaths

See para **8.7**.

With some exceptions, e.g. s 98, a beneficiary's entitlement to a gift under a will depends on his surviving the testator, and if he predeceases the testator the gift will lapse. Thus, there is a particular difficulty that arises when a testator and a beneficiary die in circumstances, for example, a car crash or an airline disaster, in which it is not clear who died first.

Section 5 of the Succession Act, 1965, as amended, provides that where, after the commencement of the Act, two or more persons have died in circumstances rendering it uncertain which of them survived the other or others, then for the purposes of the distribution of the estate of any of them, they should be deemed to have died simultaneously.

Where joint tenants die in circumstances in which it is unclear which died first, the effect of s 5 of the Succession Act is that the property held jointly is deemed to have been held as tenants in common in equal shares and will pass to their respective estates.

Therefore, in the case of testators who benefit each other by their wills and who die simultaneously in circumstances which make it uncertain which of the two is the survivor, by being presumed to have died simultaneously, the gifts to each other in their wills will lapse. If both make each other in their wills universal legatees and devisees, then an intestacy will ensue and their estates will be distributed accordingly. For this reason, spouses often include a '*commorientes* clause' when making similar wills.

Lapse and spouses—commorientes clauses

It is quite common for husbands and wives, when leaving all of their property to each other, to insert a *commorientes* clause. This provides for the eventuality of both spouses dying at the same time or within a very short time of the other and for an alternative distribution of estates, often in trust for the children of the married couple.

Take, for example, the situation of a childless husband and wife who are involved in a common accident. If the husband dies immediately, having by his will left all his property to his wife, and his wife then subsequently dies a couple of days later, it is possible that the testator's estate will be distributed under the terms of his wife's will to his in-laws. This may not be what the testator would have anticipated or wanted.

In order to cover the situation of simultaneous or 'near in time' deaths of spouses and in order to avoid any ambiguity, it is usual for a *commorientes* clause to be inserted in the will of married persons. The usual procedure is for a testator to leave all his property to his spouse on the condition that she survives the testator for a stated period (usually thirty days).

If the surviving spouse survives the testator by the stated period, the benefit will vest in the surviving spouse.

If the surviving spouse does not survive the testator by that period, alternative provisions can be made under the testator's will.

For an example of a *commorientes* clause, see the precedent will at para **2.17**.

2.9.2.3 Words of severance

The drafting of a residuary clause requires the consideration of the appropriate words of severance. Words of severance have been dealt with at para **2.7.3.1** but such words are especially important at the residue stage and need to be considered again here.

If a residuary benefit is left to a number of people jointly, then in the event of the death of any one of those persons before the testator the survivors will receive the entire benefit between them. If, however, words of severance such as 'in equal shares' or 'between' are used, this can result in a partial intestacy should any one of the beneficiaries predecease the testator without a suitable 'gift over' clause or alternative provision, or where s 98 does not apply.

2.9.2.4 Precedent clauses

A sample of a residuary clause where there is an absolute bequest to the children of the testator with alternative provision to the spouse of the child who predeceases the testator, and, in the event that the child dies without a spouse, to the children of that child of the testator, would be as follows, as per Spierin, *Wills—Irish Precedents and Drafting*, 3rd edn (2020):

> 'I GIVE DEVISE AND BEQUEATH all the rest, residue and remainder of my estate of every nature and description and kind, wheresoever situate, to my children in equal shares.
>
> In the event that any child predeceases me leaving a spouse, then I DIRECT that the share of that child shall pass to his/her spouse.
>
> In the event that any of my children predecease me without leaving a spouse (or leaving a spouse from whom he/she is judicially separated by agreement, or who is in desertion of him/her at the date of my death, however long that desertion may have been at the date of my death, or who would be otherwise unworthy to succeed to the estate of my child by virtue of the provisions of Section 120 of the Succession Act 1965), but leaving children, then I give the share of that child to his/her children and if more than one, in equal shares.
>
> And in the event that any of my children dies leaving no spouse (or leaving a spouse from whom he/she is judicially separated by agreement, or who is in desertion of him/her at the date of my death, however long that desertion may have been at the date of my death, or who would be otherwise unworthy to succeed to the estate of my child by virtue of the provisions of Section 120 of the Succession Act 1965), and no children, then the share of that child shall pass to my children living at my death in equal shares.'

It is important to remember that this example refers to this specific instruction only. It often arises that the testator wishes the property to be held in trust for grandchildren and not to go to a spouse of a predeceased child. In each case, specific informed instructions must be taken, and the will must be drafted exactly in accordance with these instructions.

2.10 Enabling Clauses: Advancement, Appropriation, Apportionment, Charging Clause for Executors/Trustees

There are a number of miscellaneous matters that should be addressed in every will. The following is a brief summary of these. These provisions are normally dealt with by way of miscellaneous headings at this stage of the will.

2.10.1 ADVANCEMENT

See para **4.6.4.4**.

2.10.1.1 Applicable legislation

Section 63(1) of the Succession Act states:

> 'any advancement made to the child of a deceased person during his lifetime shall, subject to any contrary intention expressed or appearing in the circumstances of the case, be taken as being so made in or toward the satisfaction of the share of such child in the estate of the deceased or the share of which such child would have taken if living at the death of the deceased and as between the children shall be brought into account in distributing the estate.'

Where children are concerned, it is important to obtain instructions from a testator as to whether they wish for their children to start off with a 'clean slate' on death or whether they wish for previous gifts or advancements to the child to be taken into account. Specific instructions need to be obtained as to whether any capital advances, for instance cash advances, shares in the family business, or transfers of property, should be taken into account in the ultimate distribution on death.

Note that the value of the advancement should be reckoned as at the date of the advancement under s 63(2). However, the will can provide for the advancement to be valued in a different way, for example by applying the consumer price index to the sum originally advanced. Instructions are required on this point. Note also the duty to advise a testator that advancement is only taken as being in or towards satisfaction of the share of such child in the estate and does not therefore affect any specific legacies to such child. It would therefore be taken into account in the distribution of the residue or assets on intestacy.

Under s 63(5) the onus of proving that the child has been made an advancement shall be on the person so asserting, unless the advancement has been expressed in writing by the deceased. The provision is to relieve a child of any obligation to prove negatively that every asset he acquired was not a gift by way of advancement.

2.10.1.2 Best practice and common errors

1. Practitioners should take care to calculate the advancement correctly, remembering that *not all gifts* are advancements. See s 63(6) for a definition of 'advancement'.
2. It has happened in the past that the prior advancement is included for the purposes of calculating the spouse's legal right share, which is, of course, an error.
3. There is no declaration in the will or otherwise that it is to be excluded and the factual position is unclear on death, resulting in beneficiaries being in conflict with each other.

2.10.1.3 Precedent clause

If a testator wishes for children to start off with a clean slate on death, the following provision should be inserted in the will:

'I declare that no advancement within the meaning of Section 63 of the Succession Act shall be brought into account in the distribution of my estate.'

2.10.2 APPROPRIATION

2.10.2.1 Applicable legislation

- Section 55 of the Succession Act, 1965.
- Section 56 of the Succession Act, 1965.

2.10.2.2 Best practice and common errors

1. Not inserting a clause permitting appropriation.
2. Inserting a clause permitting appropriation but failing to put in the relevant provision allowing it to be carried out without serving the notices or obtaining the consents. There is no point in just stating that the executors shall have the power to appropriate under the Act, because they have this power anyway.

Under s 55 of the Succession Act, the personal representatives may appropriate any part of the estate of a deceased person not specifically bequeathed to any beneficiary in its actual condition and state of investment at the time of appropriation in or towards satisfaction of any share in the estate, whether settled or not, according to the respective rights of the person interested in the estate. The power of appropriation is strictly limited by s 55. See para **3.8.1.2**.

It is important to note, however, that appropriation of property to satisfy a benefit under a will or trust is not exempt from stamp duty unless the disposition (i.e. the will) gives a specific power to the executors to so appropriate. If this power is not expressly given in the will, the appropriation is subject to stamp duty as a conveyance or transfer on sale. It also has capital gains tax consequences. See Chapter 12 of the CAT Lecture Notes (see Preface) for further details.

This is a problem that can be overlooked in practice and it is extremely important to include a power to appropriate in the will, without serving any of the appropriate notices or obtaining any of the required consents.

2.10.2.3 Precedent clause

An example of a proper appropriation clause would be as follows:

'I direct that my executors and/or trustees can exercise the power of appropriation conferred upon them by Section 55 of the Succession Act, 1965 without serving any of the required notices or obtaining any of the required consents.'

2.10.3 APPORTIONMENT

There are statutory and common law rules of apportionment which are discussed in detail in the Trusts Lecture Notes (see Preface) at para 1.6.3. It is common practice to insert in the will a clause excluding these rules when creating a will trust or settlement.

2.10.3.1 Best practice and common errors

1. The failure to insert the clause may lead to difficult and time-consuming calculations in apportioning each and every item of income.

2. Where a will creates a life estate, it is usual to include a declaration to exclude the technical rules in relation to apportionment. This saves a practitioner from having to apportion each and every dividend that might arise between the pre-death and post-death periods or indeed during the currency of the life interest.

2.10.3.2 Precedent clauses

An example of a proper apportionment clause would be as follows:

'All income received after my death shall be treated as income of my Estate regardless of the period to which it relates and the statutory rules concerning apportionment and the rules in Howe v Dartmouth and Allhusen v Whittle shall not be applied.'

Or:

'The statutory and equitable rules of apportionment shall not apply to this settlement and the trustees shall be permitted to treat all dividends and other payments in the nature of income received by them as income at the date of receipt irrespective of the period for which the dividend or other income is payable.'

2.10.4 CHARGING CLAUSE

2.10.4.1 Applicable legislation

Section 82 of the Succession Act, 1965 states:

'(1) If a person attests the execution of a will, and any devise, bequest, estate, interest, gift, or appointment, of or affecting any property (other than charges and directions for the payment of any debt or debts) is given or made by the will to that person or his spouse, that devise, bequest, estate, interest, gift, or appointment shall, so far only as concerns the person attesting the execution of the will, or the spouse of that person, or any person claiming under that person or spouse, be utterly null and void.

(2) The person so attesting shall be admitted as a witness to prove the execution of the will, or to prove the validity or invalidity thereof, notwithstanding such devise, bequest, estate, interest, gift, or appointment.'

38 BASIC ELEMENTS OF A WILL AND MUTUAL WILLS

2.10.4.2 Best practice and common errors

1. When is the solicitor also a beneficiary?

    Where a solicitor is an executor and there is a charging clause then he is also considered to be a beneficiary under the will.

2. Why can charging clauses be a problem?

    It often occurs in practice that a testator wishes to appoint his solicitor as his executor. There is no problem in him so doing. However, what then frequently happens is that:

    (a) the solicitor fails to include a charging clause in the will

    or

    (b) he does remember a charging clause but then witnesses the will.

3. Necessity for charging clause

    The general rule in law is that a trustee cannot profit from his office and thus is not entitled to charge fees.

    In such circumstance, as an executor is a trustee of the estate for the beneficiaries, he will not be entitled to charge a professional fee for work done in relation to the estate. The executor will only be entitled to out-of-pocket expenses unless the beneficiaries, being of age and sound mind, permit costs to be charged.

4. Section 150 and charging clauses

    Section 150 of Legal Services Regulation Act, 2015 covers the solicitor's duty to inform a client in writing of fees to be charged. The insertion of a charging clause should of course be discussed with the testator and explained to him. In other words, what the solicitor intends to charge or the basis on which the solicitor intends to charge for the administration should be explained to the testator and a note of the testator's agreement to the charges or basis for charges made in the attendance. Section 150 is discussed in greater detail at para **15.7**.

5. Witnessing such a will

    The impact of s 82 of the Succession Act on charging clauses is not often truly appreciated. Even where a charging clause is included in the will, a solicitor still may not be entitled to charge for work done if he witnesses the will. It is imperative that the solicitor and no member of the practice (being a partner of the practice) witness the will. Neither should a spouse or civil partner of the solicitor or a spouse or civil partner of any partner in the practice witness the will.

    This is because a charging clause is regarded as a legacy, albeit a conditional legacy, and therefore is subject to the ordinary rules governing bequests under a will including the rule that an attesting witness may not take a gift under the will.

    Therefore, if a solicitor, his spouse, or a partner in the firm attests the will he is not permitted to receive payment for his services under the charging clause (see *Re Pooley* (1888) 4 Ch D 1). All he will be entitled to receive is out-of-pocket expenses (see *Re Barker* (1886) 40 Ch D 1).

6. Status of a charging clause and abatement

    A further point to note in relation to solvent but illiquid estates, i.e. where there are sufficient funds to pay debts and liabilities but perhaps not sufficient funds to pay all bequests in full, is that, because a charging clause is regarded as a legacy, it will abate with other legacies. Therefore, if there is any doubt about the sufficiency of funds to discharge legacies, it should be provided in the will that the charging clause is to take priority over all other legacies and bequests.

2.10.4.3 Precedent clause

An example of a clause providing that the charging clause is to take priority over all other legacies and bequests is as follows:

> 'Any Executor or Trustee who for the time being is a person engaged in the profession or business shall be entitled to charge and be paid in priority to all other dispositions contained herein all usual professional and other charges for business done by him or his firm in connection with proving hereof or the execution of the trusts hereof whether in the ordinary course of his profession or business or not and including business which an executor or trustee not being engaged in any profession could have transacted personally and said fees, VAT and outlay are to be discharged in priority to other legacies.'

2.11 Powers of Trustees

Powers of trustees will be dealt with in Chapter 2 of the Trusts Lecture Notes (see Preface).

2.12 Date of Will

It is surprising how often a simple matter such as the date of the will can be overlooked. The date can be inserted either at the top of the will or at the foot, just above the signature. Normally, when the will is being drafted prior to execution, the date of the will is left blank as follows:

Either:

> '**THIS WILL** is made the   day of   20   ' *[at the top of the will]*

Or:

> 'In witness hereof I have subscribed my name this day of 20'   *[just above the signature]* and the dates inserted by hand when the will is executed.

It is advisable that the will should contain the date just before the signature so that it is less likely to be overlooked in the act of execution. In the event of the will being undated, an affidavit from an attesting witness will be required, confirming the date of the execution of the will, and this can cause delays and difficulties in attempting to extract probate. Usually the month and year are typed on the face of the will but the day left blank and filled in by hand.

2.13 Signature of Testator

2.13.1 APPLICABLE LEGISLATION

Section 78 of the Succession Act, 1965 states:

> 'To be valid a will shall be in writing and be executed in accordance with the following rules:
>
> (1)   It shall be signed at the foot or end thereof by the testator, or by some person in his presence and by his direction.'

2.13.2 BEST PRACTICE AND COMMON ERRORS

2.13.2.1 Sending a will out for execution

It is not uncommon in practice for a will which has been sent out to a testator for execution to be dated and signed by the witnesses but the testator fails to sign. Obviously, if a testator is signing in a solicitor's office, the question of the signature of the testator should not arise, but solicitors should be particularly careful if wills are sent out by post or executed outside the office that when they are returned a check for the essential elements is made, for example, insertion of date, insertion of signature, and signature of two witnesses.

2.13.2.2 Weak signature

In a case where a signature is weak, the Probate Office may require further evidence as to its execution; if it appears likely that it might be necessary for an affidavit of due execution to be sworn and left with the will, it could be advisable for this to be done at the outset. Affidavits of due execution are dealt with at para **7.4.11**.

2.14 Attestation Clause

The final element in any will (and it should always be the final element, in that no further writing should be inserted after the signature) is the attestation clause. It is interesting to note that there is nothing in the Succession Act requiring a form of attestation to any will, and the absence of an attestation clause is not fatal in itself to a will.

2.14.1 APPLICABLE LEGISLATION

The Rules of the Superior Courts, 1986, O 79, r 6 state:

> *'If there be no attestation clause to a Will presented for probate, or administration with Will annexed, or the attestation clause thereto be insufficient, the Probate Officer shall require an Affidavit from at least one of the surviving witnesses, if they or either of them be living, to prove that the statutory provisions in reference to the execution of Wills were in fact complied with. A note signed by the Probate Officer shall be made on the engrossed copy Will annexed to the probate or administration to the effect that Affidavits of due execution, or as the case may be, have been filed.'*

2.15 Signature of Witnesses

It is vital that the attestation clause sufficiently cover the requirements in s 78 of the Succession Act which deals with due execution of wills.

Interestingly enough, there is no actual requirement set out in legislation as to the capacity of a witness. Obviously, however, it would be more prudent that the witnesses are both of age and have capacity, not least as they may need at some time in the future to swear an affidavit in relation to the execution.

2.15.1 APPLICABLE LEGISLATION

Section 78

> *'(2) Such signature shall be made or acknowledged by the testator in the presence of each of two or more witnesses, present at the same time, and each witness shall attest by his signature the signature of the testator in the presence of the testator, but no form of attestation shall be necessary nor shall it be necessary for the witnesses to sign in the presence of each other.'*

It is surprising how often confusion can arise in practice as to the necessary elements. First, the testator must sign or acknowledge his signature in the presence of two witnesses, who must be present at the same time. Each of those witnesses must in turn attest by their signature the signature of the testator in the presence of the testator.

Note, however, that it is not absolutely necessary for the witnesses to sign in the presence of each other, although in practice this may well happen. It is vital for practitioners to know by heart a valid form of attestation should a will need to be drawn up in an emergency situation, where, for instance, a solicitor may not have access to precedents.

Section 82

> *'If a person attests the execution of a will, and any devise, bequest, estate, interest, gift, or appointment, of or affecting any property (other than charges and directions for the payment of any debt or debts) is given or made by the will to that person or his spouse, that devise, bequest, estate, interest, gift, or appointment shall, so far only as concerns the person attesting the execution of the will, or the spouse of that person, or any person claiming under that person or spouse, be utterly null and void. The person so attesting shall be admitted as a witness to prove the execution of the will or to prove the validity or invalidity thereof, notwithstanding such devise, bequest, estate, interest, gift, or appointment.'*

It is vital that the witness to a will is not a beneficiary under the will or the spouse or civil partner of a beneficiary under the will. The possibility for abuse should a witness to a will also be a beneficiary or the spouse or civil partner of a beneficiary is obvious and this is a long-standing principle going back to the (now repealed) Wills Act, 1837.

A number of issues arise for solicitors:

1. Should a solicitor allow a beneficiary (or the spouse or civil partner of a beneficiary) to witness a will, this is potentially negligent and the disappointed beneficiary may well have an action against the solicitor. This risk is all the greater when a will is sent out for execution and return. See para **5.9.1.9**.

2. The beneficiary must be married or a civil partner at the time of execution and witnessing for the section to apply. Should a witness subsequently marry or enter into a civil partnership with a beneficiary, this will not invalidate the bequest. See *Thorpe v Bestwick* (1881) 6 QBD 311.

3. See para **2.10.4** for the effect of s 82 on charging clauses.

2.15.2 PRECEDENT CLAUSES

The following clauses are in order:

1. *'Signed by the testator in our presence and signed by us in the presence of him and of each other.'*

2. *'Signed by the said testator as and for his last Will and Testament in the presence of us who at his request and in his presence and in the presence of each other have hereunto subscribed our names as witnesses.'*

2.16 Conclusion of Basic Elements

The insertion in a will of the 'building blocks' described in this chapter will not guarantee a valid will reflecting the testator's intentions; however, their consideration should help to focus the practitioner's mind and lead to that result.

2.16.1 PHYSICAL CONDITION OF WILL/WILL PRINTED ON SINGLE SHEETS WITH WRITING ON ONE SIDE ONLY

The will should not be damaged or marked in any way after execution. If it is, an affidavit of plight and condition will have to be executed, incorporating an affidavit of due execution. This will be dealt with in **Chapter 7**.

42 BASIC ELEMENTS OF A WILL AND MUTUAL WILLS

Wills prepared on single sheets (A4 on a PC, for example), with writing on one side only, should be bound in the traditional methods. These include:

(a) ribbon or tape;

(b) staples covered over by heavy adhesive material;

(c) brass eyelets.

Each page containing written material should be numbered in the following manner. In the case of a will consisting of ten separate sheets with writing on one side of each sheet, each written page should be numbered *'Page 1 of 10'*, *'Page 2 of 10'*, and so forth.

The suggested attestation clause would read as follows:

'Signed and acknowledged by the above-named Testator as and for his last Will and Testament in the presence of us both present at the same time who in his presence at his request and in the presence of each other have hereunto subscribed our names as witnesses this Will having been printed on the front side only of the foregoing 10 sheets of A4 paper.'

The use of the word 'foregoing' in this context can be potentially confusing. The interpretation of the Probate Office is that anything appearing before the use of the word is 'foregoing'. Therefore, one would say *'the foregoing three pages of A4 paper'*, even when the clause is contained on the third page, and in normal English usage there would be only two foregoing pages. Also, if using a backing page, the word-processing program will count the backing page as a page and this should not be used in the number of 'foregoing' pages.

2.17 Precedent Will Illustrating Basic Components of a Will

[Notes on the left are for explanatory purposes only, do not form part of, and should not be included in the will.]

Testator's name, address, and revocation clause	I, JOHN JONES of 15 Anglesea Road, Ballsbridge, Dublin 4, make this as and for my last Will and Testament hereby revoking all former Wills and other testamentary dispositions at any time heretofore made by me.
Conditional appointment of spouse as executrix and universal legatee & devisee	If my wife, Helen Jones, survives me by a period of thirty days, I give, devise and bequeath the whole of my estate of whatsoever nature and wheresoever situate to her and appoint her my executrix and I direct her to pay all my debts, funeral and testamentary expenses.
Commorientes clause	If my wife does not survive me by thirty days, then and in that event the following provisions shall apply:
Appointment of executors	I appoint my sisters, Mary Jones of 10 Seaview, Taylor's Hill, Galway and Anne Jones of 2, The Brambles, Sutton, Dublin, to be my executrices and I direct them to pay all my debts, funeral and testamentary expenses.
Charging clause	I declare that any of my executrices who is/are engaged in a profession shall be entitled to be paid fees for work done by her or her firm on the basis that she/they were not my executrices/not one of my executrices but employed to act on behalf of my executrices.
Appropriation clause	I direct that in addition to all statutory powers that my executrices may have they shall have the power to exercise the power of appropriation under section 55 of the Succession Act, 1965 without serving any of the notices or obtaining any of the required consents.

BASIC ELEMENTS OF A WILL AND MUTUAL WILLS

Legacies

1. Pecuniary (to a minor with receipt clause)

To my niece Anne Jones, daughter of my said sister Mary Jones, I give and bequeath the sum of One Thousand Euro (€1,000) and should I die before she attains the age of 18 I direct that the receipt of her mother shall be a full and final discharge for my executrices.

2. Charitable

To the Irish Society for the Prevention of Cruelty to Animals, ISPCA Head Office C/o National Animal Centre, Derryglogher Lodge, Keenagh, Co. Longford, Registered Charity Number 20008734, I give and bequeath the sum of Five Hundred Euro (€500) for the general charitable purposes of the said Society. The receipt of the Honorary Treasurer for the time being of the said Society shall be sufficient receipt to my executrices for payment of the said sum.

3. Masses

To the Superior for the time being of The Order of St Augustine—Irish Province, St Augustines, Taylors Lane, Ballyboden, Dublin 16, Registered Charity Number 20014926, I give and bequeath the sum of One Hundred Euro (€100), such sum to be used for the celebration of Masses for the repose of my soul, and the souls of my relatives and friends at the usual stipend and I direct that the receipt of the said Reverend Father Superior shall be sufficient receipt to my executrices for payment of the said sum.

Negation of advancement (s 63 clause)

I declare that no advancement within the meaning of section 63 of the Succession Act shall be brought into account in the distribution of my estate.

Negation of Status of Children Act, 1987 clause

I further declare that this Will or any codicil hereto shall be construed as if the provisions of the Status of Children Act, 1987 do not apply.

Residuary clause between children as tenants in common

As to all the rest residue and remainder of my estate of whatsoever nature and wheresoever situate I give, devise and bequeath the same to my children in equal shares for their own use and benefit absolutely.

Substitutionary clauses, i.e. 'gift over' of share of residue

Where child dies leaving children

In the event of any of my children predeceasing me leaving a child or children him or her surviving then and in that event I give, devise and bequeath the share of that predeceased child to the children of such child on reaching the age of eighteen years and if more than one in equal shares for his, her or their benefit absolutely.

Where child dies without leaving children

In the event of any of my children predeceasing me without leaving a child or children him or her surviving then and in that event I direct that the share of that child shall pass to my remaining children in equal shares for their own use and benefit absolutely.

Testatum

In witness hereof I have hereunto signed my name this _____ day of _____ 20 _____

Signature of testator

John Jones

Attestation clause

Signed and acknowledged by the above-named Testator as and for his last Will and Testament in the presence of us both present at the same time who in his presence and at his request and in the presence of each other have hereunto subscribed our names as Witnesses.

Note: If the will is printed on single sheets of paper, one side only, e.g. on a PC, the attestation clause should include	This Will having been printed on the front side only of the foregoing three pages of A4 paper.	
Witnesses' signatures	*Mary Murray*	*John Murray*
Addresses	16 Anglesea Road, Ballsbridge, Dublin 4	16 Anglesea Road, Ballsbridge, Dublin 4
Descriptions	Software Engineer	Company Director

2.18 Mutual Wills

Mutual wills are two testamentary documents made by two persons/testators, each giving the other rights in property as identical as possible, for the purpose of carrying out the intention of the two testators. Wills in this manner are most likely to be made by second spouses/civil partners in favour of each other and their or either of their children. It is not necessary that the parties receive a benefit under the wills in order for a court to determine that mutual wills have been made by the testators.

In order for wills to be 'mutual wills' there must be a contract or express agreement between the testators to that effect, namely the manner in which the assets of both and each deceased will devolve on death, and it must be intended that the agreement as to the devolution of the property as per the terms of the wills is enforceable after the death of the first testator to die. As a result of the prior agreement, the effect of a mutual will can be a restriction on the surviving testator from dealing with his or her own property/assets and the property/assets inherited from the first testator.

While there is no reported Irish case on mutual wills, the commentary in the various Irish textbooks raises no issue on whether the doctrine of mutual wills as developed in England and other jurisdictions would be applicable in Irish law. As the doctrine of mutual wills appears to be based upon equitable principles and the doctrine of the constructive trust, it is likely that the Irish courts would endeavour to enforce such a binding agreement insofar as that may be practicable and in accordance with law.

Mutual wills at present are still relatively uncommon in Ireland. However, as the number of second relationships increases, they will become more common.

However, there is a strong argument that it would be unwise to engage at all in the process of making mutual wills, and for further information on this subject see Stephenson Solicitors' 11th Lecture, *Second Time Around—Spouses/Partners and Property*, pp 62–70.

Mutual wills presently give rise to some misunderstanding. Where a husband and wife or civil partners decide to make almost identical wills, sometimes known as 'matching wills' or 'mirror wills', this in itself does not confer upon such wills the status of 'mutual will'. There must be an element of contractual arrangement. Raymond J Friel (BCL, LLM, Barrister at Law), in his article entitled 'Creation and Enforcement of Mutual Wills' ((1996) 1 *Conveyancing and Property Law Journal* 2), correctly points out that in order to overcome the issue of consideration arising, the agreement to create mutual wills should be made under seal, as a contract made under seal does not require consideration. This is a point well worth noting if you are ever asked to draft mutual wills for clients.

The mutual wills of the testators may be comprised in a joint will (see *In re Hagger* [1930] 2 Ch 190) or they may consist of two separate wills (see *In re Green* [1951] Ch 148). The latter is the more common arrangement. There are apparently no Irish cases decided in relation to mutual wills. However, it is clear that there is a problem in enforcing a contract by which the ultimate beneficiary was not a party. The enforcement of the agreement between the testators is, of course, a matter for the equitable jurisdiction of the court. In the case of *Dufour v Pereira* (1769) 1 Dick 419; 21 ER 332, Lord Camden did indicate (2 Hargr Jurid Arg at 310) that the following elements must be present:

1. It must first be established that an agreement existed between the testators to make mutual wills.
2. If consideration is sought for the agreement, it is found by the first testator dying without revoking his will in pursuance of the agreement (this was reinforced in *Re Dale* [1993] 4 All ER 129).
3. There must be some form of agreement between the two testators that a named beneficiary will obtain a particular bequest.

Lord Camden proceeded to say:

'He that dies first does by his death carry the agreement on his part into execution. If the other then refuses, he is guilty of a fraud, can never unbind himself, and becomes a trustee of course. For no man shall deceive another to his prejudice. By engaging to do something that is in his power, he is made a trustee for the performance, and transmits that trust that claim under him.'

However, of course, bear in mind that the testator to a mutual will may 'unbind himself' during his lifetime, simply by giving notice to the other party that he is no longer bound by the mutual arrangement.

Because, as with any other type of will, the execution of a mutual will is a revocable act, it may be revoked by due consent by one party only, if he gives notice.

However, note that the power to revoke becomes inoperative on the death of one of the testators, as Lord Camden went on to say:

'to affront the survivor (who has deluded his partner with this Will upon the faith of persuasion that he would perform his part) may legally recall his contract, either secretly during the joint lives, or after his death I cannot allow.'

Clearly, therefore, the essence of a mutual will is that there is clear evidence of the existence of the agreement to make mutual wills. Identical provisions and simultaneous executions of wills will not give rise to any presumption in favour of mutual wills. For example, one of the most common wills you will make is where a husband and wife make 'mirror' wills leaving everything to the survivor with gift over to the children. These are not necessarily mutual wills.

An easy way of showing the testators' intention is to have them make declarations, either in the will or in a document to be kept with the will, of their agreement to make mutual wills. Of course, an intention to be bound by a previous arrangement may also be gathered from the survivor accepting any benefit given to him by the deceased testator's will.

However, the leading English case in the area, *Re Noit Dale* [1993] 4 All ER 129, would suggest that such a benefit is not necessary.

In this case, on 8 September 1988, Mr Norman Dale and Mrs Monica Dale made wills each leaving all real and personal property in favour of their children, a son and daughter, in equal shares or to the survivor of them. Mr Dale died on 9 November 1988 without having altered or revoked his will and probate was granted to his son and daughter in August 1990. In July 1990 Mrs Dale made a new will, leaving £300 to her daughter and the residue (worth approximately £19,000) to her son, and appointing her son executor. She died on 30 November 1990 and probate was granted to her son in June 1992.

The daughter sued for enforcement of the mutual will. The defence pleaded that Mr and Mrs Dale did not receive anything from each other, i.e. that there was no consideration and thus no obligation. The court found that there was in fact a mutual will, as sufficient consideration could be found from the performance of the promise by the execution of the will itself and the detriment caused to Mr Dale by his failure to revoke the mutual will despite his right to do so. Whether or not mutual wills have been made will be a matter of fact in each case.

2.18.1 APPLICATION OF MUTUAL WILLS

A constructive trust becomes operative from the date of death of one of the testators, once the agreement between them has been shown to exist. This not only renders his will effective but makes the agreement binding on the surviving testator. Therefore, any new will, made by the surviving testator, can only be effective in so far as it complies with the newly created trust, and the surviving testator's personal representative will be bound to administer the estate of the surviving testator subject to the trust.

Most interestingly, the constructive trust arising out of the agreement to make mutual wills will continue notwithstanding the revocation of the surviving testator's will by subsequent marriage. See *Re Cleaver* [1981] 1 WLR 939. See also *Re Goodchild* [1996] 1 All ER 670.

Mutual wills had for a period of time become quite archaic. However, given the modern tendency towards second and even third families, they are likely to become more popular and, if not handled correctly, are likely to cause immense problems in the administration of estates.

2.18.2 PRECEDENT CLAUSE IN RESPECT OF MUTUAL WILL

Mutual wills are wills made on foot of an agreement as just described. The wills are made in the normal and usual manner, complying with the provisions of the Succession Act, 1965.

The wills would follow the usual format, revoking former wills and testamentary documents, appointing executors and trustees if necessary, directing the discharge of the debts and expenses of the testator, and providing for the devolution of the assets and estate of the deceased in a normal and regular format.

It is not necessary that the mutual wills confer a financial benefit on the other party to the agreement, although in the case of mutual wills between husband and wife or cohabiting persons, one would imagine that in the normal course each partner/spouse would seek to confer a benefit on the other.

Mutual wills are revocable in the normal manner and as provided for in the Succession Act, 1965, unless there is an express agreement between the parties that the wills are not revocable. A subsequent marriage/civil partnership in any event would revoke a prior will, whether mutual or not and whether there is an agreement not to revoke or not. The issue will then arise as to how a court will enforce the agreement. Mutual wills can be revoked during the lifetime of the parties and on notice to the other party to the agreement. This would bring the agreement to an end and no issue would therefore arise on the death of the testators.

The other matter to consider if ever asked to draft mutual wills, and assuming that the formalities are properly carried out, is whether the wills should contain a clause reciting the agreement or contract of the testator and the other party on the face of the will.

There is no reason why a clause should not be inserted in the will reciting that there is a pre-existing agreement in relation to the making of the will in those terms with another named party. In fact, as this would make it clear from the will that it is part of an agreement in relation to the devolution of certain property, there would be distinct advantages in doing so.

As previously stated, if asked to make mutual wills, the agreement to do so should be in writing, made under seal, and retained with the wills of the parties.

This precedent declaration is incorporated into the revocation clause, but could also be a separate clause in a will:

> *'I hereby revoke all former will and testamentary dispositions heretofore made by me and I declare this to be my last will and that I have agreed with [name] that I shall not amend my will after the death of [name] if it is then unamended and unrevoked.'*

CHAPTER 3

THE LEGAL PERSONAL REPRESENTATIVE

3.1 The Role of a Legal Personal Representative

Where a will appoints a person as an executor (executrix, if female), that person is the person entitled to take out the grant of probate to the estate of the deceased. This chapter will refer to the executor, but everything said equally applies to an executrix.

The executor's powers and duties arise at the date of death of the deceased. From the date of death the executor can issue proceedings and enter into contracts to sell land but cannot obtain judgment or execute a deed of assurance transferring the land until he has extracted the grant of probate.

The appointment may, preferably, be express ('*I appoint X to be my executor*') or implied, i.e. 'by tenor' (see para **3.3.1**).

The appointment of an executor can be limited to a certain part or asset of the estate (see para **2.4.3**) or substitutional, and can be absolute, not contingent (see *In the Goods of Martin* (1955–56) Ir Jur Rep 52).

An administrator (administratrix, if female) is the person who extracts the grant in an intestate situation or in a testate situation when there is no executor extant for whatever reason, for example, the executor is dead or none was appointed. An administrator's powers and duties arise only when the grant of representation has issued to him.

The generic term 'legal personal representative' or simply 'personal representative' includes both executors and administrators.

The role of a personal representative is quite onerous and a testator should consider very carefully the responsibility, and indeed the burden, that he may be placing on a prospective executor; not least for this reason but also, to avoid a will annexed situation arising (see **Chapter 8**), it is preferable to appoint more than one executor.

Once a personal representative undertakes the administration, his role as a personal representative never ceases and he will always be the personal representative of that estate. It is important, therefore, that a personal representative discharges his duties correctly and ensures that he has all appropriate clearances and discharges to protect his position. In any administration it must be kept in mind that the client is the executor/administrator, and he must be advised fully on how to discharge his duties.

3.2 Who Can be Appointed an Executor?

In essence, a testator can appoint anybody or even an institution as an executor. For example, a minor or someone who lacks mental capacity could be appointed executor. Similarly, the Royal National Lifeboat Institution (or preferably the appropriate officer of the

48 THE LEGAL PERSONAL REPRESENTATIVE

institution) could be appointed executor. However, while anybody may be appointed, not everybody is suitable.

In advising a testator, it is important to check:

1. That a prospective executor will have the capacity to act;
2. That the testator has asked the prospective executor if he will act, as the executor is under no obligation to undertake the administration on the death of the testator. A willingness to act is always helpful;
3. That, if it is a sole executor that executor is not residing out of the jurisdiction, as such an executor may have to appoint an attorney to extract a grant in this jurisdiction. Further, since the Finance Act, 2010 (3 April 2010), where a sole executor is not resident, it is important to understand that the solicitor being appointed also acts as an agent and will have a liability for inheritance tax, which is an added complication. See CAT Lecture Notes (see Preface). At the very least, one of the executors should, where possible, be resident in this jurisdiction;
4. Whether a special executor needs to be appointed, e.g. for a literary estate. See para **2.4.3**;
5. Whether it is appropriate to appoint a substituted executor;
6. That if an institution is being appointed as an executor, that that institution is a corporation within the meaning of s 30 of the Succession Act. See para **2.4.2** at point 6.

As previously stated, while only one executor is necessary, it is prudent for many reasons—one to watch the other, in case of disability, if the executor predeceases, etc—to appoint two executors, or at least a substitute executor. See para **2.4.3**.

3.2.1 CAN A FAMILY MEMBER BE AN EXECUTOR?

There is nothing whatsoever to prevent a family member, who may also be a beneficiary, from acting as executor. However, it is important to ensure that a conflict of interest does not arise for the executor in his capacity as a beneficiary or any other capacity, e.g. creditor. An executor must be impartial in carrying out his duties. An executor in such a position should be advised to see another solicitor for independent legal advice in his capacity as anything else other than the legal personal representative.

3.2.2 CAN A TRUST CORPORATION BE APPOINTED AS AN EXECUTOR?

It is possible for a trust corporation to be appointed as an executor by a will; however, it must be a trust corporation within the meaning of s 30(4) of the Succession Act, 1965. Under s 30(1) the High Court may:

'a) *where a trust corporation is named in a will as executor whether alone or jointly with another person, grant probate to the corporation either solely or jointly with another person, as the case may require, and*

b) *grant administration to a trust corporation either solely or jointly with another person, and the corporation may act accordingly as executor or administrators as the case may be.*'

Note under subsection (2) that representation shall not be granted to any person on behalf of a trust corporation. Subsection (4) defines a 'trust corporation' as:

'(a) *a corporation appointed by the High Court in any particular case to be a trustee;*

(b) *a corporation empowered by its constitution to undertake trust business and having a place of business in the State or Northern Ireland, and being—*

  (i) *a company established by act or charter or*

  (ii) *an Associated Bank under the Central Bank Act, 1942, or*

THE LEGAL PERSONAL REPRESENTATIVE

(iii) *a company (whether registered with or without limited liability) within the definition contained in the Companies Act, 1963 or within the meaning of the corresponding law of Northern Ireland, having its capital (in stock or shares) for the time being issued of not less than two hundred and fifty thousand pounds (€320,000), of which not less than one hundred thousand pounds (€130,000) has been paid up in cash, or*

(iv) *a company (registered without limited liability) within the definition contained in the said Companies Act, or within the meaning of the said law of Northern Ireland, one of the members of which is a corporation within any of the previous provisions of this paragraph, or*

(c) *a corporation which satisfies the President of the High Court that it undertakes the administration of any charitable, ecclesiastical or public trust without remuneration, or that by its constitution it is required to apply the whole of its net income for charitable, ecclesiastical or public purposes and is prohibited from distributing, directly or indirectly, any part thereof by way of profits, and is authorised by the President of the High Court to act in relation to such trusts as a trust corporation.'*

Provided that a trust corporation qualifies under s 30, an official of the trust corporation swears the necessary schedule of assets and oath, etc, necessary to obtain the grant. The corporation must lodge a copy of the resolution authorising such official to swear the affidavits necessary (see O 79, r 19).

In the event of the appointment of a trust corporation by will, ensure that such trust corporation will be entitled to charge for trust business undertaken, and that there is a proper charging clause in the will.

See also para **2.4.3** for precedent.

3.2.3 CAN A MINOR BE AN EXECUTOR?

In law, while a minor can be appointed, if the testator dies before the minor reaches the age of majority the minor cannot act (see s 32 of the Succession Act, 1965, as amended by the Age of Majority Act, 1985). In practice, it is not advisable to appoint a minor in the event of it being any way likely that the minor may need to act as an executor. However, s 32 does go on to provide that where a minor is sole executor of a will, administration with will annexed shall be granted to his guardian or to such person as the High Court thinks fit. See para **11.1.4.9**.

However, this only applies until the minor attains the age of eighteen years (formerly twenty-one years, prior to the coming into force of the Age of Majority Act, 1985) and he applies for and obtains a grant of probate or letters of administration with will annexed; on his attaining that age, and not before, probate of the will may be granted to him. An administrator appointed under s 32 has all the powers of a general administrator except that his administration is limited until such time as the minor reaches the age of eighteen.

Where a minor is not the sole executor of the will, probate may be granted to the other executor/s who are of age, reserving the right of the minor executor to take probate on attaining full age.

3.2.4 CAN A CHARITABLE BODY BE AN EXECUTOR?

In the event of the appointment of a charity as an executor, you may find that such charity is not a trust corporation within the meaning of the Act; in particular, under s 30(4)(c) it may not be a trust corporation appointed by the High Court in any particular case to be a trustee. A list of approved charitable trust corporations is available from the Probate Office. It may be necessary for the charity to take out a grant through a nominee, and such resolution appointing the nominee is lodged with the probate papers and referred to in the oath of executor. (See also para **2.4.3** for precedent.)

In the event of the appointment of a charity as an executor, ask the testator if the charity is a trust corporation. See para **3.2.2**.

For the same reason, it is not advisable to have a charity as a sole residuary beneficiary as, if the executors appointed do not act for some reason, such a charity would be the next entitled to extract the grant. See the article by Úna Burns entitled 'A Different Type of Legal Personal Representative' in the *Parchment*, Autumn 2012, for further information on the problems this can cause post-death.

3.2.5 CAN A PROFESSIONAL BE AN EXECUTOR?

It is often the case that a solicitor or accountant or other professional person is to be appointed as an executor. In this instance, always insert (having taken the testator's instructions) a charging clause, as an executor is not entitled to be paid for his services as of right. In the event of a solicitor being appointed and there being no charging clause in the will, specific consent for the charging of the firm's fees has to be sought from all persons from whose share of or benefit in the estate the fees are to be paid. An executor is entitled to out-of-pocket expenses, but in the absence of a charging clause or consent of all appropriate parties he would not be entitled to raise professional fees for time expended etc on the administration. This has been discussed at paras **2.4.3** and **2.10.4**.

3.2.6 CAN A PERSON UNDER A DISABILITY BE AN EXECUTOR?

A grant of representation will not be given to a person who is mentally incapable of managing his affairs. A person must have testamentary capacity to act as an executor.

Where there are two or more executors, those capable may prove the will and the power may be reserved for the incapable executor. The Rules of the Superior Courts, O 79, r 26 provide:

'A grant of administration (which includes administration with will annexed) may be made to the committee of a person of unsound mind for such person's use and benefit.'

Order 79, r 27 goes on to provide:

'In the case where a person of unsound mind has not a committee appointed by the Court, a grant may issue to such person as the Probate Officer may by order sign with the consent of the Registrar of Wards of Court.'

If the executor is suffering from a mental or physical disability, he may be unable to act in person but if he has capacity could do so via a power of attorney. See **11.1.4.8** and note the Rules of the Superior Courts, 1986, O 79, r 23, which states:

'In the case of a person residing out of or about to leave the jurisdiction of the court, or who, in the opinion of the Court or Probate Officer is suffering from a severe continuing physical disability, administration or administration with the will annexed, may be granted to his [the personal representative's] attorney acting under a Power of Attorney.'

For fuller detail and precedent applications/oaths see also Stephenson Solicitors' 19th Seminar, *Legal Personal Representatives: The Good, the Bad and the Indifferent*, pp 81–96.

3.2.7 CAN AN UNNAMED PERSON BE APPOINTED AS AN EXECUTOR?

A person may be designated by name or by office, e.g. the Minister for Justice or the Bishop of Kerry. If this is the case it is the person holding that office at the date of death of the testator who is the executor unless the will overrides this.

Conversely, when it is a firm of solicitors who is appointed as executor, the Probate Office practice is to admit only those who were partners at the date of execution of the will, unless the will states differently. This is one of the rare exceptions to *'the will speaks from the date of death'*. Another example is s 82 of the Succession Act. See para **2.15.1**.

THE LEGAL PERSONAL REPRESENTATIVE

3.3 How is an Executor Appointed?

An executor is usually specifically appointed in a will as an executor (see **2.4.3** for precedent). However, an executor may also be appointed, not expressly in the will, but by implication, i.e. according to tenor.

3.3.1 WHAT IS AN EXECUTOR ACCORDING TO TENOR?

This right of executorship also accrues to the person or persons who are constituted executors according to the tenor of the will by virtue of the functions assigned to them by the will.

For example, the testator omits to appoint X as executor but nevertheless gives him a function which indicates that he intends him to act in this capacity, for example, authorises him to pay his debts. The latter designation is called 'executor according to the tenor' or as referred to in older texts, an executor de son tort. It will also be accorded to persons who are given authority in foreign wills where they apply for a grant of Irish probate—see Rules of the Superior Courts, O 79, r 5(8)(c).

In the event of no executor being appointed, whether by oversight or otherwise, the order of individuals entitled to extract a grant is strictly determined by O 79, r 5 of the Rules of the Superior Courts. In that event it is usually—but not always—the person entitled to the residue of the estate who would be the person next entitled to so extract a grant. This is covered in detail in **Chapter 8**.

3.4 How Many Executors Can Be Appointed?

There is no limit on the number of executors that can be appointed, but note that the Rules of the Superior Courts provide that no grant of administration (note there is no reference here to a grant of probate) shall be made jointly to more than three persons unless the Probate Officer otherwise directs (see O 79, r 5(14)).

It is always wise to appoint more than one executor and there is nothing to prevent the appointment of a substitute executor in the will, for example if an executor is not able to act at the time of the death. It quite often arises that elderly couples each appoint the other as the sole executor. On the death of the first, the survivor is also often quite elderly and infirm and difficulties can arise if a second executor, or indeed the question of a substitute executor, has not been considered. However, the words '*I appoint X or Y as my executor*' should never be used as this has been held to be void for uncertainty.

3.5 Does an Executor Have to Act?

An executor, once appointed, is not bound to act even if he had agreed to accept the office pre-death (see *Hargraves v Wood* (1862) 2 Sw & Tr 602).

An executor has a choice to accept, reserve, or renounce the executorship.

3.5.1 ACCEPTANCE

It is important to note, that in the event of an executor accepting his appointment as an executor, once a grant of probate issues, such executor cannot subsequently turn back and seek to renounce without the consent of the High Court. See para **3.5.3.1**.

Indeed, it is particularly important to explain to an executor who is also a trustee that acceptance of executorship automatically is an acceptance of the trusteeship.

Always be careful to explain the practical consequences of acceptance or renunciation to the prospective executor. This is especially important where the executor may be a creditor of the estate, a qualified cohabitant, or a child who wishes to make an application for redress from the estate.

3.5.2 RESERVATION

The person who reserves his right to act does not have to execute any document (as would be necessary for a renunciation—see para **3.5.3**) and can come back into the administration at a later date and take out a subsequent grant. It is considered good practice, however, to obtain a letter from such an executor confirming his wish to reserve his rights. In the UK, such a letter of confirmation from an executor reserving his rights is necessary for production to the court in order to obtain a grant. This may happen in practice where there is a conflict of interest and an executor may wish to reserve. No such requirement yet exists in Ireland—it is sufficient to state the fact in the oath of the executor. However, it is the practice where a bank's rights are being reserved to obtain a letter from the bank consenting to their reservation. In practice, banks rarely reserve but in recent times always renounce.

3.5.3 RENUNCIATION

In the event of an executor renouncing his right to act, his right in respect of the executorship shall wholly cease, as outlined in s 17 of the Succession Act, 1965. In the event of an executor wishing to renounce, he must execute a form of renunciation, which must be exhibited in the oath of executor filed in the Probate Office. For the wording for this see para **7.2.2.2**.

When advising an executor on the question of renunciation, it is important to state that he cannot, without the court's consent, come back into the administration at any stage in the future. A renunciation, once executed and the grant extracted, is final. Order 79, r 38 of the Rules of the Superior Courts provides that a person who renounces probate in one character shall not be allowed to obtain representation in another character unless the court shall otherwise order.

It is rare but possible for an executor who has renounced to withdraw that renunciation (see s 18(1)), but to do so he must have leave of the court and it is only given where it is to the benefit of the estate or beneficiaries to do so.

However, in the event of a person wishing to act as a trustee but not as an executor, the renunciation of his role as an executor will not prejudice his acceptance of the trusteeship of the will, though if a person acts as an executor he is presumed to have accepted the trusteeship and cannot subsequently disclaim. In the event of his wishing to back out, he must retire, and this is provided for in ss 10 and 11 of the Trustee Act, 1893.

3.5.3.1 Where an executor has intermeddled and then seeks to renounce

In a case where an executor has intermeddled in the estate of a deceased person but then is not in a position to extract probate, the executor cannot then renounce without the permission of the court.

The standard form of renunciation confirms that the person seeking to renounce has not intermeddled in the estate of the deceased. Certain actions of an executor can be deemed as acts of intermeddling in the estate of a deceased person. In the current climate it is possible that engaging with creditors of the estate of a deceased person with regard to the liability of the estate of the deceased could be deemed to be an act of intermeddling.

3.5.3.2 What if the executor does not accept, reserve, or renounce?

Sometimes, for various reasons, an executor may not take any action. In that case, use of the citation process is an option. See para **11.6**.

3.5.4 CAN AN EXECUTOR BE REMOVED?

As can be seen under the provisions of ss 26(2) and 27(2) of the Succession Act, 1965, statutory power is given to the court to revoke, cancel, or recall grants of representation (see para **11.2**).

This arises where there has been a fundamental error with regard to the issue of the grant, or, subsequent to the issue of the grant, events make it necessary for the grant to be revoked in order to ensure the proper administration of the estate.

These sections are also the relevant sections to consider if a grant has been extracted but the personal representative is not progressing the administration of the estate of the deceased in a timely fashion or correctly.

In addition, s 62 of the Succession Act, 1965 sets the time allowed for the distribution of the estate of a deceased person.

Section 62 'Executor's Year'

> '(1) The personal representatives of a deceased person shall distribute his estate as soon after his death as is reasonably practicable having regard to the nature of the estate, the manner in which it is required to be distributed and all other relevant circumstances, but proceedings against the personal representatives in respect of their failure to distribute shall not, without leave of the court, be brought before the expiration of one year from the date of the death of the deceased.
>
> (2) Nothing in this section shall prejudice or affect the rights of creditors of a deceased person to bring proceedings against his personal representative before the expiration of one year from his death.'

See *Shaughnessy v Shaughnessy* [2016] IEHC 303, where the 'executor's year' was fully explored.

3.5.4.1 When will a court remove an executor?

The case law relating to applications seeking to remove a personal representative who is not performing his functions suggests that the court requires 'substantial grounds' for the revocation of a grant and will not revoke a grant merely on the grounds that it would be convenient to do so. This is particularly the case for an executor because the executor was chosen by the testator. There must be 'serious conduct or serious misconduct' before an acting executor would be removed, as can be seen from the case of *Dunne v Heffernan* [1997] 3 IR 431.

In the case of *Re Flood, Flood v Flood* [1999] 2 IR 234, Judge Macken did remove an executor, but applied the principle as stated by the Supreme Court in *Dunne v Heffernan*. In that particular case there was a clear conflict of interest. The executor to be removed was claiming a beneficial interest in certain moneys which prima facie formed part of the estate. In those circumstances, the judge held that she could not allow the executor to proceed, because there was a clear conflict of interest.

In the past it has been held that a conflict arising for the executor will be a sufficient ground for the removal of the executor, and the revocation of the grant issued to him, by the court.

It would be normal practice that the application would be made by one of several existing personal representatives or by a beneficiary of the estate to have the executor with the conflict removed and the grant revoked. The person making the application must have *locus standi* to do so and must have some interest in the proper administration of the estate.

Therefore, the person could be the executor himself, the other joint executors, or a beneficiary or creditor of the estate of the deceased. See also *Scally v Rhatigan (No 2)* [2102] IEHC 140, where Laffoy J removed the only surviving executor, in this case the testator's solicitor, as she believed that there was a clear conflict of interest.

In an appropriate case the application to remove the executor and revoke the grant can be made by originating Notice of Motion, grounded upon affidavit before the Probate Judge, in the non-contentious Probate List. If, however, it appears that the executor/personal representative sought to be removed will resist the application, it would seem to be appropriate that the application be made by Special Summons where, as an alternative, the applicant/plaintiff would seek orders in relation to the administration of the estate or orders directing the personal representative to administer the estate. Rules of the Superior Courts, O 3 sets out the type of relief which can be sought by the Special Summons. The procedure is intended to dispose of such proceedings in a summary manner based upon affidavit evidence.

It is interesting to note that there does not always have to be actual misconduct by the executor to be removed. In the English case of *Angus v Emmott* [2010] EWHC 154 (Ch), the Deputy High Court Judge came to the conclusion that even though there had been no misconduct on the part of the personal representative, a situation had been reached:

> *'in which there is such a degree of animosity and distrust between the executors that the due administration of Mr …'s estate is unlikely to be achieved expeditiously in the interests of the beneficiaries unless some change is made.'*

The court held in that case that the safest and most appropriate course to ensure the administration of the estate in the interests of all of the beneficiaries was to remove the executors and replace them with a professional executor who could take an independent view in progressing the administration of the estate.

The following day, the English High Court, in *Kershaw v Micklethwaite* [2010] EWHC 506 (Ch), gave judgment in a dispute involving the claim by a son of the deceased that some or all of the executors named in her will should be removed. There was a list of complaints made by the potential beneficiary, and in addition to those complaints, the son stated that the relationship between him and the executors, who were his sisters, had broken down and he lacked confidence in their competence to deal with the estate. The court rejected the suggestion that an executor could be removed more readily than a trustee. The court held that it would not be induced to remove a trustee by reason of every mistake or neglect of duty or inaccuracy of conduct. The court also held that it did not consider that friction or hostility between an executor and a beneficiary was of itself a reason for removing an executor and said:

> *'[T]he poor relations between the parties need not and should not either prevent or impede substantially the administration of the estate.'*

The court took into consideration the fact that the executor had been appointed by the testatrix herself and the judge also held that costs were a factor weighing against the removal of the executors. The court considered that changing the existing personal representatives and appointing a fresh professional executor could be expected to increase the costs of administration significantly, to the detriment of the beneficiaries, including the claimant.

In the case of *Alkin v Redmond and Whelan* [2010] WTLR 1117, Bompas QC, sitting as a Deputy High Court Judge, dealt with an application to remove the two executors of the estate of the deceased, who was a retired solicitor. The court considered the principles applicable to the removal of executors. The court was satisfied that the principles described by Lord Blackburn in the case of *Letterstedt v Broers* (1884) 9 App Cas 371 should prevail. That was a decision of the Privy Council which concerned the equitable jurisdiction of the court to remove trustees. Lord Blackburn had quoted a passage from Story's *Equity Jurisprudence*, s 1289 as follows:

> *'But in cases of positive misconduct, courts of equity have no difficulty in interposing to remove trustees who have abused their trust; it is not indeed every mistake or neglect of duty, or inaccuracy*

of conduct of trustees, which will induce courts of equity to adopt such a course. But the acts or omissions must be such as to endanger the trust property or to show a want of honesty, or a want of proper capacity to execute the duties, or a want of reasonable fidelity.'

Having quoted the passage, Lord Blackburn went on to say:

'It seems to their Lordships that the jurisdiction which a court of equity has no difficulty in exercising under the circumstances indicated by Story, is merely ancillary to its principal duty, to see that trusts are properly executed ... and therefore, though it should appear that the charges of misconduct were either not made out or were greatly exaggerated, so that the trustee was justified in resisting them, and the court might consider that in awarding costs, yet if satisfied that the continuance of the trustee would prevent the trust being properly executed, the trustee might be removed. It must always be borne in mind that trustees exist for the benefit of those to whom the creator of the trust had given the trust estate ... If it appears clear that the continuance of the trustee would be detrimental to the execution of the trust, even if for no other reason than that human infirmity would prevent those beneficially interested, or those who act for them, from working in harmony with the trustee, and if there is no reason to the contrary from the intentions of the framer of the trust to give this trustee a benefit or otherwise, the trustee is always advised by his own counsel to resign, and does so, if, without any reasonable grounds he refuses to do so, it seems to their Lordships that the court might think it proper to remove him ... It is quite true that friction or hostility between trustees and the immediate possessors of the trust estate is not of itself a reason for the removal of trustees. But where the hostility is grounded on the mode in which the trust had been administered, where it has been caused wholly or partially by substantial overcharging against the trust estate, it is certainly not to be disregarded.'

It therefore can be seen that while the courts are slow to remove executors, they will do so where it appears necessary for the property administration of the estate of a deceased person.

See also *Philip Davies and Joan Davies v Marian Hutchinson* [2017] IEHC 693.

3.6 The Role and Duties of an Executor

Before dealing with the powers of an executor in detail, it is necessary to review their role and duties. This is not an exhaustive list and will vary from case to case. It is recommended that an outline of the role and duties of the executor be supplied to each executor of each estate on which a solicitor advises.

3.6.1 THE ROLE OF AN EXECUTOR

Here, in letter format, is a very general example of the type of letter that should be sent to an executor, outlining his role very simply.

'Your function as an executor is to extract a grant of probate to the estate and to administer the estate of the deceased.

As executor, your powers and duties date from the death of the deceased.

From the date of death the whole estate devolves or passes to you as executor. You have very wide powers under general law, apart from any powers given to you under the will. As explained previously [practitioners should ensure that this has in fact been spelled out to their clients], an executor may renounce the executorship but once you decide to take on the role of executor you cannot then renounce it at a later stage.

The duties of a personal representative last for life; therefore, your obligations as executor are ongoing.

The following is a simple set of guidelines on the powers and duties of executors. It is, necessarily, set out in very brief and summary form. [A summary of an executor's duties is set out below and could be included with the letter but, of course, they should be made personal to the individual circumstances of the case. Some examples of individual cases are also listed below.] It is hoped it will be of assistance to you.

We shall be guiding and advising you on all matters in relation to the administration of the estate and we will be undertaking all your tasks which we are able to undertake.

We will of course be instructing you fully on all those duties or tasks which you alone can perform. Likewise, we will explain fully all documents and declarations which you are required to sign.

If you have any questions at all arising out of this or, indeed, if you have any queries on any matter during the course of the administration, please feel free to contact us at any stage.'

3.6.2 THE DUTIES OF AN EXECUTOR

[See Brady, *Succession Law in Ireland*, 2nd edn (1995), p 251, para 9.11.]

3.6.2.1 Disposal of the body

Disputes about burial can be the most fraught disputes that practitioners are ever likely to encounter and the most difficult to deal with, as the dispute is fuelled by emotion or occasionally political necessity: see for example the case of Frank Stagg. (Stagg was a member of the IRA who died on hunger strike in England in 1976. On the return of his body to Ireland, it was seized by the State and buried under concrete so he could not be given a republican funeral.) The reality of the law in this area is not of much assistance, as it is often not what the family and friends of the deceased would expect but is based on what they perceive as archaic rules, which can be difficult for those grieving to accept.

The problem is exacerbated by the fact that the resolution of the dispute is, by its very nature, one where time is of the essence.

If involved in a dispute it is, as always, essential to know the law in this matter, but better still to be able to assist in reaching an agreement. Indeed, many of the most recent cases in Ireland and in England, including injunctive applications, have not proceeded to full hearing but have been settled.

The law in this area is essentially case driven. It was established by the seminal case of *Williams v Williams* [1882] 20 Ch D 659 that there is no property in a corpse. For example, it cannot be the subject of property transactions, nor can it be bought, sold, stolen (that is to say, it can be stolen but such an act does not constitute theft), or criminally damaged or seized by the deceased's creditors or indeed by the Inland Revenue as security for the deceased's debts. See *R v Fox* (1841) 2 QB 246 and *Bourne (Inspector of Taxes) v Norwich Crematorium Limited* [1967] 2 All ER 576.

Further, as the body does not constitute property it does not therefore form part of the deceased's estate and cannot pass under the deceased's will or under the law of intestacy.

Therefore, it is important to advise the testator that any direction contained in the will as to the disposal of a body is unenforceable. If the testator insists on inserting such a direction in the will, while it may have persuasive value and may indicate the deceased's wishes, it has no legal consequence.

Oddly enough, while it is not possible to have 'rights over a corpse' the law does impose responsibilities on certain categories of persons, primarily but not exclusively on the personal representative, in respect of corpses. There is, in effect, a type of hierarchy of people who are under a duty to dispose of the body and for this purpose those persons might be said to have a right to the possession of the corpse.

As you might expect, it has been long established that the primary duty to dispose of a deceased body falls on the deceased's personal representative and thus they have a right to possession of the corpse and to decide how it should be buried. The English case of *Leeburn v Derndorfer* (2004) WLTR 867 extended this right to properly dispose of the deceased's ashes after cremation. However, as can be seen from the Stagg case, authority is one thing and possession is another.

Where there is no personal representative, then the person with the highest right to extract the grant can take possession of the corpse. There has in fact been a case where the deceased's separated wife was entitled to possession of her husband's corpse over and above the right of his cohabitant when he died, as it was the separated wife who was entitled to extract the grant. For the same reason, there is another case where the deceased's adoptive parents were given the right to decide on the burial rather than the deceased's biological parents.

In relation to children, not surprisingly it has been established that where the parents are married they are equally entitled to their deceased child's body and it is clear that conflict could arise in these circumstances in which the law would not assist at all as there is equal entitlement.

The obvious exception to all of these situations is that the coroner's right to the body supersedes all other rights when he is enquiring into the cause of death.

While, as we have seen, the personal representatives have a duty to dispose of the body, they are effectively deemed to take possession of it as trustees, and in theory therefore they should dispose of it in a way that they deem appropriate but with regard to any express wishes of the deceased and the claims of relatives and others with an interest.

However, as it is a form of trust this is not a legal obligation but in effect a moral one, and therefore they can and do, as can be seen from case law, act contrary to family members' wishes.

Indeed, the issue is further complicated in that where there is more than one personal representative, one of them can act unilaterally and in effect dispose of the deceased's body in a way that is in opposition to the wishes of the other personal representative. Thus, while there is a clear hierarchy for those responsible for the body, conflict or disputes can arise where two or more people are equally entitled and disagree as to the right course of action, not to mention where family members are in opposition to the views of the personal representatives.

Ideally, this issue should never have to be referred to court. However, should the dispute proceed to court, the factors that the court will consider are the length of time since the death and the need for the disposal of the body without further delay, the reasonableness of the proposed arrangement, and the wishes of those who are opposing the arrangement proposed.

The court in essence takes a very practical approach and tries to '*weigh the competing claims and arrive at what one would truly call a legal judgment*' (*Dodd v Jones* [1999] SASC 458).

For further information on disputes relating to bodies see Stephenson Solicitors' 16th seminar, *Probate Disputes in the Administration of Estates*.

3.6.2.2 Valuation and protection of assets

The next duty of an executor is to ascertain the precise value and extent of all the deceased's assets. At this stage the executor has the right to pay, or take releases of, debts owing from the estate. An executor may also sell or otherwise dispose of, at his discretion, the goods and assets of the testator before the grant of probate issues. However, certainly in relation to assets such as land or stocks and shares, it would be difficult to do so without the grant and, in practice, sales of assets will usually occur after the grant issues.

The executor must ensure that the assets of the estate are properly protected. It follows that there is a duty to see that all assets normally requiring insurance, such as a house, land, or other valuable items—for example, jewellery, house contents, and car—are insured with a reputable insurance company. However, amazingly, no such power is given to an executor in the Succession Act.

3.6.2.3 Ascertain all liabilities and the beneficiaries

An executor must ascertain all outstanding debts, taxes, etc and check that there are no claims outstanding against the estate. All of the beneficiaries must also be ascertained.

58 THE LEGAL PERSONAL REPRESENTATIVE

An executor must also make enquiries from all relevant beneficiaries in relation to prior gifts or inheritances received by them in order to complete the 'beneficiary screen' section of the revenue form SA.2. See para **6.9.7**. It is essential to obtain details of all relevant beneficiaries' PPS numbers.

3.6.2.4 The Statement of Affairs (Probate) Form SA.2

When all enquiries have been made (and these can be numerous and complex), a schedule or list of all the assets and liabilities of the deceased must be prepared. This is an official document known as a Statement of Affairs (Probate) and it must be sworn by the executor along with several other relevant documents and declarations. If dealing with a death post 17 June 1993 but prior to 6 December 2000 probate tax returns are also made and probate tax is paid at this stage. If dealing with a death between 17 June 1993 and 6 December 2000, probate tax may be applicable. Probate Tax has been repealed, however the tax may still arise in one circumstance. Where a spouse died between 17 June 1993 and 6 December 2000 leaving their estate to their spouse for life, probate tax was deferred until the death of the surviving spouse. On the death of this surviving spouse, probate tax may be payable. See Stephenson Solicitors' 35th Seminar, *Home is Where the Heart is*.

3.6.2.5 Extract the relevant grant and collect in the assets

When all the relevant papers have been lodged in the Probate Office, the grant of representation issues. Prior to 14 June 2010, it was the practice (and still is for deaths prior to 5 December 2001) to ~~first file the Inland Revenue affidavit~~ SA.2 in the Revenue Commissioners and, once the certified Inland Revenue affidavit was returned to the filing solicitor, to then lodge same with the other probate papers in the Probate Office. Current practice is to file one original Inland Revenue affidavit and one copy with the rest of the probate papers. See **Chapters 6** and **7** for further details.

The executor is then in a position to collect in all the deceased's assets. It is at this stage that assets not being specifically given to named beneficiaries would be sold where appropriate.

3.6.2.6 Pay the expenses and debts of the estate and obtain tax clearances

The executor is obliged to pay the funeral expenses and all other outstanding debts of the deceased.

The executor is then required to distribute the assets to those entitled, while ensuring that taxes due by the estate are paid. These taxes include all taxes due by the deceased prior to his death and all taxes arising out of the administration of the estate itself. Ensure that all relevant clearance certificates/letters of comfort are obtained prior to distribution. See para **12.5.2** for further information re ascertainment of debts by an executor and the use of a s 79 notice.

Since the coming into force of the Finance Act, 2010 the personal representative is no longer secondarily liable for payment of capital acquisitions tax unless the beneficiary resides outside the jurisdiction. It is essential that the personal representative is aware of when he does have responsibilities in this area and of his responsibilities in relation to all other taxes both arising before and after the death of the testator. Where the personal representative is secondarily liable for payment of capital acquisitions tax, he should ensure that it is fully discharged prior to distribution.

3.6.2.7 Prepare administration accounts

Finally, the executor must furnish an administration account, that is to say, an Estate Account, Cash Account (possibly a Cash Capital and Cash Income Account, depending on the complexity of the estate), and a Distribution Account wherein he accounts for all monies received and all monies distributed during the administration period. See para **15.8**. For fuller detail on Estate Accounts and solicitors' obligations re same see Stephenson Solicitors' 31st Seminar, *The Probate Dance—In and Out and All About*.

3.6.2.8 Duty for life

The duties of the personal representative are for life. For example, if an asset is discovered after distribution is complete, it is the duty of the personal representative to dispose of that asset as per the will or rules of intestacy. An amended schedule of assets may be required.

3.6.2.9 Relevant points for executors

The following points are of relevance to executors and are mentioned here, as they are the queries most frequently raised by personal representatives:

1. The general rule is that an executor sufficiently discharges his duty where he takes all precautions which an ordinary prudent person would take in managing similar affairs of his own. The office is a personal one, the testator having chosen him for his trustworthiness.

2. An executor may not delegate his authority but he may employ other persons, experts in their own fields, to help him. He will not be liable for their mistakes or negligence, provided that they are employed only to do acts within the scope of their profession or expertise.

3. The office of executor is gratuitous, i.e. the executor is not entitled to receive fees or to profit from carrying out his duty. However, neither should he incur a loss, so all expenses properly incurred during the administration period are recoverable by him.

4. There is no obligation on an executor to give a copy of the will to anyone before it is admitted to probate, or to inform a beneficiary of his interest. (If required, an executor must give any information to a beneficiary in relation to his interest in the estate, and in the normal course he will do so in any event.) However, it should be noted that once the will is 'proved' (i.e. admitted to probate) and the grant issued, a copy of the will is contained in the grant of probate and the will becomes a document of public record which anyone is entitled to inspect and of which anyone can obtain a copy.

3.7 How to Advise an Executor of a Ward of Court

There is an excellent CPD lecture by James Finn, the Registrar of Wards of Court, of 29 September 2011 entitled *Wards of Court*, which deals with wards of court in general and also with the duties owed by the executor of a ward of court.

His advice may be summarised as follows:

The Wards of Court Office must be immediately notified of the death of the ward. Where the will is in court (see O 67, r 87), the Registrar will open the will for the purposes of ascertaining the executor and checking if the ward has left instructions regarding the disposal of his body. They then send the will to the Probate Office and direct the Accountant of the Courts of Justice to suspend all payments of the funds in court. The committee ceases to act on the ward's behalf when the ward dies. At the death of the ward, the committee must lodge a statement of facts with the Registrar, and this leads to the dismissal of the wardship (O 67, r 89). The statement of facts is sworn by the committee and is filed in the Office of the Wards of Court. It should contain:

1. the date and place of death of the ward, his marital status, and whether he died testate or intestate;
2. names, addresses, and relationship of the next of kin to the deceased;
3. name and address of the deceased's personal representative;
4. list of the deceased's assets;
5. any claims against the estate;
6. whether the estate is solvent or insolvent.

Following the filing of the statement of facts, the solicitor for the committee will appear before the Registrar for the purpose of having the matter dismissed from wardship. It is not necessary for the grant to issue before the statement of facts may be filed, nor is it necessary for the personal representative to wait until the wardship is dismissed before obtaining a grant. The personal representative of a ward must not intermeddle with the estate without the leave of the court until the wardship matter is dismissed. Remember that funds can be released by the Wards of Court Office without a grant of representation where the ward's total assets do not exceed €25,000 since 28 December 2012 and €6,500 prior to that (O 67, r 92, as amended), and where he has died intestate.

Once the statement of facts is filed, where a committee has been in receipt of income and the final committee account filed, a dismissal order will issue, and thereafter the administration proceeds in the usual manner. Obviously, such a personal representative will not have the original will to exhibit in the oath of executor, so he, or any other person entitled to prove the ward's will, must bespeak a copy of the original will from the Probate Office. See also Stephenson Solicitors' 19th Lecture, *Legal Personal Representatives: The Good, the Bad and the Indifferent*, pp 82–91 for further information and precedent oaths on advising the executor where the deceased was a ward of court and also where the executor or the next of kin entitled to extract a grant on intestacy is a ward of court.

3.8 The Powers of an Executor

An executor's powers can arise both by statute and/or by will.

To draft a will, it is essential that the statutory powers of an executor are understood so that, given the particular potential assets and beneficiaries of a testator, the executor is given whatever additional powers he might require in the will.

3.8.1 POWERS OF EXECUTOR CONFERRED BY STATUTE

It is important to note that an executor derives his title and authority from the will, and the assets in the estate automatically vest in an executor on death. On the other hand, an administrator derives his title from the date of the grant of administration. Thus, clearly an executor has more power pre-grant than an administrator does, which is another reason why one should make a will (see para **1.1.4**).

The Succession Act, 1965 confers wide powers on an executor to deal with the assets in the estate and these can be summarised as follows. In each case the specific sections should be referred to. At the outset it should be noted that where probate is granted to one or two or more persons named as executors, whether or not power is reserved to the other or others to prove, all the powers which are by the Succession Act, 1965 or otherwise conferred by law on the personal representative may be exercised by the proving executor or executors or the survivor or survivors of them and shall be as effectual as if all the persons named as executors had concurred therein (s 20(1)).

However, a single personal representative cannot act as a trustee of the settlement until at least one other trustee has been appointed. A single personal representative does not appear to have the power to appoint the trustees himself. However, where this arises where land is settled by will (e.g. '*to my wife, Mary for life, with remainder to my son, John*') and the testator omits to appoint trustees (see Trusts Lecture Notes (see Preface) at para 2.10.2) the Land Act, 2009, s 19 can assist.

3.8.1.1 Power to sell (section 50)

Section 50 confers a power on a personal representative to sell the whole or any part of the estate of a deceased person for the purpose not only of paying debts but also of distributing the estate among the persons entitled thereto. Note that in the event of a sale for the purpose of distribution, the personal representative shall, as far as is practicable, give effect to the wishes of the persons of full age entitled to the property proposed to be sold or, in the case of dispute, of the majority of the beneficiaries (according to the value of their combined interests). However, a purchaser is not concerned to see that the personal representatives have complied with such wishes: see s 51.

By virtue of s 51, a purchaser is protected from debts and liabilities of the deceased and from all claims of any person entitled to any share in the estate of the deceased. A purchaser is also protected where a grant has been revoked (s 25).

The Irish case of *Molyneux v White* (1894) 13 LR IR held that an executor could not give a good title to a purchaser without proof that there were unpaid debts when thirty-seven years had elapsed between the date of death and the date of sale. However, s 51 of the Succession Act, 1965 did not limit in any way the protection of a purchaser where time has elapsed. Kenny J, in the case of *Shiels v Flynn* [1975] IR 296, stated that in the case of persons who died after 1 June 1959 *Molyneux v White* was no longer good law. This tied in nicely with the wording of s 51.

In the later case of *Crowley v Flynn* [1983] ILRM 513, Barron J stated that where there is a lapse of twenty years, the purchaser is put on inquiry as to the reason for the sale. He relied on *Molyneux v White*. Professor Brady refers to the fact that Barron J made no mention of *Shiels v Flynn* and thus some uncertainty was introduced. There was further no reference to s 61 of the Succession Act, which states:

> *'A purchaser from personal representatives shall be entitled to assume that the personal representatives are acting correctly and within their powers.'*

The Civil Law (Miscellaneous Provisions) Act, 2008 amends the Succession Act in a number of respects, clarifying, amongst other issues, the following:

Section 3(1) of the Succession Act, 1965 defined the word *'purchaser'* as meaning *'a grantee, lessee, assignee, mortgagee, chargeant or other person who **in good faith** [author's emphasis] acquires an estate or interest in property for valuable consideration'*. There was always a doubt, because of the inclusion of the words *'in good faith'*, as to whether a purchaser from an executor was fully and effectively protected.

Section 67 of the 2008 Act amended the definition of *'purchaser'* by deleting the words *'in good faith'*. This removes any doubt.

3.8.1.2 Power to appropriate (section 55)

The personal representative has the power to appropriate any part of the estate of a deceased person in its actual condition or state of investment at the time of appropriation in or towards satisfaction of any share in the estate, whether settled or not, according to the respective rights of the persons interested in the estate. However, this power is subject to the provisions of s 55 of the Succession Act, 1965. A power to appropriate can, in practice, be useful and may facilitate an executor, but the executor must adhere closely to the provisions of s 55 unless the will specifies otherwise. Note the following points in connection with an appropriation under s 55:

(a) The assets which may be appropriated consist of any part of the estate of a deceased person in its actual condition or state of investment at the time of appropriation.

(b) An appropriation cannot be made under s 55 which would affect prejudicially any specific devise or bequest, but there is an exception to this and that is in a case to which s 56 applies. See para **4.5.7**.

(c) Appropriation cannot be made under s 55(3) until notice of the intended appropriation has been served on all parties entitled to share in the estate (other than persons who may come into existence after the time of the appropriation or who cannot after reasonable enquiries be found or ascertained at that time).

(d) In the event of any of these parties being disgruntled by the proposed appropriation, they may within six weeks from the service of such notice apply to the court

62 THE LEGAL PERSONAL REPRESENTATIVE

to prohibit the appropriation. Note that the court's role is supervisory only, and it can only prohibit the appropriation and cannot seek to enforce it.

In the case of *H v O* [1978] IR 194 the Supreme Court set down principles which would be adopted by the court on an application to prohibit an appropriation under subsection (3). Henchy J stated as follows (at 206):

> 'It must be assumed, having regard to the tenor, the scope and the purpose of the Section, that the Court should prohibit an intended appropriation only:
>
> (i) when the conditions in the section have not been complied with; or
>
> (ii) when, notwithstanding such compliance it would not be just or equitable to allow the appropriation to take place, having regard to the rights of all persons who are or will become entitled to an interest in the estate; or
>
> (iii) when, apart from the section, the appropriation would not be legally permissible.'

(e) Subsection (4) provides that an appropriation under s 55 cannot be made except with specified consents:

  (i) when made for the benefit of a person absolutely and beneficially entitled in possession, the consent of that person; and

  (ii) when made in respect of any settled share, the consent of either the trustee thereof if any (not being also the personal representative) or the person who may for the time being be entitled to the income.

(f) If the person whose consent is required is an infant or of unsound mind, consent can be given on his behalf by his parents or a parent, guardian, committee, or receiver or in the case of an infant if none is available, by the court on an application by his next friend (subsection (5)).

(g) Subsection (6) provides that no consent shall be required on behalf of a person who may come into existence after the time of appropriation or who cannot after reasonable enquiries be found or ascertained at that time. However, there is a certain protection afforded to these people in subsection (12) in that there is a direction that the personal representative must have regard to the rights of persons who may come into existence after the date of appropriation, or who cannot after enquiries be found or ascertained at the time of appropriation and of others whose consent is not required.

(h) An appropriation made pursuant to s 55 binds all persons interested in the property of the deceased whose consent is not made requisite unless the court on an application made to it under subsection (3) otherwise directs (subsection (11)).

(i) In relation to a subsequent purchaser from an individual to whom property has been appropriated, such appropriation is deemed to have been made in accordance with the requirements of s 55 and after all requisite notices and consents, if any, had been given. This provides a certain protection to purchasers (see subsection (14)).

(j) Note that s 55 applies whether the deceased died intestate or not and whether before or after the commencement of the Succession Act. This extends to all property over which a testator exercises a general power of appointment (s 16).

(k) The question of the valuation of property at the time of an appropriation can cause some difficulty. The correct view appears to be that the assets should be valued at the date of the appropriation, and this underlines the requirement to treat the question of an appropriation seriously and quickly. In order to protect the personal representative, the written consent to an appropriation should refer to the value of the assets for appropriation purposes.

The section was considered by Finnegan J in the High Court case of *Messitt v Henry* [2001] 3 IR 313. There, the deceased died intestate. He was a bachelor and survived by one sibling, the personal representative, and a number of nephews and nieces who were the issue of a predeceased sibling. The estate principally comprised a cottage and lands at Enniskerry, County Dublin.

The personal representative, who had been born in the cottage concerned, wished to appropriate the cottage and some surrounding land in satisfaction of her half share of the estate. She took advice from a reputable auctioneer and was advised as to a suitable subdivision of the lands, which would, in the opinion of her valuer, not prejudice the entitlement of the children of the predeceased sibling. Correspondence ensued between the solicitor having carriage of the administration and the issue of the predeceased sibling and their solicitor. A notice of appropriation was served which was objected to and an application was brought before the court, arising out of the objection.

The court accepted the bona fides of the personal representative seeking to appropriate the cottage and surrounding lands and took into account her sentimental attachment to the cottage and lands when assessing those bona fides. The court heard evidence of valuers adduced on behalf of the personal representative and on behalf of the other beneficiaries. It preferred the evidence of the valuer who gave evidence on behalf of the beneficiaries. He held that in the subdivision proposed by the personal representative there was a disparity, and that on that subdivision the personal representative would be acquiring 55 per cent of the estate, whereas the other beneficiaries would have their benefit reduced to 45 per cent of the estate. In such circumstances he prohibited the appropriation.

The court applied the principles laid down by the Supreme Court in *H v O* and held that the personal representative in exercising the right of appropriation nevertheless acts as a statutory trustee and it was imperative that the appropriation would not prejudice the interest of the other beneficiaries.

In the correspondence which passed between the respective solicitors, there was considerable detail relating to the liabilities of the estate, and the notice of appropriation made no reference to the apportionment of the liabilities. The court held that it could only have regard to the notice that issued pursuant to s 55 and not to the correspondence, and as the notice was silent as to liabilities it might suggest that there was not to be an equal apportionment of the liabilities and, to this extent, would further prejudice the other beneficiaries.

The court in *Messitt v Henry* appears to have approached the case as a mathematical exercise, which might not be the intention of the section. The court, for example, refused to take into account that, on the appropriation, the sister of the deceased would be entitled to claim agricultural relief which would have resulted in a saving of capital acquisitions tax for her in excess of IR£90,000 (€114,290).

It is imperative in appropriation cases, therefore, that it be impressed upon any valuer the importance of being very accurate in respect of the valuations and, if necessary, to err on the side of caution by according, perhaps, a slightly greater benefit to persons who might claim to be prejudiced by the appropriation. It is fair to say that in cases of this sort there may well be a family history whereby persons will object to appropriation so that a particular person does not obtain a particular piece of property, and it would be very important therefore that the valuer give very clear and precise advice. No service will be done to a client if the value is either inflated or deflated. The valuation should be as accurate as possible, accepting, of course, that valuation is not an exact science.

Care should be taken in relation to the drafting of the notice of appropriation to include all matters relevant to the appropriation, such as the apportionment of liabilities where that arises.

Stamp duty and appropriation

It is important to note that appropriation of property to satisfy a benefit under a will or trust is not exempt from stamp duty unless the disposition (i.e. the will) gives a power to the executors to so appropriate. If the power is not expressly given in the will, the appropriation is subject to *ad valorem* stamp duty as a conveyance or transfer on sale, whereas only nominal stamp duty is payable if a specific power to appropriate is contained in the will.

64 THE LEGAL PERSONAL REPRESENTATIVE

The power to appropriate is an area that can be overlooked in practice and it is therefore very important to include such an appropriation at the will-drafting stage. For further discussion on this, see Bohan, *Capital Acquisitions Tax*, 4th edn (2013), para 9.48.

In addition to stamp duty, please note the provisions of s 55(17) of the Succession Act:

> *'Where any property is appropriated under the provisions of this section, a conveyance thereof by the personal representatives to the person to whom it is appropriated shall not by reason only that the property so conveyed is accepted by the person to whom it is conveyed in or towards the satisfaction of a legacy or a share in residuary estate be liable to any higher stamp duty than that payable on a transfer of a personal property for the like purpose.'*

Under a deed of family arrangement (see para **15.3**) or a variation of the terms of the will or shares on intestacy, stamp duty liability can arise in any document completed for the purpose of passing any interest in land. One should ensure that such stamp duty is paid and that there is no collusion with the beneficiary for the non-payment of same.

Note: where an appropriation has been made in favour of a surviving spouse and the surviving spouse has made a payment into the estate to cover the excess in value of the property appropriated by his share in the estate (s 56(9)), the protection of s 55(17) as outlined earlier against payment of stamp duty may not extend to at least the equality money paid, since the conveyance would then be, in part, a sale.

3.8.1.3 Power to appropriate under section 56

The question of appropriation under s 56 is dealt with extensively at para **4.5.7**.

3.8.1.4 Power to appoint trustees for a minor beneficiary (section 57)

Section 57 enables the personal representatives to appoint trustees where a minor is entitled to any share in the estate of a deceased person and there are no trustees appointed able and willing to act. Section 58 confers powers on such trustees to deal with the property. Please note that s 58(2) of same has been repealed by the Land and Conveyancing Law Reform Act, 2009. See Spierin, *The Succession Act 1965 and Related Legislation: A Commentary*, 5th edn (2017), pp 175–7.

3.8.1.5 Power to lease (section 60)

Under s 60 the personal representatives are given wide powers to lease property where this is reasonably necessary for the administration of the estate. Note, however, that the powers of leasing of an executor may be enlarged, varied, or indeed restricted by the will of the deceased.

3.8.1.6 Power to mortgage (section 60(3)) and to complete transactions (section 60(4))

Section 60(3) confers authority on the personal representatives from time to time to raise money by way of mortgage or charge for the payment of expenses, debts, and liabilities, and any legal right and, with the approval of all the beneficiaries being *sui juris* or the court (but not otherwise), for the erection, repair, improvement, or completion of buildings, or the improvement of lands forming part of the estate of the deceased.

Section 60(4) confers authority on the personal representatives to complete any transaction which the deceased commenced prior to his death but which is not completed at the date of death.

3.8.1.7 Power to compromise (section 60(8))

Section 60(8) enables the personal representatives to settle claims and disputes without personal liability for loss, provided, however, that they have acted in good faith. For example, they can allow time for payment of any debt or compromise, compound, abandon, or submit to arbitration or otherwise settle any debt, account, dispute, claim, or other matter relating to the estate of the deceased.

Please note that this power to compromise does not extend to s 117 applications taken against the estate. See the judgment of Laffoy J in *Re the Estate of MK Deceased* [2010] IEHC 530. In such cases, the consent of the beneficiary adversely affected by the settlement should be obtained.

In the present economic climate, but always of relevance, is dealing with creditors of an estate. Section 49, while not a complete panacea, is helpful in protecting an executor (see para **12.5.2**).

The full effect of the Personal Insolvency Act, 2012 on an estate, be it as a debtor or a creditor, has complicated the position for executors, and how best to deal with the estate of an individual who is the subject of a debt relief notice, debt settlement arrangement, or personal insolvency arrangement remains to be seen. In particular, the need to advise the personal representative when a debtor seeks personal insolvency arrangements on his power under the legislation is more pressing than ever. Where a debt is owed to the estate, the executor should take particular care if settling the debt for less than the full amount owed. It may be advisable to seek a form of clearance or indemnity from those beneficiaries affected. For further information on this aspect, see Stephenson Solicitors' 23rd Lecture, *Time's-a-ticking and it's Later Than You Think!*.

3.8.2 POWERS CONFERRED ON AN EXECUTOR BY WILL

Because the powers of an executor under the Succession Act, 1965 are not always seen as sufficient, it is usual to confer wider powers on an executor in the will to deal with the assets and liabilities to enable further flexibility. The will is the first place to look for powers of an executor as the powers given under statute will probably have been extended and less often may have been curtailed.

Examples of such conferred powers are as follows:

1. Power to appropriate without serving any of the necessary notices or obtaining any of the required consents.

2. Power to invest or purchase unauthorised securities.

3. Power to employ agents/managers in respect of estate assets.

However, if these and other necessary powers are not given by the will, there is nothing which can be done post-death to impute same. Thus, what powers may be required in each testator's individual will, the type/location of assets, and the type of beneficiaries must be considered and so inserted, having first taken the testator's informed instructions.

3.8.2.1 The exercise of these powers

It is often the case that not all of the executors appointed in the will act in the administration of the estate. There are many reasons why this might occur, for example, that they are abroad, or due to issues of age and/or infirmity. Accordingly, though one of the executors may be alive and available to act he may be unwilling so to do and may choose to renounce or reserve. See paras **3.5.3** and **3.5.2** respectively.

Section 20 of the Succession Act deals with this issue and makes it clear that in such circumstances the executors who do prove the will are entitled to act without reference to the non-acting executor whose rights have been reserved.

The powers of executors are normally exercised jointly and severally. While the concurrence of executors who are named in the will but who have not taken out probate is not required, disposal of any assets in the estate, for example, will always require the signature of all acting executors. From a conveyancing point of view, it is advisable that all acting executors join in a conveyance of land.

3.8.3 WHAT IS THE DIFFERENCE BETWEEN THE ROLES OF AN EXECUTOR, A TRUSTEE, AND A GUARDIAN?

The role, duties, and powers of an executor have previously been discussed. In short, the function of an executor/administrator is to extract a grant to administer the estate and he has all the powers in the Succession Act, including the power of sale of assets and whatever powers the will bestows on him.

The role of a trustee is to carry out, as per the trust deed, the wishes of the settlor. The powers and duties of a trustee are dealt with in Chapters 1 and 2 of the Trusts Lecture Notes (see Preface).

The role of a guardian is to be in effect *in loco parentis* to the child for whom he is appointed guardian. See para **2.6**. A testamentary guardian may be appointed by will and this person is the person specifically appointed by the parent to care for the minor children should the need arise. See s 7 of the Guardianship of Infants Act, 1964 as replaced by s 50 of the Children and Family Relationships Act, 2015. Such a guardian would be appointed as follows:

> *'I hereby appoint X of [address] as Testamentary Guardian of any of my children who are under the age of 18 at the date of my death.'*

It is vital not to confuse the roles of executor, trustee, and guardian. Where the testator is appointing a person in either role, it is important that the provision appointing such persons is clear and certain and the duties and obligations of all roles are clearly explained and differentiated.

Confusion is most likely to occur when one person combines all three roles. For the distinction between personal representatives and trustees see Trusts Lecture Notes (see Preface) at para 1.9.

It is less likely that the role of a guardian will be confused with that of a personal representative or trustee as, while they can be the same person, they rarely are. Much depends on the specific circumstances of the case and the testator's instructions.

CHAPTER 4

WILL DRAFTING—THE RIGHTS OF SPOUSES/CIVIL PARTNERS, COHABITANTS, AND CHILDREN

4.1 Introduction

After examining the basic elements of will drafting, closer examination must be made of the legislative provisions affecting a testator's capacity to dispose of his property freely by will. These provisions should be at the forefront of a practitioner's mind in advising a testator and their full effects must be explained in detail to the testator. As has been outlined in previous chapters, a female testator is a testatrix. All references to testator apply equally to a testatrix unless specifically stated not to.

The testamentary freedom of a married testator is curtailed by the provisions of Part IX of the Succession Act, 1965 (hereinafter referred to as 'the Succession Act'). It is restricted to an even greater extent where the testator is both married and a parent, and indeed is further restricted by the provisions of Parts 8 and 15 of the Civil Partnership and Certain Rights and Obligations of Cohabitants Act, 2010 (hereinafter referred to as the 'Civil Partnership Act') where the testator is a civil partner or qualified cohabitant.

The status of the surviving spouse in Ireland is well established and was clearly set out in the Succession Act. There have been few changes to this position in the past fifty years. There have, of course, been some refinements made to same, most notably under Family Law legislation, in particular under s 14 of the Family Law Act, 1995 and under s 18 of the Family Law (Divorce) Act, 1996. Of course, following the Marriage Act, 2015 (hereinafter called the 'Marriage Act') there is a major change to marriage (see para **2.3.1**); however, the definition of a 'spouse' did not change and thus references below to spouse will include spouses of the same sex.

Six months after the Marriage Act was commenced (16 November 2015) it was no longer possible for an Irish civil partnership to be entered into. Existing civil partnerships are not affected and continue to be valid.

Since the Civil Partnership Act was enacted on 1 January 2011, slightly more than 2,100 civil partnerships have been registered in Ireland. While some of these have been dissolved there remain a substantial number of existing civil partnerships and a number of civil partnerships entered into in foreign jurisdictions which are recognised here (see para **4.2.1**). Although a number of people in civil partnerships may choose to dissolve their civil partnership and possibly enter into a same-sex marriage (either with each other or with someone else), some will not and thus there will still be a number, albeit dwindling, of civil partnerships in existence. Thus, for some time to come, the legal issues and tax law in relation to civil partnerships will continue to be relevant.

4.1.1 CIVIL PARTNERSHIP ACT

The Civil Partnership Act came into force on 1 January 2011 and at that time reflected, in succession terms, the changes in Irish society since 1965 and the fact that there were a number of same-sex couples and non-married couples who needed legal recognition. The Civil Partnership Act amended the Succession Act and thus references to sections of that Act must be read in light of this. For example, in general, where there is a reference to a spouse in the Succession Act it is now amended by inserting the words 'or civil partner' after 'spouse'. Thus, it is more important than ever, when referring to the Succession Act, that it is the most recent version that is consulted.

The Civil Partnership Act gave a civil partner rights very similar to, but not exactly or precisely the same as, those of a surviving spouse. As we will see, where a deceased civil partner has children, the legal right share of the surviving civil partner, while similar to that of a surviving spouse, is not exactly the same. For example, where the testator leaves a child or children surviving, the surviving civil partner, unlike a surviving spouse, has no guarantee of a legal right to a one-third share of the estate nor indeed the two-thirds share on intestacy where the deceased leaves a child. See ss 117(3A) and 67A(3) of the Succession Act as inserted by the Civil Partnership Act.

This 'flaw' in the Civil Partnership Act was remedied by the Marriage Act (see ss 67 and 69) and a spouse can now be of the same sex.

Further, the Civil Partnership Act gives a right of redress to cohabitants that is more akin to the right of a child to take a s 117 action than the rights of a surviving spouse, yet it is not the same as either.

4.1.2 TAKING INSTRUCTIONS RE SPOUSES, CIVIL PARTNERS, AND COHABITANTS

Nevertheless, any practitioner taking instructions for a will needs to establish the 'civil status' (formerly marital status) of the testator, i.e. is the testator single, engaged, married, deserted, separated, divorced, widowed, a civil partner, a surviving civil partner, a civil partner whose civil partnership has been dissolved (i.e. a 'divorced' civil partner), a cohabitant, or a qualified cohabitant. In other words, a key issue for practitioners when taking instructions for a will is to establish the civil status of the client and to be able to advise accordingly. See para **5.2** for a Precedent Instruction Sheet for a will, and in particular the sections relating to spouses, civil partners, and cohabitants.

The difficulties of so advising are all too apparent when the fact is that more than one civil status can apply to the same testator at any one time—for example, it is possible to have an ex-spouse and a current civil partner simultaneously, or indeed an ex-spouse, an ex-civil partner, and a cohabitant simultaneously or a civil partner and a cohabitant. Further, while it is not possible to have a spouse and a civil partner simultaneously, it is eminently possible to have a spouse (albeit one who qualifies for divorce: see s 172(6) of the Civil Partnership Act) and a cohabitant simultaneously.

It has been suggested by many that the provision of registration of same-sex civil partnerships and the protection of vulnerable cohabitants should have been dealt with by way of two separate acts, as what has been enacted could be considered to be a very unhappy 'marriage' of two fundamentally different relationships.

The problem lies in the fact that to become a civil partner a positive act was required, and neither party to a civil registration could be in any doubt that their legal status had now changed. However, one can be, or can have been, a cohabitant without taking any positive step and thus without ever being aware that one's legal status has changed. This makes advising a client very difficult, not least as they themselves may be completely unaware of their civil status, and detailed (and what will often appear very intrusive) queries by the practitioner will be required. See Stephenson Solicitors' 29th Seminar, Do Ask—Do Tell, pp 23–7.

This chapter does not deal with the Civil Partnership Act in general, but merely its provisions in relation to succession law; therefore, the relevant sections of the Civil Partnership Act should be read in detail for a full understanding of that Act.

There have been many commentaries and lectures on this subject which can also usefully be consulted, for example:

1. Paula Fallon's CPD/STEP Lecture, *The Civil Partnership and Certain Rights and Obligations of Cohabitants Act 2010*, 30 September 2010;

2. Stephenson Solicitors' 17th Lecture, *Will Drafting for the New Decade: Applying New Legislation and Updating Old Skills*, pp 54–64, 23 April 2010 and Stephenson Solicitors' 18th Lecture, *Administering Estates in the New Decade: New Forms, Case Law and Legislation*, pp 32–53, 19 November 2010. Indeed, the authors are indebted to Anne Marie Maher BL, who dealt with the Civil Partnership Act in that lecture, for some of the material in this section of the chapter.

The Cohabitation Redress Scheme applies to persons of the same sex or opposite sex living in an intimate relationship, where the parties are not married or in a civil partnership with one another.

In most situations where the testator and his spouse/civil partner are happily married/in a happy civil partnership, the testator leaves his entire estate to the surviving spouse/civil partner with a gift over to the children if the spouse/civil partner does not survive for a specified period, typically thirty days, or if the spouse/civil partner dies simultaneously with the testator (see para 2.17 'Commorientes' Clause). However, as does quite often happen, if the testator does not wish to leave the bulk of his estate to his surviving spouse/civil partner, or wishes to leave the spouse/civil partner less than they are entitled to under Part IX of the Succession Act, 1965 as amended by the Civil Partnership Act, then they must be informed of the Act's provisions in detail and the possible consequences of them. The practitioner should check whether the testator wishes to leave anything in the will to his spouse/civil partner/cohabitant, how that bequest is to be expressed, and all possible results of this bequest on the estate: for example, s 115.

Who is a spouse has long been established, but given the fact that the Civil Partnership Act is relatively new, who is a civil partner under the legislation needs to be addressed before the discussion of the rights of surviving spouses/civil partners can be considered.

4.2 Who is a Civil Partner in Ireland?

Civil Partnership Registration only applied to persons of the same sex and provided for the same-sex couple, on registration, to become civil partners. This new legal status (which already is no longer a possibility since the Marriage Act 2015) conferred on civil partners statutory rights and obligations, automatically conferred upon each of the civil partners on registration.

A civil partner is defined under s 3 of the Civil Partnership Act, 2010 as follows:

'*A civil partner is either of two persons of the same sex who are—*

(a) parties to a civil partnership registration that has not been dissolved or the subject of a decree of nullity, or

(b) parties to a legal relationship of a class that is the subject of an order made under section 5 that has not been dissolved or the subject of a decree of nullity.'

Therefore, to enter into a civil partnership, the parties had to be:

- over eighteen years;
- of the same sex;

- unmarried and or unregistered; and
- unrelated to each other (i.e. not within the prescribed prohibited degrees of relationship—see s 26 of the Civil Partnership Act for the new third schedule to the Civil Registration Act, 2004).

The Civil Partnership Act provided for registration of a civil partnership in the same way as registration of a marriage, and in this regard the Civil Partnership Act made significant amendments to the Civil Registration Act, 2004 to extend civil registration to include civil partnerships.

As with marriage, a will made prior to entry into civil partnership was revoked by that civil partnership, except a will made in contemplation of entry into that civil partnership, whether so expressed in the will or not. Section 79 of the Civil Partnership Act amends s 85(1) of the Succession Act to include the registration of a civil partnership. However, as is the case with divorce, dissolution of a civil partnership does not revoke a will.

Note however that under s 16 of the Marriage Act, 2015 the wills of existing civil partners who marry each other will not be automatically revoked.

4.2.1 IS A FOREIGN CIVIL PARTNERSHIP RECOGNISED?

The recognition of same-sex relationships registered outside Ireland is dealt with under s 5 of the Civil Partnership Act, which states as follows:

> 'The Minister may, by order, declare that a class of legal relationship entered into by two parties of the same sex is entitled to be recognised as a civil partnership.'

This applies, provided the legal relationship was exclusive in nature and complied with requirements set out under s 5(1). The Minister made such orders by way of SIs 648/2010, 649/2010, 505/2012, 490/2013, and 212/2014, the latter taking effect on 23 May 2014. Clearly this is an evolving area of law and thus it is important, when considering the validity of a foreign civil partnership, to check the most recent statutory instrument in this area.

In a similar manner, under s 5(4) the Civil Partnership Act provides for the recognition of foreign dissolutions, and these will be recognised as dissolutions under s 110. It is important to note in relation to this that the recognition of foreign civil partners' relationships/dissolutions is not retrospective.

Note however, that s 11(6), (7), (8), (9), and (10) of the Marriage Act, 2015 amend or revoke these SIs so that no foreign civil partnership will be recognised six months after the repeal of the Civil Partnership Registration (s 12). This took effect from 16 November 2015 and so foreign civil partnerships registered after 16 May 2016 will not be recognised.

Same-sex marriages will be recognised as marriages here from the later of the date of the commencement of s 11 or the date of the marriage.

There is no 'backdating' of the recognition.

4.2.2 HOW CAN A CIVIL PARTNER CEASE TO BE A CIVIL PARTNER FOR SUCCESSION ACT PURPOSES?

The rights of a civil partner can be extinguished in various ways, such as by:

1. grant of Decree of Nullity (see s 107 of the Civil Partnership Act);
2. grant of Decree of Dissolution (see s 110 of the Civil Partnership Act);

    Note that a will made after the registration of a civil partnership is not automatically revoked by the dissolution. However, a marriage by a civil partner will revoke a will unless of course it is made in contemplation of said marriage or it is a marriage of civil partners to each other (see para **2.3**).

3. renunciation (see s 113A of the Succession Act);
4. unworthiness to succeed (see s 120 of the Succession Act, as amended).

However, if any of these apply, full details should be taken and a copy of all renunciations/decrees/orders should be obtained. It should also be noted that there are a number of possible ancillary reliefs available which may have been granted on dissolution. Indeed, somewhat analogous to the rights of a former spouse under s 18(4) of the Family Law Act, 1995, an ex-civil partner can, on the death of the other, bring an application for provision to be made from the estate of the deceased civil partner (see s 127 of the Civil Partnership Act) but, again similar to s 18 of the Family Law Act, 1995, under s 127(11) of the Civil Partnership Act this right can be blocked.

4.3 Spouses'/Civil Partners' Rights

The legal right of the spouse/civil partner and provision for children applies where a **testator** dies on or after 1 January 1967, the date of commencement of the Succession Act, 1965. See ss 109(1) and 2 of the Succession Act, 1965. Note also, for deaths after 14 June 1988, the rights accorded to marital children are conferred on non-marital children, regardless of when the deceased made his will.

4.4 Death 'wholly or partly testate'

Section 109

> 'Where, after the commencement of this Act, a person dies wholly or partly testate leaving a spouse/civil partner or children or both spouse and children, the provisions of this part shall have effect'.

Therefore, this part of the Act only applies to a person who dies wholly or partly testate. It does not apply to a person who dies intestate.

4.5 The Surviving Spouse's/Civil Partner's Legal Right Share

The surviving spouse/civil partner possesses a unique importance because of the provisions of the Succession Act, 1965, as amended, designed to protect the surviving spouse/civil partner where the deceased spouse/civil partner dies testate or partially testate. These types of provisions do not exist for any other category of beneficiary, whether to protect a beneficiary from disinheritance or to ensure that a beneficiary is notified of their rights under the Act.

This protection in the 1965 Act is a blatant, but some would deem necessary, restriction on the right of the testator to leave his property to whomsoever he might wish. The rights of the surviving spouse/civil partner should be read in conjunction with the right of appropriation of that surviving spouse/civil partner in respect of the dwelling in which the surviving spouse/civil partner was ordinarily resident at the date of death. See s 56 of the Succession Act, 1965, and also para **4.5.7**.

Remember, however, that a surviving spouse/civil partner can cease to be a surviving spouse/civil partner actually and/or for Succession Act purposes in a number of ways: renunciation, separation, divorce (bearing in mind the provisions of s 18 of the Family Law (Divorce) Act, 1996: see paras **4.2.2** and **4.5.8.3**), dissolution, nullity, and s 120 unworthiness to succeed, all of which will be discussed in more detail later.

4.5.1 WHAT EXACTLY IS THE LEGAL RIGHT SHARE?

Section 109(2)

> *'In this Part, references to the estate of the testator are to all estate to which he was beneficially entitled for an estate or interest not ceasing on his death and remaining after payment of all expenses, debts, and liabilities (other than estate duty [CAT]) properly payable thereout.'*

What does this mean?

'all Estate . . . not ceasing on his death'.

This excludes:

1. trust property which the deceased held at his death as sole trustee and which vests in his personal representatives (see s 10(5)), as a testator would not have had a beneficial entitlement to such property;
2. joint property passing by survivorship, i.e. where there is a presumption of advancement which has not been rebutted;
3. property in which the deceased person had a limited interest ceasing on death;
4. *validly* nominated property (please see para **12.7**):
   - statutory: credit union, Post Office Savings Certificates;
   - non-statutory: nominated pension schemes and insurance policies.

'after payment of all expenses debts . . . other than . . . [capital acquisitions tax] properly payable thereout.'

Capital acquisitions tax is a tax payable by the beneficiaries, not the estate. This means the net estate after all just debts and expenses (consider s 47, see also para 14.5 re s 49 notice) have been paid out. Debts and expenses include funeral, testamentary, and administration expenses.

This includes testate and intestate estates: in short, everything that is available to be distributed under the will or partial intestacy or full intestacy.

4.5.2 CALCULATING THE LEGAL RIGHT SHARE AND THE RESIDUE—TWO DIFFERENT THINGS AND THUS TWO DIFFERENT CALCULATIONS

4.5.2.1 How to calculate the legal right share

The **gross estate** (which does not include joint property, life interests, nominations, etc)

Less **costs, liabilities, and expenses** (specific bequests under the will are not deducted)

Leaves the **net estate**.

Once the net estate is established, the legal right share may be calculated as a fraction of the net estate.

Please note that this is how the legal right share is calculated and pertains only to the calculation of the legal right share, **which is separate and distinct from calculating the residue.**

4.5.2.2 How to calculate the residue

In order to obtain the value of the residue the calculation would be:

The gross estate

Less bequests

Leaves the gross residue

WILL DRAFTING—THE RIGHTS OF SPOUSES/CIVIL PARTNERS

Less **debts properly payable from the residue** (Not all debts are paid from the residue, e.g. the will may dictate that debts are paid otherwise than from the residue. Also, if there is a partial intestacy then Part II of the First Schedule to the Succession Act applies and debts are first payable from the assets in the partial intestacy; see para **12.4.2.2**.)

Leaves the net value of the residue.

For how to calculate a partial intestacy see para **4.5.5.5**.

4.5.2.3 Does the testator have children?

Section 111 of the Succession Act, 1965 provides:

> *'If the testator leaves a spouse and no children, the spouse shall have a right to one half of the estate. If the testator leaves a spouse and children, the spouse shall have a right to one third of the estate.'*

Section 111(A)

> *'(1) If the testator leaves a civil partner and no children, the civil partner shall have a right to one-half of the estate.*
>
> *(2) Subject to section 117(3A), if the testator leaves a civil partner and children, the civil partner shall have a right to one-third of the estate.'*

In this instance, the extent of the share depends upon whether or not the testator leaves a child or children, unlike the share on intestacy, which depends on whether there is issue. Note that the legal right share only applies in a testate situation. A surviving spouse/civil partner on intestacy is always better provided for in that a spouse/civil partner on intestacy is entitled to two-thirds of the estate if the deceased has issue. If the deceased has no issue, the surviving spouse/civil partner on intestacy is entitled to the entire estate. However, in relation to surviving civil partners, see the possibility of diminution of their share on a successful application by a child or children of an intestate civil partner under s 67A(3).

When advising a testator, calculation of the legal right share is vital for the testator. In order for the testator to make an informed decision, accurate figures must be available to him. It is not sufficient to indicate that the legal right share will be half or one-third of the net estate, as the case may be. The testator making the will needs to know how much money is involved and how his estate will be affected if the surviving spouse/civil partner chooses the legal right share.

Similarly, post-death, the surviving spouse/civil partner will need similar advice, in terms of figures and not just fractions, in order to make an informed choice (see para **12.4.2.2**) and indeed how the legal right share, if taken, will affect the other beneficiaries (see para **12.4.2.3**).

It is crucial to remember that it is the child or children of the deceased testator, not his spouse's or civil partner's child or children, who determine whether the share is a third or a half.

4.5.2.4 Who is a child of the testator for the purposes of Part IX of the Succession Act, 1965?

- Children of the blood (whether marital or non-marital).
- Children validly adopted.

In light of the Children and Family Relationships Act, 2015, particular care should be taken to establish who is a child.

4.5.2.5 Who is not a child of the testator for the purposes of Part IX of the Succession Act, 1965?

- Stepchildren.
- Foster children.
- Children in relation to whom the deceased acted *in loco parentis*.

4.5.3 THE PRIORITY OF THE LEGAL RIGHT SHARE

Furthermore, the testator must also be advised of the priority of the legal right share.

Section 112

> 'The right of a spouse under Section 111 or the right of a civil partner under section 111A (which shall be known as a legal right) shall have priority over devises, bequests, and shares on intestacy.'

This means that the legal right share ranks in priority after the rights of creditors of the deceased and before/ahead of any other beneficiary.

The practitioner should check whether the testator's spouse/civil partner has renounced in any way. See para **4.5.9**. Under s 113 and s 113A, the legal right of a spouse/civil partner may be renounced in writing by an ante-nuptial/ante-civil-partnership-registration contract or during marriage/after registration of civil partnership. The question of a renunciation, however, will always have to be carefully scrutinised, especially if the parties met on unequal terms. In this instance it is important always to note the necessity for independent legal advice and the possibility of undue influence.

The practitioner should check whether the testator wishes to leave anything in the will to his spouse/civil partner, how that bequest is to be expressed, and all possible results of this bequest on the estate, for example, s 114.

In relation to civil partners and the legal right share please note that this is vulnerable under s 117(3A) as this amendment to the Succession Act by the Civil Partnership Act confers upon the court the power to make an order under s 117, only, however, where a court is of the view that it would be unjust not to make such an order. See para **4.6.4.1**.

4.5.4 SECTION 114 (BEQUEST IN ADDITION TO LEGAL RIGHT SHARE)

Section 114 provides that where property is devised or bequeathed in a will to a spouse/civil partner and the devise or bequest is expressed in the will to be in addition to the share as a legal right of the spouse/civil partner, the testator shall be deemed to have made by the will a gift to the spouse/civil partner consisting of:

(a) a sum equal to the value of the share as a legal right of the spouse/civil partner; and

(b) the property so devised or bequeathed.

Such provisions are very rare but do occur. Should such a situation arise, Brian E. Spierin S.C. has included a suitable precedent in his book, *Wills—Irish Precedents and Drafting*, 2nd edn (2012), p 102, para 6.55, which is repeated here:

> 'I give the sum of € to my husband/wife/civil partner of which said sum is to be in addition to the legal right share to which my said husband/wife/civil partner is entitled by reason of the provisions of Part IX of the Succession Act 1965 as amended by the Civil Partnership and Certain Obligations of Cohabitants Act 2010.'

Section 114(2) states that in any other case (in practice the vast majority of instances), a devise or bequest in a will to a spouse/civil partner shall be deemed to have been intended by the testator to be in satisfaction of the share as a legal right of the spouse/civil partner.

> 'In any other case, a . . . bequest in a will to a spouse/civil partner shall be deemed to have been intended by the testator to be in satisfaction of the legal right share.'

This is the more likely scenario, and in this case the surviving spouse/civil partner will have a choice or 'election' to make.

4.5.5 WHAT CHOICES ARE OPEN TO THE SURVIVING SPOUSE/CIVIL PARTNER?

The surviving spouse/civil partner has a number of choices, depending on whether or not there was a bequest to him or her in the will or if there is a partial intestacy.

4.5.5.1 Bequest to spouse/civil partner

If there was a bequest to the surviving spouse/civil partner in the will, the surviving spouse/civil partner has a right of election between the legal right share or the bequest under the will and a share of any partial intestacy. See para **4.5.5.3**.

The right of election does not automatically vest in the surviving spouse/civil partner and should the surviving spouse/civil partner die before election, then they are deemed to have taken under the will. See *In re Urquhart* [1974] IR 197.

4.5.5.2 No bequest to spouse/civil partner

If nothing is left in the will, then there is no election as the right vests automatically in the survivor, on the death of the spouse/civil partner or the personal representative of the survivor, should the survivor die shortly thereafter. See *Re Cummins; O'Dwyer v Keegan* [1997] 2 IR 585; [1997] 2 ILRM 401. See also paras **4.5.6** and **13.6.4.1**.

4.5.5.3 The right of election

Section 115 contains the detailed provisions governing the right of a surviving spouse/civil partner to elect between the legal right over the entire estate (not merely that bequeathed by will) on the one hand or the bequest(s) under a will *and* the share on partial intestacy on the other. The comparative benefits must be calculated and the effect of same on the other beneficiaries, see para **12.4.2.3**.

Section 115

'(1) (a) Where under the will of a deceased person who dies wholly testate, there is a devise or bequest to a spouse or civil partner, the spouse or civil partner may elect to take either that devise or bequest or the share to which he is entitled as a legal right.

(b) In default of election the spouse or civil partner shall be entitled to take under the will and he shall not be entitled to take any share as a legal right.

(2) (a) Where a person dies partly testate and partly intestate, a spouse or civil partner may elect to take either

(i) his share as a legal right or

(ii) his share under the intestacy [two-thirds if there are children, all if there are none], together with any devise or bequest to him under the will of the deceased.

(b) In default of election the spouse or civil partner shall be entitled to take his share under the intestacy, together with any devise or bequest to him under the will, and he shall not be entitled to take any share as a legal right.

(3) A spouse or civil partner, in electing to take a share as a legal right, may further elect to take any devise or bequest to him less in value than the share in partial satisfaction thereof.

(4) It shall be the duty of the personal representatives to notify the spouse or civil partner in writing of the right of election conferred by this section. The right shall not be exercisable after the expiration of six months from the receipt by the spouse or civil partner of such notification or one year from the first taking out of representation of the deceased's estate, whichever is the later.

(5) Where the surviving spouse or civil partner is a person of unsound mind the right of election conferred by this section may, if there is a committee of the spouse's or civil partner's estate,

be exercised on behalf of the spouse or civil partner by the committee by leave of the Court which has appointed the committee or, if there is no committee, be exercised by the High Court or, in a case within the jurisdiction of the Circuit Court, by that Court.

(6) *In this section but only in its application to a case to which subsection (1) of section 114 applies, "devise or bequests" means a gift deemed under the subsection to have been made by the will of the testator.'*

Therefore, where the testator dies fully testate and leaves a bequest to his spouse/civil partner, they may elect to take *either* that bequest *or* their legal right share. If they do not choose, they are deemed to take the bequest and lose their legal right share entitlements. From a financial perspective, there are other considerations. This is a straightforward calculation to make: which is worth more, the legal right share or the bequest under the will? However, monetary considerations do not always take priority. See para **4.5.10** for the effect on the will and administration of the estate if the spouse/civil partner takes their legal right share.

4.5.5.4 The right of election and partial intestacy

This possibility is covered by s 115(2):

(a) *'Where a person dies partly testate and partly intestate, a spouse or civil partner may elect to take either;*

　(i) *his share as a legal right, or*

　(ii) *his share under the intestacy, together with any devise or bequest to him under the will of the deceased.*

(b) *In default of election, the spouse or civil partner shall be entitled to take his share under the intestacy, together with any devise or bequest to him under the will, and he shall not be entitled to take any share as a legal right.'*

4.5.5.5 How to calculate a partial intestacy

This is not as straightforward a calculation. The following needs to be established before the calculation is possible:

- Value of the gross estate.
- Value of all the bequests under the will.
- Value of debts, funeral, and testamentary expenses.

How to calculate the value of a partial intestacy:

1. Subtract the value of all bequests under the will from the value of the gross estate to arrive at the value of the gross intestate part of the estate.

2. Subtract the value of debts, funeral, and testamentary expenses from the gross intestate part of the estate to arrive at the value of the net intestate part of the estate.

When these figures are established, practitioners should set the legal right share of the entire net estate against the bequest under the will and surviving spouse/civil partner's share of intestacy (all of the intestate estate if the deceased did not leave children and two-thirds of the intestate part of the estate if the deceased left children). See para **8.4**.

As noted, when calculating the value of the partial intestacy, one must first deduct all liabilities from the value of the intestate part of the estate. If this is not done there is an incorrect calculation, and this error has the effect of falsely raising the value of the partial intestacy. The legislative source for this is Part II of the Second Schedule to the Succession Act, 1965:

'Order of application of assets where the estate is solvent

1. *Property of the deceased undisposed of by will, subject to the retention thereout of a fund -sufficient to meet any pecuniary legacies.'*

4.5.5.6 Where the surviving spouse/civil partner is of unsound mind

Where the surviving spouse or civil partner is of unsound mind the election may be made by the spouse/civil partner's committee with leave of the court or, if there is no committee, by the court itself. See s 115(5).

4.5.5.7 Is property situate abroad affected by the legal right share?

As previously discussed, it applies to the net estate of the testator, that is to say all his property, both real and personal after payment of expenses, debts, and liabilities.

What is the position in relation to property situate abroad? This is a more complex situation and practitioners are referred to *Re GM: FM v TAM* [1972] 106 ILTR 82.

Movable property is, of course, governed by the *lex domicilii* and, if the testator died domicile in Ireland, would be covered by Part IX, as would immovable property situate in Ireland.

4.5.6 LIMITATION PERIODS—ENFORCEABILITY OF LEGAL RIGHT SHARE

It is necessary to discuss with the testator the time limits for claims against his estate or by his estate after his death, if only because, quite often, this may prompt the testator to disclose circumstances which otherwise he may neglect to mention.

In looking at the limitation periods, in a situation where there is either a spouse (or civil partner—remember that since the Civil Partnership Act all of this also applies to civil partners) for whom no provision has been made in a will, or a spouse who has a right on intestacy, the normal period of time for a claim under s 111 is governed by s 45 of the Statute of Limitations, as amended by s 126 of the Succession Act, 1965. Section 126 provides that no action in respect of any claims to the estate shall be brought after the expiration of six years from the date when the right to receive the share or interest accrued.

However, in a case where provision is made in a will for a spouse or civil partner, time would appear to run from when notice has been served of the right of election.

It is important to note that the right of election is not exercisable after the expiration of six months from the receipt by the spouse or civil partner of such notification or one year from the first taking out of representation of the deceased's estate, whichever is later (s 115(4)).

As noted earlier, where a spouse or civil partner dies before electing, the estate of that spouse or civil partner takes the bequest under the will. The right of election is not heritable, it is personal to the spouse or civil partner. This also applies where the spouse or civil partner dies *before* being notified of the right of election.

A practitioner may well be consulted by a surviving spouse or civil partner for advice on whether or not to elect to take their legal right share and must be in a position to be able to calculate the relative benefits under the will or on election.

Leaving a spouse or civil partner a life interest in an estate does not satisfy the requirements of s 111. If a will so provides, the surviving spouse/civil partner can elect to take an absolute one-half or one-third as the legal right share, including the life interest in partial satisfaction of that share. A surviving spouse/civil partner also receives any property held jointly with their deceased spouse by survivorship. This is not taken into account in calculating the legal right share, and the spouse/civil partner can still turn around and claim a legal right share in the remainder of the estate not jointly held. In relation to a civil partner, this, of course, is not a guaranteed share, given s 117(3A).

The right of election is a personal right conferred on the spouse/civil partner which cannot be subsequently exercised by their personal representative, should the surviving spouse/civil partner die before election. See the case of *Re Urquhart* [1974] IR 197.

In any instance where the question of election arises, it is vital to ensure that the surviving spouse/civil partner obtains independent legal advice to ensure that they are fully aware of what is involved in such an election. Practitioners should note also that a spouse/civil partner, in electing to take the legal right share, may further elect to take any devise or bequest to them less in value than the share in partial satisfaction thereof (see subsection (3)). This would include a limited interest in any part of the estate, which would have to be valued.

Practitioners should note the Supreme Court decision in *Re Cummins; O'Dwyer v Keegan* [1997] 2 ILRM 401. The facts of this case were as follows.

Thomas Cummins and Kathleen Cummins were husband and wife. Thomas Cummins died on 2 February 1995 and at the time of his death his wife was in a coma. She died later on the same day, without either regaining consciousness or becoming aware that her husband had died. The couple had no children. They both died testate.

The wife left a substantial estate of approximately £370,000. The husband's estate amounted to approximately £2,400,000. The husband made no provision for his wife in his will. The issue arose as to what interest, if any, the wife acquired in her husband's estate under the provisions of Part IX of the Succession Act by reason of his predeceasing her. She had not renounced her rights under that Part in accordance with the provisions of s 113, nor had she been disentitled to succeed by virtue of the provisions of Part X of the Act.

A residuary legatee of the wife's estate claimed that the wife's interest included the legal right under s 111 of the Act. Accordingly, the wife's executors commenced proceedings in which they sought from the court determination of the following question: 'whether by virtue of the death of her husband Thomas Cummins, Kathleen Cummins acquired a half share in the estate of her husband.'

In the High Court Kelly J rejected the claim by Kathleen Cummins's relative that Mrs Cummins was entitled under the Act to a legal right of one-half of her husband's estate. In the Supreme Court Barron J considered the net issue, i.e. whether the right given by s 111 of the Succession Act creates an interest in the property comprising the appropriate share in the estate of a deceased or merely a right personal to the widowed spouse to elect to take such interest. Part IX of the Act gives the widowed spouse a right to share in the estate of the deceased spouse notwithstanding testamentary dispositions to the contrary.

Barron J considered s 111(2):

> 'If the testator leaves a spouse and children, the spouse shall have a right to one-third of the estate.'

He considered the meaning to be given to the words *'shall have a right to'*. He determined that, first, the surviving spouse has a right to a share in the estate, and second, this right has the same quality as an interest arising under a will or a share arising on intestacy. The two latter interests vest on death. In his view, the former interest also vested. The question of election did not arise in this case as it arose in the case of *Re Urquhart*.

The court also held that the absence of any procedure for notification of the surviving spouse of her entitlement to avail of the legal right share was fatal because of the alternative interpretation upheld in the High Court. The court also noted the importance for certainty in the area of making of wills.

In his judgment, Barron J cited the view of Walsh J in the case of *Re Urquhart*:

> 'In my opinion the whole of this structure presupposes and is based upon an assumption implicit in the Statute, in addition to what is expressly stated in Section 111, that a legal right share arises on the moment of the death of the testator. Where there is no legacy or devise or where there is a legacy or devise expressed to be in addition to the legal right share, the legal share vests upon the death.
>
> But when a testator in his will makes a devise or bequest to his spouse and it is not expressed to be in addition to the spouse's legal right, then the spouse has a statutory right to take the share as a legal right, but that share does not vest until he takes it.
>
> If the spouse does not take the share as a legal right, then the legacy or devise under the will, which vested in the spouse at the death of the testator will remain vested in the spouse without taking any step in relation to it. The spouse can never have both.'

This was accepted in *O'Dwyer v Keegan* as a correct statement of law. Practitioners should note that there could be the following anomaly. Where a spouse makes provision in their will for a devise or bequest provided that the surviving spouse should survive for a period of thirty days, in circumstances where the surviving spouse dies within that period, the condition precedent in the will is not satisfied and therefore the spouse's estate is left completely unprovided for.

Re Urquhart is authority for the proposition that the legal share would not automatically vest on death as the surviving spouse has not positively asserted a claim to it. However, if the surviving spouse who dies within the thirty-day period had not been provided for at all, then the surviving spouse would automatically be entitled to a legal right share.

For further discussion on the enforceability of the legal right share and the legal right share in general, see Spierin, *The Succession Act 1965 and Related Legislation: A Commentary*, 5th edn (2017).

4.5.6.1 When is the value of the legal right share established?

There are invariably arguments about when the legal right share should be valued as the spouse/civil partner and the estate/remaining beneficiaries will each argue for a valuation date that suits them best.

This was especially true during the Celtic Tiger years, as there was, in most cases, a radical increase in value from the date of death to the date of distribution; although, in more recent times, the opposite was generally the case—the argument continues, albeit in reverse.

There are those who argue that the legal right share should be calculated on the value of the net estate as at the date of death (i.e. the values as outlined in the form SA.2) and those who argue that it should be calculated on the value of the net estate as at the date of appropriation.

- Where the value has increased, the beneficiaries will be arguing, it should be the date of death value, whereas the spouse/civil partner will want the date of distribution as the valuation date.

- Where the value has decreased, the beneficiaries will be arguing, it should be the date of distribution, whereas the spouse/civil partner will want the date of death value as the valuation date.

Unfortunately, the Succession Act, 1965 does not specify the date on which the legal right share is to be valued.

Those who argue that the date is the date of death value do so on the basis that s 109 defines an 'estate' as that to which the testator was beneficially entitled as at his death, and therefore it is the value as at the date of death that should be used.

However, all that s 109 defines is what is in the estate: see para **4.5.1**. Therefore, we must look to case law for assistance as to the valuation date.

The valuation of the legal right share, as well as other issues, was dealt with in the unreported judgment of O'Neill J in the High Court, in the case of *K v K and O'R* (delivered on 25 January 2007).

O'Neill J said that the executor

> 'had a duty to maximise the value of the estate for the benefit of the beneficiaries and to ensure a correct and just distribution of the estate in accordance with the will of the testator and in accordance with the lawful election of the first named defendant.'

In that case, the first named defendant was the surviving spouse and the value of the property, one of the principal assets of the estate, was, it was ordered, not to be valued as at the date of death but at its current value. In fact, O'Neill J went so far as to order that the property be sold so that its current value could be definitively established.

In general, it would appear (and indeed it is generally accepted) that the legal right share is valued at/on/near the date when it is being realised.

This remains a difficult area as legislation does not assist. Further, there are very few cases to aid our interpretation and those that do exist, as we can see from *K v K* and *O'R*, are not definitive, as it was not actually stated in this case that it is definitively the present value that should be taken into account; rather, it is stated that it is up to the legal personal representative to obtain the maximum value for the spouse, which right now may well be the date of death value whereas in previous years it would have been the present value.

The relatively more recent case of *S v H* (unreported) 12 March 2010, High Court, accepted that the value should be the date of death, although it is slightly ambiguous.

4.5.6.2 An example of the notification of the surviving spouse's/civil partner's right of election in a wholly testate situation

This notification should be amended accordingly where a civil partner is the notice party.

THE HIGH COURT

PROBATE

NOTIFICATION OF RIGHT OF ELECTION

WHERE DECEASED SPOUSE/CIVIL PARTNER DIES WHOLLY TESTATE

In the Estate of   , Deceased etc

To:

of:

We,   and   being the personal representatives of the above Deceased (hereinafter called 'the Deceased') late of   , who died on the day of , 20   , **HEREBY GIVE YOU NOTICE**, pursuant to section 115 of the Succession Act, 1965 (hereinafter called 'the Act') as follows:

1. By his last will (and codicil if applicable) dated the   day of   , 19/20   , the Deceased devised and bequeathed to you certain property in the following terms:

    [*here, quote from will*].

    The foregoing devise and bequest was not expressed to be in addition to your legal right share under the Act.

2. You may elect to take under section 115 of the Act either the property devised and bequeathed to you as aforesaid, or the share to which you are entitled as a legal right.

3. In default of election you will be entitled to take under the will and you shall not be entitled to take any share as a legal right.

4. The right of election conferred on you as aforesaid shall not be exercisable after the expiration of six months from the receipt by you of this Notification or one year from the first taking out of representation to the Deceased's Estate (which occurred on the   day of   20   ), whichever is the later.

Dated this   day of   , 20   .

_____

Solicitors for the personal representative

4.5.6.3 An example of the notification of the surviving spouse's/civil partner's right of election in a partly testate situation

Again, this notification should be amended accordingly where a civil partner is the notice party.

THE HIGH COURT

PROBATE

NOTIFICATION OF RIGHT OF ELECTION

WHERE DECEASED SPOUSE/CIVIL PARTNER DIES PARTLY TESTATE

In the Estate of   , Deceased.

To:

of:

We,   and   , being the personal representatives of the above named Deceased (hereinafter called 'the Deceased'), late of   , who died on the day of   , 20   , **HEREBY GIVE YOU NOTICE**, pursuant to Section 115 of the Succession Act, 1965 (hereinafter called 'the Act') as follows:

1. By his last will (and codicil if applicable) dated the   day of   , 19/20   , the Deceased devised and bequeathed to you certain property in the following terms:

    [*here, qeuote from will*].

The foregoing devise and bequest was not expressed to be in addition to your legal right share under the Act.

2. The Deceased died Intestate in respect of the following property:

    [*here, itemise the property and state its value*].

You are entitled to [specify the exact share] of such property.

3. You may elect to take, under Section 115 of the Act, either:

    (a) your share as a legal right under the Act; or

    (b) your share of the property in respect of which the deceased died intestate, together with the property so devised and bequeathed to you by the will, but you shall not be entitled to take any share as a legal right.

4. The right of election conferred on you as aforesaid shall not be exercisable after the expiration of six months from the receipt by you of this notification or one year from the first taking out of representation to the Deceased's Estate (which occurred on the day of   , 20   ), whichever is the later.

Dated this   day of   , 20   .

_____
Solicitors for the personal representative

4.5.7 SECTION 56—APPROPRIATION IN FAVOUR OF A SURVIVING SPOUSE/CIVIL PARTNER OF THE FAMILY HOME

Under s 56, where the estate of a deceased person includes a dwelling in which, at the time of the deceased's death, the surviving spouse/civil partner was ordinarily resident (colloquially, but incorrectly, referred to as the 'family home'), the surviving spouse/civil partner may, subject to subsection (5), require the personal representative, in writing, to appropriate the dwelling under s 55 in or towards satisfaction of his or her share. Section 55 is dealt with at para **3.8.1.2**; suffice it to say here that it contains the general rules on the personal representative's power to appropriate property.

The same power applies in relation to the appropriation of any household chattels. This provision was mainly brought in to allow a surviving spouse/civil partner to keep the family home if it had not been left to the surviving spouse/civil partner; but practitioners should note that it is a condition that the surviving spouse/civil partner must be ordinarily resident in the house as at the date of death of the deceased.

Note also that under subsection (3), if the share of the surviving spouse/civil partner is insufficient to enable an appropriation to be made under subsections (1) or (2), as the case may be, the right conferred by the relevant section may also be exercised in relation to the share of any infant for whom the surviving spouse/civil partner is a trustee under s 57 or otherwise.

It is a duty of the personal representative to notify the surviving spouse/civil partner in writing of the rights conferred by this section under subsection (4). In practice, the notice to surviving spouse/civil partner is normally sent out with the notification of the right to elect under s 114. See para **4.5.6.1**.

4.5.7.1 Restrictions on the right to appropriate

There are certain restrictions contained in subsection (5).

Under that subsection, a right conferred by the section is not exercisable after six months from the receipt of the surviving spouse/civil partner of such notification or one year from the first taking out of representation of the deceased's estate, whichever is the later. This ties in with similar time limits for the exercise of the right to elect to take a legal right share.

Section 5(6) goes on to say that such appropriation shall not be made in relation to a dwelling in any of the cases mentioned in subsection (6), unless the court, on application made by the personal representatives or the surviving spouse/civil partner, is satisfied that the exercise of that right is unlikely to diminish the value of the assets of the deceased, other than the dwelling, or to make it more difficult to dispose of them in due course of administration, and authorises its exercise.

The Act recognises that there will be certain instances where the spouse/civil partner's right to appropriate will have a direct effect on the overall value of the assets. Under subsection (6) the various categories of dwellings are set out and are, in short, as follows:

(a) where the dwelling forms part of a building and an estate or interest in the whole building forms part of the estate; or

(b) where the dwelling is held with agricultural land an estate or interest in which forms part of the estate; or

(c) where the whole or a part of the dwelling was at the time of the death used as a hotel, guesthouse, or boarding house; or

(d) where a part of the dwelling was, at the time of the death, used for purposes other than domestic purposes.

It is important to note that the personal representative has no automatic power to appropriate in any of the circumstances noted here without first making an application to court. The court, under subsection (10)(d), shall not make an order under that subsection in relation to a dwelling in any of the cases mentioned in subsection (6), unless it is satisfied that the order would be unlikely to diminish the value of the assets of the deceased, other than the dwelling, or to make it more difficult to dispose of them in the due course of administration.

In the case of *H v H* [1978] IR 138, Parke J considered an appeal from the High Court. With reference to s 56, Parke J agreed with Kenny J's opinion in the High Court on the onus of proof. Kenny J had held that the onus lies upon the applicant under the subsection to satisfy the court that the exercise of the right of appropriation is unlikely to diminish the value of the assets of the deceased other than the dwelling or to make it more difficult to dispose of them in due course of administration.

In accordance with subsection (8)(a):

> '*So long as a right conferred by this section continues to be exercisable the Personal Representatives shall not, without the written consent of the surviving spouse or the leave of the Court given on the refusal of an application under paragraph (b) of subsection (5) sell, or otherwise dispose of the dwelling house or household chattels except in the course of administration owing to want of other assets.*'

It is important to note also that under subsection (9) the rights conferred by this section on the surviving spouse/civil partner include a right to require appropriation partly in satisfaction of a legal right share in the deceased's estate and partly in return for a payment of money by the surviving spouse/civil partner on the spouse/civil partner's own behalf, and also on behalf of any infant for whom the spouse/civil partner is a trustee under s 57 or otherwise. There is also a hardship provision in subsection (10)(b).

In short, s 56 is the only case in which a beneficiary, being a surviving spouse/civil partner, can insist that an appropriation be made. A 'share' is defined in s 3 as including any share or interest, whether arising under a will or intestacy or as a legal right, including a right to the whole estate. Once a surviving spouse/civil partner has applied for appropriation of the dwelling, equity immediately arises in the spouse's favour, which can be enforced by his or her personal representative if the surviving spouse/civil partner dies before the administration has been completed. See the case of *Re Hamilton; Hamilton v Armstrong* [1984] ILRM 306.

In view of all of this, it is essential that the testator understands what right the surviving spouse/civil partner will have and its effect on the estate if they choose to appropriate the family home. Obviously, this will only apply where they are not a joint tenant in the family home with their spouse/civil partner. In this case it would pass to them by survivorship anyway and s 56 would be irrelevant.

4.5.7.2 Precedent notification of the right of appropriation

This notification should be amended accordingly where a civil partner is the notice party.

THE HIGH COURT

PROBATE

RIGHT OF APPROPRIATION NOTIFICATION

In the Estate of   , Deceased.

To:

of:

We,   and   being the personal representatives of the above Deceased (hereinafter called 'the Deceased') late of   , who died on the   day of   , 20   **HEREBY GIVE YOU NOTICE**, pursuant to Section 56 of the Succession Act, 1965 (hereinafter called 'the Act') as follows:

1. You are entitled to require us to appropriate to you under section 55 of the Act, in or towards satisfaction of any share of the Estate to which you are entitled the dwelling in which at the time of the Deceased's death, you were ordinarily resident, and also any household chattels.

2. If your share of the Estate is insufficient to enable an appropriation to be made as aforesaid, the right conferred on you may also be exercised in relation to the share of any infant for whom you are a Trustee under Section 57 of the Act, or otherwise.

3. The Right of appropriation conferred on you as aforesaid shall not be exercisable by you after the expiration of six months from the receipt by you of this notification, or one year from the first taking out of Representation of the Deceased's Estate (which occurred on the   day of   20   ), whichever is the later.

4. You are required to notify us in writing to appropriate the dwelling under section 55 of the Act.

Dated   this day of   , 20

_____

Solicitors for the personal representative

4.5.8 HOW CAN A SURVIVING SPOUSE/CIVIL PARTNER CEASE TO BE A SURVIVING SPOUSE/CIVIL PARTNER FOR THE PURPOSES OF THE SUCCESSION ACT, 1965?

There are at least four relatively common ways by which the surviving spouse/civil partner can cease to be considered the surviving spouse for Succession Act purposes. See para **4.2.2**.

4.5.8.1 By renunciation

Section 113 of the Succession Act, 1965 states:

> *'The legal right of a spouse may be renounced in an ante-nuptial contract made in writing between the parties to an intended marriage or may be renounced in writing by the spouse after marriage and during the lifetime of the testator.'*

Section 113A

> *'The legal right of a civil partner may be renounced in an ante-civil-partnership-registration contract made in writing between the parties to an intended civil partner or may be renounced in writing by the civil partner after registration and during the lifetime of the testator.'*

These sections of the Act are intended to, and do, make the legal right share more flexible, as they allow a spouse/civil partner to dispose of it entirely during his or her lifetime in a simple manner.

Pre-marriage/pre-registration of a civil partnership

The legal right of a spouse/civil partner may be renounced in any ante-nuptial pre-marital/ante-civil-partnership-registration contract made in writing between the parties to an intended marriage/civil partnership. Particularly with wealthy clients, it is usually incorporated into a marriage/civil partnership settlement or, less usually, in an agreement to enter into a post-nuptial/post-civil-partnership-registration settlement. This would be a very clear-cut situation and easy to deal with from an administration of estates point of view.

Post-marriage/post-registration of a civil partnership

The spouse's/civil partner's legal right may be renounced in writing by a spouse/civil partner of the testator after marriage/post-civil-partnership-registration and during the lifetime of the testator. Obviously, if it is done after the death, it is not a renunciation but a disclaimer. It must be in writing, but no contract is necessary.

Renunciation is final. There is no provision for its revocation unless there is fraud or undue influence, or if it is made by a person of unsound mind. See *JH v WJH* (unreported) 20 December 1979, High Court. A person who wishes to overturn their renunciation will have to show the court that it was obtained by fraud or undue influence or that they did not know the nature and content of the document executed. Effectively, these are the same criteria as for any document signed by someone who subsequently wishes to set it aside. Thus, where there is any doubt, it must be ensured that the person who it is claimed has renounced had independent legal advice.

Where it is claimed that any type of renunciation exists, the practitioner should proceed very carefully. It must be ensured that the renunciation is valid and that independent legal advice was obtained at the time. Renunciation agreements are most common in a separation agreement (see para **4.5.8.2**) but are becoming increasingly common in a second marriage/civil partnership situation, where the proposed surviving spouse/civil partner comes to the marriage/civil partnership with their own assets and the proposed deceased has several children. The terms of any such renunciation would need to be examined and the consequences of same explained to the testator.

4.5.8.2 By separation

Judicial Separation and Family Law Reform Act, 1989

The Judicial Separation and Family Law Reform Act, 1989 came into operation on 19 October 1989. Part I of that Act set out circumstances in which an applicant could apply for and obtain a decree of judicial separation and Part II listed the ancillary financial, property, custody, and other orders that could be applied for following the granting of a decree of judicial separation. Part II of the Act provided for such ancillary reliefs as repealed (with the exception of s 25) by the Family Law Act, 1995.

It is important to note that this does not apply to civil partners and there is no similar provision contained in the Civil Partnership Act for civil partners (see para **4.2.2**).

The separated spouse

In dealing with separated spouses (the reference to spouses and not separated civil partners is deliberate as at the time of writing there is no legislation relating to separated civil partners: see para **4.2.2**), it is important to remember for all circumstances that such a spouse is still a spouse, but one whose rights and interest may well be limited by the terms of such separation order, agreement, or otherwise. The terms of any such court order or separation agreement need to be scrutinised carefully to clarify rights on death and thus ensure that correct advice is given to a testator.

Where there is a separation without any formal agreement, this does not change the gift or inheritance tax exemption accorded by the legislation. The marriage is still recognised as valid. Where there is a legal separation, there is still no change in the legal status as a married couple and the usual exemption would still apply. With couples who are separated (and not divorced) the following must be checked.

Are any financial compensation orders in existence?

The practitioner should check whether any financial compensation order was granted under s 11 of the Family Law Act, 1995 (as amended by s 52(d) of the Family Law Divorce Act, 1996). Section 11 provides that, on the granting of a decree of judicial separation or at any time thereafter, the court, on application to it in that behalf by either of the spouses concerned or by a person on behalf of a dependent member of the family, may, during the lifetime of the other spouse or as the case may be, make certain financial compensation orders.

These extend to effecting policies of life insurance, assigning any interest in a policy of life insurance, or continuing payments under a policy of life insurance. Under subsection (2)(b), an order under this section ceases to have effect on the remarriage or death of the applicant in so far as it relates to the applicant, and under subsection (2)(c), the court shall not make an order under this section if the spouse who is applying for the order has remarried. It is important for the practitioner to check that the terms of any such order have been carried out and that it no longer affects any of the assets belonging to the deceased.

The practitioner should note further that under s 18 of the Family Law Act, 1995, which refers primarily to financial compensation orders:

> 'The Court may on application to it in that behalf by either of the spouses concerned or in the case of the death of either of the spouses by any other person who in the opinion of the Court has a sufficient interest in the matter or by a person on behalf of a dependent member of the family concerned, if it considers it proper to do so having regard to any change in the circumstances of the case and to any new evidence, by order vary or discharge an order to which this section applies.'

Are there any pension adjustment orders?

Section 12 of the Family Law Act, 1995, which deals with pension adjustment orders, provides in subsection (2) that:

> 'where a decree of judicial separation has been granted, the Court, if it so thinks fit, may in relation to retirement benefit under a scheme of which one of the spouses concerned is a member, on application to it in that behalf at the time of the making of the order for the decree at any time thereafter

during the lifetime of the member spouse by either of the spouses or by a person on behalf of a dependent member of the family, make an order providing for the payment, in accordance with the provisions of this section to either of the following as the Court may determine, that is to say:

(a) the other spouse and in the case of the death of that spouse his or her personal representative, and

(b) such person as may be specified in the order for the benefit of a person who is, and for so long only as he or she remains a dependent member of the family of a benefit consisting either, as the Court may determine, of the whole or such part as the Court considers appropriate of that part of the retirement benefit that is payable (or which but for the making of the order for the decree would have been payable) under the scheme and has accrued at the time of the making of the order for the decree and, for the purpose of determining the benefit, the order shall specify.'

Under s 11(1)(b), the court can make a financial compensation order if it considers that the forfeiture by reason of the decree of judicial separation by the applicant or the dependant, as the case may be, of the opportunity or possibility of acquiring a benefit (e.g. a benefit under a pension scheme) can be compensated for wholly or in part by so doing. In checking the pension position on death, it is vital to check, in a situation where the parties were separated, whether any such financial compensation order affects the pension.

Under s 14 of the Family Law Act, 1995:

'On granting a decree of judicial separation or at any time thereafter, the Court may, on application to it in that behalf by either of the spouses concerned, make an order extinguishing the share that either of the spouses would otherwise be entitled to in the estate of the other spouse as a legal right or on intestacy under the Act of 1965.'

The court must be satisfied that adequate and reasonable financial provision exists or can be made for the spouse whose succession rights are in question.

The practitioner should note also the possibility of such a financial compensation order affecting any pension belonging to the deceased. Under s 13 of the 1995 Act, on the granting of a decree of judicial separation or at any time thereafter, the court:

'may, in relation to a pension scheme, on application to it in that behalf by either of the spouses concerned, make during the lifetime of the spouse who was a member of the scheme ('the member spouse') an order directing the trustees of the scheme not to regard the separation of the spouses resulting from the decree as a ground for disqualifying the other spouse for the receipt of a benefit under the scheme a condition for the receipt of which is that the spouses should be residing together at the time the benefit becomes payable.'

In particular, in relation to civil partners and financial orders or pension orders, see Part 5 of the Civil Partnership Act, 2010 ss 43–52.

Can the succession rights of a separated spouse be extinguished?

Under s 14 of the Family Law Act, 1995, succession rights can be extinguished. It provides:

'On granting a decree of judicial separation or at any time thereafter, the Court may, on application to it in that behalf by either of the spouses concerned, make an order extinguishing the share that either of the spouses would otherwise be entitled to in the estate of the other spouse as a legal right or on intestacy under the Act of 1965.'

There are circumstances attached, including that the court must be satisfied that adequate and reasonable financial provision exists for the spouse whose succession rights are in question.

The practitioner should be careful as, on the death of a separated person, the surviving spouse has a right to reapply to court.

Section 15A of the Family Law Act, 1995 was inserted by s 52(g) of the Family Law Divorce Act, 1996. Subsection (1) provides as follows:

'Subject to the provisions of this section, where, following the grant of a decree of judicial separation, a Court makes an order under section 14 [re extinguishment of succession rights] in relation to the spouses concerned and one of the spouses dies, the Court on application to it in that behalf by

the other spouse (the applicant) not more than six months after representation is first granted under the Act of 1965 in respect of the estate of the deceased spouse, may by order make such provision for the applicant out of the estate of the deceased spouse as it considers appropriate having regard to the rights of any other person having an interest in the matter and specifies in the order if it is satisfied that proper provision in the circumstances was not made for the applicant during the lifetime of the deceased spouse under section 8, 9, 10(1)(a), 11 or 12 for any reason (other than conduct referred to in subsection (2)(i) of section 16) of the applicant.'

Subsection (2) states:

'The Court shall not make an order under this section if the applicant concerned has remarried since the granting of decree of judicial separation concerned.'

Can the right to reapply be blocked?

In relation to a judicial separation, there is a continual residual right vested in a separated spouse, even where the inheritance rights have been extinguished, to make an application to the court for a share out of a deceased's estate upon the death of the spouse concerned. It is possible, however, for a blocking order to be granted by the court, i.e. that either or both spouses shall not on the death of either of them be entitled to apply for a provision out of the other's estate. The court can do this if it considers it just to do so.

Section 15A(10) provides that on granting a decree of judicial separation or at any time thereafter the court may, on application to it by either spouse during the lifetime of the other spouse, if it considers it just to do so, make an order that either or both spouses shall not on the death of either of them be entitled to apply for an order under s 15A.

Is there a duty on a personal representative to notify the separated spouse?

Under s 15A(6), the personal representative of the deceased spouse shall make a reasonable attempt to ensure that notice of the death is brought to the attention of the other spouse concerned. Where a surviving spouse wishes to bring an application under this section, he or she must give notice to the spouse (if any) of the deceased spouse concerned and such (if any) other persons as the court may direct (subsection (5)).

Alan Shatter, in *Family Law*, 4th edn (1997), states at para 17.98 that:

'Having regard to the statutory prescribed provisions applicable to the extinguishment of a spouse's Succession Act, 1965 entitlements in judicial separation proceedings, it is difficult to envisage any circumstances arising in which a Court specifically determines it is appropriate to make a section 14 order but not appropriate to make an order under section 15A(10).'

Intestate succession and the separated spouse

The share on intestacy of a separated spouse may well be extinguished by a court upon the granting of a decree of judicial separation, or indeed it may have been renounced by the surviving spouse. Care must be taken in the drafting of any renunciation to ensure that it covers both testate and intestate succession.

Please note:

1. A separated spouse who has waived Succession Act rights in a deed of separation or against whom a decree of divorce *a mensa et thoro* was granted or whose Succession Act rights were extinguished by an order made pursuant to s 17 of the Judicial Separation and Family Law Reform Act, 1989 (as compared with s 14 of the Family Law Act, 1995) is excluded from making an application for a discretionary payment in the estate of the deceased spouse.

2. Practitioners should also note the anomaly that in the event of a person obtaining a separation pursuant to s 17 of the Judicial Separation and Family Law Reform Act, 1989 subsequently divorcing, the divorce in itself affords the protection of the Family Law Divorce Act, 1996 and in particular the divorced spouse is now entitled to make application for a discretionary provision under s 18 of the 1996 Act (unless precluded by a blocking order from doing so in the proceedings).

4.5.8.3 By divorce for spouses and dissolution of civil partnership for civil partners

Family Law (Divorce) Act, 1996

Note: a will is revoked by the subsequent marriage of a testator (s 81(1) of the Succession Act, 1965). However, it is not stated in the Family Law (Divorce) Act, 1996 that a decree of divorce has the same effect. In the event of the granting of a decree of divorce, a client's will must be reviewed immediately.

From a practitioner's point of view, in advising a testator or indeed in administering an estate, an extremely important provision was inserted by the Family Law (Divorce) Act, 1996.

Section 18(1)

> *'where one of the spouses in respect of whom a decree of divorce has been granted dies, the Court, on application to it in that behalf by the other spouse not more than six months after representation is first granted under the Act of 1965 in respect of the estate of the deceased spouse, may by order make such provision for the Applicant out of the estate of the deceased spouse as it considers appropriate having regard to the rights of any other person having an interest in the matter and specifies in the order if it is satisfied that proper provision in the circumstances was not made for the Applicant during the lifetime of the deceased spouse under section 13, 14, 15, 16 or 17 for any reason.'*

It is important to note that the court will not make an order under subsection (2) in favour of a spouse who has remarried since the granting of the decree of divorce. Under subsection (3), in considering whether to make an order under this section, the court shall have regard to all the circumstances including:

(a) any order under paragraph (c) of s 13(1) or any property adjustment order in favour of the applicant; and

(b) any devise or bequest made by the deceased spouse to the applicant.

In the event of such an application being brought, under subsection (5), notice of such application shall be given by the applicant to any subsequent spouse (if any) of the deceased spouse concerned, and to such (if any) other persons as the court may direct. The court has power to have regard to any representations made by the subsequent spouse of the deceased, and any other such persons.

There is an additional onus on a personal representative under subsection (6), which provides that the personal representative of a deceased spouse in respect of whom a decree of divorce has been granted shall make a reasonable attempt to ensure that notice of his or her death is brought to the attention of the other spouse concerned and, where an application is made under this section, the personal representative of the deceased spouse shall not, without the leave of the court, distribute any of the estate of that spouse until the court makes or refuses to make an order under this section.

Under subsection (7), where the personal representative of a deceased spouse in respect of whom a decree of divorce has been granted gives notice of his or her death to the other spouse concerned and

(a) the spouse intends to apply to the court for an order under this section; or

(b) the spouse has applied for such an order and the application is pending; or

(c) an order has been made under this section in favour of the spouse,

the spouse shall, not later than one month after the receipt of the notice, notify the personal representative of such intention, application, or order as the case may be, and if he or she does not do so the personal representative shall be at liberty to distribute the assets of the deceased spouse or any part thereof among the parties entitled.

There is a protection afforded in subsection (8) in that the personal representative shall not be liable to the spouse for the assets or any part thereof so distributed unless at the time of such distribution he or she had notice of the intention, application, or order aforesaid.

It is important to note, however, that under subsection (10), in the event of a decree of divorce being granted or at any time thereafter, the court, on application to it in that behalf by either of the spouses concerned, may during the lifetime of the other spouse, if it considers it just, make an order that either or both spouses shall not on the death of either of them be entitled to apply for an order under this section.

This 'blocking order' is fairly common and it is therefore likely that such provision will be included at the time of the divorce to this effect. It is very important to check that this provision has been allowed for.

In relation to civil partners, there is no 'divorce' but there can, of course, be a decree of nullity or a decree of dissolution and in such cases, obviously the order itself as with divorced spouses, should be reviewed. However, it should also be noted, as with divorce decrees, that there is the possibility on the dissolution of a civil partnership for a blocking order to be obtained. See s 127(11) of the Civil Partnership Act.

Foreign divorce

Prior to the introduction of divorce in Ireland in February 1997, many Irish people obtained divorces in foreign jurisdictions. In many cases they went and established residence in such varied places as Mexico, the Dominican Republic, and nearer to home in England and Scotland. Unfortunately, from the point of view of advising a testator or indeed administering an estate, it is frequently the case that these divorces are not capable of recognition in this country and, further, that subsequent marriages will not be recognised.

Many people seem to think that just because divorce is now permitted in Ireland, the rules have relaxed in relation to the recognition of foreign divorces, and that somehow retrospectively their own situation is now regularised. This is not correct. Essentially, the basis of recognition is that Ireland will recognise a foreign divorce if it is granted in the jurisdiction where either spouse is domiciled at the date of the commencement of the proceedings.

If there is any doubt as to who the surviving spouse will be on the basis of a foreign divorce, there is a procedure under the Family Law Act, 1995 where an application can be made to the court pursuant to s 29 of that Act for a declaration on the validity of a foreign divorce and any subsequent marriage on the strength of it. While this is obviously a tedious procedure, it should not be overlooked where there is any doubt.

The practitioner is not responsible for people who have not taken the correct steps to legalise their position but is certainly quite often left dealing with the results of it. For example, if the deceased has obtained a foreign divorce and subsequently 'remarried' without sorting out his affairs, then it is open to the 'original spouse', as indicated earlier, to make an application under s 29 of the Family Law Act, 1995 for an order that they are a lawful spouse and therefore entitled to Succession Act rights.

In relation to civil partners, unlike the ability of the Minister to issue orders under s 5 of the Civil Partnership Act in relation to recognition of civil partnerships, there is no equivalent section in relation to the recognition of foreign dissolution of civil partnerships and thus, as with recognition of foreign divorces, where there is any doubt as to the validity of a foreign dissolution an application to the courts for its recognition, or not, may be prudent.

Former spouses who entered into civil partnerships effectively lost their status as former spouses. As stated above under divorce legislation, former spouses continue to have the right to apply to the courts for maintenance and property orders. However, once they entered into a civil partnership, this changed. Maintenance orders and pension adjustment orders in favour of a former spouse lapsed if that spouse entered into a civil partnership. A property adjustment order may not be made for the benefit of a former spouse if that spouse has registered in a civil partnership.

4.5.8.4 By the application of section 120—unworthiness to succeed

Please note that the law as stated below may change in light of the Law Reform Commission's Report, *Prevention of Benefit from Homicide* (LRC 114-2015) and the draft Civil Liability (Amendment) (Prevention from Benefit from Homicide) Bill arising therefrom. For a full review see Stephenson Solicitors' 28th Seminar, *Quis custodiet ipsos custodes et al?*

While the section applies in both testate and intestate cases, in this chapter we will be looking at it from the point of view of advising a testator. In ascertaining whether a spouse/civil partner is entitled to a legal right share, s 120 of the Succession Act, 1965 must also be considered and, where applicable, explained carefully to the testator. This section precludes a spouse of a testator from asserting his entitlement to the legal right share in the following circumstances:

1. Where that spouse has been guilty of murder, attempted murder, or manslaughter of the other (except any share granted to that spouse after the act that constituted the offence in question).

2. (a) Where a decree of divorce *a mensa et thoro* has been obtained.

   (b) A spouse who has failed to comply with a decree of restitution of conjugal rights obtained by the deceased.

   (c) A spouse guilty of desertion, which is continued up to the death of the deceased spouse for two years or more. That period of two years must be continuing at the date of death and if, therefore, parties recommenced cohabitation prior to the death of the deceased spouse, then this would have the effect of nullifying any previous desertion. Desertion in this context is, pursuant to s 120(3), to include the notion of constructive desertion.

2(A). A deceased's civil partner who has deserted the deceased is precluded from taking any share in the deceased's estate as the legal right or on intestacy if the desertion continued up to the death for two years or more.

3. A person found guilty of an offence against the deceased or against the spouse or any child of the deceased (including a person to whom the deceased was *in loco parentis* at the time of the offence) which has been punishable by imprisonment for a maximum period of at least two years.

3(A). A civil partner who was guilty of conduct which justified the deceased in separating and living apart from him or her is deemed to be guilty of desertion within the meaning of subsection 2(A).

Pursuant to s 120(5), any share which a person is precluded from taking by virtue of the points noted here is distributed *'as if that person had died before the deceased'*.

Situations arise where the surviving spouse/civil partner, whom the deceased alleges has been in desertion or comes within one of the other criteria of s 120, will seek to claim their legal right share. In this instance the legal personal representatives, in order properly to protect their position and preserve the estate's assets, should seek a court order, either in the Circuit Court or in the High Court, deeming that person unworthy to succeed pursuant to the provisions of s 120.

An example of this is the 'Jack Whites case', *Re Nevin* (unreported) 13 March 1997, High Court, and subsequent related case, *Nevin v Nevin* [2013] IEHC 80, and similar cases; *Cawley v Lillis* [2011] IEHC 515 and *Cawley v Lillis* (No 2) [2012] IEHC 70 and the Law Reform Commission Report as cited above.

It is also important to note that spouses/civil partners who come within the conditions in s 120 are unworthy to succeed vis-à-vis any share of the deceased's estate as a legal right or on any share arising on intestacy. They are not, however, prevented from taking a specific benefit under the terms of the will of the testator where same has been made post the offence. Therefore, if the testator wishes, he may leave such a spouse/civil partner a bequest in the will.

Any share affected is distributed as if the person had died before the deceased. These provisions should not be ignored. In the past, when there was no legislative framework for a separation, many spouses deserted or abandoned their families, and while they might have continued to be spouses (in that a decree of divorce may not have been obtained or granted), they might have been disqualified under the provisions of s 120. Note should be taken that the testator can preclude the operation of s 120 in certain circumstances; for example, a provision made in a will after the offence of attempted murder is exempted. The provision may also be seen to operate harshly, for example where an individual is precluded from succession as a result of a manslaughter conviction following a car accident.

However, s 120 of the Succession Act only applies to the share of the estate to which the spouse/civil partner would have been entitled on testacy or intestacy and does not affect the spouse's/civil partner's entitlement to extract a grant of administration in the estate of the deceased. In the *Re Nevin* case cited earlier, Catherine Nevin was precluded from administering her husband Thomas Nevin's estate. In the first instance, while awaiting clarification as to whether Mrs Nevin would be prosecuted, she was entitled to a grant limited to collecting and preserving the assets but not in distributing the estate.

Judge Elizabeth Dunne made an interesting determination on 9 October 1998 (*McCann, Re Esther* (unreported) 8 October 1998, Dublin Circuit Court) in a case where a man was convicted of killing his wife and adopted child by arson of the family home. The family home was registered in joint names and should have passed automatically to him by the right of survivorship. Judge Dunne was influenced by the provisions of the Succession Act in relation to disqualification from inheritance and did not allow the man to take his wife's share of the property.

The judge further made an order for the sale of the property and directed that the proceeds would be divided 52.5 per cent to the deceased wife's mother and 47.5 per cent to the man. Judge Dunne said the difference would ensure that an increase in value which had arisen by virtue of the discharge of the mortgage by a mortgage protection policy would not benefit the man. The judge further ordered that he would pay his mother-in-law's costs and that an award be made under the Civil Liability Act for mental stress and funeral expenses.

The judge had earlier ordered the man to pay his mother-in-law a sum of £27,900 which had accrued from his share of a life insurance policy on the mortgage. Judge Dunne held that, although there was no specific decided case on the point, the effect of the murder was, in her view, to sever the joint tenancy. The estate of the late wife therefore remained outstanding for the benefit of the mother.

In relation to unworthiness to succeed and joint assets, see *Cawley v Lillis*, as referred to earlier. There are two judgments in this case by Laffoy J (dated 6 December 2011 and 21 February 2012), the first dealing with the substantive proceedings, i.e. the distribution of joint assets in such circumstances, the latter dealing only with the issue of costs.

In relation to costs and joint tenancies, note the recommendations made by the Law Reform Commission Report in Chapter 5, pp 76 and 79 in particular.

Brian E. Spierin S.C., in *Wills—Irish Precedents and Drafting*, 3rd edn (2020), Appendix 8, p 291, comments on the question of desertion and separation agreements. He states:

> 'Generally speaking, in separation agreements, the persons agree to live separate and apart. If there is such an agreement, any desertion that existed prior to the date of the separation agreement is set aside. Therefore, if the separation agreement makes no other provision in relation to rights under the Succession Act 1965, a spouse who was unworthy to succeed by virtue of desertion may be rendered worthy again by entering into a separation agreement.'

Note that there is or can be an interaction between s 117 cases and s 120: see *LC (a minor) v HSE* (2014) IEHC 32.

4.5.9 WHAT IS THE EFFECT ON THE WILL/ADMINISTRATION OF THE ESTATE OF THE SURVIVING SPOUSE/CIVIL PARTNER TAKING THEIR LEGAL RIGHT SHARE?

It is not sufficient for a practitioner to be able to tell a testator what a surviving spouse/civil partner is entitled to or, indeed, when acting for the spouse/civil partner, what their legal right share is in monetary terms versus their bequest under the will and share of any partial intestacy. A practitioner must also be able to inform the testator or, when acting for the spouse/civil partner, the spouse/civil partner, of the effect on the estate, on the will, and any other beneficiaries of such a choice as this might be a consideration and it certainly is information which the testator or the surviving spouse/civil partner requires to make an informed decision.

If the spouse/civil partner chooses their legal right share, it will 'blow the will out of the water', because a third or a half of the net estate, depending on whether or not the testator left children, must be given to them. If it was not envisaged in the will that this would occur, someone is going to 'lose out', in that assets which were left to somebody else will have to be appropriated. The aggrieved beneficiary does not receive compensation and inevitably there are arguments as to from which assets the legal right share should be paid. Everyone will claim that it should come from someone else's bequest. It is very important, therefore, that the testator is properly advised from where this would be paid.

The legal position is outlined here, but of course in many cases it comes down to a matter of negotiation. Please note the observations of Henchy J in *H v O* [1978] IR 194 at 204:

> '[N]owhere in the Act is there any specific statement as to how the personal representatives are to discharge the surviving spouses legal right to one-third or one-half of the estate, as the case may be. Section 112 gives the legal right priority over devises, bequests and shares on intestacy. In the general context of the Act of 1965 it must be assumed that the legislative intention was that the legal right (where elected for) is to be discharged in the same manner as if the one-half or one-third of the estate had been expressly given in the will in priority over all devises and bequests.'

This observation states the problem very neatly, i.e. it is not specifically stated anywhere in the Act how it is to be paid, but certain deductions can be made by reading the Succession Act carefully. See later in this chapter.

As noted earlier, s 112 provides:

> 'The right of a spouse under section 111 (which shall be known as a legal right) shall have priority over devises, bequests, and shares on intestacy.'

This means that the legal right share ranks in priority after the rights of creditors of the deceased.

Section 45(1)

> 'The estate, whether legal or equitable, of a deceased person, to the extent of his beneficial interest therein, and the estate of which a deceased person in pursuance of any general power disposes by his will, are assets for payment of the funeral, testamentary and administration expenses, debts (whether by speciality or simple contract) and liabilities, and any legal right, and any disposition by will inconsistent with this section is void as against the creditors and any person entitled to a legal right, and the Court shall, if necessary, administer the property for the purpose of the payment of the expenses, debts and liabilities and any legal right.'

Section 46 goes on to provide at subsections (3) and (6):

> '(3) Where the estate of a deceased person is solvent, it shall, subject to rules of Court and the provisions hereinafter contained as to charges on property of the deceased, and to the provisions, if any, contained in his will, be applicable towards the discharge of the funeral, testamentary and administration expenses, debts and liabilities and any legal right in the order mentioned in Part II of the First Schedule . . .
>
> (6) A claim to a share as a legal right or on intestacy in the estate of a deceased person is a claim against the assets of the estate to a sum equal to the value of that share.'

The effect of these sections is that the legal right share, once ascertained, is considered in a similar fashion to a debt against the estate, ranking in priority after the 'real' funeral, testamentary and administration expenses, debts, and liabilities, and before any other bequests of any nature. In other words, it is treated as if it was a pecuniary legacy, and will, in the solvent estate, be discharged accordingly. Such shares will also abate like a pecuniary legacy in relation to the payment of debts, that is to say pro rata. See para **12.4.2.3**.

The order of payment of the legal right share is to be found for solvent estates in Part II of the First Schedule to the Act and for insolvent estates in Part I of the First Schedule to the Act. If the estate is insolvent, i.e. the testator died owing more than he owned, there will be no net estate out of which to pay a legal right share, so this section will concentrate on Part II. See para **12.4.1** for abatement.

4.5.9.1 Rules as to application of assets in a solvent estate

These are set out in Part II of the First Schedule, as outlined in para **12.4.2.2**. The paragraph goes on to explain the effect on a solvent estate where there are insufficient funds to pay debts, funeral, and testamentary expenses properly payable out of residue and on the formula for calculating the amount payable by specific beneficiaries in these circumstances.

A similar effect and a similar formula for payment of outstanding legal right share will apply where there are insufficient funds to pay the legal right share out of the residue. This would be the case in most estates, unless the majority of the estate is distributed on a residuary basis.

The effect of this is that where proper provision has not been made for the spouse/civil partner, the balance, or indeed the entirety, of the legal right share will be taken from the remainder of the estate in the order outlined in para **12.4.2.2**.

The surviving spouse/civil partner can require the personal representative to pay the legal right share without making an application to court.

Similarly, under s 56 of the Act, where the legal right share is in excess of the value of the family home, such appropriation can be made in partial satisfaction of the legal right share under s 56(9). This need not be the subject of an application to the court but can be ordered by the surviving spouse/civil partner.

Otherwise, a 'hardship' application can be made under s 56(10), subject to the restrictions outlined in subsection (10)(d).

Where the family home is the subject of such an application by the surviving spouse/civil partner, the issue of the proposed beneficiary is raised. Section 56 is the only circumstance in which a specific bequest to a beneficiary can be overruled.

The Act is silent on the 'compensation' of such a beneficiary. Under normal circumstances, specific bequests are the last to adeem. In this case, the specific bequest is the first to adeem. No provision is made for compensating the beneficiary where the family home is worth less than the legal right share.

One interpretation of the effect of such appropriation is that the property is 'adeemed' as a result of the spouse's/civil partner's application under s 56. When the spouse appropriates in partial satisfaction of their legal right share, the effect of the spouse's/civil partner's electing to take the legal right share is similar to a debt against the estate. In this case, the debt was against the 'family home'. As the property does not form part of the estate after the application was made, the effect is that of ademption, and no compensation is payable.

Where the spouse/civil partner applies to the court under s 56(10), the court can make such further and other order as it sees fit. This wider power of the court enables it to deal with any consequential problems that may arise, thus avoiding the necessity of an administration suit. In this case, the property is claimed partially as a legal right share and partially by the discretion of the court.

Given this, it cannot be stated often enough that a testator must fully understand the possible effects on his estate should he choose to ignore the provisions in Part IX of the Succession Act and leave the surviving spouse nothing, or less than his or her legal right share.

4.5.10 WHAT PROPERTY WILL THE COURT CONSIDER IN RELATION TO A SURVIVING SPOUSE'S/CIVIL PARTNER'S LEGAL RIGHT SHARE OR A SUCCESSFUL APPLICATION BY A CHILD UNDER SECTION 117 OR 117(3A)?

Where a spouse/civil partner is entitled to a portion of the estate or children have a right to make a claim under ss 117 and 117(3A) of the Succession Act, 1965 against the estate of the deceased person, the court will take into account all the property of the testator wherever situate to determine the extent of the estate. However, the amount awarded by the court can only be available out of the estate of which the court has jurisdiction. See *Re GM: FM v TAM* [1972] 106 ILTR 82.

Thus, the problem can arise where there are overseas assets in a number of jurisdictions, all of which have different succession rights. The Succession Act does not adequately address the conflict of laws issue that can arise in this context of administration of estates. In such a case, the most prudent manner of proceeding is to consider each case on its merits considering the Hague Convention on the Conflict of Laws relating to the Form of Testamentary Dispositions (1961). Unfortunately, Ireland has not yet ratified the Hague Convention on the Law Applicable to the Estates of Deceased Persons (1989). When it does, there will be a more unitary approach to succession, based on the law of the state of the person's habitual residence at the time of death, subject to the right to dispute the law of the estate to be applied.

4.5.11 SECTION 121 OF THE SUCCESSION ACT, 1965—DISPOSITIONS WITH A VIEW TO DIMINISHING THE ESTATE

This section of the Succession Act does not specifically relate to spouses/civil partners; however, it could be very important to a spouse or indeed a civil partner in any given situation. Section 121 applies to a disposition of property (other than a testamentary disposition or a disposition to a purchaser for full value) under which the beneficial ownership of the property vests in possession in the donee within three years before the death of the person who made it or on his death or later.

Under s 121(2), if the court is satisfied that a disposition to which this section applies is made for the purpose of defeating or substantially diminishing the share of the disponer's spouse/civil partner, whether as a legal right or on intestacy, or the intestate share of any of his or her children, or of leaving any of his or her children insufficiently provided for, then, whether the disponer died testate or intestate, the court may order that the disposition shall, in whole or in part, be deemed, for the purposes of Parts VI and IX, to be a devise or bequest made by him by will and to form part of his estate and to have had no other effect.

This provision was brought in to prevent dispositions for the purpose of disinheriting a spouse/civil partner or children, and it is always important to have reference to such provision in your initial instructions. Note that under s 121(9):

> 'Accrual by survivorship on the death of a joint tenant of property shall, for the purpose of this section be deemed to be a vesting of the beneficial ownership of the entire property in the survivor.'

Note also that under s 121(6) in the case of a disposition made in favour of the spouse/civil partner of the disponer, an order shall not be made under this section on an application by or on behalf of a child of the disponer, who is also a child of the spouse. The same may not be the case re a disposition made in favour of the civil partner of the disponer by or on behalf of a child of that disponer.

4.6 Children's Rights

When a person dies testate, a child, unlike a spouse/civil partner, is not entitled to a specified share in a deceased person's estate as a right. However, the rights of children are significant and can vary according to the circumstances and 'type' of child. A number of facts must be established before that testator can be advised appropriately.

4.6.1 STEPS TO BE TAKEN

How to advise in this area can be broken down into a number of steps.

4.6.1.1 The first step—entitlements

When advising a testator, or indeed when acting for the legal personal representative of the estate or for a child of a deceased person, the first thing that must be established is: to what is the child entitled. See para **4.6.2**.

4.6.1.2 The second step—'type' of child

Decide what 'type' of child is being advised on, as this affects their rights under the Succession Act and indeed their tax status vis-à-vis the deceased. See para **4.6.3**.

4.6.1.3 The third step—actions a 'type' of child may take

The practitioner should consider what actions such a child may take and the effect that they have on the will and/or the administration of the estate.

The practitioner should remember that, if the legal personal representative is being advised in the area of children, it is vital that he or she is advised that it is not his or her duty to inform children of possible actions they may take against the estate. The situation would, of course, be different where a child is being advised or where the testator is being advised pre-death. See para **4.6.4**. Note also the recommendations of the Law Reform Commission in its Issue paper re s 117 of the Succession Act.

4.6.1.4 The fourth step—underage children

The practitioner should consider whether there are any underage children, and the consequences of this. See para **4.6.5**.

4.6.1.5 The fifth step—tax status of children

The practitioner should be able to advise the testator on the tax status of any children. Where the solicitor is also providing taxation advice for the estate, the taxation consequences of the 'type' of child for tax purposes should be fully understood.

4.6.1.6 The sixth step—other relevant legislation

The practitioner should consider other legislation (e.g. the Guardianship Act, 1964 as amended by the Children and Family Relationships Act, 2015) relating to children which may affect the administration of an estate of which the testator should be advised prior to making his will. See paras **4.6.3.4** and **4.6.7**.

4.6.2 TO WHAT IS A CHILD ENTITLED?

4.6.2.1 In a testate situation

What a child is entitled to in a testate situation depends entirely on the will. It is important that the testator be informed that what any child is left in the will may be affected by the legal right share of the spouse/civil partner, should they take it, and any litigation against the estate which is successful. However, in relation to the surviving civil partner, see s 117(3A).

4.6.2.2 In an intestate situation

Under s 67 of the Succession Act, if an intestate dies leaving a spouse/civil partner and issue, then the spouse/civil partner takes two-thirds and the remaining one-third is distributed among the issue in equal shares if the issue are in equal relationship to the deceased, and, if not, *per stirpes*. See para **8.4**. Practitioners should be aware of s 67A(3) of the Act, where the child of a deceased civil partner inherits.

4.6.2.3 'Issue' and 'child'

This naturally raises the question: what do the terms 'issue' and 'child' mean, for the purposes of the Succession Act?

'Issue' for the purposes of the Act extends to children (both marital and non-marital): see para **4.6.3**, adopted children and their lineal descendants: see s 26 of the Adoption Act,

1952 and s 29 of the Status of Children Act, 1987. The term does not include stepchildren or foster children.

4.6.3 'TYPES' OF CHILDREN

As noted above, a child, unlike a spouse, is not entitled to a specified share in a deceased parent's estate as a right. Nevertheless, when advising the testator of an estate it is crucial to enquire about all of the potential types of children a testator may have. For example:

4.6.3.1 Marital children

There is a presumption that a child of a marriage is a child of the husband and wife. See s 46 of the Status of Children Act, 1987.

4.6.3.2 Unborn children

Section 3(2) of the Succession Act states that descendants and relatives of a deceased person begotten before his death but born alive are regarded as having been born in the lifetime of the deceased and as having survived him; therefore in an intestacy situation, or in a testate situation where there is a bequest 'to all of my children', any such child must be taken account of.

The above section may need to be reconsidered, post the commencement of the Children and Family Relationships Act, 2015 and in particular the Regulations arising therefrom.

4.6.3.3 'Section 98' children

Where children have predeceased the deceased leaving issue, i.e. where s 98 applies to the distribution in the administration of this estate, there must be considered the importance of informing a testator of this pre-death, anticipating and, where required, forestalling the consequences of same; see para **2.7.3**.

It can happen that a child for whom a testator has made provision in his will dies before the parent. Normally, where a beneficiary predeceases the testator, the gift lapses and falls into the residue of the estate. There is, however, an exception to the doctrine of lapse and this is contained in s 98 of the Succession Act. This needs to be explained very carefully to the testator.

Section 98 of the Succession Act is frequently misapplied or confused with the *'per stirpes'* rule or completely ignored, resulting in the incorrect distribution of assets during the administration.

Section 98 essentially provides that:

- where a child predeceases a testator leaving issue (not just children but issue), and such issue are living at the time of the death of the testator, the gift shall not lapse but shall take effect as if the death of that person had happened immediately after the death of the testator;

- unless a contrary intention appears from the will.

If, therefore, a testator's child predeceases the testator, leaving two grandchildren, the benefit that would have been received by such child is preserved and will pass through the deceased child's estate, but not necessarily to the grandchildren (it only goes automatically to the grandchildren when a child predeceases an intestate parent, i.e. *per stirpes*). See para **8.4**.

Thus, in a testate (i.e. s 98) situation, if, for example, the deceased child has made a will leaving all his or her estate to his or her spouse (the son- or daughter-in-law), such benefit would be preserved and would pass to such son- or daughter-in-law.

This should have been pointed out to a testator at the time of the making of a will. In certain instances, testators might well wish to make provision for any such benefit to be preserved for their grandchildren, but specific provision would have to have been made in a testator's will for this. It cannot be done retrospectively post-death. If that was what was intended but not done in the will, there is no choice in the administration of the estate but to follow the letter of s 98.

It is vital to realise that the third criteria required for s 98 to apply, i.e. that the deceased predeceased issue, must leave issue surviving them, has nothing to do with the result of the application of s 98 and that s 98 applies only in testate estates and has nothing to do with the *per stirpes* rule which applies on intestacy; see para **8.5**.

Example of the operation of s 98

Problem

Anne gave the residue of her estate to her daughter, Joanna, who predeceased her, leaving two children, John and Mary, alive at the date of Anne's death. Anne's executor is also dead. Her daughter, Joanna, made her boyfriend, Flash Harry, the sole executor and universal legatee and devisee of her will.

Question

What happens to the gift of the residue, and who will now extract the grant with will annexed in Anne's estate?

If we apply the three conditions, which must be satisfied for s 98 to apply, the answer should emerge.

1. Did the testatrix make the gift in her will to issue?

    Yes. Anne made a bequest in her will to Joanna, who is issue.

2. Did the issue to whom the gift was given predecease the testatrix?

    Yes. Joanna predeceased Anne.

3. Did the issue to whom the gift was given leave issue alive at the date of death of the testator?

    Yes. Joanna left issue, John and Mary, alive on Anne's death.

Thus, by applying s 98, Joanna is deemed to die immediately after Anne. Under Anne's will, all her property goes to Flash Harry. The gift of the residue will go to Flash Harry as universal legatee and devisee of Joanna's will. Flash Harry, as sole executor of Joanna's estate, will extract the grant of administration with will annexed in Anne's estate.

Anyone who inherits in lieu of a predeceased child does not have the right to take an action under s 117 or an action under s 63, as the child would have. See para **4.6.4**.

4.6.3.4 Non-marital children—Status of Children Act, 1987

The Status of Children Act, 1987 applies, when the testator has a non-marital child or their issue has a non-marital child see 'section 98' children above.

Where it applies, the effect of this Act can completely alter a testator's intensions and indeed the course of the administration of an estate and must be fully understood by practitioners in this area.

The Status of Children Act was passed on 14 December 1987. A portion of the Act came into operation with effect from 14 January 1988 and a portion came into effect on 14 June 1988. The Act equalised the rights of children and amended the law relating to their status pertaining to succession and other property rights. The previous position was that any non-marital child was not entitled to share in a deceased parent's estate. Section 3(1) of the Act states:

> *'in deducing any relationship for the purpose of this Act or any Act of the Oireachtas passed after the commencement of this section the relationship between every person and his father and mother*

(or either of them) shall unless the contrary intention appears be determined irrespective of whether his father or mother are or have been married to each other and all other relationships shall be deduced accordingly.'

This does not affect children adopted under the Adoption Acts, who continue to be children of their adoptive parents (see s 3).

In construing any disposition (including a will or codicil) made after the commencement of Part V of the Act, references to relationships between persons must be construed in accordance with s 3. Part V of the Act came into effect on 14 June 1988 and only dispositions made after this date are affected. In a situation where a will was made before 14 June 1988, and the testator dies subsequently, the old rules of construction still apply. At the outset of any administration the solicitor must check whether the provisions of the Status of Children Act apply.

The provisions of the Status of Children Act have been incorporated into the taxation legislation by s 74 of the Finance Act, 1988. Section 74 has effect in relation to the Tax Acts in respect of the year 1987/88 and subsequent years of assessment or accounting periods ending on or after 14 January 1988, as the case may be, in relation to the Capital Gains Tax Acts in respect of disposals made on or after 14 January 1988, and in relation to the Capital Acquisitions Tax Act, 1976 in respect of gifts or inheritances taken on or after 14 January 1988, and in relation to the statutes relating to stamp duty in respect of any instrument executed on or after 14 January 1988. These changes are incorporated into the Taxes Consolidation Act, 1997, the Capital Acquisitions Tax Consolidation Act, 2003, and the Stamp Duty Consolidation Act, 1999, respectively.

A non-marital child now moves into a Group A threshold and a non-marital grandchild now moves into a Group B threshold. Consider the possibility of the effect of a CAT relief in such circumstances i.e. if a non-marital child of a predeceased child, is a minor, then such child will move to a Group A threshold. See para 1 of the First Part of the Second Schedule to the CAT Consolidation Act, 2003 as amended by Schedule 3 to the Finance (No 3) Act, 2011.

Thus, it is necessary to advise a testator that the Status of Children Act will apply to their will unless they specifically state otherwise. It is therefore necessary in drafting a will specifically to negative the provisions of the Act if this is what the testator's instructions are, because otherwise the Act will automatically apply.

The negation of the Act in a will does not affect the right of such issue to inherit but merely affects the definition of 'child' or 'children' or 'grandchild' or 'grandchildren', if referred to in the will. See para 2.1.7 'Negation of Status of Children Act, 1987 clause'. For instance, a bequest to *'all of my grandchildren'* will now automatically include non-marital grandchildren. However, if the testator specifically names certain children, a non-marital child would not automatically be included, but may have an entitlement under s 117.

The most important amendment to the Succession Act, 1965 is the insertion of s 4A (as inserted by s 29 of the Status of Children Act), which provides that relationships shall now be deduced irrespective of one's parents' marital status and all other relationships shall be determined accordingly. Where a person whose father and mother have not married each other dies intestate, he shall be presumed not to have been survived by his father or other person claiming through his father unless the contrary is shown. However, this is a rebuttable presumption. Prima facie, a deceased person's mother would inherit and all persons claiming through the mother (s 29(2)).

Section 30 inserted s 27A into the Succession Act. To ensure that where (for example) a single man dies intestate, this section creates a rebuttable presumption that he did not have any non-marital children or further issue tracing back to a non-marital child to ensure that the parents of the deceased can extract a grant of administration intestate.

Summary of effects of the Status of Children Act, 1987

It is clear that an application can be made under s 117 (see para **4.6.4**) by a non-marital child to the estate of a parent, irrespective of when the will was made. However, the testator must have died after Part V of the Act came into force, i.e. after 14 June 1988. Summarising what exactly is affected by the provisions of the Act, it applies to:

1. wills and other dispositions made on or after 14 June 1988;

2. deaths on or after 14 June 1988 in relation to:

    (a) intestate succession; and

    (b) s 117 applications (notwithstanding the date of the will).

Practitioners should note that s 27(7) provides that a will or codicil made before 14 June 1988 is not to be treated as having been made later merely because it is confirmed by codicil after that date.

4.6.3.5 Adopted children

Section 3(2) of the Status of Children Act, 1987 provides that an adopted person shall be deemed from the date of the adoption order to be the child of the adopted parents, not the child of any other persons. Adopted children are not entitled to any portion of their natural parent's estate; however, since the Finance Act, 2001, adopted children have Group A CAT threshold from both their adopted and their natural parents. They do not have any Succession Act rights from their natural parents but do have Succession Act rights from their adoptive parents.

4.6.3.6 Stepchildren

Unfortunately, there is no precise legal definition of the term 'stepchild' in Irish legislation. However, it is generally understood to refer to the son or daughter by a former marriage of the stepparent's spouse. In other jurisdictions, it is actually defined. For example, in Western Australia the concept of a stepparent in relation to a child is understood as being a parent who is:

1. not the parent of the child; but is

2. married to a parent of the child; and

3. treats or any time during the marriage has treated the child as a member of the family formed with the parent.

There is no actual legal obligation to provide for stepchildren. As they are not 'children' of the deceased they are not entitled to make an application under s 117 of the Succession Act and are not entitled to a share on intestacy.

A stepchild for tax purposes is deemed to be a child (i.e. Group A threshold for CAT). However, in relation to their right to extract a grant or to inherit on intestacy (see s 67 of the Succession Act), the law, at present, is that stepchildren, having no blood relationship to the deceased, have no Succession Act rights. Stepchildren have CAT Group A threshold but do not have Succession Act rights. See CAT Lecture Notes (see Preface).

4.6.3.7 Foster children

Similarly, there is no legal obligation to provide for foster children. Foster children are not entitled to make an application under s 117 of the Succession Act and are not entitled to share on intestacy. A foster child is a child who has resided with the deceased and was under the care and maintenance of the deceased at the deceased's expense for a minimum of five years before the foster child's eighteenth birthday.

Because of the case of *Boyle Deceased; O'Rourke v Gallagher* (unreported) February 2000, Letterkenny Circuit Court, which was decided on the basis of a type of proprietary estoppel (see **4.6.4.5**), not on the fact that the applicant was a foster child, some practitioners believe that foster children now have similar rights to adopted children. This is not the case. Foster children have no rights whatsoever to their foster parent's estate. They are strangers in blood to each other. Certain foster children have CAT Group A threshold since 6 December 1999; see Chapter 3 of the CAT Lecture Notes (see Preface). To repeat, they do not have Succession Act rights.

In summary, stepchildren and foster children are not the deceased's children for Succession Act purposes, although for taxation purposes they are. Given this knowledge, the testator may very well change how he directs his estate to be divided.

4.6.3.8 Children of a deceased civil partner

A child of a deceased civil partner is, of course, simply either the biological or adopted child of a deceased, but same is listed separately as a 'type of child'.

4.6.3.9 Children of a surviving civil partner

The child of a civil partner of the deceased is a stranger in blood to the deceased civil partner for Succession Act, 1965 purposes. Only one of the civil partners is the parent. The Finance (No 3) Act, 2011, which deals with the taxation consequences of civil partnership and qualified cohabitants, gives such a child a similar Group A taxation relationship as a stepchild for taxation purposes, but does not provide for succession rights. See Chapter 3 of the CAT Lecture Notes (see Preface). However, consider also who is a child under the Children and Family Relationships Act, 2015.

4.6.4 WHAT ACTIONS CAN A CHILD TAKE AGAINST AN ESTATE?

It was outlined earlier, that for Succession Act, 1965 purposes all children, with the exception of stepchildren and foster children, are children of the deceased . Therefore, this section applies only to those types of children.

4.6.4.1 Actions under section 117

The first type of action is based on s 117 of the Succession Act, 1965, which allows a child of a testator to make an application to court for provision to be made.

> '(1) Where, on application by or on behalf of a child of a testator [therefore this could not apply on intestacy], the Court is of opinion that the testator has failed in his moral duty to make proper provision for the child in accordance with his means, whether by his will or otherwise, the Court may order that such provision shall be made for the child out of the estate as the Court thinks just.'

The court is obliged to consider the matter from the point of view of a prudent and just parent, and must take into account the position of each of the children of the testator and any other circumstances which the court considers to be of assistance in arriving at the decision that is as fair as possible to the child and to the other children (see s 117(2)).

Section 117 and the surviving spouse

Under s 117(3) it is provided that an order under this section will not affect:

1. the legal right of the surviving spouse; or
2. if the surviving spouse is the mother or father of the child applicant, any devise or bequest to the spouse or any share to which the spouse is entitled on intestacy.

Section 117(3A) and the surviving civil partner

Section 117(3A)

> 'An order under this section shall not affect the legal right of a surviving civil partner unless the Court, after consideration of all the circumstances, including the testator's financial circumstances and his or her obligations to the surviving civil partner, is of the opinion that it would be unjust not to make the order.'

Section 117(3A) provides additional protection to the child of a deceased civil partner not unlike that given under s 67A(3), which applies in cases of intestacy, as the court has the power to make an order for provision for a surviving child out of the legal right share of a surviving civil partner.

This does not apply in the case of a surviving spouse and thus again there is a difference between a child of a civil partner who dies testate and the child of a married parent who issues proceedings under s 117 against the estate of a married parent. Provision cannot be made for that child from the legal right share of the surviving spouse as the legal right share is ring-fenced for the surviving spouse only, not for a surviving civil partner. So again, the Civil Partnership Act discriminates in favour of the child whose parent is a civil partner, over the child whose parent is not.

When advising a client with a child or children who is a civil partner and/or may be a civil partner at the date of death and thus perhaps survived by a surviving civil partner and child, all advice given should be considered very carefully in light of the Civil Partnership Act.

However, also now consider the effect of ss 67 and 69 of the Children and Family Relationships Act, 2015 on this 'flaw' under the 2010 Act.

Time limits for section 117

In this instance, time limits are very important. Section 117(6), which sets a strict time limit for applications, has been amended by the Family Law (Divorce) Act, 1996. The twelve-month period has been reduced to *six months* and therefore an order under this section shall not be made except on an application made within six months from the first taking out of representation to the deceased's estate.

The time limit is a strict one, which is not extended by s 127 in the case of disability, including infancy (see *MPD v MD* [1981] ILRM 179 at 182–4). Carroll J held that the extension of limitation periods set out in the Statute of Limitations and the Succession Act did not apply to claims by a child for proper supervision under s 117, since a claim under that section was not a claim under a will, but rather was made independently of the will and against its provisions; nor was it a claim on intestacy or a legal right.

To put it another way, a potential s 117 applicant aged six months, for example, or one suffering from a serious mental disability are both subject to the same statutory time limit as an adult with no disability.

This is obviously different from a personal injuries action, for example where the Statute of Limitations makes specific provisions for the time limits for the institution of proceedings where persons suffer from a disability.

Is an extension of time possible?

While s 127 of the Succession Act, 1965 extends periods of limitation in certain circumstances, it has no application to s 117 proceedings: see *MPD v MD* cited earlier and the judgment of Laffoy J in *In Re F Deceased; S1 v PR1 and PR2* [2013] IEHC 407.

What factors will be considered?

Many considerations are taken into account by the court, and these were clearly laid out in the judgment of Kenny J in *Re GM; FM v TAM* [1972] 106 ILTR 82:

> 'There is a number of criteria which must be taken into account where the moral duty to make proper provision for a child and the matter must be judged by the facts existing at the date of death and must depend on
>
> (a) the amount left to the surviving spouse or the value of the legal right if the surviving spouse elects to take this,
>
> (b) the number of the testator's children, their ages and their position in life at the date of the testator's death,
>
> (c) the means of the testator,
>
> (d) the age of the child whose case is being considered and his or her financial position and prospects in life, [and]
>
> (e) whether the testator has already in his lifetime made proper provision for his child.'

In the event of a testator choosing to exclude the applicant child where he has reason for doing so, it is important that such reasons are contained in the solicitor's attendance, as evidence may be required at a later date. The reasons may be as simple as an outline of monies provided to a child in the past. The more detail gathered at the time of the taking of instructions and the making of the will, the easier it will be to defend a s 117 application in court.

The testator may also enclose a declaration to this effect in a will, and practitioners are referred to Spierin, *Wills—Irish Precedents and Drafting*, 2nd edn (2012) at pp 104 and 198 for such declarations. Obviously, this will not prevent a disappointed child from making an application.

The test in deciding whether provision should be made is not whether the child is a dependent but whether the testator has failed in his moral duty to make proper provision. The court is not permitted to make provision for a child which interferes with the legal right share of a surviving spouse, nor with a devise or bequest to or a share on intestacy of a parent of the child (where that parent is the surviving spouse).

Therefore, if the testator has bequeathed his entire estate to a surviving spouse, a s 117 application is not available to children of that testator and spouse, nor is it available where the deceased died intestate, as the child will automatically have an entitlement on intestacy. It is a limitation that an application is not available in the case of intestacy where, for instance, there is a child suffering from a handicap or other disability. In this instance, the child does not have an opportunity to apply for greater provision than his brothers and sisters.

Application can only be made by or on behalf of a child; it is not available to a grandchild or other person to whom the testator stood *in loco parentis*. The testator may have discharged his moral duty *inter vivos* with gifts or settlements made during the testator's lifetime, and in the event of such provision having been made it is important that the solicitor drawing up the will obtain details of this at the time of the making of the will. The test is an objective one; the subjective opinion of the testator that he owed no duty, or that he had discharged such duty, is not conclusive.

Onus of proof/failure of a parent's moral duty

The Supreme Court has considered s 117 applications on several occasions, for example *EB v SS and G McC* [1998] 4 IR 527. However, the first decision was that in *C v C* [1989] 1 ILRM 815. Finlay CJ stated that the phrase in s 117(1) referring to a failure in a parent's moral duty to make proper provision for a child places a 'relatively high onus of proof' on an applicant. He further stated that there must be a positive failure in moral duty.

The facts of *EB v SS and G McC* are that the applicant made a s 117 application in relation to his deceased mother's estate. She was a widow with four children. The plaintiff's late father had a successful business. At the date of his death in 1985 he owned 56 per cent of the shares in the company, to which his widow then became entitled. In 1987 the plaintiff's mother transferred her shares in this company to her four children.

The plaintiff's shares realised a sum of approximately €275,000. He dissipated this sum within a short period of time and it had all gone by 1992. In 1992, the plaintiff's mother made a will and left a very nominal bequest to her son, whom she described as an 'eternal student'. The son had a serious alcohol and drug addiction problem. The plaintiff was in relatively straitened circumstances. The residue of her estate was left to five charities and the value of the estate was approximately €335,000.

The procedures were instituted by the plaintiff under s 117, claiming in a declaration that the testatrix had failed in her moral duty to make proper provision for the plaintiff in accordance with her means by her will or otherwise. Having regard to all the circumstances of the case, Keane J concluded that there was no breach of her moral duty to the plaintiff. He considered a number of courses that might have been open to the testatrix in making provision for the plaintiff during her lifetime, but he reiterated that the test to be applied is not which of the alternative courses the court itself would have adopted if confronted with the situation.

The true test is whether the decision by the testatrix to opt for the course of leaving unaltered the bequest to the charities constituted a breach of her moral duty, and Keane J was satisfied that it did not. He also placed considerable significance as to how the plaintiff was treated and supported by both his parents up to the time of the transfer of the shares to him.

The plaintiff had also received a very good education, but Keane J considered that the decision of the testatrix not to make further provision for him in her will may well have been prompted not merely by a concern that her money should go where she could be sure that it could do most good but also by a belief that since the provision of significant financial assistance to the plaintiff had not in the past produced the best results, it might not have been in his own interest to provide him with further funds, even through the mechanism of a trust.

Keane J further emphasised that the legislation was designed to protect children and not grandchildren. He did not agree to the extension of the ample protection which the Oireachtas afforded to children even in the middle-aged and elderly category, to grandchildren, as it would seem to bring within the scheme of the Act a category of claimants the protection of whom was not envisaged by the legislature.

Lynch J concurred with Keane J's view, with Barron J dissenting.

It is important for practitioners to note that the court is also prepared to take into account the behaviour of the plaintiff towards his parent, as was seen in *McDonnell v Norris* [1999] ILRM 270. Therefore, when taking instructions from the testator in such a possible case, it is vital that full details of all surrounding circumstances are investigated and noted.

New criteria for section 117 evolving through common law

Once the court has accepted that there has been such a 'positive failure in moral duty', it will look at the circumstances of the applicant child, the circumstances of any other children, and any other matter which it sees fit. The court must be satisfied that a need exists. In the judgment of McCracken J, in *McC(M) and N(B) v M(DH) and H(E)* [2001] 10 JIC 3104, reference was made to a passage from *Re the Goods of JH Deceased* [1984] IR 599, Barron J, where the judge referred to the necessity for the child to demonstrate that they had a particular need which the means of the testator could satisfy in whole or in part and that if no such need exists (even where no provision had been made by the testator by his will or otherwise) the court had no power to intervene. This judgment provides an excellent summary of the presently evolving position regarding the criteria for s 117 applications. It is strongly recommended that anyone practising in this area read this judgment.

When looking at the circumstances of the applicant child to determine whether the need exists, the court will take into account the financial circumstances of the spouse of that child. However, as discussed, the section will not be used to benefit grandchildren. In practice the needs criteria for obvious reasons tends to be considered first.

Relevant legal principles

The 2003 judgment of Kearns J in the case of *Re ABC Deceased; XC, YC and ZC v RT, KU and JL* [2003] 2 IR 250, included relevant legal principles which could be said to derive under s 117 as follows:

(a) The social policy underlying s 117 is primarily directed to protecting those children who are still of an age and situation in life where they might reasonably expect support from their parents against the failure of parents who are unmindful of their duties in that area.

(b) What has to be determined is whether the testator, at the time of his death, owes any moral obligation to the applicants and if so, whether he has failed in that obligation.

(c) There is a high onus of proof placed on an applicant for relief under s 117, which requires the establishment of a positive failure in moral duty.

(d) Before a court can interfere there must be clear circumstances and a positive failure in moral duty must be established.

(e) The duty created by s 117 is not absolute.

(f) The relationship of parent and child does not itself and without regard to other circumstances create a moral duty to leave anything by will to the child.

(g) Section 117 does not create an obligation to leave something to each child.

(h) The provision of an expensive education for a child may discharge the moral duty as may other gifts or settlements made during the lifetime of the testator.

(i) Financing a good education so as to give a child the best start in life possible, and providing money, which if properly managed, should afford a degree of financial security for the rest of one's life does amount to making 'proper provision'.

(j) The duty under s 117 is not to make adequate provision but to provide proper provision in accordance with the testator's means.

(k) A just parent must take into account not just his moral obligations to his children and to his wife, but all his moral obligations, for example to aged and infirm parents.

(l) In dealing with a s 117 application, the position of an applicant child is not to be taken in isolation. The court's duty is to consider the entirety of the testator's affairs and to decide upon the application in the overall context. In other words, while the moral claim of a child may require a testator to make a particular provision for him, the moral claims of others may require such provision to be reduced or omitted altogether.

(m) Special circumstances giving rise to a moral duty may arise if a child is induced to believe that by, for example, working on a farm he will ultimately become the owner of it thereby causing him to shape his upbringing, training, and life accordingly.

(n) Another example of special circumstances might be a child who had a long illness or an exceptional talent which it would be morally wrong not to foster.

(o) Special needs would also include physical or mental disability.

(p) Although the court has very wide powers both as to when to make provisions for an applicant child and as to the nature of such provision, such powers must not be construed as giving the court a power to make a new will for the testator.

(q) The test to be applied is not which of the alternative courses open to the testator the court itself would have adopted if confronted with the same situation, but rather whether the decision of the testator to opt for the course he did, of itself and without more, constituted a breach of moral duty to the plaintiff.

(r) The court must not disregard the fact that parents must be presumed to know their children better than anyone else.

These principles have been cited with approval in succeeding cases.

In summary

The test for s 117 is twofold and both must be satisfied:

1. The court must be satisfied that there was a positive failure in the moral duty of the testator. The relevant date for considering such failure is the date of death of the deceased and there is a high onus resting on the child to establish such a failure.

2. The child must establish that a need exists (as at the date of death) which the testator could have satisfied by will or otherwise but failed to do so. Again, through case law, the 'needs' element tends to be considered first.

Only then will the court look at the estate of the deceased, the benefits received by the child in the past, and any benefits under the will (if any), taking into account the position of each of the children and any other circumstances in arriving at a decision that would be as fair as possible to the applicant child and any other children. See Law Reform

Commission Report (LRC 118–2017) on s 117 for proposed changes to same. See also Stephenson Solicitors 32nd Seminar, *Stranger in a Strange Land*, for a full discussion on same (pp 7–11).

What is the effect of a section 117 application on the administration of the estate?

Where proceedings pursuant to s 117 of the Succession Act have issued, a practitioner should advise the legal personal representative to refrain from winding up the estate until such time as the applicant's case has been decided upon. However, even where there is a possibility of a claim or a claim has already been made, it might still be possible to distribute part of the estate. See the case of *H v H* (unreported) February 2001, High Court (*ex temp* judgment on an interlocutory application), where Budd J refused an application for an injunction to restrain payment out of the legal right share of the spouse where she had undertaken prior to the application to hold the balance of the estate pending the determination of the proceedings. Of course, payments which could be affected by a court order could always be made with the consent of all interested parties, or pursuant to an order of the court. See also, In the Matter of the Estate of Peter Clohessy 2017 IEHC 797. See Stephenson Solicitors 33rd Seminar, *All Kinds of Everything*, for a full discussion on same (pp 19–22).

Nevertheless, when acting for such a child and in the event of the solicitors with carriage of the administration of the estate declining to cease administering, it would be advisable to seek injunctive relief preventing the administration of the estate, pending the adjudication of the claimant's case.

The personal representative should not notify a child of his or her right to take a section 117 application

One of the most frequent questions asked in relation to s 117 is whether there is an obligation on the personal representative to notify any or all of the children of a deceased parent that they have a right to institute proceedings pursuant to s 117.

There is no such obligation. Indeed, to encourage any such claim may expose the personal representative to an action in negligence by those beneficiaries entitled to share under the terms of the deceased's last will and testament. See Spierin, *The Succession Act 1965 and Related Legislation: A Commentary*, 5th edn (2017), and see also the Law Reform Commission's Report (LRC 118–2017) re s 117 on this point.

How does a practitioner initiate an application under section 117 on behalf of a child?

While the application occurs post-death, it is important to be familiar with how the section will operate in practice, as the testator pre-death must be advised of what will occur should a child choose to take such an application.

Proceedings under s 117 of the Succession Act, 1965 in the High Court are commenced by way of special summons pursuant to O 3 of the Rules of the Superior Courts, 1986 and are grounded upon an affidavit sworn by the plaintiff.

The special summons is made returnable for the Master's Court and it is usual practice to allow the defendant time to file their replying affidavit while the matter is listed in the Master's Court.

Once the defendant's replying affidavit has been filed and all papers are in order, the matter would be transferred from the Judges List to the list to fix dates to obtain a date for hearing.

In the interim, both the plaintiff and the defendant can raise particulars on foot of the affidavit and seek voluntary discovery and, if necessary, issue motions compelling discovery.

A notice of intention to cross-examine witnesses on foot of their affidavits is usually served.

The documents required are:

1. special summons;
2. grounding affidavit of the plaintiff;

3. replying affidavit of the defendant;
4. notice for particulars, if necessary;
5. request for voluntary discovery and if necessary, motions compelling discovery;
6. notice of intention to cross-examine witnesses on foot of their affidavits.

The procedure for s 117 proceedings in the Circuit Court is governed by O 50 of the Circuit Court Rules. Proceedings are issued by way of Succession Law Civil Bill.

Thereafter, particulars can be raised and a defence filed. The procedure in respect of discovery applicable in the High Court will also be applicable in the Circuit Court.

It is important to note that under the Circuit Court Rules any proceedings issued on or after 3 December 2001 in respect of s 117 proceedings must be by way of Succession Law Civil Bill. Once the proceedings are issued, a caveat must be filed in the Probate Office and the particulars of the caveat filed must be endorsed on the Succession Law Civil Bill prior to serving.

Costs

Practitioners should note that under s 117(5) the costs of the proceedings shall be at the discretion of the court and, in the vast majority of cases where the proceedings are not frivolous or vexatious, the costs are borne by the estate. This follows the decision in the case of *In bonis Morelli; Vella v Morelli* [1968] IR 11, which found that where there are reasonable grounds to challenge the will and where the proceedings are conducted bona fide, then the unsuccessful challenger should also be entitled to their costs from the estate.

However, this is not always the case: see *EB v SS* [1998] 4 IR 527 and *Re B; K v D* (unreported) 8 December 2000, High Court. In the latter case the personal representative defending an action was denied her costs when she admitted on cross-examination that she had not seen the affidavits until the morning of the trial, despite the fact that she had sworn a replying affidavit. The judge, Kearns J, felt that the matter should never have been allowed to proceed to trial and refused the defendant executrix her costs in the circumstances.

Furthermore, the recent Supreme Court judgment of Kearns J in the case of *Elliott v Stamp* [2008] IESC 10 (while this case related to a will challenge, not s 117, the logic of same may well be followed in such cases) goes further. He stated that once an executor fully and fairly sets out the available evidence pertaining to the issues in the case (in that case, testamentary capacity), a plaintiff who elects nonetheless to maintain the claim thereafter but who loses the case may not recover the costs from the estate unless they were justified in continuing the proceedings after the disclosure has been made.

Even taking this into account, however, if a testator is excluding a child from his will and that child takes a successful s 117 application, the testator must be informed of the possible effects and costs to his estate. Should he then choose to proceed, the solicitor takes detailed notes of his instructions and the advice given and proceeds to draft the will as requested.

4.6.4.2 Actions under section 121

The second type of action that a child may take is an action under s 121 (dispositions for the purpose of disinheriting a spouse/civil partner or children) and where it is taken, it is generally taken in connection with a s 117 application.

The 'connection' between section 117 and section 121 of the Succession Act, 1965

Often when an applicant gives instructions or wishes to institute proceedings pursuant to s 117, the nature and extent of a deceased's estate is unknown.

Specifically, it is often unknown whether there were any dispositions within three years of the date of death to which s 121 could apply. Given the equally short statutory time limit applicable both to s 121 and s 117, it is increasingly common for a pleading pursuant to s 121 to be included in any s 117 proceeding.

This is to ensure that if it is subsequently discovered (it may of course already be known) that the deceased did dispose of assets within three years of the date of death and that there is an issue as to whether those assets should be included in the estate and subject to the s 117 application then it is for this reason that claim is made pursuant to this section also.

There is also the possibility of assets which are the subject of a successful s 121 application being made available for a s 117 application (see *MPD v MD*, cited at para **4.6.4.1**).

4.6.4.3 Actions under section 67A(3)

The third type of action a child may take is under s 67A(3).

Section 67A

'(1) Where a civil partner dies intestate, without issue, the surviving civil partner is entitled to the whole estate.

(2) Where a civil partner dies intestate with issue, the surviving civil partner is entitled to two-thirds of the estate, the remaining one-third being divided equally among any surviving issue in accordance with section 67B(2).'

Section 67B(2)

'If all the issue are in equal degree of relationship to the deceased the distribution shall be in equal shares among them; if they are not, it shall be per stirpes.'

It is vital to realise that these rules of intestacy are subject to a novel provision under s 67A(3), which states as follows:

'The Court may, on the application by or on behalf of a child of an intestate who dies leaving a civil partner and one or more children, order that provision be made for that child out of the intestate's estate only if the Court is of the opinion that it would be unjust not to make the order, after considering all the circumstances, including—

(a) the extent to which the intestate has made provision for that issue during the intestate's lifetime,

(b) the age and reasonable financial requirements of that child,

(c) the intestate's financial situation, and

(d) the intestate's obligations to the Civil Partner.'

Thus, the court can make further provision from the deceased's estate for an applicant child of the deceased who was in a civil partnership at the date of death, and in making such provision from the estate of the deceased, the court may interfere with the surviving civil partner's two-thirds share. There is no such provision re surviving spouses. However, also now consider the effect of ss 67 and 69 of the Children and Family Relationships Act, 2015 on this 'flaw' under the 2010 Act.

Under this section, the court, in ordering provision for an applicant child, cannot grant a child less than they would have been entitled to had no order been made, and the amount granted cannot be greater than had the deceased died intestate leaving neither a surviving spouse nor civil partner. Therefore, on application the court cannot in any way interfere with the child's intestate share; moreover, the maximum share that the court can award cannot be greater than if the parent had died without a civil partner or spouse.

Examples of section 67A(3) in operation

(a) A civil partner dies intestate survived by a civil partner and one child who brings an application pursuant to s 67A(3):

1. The surviving civil partner is entitled to two-thirds subject to s 67A(3).
2. The surviving child is entitled to one-third.
3. The court cannot grant a share to the applicant child less than their one-third share.

4. The court cannot grant a share to the applicant child more than the child would have been entitled to had the deceased died without a spouse or civil partner, i.e. assuming one child and no issue of a predeceased child, the whole estate.

5. Therefore, the child cannot be granted a share less than one-third, and as there are no other children, provision can be made out of the remaining civil partner's two-thirds share.

(b) A civil partner dies intestate and is survived by a civil partner and two children:

The surviving civil partner is entitled to two-thirds of the estate and each of the children is entitled to one-sixth share. Either of the children can bring an application pursuant to s 67A(3) to have their intestate share increased, and if one does so:

1. The court cannot interfere with the one-sixth share of the other child.

2. The court cannot grant to the applicant child less than their one-sixth share.

3. The court cannot grant a share to the applicant child greater than they would be entitled to had their parent not been married or had a civil partner at the date of death, and if the deceased had died intestate without a civil partner, each of the children would have been entitled one-half share in the estate of the deceased.

4. The court can make provision for the applicant child that cannot be less than one-sixth or more than one-half.

5. The court, in increasing the applicant child's intestate share, is reducing the surviving civil partner's two-thirds share.

It might thus appear to such a child that there was 'nothing to lose' and thus the Civil Partnership Act, 2010 may increase litigation. The position re costs of such an action under s 67A(6) shall be at the discretion of the court.

Note that there is no similar provision in the Succession Act, 1965, allowing a child in an intestate situation to apply to court seeking additional provision from the estate of their married parent. Therefore, it appears that the Civil Partnership Act discriminates in favour of children whose parents are in a civil partnership over children whose parents are married.

In short, where there is a child (or children) and a surviving civil partner, that civil partner may be treated differently to a spouse in that the surviving civil partner's intestate share is vulnerable and open to litigation by the operation of s 67A(3).

Time limits for an application made under section 67A(3)

As is the case of proceedings issued under s 117 of the 1965 Act, proceedings must be brought within six months from the first taking out of representation to the deceased's estate. See s 67A(7) of the Civil Partnership Act. This is a very short time limit and great care will need to be taken to avoid the possibility of a negligence claim arising.

4.6.4.4 Actions under section 63—advancement

The third type of action a child may take in a testate or intestate situation is where he receives a share of the estate with his sibling or siblings and this child has received a previous 'advancement'. In that case, any one of the siblings may take an action against this child, which would, of course, affect the administration of the estate and, if successful, its distribution. See later for how the distribution would be affected. The practitioner must be in a position to explain the affecting consequences of this to the testator. It is important to understand that not all gifts are advancements.

In order to explain advancement fully, its history and the wording of s 63 of the Succession Act must be examined.

The doctrine of advancement, formally known as 'hotch-pot', is a very important doctrine which has been embodied in s 63 of the Succession Act, 1965.

Formerly, the doctrine of 'hotch-pot' applied in Ireland only in case of intestacy. Under s 63 of the Succession Act the doctrine of advancement applies to both testate and intestate situations, so it can be said that it replaces the former doctrine of 'hotch-pot' and embodies the existing rule against double portions, which was in effect the part of the doctrine of advancement which applied to wills.

The whole purpose of the doctrine of advancement was and is to achieve fairness between the children of the deceased.

It is important at the time of taking instructions for a will to ascertain if a testator has made any capital advancements to a child which may be taken into account on death. If this is not done at will-drafting stage, the personal representative, should it arise, will be caught on the back foot, with no information from one of the key parties involved, i.e. the deceased parent. It should be noted that not all gifts are advancements.

When it arises

Section 63(1)

> 'Any advancement made to the child of a deceased person during his lifetime shall, subject to the contrary intention expressed or appearing from the circumstances of the case, be taken as being so made in or towards satisfaction of the share of such child in the estate of the deceased for the share which such child would have taken if living at the death of the deceased, and as between the children should be brought into account in distributing the estate.'

Advancement

'Advancement' is defined in s 63(6) as:

> 'a gift intended to make permanent provision for a child [thus not all gifts are advancements] and includes advancement by way of portion or settlement, including any life or lesser interest and including property covenanted to be paid or settled. It also includes an advance or portion for the purpose of establishing a child in a profession, vocation, trade or business, marriage portion and payments made for the education of the child to a higher standard than that provided by the deceased for any other or others of his children.'

It is presumed that the parents wish to provide equally for all their children. Therefore, if one of the children has been advanced a capital sum, which is advancement, during the deceased's lifetime, then if that child wishes to participate in the distribution in his parent's estate, he must bring the advancement into 'hotch-pot', i.e. into account.

It is important to note that s 63 applies only where no contrary intention is expressed or appears from the circumstances of the case. It is usual for most parent testators or testatrixes to express the contrary intention in the will, so that if the will provides for equal division, each child will get an equal sum irrespective of what may have been advanced to the child during the lifetime of the testator or the testatrix.

When is its value established?

Section 63(2) goes on to say that the value of the advancement shall be reckoned as at the date of the advancement, not at the date of death; there is no provision for inflation or indexation. The will can provide for the advancement to be valued in another way should the testator so wish, for example by applying the Consumer Price Index to the capital sum originally advanced.

What inheritance does it affect?

Advancement is only taken as being 'in or towards satisfaction of the share of such child in the Estate'; it does not affect any specific legacies to such a child. It would therefore be taken into account only in the distribution of the residue among children, where there are gifts to children as a class or assets passing on intestacy.

Onus of proof

Section 63(5)

> 'The onus of proving that a child has been made an advancement shall be on the person so asserting, unless the advancement has been expressed in writing by the deceased.'

Spierin, in *The Succession Act 1965 and Related Legislation: A Commentary*, 5th edn (2017), expresses the view that the purpose of this provision is to relieve a child of any obligation to prove negatively that every asset he has acquired was not a gift by way of advancement from his deceased parent.

Thus, it is clear that if a testator wishes for all children to start off with a 'clean slate' on his death, it is important to negate the effect of any advancement made in the lifetime of the testator.

Section 63(3) and (4) provide that if the advancement amounts to more than a child's share under a will or intestacy, then the child is to be excluded from the distribution. If the advancement is less than the child's share he is entitled to share in the distribution to the extent necessary to satisfy his share, i.e. he is to receive in satisfaction of this share so much only of the estate as will add to the advancement sufficient to make up the full amount of the share.

While this is stated quite clearly, it is not always easy to see immediately in practice how it will operate and, should there be a possibility of that arising, the testator needs to be informed exactly of the effect it will have on the estate. The following examples should assist.

Example 1: A straightforward example

Anne Richardson dies intestate. Most of her assets have been held jointly with her husband, Martin. She leaves a net estate worth €45,000. Martin survives her and their two children, one of whom received an advance of €10,000 during Anne's lifetime in order to enable him to start a small business.

Martin will take two-thirds of the estate, i.e. €30,000 (the doctrine of advancement applies only between the children and so will not affect the surviving spouse's share).

There is therefore €15,000 available for the two children. The child who received the advancement has to take into account his previous €10,000. He will receive €10,000 less than his brother or sister. This means that he will take €2,500 and his brother or sister will take €12,500. The method of reaching this figure (where the amounts are less convenient than in this simple example!) is:

1. add back to the amount available for distribution between all the children by the amount received by way of advancement: in this example, €15,000 + €10,000 = €25,000;
2. then 'distribute' this amount between the children: in this example, €12,500 each;
3. then deduct the amount of the advancement from the share of the child who received it: in this example, €12,500 − €10,000 = €2,500.

Example 2: A more complex example

John Black dies intestate, a widower, leaving an estate worth €90,000 and three children who had previously received €12,000, €15,000, and €33,000, respectively.

John Black deceased

It is important to note that a s 63 application can only affect the children's shared inheritance. A shared inheritance could be, for example, a universal bequest to the children, a residuary bequest to the children, or a pecuniary legacy to the children. It will not have any effect on any other bequest or devise. It is in effect a 'redistribution' of the shared inheritance. In other words, for s 63 to apply siblings must be receiving a share of an estate;

be it a shared specific bequest, a share of the residue, or a share on intestacy, and one or more of those siblings must have received an advancement.

	Total Estate	Child 1	Child 2	Child 3
Estate available for distribution prior to s 63 being applied	€90,000	€30,000	€30,000	€30,000
Add advancements as if they were part of the estate	€60,000	€20,000	€20,000	€20,000
'Notional' estate	**€150,000**	€50,000	€50,000	€50,000
Deduct actual advancements	€60,000	€12,000 (i.e. deduct actual amount received)	€15,000 (i.e. deduct actual amount received)	€33,000 (i.e. deduct actual amount received)
Amount received by each child	€90,000	€38,000	€35,000	€17,000

The effect on the will/administration of a child's application under section 117 and/or section 63 and/or section 67A(3)

A child's right to apply under ss 63, 67A(3), and 117 when appropriate and the effect on the estate of an application under ss 63 and 67A(3) have been outlined earlier.

An examination of the potential effect that a s 117 application may have on the estate is outlined here.

First, an application under s 117 cannot affect the spouse's legal right share or, where the spouse is the parent of the applicant, any bequest to that spouse. All other bequests are available to the court to redistribute, as it *'may order that such provision shall be made for the child out of the estate as the Court sees just'*. It can, of course, affect the share of the civil partner of the deceased. See **4.6.4.1**.

While a non-marital child can take a s 117 application that can affect the bequest to a spouse, to date the courts have not reduced the bequest to the spouse below the legal right share. This is not to say that the courts will not do so in the future, as they have the power to do so should the spouse elect to take his bequest under the will in lieu of his legal right share.

What is important to realise is the effect on the estate of these applications, either by a disgruntled spouse or by a child or children, or both.

While it is not possible to predict the outcome of such a combined series of applications against the estate, the courts in the past have elevated the rights of the spouse and children above the rights of any other beneficiaries. It will be interesting to see, in light of the civil partnership legislation, what the attitude of the court will be in these changed circumstances.

One possible outcome, based on the court's approach in the past, is that the estate will effectively be divided up between the spouse and children and that any other beneficiaries will be excluded from their benefits under the will.

It is of crucial importance that the practitioner advises the testator of this when giving initial advice regarding the drafting of a will. If a testator chooses to exclude his spouse and children from the will entirely, without good reason, there is every possibility that the courts will overrule such a will, possibly in its entirety.

As usual, full notes should be taken of advices given and left with the will for future reference.

For the effect of a successful action under s 67A(3), see the example at para **4.6.4.3**.

4.6.4.5 Proprietary estoppel actions

The fourth type of action which may be taken is based on the doctrine of proprietary estoppel. This type of action is taken comparatively rarely and is even more rarely successful, as the circumstances which would lead to such an action rarely arise and the burden of proof is onerous.

This doctrine broadly applies where a person has acted to his detriment as a result of the belief that he would be given a right over the other person's property and that belief is known to and encouraged by that other person. In those circumstances the court may impose what is effectively a constructive trust to protect the equity of the person who acted to his detriment. Obviously, this does not arise only in relation to children, but issue is relevant here as most of the cases taken on proprietary estoppel in relation to wills have been by children.

The leading Irish case in the area is the High Court decision of Geoghegan J in *Smith v Halpin* [1997] 2 ILRM 38. The facts of *Smith v Halpin* were that the plaintiff, who was brought up in a house on a farm in County Meath, decided to marry and asked his father to provide him with a site on the father's land. His father confirmed to him that the house and farm would be his after the death of himself and his mother and that there was no necessity for the son to have a separate house. The father suggested that the plaintiff instead build an extension to the family home, which the plaintiff did at his own expense.

In order to fund the cost of the extension the plaintiff borrowed funds, and the site of the extension was transferred into his name for the purposes of providing security for the lending institution. The father made a number of wills which pre- and post-dated the building of the extension. In his final will, he left the farmlands to his wife for her life and remainder to the plaintiff, but left the dwellinghouse to his wife for life and remainder to the second-named defendant (his daughter) subject to a right of way in favour of the plaintiff. The plaintiff sought an order directing that the remainder interest be transferred to him, based on the principle of proprietary estoppel. Alternatively, the plaintiff sought recovery of the funds spent by him on the house.

Geoghegan J stated that, in his view, if the court were satisfied that the facts of a case gave rise to a proper recourse to the principle of proprietary estoppel, then it was a matter for the court to determine how best to protect the equity and to consider what the equity was. Geoghegan J acknowledged that it was the plaintiff's clear expectation that he would have a fee simple interest in the entire house and held that the protection of the equity arising from the expenditure therefore required that a court order be made directing a conveyance of that interest to him.

Geoghegan J cited with approval the principle laid down by Cumming-Bruce LJ in *Pascoe v Turner* [1979] 2 All ER 945:

> '[T]he principle to be applied is that the Court should consider all the circumstances and the counter claimant having at law no perfected gift or licence other than a licence revocable at will, the Court must decide what is the minimum equity to do justice to her, having regard to the way in which she changed her position for the worse, by reasons of the acquiescence and encouragement of the legal owner. The defendant submits that the only appropriate way in which the equity can here be satisfied is perfecting the imperfect gift as was done in Dillwyn v Llewelyn.'

The Supreme Court decision in *McCarron v McCarron* (unreported) 13 February 1997 provides some guidance on the issue of financial detriment. In that case, the plaintiff had worked on the farm of a disabled relation for sixteen years until the relation's death. Letters of administration in the estate issued to the defendant as next-of-kin. While there was a question as to the extent of the work at some time during the sixteen-year period, there was no dispute that the plaintiff had assisted on the farm, and the High Court had accepted the plaintiff's evidence of the extent of the assistance. The Supreme Court upheld the High Court order for specific performance on the basis that there was sufficient certainty that conversations between the plaintiff and the deceased amounted to a contract to devise the deceased's land to the plaintiff in return for working on the farm. The court held that in the circumstances it was not necessary to decide on the basis of the doctrine of proprietary estoppel. However, Murphy J expressed (albeit *obiter*) the following view:

> '*I see no reason why the doctrine should be confined to the expenditure of money or the erection of premises on the land of another. In a suitable case it may well be argued that a plaintiff suffers as severe a loss or detriment by providing his own labours or services in relation to the lands of another and accordingly should equally qualify for recognitions in equity. In practice, however, it might be difficult to determine the extent of the estate or interest in land for which a plaintiff might qualify as a result of his personal efforts. Perhaps a claim of that nature would be adequately compensated by a charge or lien on the lands for a sum equivalent to reasonable remuneration for the services rendered.*'

While it is not always easy to establish proprietary estoppel, there is a large advantage to establishing an equitable interest based on this doctrine rather than making a claim under s 117. Once the doctrine is established, it prevails even over the legal right of the spouse and the claims of other children of the testator who are sharing the estate. Further, claims under the doctrine are not subject to the strict time limits imposed by s 117 (see earlier). However, in order to prove a claim of proprietary estoppel, it is necessary to adduce fairly strong evidence to establish the equity and of course there is always a risk that the courts may decide that no such equity exists. In general, re estoppel but in particular re the time limits for same, see *Cavey v Cavey* [2014] IESC 16, where the Supreme Court confirmed that a claim for promissory estoppel must be brought within the relevant period or within two years of the date of death of the deceased, whichever expires first. See also, *K v K* (2018) IEHC 615 which, apart from other issues, examined estoppel in detail.

4.6.5 UNDERAGE CHILDREN

Where there is a bequest to an underage child and there is no receipt clause or no trustees are appointed in the will or where on intestacy an underage child inherits, then the legal personal representative has a problem. Thus, when the testator discusses bequests to children with his solicitor, it should immediately be established whether there is an underage child and, if appropriate, a trust inserted in the will. Depending on the asset or the sum concerned and the age of the underage child, it may be appropriate merely to insert a receipt clause as per the precedent will at para **2.17**. See Chapter 1 of the Trusts Lecture Notes (see Preface).

If this is not done pre-death, what are the consequences? There is nobody in whom the legal personal representative may vest the asset so bequeathed or from whom he may obtain a receipt.

However, in such a case s 57 of the Succession Act is of assistance:

> '(1) Where an infant is entitled to any share in the estate of a deceased person and there are no trustees of such share able and willing to act, the personal representatives of the deceased may appoint a trust corporation or any two or more persons (who may include the personal representatives or any of them or a trust corporation) to be trustees of such share for the infant and may execute such assurance or take such other action as may be necessary for vesting the share in the trustee so appointed. In default of appointment the personal representatives shall be trustees for the purposes of this section.
>
> (2) On such appointment the personal representatives, as such, shall be discharged from all further liability in respect of the property vested in the trustees so appointed.'

Thus, where minors inherit and no trustees have been appointed, difficulties can be avoided by the appointment of individuals by the personal representatives as trustees for the purposes of s 57 as just outlined, and a court appointment is avoided. These trustees can be the same individual as the legal personal representative.

A point that can be overlooked is that, in default of appointment, the personal representatives shall be trustees for the purposes of this section. This should be carefully explained to the legal personal representatives, as they may be happy to act as legal personal representatives but not wish to take on the onerous duties of trustees.

Practitioners should note that there is a major drawback to s 57 in that it only applies to the share of an infant: it does not apply to the share of any other person who through disability or otherwise is precluded from giving a proper receipt to the executors. If the will does not provide the structure this is very limiting, and an application will have to be made to court under s 25 of the Trustee Act, 1893.

Trustees are permitted to hold property vested in them under s 57 to retain it in its existing condition or state of investment or to reinvest it in authorised trustee securities. The powers of such a trustee to invest are laid out in s 58, which gives these trustees the requisite powers to administer such a trust as follows:

'(1) *Property vested under section 57 may be retained in its existing condition or state of investment or may be converted into money and invested in any security in which a trustee is authorised by law to invest, with power, at the discretion of the trustees, to change such investments for others so authorised.*

(2) *Where an infant becomes entitled to any estate or interest in land on intestacy and consequently there is no instrument under which the estate or interest of the infant arises or is acquired, that estate or interest shall be deemed to be the subject of a settlement for the purposes of the Settled Land Acts, 1882 to 1890, and the persons who are trustees under section 57 shall be deemed to be the trustees of that settlement.*

(3) *A person who is sole trustee under section 57 shall be entitled to receive capital trust money.*

(4) *Persons who are trustees under section 57 shall be deemed to be trustees for the purposes of sections 42 and 43 of the Conveyancing Act, 1881.*

(5) *Without prejudice to any powers under the said sections 42 and 43, persons who are trustees under section 57 may at any time or times pay or apply the capital of any share in the estate to which the infant is entitled for the advancement or benefit of the infant in such manner as they may, in their absolute discretion, think fit and may, in particular, carry on any business in which the infant is entitled to a share.*

(6) *The powers conferred by subsection (5) may also be exercised by the surviving spouse as trustee of any property of an infant appropriated in accordance with section 56.*'

Additional powers, if necessary, can be found in the following legislation: the Trustee Act, 1893; the Trustee (Authorised Investments) Act, 1958; the Charities Act, 1961; the Trustee (Authorised Investments) Order, 1998 (SI 28/1998); and the Land and Conveyancing Law Reform Act, 2009.

The Succession Act also covers the situation where a minor becomes entitled to land on intestacy and there is therefore no instrument, i.e. there is no will. Prior to the coming into force of the Land and Conveyancing Law Reform Act, 2009 in December 2009, this situation was catered for by s 58(2) of the Succession Act, 1965. Section 58(2) was repealed by the 2009 Act, and since December 2009 where a minor inherits land on intestacy this is now governed by s 19 of the Land and Conveyancing Law Reform Act, 2009. This section deems a settlement to exist where a minor becomes entitled to land on intestacy.

Further, s 20 of the Land and Conveyancing Law Reform Act, 2009 and s 42 of the Conveyancing Act, 1881 confer wide powers of management on trustees and contain provisions regarding the receipt and application of income during minority. Section 43 gives trustees powers to apply the income of the property of an infant for his maintenance, education, and benefit. Practitioners should note that s 43 applies only to infants. If there is no provision in a will providing for the application of income between the age of eighteen and the date of vesting of the interest (perhaps twenty-one or twenty-three), this can result in the trustees being obliged to accumulate income and can therefore attract discretionary trust tax.

Under subsection (5), persons who are trustees under s 57 may at any time or times pay or apply the capital of any share in the estate to which the infant is entitled for the advancement or benefit of the infant in such manner as they may in their absolute discretion think fit, and may in particular carry on any business in which the infant is entitled to a share. This section is extremely important in that it allows trustees to apply capital for the benefit of an infant beneficiary but also allows the trustees to carry on any business in which the infant is entitled to a share. Taking into account that legal personal representatives have no absolute power to run a business unless it is specifically provided for in a will, this could be a very important practical power in administering an estate.

Practitioners should note also s 57(6), which provides:

> *'The powers conferred by subsection (5) may also be exercised by the surviving spouse as trustee of any property of an infant appropriated in accordance with section 56.'*

Practitioners should note that this section refers to the personal *representatives* proving the will, i.e. plural. It would appear that where there are two or more personal representatives s 57 will do away with the expense and inconvenience of an application to court for an appointment of a trustee where none is appointed by will. It is doubtful that a single personal representative can appoint a second trustee himself. However, it is frequently done in practice. See Spierin, *The Succession Act 1965 and Related Legislation: A Commentary*, 5th edn (2017).

Note that in the drafting of the Succession Act, there is reference in a number of instances to the 'personal representative' (singular) and 'personal representatives' (plural), and it is not clear in all cases whether or not the terms are interchangeable. In these circumstances there is no definitive solution but to apply to court, unless s 19 of the Land Act can assist. See Chapter 2 of the Trusts Lecture Notes (see Preface).

4.6.6 THE TAX STATUS OF A CHILD

For tax purposes, all children are considered to be the deceased's 'children' and thus fall under Group A under the capital acquisitions tax regime. However, stepchildren, children of a civil partner, and foster children are not 'children' for the purposes of the Succession Act. This should be explained clearly to the testator where it applies.

4.6.7 OTHER LEGISLATION RELATING TO CHILDREN WHICH MAY AFFECT A WILL

Three other Acts which should be borne in mind when dealing with children and the drafting of wills or the administration of estates are as follows.

4.6.7.1 Guardianship of Infants Act, 1964; Children and Family Relationships Act, 2015

It is possible for a father and mother, by deed or will, to appoint another person or persons to be the guardian or guardians of their children after their death. However, the appointment only becomes effective after the death of the testator. In practice, a testamentary guardian can act jointly with the surviving parent of the minor so long as the surviving parent remains alive, unless the surviving parent objects to his so acting.

If the surviving parent objects, or if a testamentary guardian considers that the surviving parent is unfit to have custody of the minor, the testamentary guardian has access to the court for an order under s 7 of the Guardianship of Infants Act as replaced by the Family Law and Relationships Act, 2015. It is important to note that where two or more persons are appointed to be guardians, they shall act jointly and, on the death of any of them, the survivor shall continue to act. Being testamentary guardian of a child or indeed having a role *in loco parentis* to a child does not confer on that child Succession Act rights.

4.6.7.2 Age of Majority Act, 1985

The Age of Majority Act decreased the age of majority from twenty-one to eighteen. Section 2 provides that a person attains full age when he or she attains the age of eighteen years or if the person marries before attaining that age. Practitioners should note, however, that the age for marriage has been amended by s 31 of the Family Law Act, 1995.

Under subsection (1):

> *'A marriage solemnised, after the commencement of the section, between persons either of whom is under the age of 18 years shall not be valid in law.'*

Is a child an infant or a minor?

Section 3 of the Age of Majority Act provides that a person who has not reached full age shall be described as a minor and not an infant. Practitioners should be careful to provide, therefore, that wills and documents are drafted using the word 'minor' rather than 'infant'.

4.7 Cohabitants

Part 15 of the Civil Partnership Act, 2010 sets out the 'rights' of cohabitants, but unlike civil partners it does not give automatic succession law rights to a surviving cohabitant. It sets up, under s 194, a redress scheme and allows a qualified cohabitant, on application, to seek provision from the estate of the deceased qualified cohabitant. Practitioners should read s 194 in its entirety.

4.7.1 TO WHOM DOES IT APPLY?

The qualified cohabitants redress scheme applies to opposite-sex and same-sex couples, who are not married, not in a civil partnership, and unrelated. The redress scheme is activated at the end of a relationship or on the death of one of the parties.

A cohabitant is defined under s 172 as:

> *'one of 2 adults (whether of the same or the opposite sex) who live together as a couple in an intimate and committed relationship and who are not related to each other within the prohibited degrees of relationship or married to each other or civil partners of each other.'*

It does appear that the relationship is exclusive in nature, but what is meant by 'live together' and 'intimate and committed'? These are not defined in the section and will likely lead to litigation. There are some English cases which may help to define the former and were reviewed by McCracken J in the case of *McA v McA* [2000] 1 IR 457. In that case McCracken J found that parties living under the same roof may be living apart from each other. It must be noted that this decision was in the context of marital breakdown, and it should be noted that the court decided that a married couple could equally maintain their relationship while living separate and apart.

The recent English decision of *Kotke v Saffarini* [2005] EWCA Civ 221 is instructive in this regard, dealing as it does with an unmarried couple and trying to establish when actual cohabitation or 'living together as a couple' began.

If this occurs, the Civil Partnership Act sets out a range of factors to be considered to assist in deciding as to whether or not the couple were in a cohabiting relationship at s 172(2), which states as follows:

> *'In determining whether or not two adults are cohabitants, the Court shall take into account all the circumstances of the relationship and in particular should have regard to the following:*
>
> *(a)   the duration of the relationship;*
>
> *(b)   the basis on which the couple live together;*
>
> *(c)   the degree of financial dependence of either adult on the other and any agreements in respect of their finances;*
>
> *(d)   the degree and nature of any financial arrangements between the adults including any joint purchase of an estate or interest in land or joint acquisition of personal property;*
>
> *(e)   whether there are one or more dependent children;*
>
> *(f)   whether one of the adults cares for and supports the children of the other; and*
>
> *(g)   the degree to which the adults present themselves to others as a couple.'*

Section 172(3) goes on to state:

'For the avoidance of doubt a relationship does not cease to be an intimate relationship for the purpose of this section merely because it is no longer sexual in nature.'

4.7.2 WHAT IS A 'QUALIFIED COHABITANT'?

A cohabitant is deemed to be a qualified cohabitant if certain additional requirements are met under s 172(5), which states as follows:

'a qualified cohabitant means an adult who was in a relationship of cohabitation with another adult and who, immediately before the time that that relationship ended, whether through death or otherwise, was living with the other adult as a couple for a period—

(a) of 2 years or more, in the case where they are the parents of one or more dependent children, and

(b) of 5 years or more, in any other case.'

It is anticipated that practical difficulties will arise in establishing the duration of the relationships, as unlike the situation of a marriage or the registration of a civil partnership, there is unlikely to be a record of the date when the parties started cohabiting.

Notwithstanding this, subsection (6) further provides that:

'an adult who would otherwise be a qualified cohabitant is not a qualified cohabitant if either one or both of the adults is or was, at any time during the relationship, married to someone else.'

Unless, at the time the relationship ends, the qualified cohabitant who is or was married has lived apart from their spouse for a period or periods of at least four years during the previous five years, they do not qualify. That is, they do not have to be divorced, merely eligible to divorce: see s 172(6).

Note that s 172(6) does not extend to civil partners, and thus it is possible for a qualified cohabitant to be also in a civil partnership, albeit living apart from their civil partner, and it is clear that under the legislation no minimum time period is required, as is the case of persons who were previously married.

There have been few cases on this matter at the time of writing: see *MO'S v EC Circuit Court* (unreported) 12 January 2015 which discusses this in detail in relation to an applicant seeking redress at the end of a relationship and *DC v DR* (unreported) 5 May 2015, High Court, Baker J, in relation to an application by a surviving cohabitant in relation to a deceased cohabitant.

See also *Lewis v Warner* [2016] EWHC 1786 (QB), *Parris v Trinity College Dublin* Case C-443/15 [2017] 2 CMLR 17, and *In the Matter of an Application by Denise Brewster for Judicial Review (Northern Ireland)* [2017] UKSC 8, the latter two being very informative in relation to civil partners and pensions and cohabitants and pensions.

4.7.3 WHAT PROVISION CAN BE MADE FOR A QUALIFIED COHABITANT ON THE DEATH OF THE OTHER?

Section 194 of the Civil Partnership Act allows a qualified cohabitant, on the death of the other, to bring an application before the court, seeking that provision be made for the survivor of them from the estate of the deceased (see Appendix 3 of the Act). It states as follows:

'A qualified cohabitant may, after the death of his or her cohabitant but not more than 6 months after representation is first granted under the Succession Act 1965 in respect of that cohabitant's estate, apply for an order under this section for provision out of the net estate.'

A cohabitant needs to be ordinarily resident in Ireland. See s 196 (4) of the Civil Partnership Act.

4.7.4 TIME LIMITS

Proceedings under s 194 can be instituted at any time after the death of the cohabitant, but not later than six months after a grant to the estate is extracted. However, if the relationship ended, i.e. the cohabitation ceased more than two years prior to the death, then proceedings cannot be instituted unless the conditions set out at s 194(2)(a) or (6) apply.

4.7.5 WHAT WILL THE COURT CONSIDER?

The court may make any order for provision for the applicant that the court considers appropriate having regard to the rights of any other person having an interest in the matter.

The court, in considering whether or not to make such an order, will have regard to all the circumstances, including: an order made under s 173(6), 174, 175, or 187 in favour of the applicant; a devise or bequest made by the deceased in favour of the applicant; the interests of the beneficiaries of the estate; and all the other factors set out in s 173(3).

4.7.6 WHICH PARTIES MUST THE COHABITANT NOTIFY?

Notice of proceedings under s 194 should be given by the applicant to the personal representatives of the deceased's estate, any spouse, any civil partner, or any other persons that the court may direct. The court should also have regard to any representations made by those persons.

4.7.7 WHAT CAN A COHABITANT RECEIVE?

The court, in making provision for an applicant under this section, cannot exceed a share *greater than* what a spouse or civil partner would be entitled to either on intestacy or by way of a legal right share, and where a deceased cohabitant was married at the date of death, an application brought by a cohabitant *cannot affect* the legal right share of the spouse.

4.7.8 COHABITANT VERSUS SURVIVING SPOUSE

No provision can be made for a qualified cohabitant from the legal right share of a spouse.

4.7.9 COHABITANT VERSUS CIVIL PARTNER

There is no reference made to the legal right share of a surviving civil partner versus a cohabitant. Therefore, it seems, subject to case law which will clarify the position, that provision can be made for a qualified cohabitant out of the legal right share of a civil partner, albeit such an order may adversely affect the rights of the surviving civil partner.

4.7.10 THE COHABITANT AND THE LEGAL PERSONAL REPRESENTATIVE

Where a cohabitant does not notify the personal representatives of the estate of the deceased of his intention to apply, the estate can be distributed amongst those entitled, without any liability attaching to the personal representatives.

4.7.11 CAN A COHABITANT CONTRACT OUT OF THE REDRESS SCHEME UNDER THE ACT?

Cohabitants can organise their own financial affairs and opt out of the redress scheme under Part 15, including s 194, by virtue of s 202, which states as follows:

> *'Notwithstanding any enactment or rule of law, cohabitants may enter into a cohabitants' agreement to provide for financial matters during the relationship or when the relationship ends, whether through death or otherwise.'*

Note that any such agreements are only valid under subsection (2) where the cohabitants—

1. have each received independent legal advice before entering into it; or
2. have received legal advice together and have waived in writing the right to independent legal advice;
3. the agreement is in writing and signed by both cohabitants; and
4. the general law of contract is complied with.

4.7.12 CAN A COHABITANT 'RENOUNCE'?

Section 202(3) allows that a cohabitants' agreement may provide that neither cohabitant may apply for an order for redress referred to in s 173 or an order for provision from the estate of his or her cohabitant under s 194. *But* by virtue of s 202(4) the court may vary or set aside a cohabitants' agreement in exceptional circumstances where its enforceability would cause serious injustice, and clients must be warned of this possibility.

4.7.13 WHAT IS THE STATUS OF COHABITANT AGREEMENTS SIGNED BEFORE THE CIVIL PARTNERSHIP ACT COMMENCED?

Section 202(5) states that an agreement that meets the other requirements of this section shall be deemed to be a cohabitants' agreement under s 198 even if it were entered into prior to the commencement of cohabitation.

CHAPTER 5

INSTRUCTIONS, ATTENDANCE, AND EXECUTION

5.1 The Difference between Taking Instructions and Drafting an Attendance

The difference between taking instructions and drafting an attendance, and the importance of doing both, is not always appreciated.

5.1.1 THE DISTINCTION BETWEEN INSTRUCTIONS AND ATTENDANCE

Instructions are what the client instructs a solicitor to do. An attendance is what was actually said. The former is an invaluable tool in drafting the will and in preparing the latter. Both are essential if there is a dispute of any nature at a later stage.

There follows a precedent instruction sheet for a will, which is a combination of the two. This checklist is something which is particularly useful whenever a solicitor has to draft a will in a hurry but it should always be used, albeit subtly, as a reminder mechanism.

The aim is to ensure that the will reflects the testator's informed instructions, and an instruction sheet not only ensures that the solicitor has adequate information in relation to the assets of the testator and any details of his family but also acts as a reminder to the solicitor to advise on the provisions of the Succession Act, 1965 (as amended); the Status of Children Act, 1987; the Land and Conveyancing Law Reform Act, 2009; the Civil Partnership and Certain Rights and Obligations of Cohabitants Act, 2010; the Marriage Act, 2015 and the Children and Family Relationships Act, 2015 etc; and on any relevant tax implications of the will.

By 'informed instructions' is meant the final instructions of the testator who has had the legislative and taxation consequences of his wishes explained to him. See *Doran v Delaney* (1998) 2 IR 61 (SC), where Barron J stated that 'a solicitor was not a conduit pipe'.

This point was very well and unambiguously put by Barron J in the Supreme Court in the case of *Carroll v Carroll* (1999) 4 IR 241 when he said:

> '*a solicitor or other professional person does not fulfil his obligations to his client . . . by simply doing what he is asked or instructed to do. He owes such a person a duty to exercise his professional skill and judgment and does not fulfil that by blithely following instructions without stopping to consider whether to do so is appropriate. Having done that he must then give advice as to whether or not what is required of him is appropriate.*'

In other words, it is not just enough to take the client's instructions, be able to prove same, and to act on them: the client must be given the benefit of the solicitor's professional advice even re non-essentials (in the sense that their absence will not invalidate a will e.g. gift overs to avoid lapse) and be able to prove that this was done, i.e. via the instruction sheet and attendances.

See also *Cavey v Cavey & ors* [2014] IESC 16 where the Supreme Court, as well as dealing with estoppel per se, highlighted the need for solicitors to consider and discuss with the client all aspects of the matter, not just the ones raised by the client, and indeed as is so often stated by the judge/s in such cases, the absolute need for contemporaneous notes of instructions given/taken and advices given.

If there is any doubt after the *Doran v Delaney*, *Carroll v Carroll*, and *Cavey v Cavey* cases, consider also:

Bourke v O'Donnell and Bank of Ireland [2010] IEHC 348;

Haughey v J&E Davy and Davy & ors [2014] IEHC 206; or

MC (A Ward of Court) v FC [2013] IEHC 272.

When asked to 'just draft a simple will', the extent of the care required from practitioners is heavy and practitioners need, in drafting the clauses in the will, to go beyond just what they are asked to do—practitioners are not just that 'conduit pipe'.

Many questions need to be asked, often intrusive ones, to obtain sufficient information to draft not only a valid will but a good one, i.e. a will reflecting 'the testator's intention and instructions taking into account the testator's own particular circumstances'.

The primary objectives of any person drafting a will are to 'fairly and clearly reflect the testator's instructions and to minimise the possibility of disputes after the testator has died. . .' (see Spierin, *Wills, Irish Precedents and Drafting*, 3rd edn (2020), pp 1 and 2).

In addition, clearly, it should also be a tax efficient one.

Why?

Given that a will generally has tax implications, and it is the solicitor's duty to take informed instructions and explain the tax consequences of directions in the will, it is very dangerous to agree to draft a will without considering the taxation implications of the document which is presented to the client.

There are standard, if anything is standard in a will, taxation points which will arise in respect of most wills e.g. powers of appropriation, unintentional trusts, property being left to an elderly beneficiary who may not be able to pay the tax, valuation dates, s 84 beneficiaries, s 72 assets, s 98 children, etc, not to mention applying CAT basic exemptions, or even more importantly, not negating the possibility of same by incorrect drafting. This will be considered, in detail, in the CAT materials. It is clear a testator needs tax advice on these and other issues and it would be very imprudent to ignore the obvious need for such advice.

Not every probate practitioner must be a tax expert and give advice on complex tax avoidance schemes (a client can always be referred for taxation advice), but to draft a will without being able to, at the very least, identify the taxation issues which may require advice, is imprudent.

Thus, as a minimum, it needs to be ensured that any potential substantial tax exposure for the beneficiaries under the will be identified by the practitioner, any obvious tax planning options explained to the testator, and, finally, a will drafted according to his informed instructions.

Consider the case of *Hurlingham Estates Limited v Wilde & Partners* (1997) 1 Lloyds (see below), a case which, while referring to conveyancing and the failure to give tax advice, is equally applicable to wills and CAT.

A reasonably competent solicitor will be expected to advise on CAT issues and if this cannot be done, then this inability must be put in writing to the testator in very clear terms, bearing in mind most testators will not necessarily know they need CAT advice. See *Grey v Buss Murton* [1999] PNLR 882.

If the solicitor is not giving any tax advice at all, this would have to be stressed very clearly in the retainer and any liability cap also clearly stressed. It is advised that this be acknowledged separately in writing by the client.

The English case of *Hurlingham Estates Ltd v Wilde & Partners (A Firm)* Ch D 627, Lightman J, 10 September 1996; [1997] STC 627, followed by the more recent case of *Hossein Mehjoo v Harben Barker (A Firm) and Harben Barker Limited* [2014] EWCA Civ 358 are instructive in this regard.

In *Hurlingham Estates Ltd v Wilde & Partners*, the solicitor took on a retainer for a client involving the sale of business premises. There was a tax aspect to the transaction. There was no engagement letter and the solicitor later said that he had made it clear to his client that he was not going to advise on the tax aspect.

However, the court did not accept this evidence and the judge was scathing:

> *'Mr. X, the solicitor, assumed the full role in the transaction and responsibilities to be expected of a solicitor having the conduct of it. I have no doubt that, if he had at the meeting of 29 May exposed his ignorance and unfitness to have the conduct of the matter as he should, the clients . . . would have immediately instructed someone competent instead. Mr X must have known and feared this. He entered the tax minefield armed only with a precedent book (as he frankly admitted) not knowing what to look for or the significance of anything he found . . .'*

That case laid down a test regarding the extent of a solicitor's duty.

That test was whether, taking into account the terms of the retainer and all of the circumstances which should have been reasonably known by the solicitor, that solicitor should have reasonably appreciated that the client needed advice and guidance regarding his tax liabilities.

This test has been applied in the UK in *Mehjoo v Harben Barker* where a firm of accountants acting in the sale of their client's business gave general tax advice but did not advise on a specialist point of tax law. Mr Mehjoo was non-domiciled, which had a particular tax advantage if the sale of the business was structured in a particular fashion; in this case if the situs of the shares could be moved overseas. The accountants in question were not aware of this but had advised Mr Mehjoo that there might be schemes available to reduce his tax liability, albeit that they did not specifically advise him to seek advice from a specialist in non-domiciled tax affairs.

The transaction went through, but after the event Mr Mehjoo became aware that if ownership of the shares had been transferred overseas prior to the disposal then as a non-domiciled individual owning overseas assets his capital gains tax bill would have been minimal. Mr Mehjoo sued his professional advisers for £1.4 million for professional negligence claiming that in not referring him to non-domicile specialists or drawing his attention to another scheme—known as the Bearer Warrant Scheme—Harben Barker had acted negligently.

After years of dispute, the High Court ruled in Mehjoo's favour but he subsequently lost on appeal. The Appeal Court judgment, which sets out the standard to be applied in *Hurlingham Estates Ltd v Wilde & Partners*, serves to limit the exposure of professionals where their letter of retainer sets out clearly what they are and are not advising on and when they advise their client in writing to seek specialist advice, especially in relation to tax.

Another reason why an instruction sheet is important is that the solicitor has all the necessary information to draft an attendance which, if necessary, will be capable of proving those instructions and showing that the testator had capacity, and that the solicitor had informed him of all the relevant matters, for example, s 98 of the Status of Children Act and capital acquisitions tax (CAT). As a will generally cannot be varied after death, full and clear instructions must be obtained from the client, and for this purpose the use of an instruction sheet is essential.

Sometimes it can be quite difficult to strike a balance between listening to the testator and allowing him to express his wishes re the will and chat in general, and ensuring that during the course of the interview the solicitor obtains all the relevant information. This is one of the reasons why an instruction sheet is so vital; it assists a solicitor in ensuring that he covers the necessary ground. The solicitor has a duty to advise the testator on the effect of his wishes and indeed (as will be covered in the CAT Lecture Notes; see Preface) to minimise the tax effect of such wishes, but this does not extend to forcing views on the testator as to how he should dispose of his assets. Thus, while the will should reflect the wishes of the testator and not anyone else's, it is important to get a balance, i.e. to advise the testator of the various options open to him according to his circumstances.

In addition, an instruction sheet is also vital in helping practitioners comply with best practice, which requires that instructions be taken in relation to a will not in the presence of interested third parties, particularly any prospective beneficiaries. Finally, the absence of contemporaneous notes between a solicitor and client makes an assessment of a client's capacity difficult, and in *Moyles v Mahon* [2000] IEHC 197 the court stated that, while it accepted the evidence of the solicitor in this case:

> *'It is certainly desirable that there should be a fuller note than that which exists in this case . . . it is certainly desirable to have an attendance but it is not a mandatory requirement. If one of these solicitors had died, there may be grave difficulties in certain circumstances without a contemporaneous note.'*

This begs the question, how best to obtain informed instructions?

Very few clients, if any, know exactly what information is needed or its relevance. Many questions, often intrusive ones, need to be asked by the solicitor in order to have sufficient information to draft not only a valid will but a good one. A 'good will' in this case is a will reflecting *'the testator's intention and instructions taking into account the testator's own particular circumstances'*.

5.2 Precedent Instruction Sheet for a Will

Date   **Place**   **Taken by**   **Parties present**

Time meeting commenced and terminated:

Testator's full name and address:

Former addresses:

Date of birth:

PPS number:

Occupation:

Ordinary Residence:

Domicile

- If domicile is not domicile of origin what is it?
- What evidence is there? Is an affidavit needed?
- Where a client has assets in multiple jurisdictions, especially where his habitual residence is in one of these jurisdictions, consider jurisdiction (EU Regulation 650/2012 IP/12/576—*Rules to Ease Cross Border Succession*) and apply check list as set out in '*A Rough Guide to the EU Succession Regulation*' (2016) 1 STEP 70.
- Given that, is a declaration of choice of law required?

Particulars of any instructions as to funeral/grave arrangements

Is there a previous will in any jurisdiction?   Yes/No

Where held?

If changing same—why?

Are there Foreign Assets?

- Is there a foreign will?
- Is this will to revoke it or not?

- Who is giving/has given foreign legal/tax advice?
- Ensure revocation reflects circumstances and if deviation from standard also amend residue clause.

Executors/Trustees

Preferably more than one.

Names and addresses.

Relationship to testator if any.

Substitutionary executor?

If solicitor is one or sole executor:

- Date testator informed in writing of prospective charges (attach copy of s 68 letter)
- Particular solicitor or firm in general?
- Charging clause/priority authority?
- NB. Do not witness will.

Guardians

- Names and Addresses:
  - Effect of Children and Family Relationships Act, 2015 in general and is the testator a guardian but not a parent of a child? If so, who is to be appointed as guardian in the will of said child?

Capacity

- Is the testator suffering from any illness which may have an effect on capacity?
- Is the testator on any medication or have they taken any drugs, prescribed or otherwise, in the last 24 hours including alcohol?
- If on medication, what medication and what is the effect of same on functional ability?

    Note of Solicitor's views on result of enquiries applying the *Banks v Goodfellow* (1870) LR 5 QB 549 test, *Key v Key* [2010] EWHC Ch 408 (Ch), and the functional capacity test as set out in *Scally v Rhatigan* (No 1) [2010] IEHC 475, including but not exclusively:

    1. Does the client understand that they are making a will and the effect of same?
    2. Does the client know the nature and extent of assets?
    3. Is the client aware of who their relatives are and whom they wish to benefit?

- What is the result and evidence of said result re the queries above?
- If there is some doubt (any 'red flags' as per Coy and Hedeen, *Disabilities and Mediation Readiness* in *Court-Referred Cases; Developing Screening Criteria and Service Networks* (September 2000), available at http://www.mediate.com/articles/cohed1.cfm), list reasons for same and what was done by whom in light of this and the result of any such action and conclusions reached.
- Is affidavit from physician (GP or specialist) re capacity needed/prudent?
- If there is a doubt as to capacity and if the client declines to obtain a medical report, have they been advised of the possible consequences?

Re Undue Influence

- What advices given re Ervine J in *Darby v Shanley* [2009] IEHC 459?
- Who made the appointment re drafting the will?
- Who provided, if any, written details, background circumstances, or wishes?

- Are there any particular factors suggesting particular vulnerability or susceptibility to influence?
- If so, what action was taken?
- Who else, if anybody, was present when instructions were being taken?
- What are the relationships of the main beneficiaries to the testator?
- Do we act for any of those beneficiaries in any other sphere?
- Has the testator a previous will and if so why is it being changed? Who suggested it should be? Who is or was, if not us, the testator's solicitor?

Civil/Marital Status of Testator

- Single/Married/Separated/Divorced/Widow/er/Civil Partner/Ex-Civil Partner or Surviving Civil Partner?

    Obtain proof of same.

    Is a marriage or civil partnership being contemplated (obtain full details pursuant to *Re the Estate of Noel O'Brien Deceased* [2011] IEHC 327)?

- Insert appropriate clause in will.

If testator is/was married.

- Husband's/wife's name.
- Date of marriage.
- If spouse/civil partner has predeceased obtain death certificate,
- Date of nullity/separation/divorce/dissolution—check copy of divorce or separation agreement or order for any matters affecting rights of succession or orders affecting pension or property.

Watch foreign divorces—check validity

Taking instructions where the client is or was a civil partner.

- Is or has the client ever been a civil partner?
- If so, obtain the civil partner's name and current address.
- If so, what was the date of registration of the partnership? (Obtain a copy certificate of registration.) Did the testator and his/her civil partner subsequently marry each other? If so, inform client that any previous will made either in contemplation of the civil partnership or made during the civil partnership but before the marriage is still valid and not revoked by the marriage.
- Explain in detail the rights of a surviving civil partner (legal right share) and especially how same may be reduced where the deceased civil partner had a child or children either by an application under s 67A(3) (intestate) or s 117(3A) (testate).
- Has the civil partnership been dissolved or annulled? If so, obtain copies of any decrees/orders—has the right to re-apply under s 127 of the Civil Partnership Act been blocked or any ancillary orders given?
- Has there been any renunciation of civil partnership rights or pre-civil partnership agreements? If so, obtain a copy.
- Has the client's civil partner deserted them (s 120 of the Succession Act as amended by s 87 of the Civil Partnership Act)?
- Obtain death certificate where civil partner has predeceased.
- If the client proposes to leave their civil partner less than the legal right share, or not to leave the surviving civil partner the dwellinghouse in which they are ordinarily resident, give and note full advices on the effect of these proposals.

- Watch foreign partnerships and latest additions to same under SIs 649/2010, 505/2011, 642/2011, 505/2012, 490/2013 and 212/2014.

Taking instructions where the client was or is a cohabitant.

- Explain what a qualified cohabitant is, i.e. an adult who was living as a cohabitant immediately before that relationship ended either by death or otherwise for a period of two years or more where the cohabitants are parents of one or more dependent children or over five years or more in any other case: see s 172(5).
- Explain that a person will not be considered a cohabitant if one or both parties was married to somebody else and at the time the relationship ended each person who was married had not lived apart from his or her spouse for a period of at least four years during the previous five years as per s 172(6).
- Is the testator or has he or she ever been a qualified cohabitant?
- If so, re each relationship that qualifies, obtain as full a history as possible, e.g. names and addresses/when and for how long was/is the relationship in being, what was/is the intention, was/is there financial dependency, are there one or more dependent children: s 172(2), and the residence and domicile of the testator and the cohabitant.
- Is there is a current cohabitee?
- If so, advise on the rights of same, i.e. the right to seek redress: s 194.
- In relation to prior cohabitees:
  - Did same remarry or enter into a civil partnership subsequently? If so, obtain full details, e.g. if the relationship ended more than two years ago is that cohabitee in receipt of periodical payments?
  - Did any cohabitees at any stage make an application for and obtain any orders under ss 174, 175, 176, or 187 etc, e.g. are there any maintenance/pension/property rights/attachment orders in existence? If so, obtain copies.
  - Has any agreement been entered into under s 202? If so, obtain a copy of same. If not, should an agreement be put in place now? Explain that the court may vary or set aside same: s 202(4).

Taking instructions where the client is deserted

- If so, obtain details and if necessary an affidavit from testator: s 120 in general.

Spouse/civil partner: Universal legatee provided survives one month—YES/NO

Has spouse/civil partner executed will?   Sole Executor—YES/NO

NB If spouse/civil partner is universal beneficiary, set out provisions to apply if spouse/civil partner fails to survive by one month—*commorientes* clause.

Children

- Names and addresses and residence (tax purposes) (present ages in brackets)
- Notes on children—including tax versus legal status
- Adopted/Foster/Step-Children/Non-Marital Children/Children of Civil Partner/Cohabitant
- Other close next of kin/dependents
- Paternity Order/s
- Any Orders under the Children and Family Relationships Act, 2015?
- Advice given on s 98 of Succession Act and instructions are as follows.
- Advice given on s 63 of Succession Act and instructions are as follows.
- Advice given on s 67 of Succession Act and instructions are as follows.
- Explanation of provisions of Status of Children Act instructions are as follows.

Reasons for not including dependents (spouse/civil partner/cohabitant/provision for children)

- Succession Act rights explained re spouse/civil partner/cohabitant?
- If separated, any Orders under s 9 or s 14 of the Family Law Act, 1995?
- If divorced, any Orders under s 18(10) of the Family Law (Amendment) Act, 1996?
- If civil partnership dissolved—obtain copies of any decrees/orders—has the right to re-apply under s 127 been blocked or any ancillary orders given?
- Re cohabitants—ss 174, 175, 176, or 187 etc, e.g. are there any maintenance/pension/property rights/attachment orders in existence? If so, obtain copies.
- Any Succession Act renunciation executed? If so, where is same? Was there independent legal advice? Obtain copy.
- Advice given on s 117 (watch especially children of civil partner) of the Succession Act and client's consideration of child/children, if applicable and instructions are as follows.
- If s 117 is a likely issue, consider each element of s 117 and note informed instructions are as follows.
- Should affidavit be obtained now?

NB Ensure full letter sent to client setting out advices re same and all possible consequences. If possible, get same signed by testator and ensure this copy is kept with the will.

Particulars of Assets (with approximate values)—and include liabilities thereon

Houses and contents

If foreign, consider law, tax, and revocation.

Location of deeds (check title, rectify if necessary).

Charge/Mortgages

- Is there a Mortgage/Charge?
- If so, is there a Mortgage Protection Policy?
- If not, has s 47 been explained and what are the testator's instructions re discharge of the debt?
- Has the testator availed of the Ancillary State Support 'Fair Deal' Scheme? If so, has any been repaid?
- Has a charge been registered?
- Testator's response to query as to payment of charge, i.e. vary or negate s 47.
- If no charge in place now, consider possibility of HSE charge arising post will.
- Re HSE, check which properties, if any, should be used to discharge debt first.

If property not being left to surviving spouse/civil partner has effect of s 56 and consequences to beneficiary been explained?

Shares

- Attach list if possible—location of share certificates.
- Watch ademption clause.
- Name, if appropriate, of broker.

Bank accounts

- Where? Bank and branch.
- Account number?
- Sole or joint?

Credit union

- Number and location of account and is it nominated?
- Level of nomination?

Digital assets/social media

- List of social media, i.e. online accounts:
  - o Facebook.
  - o Twitter.
  - o Instagram.
  - o Email etc.
  - o Is any agreement in place with providers?
- Passwords or location of same?
- Disposal of same? What, if any accounts are bequeathable?
  - o See Spierin: *Wills—Irish Precedents and Drafting*, 3rd edn.

Post Office/Saving bonds

- Where?
- Account number/s?
- Sole or joint?

Prize bonds

- Where?
- Sole or joint?

Re any joint assets as listed above confirm:

1. Who provided the joint property?
2. Who is on death to receive the entire?
3. The source of the joint property.
4. The relationship of the testator to the other joint holder/s.
5. Evidence to rebut or support advancement or resulting trust.
6. In relation to personalty, how is income being dealt with?
7. If bank account—what instructions given to bank, was bank mandate executed—obtain a copy of same.
8. Where mandate not available or contradicts the testator's instructions, have client confirm with the bank the position.
9. What was/is intention of deceased? For avoidance of doubt consider inserting clause in will.

Agricultural property

- Ensure land clearly identified.
- If map needed, watch attestation clause.
- Capital Acquisitions Tax Consolidation Act, 2003, s 89(3)?
- Livestock, bloodstock, plant.
- Potential for Agricultural Relief and perspective beneficiaries.
- New requirements for Agricultural Relief under the Finance Act, 2015.

Pension Scheme Benefits (Any reference)

- Section 72(60) policies—instruction required in will?
- Life assurance.
- Location of policy documents.

Any nominated accounts/policies.

Wasting assets—horses, planes etc? If so, what additional powers does executor need to be given?

Any other assets? Collectables, Antiques, Jewellery Etc. . .

Charitable Legacies

- ID fully via CRA Database.
- Explain possible effect if it's a residuary beneficiary?
- Insert receipt clause.

Pecuniary Legacies

If series of same, suggest percentage of estate/residue instead to testator and take informed instructions. Where are these pecuniary legacies to be paid from?

Residue

- Is there any division of residue?
- If so, joint tenancy or tenancy in common?
- Provision to avoid lapse of residue (watch s 91 versus s 98 if residue left to children).

Capital Acquisitions Tax

- Note gifts/inheritance post 5 December 1991 as gifts/inheritances from that date are aggregated under the CAT system.
- Has testator made gifts to beneficiaries who are to benefit under the proposed will?
- If so have appropriate returns been made to the Revenue?
- Have beneficiaries under proposed will received other gifts/inheritances known to testator from anybody else and are they aggregable?
- Has testator been advised of potential tax liability of proposed beneficiaries and any possible tax exemptions?
- Has the testator been advised of possible exemptions of any asset which attracts same, e.g. farmland?
- If the Capital Acquisitions Tax Consolidation Act, 2003, s 84 '*exemption relating to qualifying expenses of incapacitated persons*' arises or may arise has testator been advised and the appropriate clause inserted in the will to allow use of exemption?
- If s 60 (now, technically s 72 of the Capital Acquisitions Tax Consolidation Act, 2003) policy exemption arises or may arise has the testator been advised and if same exists has the appropriate clause been inserted in the will re the use of the exemption?

ID Beneficiary

- Does the testator have any relatives/friends with the same/similar name and/or address as any beneficiary or potential beneficiary? (Especially consider wording in light of *O'Donohue v O'Donohue* [2011] IEHC 511).
- If so, clarify in minute detail the identity of the beneficiary.

Is a Trust Needed?

- Most appropriate type of trust (e.g. trust for sale, discretionary/fixed trust)?
- Trustees?

- Trust fund?
- Beneficiaries?
- Charging clause?
- Settlement of residue—ultimate default trust?
- Children—receive income at 21/25? Capital at 21/25?
- Letter of Wishes?
- Is it or will it be or cease to be a Part 4 trust under the Land and Conveyancing Law Reform Act, 2009?
- Powers of trust involved—investment, advance, lend, borrow, apportionment, appropriation, manage land, run business.

Re possible *quantum meruit* claim—the helpful neighbour or estoppel

- Are any relatives, friends, or neighbours assisting the testator in any way, e.g. carrying out works, providing services to the home or land?
- If so, are they being remunerated?
- Has any promise been made to them or any other party or is there any agreement in place (consider *McCarron v McCarron* (unreported) 13 February 1997 and *Coleman v Mullen* [2011] IEHC 179).

Power of Appointment

- Does the testator have a power of appointment over any asset?
- Obtain a copy of the original document granting the power.
- Is it a general or special power—what tax advice has been given?
- Can it be exercised by will?

Testator's Accountant/Valuer/Stock Broker/Estate Agent

Names/s/Address/es

Enduring Power of Attorney (EPA)

Has one been done?

Name and addresses of attorney/s.

Name and addresses of notice parties.

Location of EPA.

If not, should EPA be prepared now?

Potential conflict with will either now or when EPA is activated—obtain informed wishes/instructions of testator if conflict should arise: e.g. should attorney have sight of the will?

Advanced Healthcare Directive(s)

Have any been made?

Location of same?

Confidentiality

Obtain from client, if applicable, permission to disclose information where it may, in the future, be suspected that abuse is occurring and/or if EPA invoked.

Terms of Retainer

Will to be engrossed/drafted by?

Actions of testator? By when?

Draft to go for approval to testator at:

Correspondence to home/office?

Telephone no.

Mobile.

Email address.

Original will to be kept by:

Solicitor/testator/bank or other?

Costs

Fees quoted €

Date Section 150 letter sent?

Execution of Will

Time, date, who was present?

5.3 Taking the Instruction Sheet Section by Section

1. Meeting and testator's basic details: a note of time and place is usually taken automatically but rarely of who arranged the meeting or what impairment the testator may have had and what was done to overcome same.

    Why is this important to ask and to take a note of?

    If there is any question post death re the will the answers to these questions will be vital.

    Also, of course, having the question there re impairment reminds us to check whether the testator can hear or see well.

    If hearing is impaired is his/her hearing aid on? Can he/she see without glasses, if not does he/she have their glasses? Can he/she read?

    The solicitor should obtain the full name and address of the testator, especially if it differs from his 'everyday' name (see para 2.2), and all former addresses (the latter can be particularly useful in tracing old accounts post-death). If the client is not actually known to the solicitor or the firm, then the requirements of any current money laundering regulations need to be considered. Of course, if the client is not known to the solicitor, it is more difficult to advise effectively, as the solicitor will not have an in-depth knowledge of the client's background and circumstances. Where the client is known to the solicitor or firm, this opportunity should be taken to check the other files in the office relating to that client to ascertain exactly what has happened previously with them. Further, the title deeds of all property owned by the testator should be obtained and scrutinised: see *Carr-Glynn v Frearsons* [1998] 4 All ER 225 and also para **5.9.1.1**.

2. The solicitor should obtain a copy of the birth certificate of the testator or if not, at least the testator's date and place of birth, as this information is usually needed post-death, especially where the testator has a life policy.

    This information is not always on the death certificate and, amazingly frequently, the relatives do not know it.

3. The obtaining of the client's PPS number at this stage will speed up the administration post-death.

    Ask the primary source—the client—what his view is of his occupation, and more importantly his tax residence/ordinary residence/domicile.

    Ask the client if he is considering availing of the EU Directive on cross border succession which came into force on 17 August 2012.

While Ireland, the UK, and Denmark opted out of the regulation, it does apply in many of the European countries where clients are likely to own holiday homes or other types of property. They can now make a will in such a country, including a declaration that Irish law is to be applied.

This chapter does not deal with the Directive in detail; see the excellent *Law Society Gazette* article by Aileen Keogan entitled 'Succession Slalom' in the December 2013 *Gazette*.

4. Funeral arrangements: it is all very well to insert directions in the will, but useless if the executors are unaware of these. It is not unheard of for a burial to have taken place when a cremation was required or, worse still, the other way around. See para **3.6.2.1**.

5. Previous wills: the solicitor should obtain instructions to obtain any previous wills to prevent confusion.

   In such cases, it is vital to discuss with the testator why he is changing his will and to note his reasons for doing so. The solicitor may obtain a great deal of information by reviewing existing wills, and it gives the solicitor a very good background to the client's attitude and changes of mind. This can be very significant if the will is subsequently challenged, and it also helps the solicitor identify problems, family disputes, etc. It is one of the indicators to mental capacity as recommended by the LRC consultation paper on the law and the elderly, and case law. It is important to remember that, while a subsequent marriage (except a marriage to one's civil partner, or a will made in contemplation of that marriage) invalidates a will, a subsequent divorce/dissolution of civil partnership does not.

   Since the Marriage Equality Act, 2015, where civil partners chose to marry each other, this marriage does not invalidate a previous will made by the said civil partners, see para **2.3**.

6. Executors: while only one is legally required, it is better to have two. The proposed executors should be aware that they are so named and should be willing to act. Of course, it is easier, if possible, to have executors living in this jurisdiction for practical purposes. Also, it may be necessary to use a power of attorney and to appoint an Irish solicitor to administer the estate for CAT purposes where the only executor available resides outside the jurisdiction.

   Clients should be advised, when making their will, that if a proposed executor predeceases them, they should change their will if they have not appointed a substitute therein. This is particularly relevant where a testator appoints a spouse/civil partner as executor. When a client dies, and their spouse/civil partner also made a will in your office, it is good practice to review the surviving spouse's/civil partner's will. If, for example, the deceased client was appointed as sole executor of that will, a replacement executor needs to be appointed to the surviving spouse's/civil partner's will as soon as possible.

   Also, any bequests to the deceased spouse/civil partner in the surviving spouse's/civil partner's will would need to be reviewed and amended as appropriate. See paras **2.4.2** and **3.2.2**.

   In relation to the statutory powers of executors/trustees, their adequacy should be considered once a full list of all assets and beneficiaries and all surrounding circumstances have been ascertained. Consider what additional powers must be given to them to allow them to do their job adequately. See para **3.8**.

7. Professional trustees and executors: the solicitor should ensure that a charging clause is inserted. If a member of the firm is appointed, make sure that a partner does not witness the will, as the right to charge for any work done is lost. If a client wishes to appoint a bank as an executor or trustee, ensure that the client is aware of the fees involved. The consent of the bank to act should also be obtained, and this will normally require furnishing it with a draft of the will. This in turn can only be done with the consent of the client. See **Chapter 3**.

8. Civil status: the solicitor should investigate the situation very thoroughly. If appropriate, seek a copy of the marriage certificates/separation agreements and any divorce certificates, separation agreements, court orders or otherwise. The solicitor should be aware of blocking orders or orders affecting pensions and property. See **Chapter 4**.

   Further, since the Civil Partnership and Certain Rights and Obligations of Cohabitants Act, 2010, all details re civil partners and/or cohabitants and any relevant documentation, for example, registration certificate/dissolution certificate, should be obtained and considered, especially re court orders on a dissolution of a civil partnership or re a cohabitant's agreement. The testator's word or understanding of a court order or agreement should never be taken as definitive. The primary source should always be consulted.

   Thus, in terms of taking instructions where there is or was a civil partner, we need to investigate the entire position, establishing to start with at least the following:

   1. Whether the testator has or ever had a civil partner.
   2. If so, the date of registration of the partnership.
   3. Whether there has been any renunciation of civil partnership rights—if so, obtain a copy of same.
   4. Whether the civil partnership has been dissolved or annulled—if so, whether there have been any orders granted. Obtain copy of dissolution/annulment/orders.
   5. If the civil partner is to be left less than the legal right share or not left the dwelling house in which they are ordinarily resident, what advice was given re the effect on the estate.
   6. Cohabitants; as a minimum, the following needs to be established:

       a. Explain what a qualified cohabitant is, i.e. an adult who was living as a cohabitant immediately before that relationship ended either by death or otherwise for a period of two years or more (where the cohabitants are parents of one or more dependent children), over five years or more in any other case (see s 172(5)). Explain that a person will not be considered a cohabitant if one or both parties was married to somebody else and at the time the relationship ended each person who was married had not lived apart from his or her spouse for a period of at least four years during the previous five years as per s 172(6).

       b. Is the testator, or has he ever been, a qualified cohabitant? If so, re each relationship that qualifies, obtain as full a history as possible, for example, names and addresses; when and for how long was/is the relationship in being; what was/is the intention; was/is there financial dependency; are there one or more dependent children (see s 172(2))?

       c. Is there a current cohabitee? If so, advise on their rights, i.e. the right to seek redress under s 194.

       d. In relation to prior cohabitees, did they remarry or enter into a civil partnership subsequently? If so, obtain full details, for example if the relationship ended more than two years ago is that cohabitee in receipt of periodical payments?

       e. Did any cohabitees at any stage make an application for and obtain any orders under ss 174, 175, 176, or 187, etc, for example, are there any maintenance/pension/property rights/attachment orders in existence? If so, obtain copies.

       f. Has any agreement been entered into under s 202? If so, obtain a copy of this. Explain that the court may vary or set this aside (s 202(4)).

       g. If not, should an agreement be put in place now?

9. Children: the solicitor should check the legal status of the child vis-à-vis the testator for both succession and taxation purposes. Not all 'children' are the children

of a testator for Succession Act purposes. For example, an adopted child has two potential sets of parents for tax purposes but only one set for succession rights. Advise on s 98 and s 63 of the Succession Act, 1965 and the Status of Children Act, 1987 and obtain all details. See **Chapter 4**.

10. Assets: the solicitor should ensure that all information, such as where assets are kept, particulars of joint property and client's intention in relation to same, foreign property, details of shares, foreign and domestic, are obtained. The name and address of the client's accountant should also be obtained, as this could prove particularly useful for the valuation of unquoted shares at a later stage.

    To avoid any post-death claims of promissory or proprietary estoppel, it would be prudent to ask at instructions stage if this is a possibility and if so, take full details and, if necessary, an affidavit from the testator.

    So many clients are now using digital means to store and access data, sometimes of a highly personal nature, sometimes of a financial nature, and thus, how to access and control such data and whether and how they may be bequeathed is becoming increasingly relevant. For example, does the testator wish to have all his accounts deleted or bequeath the accounts? Whatever the testator's wishes, the various access codes need to be recorded, while at the same time maintaining security.

    There are no easy answers in this area as the use of social media and other online accounts is a relatively new phenomenon and much depends upon the terms of service which were agreed to by the testator when the online account was created. For example, Gmail's policy is that they will only provide Gmail account content following 'an order from the US Court'. It used to be the case, prior to spring 2009, that where there was proof of death, identification, and authority, the legal personal representative could gain access to the account. It would appear that this is based on defending the privacy of the account holder, yet in most jurisdictions, certainly common law jurisdictions, the right to privacy terminates at death. The policies of other providers, such as Facebook, are not so clear cut. This is a new area for both the account providers and the account holders, and presumably rules will be created to govern it in due course. At present, however, it would appear that account holders have little ability to determine what should happen to their accounts following their death.

    Thus, it is even more important, if the account holder wishes any particular action to be taken in relation to the accounts or for those accounts to be bequeathed, that there is a record of how the accounts can be accessed that can be given to the personal representative or the proposed beneficiary. Otherwise, the legal personal representative/next of kin will be totally dependent upon the cooperation of the service provider.

    In a very informative article entitled 'The Remains of the Data', *Law Society Gazette*, January/February 2013, Damien McCallig considers the particular issues arising in these cases and quotes an interesting statistic from a 2011 survey in the UK which found that one in ten people in Britain do record passwords and online account information in their wills.

11. Disinheriting a spouse/civil partner or child: the reasons for this need to be recorded in detail. Has the client been advised on the full impact of such a decision—for example, a spouse/civil partner's legal right share and s 117 applications? See **Chapter 4**.

12. Capital Acquisitions Tax: the solicitor should ascertain whether any previous gifts or inheritances to the beneficiaries were made by the testator or if there have been any aggregable gifts from other sources. The solicitor should further ascertain whether any returns have been made regarding any taxable gifts and ensure that the client is advised of the CAT liabilities likely to arise on his death and any possible exemptions which may be available to his beneficiaries. See CAT Lecture Notes (see Preface), particularly Chapter 11.

13. Terms of the will:

    (a) The solicitor should ensure that specific items, for example jewellery, are described as clearly as possible and that if a s 56 application is likely, this is explained fully. See **Chapter 4**.

    (b) Charities: where a charity is involved, it is important at the will-drafting stage to ensure that it is sufficiently identified. Problems can arise where a charity is carelessly or incorrectly described or, for instance, where a particular charity has ceased to exist or its functions have been taken over by a similar charity. The general principle is that a charitable bequest will not fail for uncertainty. Section 47 of the Charities Act, 1961 provides a list of circumstances in which a *cy près* application of funds may be made, which has been further extended by subsequent legislation relating to charities. Since the coming into force of Part 2 of the Social Welfare (Miscellaneous Provisions) Act, 2002, the amount that can be the subject of a *cy près* application is unlimited. In order to avoid possible difficulties post-death, it is advisable at the will-drafting stage to determine the appropriate person from whom you should obtain a receipt and then insert in the will that the appropriate person (who would normally be the Secretary, Treasurer, or Superior of a charity) is the person authorised to give a sufficient receipt and discharge for the executors. See **Chapter 2** and para **13.2.7**.

    (c) Pecuniary legacies: the solicitor should advise the client of the possibility of ademption if the client wishes to name particular account numbers in his will and of abatement if there is not enough money in the estate to pay all pecuniary legacies. See **Chapter 2**.

14. Residue: the solicitor should make sure there is such a clause, and that there is an effective gift over. See **Chapter 2**.

15. Power of appointment: a testator can not only dispose of his own property by will but also exercise a power of appointment. Thus, it is vital to check whether the testator has such a power over any property when he attends with a view to making the will and whether that power is general or special. Section 93 of the Succession Act provides as follows:

    'A general devise of land shall be construed to include any land which the testator may have power to appoint in any manner he may think proper, and shall operate as an execution of such power unless a contrary intention appears from the will; and in like manner a general bequest of the personal estate (other than land) of the testator shall be construed to include any such estate which he may have power to appoint in any manner he may think proper, and shall operate as an execution of such power unless a contrary intention appears from the will.'

    It is important to note that this section covers a general power of appointment and not a special power of appointment. The section will not apply where, for instance, the objects of the power are a limited class such as the testator's children (which would need the exercise of a special power of appointment) or where certain persons are excluded from being objects. The solicitor should check that the power of appointment is capable of being exercised by will and that it is not a power limited to being exercised by a deed. A general power of appointment includes every power, right, or authority, whether exercisable only by will or otherwise, which would enable the holder thereof to appoint or dispose of property to whomsoever he thinks fit or to obtain such power, right, or authority, but exclusive of any power exercisable solely in a fiduciary capacity under a disposition not made by himself or exercisable by a tenant for life, or as a mortgage.

    See also ss 10(4) and 45(1) of the Succession Act, 1965, which provide that property subject to a general power of appointment is included in the real and personal estate of a deceased person and is available to satisfy creditors, respectively.

    A special power of appointment, by contrast, will limit the class of persons in whose favour an appointment can be validly made:

136 INSTRUCTIONS, ATTENDANCE, AND EXECUTION

Section 45(1)

> 'The estate, whether legal or equitable, of a deceased person, to the extent of his beneficial interest therein, and the estate of which a deceased person in pursuance of any general power disposes by his will, are assets for payment of the funeral, testamentary and administration expenses, debts (whether by specialty or simple contract) and liabilities, and any legal right, and any disposition by will inconsistent with this section is void as against the creditors and any person entitled to a legal right, and the court shall, if necessary, administer the property for the purpose of the payment of the expenses, debts and liabilities and any legal right.'

If, after enquiries, the solicitor finds out that the testator does have such a power and he has checked the relevant instrument, then the solicitor should advise the testator on the implications of exercising such a power by will. The testator may have exercised such a power during his or her lifetime. An example of this would be where a testator, under the terms of a parent's will, received a life interest in certain property, the 'trust fund'. This life interest could have been coupled with the power to appoint the trust fund by will among the testator's children.

Failure to exercise this power of appointment in the testator's will could lead to the trust fund devolving under the terms of the testator's parent's will to a third party, which could be contrary to what the testator would have intended. Many testators are not aware of the necessity to exercise the power specifically by will and may assume, unless advised correctly, that the 'trust property' will automatically be included in the residue of their estate. A general power of appointment may be validly exercised by a will which was made before the creation of the actual general power of appointment. Therefore, if a document comes into existence whereby a testator is given a general power of appointment, check the provisions of any existing will to see if the exercise of such power has been dealt with or should now be dealt with in any future will. Section 93 will not operate if a contrary intention is expressed in the will, so if the testator wishes to exclude the operation of s 93 this must be specified clearly. In the event of a testator having a power of appointment, it is vital to obtain a copy of such instrument conferring the power and to peruse its terms. See also s 98 of the Finance Act, 2012 and the changes made to the taxation of assets under power of appointment.

16. Capacity: assess and note same. See para **5.4.2**.
17. Terms of retainer, i.e. the requirements of the client, the legal services needed to satisfy those, the action to be taken by the firm, the terms of business offered by the firm (see Law Society Recommended Terms and Conditions (2015 edn)), what is needed from the client both in terms of actions and information and any applicable time limits, the nature of any follow up work that may be required, when the fee advice will be sent to the client, when a draft will/engrossment is to be provided, etc. See para **5.9.1**.

5.4 Taking Instructions in Special Cases

When taking instructions in all cases, but especially in relation to the ill, the elderly, or where there is any doubt of mental capacity, two issues in particular need to be considered:

1. mental capacity; and
2. outside influences.

Just because a client is elderly or ill, or both, does not mean that they lack mental capacity, but with the elderly and the vulnerable, and with those where there is any doubt of mental capacity, extra care needs to be taken. The elderly are vulnerable to a number of issues and this has been recognised by several institutions.

The Law Reform Commission has recognised the problem and states on its website:

'It is coming to be recognised that there is a need to provide adequate legal safeguards for vulnerable groups in our society, that is, citizens who are themselves unable to vindicate their legal rights, whether because of advanced age, ill-health, mental incapacity, lack of education, or lack of familiarity with our legal structures.'

The Commission has now issued two papers and one report on this subject, namely *Consultation Paper—Law and the Elderly* (LRC CP 23-2003), *Consultation Paper—Vulnerable Adults and the Law* (LRC CP 37-2005), and *Report—Vulnerable Adults and the Law, 2006* (LRC 83-2006).

The Assisted Decision Making (Capacity) Act, 2015 has been passed but had not yet been commenced at the time of publication of this book. While the functional test as set out in the Act re capacity does not apply to wills (see s 140), nevertheless practitioners should familiarise themselves with the Act when it comes into force and with the Regulations to be published with the Act.

The Law Society also recognises this need and deals with it in its *A Guide to Good Professional Conduct for Solicitors*, 3rd edn (2013). Chapter 02, Part 2.2 of the Guide deals with clients lacking mental capacity, and duress or undue influence, at pp 12–13, and practitioners should be familiar with this.

In addition, the Law Society has issued several practice notes/guidelines on dealing with vulnerable clients and particular attention is drawn to the following:

- 'Do Not Go Gentle—Cherishing the Elderly Client', *Law Society Gazette*, December 2008
- 'Joint Bank Accounts—Guidelines for Solicitors', *Law Society Gazette*, December 2008
- 'Drafting Wills for the Elderly Client—Guidelines for Solicitors', *Law Society Gazette*, January/February 2009
- 'Administration of Estates—Guidelines for Solicitors', *Law Society Gazette*, March 2009
- 'Gifts: Acting for an Elderly Client—Guidelines for Solicitors', *Law Society Gazette*, April 2009
- 'Enduring Powers of Attorney—Guidelines for Solicitors', *Law Society website*, 19 June 2009
- 'Acting for the Vulnerable Client', *Law Society Gazette*, January/February 2011
- 'Transactions Involving Older/Vulnerable Clients—Guidelines for Solicitors', *Law Society Gazette*, April 2012
- 'Enduring Powers of Attorney—Guidelines for Solicitors', *Law Society website*, July 2016

Many of these are available on the Law Society Probate, Administration and Trusts Committee resources page:

http://www.lawsociety.ie/Solicitors/Representation/Committees/Probate-Administration-and-Trusts/.

There is an excellent lecture by Padraic Courtney and Elaine Rogers entitled *Guidelines and Best Practice*, which was part of *Managing Your Third Age Client—Updates, Guidelines and Precedents*, a seminar held jointly between the Law Society and Solicitors for the Elderly Ireland on 18 October 2012.

Solicitors for the Elderly Ireland have given many lectures on the issue of capacity and how best solicitors can assist clients in this area. A particularly good leaflet entitled *Why am I Left in the Waiting Room?* is available on their website: http://www.solicitorsfortheelderly.ie/.

The Law Society of England and Wales and the British Medical Association have also published a very instructive book entitled *Assessment of Mental Capacity—Guidance for Doctors and Lawyers*, 2nd edn (1995) (there is a later, third edition in 2010, but this is based on the new Mental Capacity legislation in Britain which is not currently relevant to Ireland) and it states as follows:

'There is a legal presumption of capacity unless the contrary is shown. Whether a client has capacity is a matter of law. Different levels of capacity are required for different activities. If there is a doubt

about a client's mental capacity, it is advisable for the lawyer to seek a medical opinion. Medical practitioners should be asked to give an opinion as to the client's capacity in relation to the particular activity or action in question, rather than a general assessment of the client's mental condition. In order to do this, the lawyer has a responsibility to explain to the doctor the relevant legal test of capacity. It should not be assumed that doctors automatically understand what is being asked of them.'

Indeed, this need has been recognised by financial institutions and the Central Bank has amended its code on consumer protection by including the vulnerable consumer. It states as follows:

'Identification of a consumer's vulnerability or otherwise will require the exercise of judgement and common sense and should be based on a consumer's ability to make a particular decision at a point in time.'

There are many useful textbooks on capacity, in particular, Hoare's *Probate Practitioner's Handbook*, 6th edn (2010), which contains a useful checklist entitled *'The Association of Contentious Trust Probate Specialist's Checklist'*, and Casey, Brady, Craven, and Dillon, *Psychiatry and the Law* (2010).

5.4.1 MENTAL CAPACITY

This paragraph does not deal with mental capacity in general or with the Assisted Decision-Making (Capacity) Act, 2015 in particular. At the time of writing this Act has not yet been commenced but it should be noted that s 140 excludes wills from its provisions. The new Act, when commenced, will make no appreciable difference to assessment re testamentary capacity. This paragraph focuses on legal capacity from the perspective of taking instructions re wills from vulnerable adults or where there is a query re capacity, which is not to say that capacity should not always be assessed in any event.

Traditionally, mental capacity has been seen in very black and white terms—either one had capacity or one did not. However, as can be seen from the Law Reform Commission reports and papers, it was accepted that a new approach to capacity was required, as is seen in the Assisted Decision Making (Capacity) Act, 2015 (but, as noted above, s 140 confirms that it does not apply to will-making). It is not intended here to review the reports, suffice it to say, and very briefly put, that the Law Reform Commission in making its recommendations considered three possible approaches to capacity.

(a) Outcome approach

Under the outcome approach, capacity is determined by the content of the individual's decision, so that a decision which does not conform to normal societal values (or the values of the assessor) might be deemed to be evidence of incapacity. The outcome approach is often used by doctors, e.g. the Mini Mental State Examination (MMSE). The Law Reform Commission concluded that the outcome approach was generally not satisfactory.

(b) Status approach

The status approach to capacity involves making a decision on a person's legal capacity based on the presence or absence of certain characteristics. It involves an 'across the board' assessment of a person's capacity based on disability, rather than the person's capacity in relation to a particular decision being made at a particular time.

The status approach is still used in the Wards of Court system and, in respect of EPAs, the Powers of Attorney Act, 1996 deals with a broad assessment of capacity. This approach was also rejected by the Law Reform Commission subject to the acceptance of existing provisions as safeguards for EPAs.

(c) Functional approach

The functional approach assesses capacity on an 'issue specific' basis. Indeed, the question of legal capacity generally arises in specific contexts, such as making a will, the capacity to make a gift, to marry, or to consent to medical treatment.

The circumstances are 'issue specific', therefore a decision on legal capacity in relation to one issue will not necessarily be decided in the same manner in relation to another issue.

The functional approach is the approach recommended by various consultation papers of the Law Reform Commission and indeed adopted in the mental capacity legislation.

Following the functional approach to capacity, which is based on a time- and issue-specific basis, it is clear that the capacity of an individual is very much a variable concept in that one could, for example, have the capacity to marry but not to make a will, or to make a will but not to make an EPA.

This is because capacity is not a global concept to be applied to all acts of a particular person at one particular point in time but is dependent upon their understanding of the 'nature and consequences' of any particular decision. Thus, each particular act needs to be assessed independently.

In addition, the ability to understand the nature and consequences of any particular decision and thus capacity, in relation to a particular act, must be assessed 'in the context of available choices at the time the decision is to be made', not in the abstract.

In addition, where there is any doubt as to an individual's capacity, *'whether that person has capacity shall be decided on the balance of probabilities'*. See Laffoy J's view in *Scally v Rhatigan (No 1)* [2010] IEHC 475, when she stated that the court must be satisfied on the *'balance of probabilities'*. In this case, Laffoy J reviewed the law in general on the issue of capacity including the case law and thus it is a seminal case in the area which should be read in detail. In this case, she was satisfied that, despite severe physical and cognitive disabilities, the testator did have testamentary capacity in the particular circumstances. The following issues should, she said, be considered by the court:

- Evidence of family members of the testator.
- Evidence of the circumstances under which the will was made.
- Medical evidence of the deceased's physical and mental condition.
- Evidence of the practice of the solicitor who drafted the will in assessing capacity.

This final point is vital and a detailed note of same should be made contemporaneously. See *Moyles v Mahon* [2000] IEHC 197.

5.4.2 CAPACITY TO MAKE A WILL

Section 77 of the Succession Act, 1965, which is the primary legislation in relation to will making in this area, states, as to who may make a valid will, as follows:

'(1) To be valid a will shall be made by a person who . . . (b) is of sound disposing mind.'

While the statute is clear, *'sound disposing mind'* is not defined, and as the test for testamentary capacity, as we shall see later, is a legal not a medical one, it can prove difficult for practitioners to assess this as there is currently no definition of capacity.

While the Assisted Decision-Making (Capacity) Act, 2015 does provide a statutory definition of capacity, which will assist, it does not provide a definition of incapacity. Therefore, on occasion, legal practitioners, with the assistance of medical practitioners and in the absence of a definition of incapacity, will be required to assess and declare incapacity based on the absence of capacity as defined in the statute.

However, there is some assistance in case law and certain general points re testamentary capacity can be stated.

5.4.2.1 Presumption of capacity and burden of proof

Where a will is formally valid there is a presumption both of due execution and of testamentary capacity (*Re Glynn Deceased* [1990] 2 IR 326).

140 INSTRUCTIONS, ATTENDANCE, AND EXECUTION

There is a presumption of soundness of mind (presumption of capacity), but note however that once incapacity has been established, by acceptable evidence, it is presumed to continue until the contrary is proved (presumption of continuance).

If there is a challenge to a will which is based on the state of knowledge or health of the testator, the onus is on the person who challenges the will, i.e. the person who alleges lack of capacity must prove the case. See *Vaughan v Vaughan* [2002] EWHC 699.

The mere fact that the testator is very elderly will not in itself rebut the presumption of capacity. While there is a minimum age for capacity to make a will (see s 77 of the Succession Act, 1965) there is no upper limit for the making of a will. See the case of *In Re Helena Blackhall Deceased* (unreported) 1 April 1998, Supreme Court.

In this instance, the testatrix was in her nineties when she executed her will and her soundness of mind was challenged. In all the circumstances, the court held that there was nothing to suggest that she was not of sound mind and understanding as at the time of the execution of the will and that there was not sufficient evidence to rebut the presumption of her mental capacity.

The fact that a testator may have a mental illness does not mean he may not have capacity to make a will. See the judgment of Peter Kelly J (now President of the High Court) in *O'Donnell Deceased* (unreported) 24 March 1999, High Court, where a paranoid schizophrenic was deemed to be of sound disposing mind. Indeed, even if a testator suffers from insane delusions (see *De Souza Wearen v Gannon* (unreported) 20 February 2004, High Court) he can be found to have capacity to make a will.

The fact that a testator's proposed disposition of his assets on his death is not 'reasonable', or at least what the majority of us would consider reasonable, does not mean he is not of sound disposing mind. In effect, he can be *'as odd as bedamned'* because, as was so beautifully stated in *Bird v Luckie* (1850) 8 Hare 301, the law does not require a testator to behave *'in such a manner as to deserve approbation from the prudent, the wise, or the good'*.

5.4.2.2 Test for testamentary capacity

The test for testamentary capacity was laid down in the case of *Banks v Goodfellow* (1870) LR 5; QB 549. The case provides a test, which has three principles or elements. While this is clearly a very old case, it has been reaffirmed time and time again: see *Richards v Alan* [2001] WLTR 1031, the *O'Donnell* case cited at para **5.4.2.1**, *Flannery v Flannery* [2009] IEHC 317, and, most comprehensively, in *Scally v Rhatigan* [2010] IEHC 475.

All practitioners taking instructions from testators should be clearly aware of the requisite elements and be sure that each element is satisfied and thus that the testator has testamentary capacity.

The requisite elements are as follows:

1. The testator must understand that he or she is making a will, a document that will dispose of assets on death. The testator, however, need not understand the precise legal effect of the provisions in the will.

2. The testator must be capable of knowing the nature and extent of his or her estate.

3. The testator must be able to give consideration to those persons who might be expected to benefit from his or her estate and decide whether or not to benefit them.

A practitioner should record the testator's mental position in a detailed attendance or, if appropriate in the circumstances, in an affidavit.

Be aware that it is the practice of the Probate Office to require an affidavit of mental capacity in any case where a testator dies in a mental institution notwithstanding the date of execution of the will. If a medical affidavit certifying capacity is provided and this is not contested by any party then this normally satisfies the Probate Office. Where such a medical affidavit is not available, it will accept an affidavit from the solicitor who drew up the will and also from the attesting witnesses.

Therefore, it would be wise, where there is any doubt re capacity, for the solicitor to arrange to have the client's doctor confirm the testator's mental capacity and if necessary, have the doctor swear an affidavit of mental capacity at the time of the making of the will. See Appendix 4 of Spierin, *Wills—Irish Precedents and Drafting*, 2nd edn (2012), pp 257–9 for this. While all the guidelines referred to here are very useful, ultimately it is the decisions of the legal and medical practitioners that are all important, and in particular the former.

The responsibility by non-medical practitioners to assess mental capacity is an extremely onerous one with which, frankly, we need all the help we can get from our medical colleagues.

5.4.2.3 Working with medical practitioners

It could be argued that where the legal profession sometimes falls down is that the exact level of capacity required for each activity is not clearly communicated to the medical adviser. Medical practitioners should be asked to give an opinion as to the client's capacity in relation to the particular activity or action in question, rather than a general assessment of the client's mental condition. In order to do this, the lawyer has a responsibility to explain to the doctor the relevant legal test of capacity in relation to the making of a will. It should not be assumed that doctors automatically understand what is being asked of them in any particular circumstance.

Thus, when seeking a medical opinion re capacity, in order to help medical practitioners to help solicitors, it is essential to be specific as to what exactly is needed.

An accurate assessment of capacity depends upon absolute clarity of both the solicitor and, if involved, the doctor, particularly in relation to the difference or the relationship between legal and medical understanding of capacity.

Quite often the question arises as to which doctor should be approached for his opinion/ to carry out his assessment, and obviously it must be a doctor who has experience in relation to assessing capacity. On the other hand, the local family GP, while not having specialist knowledge, may well have known the testator for years and be best placed to provide the opinion. In the author's experience, especially where a case is borderline or where there is fluctuating capacity and lucid intervals, the local GP is often reluctant to make an assessment and provide an opinion. Thus, whether it should be the local GP or a specialist geriatrician must be considered in light of the circumstances of each case.

Unfortunately, quite often a testator, especially one whose faculties are slipping and who is aware of that, may refuse to attend a doctor and allow an assessment to be made and that can cause difficulties in practice.

There are cases suggesting that a solicitor may be liable for a successful challenge to a will where they have not obtained a medical opinion (see *Re Simpson* (1977) 121 Sol Jo 224, *Re Morris* [2001] WTLR 1137, and *Worby v Rosser* [1998] EWCA Civ 1438). However, it should be noted that the solicitor in each of these cases did not focus on capacity. See the Law Society eZine, April 2019, issue 83 issued by the Mental Health and Capacity Task Force for a precedent letter for solicitors to use when asking a doctor to assess a client's capacity.

What to do when there is a doubt re capacity but the testator will not attend a doctor

There are two New Zealand cases—*Ryan v Public Trustee* [2000] 1 NZLR 700 and *Public Trustee v Till* [2002] WTLR 1169—which address this issue but, unhelpfully, reach different conclusions.

In the former case, the public trustee was sued successfully for failing to prepare a will for an elderly testatrix whose capacity was in doubt.

In the latter case, a solicitor was held to be in breach of his duty of care where he drew up the will of an elderly client who was later found to lack testamentary capacity. The judge in that case said that a solicitor had a duty to consider and advise on the question of capacity but this is circumscribed by his retainer and the fact that the solicitor cannot make enquiries unless authorised to do so by the client.

It is a far from ideal situation where there is a doubt about capacity but the client declines to be assessed.

There is no one correct answer to this question which is appropriate to all circumstances and it is an issue where there is not always consensus between solicitors as to the appropriate course of action. One suggested practice is to ensure that the testator is given clear advice of the possible dangers if there is a challenge to the will and a note made of this advice, which should be given in writing. In addition, having applied, at least, the *Banks v Goodfellow* test (which has been expanded judicially by the *Key v Key* case, see para **5.4.2.4**, and by society's changing attitude to mental capacity) solicitors should note their conclusions re capacity on the file and then go ahead and make the will.

In such circumstances a simple statement such as *'In my opinion, the testator had full capacity and clearly understood . . .'* is not what is needed, but rather an extensive note of why precisely there were doubts, what investigations were made, and the result of those investigations. Although the testator is the client, the solicitor almost has two roles here; he is advising the client but is also an objective observer. It should be borne in mind that such a case may well result in a High Court action post-death where the solicitor's actions will be scrutinised and any comments or choices which the solicitor has made will be viewed from the great perspective of hindsight.

In a case where there is a difficulty or dispute over the mental capacity of an individual, and there is no medical or other evidence available, it may be necessary to make an application to court for the will to be proved, and this is where a good attendance is invaluable.

5.4.2.4 Best evidence

The importance of evidence in challenges to the will on the basis of alleged lack of capacity is crucial, and medical evidence, while compelling, is not the only source of evidence considered.

Obviously, close family members and friends of the deceased (or indeed care workers) have great opportunity to observe the deceased, and their evidence may be very useful. However, quite often it is not disinterested and, in general, the evidence of an independent solicitor is the best evidence.

Further, it has been judicially recognised that the best form of evidence from the independent solicitor is contemporaneous attendance notes. See *Moyles v Mahon* [2000] IEHC 197, where the court stated that *'it is certainly desirable to have an attendance but it is not a mandatory requirement. If one of these solicitors had died there may be grave difficulties in certain circumstances without a contemporaneous note.'*

In the case of *Key v Key* [2010] EWHC 408 (Ch), the *Banks v Goodfellow* test was slightly extended where the judge found that a man in his late eighties, whose wife of sixty-nine years had recently died, lacked capacity. Briggs J went on to say that while this was not a case where you could point to any one of the tests in *Banks v Goodfellow* and say this had not been satisfied, nevertheless it was clear that Mr Key was not capable in the week following his wife's death to exercise the necessary decision-making ability of a testator.

He continued by saying that such a conclusion *'involves a slight development of the Banks v. Goodfellow test taking into account decision making powers rather than just comprehension . . . it is necessitated by the greater understanding of the mind now available from modern psychiatric medicine'*.

This case was considered by Mary Laffoy J in the decision of *Scally v Rhatigan* [2010] IEHC 475. As the judge in this case reviews the case law on capacity in relation to Irish and English law, it is a seminal case in this area and should be read by practitioners. Another interesting case, particularly in relation to medical evidence, is *Flannery v Flannery* [2009] IEHC 317.

5.4.2.5 The extent of capacity required

Capacity need not be perfect, that is to say, a testator's capacity can be impaired to some extent but a testator can still retain testamentary capacity; see *Barrett v Kasprzyk* (unreported) 3 July 2000, and *Ewing v Bennett* [2001] WTLR 249.

5.4.2.6 Test for testamentary capacity: medical or legal?

However, as noted earlier, the key point here is that the test is a legal one and not a medical one. In *Richmond v Richmond* (1914) 111 LT 273 the court stated that *'it is for the court to decide, although the court must have evidence of experts in the medical profession who can indicate the meaning of symptoms'*.

Further, in the case of *Re Glynn Deceased* [1990] 2 IR 326, Hamilton J preferred the evidence of the persons who attended upon the deceased to take his instructions, who said that the deceased had mental capacity, against the evidence of two medical witnesses who said that the testator did not have mental capacity. This view was upheld by the Supreme Court.

In short, testamentary capacity is a legal test and while medical evidence/affidavits may be very helpful (as we considered earlier) there is no question that the test re capacity to make a will is a legal one. Due to the fact that in relation to an EPA doctors must give an assessment for capacity (Part E of an EPA), some practitioners and indeed doctors believe mental capacity is a medical test. However, this belief is erroneous: there is no question that it is a legal test.

5.4.2.7 When is capacity needed?

It should be remembered that capacity is needed when instructions are given and also when the will is executed (however, see the *Parker* exception below; Lush, *Elderly Clients: A Precedent Manual* (1996); and *Re Simpson Deceased* (1977) 121 SJ 224).

In cases of borderline capacity, a doctor or anyone else making an assessment should immediately make a record of his or her examination and findings.

If a testator lacks testamentary capacity at the time the will is executed, that will is invalid as a general rule. It is possible however, according to *Parker v Felgate* (1883) 8 PD 171, that the testator was of sound disposing mind at the time of giving instructions for the will, that is, a will may be valid even though the condition of the testator has deteriorated between the instructions and the execution to such an extent that testamentary capacity is absent when the will is executed. In order for such a will to be valid, the following conditions must be met:

1. The testator actually had soundness of disposing mind at the time of giving instructions.
2. The will was actually prepared in accordance with the instructions.
3. At the time of execution, the testator understood that he was signing a will for which he had given instructions regardless of whether he can remember the instructions or could have understood the will if it were read over to him.

The *Parker* exception, which is very much the exception and not the rule, is part of Irish law and was applied in *Re Glynn Deceased* [1990] 2 IR 326 and more recently in *Perrins v Holland* [2010] EWCA Civ 840.

5.4.2.8 Fluctuating testamentary capacity and lucid intervals

It is also possible for a will to be executed by a testator during a lucid period. For further discussion on this point see Brady, *Succession Law in Ireland*, 2nd edn (1995), pp 72–82. See also *Richards v Allan* [2001] WTLR 1031. However, clearly establishing that a will was made in a lucid interval could be difficult, and if a practitioner is dealing with such a case, great care needs to be taken.

Quite often, a testator tries to hide their failing abilities or mental difficulties/incapacity and, perhaps with the aid of a close relative (often a beneficiary!), has learnt a list of their assets and a list of those to whom they wish to bequeath those assets. Practitioners should be aware of this.

5.4.3 TAKING INSTRUCTIONS WHERE THE CLIENT IS ILL/IN IMMINENT DANGER OF DEATH/IN HOSPITAL OR NURSING HOME OR PSYCHIATRIC INSTITUTION/IS A WARD OF COURT

Assessing capacity may not be easy at the best of times but there are times when it is more difficult than others; for example, when a practitioner is called out to a hospital or to the home of a client who is seriously ill or even dying, or where there is clearly a definite incapacity at some level.

These are very difficult circumstances under which to draft a will and the solicitor in such a situation must exercise extreme caution and extreme speed (particularly in an imminent death situation), but unfortunately the two are not very compatible. Obviously, at least the test in *Banks v Goodfellow* (see para **5.4.2.2**) must be applied but there are some additional factors which need to be considered.

The practitioner must ensure the following:

(a) He is satisfied that the testator is capable of giving instructions re a will (bearing in mind that one may have capacity for one activity but not for another) and that once the will has been prepared (which would be immediately: see *Gartside v Sheffield* [1983] NZLR 37), the testator is able to read it or at least understand it when it is read over to him. However, see the *Parker* exception discussed at para **5.4.2.7**.

(b) The attestation clause covers the circumstances. For example, if the testator is too feeble to sign then the attestation clause needs to reflect that, and state who signed it at his or her request. See para **7.4.11.8**.

(c) Further, if possible, a brief medical report on the condition of the patient/medication being taken should be obtained there and then, and if that is not possible, as soon as possible.

While it is necessary when dealing with a testator who is vulnerable due to age or illness to ensure that a doctor has satisfied himself as to the capacity and the understanding of the testator (it is very important that a contemporaneous record is made: see Laffoy J's comments on this in *Scally v Rhatigan* [2010] IEHC 475), this does not of itself decide on the validity or invalidity of a will (mental capacity being a legal test) but it certainly helps to minimise a post-death dispute, if not avoid it altogether.

(d) At least two independent witnesses are obtained (it is particularly difficult to persuade members of the medical profession to act as witnesses in these matters and therefore it may be wise to ensure that witnesses are there) and that the will is prepared there and then and complies fully with all statutory requirements. Electronic devices (such as PCs or iPads) are generally not allowed into intensive care units and thus an ability to handwrite a will without access to precedents or to a printer, while a disappearing skill, is still a vital one.

(e) Where the illness necessitating the hospital stay is terminal and/or serious, it would be very prudent not to delay at all in the preparation of the will as, depending on the circumstances, any delay may be considered too much of a delay: see *White v Jones* [1995] 1 All ER 691; *The Estate of Mary Francis Collins Deceased; Collins v Bank of Ireland* (unreported) 27 March 1996, High Court; and *X v Wollcombe Young* [2001] WTLR 308.

(f) While always of importance, particularly in these circumstances, a clear and comprehensive set of attendance notes should be made re the taking of instructions and the execution contemporaneously and these should be kept with the will.

5.5 What is the Absolute Best Practice when Taking Instructions for a Will in Relation to Mental Capacity?

The requirement to apply a functional approach to capacity will give statutory effect to the current common law position on the commencement of s 3 of the Assisted Decision Making (Capacity) Act, 2015. The requirement for the functional approach is fully reflected in the Medical Council's *Guide to Professional Conduct and Ethics for Registered Medical Practitioners* (see para 5.1 of the *Guide*) and the functional approach to capacity is also reflected in the HSE National Consent Policy (see 8th edn, 2016, Chapter 3, Part 10).

In essence, people making a will should be able to understand:

'that they will die;

that the will shall come into operation on their death, but not before;

that they can change or revoke the will at any time before their death, provided they have the capacity to do so;

who the executor is or who the executors are (and perhaps why they should be appointed as executors);

who gets what under the will;

whether a beneficiary's gift is outright or conditional;

that if they spend their money or give away or sell their property during their lifetime, the beneficiaries might lose out;

that a beneficiary might die before them;

whether they have already made a will and, if so, how and why the new will differs from the old one . . .

the extent of all the property owned solely by them;

the fact that certain types of jointly owned property might automatically pass to the other joint owner, regardless of anything said in the will;

whether there are benefits payable on the death which might be unaffected by the terms of their will . . .

that the extent of their property could change during their lifetime.'

The Commission went on to make various recommendations, in particular on p 19 of the report:

'that the Guidelines for Solicitors should also note that contemporaneous notes be made by Solicitors regarding the details of the meeting with a client when the issue of testamentary capacity is an issue.'

In other words, if there is ever any doubt about the burden placed on solicitors it has been clarified by the report. Take a second look at that list. It is quite comprehensive and that is the minimum required.

5.6 Outside Influences

With all clients practitioners need to consider outside influences, but there is a particular need to do so when dealing with elderly clients.

The elderly are vulnerable to outside influences. In the same way as children are vulnerable to detrimental actions by other individuals, the elderly are also vulnerable. However, children do not normally hold assets which can be of advantage to a third party. The possibility of undue influence is always in the background and it is not an easy situation for solicitors to police, especially as often you will find that a testator in such circumstances for various reasons does not want to 'upset the apple cart' and to a certain degree nearly colludes in the situation. It is important that practitioners are always aware of the possibility of such undue influence and follow strict guidelines in ensuring that elderly clients are always interviewed on their own and are not being influenced.

5.6.1 PRESUMED UNDUE INFLUENCE

Practitioners should also be aware of situations where there is a presumed question of undue influence. Presumed undue influence can arise where a relationship of trust and confidence existed between the parties. These relationships include those between solicitors and their clients or medical advisers and their patients. There is also another class of relationships where undue influence can arise, and that is where an individual reposed trust and confidence in the wrongdoer.

It has been found that it is not necessary to prove that coercion has occurred. The existence of the relationship alone can be deemed sufficient to establish that the plaintiff could not have brought an independent mind to bear so as to consent freely to the transaction.

However, it is important to realise that a claim of undue influence should not be pursued where there is merely suspicion, not positive proof (see *Elliot v Stamp* [2008] IESC 10). It will have to be shown that the volition of the testator was positively overpowered.

See also *Lambert v Lyons* [2010] IEHC 29, where the court held that the righteousness of the transaction would be established by showing the testator knew and approved the contents of the will *and* by the thoroughness of the instructions given/taken by the solicitor. This point was also raised in *Re Corby* [2012] IEHC 408. A key UK case in this area, *Gill v RSPCA* [2009] EWHC B34 (Ch), in which James H Allen QC considers in detail undue influence, is worth reading. Interestingly, leaving aside undue influence for the moment, this case also shows the effect of refusal to mediate and could be said to be in effect the equivalent of *Elliot v Stamp* [2008] IESC 10 but relating to mediation. See also *Carroll v Carroll* [1999] 4 IR 241.

The question of independent advice has been recognised judicially as tending to rebut the presumption of alleged undue influence. In the case of *Carroll v Carroll*, in which the doctrine of undue influence was considered, Denham J acknowledged the importance of independent legal advice in seeking to rebut the presumption of undue influence and quoted from Dr Hilary Delany's book, *Equity and the Law of Trusts in Ireland*, as follows:

> 'The manner in which this presumption may be rebutted relates to two main issues: first the question of whether independent legal advice has been received and secondly whether it can be shown that the decision to make the gift or transfer was a "spontaneous and independent act" or that the donor "acted of his own free will".'

The judicial view is that independent legal advice is vital in assisting elderly individuals.

See also SI 375/2012—*Implementation of Conveyancing Conflicts Task Force Report* for further discussion on the need for independent legal advice.

To assist the elderly in weighing up the pros and cons of a proposed course of action places a great legal obligation on solicitors in giving such advice. In looking at the case of *Gregg v Kidd* [1956] IR 183, Budd J gave some practical guidelines as to how a solicitor should advise a vulnerable person and these are worth repeating in their entirety as they have so well survived the test of time.

> 'To begin with he should appraise himself of the surrounding circumstances insofar as he reasonably can: if he does not do this he can never put himself in a position to advise his client fully and effectively.
>
> He would need to discover the nature of the donor's illness so that to be able to estimate in some reasonable degree the nature of his incapacity.
>
> He would need to know how far his reasoning capacity was affected and how far he was capable of comprehending the manner in which the proposed transaction would affect his own interest and his future and to what extent he was confident to come to a rational decision.

> *Without knowing all that, he could not be said to have sufficient knowledge of his client to enable him to judge the nature of the advice he should give him and the degree of protection he would require.'*

The principles applicable in cases of undue influence were considered by Costello J in *Kavanagh; Healy v MacGillicuddy & Lyons* [1978] ILRM 175, where it was stated that evidence of the most cogent kind is required where undue influence and duress are alleged. Interestingly, where proceedings have been instituted on this particular point, the person against whom the charge of undue influence is made should also be made a defendant to the proceedings.

This care is equally required in relation to codicils: see *In Re Corboy* [1969] IR 148 and **Chapter 2**.

5.7 Taking Instructions Regarding an Elderly Beneficiary

The treatment of elderly beneficiaries at will-drafting stage is also an area of concern. It is to be hoped that the concepts of rights of residence and maintenance are losing favour as they rarely confer any comfort and, in the writer's view, only lead to difficult conveyancing issues. The better practice is to utilise the concept of a life interest in dealing with elderly spouses notwithstanding the legal right of the surviving spouse and to favour the concept in certain circumstances where there is an element of vulnerability, and the questions of protection and management are a necessary consideration.

It is not uncommon to come across situations where a surviving spouse/civil partner has no wish to be proactive in making all financial decisions and is delighted with the concept of this type of trust. Where the use of this life interest falls into difficulties is where it is simply not set up properly. Practitioners can tend to overlook that where they set up a limited interest and land is involved, they are creating a settlement under the Land and Conveyancing Law Reform Act, 2009 (which largely repealed and replaced the Settled Land Acts, 1882 to 1890). One scenario that occurs on many occasions is the creation of a life interest in a will but with no appointment of trustees. Perhaps the full implications of the fact that a trust was arising has not occurred, but some help can be obtained from s 19 of the Land and Conveyancing Law Reform Act, 2009.

5.8 Attendances

5.8.1 ATTENDANCES REGARDING INSTRUCTIONS

Immediately after meeting with the testator, and prior to drafting the will, an attendance should be prepared by the solicitor with the aid of the instruction sheet, and a copy of the attendance kept on file.

As an absolute minimum, an attendance should contain the following:

1. The date and time of the meeting, and the parties present at same (note that the testator should be alone; other people would include office staff, e.g. a trainee solicitor).

2. The instructions of the testator on the nature and extent of his estate, his wishes on its disposal, and the reasons given by him, if any, for said disposals. Be sure, where the bequest is likely to be contentious, to obtain reasons.

3. All advices on spouses/civil partners (divorce/dissolution/separation/unworthiness to succeed/renunciation of rights) and children.

4. All advices on tax.

5. If there was a previous will, its whereabouts. What is the reason for altering the will? Why is the testator not attending with the practitioner who drew up the

148 INSTRUCTIONS, ATTENDANCE, AND EXECUTION

previous will? Where there is a will in another jurisdiction, as is increasingly prevalent these days, any and all advice given on that, and preferably obtain a copy of same.

6. The (hopefully subtle) queries to ascertain that the testator had testamentary capacity. Where the doubt is of such magnitude that a medical examination is required, make a note of this.

7. What actions or planning the client requires from his solicitor.

8. What actions or planning needs to be done by the client. Inform the client of this in a follow-up letter.

9. Any other issues discussed particular to the testator.

5.8.2 ATTENDANCE REGARDING EXECUTION

This attendance should obviously indicate how, when, and where the will was executed, and the witnesses present. It is also helpful to note where the original will is stored. If anything unusual happens during the execution, a note should be made of this.

Should there be any likelihood of a query being raised in the Probate Office (e.g. a stroke victim signing with a scrawl, somebody else signing on behalf of a blind testator), then the attendance should note this, and if the attestation clause itself does not refer to the problem, affidavits of attesting witnesses should be obtained there and then and kept with the will.

A very basic precedent would be as follows:

Attendance on the execution of will

'The Testator/rix client attended at these offices today. Present in the room at all times were myself (solicitor) and (trainee solicitor) [for example] and the Testator/rix client.

I read the will over to the Testator/rix client and asked if this was an accurate representation of his/her wishes. It was. It was clear to me that the Testator/rix client understood the nature and effect of the will and was fully mentally capable as [complete as appropriate]

I then asked the Testator/rix client to execute his/her will. This was done in my presence and in the presence of. We then witnessed the will in the presence of the Testator/rix client.

The original will is being stored in the offices of

Dated the   of 20   '

5.9 The Solicitor's Duty of Care

The duty of care in the area of will drafting is an extensive and really onerous one and furthermore one that the courts seem willing, as can be seen in the cases above, to extend.

It is important to realise that just because a solicitor does not accept payment for drafting a will, this does not mitigate liability in any way (see *Finlay v Murtagh* [1979] IR 249).

It is not possible to eliminate all liability, no matter how careful a practitioner is in the drafting of a will. However, by judicious risk management it should be possible to reduce it.

5.9.1 RISK MANAGEMENT

Unfortunately, any defect or lack of clarity in a will frequently does not come to light until after the testator's death.

5.9.1.1 To whom and to what extent is a solicitor liable?

The short answer is: to everybody, for everything! This statement is not quite as cynical as it sounds, as can be seen from the cases discussed below.

The position in both Irish and English law was that while a solicitor owed a duty of care to his client based on his contract of retainer, he did not owe such a duty to a beneficiary under his client's will, and accordingly a disappointed beneficiary had no legal redress against a solicitor who had failed to ensure that the will had been validly executed: *Robinson v Fleming* (1861) 4 Macq 167.

However, the position has been altered in both Ireland and England, and now an extremely onerous duty of care is placed upon a solicitor on the taking of instructions in the preparation of a will and its drafting. See *Burke v O'Donnell and Bank of Ireland* [2010] IEHC 348.

The position was altered initially in England by the case of *Ross v Caunters* [1980] Ch 297 (on the equivalent of Irish s 82 of the Succession Act, 1965), and confirmed by a series of decisions, most notably in *White v Jones* [1995] 2 AC 207 and *Worby v Rosser* [1998] EWCA Civ 1438.

Ross v Caunters was very rapidly followed in Ireland in the case of *Wall v Hegarty* [1980] ILRM 124. In this case, the plaintiff was the executor named in a will which had been improperly attested. The defence admitted that the signature of the testator had not been fully authenticated by two witnesses and that the signature of one witness had been added subsequently in the solicitor's office.

Referring to and approving of the decisions in *Ross v Caunters, Hedley Byrne & Co v Heller* [1964] AC 465, and *Donoghue v Stephenson* [1932] AC 562, Barrington J held that the plaintiff in this case could recover three sets of damages from the solicitors of the testator:

- loss of the legacy, i.e. the £15,000 involved;
- the expense of proving the will;
- interest on the abortive legacy as and from the end of the executor's year.

It is clear from this that any solicitor engaged in the preparation and execution of a will owes a duty not only to his client (the testator) but also to any intended beneficiaries. It cannot be stressed strongly enough that if a solicitor fails to draft a valid will which accords with the instructions given by his client, then he will be potentially liable as follows:

1. to the client for breach of contract; this is likely to cause only nominal damages but, even more importantly;
2. to a beneficiary whom the testator had intended should benefit in tort.

In the case of *White v Jones* [1995] 2 AC 207 the House of Lords explained why the extension of the duty was necessary; failure to recognise the extension of the duty of care of a solicitor to beneficiaries would result in injustice. In this case the testator was seventy-eight and there was a delay of forty-four days from instruction to death.

In essence, the liability of solicitors in will drafting, especially in England, but increasingly in Ireland, has grown radically. The more cynical among us, but perhaps the more realistic, might say that we are now responsible for everything. One final case illustrates this point and indeed indicates that merely following the testator's instructions precisely may not be sufficient: *Carr-Glynn v Frearsons* [1998] 4 All ER 225.

The testatrix, aged eighty-one, consulted a solicitor to make a will leaving her interest in a property to her niece. She owned the property with her nephew and was uncertain whether she owned it as beneficial joint tenant or tenant in common. Her solicitor prepared a will and advised her that the gift of the property could not take effect if she held it as a beneficial joint tenant. The solicitor asked if the testatrix wanted her to obtain and check the deeds. The testatrix said that she would do it herself.

The testatrix did not do so. There was a suggestion in the evidence that she may have felt embarrassment in getting her nephew's authority to inspect the title deeds. On her death, the gift of the property could not take effect, as it had been held as beneficial joint tenants.

Chadwick LJ focused on two issues:

1. Did the solicitor's assumption of responsibility to an intended beneficiary in connection with the preparation of a will extend to service of a notice of severance without which the relevant provision in the will cannot take effect?
2. Could the assumption of responsibility extend to a beneficiary in a case such as this where the estate itself has a remedy? (The estate had suffered a loss as a result of the failure to sever. However, the beneficiary of any claim made on behalf of the estate would have been the residuary legatee, not the disappointed niece.)

The court answered 'yes' to both of these questions.

Therefore, now not only does a solicitor have a responsibility to an intended beneficiary, but this responsibility extends to something not part of the will itself. The Court of Appeal found that the solicitor was guilty of lack of care in failing to ensure that the elderly testatrix severed the joint tenancy; it decided that rather than waiting for the deeds, the solicitor should have prepared a notice of severance and advised that it be served immediately. Many practitioners would find this decision harsh (to say the least) and consider that explaining the problem to the client and waiting until it was known whether or not the property was held as beneficial joint tenants was perfectly reasonable. However, this case has been approved in subsequent decisions in England.

This case (at the very least) shows how much the solicitor must explain to a client how far down the road he must go, and the frightening extent of his liability.

The duty of care is that of a reasonably careful and skilful solicitor—see *Roche v Peilow* [1986] ILRM 189—and further it is not necessarily adequate to follow 'common practice' or even Law Society practice notes, and solicitors must be proactive in discharging the duty.

One light in this area is, paradoxically, the case of *Darby v Shanley* [2009] IEHC 459, where the court saw there was a breach of duty, but also noted that even if there is a breach of duty, loss or damage must result for liability to be imposed. Scant comfort, but some.

In order to reduce somewhat the risk in the drafting of a will, the following guidelines, at the very least, should be applied.

5.9.1.2 Retainer and instructions

The practitioner should take proper and full instructions (preferably on an instruction sheet and these should be kept with the will).

It is vital in each and every case that the solicitor takes the appropriate steps to clarify the extent of his retainer. Where there is a dispute between solicitor and client as to the terms of the retainer, prima facie it is the client's version which should prevail: see *X v Wollcombe Younge* [2001] WTLR 308.

The testator must be interviewed alone, and no question of undue influence should arise: see Brady, *Succession Law in Ireland*, 2nd edn (1995), p 82. The instructions of the testator should be taken in the absence of anyone who may stand to benefit under the will, or who may have influence over the testator.

The solicitor should satisfy himself that the testator is of sound disposing mind. If in any doubt, the solicitor should seek a medical report on the question of the capacity of the testator from his doctor. This is especially important in a case where a client is elderly or in hospital. See para **5.4.1**.

Be aware, however, that following the testator's instructions is not always sufficient—see the case of *Carr-Glynn v Frearsons* [1998] 4 All ER 225 at para **5.9.1.1**.

5.9.1.3 Attendance

The solicitor should ensure that full and adequate attendance notes are taken in relation to the instructions received from the testator and again ensure that these are kept with the will, for example, on the Status of Children Act, 1987; the spouse's legal right share (see *Darby v Shanley* [2009] IEHC 459); s 117 of the Succession Act; the Civil Partnership and Certain Rights of Cohabitants Act, 2010 and any relevant tax advice. When attending an elderly client or a client who has suffered a serious illness, the 'golden rule' which should always be observed is: have a medical practitioner, who satisfies himself of the capacity and understanding of the testator, witness or approve the making of the will. The solicitor should record and preserve his examination and findings, as judge after judge in case after case has stated.

The danger is that a solicitor who has not taken appropriate steps to check capacity may be liable to the estate for the cost of an action to establish the invalidity of the latest will. See *Corbett v Bond Pearce* [2001] EWCA Civ 559, where it was held that a solicitor who had not taken appropriate steps to check capacity (extensive) would not only be exposed for the loss (if any) to a beneficiary but also liable to the estate for the cost of an action to establish the invalidity of the latest will.

The importance of a solicitor having clear and contemporaneous attendance notes of what steps were taken to establish capacity, and to explore any changes from earlier wills, and whether instructions were taken in the absence of those likely to benefit, cannot be overstressed. In numerous cases where there have been real doubts as to any of these matters, the courts have commented very favourably on the quality of the solicitor's attendance notes and on the efforts made by the solicitor to establish capacity.

The solicitor should note: instructions and attendance are not the same. Instructions are what the testator tells the solicitor and attendance notes are what was said, including what the solicitor told the testator. See para **5.8**.

5.9.1.4 Receiving a benefit

It is absolutely unethical for a solicitor to take a benefit under a will of a testator whom he is advising, without insisting on the testator obtaining independent legal advice.

See para 3.5 of *A Guide to Good Professional Conduct for Solicitors*, 3rd edn, which deals with bequests or gifts by client to solicitor, staff, or family and with wills for parents.

In the English case of *Re A Solicitor* [1975] QB 475, a solicitor who was a beneficiary under a will was struck off the Register of Solicitors for not insisting that his client obtain independent legal advice or alternatively insisting that he forgo the benefit.

If a parent asks a solicitor son or daughter to make a will for them, there is endless potential for a conflict-of-interest situation to arise between the solicitor and his or her siblings. The solicitor must consider whether independent advice is essential.

5.9.1.5 Confidentiality

A solicitor has a professional duty to keep confidential all matters coming within the solicitor–client relationship, including the existence of that relationship. These matters can only be disclosed with the consent of the client or by the direction of a court.

Pre-death

A will is a confidential document, and its contents, or even the fact that a will has or has not been executed, should not be disclosed to any person. For example, if a client says to you that he will be sending his parents in to make a will with you and asks you a fortnight later if they have been in, you cannot say yes or no.

This is not to be confused with advising the testator to inform the executor or relevant next of kin that he has made a will and its location. Solicitor–client confidentiality can be waived by the client, never by the solicitor.

Post-death

As can be seen, a will is absolutely confidential between a testator and his solicitor. On the death of a testator, confidentiality passes to the legal personal representative and can only be waived by the legal personal representative. Remember, therefore, that where you are dealing with an administrator (presumably with will annexed) as opposed to an executor, the administrator's powers only arise from the date of grant of letters of administration with will annexed.

A solicitor should not, therefore, without the consent of the personal representative, disclose any information about the will or indeed about the testator's affairs. See para 4.4 of *A Guide to Good Professional Conduct for Solicitors*, 3rd edn, which deals with: Disclosure of testator's affairs; Supplying a copy of the will; Supplying copy of executor's or administrator's account; Testator's solicitor; and Wills from an acquired practice.

However, practitioners are frequently asked by beneficiaries and occasionally other parties to supply a copy of the will. Strictly speaking therefore, a solicitor should not supply a copy of, or extract from, a will to a beneficiary unless so directed by the executor. However, it may well be appropriate to avoid unnecessary complaints to the Law Society of paranoia on behalf of a beneficiary to supply a copy of the will, and it is the normal practice in the initial letter to the beneficiary (see para **6.8.4.2**) to supply an extract of the relevant part of the will; an executor should be so informed of this, and his consent obtained.

5.9.1.6 Taking instructions from the testator's family

The solicitor should never take instructions from third parties. If, because of any force of circumstance or pressure from a client, a solicitor feels tempted to do so, he should remember that the courts have been absolutely scathing about solicitors who take such instructions without seeing the client face to face.

5.9.1.7 Duty to act expeditiously

Once a solicitor has received instructions for a will, it is essential that he acts as soon as possible in preparing a draft and arranging for the will to be signed.

While it is established that a solicitor should not delay in the preparation of the will once the instructions are received, the question arises as to what amounts to a delay.

Obviously, where the testator is frail or in ill health or—as often is the case—both, then there is a particular urgency for a solicitor to deal with the matter. See the case of *Gartside v Sheffield* [1983] NZLR 37, where a disappointed beneficiary sued a firm of solicitors who failed to act properly in arranging the execution of a will for an eighty-nine-year-old testatrix who was in frail health. The inevitable happened and she died within seven days after giving instructions, and no new will had been drafted. The New Zealand Court of Appeal held a duty of care was owed to the beneficiary to deal with matters with reasonable expedition.

What is reasonable expedition varies depending upon the circumstances.

Practitioners should see the House of Lords case of *White v Jones* [1995] 1 All ER 691 and subsequent case law, where it was held that a firm of solicitors was liable to compensate beneficiaries where they were omitted from a will which had not been drafted expeditiously in accordance with the testator's instructions.

The testator had quarrelled with his two daughters (they were the plaintiffs). He executed a will in March 1986, cutting them out of the estate. However, in June 1986 he was reconciled with them and he sent a letter to his solicitors instructing them that a new will be prepared, including gifts of £9,000 to each of his two daughters.

The solicitors failed to do so before the testator died on 4 September 1986. In the majority decision it was held that the intended beneficiaries under the will were reasonably foreseeably deprived of a legacy by the solicitors' negligence and the solicitors were held liable for the loss of the legacy to the beneficiaries.

It was clear from this case and other Irish cases (*The Estate of Mary Frances Collins Deceased; Collins v Bank of Ireland* (unreported) 27 March 1996, High Court) that where a testator is in frail health there is a particular urgency for a solicitor to deal with the matter. See Brady, *Succession Law in Ireland*, 2nd edn (1995), Chapter 2, pp 83–8.

In the English case of *X v Wollcombe Young* [2001] WTLR 308, five days' delay was the issue. The instruction was taken on 26 June and the testatrix died on 1 July.

The testatrix was in hospital, suffering from terminal liver cancer. She asked a solicitor she had not met before to visit her. She explained that she wished to make various changes to her will. The principal change was to substitute her grand-niece, X, as residuary beneficiary in place of the existing charity.

The solicitor, Mr P, called on the following day (Thursday, 26 June). His attendance note recorded that the testatrix was lucid and aware of what she was doing. She told him that she was probably being moved to a hospice on Monday, 30 June and that she would get a message to him in the following week to confirm her whereabouts so that he could bring the will for execution.

Mr P went back to the office but, as his probate clerk was away, the will was not started. On Monday 30 June he discussed the matter with the clerk and the bulk of the work was carried out on 1 July. It was intended that it would be ready for signature on Thursday 3 July. Unfortunately, the testatrix died on the morning of 1 July after a rapid worsening of her condition late on 26 June.

It was alleged by X that she had suffered loss as a result of two cumulative or alternative breaches. First, Mr P should have prepared a codicil, as a holding operation, immediately substituting X as a residuary beneficiary. Second, Mr P should have produced the new will for signature by Monday 30 June at latest.

The judge, Neuberger J, suggested that seven days would be a sufficiently short period *'in most cases'*. Where the client was *'elderly or likely to die anything other than a hand written rough codicil prepared on the spot for signature may be negligent. It is a question of the solicitor's judgment based on his assessment of the client's age and health.'*

Thus, the best advice is do not delay at all, and practitioners are referred to the cases of *Hooper v Fynmores* (Times of London, 19 July 2001); *Sherrington v Sherrington* [2005] EWCA Civ 326; *Smith v Claremont Haynes & Co* (Times of London, 3 September 1991); and *Corbett v Newey* [1996] 3 WLR 729.

A 'cooling off' period, as it were, is not required: see *Darby v Shanley* [2009] IEHC 459.

In addition, the solicitor should note the warnings from the DSBA in the *Parchment*, March 1998, p 7:

> *'Many solicitors' offices will be familiar with the file containing unsigned wills. You know the ones where the client said they would come in and sign but kept putting it on the long finger. Warning: In the event of premature death on the part of the client, the solicitor may be exposed to an action if the members of the deceased's family feel aggrieved that the solicitor failed to obtain a signature. Action: Write to the clients and advise that these draft documents will be destroyed within 28 days if they do not call to sign.'*

5.9.1.8 Duty on a solicitor to give tax advice

A solicitor preparing wills for clients should at the very least be able to give tax advice to a testator on inheritance tax issues. If the solicitor is not able to give basic tax advice, this should be explained to the testator, who can then decide whether he wishes to instruct an alternative solicitor or an additional solicitor to advise on tax.

There are not many cases on this point but there is a leading UK case, *Cancer Research Campaign v Ernest Brown & Co* [1997] STC 1425, where Harmon J confirmed that while tax advice is a requirement, under a solicitor's general duty of care it is not required to advise the testator on tax avoidance schemes. As he puts it:

> *'I do not doubt the solicitor, in considering the will, must consider what inheritance tax complications that the testator will cause by the bequest for which he has given instructions. But I refuse to hold . . . that there arises a duty to inform the intended testator about tax avoidance schemes in connection with some quite other estate . . .'*

See also the cases set out at para **5.9.1.2**.

5.9.1.9 Execution and return

It is an absolute minimum, but not in itself sufficient, that the statutory requirements for the making and execution of wills are adhered to. In *Wall v Hegarty and Callanan* [1980] ILRM 124 a firm of solicitors was held negligent where a will was not properly attested.

In *Ross v Caunters* [1980] Ch 297 it was held that where a testator wished to benefit a particular person his solicitor was negligent for failing to point out to the testator that neither that person nor his spouse should witness the will. The court held that the solicitor failed to take reasonable care to ensure that such person or his spouse did not witness the will, and as that person was therefore precluded from the benefit, the solicitor was liable in damages to that person.

Preferably, solicitors should never send a will for execution by post. If a solicitor feels that he absolutely has to, great care must be taken when doing so and in such cases the requirements for the signing of the will must be set out very clearly. The solicitor should make absolutely sure that he fully explains the rule on failure of a gift to a beneficiary when the spouse/civil partner of the beneficiary witnesses a will, as discussed at para **2.15**.

There is a strong argument that one should never send a will out to be executed by post, as no matter how well a letter of instruction re execution is worded, inevitably there is a problem. See the English case of *Esterhuizen v Allied Dunbar* [1998] 2 FLR 668.

The testator (T) was a shy widower living a reclusive life who was befriended by Mrs E. T told Mrs E that he wanted to make a will but was worried about the cost. Mrs E arranged for F, who worked for Allied Dunbar and had been trained to deal with wills, to visit T. F did so and took instructions for a will to leave everything to Mrs E and her daughter, which was duly prepared by Allied Dunbar's will-writing department.

F returned to T with a will and written instructions on how to execute it. F proposed to witness the will but there was nobody available to act as a second witness. F walked around the close where T lived, but it was the middle of the day and the close was deserted. F offered to drive T to a local petrol station to find a second witness but T was unenthusiastic about the suggestion and told F to leave the will with him. F agreed and said he would contact T in a week to check whether the will had been witnessed.

F telephoned and visited a week later. T had still not executed the will. There was some dispute about precisely what was said but F again left T with the will unsigned. F telephoned Mrs E to explain that the will had not been signed. T eventually had the will witnessed by one electrician who was visiting the house. He showed the will to Mrs E, who expressed doubt as to its validity because it had only one witness. T appeared surprised.

T became ill and was admitted to hospital. He told Mrs E that he was worried about the will. Mrs E arranged for a solicitor to visit T but, by then, he was too ill to give proper instructions. On T's death his estate passed on intestacy to his next of kin.

Longmore J said:

> 'It is in my judgment not enough just to leave written instructions with the testator. In ordinary circumstances just to leave written instructions and to do no more will not only be contrary to good practice but also in my view negligent.'

One possible solution would be that the solicitor should give, in writing, an offer in the following terms:

- the client can visit the solicitor's office for execution; or
- the solicitor can visit the client's house with a member of staff; or
- the client can make his own arrangements as per the solicitor's comprehensive written instructions.

Once the will has been executed by the client and returned to the solicitor, the thorny question which then arises is:

5.9.1.10 Should the solicitor inspect the will after execution outside the office?

In the English case of *Gray v Richards Butler (A Firm)* [2002] WTLR 143 there is a clear assumption that a solicitor has a duty to examine a will returned post-execution. This view was also accepted in the English case of *Ross v Caunters* [1980] Ch 297, where it was held that the solicitors had breached their duty by not checking the will after execution, not noticing that one of the witnesses was a spouse of a beneficiary, and not bringing that fact to the attention of the testator.

5.9.1.11 Storage and copy wills

It is best practice to send a copy of the executed will to the client, setting out in writing advices given, and to scan a copy and put a copy on file, thus decreasing the likelihood, if the original is mislaid, that a copy of the executed will not be available.

The original will should be properly stored and indexed. See the extract from the *Law Society Gazette* of November 1995.

Extract from Law Society Gazette, November 1995: long-term storage of documents

'Rough handling and folding of the paper is not recommended.

Where the long term storage and preservation of legal documents, eg. wills, is involved generally one should follow professional archival principles in the creation and care of records which must be permanently preserved by:

a) *printing on acid free paper*

b) *binding should follow accepted archival methodologies*

c) *storage should be of a reasonable standard in acid free covers and boxes, and*

d) *in an environmentally controlled area.'*

5.9.1.12 Review of a wills safe

Once the will has been correctly drafted, executed, and stored correctly, can a solicitor then relax or is there a further duty of care? Dealing with the first question, there are two schools of thought:

1. The first is that the solicitor should review the wills safe regularly, in the light of legislative changes, particularly changes to tax legislation, and write to clients explaining the effect of this and if appropriate advising them to attend to draft a new will.

2. The second is that this is an enormous amount of work and if not done thoroughly and completely correctly each and every time there is a change (and to what extent should the solicitor pursue the client?), the solicitor is increasing his liability by having done it once.

Best practice would seem to be as follows.

On the execution of the will the solicitor should immediately write to the client, putting the onus on him to review his will in the light of legislative and personal life changes. It is expecting a great deal of the client to ask him to keep up to date with changes in legislation, particularly tax legislation. In the event of a significant change in tax legislation, it can be argued that the solicitor should write to the client for whom he holds a will, explaining its effect and if appropriate advising him to attend to draft a new will.

Examples from legislative changes will serve as an example of the necessity for this:

The Land and Conveyancing Law Reform Act, 2009 made fundamental changes to the powers of trustees vis-à-vis the life tenant of 'Settled Land Act type trusts'. Should the solicitor write to all clients who have made will trusts, informing them of the changes and inviting them to review their wills in light of the changes? Also, changes were made to the position of EU entitlements by SI 639 of 2017 and the question could be asked, should the solicitor should write to all former clients informing them of the changes and inviting them to review their wills in light of those changes?

This is ignoring any wills drafted in a manner to minimise taxation, which would have to be reviewed in light of changes to the taxation regime; in particular, anti-avoidance legislation.

For example, the Finance Act, 2015 made significant changes to agricultural relief and whether a beneficiary would qualify for the relief. Again, should the solicitor should write to all former clients, informing them of the changes and inviting them to review their wills in light of the changes? Dwellinghouse exemption was substantially changed in the Finance Act, 2016, Finance Act, 2017, and again in the Finance Act, 2019. Should the solicitor write to all clients who had left a dwellinghouse to a beneficiary in the hope of availing of the relief?

3. In light of the changes to dwellinghouse relief contained in the Finance Acts in 2016, 2017, and 2019, should the will be reviewed?

Changes in legislation are not the only reason for reviewing wills. The most common reason for a will needing review is that it was prepared at a time when the testator's children were minors and it provides for a discretionary trust that is now not relevant. In this case the testator will be aware of the contents of the will trust, and the age of his children, but may still have failed to take any initiative to update it. Notwithstanding that the actual responsibility may lie with the testator, it would be difficult for a solicitor to explain to a set of beneficiaries why a 6 per cent discretionary trust tax liability (3 per cent if appointed out within five years: see para 12.4 of the CAT Lecture Notes (see Preface)) needs to be paid which could so easily have been avoided.

Obviously, if a client attends on his solicitor in order to administer the estate of a spouse/civil partner or close relative or to conduct a major transaction—the sale of real or business property, for example—the solicitor should advise the client to review the terms of his will, to ensure that the will is compatible with the client's current financial and family position.

If, for example, there is a clause in the will specifically devising a named property to a beneficiary and the solicitor who prepared the will subsequently acted in the sale of the house and acted in the purchase of another on behalf of the client and never advised the client to change his will, there is every possibility that the disappointed beneficiary will sue the solicitor in negligence.

At the very least, the solicitor should inform every client post the execution of his will to come back to the solicitor to review his will in light of any changes in personal circumstances.

CHAPTER 6

ADMINISTRATION OF ESTATES: PROBATE PRACTICE AND PROCEDURE

6.1 Introduction and Overview

The late Eamonn Mongey BL, in his invaluable book *Probate Practice in a Nutshell*, first published in 1980, provided a flowchart to describe the steps in administering an estate. This flowchart (at **Figure 6.1**), slightly amended and expanded, is reproduced in this chapter with his kind permission.

FIGURE 6.1

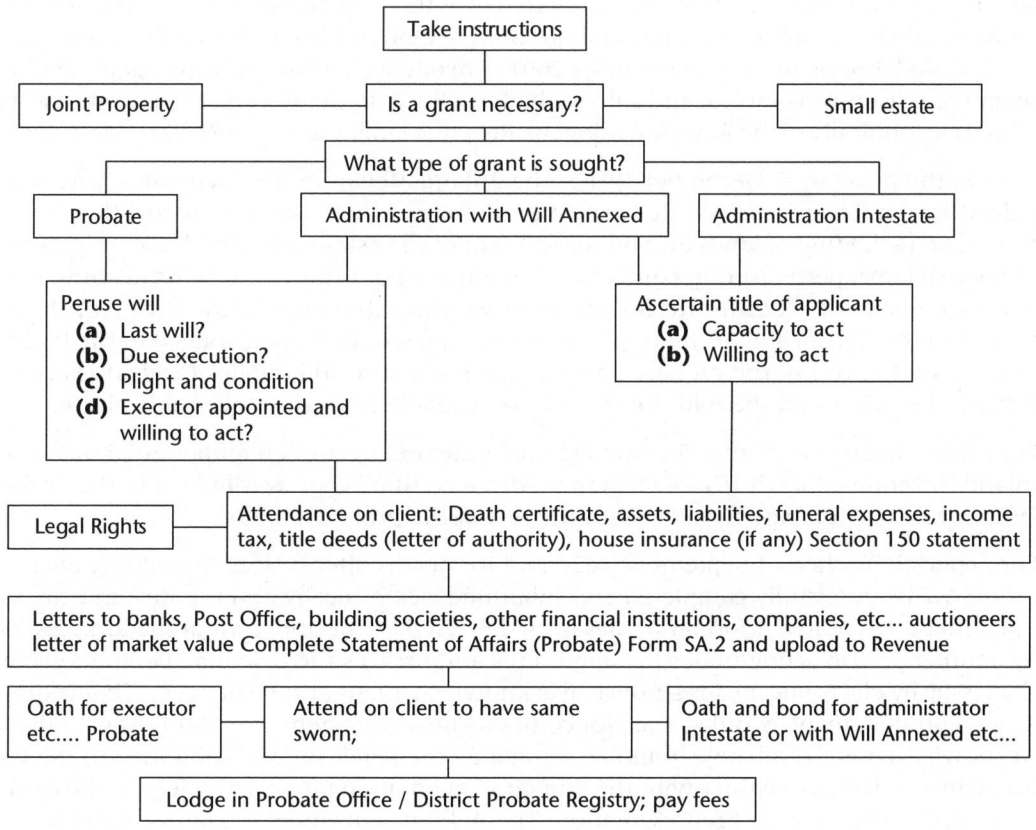

158 ADMINISTRATION OF ESTATES: PROBATE PRACTICE AND PROCEDURE

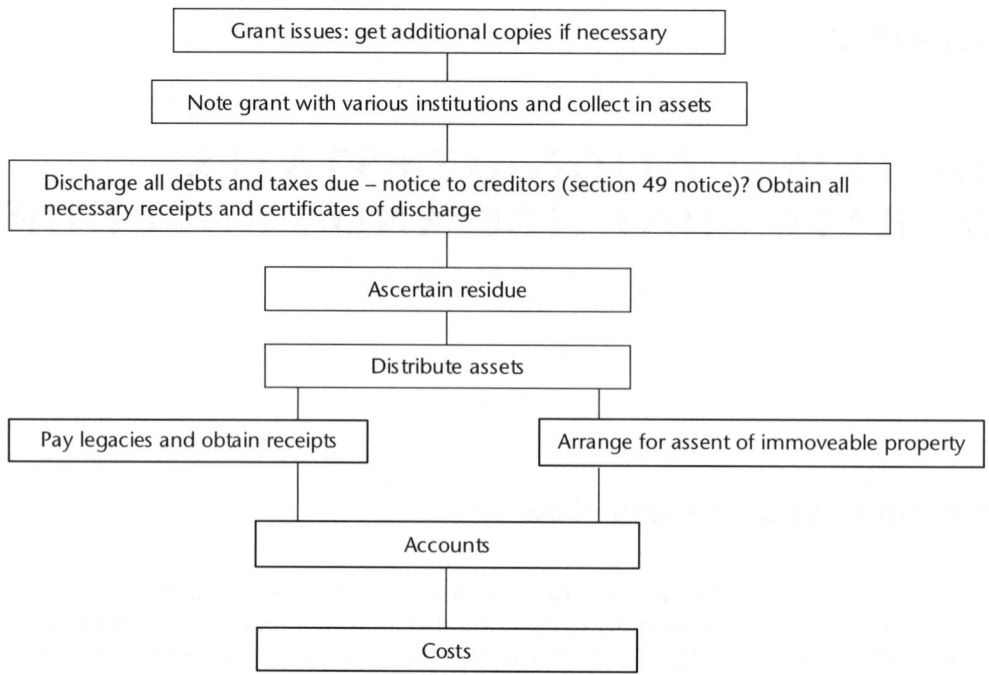

The purpose of this chapter is to outline the steps involved in administering an estate following notification of death, through receipt of instructions from the personal representative to the preparation of the Statement of Affairs (Probate) Form SA.2. The form SA.2 replaces the Inland Revenue affidavit (form CA24 also referred to as the 'schedule of assets') and is now used for applications for Grants of representation submitted on or after 14 September 2020 where the deceased died on or after 5 December 2001. Anyone seeking to apply for a grant of representation must now complete and submit the form SA.2. to the Revenue. This must be submitted electronically to the Revenue using the Revenue Online Service (ROS) or My Account.

For deaths prior to 5 December 2010, the Inland Revenue affidavit form CA24 was lodged in duplicate with the Revenue Commissioners for assessment together with a form CA6 (Schedule of lands and buildings) where the estate contained real or leasehold immoveable property. In due course the Revenue would return these forms duly certified together with a Certificate for the High Court. Subsequently the forms CA24 and CA6 with the Certificate for the High Court attached would then be lodged in the Probate Office with the rest of the probate papers. This procedure still applies for deaths prior to 5 December 2001 and the 'old' form CA24 is available from the Revenue website.

For deaths arising on or after 5 December 2001 and before 14 September 2020 the sworn Inland Revenue affidavit (CA24) together with a certified copy was lodged in the Probate Office or District Probate Registry with the rest of the probate papers.

For applications after 14 September 2020 and for deaths after 5 December 2001, once the form SA.2 is successfully completed and submitted electronically and the Revenue are satisfied that the required information has been delivered by the applicant in the form SA.2 or by another person acting under the applicant's authority as the case may be, the Revenue shall issue by electronic means a notice of acknowledgement of such delivery. This acknowledgement document is called the Notice of Acknowledgement (Probate). The Notice of Acknowledgement (Probate) should be printed by the applicant and submitted to the Probate Office or District Registry with the other documentation necessary to lead to the issuing of the appropriate grant of representation. The Acknowledgement contains certain key information from the form SA.2 submitted to the Revenue that the Probate Office requires.

6.1.1 STEPS IN ADMINISTERING AN ESTATE (PRE-GRANT)

Having ascertained the type of grant necessary and having first completed and submitted the form SA.2 electronically on ROS, once the Notice of Acknowledgement (Probate) is generated, the solicitor acting for the personal representative will then complete the rest of the necessary papers for lodgement in the Probate Office to obtain the necessary grant of representation. For these purposes the phrase 'personal representative' will be used as a generic term to include executors and administrators either on intestacy or with will annexed. Similarly, the phrase 'grant of representation' will be used as a generic term to include grants of probate, administration intestate, and administration with will annexed. At all times the distinction between the particular roles will be highlighted.

It is worth noting that the Probate Office will not issue a grant of representation until the expiry of fourteen days after death (O 79, r 33 of the Rules of Superior Courts, 1986).

6.1.2 OVERVIEW OF CHAPTERS 7 TO 11

Chapters 7 to 10 will go on to deal with the various types of grants that can be applied for, depending on the circumstances.

Chapter 7 will deal with applying for a grant of probate. This is the most common type of grant applied for and is applicable when there is a will in existence and an executor (or executors) willing to act.

Chapter 8 will deal with applying for a grant of administration intestate. This arises when the deceased died intestate; that is, without leaving a valid will. There is a precise order of persons entitled to take out such a grant which is outlined in O 79, r 5(1) of the Rules of the Superior Courts. The division of the estate is governed by the Succession Act, Part VI.

Chapter 9 will deal with applying for a grant of administration with will annexed. This type of grant arises where there is a valid will in existence but where somebody other than the executor applies for the grant, the executor(s) usually either having predeceased, or survived and died without extracting a grant or being unwilling or unable to act. Such a person, when appointed, is the administrator of the estate. The order of entitlement to extract these grants is contained in O 79, r 5(6) of the Rules of the Superior Courts.

These three types of grants constitute the majority of grants of representation issued by the Probate Office.

Chapter 10 will deal first with *de bonis non*, or secondary, grants. These arise where a grant (of either probate, administration with will annexed, or administration intestate) has issued but the person appointed (either the executor or administrator) has died without completing the administration of the estate. **Chapter 10** will then go on to deal with limited and special grants which arise in particular situations.

Chapter 11 will deal with non-contentious probate applications. These are situations where a particular order of the Probate Officer is necessary before a grant can be applied for. In some cases, the Probate Officer does not have the authority to make the necessary order and an application to the High Court is necessary.

6.1.3 FURTHER STEPS IN ADMINISTERING AN ESTATE (POST-GRANT)

The administration of the estate will then follow the remaining portion of the flowchart reproduced above.

Post-grant steps will be dealt with in **Chapters 12** to **15**.

Chapter 12 will deal with post-grant steps including collection of assets, payment of liabilities, and assets falling outside the estate.

Chapter 13 will deal with different types of beneficiaries focusing on spouse's/civil partner's/qualified cohabitant's and children's rights from the perspective of the personal representative.

Chapter 14 will deal with the obligations, duties, and claims on the estate focusing on taxation both pre-death and post death.

Chapter 15 will deal with assets of land, distribution of the assets, estate accounts, finalising matters, and closing the file.

6.1.4 GENERAL NOTES ON ADMINISTRATION OF ESTATES

Administration of estates forms a part of most legal practices. It is an area which demands a high duty of care from the practitioner and requires expertise and knowledge of the Succession Act, 1965, the Trustee Acts and the Land and Conveyancing Law Reform Act, 2009, the Capital Taxes Acts and amending Finance Acts, the Charities Act, 2009, and family law legislation including the Civil Partnership and Certain Rights and Obligations of Cohabitants Act, 2010. In the course of administering any estate, small or large, one will encounter a wide range of issues.

Frequently, one can come into contact with a surviving spouse or civil partner or some members of the immediate family who will also be the personal representative. It is important to remember at all times that one's client is the personal representative who will be dependent on the practitioner for advice and direction throughout the administration.

The area of probate and administration of estates has become one of the most contentious and difficult areas of practice. It therefore calls for a sensitive, yet sensible 'professional approach'.

As with all areas of practice, time is of the essence in administering an estate and delay can often be a contributory factor when problems arise.

6.1.4.1 Taxation issues

When commencing any administration file, one is also commencing a tax file.

Capital acquisitions tax, capital gains tax, income tax local property tax, and stamp duty implications may all arise in dealing with the estate. In addition, the Local Government (Charges) Act 2009 imposed on owners of certain residential property a liability to pay an annual charge (known as NPPR) to the local authority in whose area the property was situated. The charge applied from July 2009 to March 2013 inclusive. Accordingly, a certificate of exemption or receipt from the local authority may be required in the sale of the deceased's dwellinghouse. Payment of Local Property Tax may also be required for any residential property owned by the deceased. Practitioners should be aware of where tax liabilities arise and ensure that taxes are discharged within the relevant time limits. The tax implications are dealt with in detail in the CAT Lecture Notes (see Preface), but the necessity for obtaining the relevant clearance certificates is dealt with in **Chapter 14** of this book.

6.1.5 STAGES OF THE ADMINISTRATION OF AN ESTATE

The administration of an estate, therefore, falls naturally into four main stages:

1. Taking instructions and collecting information about the estate.

2. Preparation of the papers to lead to a grant of representation, having same sworn by the personal representative and sent to the Probate Office.

3. After the grant has been issued, the collection of assets and payment of outstanding debts.

4. Distribution of the estate in accordance with the wishes of the testator, if there is a will, and or otherwise in accordance with statute (see First Schedule, Parts I and II of the Succession Act). In the case of immovable property, the appropriate deed of assent must be prepared to vest the property in the beneficiary/beneficiaries. In some cases, this may involve the drafting of a deed of family arrangement. The last stage includes deciding the share to which each beneficiary is entitled and the preparation of the necessary accounts of the administration, to include receipts from all taxes (income tax, capital acquisitions tax, capital gains tax, including necessary letters of no audit in the case of non-resident beneficiaries) and also social welfare and nursing home care legislation (if applicable).

6.2 Immediate Tasks of the Practitioner on Notification

On receipt of instructions, i.e. on being notified that a person is dead and that the personal representative wishes to engage the firm, the collating and processing of the information necessary to proceed to the administration stage needs to be carefully managed. Prior to the first meeting with the personal representative, there are a number of issues that the practitioner needs to keep in mind.

It is better not to rush into a meeting within days of the death or notification, and the more preparation the solicitor can engage in prior to the meeting, the more productive that meeting will be.

It is useful to make telephone contact prior to the initial meeting in order to appraise oneself of the level of knowledge that the personal representative has about the affairs of the deceased and whether the personal representative will be able to assist. Identify as early as possible a situation where the personal representative will be relying on the solicitor entirely to collect the information and look after all aspects. An elderly or vulnerable personal representative will need considerable guidance and time, whereas a professional person may be of substantial assistance in certain aspects of the administration. A personal representative who is willing and able to assist with time-consuming and personal matters can be invaluable.

The following are suggestions of areas where the personal representative might be usefully employed:

- collecting the financial information and assets from the deceased's home, details of accounts, share certificates, etc;
- obtaining the death certificate;
- obtaining up-to-date details of the beneficiaries to include their names, addresses (including eircode/postcode), date of birth, country of residence and ordinary residence, domicile, contact phone number and email address, and a list of family members with, if possible, their PPS numbers;
- arranging insurance on the dwelling, contents, and other insurable items of the deceased;
- organising the funeral and the headstone/engraving and requesting that the account be sent to your office;
- removing valuables from the deceased's home and arranging for their safekeeping;
- clearing the house where necessary and arranging for the sale of contents if appropriate;
- disposing of the deceased's car and cancelling the car insurance;
- cancelling health insurance and obtaining any refund, if applicable.

These matters can be discussed on the telephone with the personal representative prior to the first meeting and if some or all of these tasks can be delegated to the personal representative prior to a meeting, the task of collecting the balance of the information will be so much easier.

You need to establish if all of the appointed executors are going to act or, in an intestacy situation, if the person entitled to extract the grant is available and has the capacity to so act.

You are now at the stage where you can commence the instruction sheet and, with this knowledge, arrange the initial meeting with the personal representative. In an ideal world this should take place as soon as is reasonable after the date of death. When this preliminary work is done you should be aware of any problems likely to arise.

6.2.1 KEEP ACCURATE RECORDS

It is important, as in every area of practice, to keep accurate records of attendances on clients and the instructions received, particularly in intestate cases, where beneficiaries are not listed as in a will, and where details of next of kin are required. These may be valuable later; especially for one's own purposes should a dispute arise. It is also helpful to prepare a family tree. Where the deceased was not a client of the office, this task is more difficult.

6.2.1.1 Estate accounts

When commencing work on an administration of an estate it is vital to understand the importance of being able to provide ultimately comprehensive and user-friendly estate accounts.

Estate accounts are dealt with in detail in **Chapter 15** but the keeping of accurate accounts should be planned for, started, and maintained throughout the administration.

In particular, a contemporaneous, detailed, and accurate account of all transactions carried out during the administration of the estate should be maintained from the outset as it makes the preparation of final accounts a much simpler process.

6.2.2 CHECK THE PURPORTED WILL

Any purported testamentary instruments and other scripts should be preserved very carefully. Check that the document held, and which purports to be the last will, is actually the last will of the testator and that there is no subsequent will or codicil. The older the will is, the higher the possibility that there is a subsequent will. If there is an attendance note and/or an instruction sheet with the will, these should also be read carefully, as they may prove enlightening.

Read the will as a whole to ensure that it is valid and that difficulties will not be encountered when the will goes to probate. On reading the will, if there are difficulties, these should be noted and brought to the attention of the personal representative. Under no circumstances should you proceed without the written instructions of the personal representative. Where necessary, relevant affidavits of plight and condition or of due execution should be prepared and executed for submission to the Probate Office when lodging all other papers. These are outlined at paras **7.4.10** and **7.4.11**.

On perusal of the will, any will trusts, including trusts for minor children, should be noted.

As outlined in Chapter 1 of the Trusts Lecture notes (see Preface), the personal representatives will discharge their duties by vesting the property concerned in the appropriate trustees. The personal representatives are given the power by s 57 of the Succession Act, 1965 and s 19 of the Land and Conveyancing Law Reform Act, 2009, to appoint trustees of the share of an infant entitled under a will or on intestacy, where there are no other trustees able and willing to act and to vest the share in such trustees. The personal representatives are thereby discharged from all further liability in respect of the infant's share.

Ascertain what other documents are held on behalf of the deceased, particularly if there are any other documents left with the will, and, if so, check their importance.

Prior to the initial interview you should request the personal representative to bring with them whatever information/documentation the family has in its possession in connection with the affairs of the deceased.

6.2.3 WHERE APPARENTLY THERE IS NO WILL

Where there is no will produced, ensure that none is in existence. Full enquiries should also be made to the extent that common sense and circumstances suggest. Often, the family may not have knowledge of the existence and/or location of a will and you may have to circularise a letter or email to colleagues in the appropriate areas to establish the position. It may be necessary to advertise in a national newspaper, the *Law Society Gazette*, or other appropriate papers or journals, including perhaps overseas, seeking information from anybody having knowledge of a will.

As a matter of common courtesy, if one in practice receives such a request, one should answer such enquiry promptly and without charging a search fee.

6.2.4 BURIAL DIRECTIONS OR OTHER URGENT MATTERS

Matters requiring urgent attention should be addressed. The deceased may, for instance, have left directions concerning disposal of his body or the use of organs for transplant or specific burial arrangements. These directions should be communicated to the personal representative or the next of kin as quickly as possible to ensure that the wishes of the deceased are observed. However, should there be any dispute as to the disposal of the body the personal representative does not have the final decision. It is usually left to the immediate family.

6.3 Is it Necessary for the Solicitor to Extract a Grant?

Prior to the initial meeting with the personal representative, the solicitor should investigate as to whether a grant of representation is necessary.

The general rule is that if a person owns significant assets in Ireland at death it will be necessary to extract a grant to administer those assets. The grant which issues will allow you to administer the assets in this jurisdiction.

However, it is important to realise that there is no legal requirement that a grant must be extracted simply because the person died with assets in the State. It will depend on the value of the estate: see paras **1.1.2** and **4.5.11** for a list of assets falling outside the estate.

There may not be a need to extract a grant in the following circumstances.

6.3.1 JOINT TENANCIES

If the property is immovable property and is jointly owned and it passes to the surviving joint owner by survivorship, then a grant is not necessary to pass title. What is necessary, however, is to ensure that the death certificate of the deceased joint holder is placed with the title deeds if unregistered; if the property is registered in the Property Registration Authority, the Land Registry section should be notified. A statutory declaration is filed with them exhibiting the death certificate of the deceased joint owner. The declaration contains an averment that the joint tenancy was not severed. The appropriate form to use is Form 47 in the Land Registry Rules. The folio is then updated to record the amended ownership. See para 14.7.2 of the *Conveyancing* OUP manual.

Further, while required to be noted on the form SA.2, nevertheless assets owned as joint tenants are not part of the estate of the deceased except where there is a resulting trust to the estate. See para **6.6.7**. However, *note* that there may still be a liability to capital acquisitions tax.

For joint accounts other than current accounts, a certificate of clearance from the Revenue Commissioners is required presently where the sum exceeds €50,000, except in the case of a spouse. Financial institutions are prohibited by law from releasing funds from joint accounts in excess of €50,000 without an IT8 letter of clearance except where the account is held jointly with a surviving spouse or civil partner. The form SA.2 has an additional feature allowing a request to be submitted for IT8 account clearance. On entering details of any jointly held bank, building society, credit union, or An Post account the applicant is presented with an option to request IT8 clearance for the account. On successful submission of the form SA.2, the Revenue will correspond directly with the applicant regarding any request for IT8 clearance.

For further details on the CAT implications of joint property, see CAT Lecture Notes (see Preface).

6.3.2 NOMINATED GRATUITIES

If the deceased was entitled only to a death-in-service benefit, then a grant may not be necessary to access those funds because the trustees of the pension scheme may have the power to appoint the funds directly to a specified beneficiary or under a nomination by the deceased. See CAT Lecture Notes (see Preface).

6.3.3 SMALL ESTATES

In the case of very small estates where the proposed beneficiaries are clearly identified, it is occasionally possible for assets comprised in the estate to be realised without obtaining a grant.

Generally, if the total cash assets in the estate are less than €25,000, financial institutions may be persuaded to release monies without a grant (e.g. Ulster Bank will release up to €31,000 and Bank of Ireland up to €35,000), but on the appropriate indemnity being signed by the executor, or all those entitled on intestacy or all the residuary beneficiaries if there is a will but no executor available to act. The death certificate will have to be produced. The requirements of each financial institution vary and should be confirmed with the individual institution in each case. Sometimes the financial institution will release sums to pay for the funeral and/or 'refreshments' up to a certain amount. Again, the requirements of each financial institution vary and should be confirmed with the individual institution in each case.

Ireland State Savings (An Post) will release the monies contained in a savings account if the amount does not exceed €6,348.69. They will require a claim form, death certificate, Post Office deposit book, certified copy will where the deceased died testate, and sworn indemnity.

Under s 23 of the Credit Union Act as amended by the Credit Union Act, 1997 (Alteration of Financial Limits) Regulations, 2006 (SI 546/2006), the directors of a credit union can pay out up to €15,000 to the persons entitled without the need for a grant. Similarly, under r 15 of the Savings Certificates (Seventeenth Issue) Rules, 2007 (SI 827/2007), An Post may pay out up to €10,000 of savings certificates to the persons entitled without the need for a grant.

Where the figure is slightly in excess of this but not substantially, it is worth contacting the financial institution involved and discussing the position. While transfers of personalty (i.e. movables, cash, cars, etc) can be vested orally or by implication (where possession is simply transferred), transfers of land must be vested by a deed of assent in writing. Assents will be dealt with in **Chapter 15**.

6.3.4 PERSONAL APPLICATION

A personal representative may also attend personally at the Probate Office, High Court, where every assistance is given in making a personal application. This includes the completion of the Statement of Affairs (Probate) Form SA.2 online using the My Account facility and completing all papers to extract the appropriate grant.

Where the estate is small and it would be uneconomical to administer the estate on behalf of the personal representative, often the best advice to the personal representative may be to make use of this service. The client, so advised, may well return to the firm in the future.

6.3.5 SUMMARY

It is not only bad practice to take out a grant when it is not necessary; it may be negligent to do so. In all cases the solicitor should therefore sit down with the proposed executor/administrator, having established what/where the assets of the estate are, to see whether it is really necessary.

6.4 Where a Grant is Always Necessary

Having discussed the circumstances where it may not be necessary for the client to go to the expense and delay of extracting a grant, given the nature of the estate, it is necessary to look at the situations where a grant is always necessary.

6.4.1 REALTY (FREEHOLD LAND)

A grant must always be obtained where the deceased died possessed of realty in his sole name. Section 52(2) of the Succession Act empowers *'his legal personal representative'* to transfer such land by assent in writing.

6.4.2 WHERE A GRANT MAY BE NECESSARY EVEN THOUGH THERE ARE NO ASSETS

Conversely, there may be occasions where, although there are no assets in this jurisdiction, it is necessary to extract a grant of representation. Section 29 of the Succession Act provides for such a situation and allows that a grant of representation in respect of the estate of the deceased may be extracted notwithstanding that the deceased left no estate in this jurisdiction. Some examples of this would be:

- where it is necessary to obtain a grant for the purpose of making or perfecting title;

- where the estate has been completely administered but a *de bonis non* grant becomes necessary, for example, where the last surviving trustee of a settlement dies leaving no estate but the only person entitled to appoint new trustees is his personal representative; or

- where a mortgage has been redeemed and there has been no reconveyance by the mortgagee who died without any estate and the mortgagor may wish to constitute a personal representative of the mortgagee to obtain a proper reconveyance.

These do not happen very often.

6.4.3 THE ESTATE OF A WARD OF COURT

It is not always necessary to apply for a grant of administration to the estate of a deceased ward. It is usually necessary to do so when the estate is solvent, but not when it is insolvent, unless it includes property such as land, which cannot be sold by anyone other than the personal representative. If the ward dies intestate and his total assets do not exceed €25,000 since 28 December 2012 (Rules of the Superior Courts (Funds in Court), 2012 (SI 488/2012)), formerly €6,500 (Rules of the Superior Courts (No 4) (Euro Changeover), 2001 (SI 585/2001)) in value, the President of the High Court has discretion to direct that the residue of the funds be paid out to the person who would be entitled to obtain letters of administration under the Succession Act, 1965. In fact, if a grant is applied for unnecessarily, the costs of obtaining it may not be allowed by the Wards of Court Office. See para **3.7**, which deals with advising the executor of a ward of court.

6.4.4 DISTINCTION BETWEEN PERSONAL REPRESENTATIVES AND TRUSTEES

While the role of personal representative has been dealt with in **Chapter 3** and the role of a trustee in Chapter 1 of the Trusts Lecture Notes (see Preface), it is opportune at this stage to distinguish between the two roles. Sometimes the same client may be the personal representative and the trustee, and it is important for both the solicitor and the client to be able to distinguish between the separate roles.

6.5 Preparing for the Initial Interview with the Personal Representative

6.5.1 INTRODUCTION AND ISSUES THAT MAY ARISE

The first meeting with the personal representative is extremely important on two counts: first, to extract as much information as will be required in the course of the administration and second, to advise the personal representative of the onerous duties applicable to such a role. It is advisable to allow sufficient time for this meeting.

Frequently, the personal representative is the surviving spouse/civil partner, who may still be very distressed and emotional and will depend entirely on the solicitor for guidance throughout the administration. On a practical note, one has to be discreet and show a little patience, understanding, and compassion. Try not to refer to the deceased as 'the deceased' in communicating with members of family. When dealing with administration it is second nature for us as practitioners to do so but family members may find this distressing.

Personal representative	*Trustee*
1. Appointment Executor—by will. Administrator 1) entitlement on intestacy/ will annexed situations 2) appointment by court.	**1. Appointment** By settlor/personal representatives of settlor (s 57). By existing trustees (and their personal representatives). By the court.
2. Number Only one need be appointed.	**2. Number** Two trustees are normally appointed, as two are necessary to give a receipt for capital monies under the LACLR Act, 2009 (unless the settlement authorises otherwise). See s 58(3) of the Succession Act.
3. Receipts One may give a valid receipt for all property except for property held under a 'Land Act' trust.	**3. Receipts** All trustees must join in giving valid receipts, unless otherwise provided in the deed of settlement.
4. Retirement A personal representative cannot retire once he has proven the will, nor can he transfer his duties to another.	**4. Retirement** A trustee can appoint other trustees and can then retire from the trust.
5. Extent of powers A personal representative has wide powers given by common law and statute, as well as any additional powers given under the will. Personal representatives may be trustees of a 'Land Act' trust under the LACLR Act, 2009 until trustees are appointed.	**5. Extent of powers** Trustees are given wide powers under the LACLR Act, 2009 (where there is a 'Land Act' trust), Conveyancing Acts, the Trustee Acts and the Succession Act. However, these are not as wide as the powers of personal representatives, particularly when the assets are not land.
6. Succession A personal representative of a personal representative does not succeed him (a *de bonis non* grant is necessary). Section 19 of the Succession Act, 1965 abolished the chain of executors.	**6. Succession** The personal representative of a trustee can act as trustee in his place unless and until he appoints someone else in his stead.

ADMINISTRATION OF ESTATES: PROBATE PRACTICE AND PROCEDURE

Often, a surviving spouse/civil partner may not have access to any assets of the deceased until such time as the grant of probate/grant of administration is obtained. Therefore, it is important to check with the surviving spouse/civil partner what income is available pending the issue of the grant. If no provision has been made this may result in hardship and underlines the necessity for obtaining a grant as soon as possible.

Nowadays, thankfully, people are more aware of life insurance and assurance and other means of providing for surviving spouse/civil partner/children immediately on death.

Prior to the first meeting with the personal representative, one will have asked them to bring all information and documentation in connection with the deceased that they may have in their possession.

One should now obtain clear and comprehensive instructions with the assistance of the instruction sheet and hard copy of the Statement of Affairs (Probate) Form SA.2. There are excellent Revenue guidelines on the use and completion of the form SA.2 available on the Revenue website.

6.6 Instruction and Progress Sheet Combining Questions Raised in the Form SA.2

The precedent instruction sheet should be used as a guideline and should also be used in conjunction with a hard copy of the form SA.2. If kept at the front of the file, it serves as a useful method of recording information and detailing changes in assets throughout the administration.

The retrieval of information from a large and bulky administration file can be time-consuming and matters such as the collection of assets can be overlooked if a proper record is not kept. The instruction sheet can also be added to or amended to take account of the individual circumstances of any given administration as the administration progresses. The form should be used in this flexible way, added to as appropriate, and amended if necessary to suit the individual facts of the particular case.

Having a record at the start of the file can be time saving as the administration progresses.

6.6.1 SAMPLE SHEET

Instruction and Progress Sheet of _____ Deceased

Name [*check death certificate and will: any difference will need to be explained*]	
Address [*check death certificate and will: again, any difference needs to be explained*] eircode.	
Date of death [*see death certificate*]	
Surviving relatives [*attach list; include in the case of intestacy relatives of the full and the half-blood*]	
Occupation [*'retired' will not do: must be 'retired occupation'*]	
Residence/ordinarily Residence *at date of Death* [Caution: *confirm with family; may have tax implications*]	
Domicile at death and Domicile of origin	
Date of birth [*check birth certificate*]	

Death certificate obtained Yes/No Coroners Interim Certificate of fact of death	
Civil status [*check it is correct on death certicate*] married/single/legally separated/widow/er/divorced/civil partner/surviving civil partner/former civil partner/minor child *Qualifying cohabitee?*	
Place of death	
Date of Irish grant	
Date of foreign grant (if any)	
Valuation date(s)	
Date of ascertainment	
PPS no of deceased [*this number is required for ALL Revenue forms*]	
Revenue file no [*only use when deceased did not have a PPS no*]	
Social welfare claim no	
Surviving spouse/civil partner? [*consider fresh will*]	
Did deceased leave a will? Yes/No	
Will all named executors act/reserve right/renounce right?	
Location of will	
Date of will/Date of any codicils	

If YES above then complete the following section (Testate)

Executor appointed/alive? *Yes/No*	
Executor no 1 name:	Relationship to deceased
Address	
Occupation	Mobile no
Phone no	Email:
Fax no	PPS no

Executor appointed/alive? *Yes/No*	
Executor no 2 name:	Relationship to deceased
Address	
Occupation	Mobile no
Phone no	Email
Fax no	PPS no

ADMINISTRATION OF ESTATES: PROBATE PRACTICE AND PROCEDURE

If there is no will or if the executor cannot act, then complete the following section (Intestate; Will annexed; *De bonis non*)

ADMINISTRATOR no 1 [*check entitlement*]	
Administrator no 1 name:	Relationship to deceased
Address	
Occupation	Mobile no
Phone no	Email
Fax no	PPS no

ADMINISTRATOR no 2 [*check entitlement*]	
Administrator no 2 name:	Relationship to deceased
Address	
Occupation	Mobile no
Phone no	Email
Fax no	PPS no

Assets [*We recommend that in time a copy of the completed form SA.2 as submitted to and accepted by the Revenue is printed and is attached to the instruction sheet.*]

		Value at date of death (€)	Grant noted Y/N	Value at and date of collection (if applicable)
1.	Bank accounts IBAN BIC and account numbers			
	1.			
	2.			
	3.			
2.	Building society			
3.	Post Office			
	1. Account			
	2. Savings certificates (total value)			
	3. Index-linked bonds			
4.	Prize bonds			
5.	Credit union			
6.	Cash in house			
7.	Household goods			
8.	Car			
9.	Real/leasehold property [*attach valuation/location of title deeds*]			
10.	Shares/securities (total value) [*attach valuation*]			
11.	Government stock (if not included in value of shares above)			

		Value at date of death (€)	Grant noted Y/N	Value at and date of collection (if applicable)
12.	Insurance policies s 72/73			
13.	Pension/gratuities: State pension/ Assistance			
14.	Medical insurance payments			
15.	Other			
	Total to be carried forward to schedule of assets	€		

	Foreign assets Currency	Value at date of death (€)	Grant noted Yes/No	Value at and date of collection (if applicable)
1.	Bank accounts			
	1.			
	2.			
	3.			
2.	Shares [attach list]			
3.	Property			
	Total to be carried forward to schedule of assets	€ [This figure is not included in the gross value of the Irish estate]		

Rate of exchange at date of death =

[Always check the currency/currencies in which you are dealing, and the rate of exchange. You may have a number of different rates during the administration. Keep an eye on these.]

Debts

[Include only debts as at date of death; keep a separate record of administration debts.]

Name and address of creditor	Amount (€)	Date paid	Receipt Yes/No
Name of funeral directors			
Funeral expenses and wake expenses and headstone			
Utilities			
Amount due to financial institutions			
Mortgage owing			
Fair deal/nursing home fees			
Liabilities owing to Revenue			
Any personal loan owing by the deceased			
Other pre-death expenses			
Total	€		

ADMINISTRATION OF ESTATES: PROBATE PRACTICE AND PROCEDURE

Joint property/joint assets

[If deceased held property jointly with another, obtain full detailed answers to questions raised in the Asset Detail Screen under the heading 'how is the property held' in the form SA.2 and insert appropriate details. The options provided under this heading for selections are as follows:

1. *Solely by the deceased.*
2. *Joint tenant and*
3. *tenant in common.]*

BENEFICIARIES RECEIVING A BENEFIT EXCEEDING €12,000.

Name	*Resident/Ordinarily Resident or Non-resident?*
Address to include Eircode/Postcode.	Tax liability? Yes/No [*insert amount*]
PPSN Date of Birth	Date of CAT clearance
Legacy/share	Date of payment
Relationship: Group threshold for CAT purposes Details of all prior benefits whether from this Group threshold or otherwise received since 5 December 1991	Receipt

Name	*Resident/Ordinarily Resident or Non-resident?*
Address to include Eircode/Postcode	Tax liability? Yes/No [*insert amount*]
Date of Birth PPS no	Date of CAT clearance
Legacy/share	Date of payment
Relationship: Group threshold for CAT purposes Details of all prior benefits whether from this Group threshold or otherwise received since 5 December 1991	Receipt

Name	*Resident/Ordinarily Resident or Non-resident?*
Address to include Eircode/Postcode	Tax liability? Yes/No [*insert amount*]
PPS no Date of Birth	Date of CAT clearance
Legacy/share	Date of payment
Relationship: Group threshold for CAT purposes Details of all prior benefits whether from this Group threshold or otherwise received since 5 December 1991	Receipt

If the deceased was a life tenant or if there is a trust contained in the will, complete this section:

- trust property;
- life tenant, specific;
- trustees;
- trust instrument;
- who is dealing with tax?
- who takes income/capital?
- requirement for inheritance tax returns?

If the deceased owned **real/leasehold property immovable property**, complete this section. [Use additional sheets if necessary.]

Location of property
Location of title deeds
[Obtain originals, always check title from originals, inspect originals if bank/building society will not release.]
Who will prepare valuation? Name
Address
Phone/fax no/email address
Tenure or interest of deceased
Area
Rateable valuation insurance: date of renewal
Value at date of death [*For insertion at page 2*]
Is property subject to: • Life interest? • Right of residence? • Annuity, etc.?
Any: • Mortgage? • Local Government household charge/NPPR charge? • Local Property Tax (please provide LPT ID Number)? • Domestic Water Charge? • Registration of Septic Tank • Mortgage protection policy/endowment policy? • HSE Nursing Home Support Scheme 'Fair Deal charge'? • Equity Release Scheme?
Full details
Date of vesting
Date of sale

General notes re:

- property, boundaries,
- planning permission, etc. [attach map if necessary]

Miscellaneous

Name of accountant	Telephone/fax no
Address	Email
Name of tax adviser	Telephone/fax no
Address	Email

Inspector of Taxes/District no

Address

PPS no

Clearances re taxes of the deceased/personal representative

	Pre-death	Post-death
Income tax		
Capital gains tax		
CAT		
Inheritance tax/Gift tax		
All necessary certificates of clearance/receipts obtained? Yes/No		
Probate tax		
Discretionary trust tax		
NPPR/LPT		
Nursing Home Support Scheme Discharge from both the Revenue and the HSE.		
Social welfare (s 339)		
UK inheritance tax (IHT)		

Civil Status

If deceased was cohabiting with another, complete this section

When did the cohabitation commence?

Did it end within two years of death of deceased?

Were any orders made or applied for under ss 173 to 175 or 187 of the Civil Partnership legislation?

If there are any agreements in place re cohabitation, where are they stored?

If deceased was separated/divorced, complete this section

If deceased separated:

1. Is there a separation agreement in existence? If so, obtain a copy.
2. Was a separation order made by the Irish courts under the 1989/1995 Acts? If so, obtain a copy.

3. What orders (if any) were made by the court under:
    a. s 17 of the Judicial Separation and Family Law Reform Act, 1989?
    b. s 14 of the Family Law Act, 1995?
4. Was notice served on the separated spouse under s 15A of the Family Law Act, 1995?

If deceased divorced:

1. Was deceased divorced in:
   - Ireland?
   - Foreign jurisdiction?
2. Has a copy of the relevant court order been obtained?
3. What order (if any) was made under s 18(10) of the Family Law (Divorce) Act, 1996?

If no order made under s 18(10):

1. Has notice been served on the spouse?
2. Has spouse remarried?

If deceased divorced in foreign jurisdiction:

Has declaration of marital status been sought/obtained?

If deceased was a civil partner, complete this section

Civil partner's name and current address

Date of registration of the civil partnership

Has the civil partnership been dissolved or annulled?

Date of dissolution or annulment of same

Copy of any dissolution or annulment order

Miscellaneous notes re administration

6.6.2 GENERAL NOTES ON COMPLETING THE INSTRUCTION SHEET

The following is a summary of the main benefits of using such a form with annotated notes.

- Vital information about the deceased is available on the first page. This is useful for telephone enquiries and the completion of the Revenue forms.
- PPS numbers of the deceased and all beneficiaries are accessible to you.
- Ascertaining if there is possible CGT liability.
- Includes valuation dates for CAT.
- Appending a copy of the valuation of shares eliminates error in transcription. Sale of shares—gain/loss.
- Notes when any clearance is received from either the Revenue Commissioners and/or Department of Social Protection and/or HSE.
- The use of the instruction sheet allows a third party, unfamiliar with the estate, to quickly familiarise themselves with the file.
- It can be used as a risk management tool.
- It gives details of beneficiaries.

ADMINISTRATION OF ESTATES: PROBATE PRACTICE AND PROCEDURE

- It provides a vital diary when one commences the collection of assets.
- It highlights the existence of trusts and the appropriate clearance for the trustees.
- It records the payment of legacies and the necessary receipts.
- In completing and updating the form, the risk of omitting or excluding any aspect of the estate is reduced.
- The instruction sheet can be altered or extended in any way, depending on the estate.

6.6.2.1 Use of the instruction sheet by reference to the Statement of Affairs (Probate) Form SA.2

One should take instructions by reference to the Statement of Affairs (Probate) Form SA.2. This form is dealt with in greater detail at **6.9**. The form SA.2 was introduced on 14 September 2020 and is to be used for applications for grants of representation to include nominal and secondary *de bonis non* grants where the deceased died on or after 5 December 2001. The form SA.2 lists the personal details of the deceased, details of the beneficiaries receiving a benefit in excess of €12,000 and the value of the benefit taken, and details of all the assets of the deceased as defined in s 10 of the Succession Act. Assets held jointly with other persons and all liabilities owing at the date of death must also be included. Details of assets passing outside the will or intestacy should also be included.

The completion of the particulars required by the form SA.2 and the replies to the questions submitted will solicit all information required for the administration of the estate. No other checklist/instruction sheet is suitable unless it contains the same questions as are in the form SA.2.

Much of the information required for this instruction sheet is just as applicable to completing the form SA.2.

6.6.3 PAGE ONE OF THE INSTRUCTION SHEET AND THE FORM SA.2: DECEASED DETAILS

Personal details of the deceased are required to include their name, last known address (including eircode), personal public service number (PPS), occupation, and the deceased's domicile at death and domicile of origin. It must be indicated if the deceased was resident or ordinary resident in the State at date of death. If the deceased was not resident or ordinary resident in the State at the date of death their country of residence at the date of death must be shown. The date, place, and cause of death; the age at death; and date of birth of the deceased person as appearing on the death certificate are required. Details of the deceased's civil status/marital status must be selected from a number of options presented. Details of the deceased's surviving relatives can be selected by ticking the appropriate check box under each presented category to include the number of surviving children if applicable. Details of remoter relatives (if any) are also required.

6.6.3.1 PPS numbers

The Social Welfare Act, 1998, which came into effect on 5 February 1999, provided for the introduction of Personal Public Service numbers.

These numbers are now traced or allocated only through the Department of Employment and Social Protection and will be required for the deceased and all beneficiaries, whether resident in Ireland or not.

Anyone requiring a PPS number can call in to their nearest Department of Employment and Social Protection local or branch office. They will be required to produce a valid ID, for example, 'long form' birth certificate, passport, and other supporting documentation. See http://www.welfare.ie for details.

When PPS numbers were originally introduced, wives of taxpayers who were not working themselves were issued with their husband's PPS number with a W suffix. This practice was changed shortly afterwards, and Revenue will not accept this number in respect of CAT. In such cases, a new PPS number should be sought from Client Identity Services, Department of Employment and Social Protection, Shannon Lodge, Carrick on Shannon, County Leitrim, directly by telephone at 1890 927999/01 7043281 or email at cis@welfare.i.e.

Where a PPS number is required for a person who is deceased or a beneficiary who is overseas, solicitors or executors can contact Client Identity Services in the Department of Employment and Social Protection. Identity information will be required before numbers will be issued.

It is important to explain at the earliest possible stage to all beneficiaries, to include non-resident beneficiaries, that a PPS number from the Department of Employment and Social Protection in Ireland will have to be issued to them before form SA.2 can be completed. Irish born non-resident beneficiaries may already have a PPS number, which should be investigated. This may be perplexing for foreign national beneficiaries, and it must be explained to them that their own State's national insurance (UK), social security (US), or similar number will not suffice. They should apply for a PPS number to Client Identity Services and this should be done as early as possible in the process to avoid delays in submitting the form SA.2. During 2020, significant delays were being incurred in the provision of PPS numbers for non-national beneficiaries and while this has eased, the importance of applying for an Irish PPS number should be stressed to non-national beneficiaries.

In order to avoid delays in processing the SA.2 inheritance tax returns etc, it is imperative that all PPS numbers are correctly entered on the relevant forms, as the Revenue will return incomplete forms, thus causing delay.

Where a PPS number is not available for a beneficiary of the estate, the form SA.2 contains a facility to allow an applicant to give an undertaking that they will not distribute any property passing under the estate to that beneficiary until the PPS number is provided to the Revenue on an amended form SA.2 return. An undertaking can only be given for one beneficiary per application. To avail of this facility the appropriate box must be ticked to indicate that a PPS number is not available and the screen instructions must be followed. It is recommended that the solicitor for the estate should not give undertakings of this nature unless absolutely necessary and only on the irrevocable authority in writing of the personal representative and the beneficiary. See **Chapter 14**, para **14.1** on undertakings.

6.6.3.2 Death certificate

At an early stage an official copy of the death certificate should be obtained from the local health office in the local health area in which the person died or from the Registrar General in Lombard Street, Dublin 2. It is also possible to apply online at http://www.certificates.ie for copies of the death certificate.

Since 2007, the hospice, hospital, GP, or nursing home, etc *does not* automatically register a death. Quite often the personal representative will have a medical certificate showing cause of death but may not have registered this as yet. Ensure that the next of kin, or the relevant informant (where no next of kin is available), registers the death at the earliest possible opportunity by completing a death notification form and presenting same at any Civil Registration Office. This should be done within three months of death (s 37 of the Civil Registration Act, 2004). We as practitioners cannot apply for the death certificate. Further useful information on the death certificate is available online at http://www.hse.ie/eng/services/list/1/bdm/registeradeath/.

On receipt of the death certificate, it is important to make sure that the details on it are correct. The death certificate contains the following: deceased's name, date and place of death, civil status, occupation, age at last birthday, cause of death, name and address of person who registered the death. It is not unknown for the deceased's name, date of death, or other information on the certificate to be incorrect. If any amendments are necessary, these should be dealt with at once. See also para **7.4.1** in this regard. The issue of a death certificate may be delayed, for example, where an inquest is pending.

It is also not unusual for a person to be known by a number of names, all of which will have to be covered in the form SA.2 as well as in all probate papers.

ADMINISTRATION OF ESTATES: PROBATE PRACTICE AND PROCEDURE

Check the place of death and cause of death. If the place of death is a mental institution or if one of the causes of death listed is a mental illness, an affidavit of mental capacity will be required.

6.6.3.3 Relatives surviving

The names, addresses, PPS numbers, and ages (if under eighteen) of all relatives who have survived the deceased should be collated at this early stage. Also of crucial importance is their relationship to the deceased and any benefits accruing. In particular, if the deceased was married or a civil partner, check whether the surviving spouse/civil partner is the legal spouse/civil partner—check the marriage/civil partnership certificate. If there is a surviving spouse/civil partner, check whether he or she has a will, and if so advise that a new will may be necessary and should be attended to immediately.

Where there is a spouse/civil partner and/or children, the solicitor must consider s 121 of the Succession Act. Did the deceased make any disposal within three years of death that may be challenged under s 121? See para **4.5.11**.

If any of the beneficiaries is/are minor, careful consideration should be given to the consequences. See paras **3.8.1.4** and **4.5.10**.

Are there any issue of a predeceased child who may derive a benefit under s 67(2) (1) the *per stirpes* rule? In addition, careful consideration should be given to the consequences of s 98 which is one of the exceptions to the doctrine of lapse as outlined in s 91 For further detail on the effects of s 98, see para **4.6.3.3** and for further details of its taxation implications, see CAT Lecture Notes (see Preface).

6.6.3.4 Domicile at death

Where the domicile of the testator is in doubt, the Revenue Commissioners may place the onus on the executors to establish the domicile of the testator. A person may be resident in more than one country but, generally, at any given time can only be domiciled in one. When an individual is born, they acquire a domicile of origin, and this remains with them throughout their life unless it is replaced by a domicile of choice. A person may acquire a domicile of choice where they move to another country with the intention of residing there permanently. If a domicile of choice lapses as a result of permanently leaving the country in which the domicile of choice exists, the domicile of origin is reactivated until replaced by another domicile of choice.

In *Revenue Commissioners v Matthews, Exham and Clarke* (1954) 92 ILTR 44 it was held that when the principles of law relating to domicile are not in dispute, the issue involves their application to the special facts of the case, and the correct inference to be drawn from the facts. The question of domicile becomes a question of fact. The only real difference in law between the two cases of acquiring a domicile of choice and holding domicile of origin in abeyance on the other hand, is that less evidence is required to establish the act of abandoning the domicile of choice than is required to demonstrate the acquisition of a domicile of choice.

It is important to take full instructions and ensure that the answer provided is in accordance with the stance the deceased had already taken with the Revenue Commissioners. Where a domicile of the deceased other than Ireland is claimed, full supporting documentation will be required.

See also CAT Lecture Notes (see Preface).

6.6.3.5 Social welfare claim number

If the deceased was a recipient of any social welfare (non-contributory) payment, the Department of Employment Affairs and Social Protection, College Road, Sligo, F91 T384 should be advised of the death. It must be informed prior to the proposed distribution of the estate. (This must be done at least three months prior to distribution.) See **Chapter 14** for further details.

6.6.3.6 Date of grant etc.

This information can be inserted as the administration progresses.

6.6.3.7 Did the deceased leave will: executors, location, date?

Where the deceased left a validly executed will and there is/are executor(s) willing to act, the grant of representation required is a grant of probate and the following section (testate) is completed.

6.6.4 EXECUTORS/ADMINISTRATORS

The information required regarding executors/administrators (executrix/administratrix if female) should be readily attainable.

If there is no will or there is no executor willing or able (or alive) to act, then it is necessary to ascertain who is entitled under the Succession Act to administer the estate. For cases where there is no will (intestacy), s 27(3) and O 79, r 5(1) set out the order of entitlement to extract such a grant on intestacy. Intestacy is dealt with in detail in **Chapter 8**.

For cases where there is a will but no executor available, the appropriate grant of representation is a grant of administration with will annexed. Section 27(3) and O 79, r 5(6) set out the order of entitlement to extract such a grant. Grants of administration with will annexed are dealt with in **Chapter 9**.

6.6.5 (IRISH ASSETS) COVER SCREEN

In the assets cover screen of the form SA.2, details of all property passing through the estate, whether under the deceased's will or on intestacy, and all property passing outside the estate by survivorship or nomination should be entered. Details of the following assets should be included, all of which are dealt with below in greater detail to include: property in the State (houses apartments, lands buildings, etc), bank/building society accounts, credit union/An Post accounts, cash, household contents, cars/boats, insurance policy/mortgage protection policy/annuity, superannuation/capital sum or ex gratia payments, agricultural assets/business assets, stocks/shares/securities, dividends, debts owing to the deceased, unpaid purchase money of property contracted to be sold in the deceased's lifetime, and other assets (any asset not covered under the above headings).

On selecting a 'property type' and selecting 'next' the applicant will be brought to an 'asset detail' screen to enter the full details of the property. Where there are two or more properties within the same category the applicant should be able to select 'add property' to enter the full details of any additional properties. It is worthwhile dealing with each asset and type of asset individually.

6.6.5.1 Bank and building society accounts

Most people have a bank and/or building society account and dealing with these is relatively straightforward. The personal representative should be able to supply details of the financial institutions where the deceased banked, together with the appropriate branch, the BIC and IBAN number of the account. The applicant should indicate if IT8 clearance is required for account clearance if applicable.

Armed with this information, it is necessary to write to the Bereavement/Deceased Support Section of each financial institution, requesting the following information:

- A certificate of the balance standing to the credit (or debit if overdrawn) of each account as of the date of death.

- A certificate of interest on any interest-bearing account from the date of commencement of the last tax year to the date of death.

ADMINISTRATION OF ESTATES: PROBATE PRACTICE AND PROCEDURE

- A certificate of interest due and unpaid on any loan/overdraft account from date of commencement of last tax year to date of death.

- Confirmation as to how the account was held i.e. solely by the deceased or jointly with others.

- Confirmation that the institution does not hold any items for safekeeping for the deceased. If so, inspect immediately. It is important to locate the receipt provided for any such items.

Should there be a large amount of money to credit in a current account, this should be transferred to a deposit account, so that it may earn interest pending completion of administration.

The letter should also request the appropriate withdrawal forms/application for repayment forms from both bank and building society, so that when the grant is available, completed forms and the grant can be sent to the institutions for a speedy withdrawal. It should have been confirmed with the client whether all sums should be payable to the solicitors or to the executor personally. Opinions vary, but as the solicitor has to provide an account to beneficiaries for all sums received and paid out (see para **17.6**) it is often more appropriate, particularly where large sums are involved, that the solicitor control the accounts as they are paid in. In that case, the written authority of the personal representative will be necessary, and this authority is usually contained in the repayment form. In practice the funds are electronically transferred to the estate solicitor's client account. See para **6.8.3**.

Joint accounts will be dealt with specifically at para **6.6.7**.

6.6.5.2 Ireland State Savings/Post Office savings accounts/savings certificates/index-linked bonds

Similarly, once the assets are identified, a letter should be sent to An Post, seeking details, particularly of the current value of the various assets held (as these will differ from the face value of certificates held by the deceased). Similarly, encashment forms should be requested at this stage.

It should be noted that whilst 'State Savings' is a brand name used by the NTMA (National Treasury Management Agency) to describe the range of savings products they offer to personal savers, An Post acts as their agents in relation to the sale and administration of these products. NTMA do not administer these State savings products and solicitors should not address any correspondence to them.

One very important point when dealing with savings certificates is nominations. A valid nomination will pass the savings certificates outside the terms of the will. Funds nominated under the Savings Certificates Rules provide that a person aged sixteen and upwards and holding a certificate may nominate any person to receive any sum payable in respect of a certificate due to such holder on his demise. See 'Nominations' at para **6.9.6.2**.

6.6.5.3 Prize bonds

A surprising number of people hold prize bonds, which are entitled to be included in draws for a period of twelve years post-death. They can be included at face value but it is best practice to write to FEXCO DAC (State Savings, Prize Bond, Fexco Centre, Killorglin V93 WN9T, Co Kerry), enclosing proof of death, to confirm the correct amount of prize bonds and to obtain the appropriate encashment or transfer form.

6.6.5.4 Credit unions

Many credit unions operate a form of life savings insurance which can lead to a multiple of the amount saved being paid to the estate on the death of the credit union member.

Under s 21 of the Credit Union Act, 1997, as amended by the Credit Union Act, 1997 (Alteration of Financial Limits) Regulations, 2006 (SI 546/2006), a member of a credit union can nominate up to the limit of €23,000 from his savings/shareholding and this nomination will pass outside the terms of the will. Again, see 'Nominations' at para **6.9.6.2**. It is important to establish if any person benefited under a nomination at any time made by the deceased. It is also important to obtain details of all credit union accounts to include the name and address of the Credit Union, IBAN or member number of the account, and details of how the title was held i.e. solely by the deceased or jointly with others. It should also be indicated if IT8 clearance is required for the account.

6.6.5.5 Cash assets/cash in house

Any cash assets need to be accounted for, and these may include large sums of cash in the house, foreign currency, and/or uncashed traveller's cheques. Foreign currency should be valued at the exchange rate as at the date of death. Consideration should be given to changing the foreign currency immediately.

In some rare cases, securities in the form of bearer securities may be present. These are securities payable to the bearer and are treated as being in the nature of cash. No formal transmission is needed on death to transfer to the personal representative and the documentation evidencing the bearer security should be kept very securely.

Any 'cash' of this nature should be lodged to the executor's account as soon as practicable. The opening of an executor's account will be dealt with at para **6.8.3**.

6.6.5.6 Household contents

In many cases, household contents will be the normal everyday household chattels (as defined in s 56(14) of the Succession Act) and will often be the subject of a bequest, along with the devise of the house in the will. Difficulties can arise where there are valuable items in the house which have not been adequately defined, for example, paintings, jewellery, and antiques.

Where any household contents are to be sold, an accurate valuation of them should be obtained as early as possible. In any event, if they pass under the will they should be valued, as they are an asset of the estate. The formality of the valuation will depend on the value of the item.

6.6.5.7 Car

One very important point that can be overlooked with a car is insurance. If the insurance policy was in the name of the deceased only and a spouse/civil partner and/or children were 'named drivers' under that policy, the policy will lapse on the death of the deceased. Therefore, it is crucial that insurance be obtained for the car immediately. If the car is to be sold or transferred under the terms of the will, it should be valued accurately, the insurance cancelled, and any refund lodged to the executor's account.

6.6.5.8 Real/leasehold property

In most estates this is the single largest asset, if not the primary asset. As with the car, insurance is critical. The property should be insured for its full reinstatement value and the insurance company should be informed of whether the house is occupied or not. If not, then only fire insurance will be available. Any valuable contents should be removed from the house for safekeeping elsewhere. Alternatively, some form of caretaker's arrangement can be entered into, but the instructions of the personal representative should be taken on this matter.

Details of all Irish property (Lands and Buildings) both real and leasehold under the following options must be included in the form SA.2:

1. The property type i.e. residential, agricultural, development land, commercial property, single site, industrial property, offices, leased property, retail property.

2. The address of the property including eircode and the Folio number of the property. If the property is unregistered freehold or leasehold, type 'none' under the query requiring a Folio number.

ADMINISTRATION OF ESTATES: PROBATE PRACTICE AND PROCEDURE

3. The value of the property at the date of death.

4. The tenure of the property whether freehold or leasehold. If leasehold the date of the lease and the length of term must be included.

5. Details of how the property was held i.e. solely by the deceased, joint tenancy, or a tenancy in common.

It is worth noting the terms of s 10 of the Succession Act:

> '[T]he real and personal estate of a deceased person shall on his death, notwithstanding any testamentary disposition, devolve on and become vested in his personal representatives.'

First, any real and leasehold (personal) property of the deceased needs to be accurately identified, preferably by means of examination of title and by comparison of title to the actual property. It is often the case, particularly with properties passed down through families, that the property may not be registered in the name of the deceased at all.

It is also essential to check whether there are any disputes in relation to the property. In consulting a professional adviser, ensure that they are informed of the extent of the deceased's interest in the property. It may be that the deceased had given rights to others, for example, right of residence; if so, this should be taken into account. If the property was held jointly by the deceased with another, the property may pass by survivorship outside the terms of the will. See 'Joint property' at para **6.6.7**. Should the property be subject to a mortgage or charge including a charge in favour of the Health Service Executive (HSE), one should be aware of the implications of s 47 of the Succession Act and of any contrary intention appearing in the will, as dealt with at para **2.7.6**.

The valuation of any property must be the open market value as at the date of death and copy valuations should be obtained. Where there is more than one property, they should be valued separately. Where the grant is by way of letters of administration with will annexed/grant of administration (intestate) or a *de bonis non* grant, it will be necessary to obtain an auctioneer's letter of current market value of the property where the application for the grant of representation is lodged more than one year from the date of death. However, if the papers are lodged within twelve months of the date of death, no proof of current market value is required; this will be dealt with in **Chapter 8**.

It is strongly recommended that reputable, professional valuers are engaged, as there are severe penalties and potential capital gains tax implications for undervaluation. See CAT Lecture Notes (see Preface).

If the property comprises a wind or solar farm or contains trees/underwood, a specialist will be required for these.

6.6.5.9 Stocks/shares/securities quoted

Dealing with stocks and shares can be problematic and there are a number of issues to be considered. In this section of the SA.2 (asset detail screen) details of all quoted stocks, shares in Corporate Bodies registered in the State, and securities held in Ireland must be included.

Engage a firm of stockbrokers

One should never attempt to value shares, but should instead always engage a stockbroker, possibly the stockbroker that the deceased engaged. It is essential to have full details of the deceased's entire shareholdings and confirmation that all the relevant share certificates are available. If in doubt about any shareholding, the most recent dividend counterfoil should provide details of the number and designation of shares. If this is not available, consult the stockbroker who is preparing the valuation or contact the Company Registrar directly, in order to clarify details of each holding.

The actual value of the stocks and shares is the price at which they can be sold on the Stock Exchange. If one reads the *Financial Times*, one normally finds two prices for any given day: a minimum and a maximum. This is because the price of the share may vary during the course of the day.

The value to be inserted here and later in the form SA.2 is one-quarter up from the minimum to the maximum. However, as noted, it is advisable to have a firm of stockbrokers give a proper valuation. Most stockbroker firms will provide the valuation in a format appropriate to the form SA.2.

Interest on securities

It is important to note also that interest is paid on securities of stocks and shares by means of dividend warrants. There is one case in which a dividend should be included, even though it has not been paid, and that is where a security is quoted *ex-dividend*.

Stocks and shares are quoted either *cum dividend* or *ex-dividend*. Where they are quoted *cum dividend*, it means that if you buy you are entitled to receive the next dividend paid by the company. Where they are quoted *ex-dividend* the person selling the share is entitled to the dividend. Quite often the deceased may have held a number of shares in different companies. Once details of the various holdings are obtained it is useful to record details on a separate sheet. It is also useful to record the number of shares held by the deceased with each company and the value as at the date of death for insertion in the form SA.2.

When you have received the valuation from the stockbrokers, they will state whether any of the quotations are *ex-dividend* and, if they are, they will send particulars of any dividend declared but not yet paid. The whole of this dividend must be included in the form less income tax at the current rate.

Dealing with the shares

Where there are UK shares it may be necessary to extract a UK grant of representation. Where there are UK shares it may be necessary to extract a grant of representation in England and Wales or in Northern Ireland or a grant of confirmation in Scotland. This grant cannot issue until after the Irish grant has issued. On the issue of the Irish grant, the duty of the personal representative is to encash or transfer those shares, depending on the contents of the will. It is not their duty to 'play the market' in the hope that the shares will increase in value. This will be dealt with at para **6.7.2**.

Stock transfer forms will be required when dealing with any such holding and should be requested from the Registrar when enquiring as to the nature and extent of the shareholding. If shares are to be sold it is helpful to record the sale price or the value at the date of transfer *in specie*. It is of vital importance that all contract notes are retained where shares are sold in the event of a capital gains tax implication on a sale of shares during the administration. These can be useful as an indication as to whether there has been a capital gain or loss. Obviously, more detailed figures will be required for capital gains tax computation, but this helps to identify the fact of a gain or loss. Again, if selling shares through a firm of stockbrokers all the relevant information will be provided in the appropriate format.

UK shares (small UK estates)

The UK inheritance tax threshold currently stands at £325,000 for an individual and £650,000 for a couple for the UK tax year 2020/21 and the rate of tax is 40 per cent. A main residence nil rate band was introduced in 2017 and gives those who pass on a main residence to their children an extra £175,000 (since April 2020) tax free (in addition to the £325,000 that can be passed on tax free). As noted earlier, it may not be necessary to extract a UK grant (for the purposes of this short note, we refer to a 'UK grant'; however, practitioners should be aware that the UK comprises four separate jurisdictions: England and Wales, Scotland, Northern Ireland, and the Isle of Man) to deal with shares if they are the only UK asset and are under this threshold.

There is a procedure for dealing with small quantities of UK shares; however, it is limited, and practice varies from registrar to registrar. See para **12.3.5.4** for further details on dealing with small estates. The most frequently used registrars are Computershare, Equiniti, and Capita IRG. Computershare deals with Vodafone shares, which are the most commonly held UK shares. They are also the easiest registrars to deal with as they will recognise Irish grants accompanied by a specific small shares declaration/affidavit.

Government stock

Some of the deceased's holdings of stock may be in the form of government stock. If so, there are certain tax avoidance considerations that may be of assistance. The CAT Lecture Notes (see Preface) give further details.

6.6.5.10 Insurance policies

Details of insurance policies need to be examined very carefully. Contact should be made with the relevant insurance companies to ensure that all the facts, especially the value of the policy and the beneficial ownership of the policy, are to hand. Any insurance policy or a copy thereof should be sent to the insurance company which issued the policy, together with the premium receipt book, if applicable, and death certificate. The company should be requested to furnish a valuation of the policy at date of death, together with the— appropriate claim form for completion by the personal representative.

In particular, the single most important issue is beneficial ownership of the policy. An insurance policy taken out by and paid for by the deceased may not necessarily fall into the estate. Examples of such policies are 'key man' policies taken out by individuals to benefit business partners. Similarly, the policy may be for the benefit of a family member or such other person as the deceased may wish to provide for. There are CAT considerations when dealing with these policies. Conversely, somebody else may have had an insurance policy taken out on the life of the deceased and for which they paid the premiums. This policy will not form part of the estate. There will not be a CAT liability on such a premium. These are currently used where co-owners of property who are not married to each other insure each other's lives in order to have sufficient money to pay any CAT liability arising on the death of one of the co-owners.

Section 72/73 Life Assurance policies

Section 72/73 life policies are insurance policies taken out under s 72 or 73 of the Capital Acquisitions Tax Consolidation Act, 2003 (formerly and popularly known as 'section 60 policies' as they were introduced by s 60 of the Finance Act, 1985) and are used specifically to pay any CAT or other taxation liability arising on death (s 72) or by an *inter vivos* transfer (s 73). Section 72 and 73 provide for an exemption from Capital Acquisitions Tax in respect of the proceeds of qualifying policies where certain conditions are met. Any value in a section 72/73 policy that is over the value of the tax due on an inheritance should be recorded as an additional benefit for the beneficiary in the form SA.2.

A policy must meet the following conditions to be a 'qualifying insurance policy':

1. it must be in a form approved by the Revenue and specifically taken out to insure against CAT;
2. the annual premiums should be paid by the insured person; and
3. it must be taken out under ss 72 or 73 CATCA 2003 to pay 'relevant tax' (such as inheritance or gift tax and payable in respect of a benefit taken from the insured person).

The proceeds of a section 72 policy must be taken on or after the death of the insured person and not later than one year after the death. Any proceeds of a section 72 or 73 policy that are not used to pay relevant tax are subject to CAT as an additional inheritance or gift. They are less popular now than in previous years but are still an issue. Please see CAT Lecture Notes (see Preface) for further details.

6.6.5.11 Pensions

A number of matters arise under the heading of pensions. Any pension belonging to the deceased is usually a valuable asset in the estate if pension rights survive on death. It is necessary to check if the entitlement to the pension died with the deceased or whether the surviving spouse/civil partner and/or children are entitled to any benefits on death. A copy of the pension scheme will have to be reviewed, and where necessary the details need to be clarified with the pension company.

The deceased may have been in receipt of a pension that was underwritten in trust and may have nominated beneficiaries of this policy during his lifetime. The pension company may have full discretion as to the payee. It is normally the surviving spouse/civil partner and/or dependent children. The pension may not be an asset in the estate. In this scenario it is important to ascertain whether the pension falls into or out of an estate. Pensions will be dealt with in greater detail at para **6.9.6.3**, when dealing with completing the Statement of Affairs (Probate).

Civil/public service gratuities

Death gratuities of serving civil servants and arrears of pensions of retired civil servants are payable from the Pay-Master General's Office on production of a grant of probate/administration. Details of any amount payable should be ascertained at this stage. It is worth noting that if the amount payable is under a certain figure and it was not necessary to extract a grant of probate, the amount will be paid on completion of a statutory declaration giving particulars of death, next of kin, etc. Payment is made by way of warrant to be signed on the face by the payee.

It is also worth noting that various branches of the Public Service, for example, the Garda, have their own organisation/union, which may make a payment on the death of the deceased member. Some of these payments are payable directly to next of kin, while others are paid to an executor/administrator. Enquiries as to the requirements for obtaining the payment should be made to the association/organisation/union concerned.

6.6.5.12 Bereavement grant

The bereavement grant of €850 from the Department of Social Protection was payable where the deceased or his spouse was an insured person. It was abolished on 15 October 2013 for deaths on or after 1 January 2014. The bereavement grant was payable to the person who paid the funeral expenses.

6.6.5.13 Health insurance or other medical entitlements

Issues that arise under this heading are the cancellation of the health insurance premium and receiving an apportioned refund.

If the deceased was discharging significant medical bills, these may be set off against income tax for that year and a form MED 1 will need to be completed. This could be done by the accountant acting in the estate, if there is one. Where the deceased had not completed the MED 1 form(s) for previous years, this can now be done when finalising the income tax affairs of the deceased.

6.6.6 FOREIGN ASSETS AND DEBTS OF THE ESTATE

Foreign assets usually fall into two types: UK shares and/or immovable property abroad. It is necessary to establish the extent and location of the foreign assets and, where necessary, their value in euro. In all cases the relevant rate of exchange is that as at the date of death. It will also be necessary to establish whether the deceased made a will in any other jurisdiction and, if so, to obtain a copy of the will (and a certified translation if necessary). There may be taxation considerations for having property in another jurisdiction. For practical purposes, it will be necessary to check requirements to have the assets released, particularly if a foreign grant is necessary. For UK grants it should be noted that date of birth is required. An Irish birth certificate may also be needed if the date of birth is not included in the Irish death certificate. Previously the Irish death certificates gave age at death, but not date of birth, which would not be accepted by the UK Probate Office. The current form of death certificate includes date of birth.

Details of all assets which the deceased owned outside the State are included in the form SA.2 to include:

1. The type of property/asset.
2. The location of the asset.
3. Details of how the property was held i.e. solely by the deceased, in a joint tenancy or under a tenancy in common.
4. The value of the asset in Euro at the date of death of the deceased.
5. All foreign debts and the location of the debts to include amounts owed by the deceased to persons or other bodies outside the State, debts contracted to be paid outside the State, and any funeral expense payable outside the State.

It is important to note that where a grant of administration is necessary, the value of the foreign assets will not be included in the gross value of the estate in the oath or bond, as the Probate Office does not have any responsibility for foreign assets.

6.6.6.1 Debts of the estate

At this early stage, it is important to ascertain all pre-death debts owed by the deceased. These will include outstanding utilities, credit card bills, store card bills, loans and mortgages, etc. All debts should be established and where a doubt exists as to any potential debts, it is possible to publish a 's 49 notice', which will be discussed in more detail in **Chapter 12**. If the deceased was the holder of any credit cards or store cards, one should consider discharging all sums due immediately, as these attract a higher rate of interest. Where there is a mortgage on the property, first check if there is a mortgage protection policy in place and whether the proceeds are sufficient to pay the mortgage. Also check whether there is a specific direction in the will as to whether the mortgage is to be paid out of the residue or whether the property is taken subject to the mortgage (s 47 Succession of the Act).

The following is a list of the possible categories of debts to be included in the form SA.2:

1. tax owing to the Revenue;
2. creditors;
3. funeral expenses payable in the State;
4. utilities (total amount);
5. amounts owing to financial institutions;
6. personal loans owing by the deceased;
7. mortgage owing (that has not been met by way of mortgage protection policy or other arrangement);
8. fair deal/nursing home fee; and
9. other debts or liabilities at the date of death.

With the exception of funeral expenses, no other costs arising after the date of death may be deducted.

6.6.7 JOINT PROPERTY

A major distinction has to be made between property held in joint names (i.e. real or leasehold property) and property held by way of a joint deposit. In most cases joint property passes by survivorship outside the terms of the will and thus does not technically form part of the deceased's estate. Where immovable property is concerned, this is almost always the case unless the deed creating the joint tenancy states otherwise. Where joint accounts are concerned, the presumption of advancement must be borne in mind.

The form SA.2 contains a reminder to the effect that that where money or other property in joint names was provided by the deceased this may, depending on the actual or legally presumed intention, have given rise to resulting trust in the deceased's favour. Questions are raised, such as, 'What was the purpose of putting the property into joint names?', 'By whom was the property provided?', 'How was the income from the property dealt with or enjoyed?' Based on the replies received to these questions the property may or may not form part of the deceased's estate. However, the value of the benefit passing may be taxable.

In addition, the form SA.2 contains a facility for requesting IT8 clearance for jointly held bank or other accounts. This is dealt with at **6.3.1** and **6.6.7.6**.

6.6.7.1 Presumption of advancement

The relationship between the account holders may be such as to give rise to a presumption of advancement. In other words, where property is transferred into joint names by a sole account holder, the relationship of the joint account holders may be such as to give rise to the presumption of advancement—the transaction being treated as an intention to make a gift unless it can be shown that the original joint tenant intended otherwise. If a presumption of advancement is established this may negative the imposition of a resulting trust in favour of the estate of the deceased and the surviving account holder may become entitled to the proceeds of the account.

The relationships that can give rise to a presumption of advancement are limited to the following:

- husband transferring property to a wife;
- father transferring property to a child;
- widowed mother transferring property to a child.

The presumption of advancement does not apply in respect of a transfer of property from a wife to husband, nor does it apply to a transfer of property from a mother to a child.

The form SA.2 requires the applicant to indicate whether the property is held jointly or as a tenancy in common.

6.6.7.2 Cohabiting couples

Where cohabiting couples hold property jointly and there is no presumption of advancement, the presumption of a resulting trust can arise. The presumption of a resulting trust is rebuttable, based on the facts available. The legal status of certain 'qualified' cohabiting couples has been altered by the civil partnership legislation and practitioners are referred to para **4.7**. It should be definitely ascertained whether such a qualified cohabitation was in existence at the date of or within two years of the death and any court order or cohabitation agreement should be sought and perused carefully.

It is to be hoped that at the time the property was purchased or at the will instruction stage, full records have been kept as to the intention of the parties. Also of significance will be the payments made by the respective parties towards the purchase of the property.

Where there has been a partial contribution to the purchase or acquisition by the survivor, the value for inheritance tax purposes can be difficult to quantify. The Finance (No 3) Act, 2011 deals with the taxation of civil partners and qualified cohabitants, and practitioners should make themselves aware of its provisions. See CAT Lecture Notes (see Preface). Prior to the introduction of family law legislation dealing with the division of assets, there were cases involving the ownership of the family home where one spouse purchased it, and where indirect contributions were made by the other spouse. These cases are still relevant to cohabiting couples: see the case of *Lynch v Butterly* (unreported) 26 July 1996, High Court. This case deals with cohabitees and the division of property. As noted, the civil partnership legislation provides some measure of redress for a surviving cohabitee outside the traditional framework.

6.6.7.3 Taxation and joint tenancies

Taxation consequences will arise on the passing of property by survivorship. The taxation of a joint interest is contained in s 13 of the Capital Acquisitions Tax Consolidation Act, 2003, as outlined in the CAT Lecture Notes (see Preface). Where property is in joint names, but the survivor did not provide his own original one-half share, the question of gift tax on the original purchase or transfer can arise, or the beneficiary can be deemed to receive an inheritance of the entire property on death.

One should alert the personal representative and also the beneficiary involved to this. A major inheritance tax relief for cohabiting couples is available under s 86 of the Capital Acquisitions Tax Consolidation Act, 2003, which provides for a 'dwellinghouse exemption' as outlined in the CAT Lecture Notes (see Preface). Again, the taxation considerations for civil partners and qualified cohabitants must be considered. While civil partners have the same tax status as a spouse of the deceased, a cohabitant (qualifying or otherwise) has a Group (C) threshold for CAT purposes. There is an exemption where a court order makes an award to a qualifying cohabitant out of the estate of the deceased cohabitant.

6.6.7.4 Disputes over the joint tenancy

A joint tenancy can be severed during the lifetime of the joint tenants. Should a dispute arise, evidence of the severance and the circumstances surrounding it will be required.

The testator may have sought to avoid the provisions of s 121 of the Succession Act, 1965 by placing property in the joint names of himself and another. The legislation specifically refers to joint tenancies in s 121(9) and deems the accrual by survivorship to be a vesting of the beneficial ownership.

6.6.7.5 Joint accounts

Where a bank account is in joint names, full details of same must be disclosed. As discussed when dealing with real or leasehold property, the presumption of advancement or the presumption of resulting trust may arise. In each case the presumption may be rebuttable based on the facts.

On the death of the original joint account holder, it is extremely important that the true intention for the opening of any joint account is ascertained.

Where a joint account is held under a joint tenancy in a financial institution the intention of the parties on opening or placing the account in joint names will determine whether the funds in the account should pass to the surviving joint holder or form part of the deceased's estate.

A solicitor who is advising in the administration of an estate should make sure that full enquiries are made and that there is no attempt either to facilitate fraud or frustrate the wishes of the deceased joint account holder.

Following the decision in *Lynch v Burke and Allied Irish Banks Plc* [1996] 1 ILRM 114 (see below) it is important to establish the intention of the deceased when opening the joint account.

Is it a joint account for the original owner's benefit only?

- Is it a joint account where there is an intention that both parties should enjoy the benefit of the joint account, i.e. to confer a gift on the joint account holder either at the date of the opening of the account or on the death of the original account holder?

- If the account is placed in the joint names by a husband with his wife or by a father to his child, is the intention to make a gift to the wife or child?

If there is no clear evidence of intention to make a gift to the surviving joint account holder then the equitable principle of the presumption of a resulting trust will apply. If there is an argument to the contrary, then the onus of rebutting the presumption of a resulting trust lies with the surviving joint account holder.

Frequently a joint account holder converts an account into a joint bank account for their convenience. This often arises where the original account holder is suffering from physical incapacity due to old age and infirmity. They convert an existing account in their sole name to a joint bank account solely so that the other account holder can carry out transactions such as lodgements and the payment of bills on their behalf. In this case, on the original account holder's death, the joint account results back to his estate. Care must be taken when dealing with these situations.

Where the presumption of advancement is successfully rebutted, it is only the amount paid into the account by the deceased himself which will be included. In some cases, it is impossible to discover how much was paid into the account by (for example) the husband and how much by the wife. In that scenario, it is best to put down half the total amount in the bank account at the date of death.

The effect of case law and in particular *Lynch v Burke and Allied Irish Banks Plc* [1996] 1 ILRM 114, O'Flaherty J, radically changed the law pertaining to joint deposits. One now should look at the contractual relationship of the parties with the bank. Each case has to be considered on the facts.

For example, accounts may have been placed in joint names for the payment of utilities by the joint account holder on behalf of the other joint account holder, who originally held the account solely for their lifetime with an understanding that whatever balance would form part of the estate of the original sole holder on his or her death. O'Flaherty J concentrated on the legal effect of the opening of deposit accounts in joint names. He emphasised that by the joint account holder's presence and signature it was manifest that she was party to the contract. He further stated that since the deceased and the joint holder contracted jointly with the bank, it would seem right that the bank should be liable to both, in accordance with the terms of the contract. There was sufficient mutuality of interest between the deceased and the surviving joint account holder to justify this assessment of the legal situation.

O'Flaherty J laid significant emphasis on the contractual aspects of the case and summarised that the surviving joint account holder must be regarded as entitled to claim as a party to the contract under the actual terms of the contract. He relied, *inter alia*, on the case of *McEvoy v Belfast Banking Corporation* [1934] NI 67 and the Australian case *Russell v Scott* (1936) 55 CLR 440.

O'Flaherty J believed that at law the niece (the surviving account holder) had a legal interest in the money on deposit either by reason of the contractual relationship of the parties or in the alternative as a gift (which admittedly was not a completed gift in the conventional sense, but one nevertheless that should be upheld as being a gift subject to a contingency): the death should not disqualify it from being a proper gift.

In this case, both the High Court judge (O'Hanlon J) and the Supreme Court judge stated that there could be no other interpretation of the deceased joint bank account holder's intention but that she intended the surviving joint account holder to succeed to the estate. This is the standard of proof required when hoping to rely on *Lynch v Burke*.

Banks and building societies may not have full records of the 'intention' of the deceased in placing deposits in joint names. There should be a 'Personal Joint Account Mandate' completed by all parties. In the case of dispute, this may be difficult to establish. To establish the contractual relationship between the depositors and the financial institution, as envisaged by *Lynch v Burke*, will not be straightforward, especially if there is a lack of clarity about the contractual relationship or otherwise of the joint deposit holders to each other. It is to be hoped that this would have been fully considered at the will preparation stage and that an attendance is in existence. See para **2.7.9**.

6.6.7.6 Requesting IT8 clearance for jointly held bank or other accounts

Financial institutions are prohibited by law from releasing funds from joint accounts in excess of €50,000 without an IT8 letter of clearance. This does not apply to accounts held jointly with a surviving spouse or civil partner. On entering details of any jointly held bank, building society, credit union, or An Post account the form SA.2 presents the option to request IT8 clearance for the account(s). On successful submission of the form SA.2 the

Revenue will correspond directly with the applicant regarding any requests for IT8 clearance. Where a joint holder of an account wishes to personally request IT8 clearance, they may do so by submitting a paper form CA4 to the National Capital Acquisitions Tax (CAT) Unit.

6.6.8 BENEFICIARIES DETAILS

For both your instruction form and for the SA.2, the information required in relation to each beneficiary is their names, addresses including PPS numbers, their dates of birth, their relationships to the deceased, the applicable threshold applying to the inheritance, and details of the current benefit to be received. Details of any 'assigned' benefits i.e. benefits passing by survivorship or nomination should be included. Details of all prior benefits taken by each beneficiary from any source since 5 December 1991 must also be provided.

Much of this information will have been gathered under the heading of 'relatives surviving', but beneficiaries who are not relatives will be included here. Their residence status is also required and it must be indicated whether they are resident or ordinarily resident in the State.

Spouses or civil partners are not listed as beneficiaries in the beneficiaries section of the form SA.2. If there are assets held jointly by the deceased and their surviving spouse/civil partner, these are not listed in the assets section of the form SA.2.

Three questions are posed in the form SA.2 under the 'beneficiary details' section. Beneficiary's details must be provided where their current benefit exceeds €12,000 excluding benefits taken by a spouse or civil partner.

The three questions posed are as follows:

1. The spouse/civil partner is the sole beneficiary. Yes/no.
2. All the beneficiaries' benefits are less than €12,000. Yes/no.
3. The full estate has been donated to charity. Yes/No.

If the answer to any of the above three questions is 'yes' the beneficiary details are not required and the applicant can then proceed to the 'asset cover' section of the form SA.2.

Where there is a charitable bequest in the will, the charity is not listed as a beneficiary in the beneficiary section of the form SA.2. Instead, in the mandatory questionnaire section an additional question has been added as follows:

Was a charitable donation bequeathed under the will of the deceased person?

If the answer provided is 'yes' the following details are required:

1. the name and address of the charity;
2. the charity registration number (if applicable); and
3. the value of the donation for distribution.

Also contained in the instruction sheet are the date of payment to the beneficiary and any payment of CAT on behalf of a non-resident beneficiary, which details will be available in the course of the administration.

See precedent letter to beneficiaries and letter for completion and return by beneficiaries at para **6.8.4.2** and Part 8 Summary of Benefits at para **6.9.7**.

6.6.9 TRUSTS

6.6.9.1 Where the deceased was a life tenant of a trust

If the deceased was a life tenant of any trust, one should obtain the trust instrument at this stage, and details of the beneficiaries who will now benefit on the life tenant's death. It is also important to identify the trust assets clearly. Practitioners should note that there is a particular requirement to lodge returns with the Revenue Commissioners within four months of the date of death of a life tenant. See CAT Lecture Notes (see Preface) for more details.

6.6.9.2 Trusts created by the will

Identify any trust created in the will and the identity of the trustees. Check that all the trustees are still alive. Check the class of beneficiaries and the assets to be placed in trust.

Where there is a trust of land under the LACLR Act, 2009, it is important to ensure that there are two trustees to give a valid receipt in respect of monies under the LACLR Act, 2009.

Check the powers of trustees in the will and consider their sufficiency of same. See Chapter 1 of the Trusts Lecture Notes (see Preface) for more detail on statutory and non-statutory powers of trustees.

In particular, did the deceased have a business? If so, enquire as to how the business is to be run and whether the personal representatives or the trustees have sufficient powers to manage the business during the administration period. Is it necessary to extend the powers to enable them to do so?

Offshore trusts

Be aware of any offshore trusts. The personal representative, in completing the Statement of Affairs (Probate), is faced with a difficult situation and, should full disclosure not be made, he, the personal representative, could be guilty of a criminal offence.

6.6.10 MISCELLANEOUS DETAILS

During the course of an administration you, the solicitor, may be consulting other professionals, such as accountants, auctioneers and valuers, stockbrokers and tax advisers, etc. It is useful to record their names, telephone numbers, fax numbers, email addresses, and indeed the name of the person with whom one is in contact, in the event of dealing with a large firm. All this information should be placed in a convenient place on the file for easy reference purposes.

6.6.11 TAX CLEARANCES

This page on the instruction sheet also refers to the various clearance certificates. First, income tax both pre-death and post-death. It also deals with capital gains tax (if applicable) and discretionary trust tax (if applicable). Where CAT is paid on behalf of a non-resident beneficiary, 'clearance' as such is not provided, but a receipt will be made available. There is also a procedure set out for informing the Revenue Commissioners of your intention to distribute to a non-resident beneficiary. See CAT Lecture Notes (see Preface).

It is helpful to note the name and address of the deceased's Inspector of Taxes.

6.6.12 IF THE DECEASED WAS SEPARATED/DIVORCED

Where the deceased was separated or divorced, full details, including copies of all court orders, separation agreements, and notices served, etc, must be obtained, particularly if the deceased was divorced in a foreign jurisdiction. This matter has been discussed in **Chapter 4** and is expanded upon significantly in **Chapter 13**, dealing with spouses/civil partners/qualified cohabitants and children.

6.7 The First Meeting with the Personal Representative

During the initial meeting with the personal representative, as much of the information to be inserted in the instruction sheet as possible should be collected. It is not unknown for a personal representative to present you with a large bundle of papers in total disarray and disclaim all knowledge of the deceased's affairs. In such circumstances a sensible approach should be adopted, and the appropriate enquiries made in order to acquire an accurate picture of the estate as a whole.

Obviously, no matter how organised the personal representative is, not all the information will be available, and the solicitor will have to write to the various financial and other institutions to obtain that information. Prior to doing so, certain formalities will have to be entered into; these will include sending a s 150 letter/terms of engagement letter to the client, the personal representative, and obtaining written authority to act. These matters are covered at para **6.8**.

In addition, the solicitor must bear in mind their obligations when dealing with clients in the context of Anti-money laundering legislation. The Law Society has provided guidelines outlining the procedures to be followed and the requirements to help prevent money laundering as follows:

- Verifying the clients identity, reviewing and copying client's photographic identity documents, and a utility bill verifying the client's current permanent address reporting any suspicious transactions.

Information that the solicitor and the personal representative should be able to ascertain between them at the meeting would include:

- whether there is a will or intestacy, or indeed a partial intestacy;
- if there is a will, whether all executors are willing and able to act and, similarly, if the deceased died intestate, whether there are administrators willing and able to act;
- identity and contact details for the personal representatives willing and able to act;
- who the beneficiaries are, based on whether there is a will, intestacy, or partial intestacy;
- what approximately, based on the information available regarding the estate, each beneficiary is likely to receive;
- in particular, if there are specific bequests, whether the items in question have been adeemed, or whether they are still in existence;
- who is entitled to the residue of the estate and/or a share on intestacy;
- which family members have survived the deceased and what are their benefits and entitlements;
- whether there are any trusts created by the will;
- whether there are any assets that fall outside the estate, whether as joint property, property nominated by the deceased, or property subject to a power of appointment by the deceased.

6.7.1 POTENTIAL BENEFICIARIES

Beneficiaries are entitled to be informed of the nature of the benefit to be received by them. They are not entitled to sight of the will until the appropriate grant of representation has issued.

The information required on potential beneficiaries will include, as discussed earlier, name, address, relationship to deceased, PPS number, and, for tax purposes, any prior benefits received since 5 December 1991. In para **6.8.4.2** there is a precedent letter to send to each beneficiary, together with an acknowledgement for completion and return by the beneficiary giving details of prior benefits.

6.7.1.1 Powers of appointment

It should be clear whether the deceased exercised a power of appointment in the will. If so, a copy of the instrument by which the deceased had such a power of appointment will have to be obtained. Powers of appointment have been covered in para **5.3** at point 15 and will be covered in greater detail while reviewing the Statement of Affairs (Probate).

It is important to investigate the taxation implications which will result on the exercise of a power of appointment by the deceased (s 10 of the Succession Act). For further details on the taxation implications of the power of appointment, see CAT Lecture Notes (see Preface).

6.7.2 PROTECTION OF ASSETS

6.7.2.1 Business assets

If, in relation to a deceased's estate, there is no authority conferred by the will to carry on the deceased's business, the personal representative should take the precaution of obtaining an indemnity from the beneficiaries before carrying on any business. This should be done even when the business is kept open for an extremely short time to fulfil existing orders. Where all the beneficiaries are not *sui juris*, this can give rise to difficulties.

A personal representative who improperly and without authorisation, either by law or under the will, carries on the business of the deceased, may be made liable to the deceased's estate or creditors for losses incurred.

If there is no authority to carry on the deceased's business under the terms of the will, it is incumbent on the personal representative to dispose of the business and to realise it as soon as is reasonably practicable.

However, if it would be good business management to carry on the business for a short period of time pending its early disposal, it would be advisable to obtain the beneficiaries' consent in writing. In the form of consent, it would be prudent to ensure that the personal representative is released and indemnified from any potential liability by taking this course of action.

6.7.2.2 Other assets

If particular assets are bequeathed by way of specific legacy, for example, jewellery or furniture, the simplest way of protecting the asset is to arrange for the legatee to take it.

However, there may be tax implications, valuation dates, administration and testamentary expenses, or partial insolvency/insolvency of the estate where all legacies may have to be abated. All these issues should be carefully considered prior to distributing assets, even where they require safekeeping—a legatee who has taken possession of an asset, for example, jewellery or a painting, may not want to return it to the personal representative. The personal representative should always obtain the appropriate receipt and indemnity on any distribution.

The duty to safeguard the assets in an estate falls upon the personal representative, but it is the duty of the practitioner to take care to give proper advice and at all times to assist the personal representative. Section 24 of the Succession Act, 1965 applies. It is important to impress on the personal representative the importance of protecting assets.

The personal representative is under no duty to appreciate the value of an asset, but he has a duty to prevent the asset from perishing.

The personal representative should be advised to take whatever immediate steps are necessary, in the circumstances, to safeguard the assets.

A prudent personal representative will ensure that all assets requiring to be insured are so insured, for the market value or reinstatement value, from the date of death to the date of distribution. In cases where a substantial premium will arise, the consent of the appropriate beneficiaries should be obtained. The personal representative should check, at the outset of any administration, that all assets requiring to be insured are so insured, even if the deceased did not so insure.

It may be necessary to remove valuables from a house for safekeeping, where a house is vacant on a death. It is necessary to check that insurance on a house is in existence at death and is continued until the asset is transferred to the person entitled or sold in the course of administration.

Normally, where a property is vacant, only fire insurance will be available and the personal representative should notify the insurance company of such vacancy. If insurance cover is not possible, advise the personal representative to make arrangements for a caretaker, if appropriate.

All relevant insurances should be checked immediately after death. If one considers that insurance is non-existent or inadequate, one should advise the personal representative to obtain adequate insurance.

6.8 Initial Steps to be Taken after the First Meeting with the Personal Representative

At the conclusion of the first interview, ensure that the original will has been returned to the will safe. Having concluded your initial interview with the personal representative, you will first write to the personal representative enclosing the following:

1. a copy of the attendance prepared following the meeting;
2. a copy of the notes on the role and duties of the personal representative;
3. the appropriate terms of engagement letter, advising of the work to be undertaken, and s 68 letter;
4. authority to act (to be signed by the personal representative and returned to you forthwith).

It is good practice to send the client a note of what was discussed at the meeting and the notes referred to on the role and duties of the personal representative for future reference. The first section, 'The role of an executor', in particular could be incorporated into letter form, which could then be personalised for each individual client and is included as a precedent at para **3.6.1**. The headings would, of course, be removed.

The practitioner should also get the personal representatives' written authority to act.

The Law Society has always taken the view that a copy of the s 150 letter should be sent to those beneficiaries liable to pay the costs, and complaints from beneficiaries who were not liable to pay costs that they did not receive a s 150 letter were not entertained.

This was the view of the High Court in *Condon v Law Society of Ireland* [2010] IEHC 5 and *Sandys v Law Society of Ireland* [2015] IEHC 363; however, the decision of the Court of Appeal in *Sandys v Law Society of Ireland* [2016] IECA 395 does not support this view. 'Client', for the purpose of s 68, in the view of the Court of Appeal is limited to the client giving instructions. In the cases outlined above, the 'client' giving instructions was a solicitor executor and, following the judgment, is not obliged as solicitor to furnish those beneficiaries with a copy of the s 68 letter. The issue of whether a solicitor executor should furnish himself with a s 68 letter was not before the Court. The judgment states at [57]:

'If, in accordance with this construction, a firm of solicitors provides a s. 68 letter to executors, or in the case of a sole practitioner, perhaps to himself at the commencement of the administration of an estate, there may be a separate question as to what obligation he or she owes as executor to furnish

> *the s.68 letter at the time it is issued to any beneficiary who will ultimately in reality be paying those costs in the sense that they will come out of that person's entitlement under the estate.'*

Section 150 of the Legal Services Regulations Act, 2015 (the LRSA, 2015) came into effect on 7 October 2015 as per the Legal Services Regulations Act, 2015 (Commencement of Certain Provisions) (No 2) Order, 2019 (SI 502/2019) art 2(a).

This Order also commenced s 5 of the SLRA, 2015 which repealed s 68 of the Solicitors (Amendment) Act, 1994 (The 1994 Act). We as solicitors are obliged to send s 150 letters to our clients and the new regime is under the umbrella of the Legal Services Regulatory Authority (the Authority).

While it is not clear whether a solicitor executor is obliged to provide a copy of such s 150 letter as executor, it remains the view of the Law Society that it is best practice to keep those beneficiaries who will ultimately bear the costs of administration informed of the likely costs from the outset.

Solicitors acting in the administration of an estate should advise the executor that it is best practice to furnish a copy of the s 150 letter to that beneficiary or those beneficiaries paying the costs. Similarly, a solicitor executor should be aware that it is best practice to furnish the beneficiary or beneficiaries paying the costs with a copy of the s 150 letter. These beneficiaries may include the residuary beneficiaries and/or those entitled on intestacy. As soon as it becomes obvious that any other class of beneficiary is likely to have to contribute to the costs, a copy of the s 150 letter should be sent to those beneficiaries.

At the outset, it is important to identify the costs involved in administering the estate. This is of concern not only to the solicitor involved but to the client, the personal representative. In discussing the costs, explain as fully as possible how costs will be calculated.

The Law Society precedent terms and conditions of business are available on the members' section of its website and contain much useful information in this regard.

It should be perfectly clear to the personal representative exactly what work will be included in the estimate. In particular, the solicitor should be precise as to whether additional work, for example, conveyancing, income tax returns, litigation, beneficiary CAT returns, and undertakings, will give rise to an additional charge. Obviously, calculating and filing beneficiary CAT returns are not charged to the estate, but is a separate item charged to the beneficiary in a personal capacity, and in such cases a separate s 150 letter should be sent to that beneficiary. However, where there are non-resident beneficiaries and/or personal representatives, the solicitor owes a duty of care to the estate to ensure that CAT is paid, as the estate would be secondarily liable in those cases: see paras 5.6 and 12.2.3 of the CAT Lecture Notes (see Preface).

Again, in this regard p 11 of the precedent terms and conditions states as follows:

> *'If we act for you in an application for a Grant of Probate/Administration and we are responsible for the payment of capital acquisitions tax, we will ask you to sign the authority in the section for details at the end of this document. By signing this form you are giving us permission to pay the tax for you. We also need you to indemnify us. This means that you agree to pay us back in full for any loss we suffer due to something you do, or omit to do, or some wrong-doing on your part.'*

The specific precedent authority states as follows:

Capital acquisitions tax

Because you are acting as my/our solicitors in the application for a Grant of Probate/Administration in the estate of [*Name of deceased*]

I/we appoint you my/our agent for the Taxes Consolidation Act, 1997, the Capital Acquisition Tax Consolidation Act, 2003 and the Finance Act, 2010.

I/We direct you to pay my/our liabilities under the capital acquisitions tax arising out of the inheritance from the estate of [*Name of deceased*]

I/We promise to keep you as our solicitors until the Revenue Commissioners release [*Firm name*] from its legal obligations.

I/We hereby indemnify [Firm name] and all their partners and their executors, administrators and anyone to whom their rights are transferred from any loss arising out of my/our acts or default.

Signed:..

Witnessed:..

Date:..

It is advisable to clarify that if any unexpected difficulties arise, or if there is litigation involved, the question of costs will have to be reviewed. What may seem straightforward and uncomplicated may have difficulties that are not apparent at the outset. This emphasises the need to ascertain value, extent, and any potential pitfalls at the earliest opportunity.

6.8.1 PRECEDENT LETTER (SECTION 150)

Letter giving the client the estimate of charges:

Re:

Dear

Thank you for your instructions in connection with the above matter. We are pleased to act for you.

The law requires solicitors, as soon as is practicable after taking instructions, to set out an estimate of charges which the solicitor intends charging, where the provision of actual charges is not in the circumstances practicable, as is the position in this case.

In addition to the professional fees and miscellaneous charges payable to us, there will be items of outlay payable to third parties, including government agencies, which must be discharged by you.

For this reason and as discussed with you, we set out below an estimate of the charges for the work which we have agreed to do for you. In the event of our having to carry out additional work, further charges may be incurred. A supplementary estimate will be furnished to you in advance of any such additional charges.

The professional fee for the administration of the estate covers completing the Inland Revenue affidavit together with all probate papers necessary to lead to the extraction of the grant of representation, and all non-contentious work in relation to the distribution of the assets and the completion of the administration of the estate, except the vesting of the immoveable property in the beneficiaries of the conveyancing fees on the sale of same.

We currently make the following estimate:

Administration of estate

1. Professional fee

Professional fee for the administration of the estate in the region of   €

Miscellaneous charges in respect of postages, phones, faxes and photocopying   €

2. Outlays payable to third parties, for example:

* Auctioneers' valuation fee   €

* Stockbrokers' probate valuation fee   €

* Discharging NPPR and any outstanding Household Charge with local authority

* Discharging Local Property Tax

3. Taxes and outlays payable to government agencies, for example

Probate fee €

Death certificate €

The professional fee and miscellaneous charges attract VAT

VAT on professional fee @ 23% €

VAT on miscellaneous charges @ 23% €

*

*

[*List other items of outlay and exact amounts, where possible]

[Delete if not applicable]

Vesting the property in the beneficiary/ies and/or sale of the property

1. Professional fee on Deed of Assent AND/OR €

Estimated professional fee in relation to a proposed sale in the region of €

2. Outlays payable to third parties

[Vendors]

† Fees to lending institution to take up title deeds €

Fee to local authority for letter re roads and services €

Commissioners'/Practising Solicitors' fees for swearing €

† Fees to lending institution for release of mortgage €

*

*

3. Taxes and outlays payable to government agencies

The professional fee and miscellaneous charges attract VAT

VAT on professional fee @ 23% €

VAT on miscellaneous charges @ 23% €

[Vendors]

Property Registration Authority fees for copy folio and filed plan €

Property Registration Authority fees for registration of discharge €

Property Registration Authority fees for registration of Assent €

Negative search fee €

Property Registration Authority fees on form of release/vacate/discharge €

*

*

[*List other amounts of outlay and exact amounts, where possible]

† This is an estimate and may vary.

We have endeavoured to include all the items of outlay likely to occur. However, additional items may occur in any particular case. If this happens in your case, we will inform you immediately.

Inheritance tax returns

If an inheritance tax return (form IT38) is made on behalf of a beneficiary, the following charges will be made.

€

€

€

1. Professional fee

Professional fee   €

Miscellaneous charges in respect of postages, phones, faxes and photocopying   €

2. Taxes and outlays payable to government agencies

VAT on professional fee @ 23%   €

VAT on miscellaneous charges @ 23%   €

We enclose herewith for your information an explanatory pamphlet concerning legal charges, published by the Law Society of Ireland, the governing body for solicitors in Ireland.

If you have any queries in relation to these matters, the writer will be happy to assist you.

Once again, thank you for your instructions.

Yours sincerely,

6.8.2 PRECEDENT LETTER GIVING AUTHORITY TO ACT (TO COMPLY WITH SOLICITORS' REGULATIONS)

[Solicitors]

3 Blackhall Mews
Blackhall Place

Dublin 7
2 October 20

Re: John Black deceased

I, Niamh O'Keeffe as personal representative of John Black, deceased hereby authorise you to act on my behalf in administering the estate of the said John Black deceased.

I understand that the fees ordinarily payable for this work will be in accordance with your letter to me, pursuant to s 150 of the Legal Services Regulations Act 2015 which I now sign and return herewith as requested by you.

Yours sincerely

Niamh O'Keeffe.

6.8.3 OPENING AN EXECUTOR'S/ADMINISTRATOR'S ACCOUNT

It is usually necessary to open an executor's/administrator's account with a bank. Alternatively, all sums can be lodged in the firm's client account in the name of the deceased. This is a matter for discussion with the client. Where a 'stand-alone' executor's account is opened, usually, this will be with the bank where the solicitor banks or where the deceased already had an account. The personal representative's instructions should be taken on this, or the personal representative may wish the account to be with a particular bank. Depending on the circumstances of the estate, an overdraft facility may be necessary and this should be agreed with the bank, pending the issue of the grant in order to discharge immediate liabilities. It is possible to negotiate with the bank that credits in the deceased's own accounts at death are set off against the personal representative's overdraft.

An authority to do this will be necessary and a precedent authority is included here.

6.8.3.1 Precedent authority to open executor's account

EXECUTOR'S/ADMINISTRATOR'S UNDERTAKING

Dated the   day of   20

TO Allied Irish Banks Plc/The Governor and Company of the Bank of Ireland

……….. Deceased

I/We intend to apply forthwith for grant of probate/letters of administration of the estate of the above named deceased and I/we have to request you to open an account in my/our name(s), the cheques on which will be signed by me or all/both of us.

For the purpose of paying the various duties and expenses, I/we shall require accommodation to the extent of (say   Euro)

and in consideration of your permitting me/us to withdraw to this extent, I/we authorise and request you to hold the moneys to the credit of the deceased on current account and/or deposit account as set-off and I/we hereby charge with such repayment any cash and securities in your hands belonging to the deceased *Provided Always* that nothing hereinbefore contained shall be construed as limiting my/our personal liability for any moneys advanced by you to me/us.

I/we undertake to repay the Bank on demand, or out of the first moneys received by me/us out of the estate of the deceased, any advance made or which may be made to me/us.

WITNESS to the Signature of

Witness..

Address..   ....

Occupation...

WITNESS to the Signature of

Witness..

Address..   ....

Occupation...

Note: Caution should be exercised in giving any undertaking. It will be absolutely necessary to ensure that there will be funds available before giving any such undertaking.

6.8.4 LETTERS TO ESTABLISH VALUE OF ESTATE

There now follow precedent letters which are written to the various financial institutions, company registrars, etc, in order to ascertain precise date-of-death valuations for the various accounts, stocks and shares, etc held by the deceased.

6.8.4.1 Precedent letter to financial institutions

This form of letter can be used when writing to banks, building societies, or other financial institutions where the deceased held an account.

When writing to Bank of Ireland or Allied Irish Banks, the practitioner should write directly to their specialist departments that deal with deceased account holders/customers at the following addresses:

Bank of Ireland	AIB Bank	Ulster Bank Ireland DAC
Bereavement Support Unit,	Deceased Account Unit	Estates and Closure Team
PO Box 365,	4th Floor,	Ulster Bank Ireland Ltd
Dublin 18	1 Adelaide Road,	Danesfort
DX 68 Cabinteely	Dublin 2	Stranmill Road
	DX 236 Dublin	Belfast
		BT9 5UB

Otherwise, you will be writing to the manager of the local branch of the financial institution.

The Manager

Re: Deceased late of Account no:

Dear Sir/Madam,

We regret to inform you of the death of

who died on the   day of   20.

We confirm that we are the solicitors who are acting in the administration of the estate and we enclose solicitors' copy of the death certificate for noting in your records and return. We understand that the deceased held the above account(s) with your branch and we shall be obliged if you would confirm the balance(s) in the account(s) as at the date of death together with interest. Kindly confirm the BIC and IBAN account details. Kindly also let us have the usual certificates of interest in regard to the accounts.

Please confirm that the deceased did not hold any other accounts either solely or jointly with any other person(s) with your bank. Kindly also advise if you hold any items in safekeeping or safety deposit box on behalf of the deceased.

Please also forward withdrawal forms for completion by the executor/administrator in due course.

Please let us know your further requirements if any.

Yours faithfully,

Note: In due course the building society/bank will require the original passbook, an official copy of the grant of probate/administration, and a withdrawal form duly completed by the personal representative.

A similar letter would be sent to An Post as per the following example and this form of letter can also be adopted in relation to other assets.

Precedent letter to An Post regarding savings certificates or savings bonds

An Post

Deceased's Section,

Saving Certificates/Bonds Section
GPO,

Dublin1

Re Estate of

Dear Sir/Madam,

We regret to inform you of the death of   who died on the   day of 20.

We confirm that we are the solicitors who are acting in the administration of the estate and we enclose a copy of the death certificate for noting in your records and return.

We currently hold the following savings certificates/bonds on behalf of the deceased [*here insert details of the documentation held*]

We should be obliged if you could confirm if the above represents the true holdings of the deceased as at the date of death.

We require a certificate confirming the value of the above as at the date of death together with interest payable.

Please forward a repayment form for completion by the executor/administrator in due course.

Yours faithfully,

Note: In due course An Post will require the original savings certificates/bonds to be lodged with it, together with the original grant of probate and the repayment form duly completed by the personal representative.

Precedent letter to company registrar

To be used especially in cases where there is some doubt as to the deceased's shareholding.

The Registrar,   Plc

Re: Deceased

Re: Holding of

Dear Sirs,

We regret to inform you of the death of

who died on the   day of 20   . We confirm that we are the solicitors who are acting in the administration of his estate.

We currently hold certificates over a holding of   shares

ADMINISTRATION OF ESTATES: PROBATE PRACTICE AND PROCEDURE

[Here insert details of share certificates and the holding].

We shall be obliged if you would confirm the deceased's shareholding as at the date of death.

As all dividends are currently mandated to the deceased's home address we should be obliged if you would retain further dividends until such time as a grant of probate has been noted with you.

Yours faithfully,

Note: In due course a registrar will require the original certificates together with the grant of probate/administration to be lodged in order that the interest of the executor/administrator can be noted on same. If you wish to transfer the shares directly into the names of the beneficiaries, stamped and signed stock transfer forms will have to accompany the correspondence in due course.

6.8.4.2 Precedent initial letter to beneficiary

This letter informs the beneficiary of the nature of the benefit and requests the beneficiary to complete, sign, and return the attached letter detailing PPS number, date of birth, residence, and any prior benefits. If there is any doubt over residence, full instructions should be taken and the CAT Lecture Notes (see Preface) should be reviewed.

Re: Estate of

Deceased   late of

Dear

We were sorry to learn of the death of

(who had been a long-standing client of this firm).

We confirm that we have been instructed by the executor/administrator to act in the administration of the estate.

Under the terms of the will of

he made the following devise and/or bequest: 'to   AB   of

in the following terms—Recite the bequest verbatim from the will

[OR

*Where the deceased died intestate (see **Chapter 8**) the following sentence should be substituted for the above:*

As the deceased died intestate you are entitled to a distributive (fraction) share in his/her estate.]

*Where there is a partial intestacy, see **para 12.1**, a combination of both may be required;*

The executor/administrator will be in a position to vest in make payment of the bequest and/or share once the grant issues subject, however, to there being sufficient assets in the estate to discharge all debts, testamentary expenses and liabilities (both ascertained and as yet unascertained).

You may be liable to capital acquisitions tax (CAT) and you may need to submit a CAT return.

We need you to confirm whether you are resident, ordinary resident or non-resident in Ireland in the current tax year/tax year in which the death of the late occurred. If you are non-resident, then payment of any bequest to you is subject to confirmation that all CAT has been paid and a return filed on your behalf.

If you wish, we can calculate the CAT payable (if any), file the appropriate CAT return (if necessary) and pay this tax (if any) on your behalf. Please contact this office if you wish us to apply for this on your behalf.

Meanwhile the Revenue Commissioners will require information from you of any previous gift or inheritance received by you since 5 December 1991. We enclose a letter of confirmation to be signed by you to this effect.

In the event of you having received a previous gift or inheritance please confirm details of same including the disponer, the amount, the date of the gift/inheritance, and the Revenue File Number (if applicable). The Revenue require this information at an early stage and any delay in giving of such information could result in delays with the administration and payment of the bequest to you. Please return the enclosed form of letter duly completed by you to include your PPS number.

If the Grant of Representation issues or the valuation date for CAT purposes arises before 31 August 20 Inheritance Tax returns must be filed and the tax paid before 31 October 20 to prevent surcharges and interest from applying.

Yours sincerely,

Note: If you apply for tax clearance for a beneficiary, you are entitled to charge that beneficiary separately for that legal service.

Precedent letter for completion and return by beneficiary

Form of Confirmation for the Revenue Commissioners

RE: Capital acquisitions tax

To: The Revenue Commissioners

       Relevant Inspector of Taxes

Re: Estate of   Deceased's PPS no:

       Late of

       Date of death

Re: File no

Dear Sir/Madam,

I   off   being a beneficiary in the estate of   deceased who died on the   hereby confirm that I have not received any previous gift or inheritance since 5 December 1991 from any source of any disponer (including the said deceased).

Or [*delete if the following section is not applicable*]

I received a gift/inheritance since 5 December 1991 (other than the present inheritance) and the following are the details:

(a) [name of donor/date of death of donor (if applicable)]

(b) [date of gift/inheritance]

(c) [the amount or value of gift]

(d) [Revenue file number (if applicable)]

(e) [my relationship to the donor].

My PPS number is _____ (We must have this to process your clearance whether or not you have received a previous gift or inheritance).

My date of birth is:

Permanent residence is _____ (Country).

Ordinary residence is _____ (Country).

Permanent domicile is _____ (Country).

Relationship to the deceased:

Dated this   day of   20

Signature of beneficiary

Witness _____

Address _____ Occupation _____

6.9 Statement of Affairs (Probate) Form SA.2

Prior to 14 September 2020 an Inland Revenue affidavit form CA24 was required when applying for all primary grants of representation. The CA24 contained an account of the deceased's person's estate outlining, *inter alia*, the assets and liabilities valued as at the date of death of the deceased. The form CA24 was lodged in the Probate Office/District Probate Registry with all other documents necessary to lead to the issuing of the required grant of representation. The process was replaced for applications for grants of representation filed on or after 14 September 2020 in respect of deaths on or after 5 December 2001. The CA24 was replaced with the completion and submission to the Revenue on ROS of a new online version of the CA24 called the Statement of Affairs (Probate) Form SA.2 (the SA.2).

Section 63 of the Finance Act, 2019 provided for an amendment to s 48A of the Capital Acquisitions Tax Consolidation Act, 2003 (CATCA 2003). Section 48A provided for the electronic delivery of information to the Revenue as part of the Probate application process. By virtue of the Capital Acquisitions Tax (Electronic Probate) Regulations, 2020 (SI 341/2020), which was published on 15 September 2020, the Revenue Commissioners in exercise of powers conferred on them by s 48A(3) (inserted by s 63 of the Finance Act, 2019) of the CATCA 2003 made regulations outlining the information, relevant supporting documentation, and will (in the case of testate deaths) to be delivered by electronic means to the Revenue Commissioners.

From 14 September 2020, intermediaries such as solicitors or agents and personal applicants such as executors or administrators of an estate wishing to obtain a grant of representation from the Probate Office or District Probate Registry are required to firstly deliver to the Revenue a form SA.2. Once the form SA.2 is completed and successfully submitted electronically to the Revenue, a Notice of Acknowledgement (Probate) will be generated. Where the Revenue are satisfied that the required information has been delivered by an applicant or by another person acting under the applicant's authority, they shall issue, by electronic means, a notice of acknowledgement of such delivery. The notice of acknowledgement shall contain such information as the Probate Office may require to perform its functions under Part IV of the Succession Act 1965. This Notice of Acknowledgement must be presented to the Probate Office/District Registry together with any other documentation required in order to proceed with the application for a grant of representation.

The Probate Office are obliged to notify the Revenue Commissioners as soon as practicable by electronic means:

1. If a will delivered to them with the SA.2 corresponds to the will delivered to the Probate Office.

2. Of the date on which the grant of representation was granted, and where a grant of representation was granted but was subsequently revoked, of the date on which it was revoked.

As noted at para **6.1**, since 14 September 2020 a form SA.2 must be submitted electronically to the Revenue on ROS in any current application for a grant of representation for any person who died on or after 5 December 2001. For deaths prior to that date the appropriate Inland Revenue Form required is the form CA24.

In summary, the form SA.2 should contain the deceased person's details, the contact details of the person submitting the application, the applicant's details, the beneficiaries' details, a full account of the deceased person's assets and liabilities valued as at the date of death, information on any assets passing outside the will or intestacy, for example jointly held property, property passing under a nomination, and replies to the questions raised in the mandatory questionnaire, which includes questions about charitable bequests, discretionary trusts, limited interests, etc which are dealt with later in the chapter.

When delivering the required information to the Revenue in the form SA.2, the applicant, or another person acting under the applicant's authority, must make a declaration that the information delivered is full, correct, and true to the best of the applicant's knowledge or belief.

The form SA.2, in addition to incorporating the functions of other forms such as the revenue IT8 (see below), has a procedure allowing for amendment instead of having to swear a new affidavit.

1. A corrective affidavit CA26 is now an amended return. Prior to the introduction of the online form SA.2 where a material error or omission was made in the old Inland Revenue affidavit CA24, a corrective Affidavit CA26 had to be sworn. Now the form SA.2 as submitted can be amended online.

2. The ability to apply for a secondary or subsequent *de bonis non* grant. The form A3 is now incorporated in to the form SA.2 and is applicable for deaths on or after 5 December 2001 where a *de bonis non* grant is required. (See **Chapter 10**).

3. The ability to request an IT8 for joint account clearance although the paper form CA4 is still available.

4. An upload feature to supply documentation to include wills, codicils, the primary grant of representation where a second grant is applied for, and supporting documentation.

There are a number of issues that must be addressed when completing the form, which is for the most part self-explanatory. Many of the issues raised have already been dealt with when detailing the contents of the instruction and progress sheet at para **6.6**. Also of benefit is the Revenue Commissioners' *Guide to Completing a Statement of Affairs Probate) Form SA2*. However, there may be other issues which require clarification.

6.9.1 GENERAL INFORMATION RE THE FORM SA.2

This section requires information relating to the deceased person and has been already dealt with at para **6.6.1**. All of the general information regarding the deceased should be readily to hand.

The contact details of the person to be contacted in respect of any queries regarding the form would usually be those of the solicitor for the applicant. Their name, firm's name, address, phone number, email address, and the solicitor's reference is required. Their Transaction Advisory Identification Number (TAIN) should be given (if applicable). This is issued by the Revenue Commissioners where the solicitor has registered as a tax advisor.

6.9.2 DETAILS OF THE APPLICANTS

In this section details of the person(s) making the application should be entered. There can be up to four applicants. The applicant is usually the executor or the nearest next of kin entitled on intestacy or, in the case of an administration with will annexed grant, the residuary legatees and devisees. Their names, addresses, occupations, relationships to the deceased person, contact phone numbers, and the type of grant required from the presented options must be provided. These include a grant of probate, administration with will annexed, administration intestate, a nominal grant, or a *de bonis non*/secondary grant.

In some cases, a nominal grant may be sought, for example a creditor's grant to stop the Statute of Limitations running. In that case, this should be explained by the applicant.

6.9.3 DECLARATION

Regulation 6 of the Capital Acquisitions Tax (Electronic Probate) Regulations, 2020 requires the applicant(s), or another person acting under the applicant's authority, to make a declaration through the online 'sign and submit' facility that the form SA.2 has been fully and correctly completed and all the particulars requested have been supplied and are true and correct to the best of the applicant's knowledge or belief. The applicant attesting to the accuracy of the information given, gives an undertaking to submit an amended Statement of Affairs (Probate) Form SA.2 where it appears that a material error or omission has been made. Where the solicitor is submitting the application on behalf of an applicant, this is not a 'solicitor's undertaking' and Revenue have confirmed to the Law Society that it will not be interpreted as such. It is the applicant who is bound by the declaration and undertaking and not the solicitor submitting on behalf of an applicant.

The importance of this must be pointed out to the personal representative(s).

6.9.4 PROPERTY IN THE STATE FORMING PART OF THE ESTATE: THE ASSET COVER SCREEN

Most of these items have been dealt with already at para **6.6** or are covered in the Revenue Commissioners' Guide to completing a Statement of Affairs (Probate) Form SA.2 and above. In this section of the form SA.2 details of all property passing through the estate under the will or on the intestacy of the deceased and all property passing outside the estate by survivorship or nomination are included. The various categories of assets are listed in the asset cover screen. They include the following:

- property in the State (land and buildings);
- bank/building society accounts;
- credit union/An Post accounts;
- cash;

- household contents;
- cars/boats;
- insurance policy/mortgage protection policy;
- superannuation/capital sum or ex gratia payments;
- dividends;
- debts owing to the deceased;
- unpaid purchase money of property contracted to be sold in the deceased's lifetime;
- other assets (any asset not covered under the above headings).

On selecting a 'property type' on the 'asset cover screen', by ticking the box 'yes' you will be brought to the 'asset detail screen' to enter full details of the property. Where there are two or more properties within the same category, for example two bank accounts, the applicant presses the 'add property' option to enter details of any additional properties.

Based on the details provided in the asset detail screen, the online application will either categorise an asset as passing through the estate and *include* the value of that asset in the estate totals at the end of the asset cover page or categorise an asset as passing by survivorship/nomination and *exclude* the value of the share of this asset from the estate totals at the end of the asset cover page. However, the value of the share of these assets will be populated automatically as 'assigned benefits' in the 'beneficiary benefits' section.

As noted, all consideration is to be rounded up or down to the nearest euro. The value entered for each asset should be its total value in euro at the date of death of the deceased person. As discussed earlier, the estate of the deceased is defined in s 10 of the Succession Act. The entire estate is listed here, regardless of any potential actions under Part IX of the Act and/or civil partnership legislation, or s 56 applications by spouses or actions under the Family Law Acts.

Some individual items need further explanation.

6.9.4.1 Business assets

Where a deceased was running a business, one should include the value of any stock in trade, book debts, cash held as working capital, and tangible assets, together with goodwill, if it has any value. Only where the estate is very small should the personal representative consider giving these values. Professional valuers will have to be instructed where the estate is substantial. Partnership property needs to be looked at very carefully.

If the deceased was a partner in a business, the following issues arise for the personal representative.

Partnerships

Obtain a copy of the partnership agreement. There may be partnership assets that were held by the partners, such as land or buildings, and the agreement may contain provisions as to how these assets are to be dealt with on death. There may be options for the surviving partners to purchase the property on death, and the personal representative needs to be fully aware of any notices or obligations that need to be attended to.

There may be undrawn profits or liabilities in the partnership attributable to the deceased partner and which will need to be included in the schedule of assets.

The deceased may have an original capital sum invested in the partnership, the repayment of which may be governed by the partnership agreement.

Any pension or life insurance policies connected with the partnership need to be identified straightaway. Partners often insure each other's lives, and the proceeds of such a policy, if paid to the surviving partners, will not form an asset in the estate.

It is a duty of the personal representative to file and prepare any outstanding tax returns relating to income up to the date of death. The personal representative must identify the income accruing to the deceased from every source. Under s 108 of the Taxes Consolidation Act, 1997 each partner is deemed to carry on a separate trade. The death of a partner does not result in a discontinuance of the partnership so long as there is a minimum of two partners remaining. The precedent acting partner needs to be furnished with a request by the personal representative for details of the profits and losses and capital allowances available to the deceased for the period from the date of the last set of accounts to the date of death.

6.9.4.2 Unquoted (private company) shares

While it is relatively straightforward to deal with quoted shares in public companies, a number of issues have to be dealt with when valuing private company shares. This is a very difficult area, and the existence of private company shares in an estate is becoming increasingly more common as more people are self-employed and moving away from the traditional structure of employment.

The valuation of private company shares requires considerable skill and experience. It requires knowledge of the valuation rules for capital acquisitions tax, capital gains tax, and stamp duty. The valuation is generally negotiated with the Revenue and the procedure can take some time if the shareholding is valuable. While it is not intended to go into the taxation issues in detail in this chapter (see CAT Lecture Notes (see Preface)), these issues have to be highlighted.

Private company shares are not in any way similar to (or as straightforward as) shares quoted publicly. The shares in a private company may never have been sold, and this may be the first time that the value has stood to be tested by the Revenue. The most immediate requirement is to engage an efficient accountant who is familiar with the business of the company and who is also fully briefed in the method of valuing shares on death. This is an area where the personal representative will need professional help; do not delay in seeking to retain the best adviser possible.

Put in hand a Companies Office search and check the shareholding of the deceased and the identity of the directors. Check that the company has all returns up to date. If not, the company may be 'struck off', whereupon it may be necessary to bring a High Court application to reinstate it.

As with all assets, check that any real property comprised in the company is adequately insured.

Section 26 of the Capital Acquisitions Tax Consolidation Act, 2003 deals with the value of property for tax, and s 27 specifically deals with shares in private trading companies.

Section 26 states that shares are valued on the following bases:

1. earnings basis;
2. asset valuation;
3. dividend yield;
4. capitalisation of profits/price–earnings ratio.

Section 27 provides that shares in such companies will be valued on a market value share basis, rather than on a winding-up basis, and also deals with the valuation of a controlling interest in connected companies. The market value is directly related to the concept of *control*. Section 27(4) defines 'control' in a company as being the control of not more than five persons if any five or fewer persons together exercise or are able to exercise or are entitled to acquire control, whether direct or indirect, of the company. For this purpose, the shareholding of family members is critical in assessing if there is control.

The forms that are submitted to the Revenue with the Statement of Affairs (Probate) are Forms Q6 and Q7, which contain all the details to support the method of valuation.

It is also necessary to do the following:

Obtain a copy of any shareholder agreements in place and consider the provisions covering the death of a shareholder. Identify the successors to the shares, their relationship to the deceased, and the availability of any reliefs for them. In particular, consider the question of the availability of business relief and advise the personal representative and the beneficiaries of the possibility of clawback of any business relief. Valuation of private company shares, business relief, and clawback are dealt with in detail in the CAT Lecture Notes (see Preface).

6.9.4.3 Liabilities

In this section details of all debts owing by the deceased at the date of death to Irish residents or other bodies and funeral expenses payable in the State should be included. With the exception of funeral expenses, no other costs arising after the date of death may be deducted. The following debts may be included:

- liabilities owing to the Revenue;
- creditors;
- funeral expenses payable in the State;
- utilities e.g. gas, electricity;
- amounts owing to financial institutions to include any outstanding mortgage that has not been met by way of mortgage protection policy or other arrangement;
- nursing home support scheme (fair deal)/nursing home fees.

Be careful about debts. While the personal representatives have power to settle or compromise debts under s 60(8) of the Succession Act, any debt due to the deceased is an asset and if a debt is forgiven, this can trigger a taxable event.

6.9.4.4 Stocks, shares, and securities

These are for quoted shares and, if a portfolio, a statement from the relevant agent or stockbroker should be obtained.

6.9.4.5 'Other' Assets

Sometimes there are assets of the deceased which do not fit neatly into any of the categories outlined above. For example, an antiques collection would not come under 'household contents' and a collection of rare or historical coins would not come under 'cash'. These are listed here and valuations provided.

Total asset value summary

Note that the figure for total gross Irish estate in the asset summary is the figure to be brought forward to the oath and any administration bond will also be based on this figure.

6.9.4.6 Irish debts, funeral expenses

Issues to be raised here include the following:

- Income tax or capital gains tax liabilities arising pre-death are dealt with in this section.
- While reasonable funeral expenses (including cost of a tombstone and a reasonable funeral meal) are allowed, refund of air fares paid for family to travel is not an expense on the estate.

This provides a figure for total Irish debts, which, when subtracted from the total gross Irish estate, gives a figure for total net Irish estate. Probate fees are based on the figure for total net Irish estate. These figures are also reproduced on the face of the relevant grant of representation.

6.9.5 PROPERTY OUTSIDE THE STATE

In this section details of all assets which the deceased owned outside the State are included: the type of asset or property; the location of the asset and details of how the property was held—whether solely by the deceased or jointly or as a tenant in common; the value of the asset in euro at the date of death; details of any foreign debts and the location of the debt (include amounts owed by the deceased person to persons or bodies outside the State and debts contracted to be paid outside the State, and any funeral expenses payable outside the State, but do not include debts payable in the State or charged on Irish property).

Once all property abroad has been identified and valued, the question arises whether the will covers these assets. For example, under the forced heirship rules of many continental countries that follow the Napoleonic Code, the discretion of the testator is extremely limited. For practical purposes, it will be necessary to check requirements to have the assets released, particularly if a foreign grant is necessary. As mentioned earlier, in all cases the relevant rate of exchange is that as at the date of death where the deceased was domiciled in Ireland and resident/ordinarily resident in Ireland, or non-domiciled but resident/ordinarily resident in Ireland for the previous five years. If any doubt arises as to domicile or residence/ordinary residence, investigate the facts and the legislation very carefully.

It is important to note that where a grant of administration is necessary, the value of the foreign assets will not be included in the gross value of the estate in the oath or bond.

It should be noted that the Revenue has reporting requirements under double taxation treaties with the US and the UK, respectively.

6.9.6 ASSET DETAIL SCREEN

This part is a 'catch-all', designed to alert the Revenue Commissioners to any taxable benefit arising as a result of the death of the deceased which does not form part of his estate.

6.9.6.1 Property held jointly or as tenants in common

When directed to the asset detail screen from the asset cover screen further details of the property must be entered. You will be required to identify how the deceased held the property—whether solely, jointly, or as a tenant in common.

Further questions are raised in relation to each joint property, whether immoveable property or a bank account. Joint property has been discussed, and if the solicitor preparing the form SA.2 is the solicitor who took instructions for a will as per para **2.7.9**, this information should be forthcoming. However, it is possible that property, or more usually a bank account, was placed in joint names after the will was executed, and in that case, full details should be ascertained and should be attached.

6.9.6.2 Nominations

Nominations fall into two broad categories: statutory and non-statutory. Even though the asset passes outside the will, it still falls within the scope of CAT and will be aggregated with any other benefit received from the estate. Nominations need to be looked at in the context of separation/divorce.

It is possible to nominate funds under certain occupational pension funds. The trustees of such funds give the members powers to nominate those persons whom they wish to benefit and to receive the funds on death. Difficulties arise if the nominated parties are not members of any specified qualifying class of beneficiaries, according to the fund. Pensions in general will be dealt with later in this chapter.

Statutory nominations

To execute a valid will, a person must be aged eighteen. However, any person over the age of sixteen has the power to make a statutory nomination, although this power is limited to funds held in a credit union and National Savings certificates. In the context of an administration, it is interesting to note that a renunciation or extinguishment of Succession Act rights does not of itself automatically revoke a nomination.

Savings certificates prior to and including the eleventh issue were and can be the subject of nomination. The twelfth issue and thereafter may not be nominated. The eleventh issue ceased on 25 January 1994. The maximum amount that could be nominated under the then applicable savings certificates rule was €76,184/IR£60,000. Post Office savings accounts can also be nominated. However, savings bonds cannot be nominated.

Under the Savings Certificates Rules, it was only possible to have one nomination, but this nomination could be in favour of more than one person. Any nomination under the Savings Certificates Rules would not be revoked by any will of the deceased, or by any event other than those specified in the rules.

A nomination under the Credit Union Act, 1997 can be revoked before death. It can also be revoked by marriage, just like a will. The civil partnership legislation does not seem to provide for revocation of a nomination under the Credit Union Act, 1997 by the subsequent entry into a civil partnership.

However, a will does not in itself revoke a statutory nomination, as it is not a testamentary disposition.

There is a statutory limit on the amount that can be passed by way of nomination under the Credit Union Act, 1997. Section 21(3), as amended, imposes a limit of €23,000. Any nomination in excess of this figure will revert to and be an asset of the estate.

If you have a figure of less than €15,000 in a credit union account, s 23 of the Credit Union Act, 1997, as amended, provides that it can be paid directly to '*such persons as appears to the Board*' (on such evidence as it considers satisfactory) to be entitled by law to receive it without the necessity for letters of administration or probate of any will.

6.9.6.3 Superannuation scheme/policy of insurance

Insurance policies and pensions were mentioned at paras **6.6.5.10** and **6.6.5.11**, respectively.

Any pension belonging to the deceased is a valuable asset of the estate where pension rights survive on death. This can often be a point of conflict if there is any doubt over the status of the surviving spouse/civil partner/cohabitant as the person entitled.

You need to check whether the entitlement to the pension died with the deceased or whether the surviving spouse/civil partner/cohabitant and/or children are entitled to any pension benefits on death. The cohabitant in this case need not necessarily be a qualified cohabitant as defined in the Civil Partnership and Protection of Qualified Cohabitants Act, 2010. Many pensions are in the form of a trust, and the trustees of the pension fund may have a wide discretion as to the payment of any proceeds out of the fund. You need a copy of the pension scheme and, once you have checked this, the details need to be clarified with the pension company.

The deceased may have been in receipt of a pension that was underwritten in trust and may have nominated beneficiaries of this policy during his lifetime. The pension company may have full discretion as to the identity of the payee, but it is normally the surviving spouse and/or dependent children. The pension may not be an asset in the estate. You should ascertain whether an asset falls into or out of an estate. The implications for the applicant in a s 117 action, or an election by a surviving spouse, for example, could be enormous.

There are a number of structures through which a person may make provision for retirement. One method is by means of membership of an occupational pension scheme. This is a scheme which can be approved by the Revenue Commissioners under Chapter 1 of the Taxes Consolidation Act, 1997. Any contributions made are made on a tax-free basis, and income and gains earned by the pension fund are tax-free. Any lump sum payable in the event of death in service is paid on a tax-free basis.

Another method is by way of a retirement annuity contract. These are often taken out by the self-employed. The contract provides a sum to purchase an annuity on retirement.

The Finance Act, 1999 introduced new options on retirement, by the amendment of the Taxes Consolidation Act, 1997, in that a member of a pension fund or a retirement annuity contract can invest the fund in an AMRF (Approved Minimum Retirement Fund) or an ARF (Approved Retirement Fund).

The basic structure for the taxation treatment of an ARF on death was introduced in the Finance Act, 1999 and this was changed in s 23 of the Finance Act, 2000 and again in 2013. The consequences of such a fund passing on death are dealt with in the CAT Lecture Notes (see Preface).

As from 15 September 2003, all employers must either give employees who are excluded from a company pension scheme access to a Personal Retirement Savings Account (PRSA) or alternatively change the rules of their company scheme to include employees with more than six months' service.

6.9.6.4 Mandatory questionnaire

In this section additional information is required in respect of the estate of the deceased.

- **Was the deceased person in receipt of any social welfare payments?**

    The question of social welfare benefits has nothing to do with tax. The purpose is to minimise fraud in claiming non-contributory social welfare payments, which are means tested. If the deceased was ever the recipient of any non-contributory social welfare payment, this question needs to be dealt with. The claim number must be entered in the box provided if the answer to the question provided was 'yes'. This is covered in detail in **Chapter 14**.

- **Has the Department of Social Protection any claim against the estate of the deceased?**

    The personal representative should contact the Department if the deceased was in receipt of social welfare payments. This should happen at least three months prior to the distribution of the estate.

- **Was the deceased in receipt of payments under the Nursing Home Support (Fair Deal) Scheme? If yes, please indicate if the HSE has any claim against the estate of the deceased.**

    The Nursing Home Support Scheme is covered at paras **2.7.6** and **14.4** and covers situations where the deceased availed of 'Ancillary State Support' under the Nursing Home Support Scheme Act, 2009 (the 2000 Act), as the Revenue Commissioners are collection agents under the Act. It is imperative to contact the HSE advising them of the death as soon as possible. One should contact them at: The HSE, Nursing Home Support Scheme, Block 6, Central Business Park, Clonminch, Tullamore, County Offally, R35 F8KO. In due course a copy of the Schedule of Assets (form CA24) or the Notice of Acknowledgement Probate must be sent to them pursuant to the provisions of the 2009 Act.

    Yes/No/Not yet ascertained

    As can be appreciated, it may not be clear at this stage whether (for example) a spouse/civil partner, the HSE, or the Department of Social Protection have a claim against the estate, particularly when a spouse has at least a year from the date the grant issues to make a claim against the estate. For this reason an additional box of 'Not yet ascertained' is available to tick for this question.

- **Was the deceased survived by a spouse/civil partner? If yes, state the position as to election under s 115?**

    Spouses' and civil partners' rights have been covered in detail in **Chapter 4** and are dealt with again in the context of administrating an estate in **Chapter 13**. Obviously, the question of election by a spouse or civil partner will affect the amount to be received by any of the other beneficiaries. It is important to establish the position on election and, if it is applicable, diarise ahead to serve the necessary election notice (legal right share of spouse: s 115 of the Succession Act).

- **Was a charitable donation bequeathed under the will of the deceased?**

If the answer provided is yes, the following details must be provided.

(i) the name and address of the charity;

(ii) the Charity Registration Number (if applicable);

(iii) the value of the donation for distribution.

- **Was the deceased at the date of her or his death the owner of a limited interest (e.g. an annuity, right of residence, or an interest for life or otherwise in a house, land, or securities)?**

This is to ascertain whether, on the death of the deceased, any taxable benefit is received by anyone else of a further limited or remainder interest in the property over which the deceased had a life interest. If there is such a trust, it is important to ascertain if there is any unpaid trust income to the date of death, as these monies will form part of the deceased's estate.

- **Did any person on or after 5 December 1991, further to a disposition (transfer or settlement) at any time by the deceased person take a benefit from the deceased not included elsewhere?**

The purpose of this question is to extract what taxable gifts the deceased made during their lifetime on or after 5 December 1991 and to establish whether tax has been paid on such gifts and other benefits. If any of the same beneficiaries now take a further inheritance from the deceased, identify how much of any tax-free threshold has already been availed of. This information will be included later in the form SA.2 beneficiary benefits section.

- **Did the deceased at any time make a disposition subject to a power of revocation or by way of surrender of a limited interest or allowing the use of any property free of charge or for other than full consideration?**

Where a disponer has made a gift and reserved to himself a power of revocation and dies without having revoked the gift, on the disponer's death the beneficiary becoming entitled may be liable to CAT (s 39 of the Capital Acquisitions Tax Consolidation Act, 2003).

The release of a limited interest for less than full consideration can give rise to four taxes: inheritance tax, gift tax, capital gains tax, and stamp duty.

Free use of property (including interest-free loans or loans for less than market rate) is an annual gift subject to the small gift exemption and will be aggregated with other benefits taken on death (s 40 of the 2003 Act).

The taxation consequences of these are covered in the CAT Lecture Notes (see Preface). At this stage, full particulars should be ascertained and disclosed to the Revenue Commissioners.

- **Did the deceased person create a discretionary trust?**

Discretionary trusts are dealt with in Chapters 1 and 2 of the Trusts Lecture Notes (see Preface). The taxation consequences are outlined (briefly) in Chapter 10 of the CAT Lecture Notes (see Preface). Briefly, when a trust is a discretionary trust the assets in the trust are subject to Discretionary Trust Tax (DTT) charges during the lifetime of the trust. DTT becomes chargeable when the settlor dies and when the youngest 'principle object' (generally the spouse/civil partner, child, or child of a predeceased child) reaches the age of twenty-one years. DTT is chargeable as follows:

> o an immediate one-off 6 per cent charge on the value of the assets in the trust on the valuation date, assuming that there are no principal objects under the age of twenty-one years; and

ADMINISTRATION OF ESTATES: PROBATE PRACTICE AND PROCEDURE

○ an annual 1 per cent charge arising on 31 December of each year (but not within twelve months of the initial 6 per cent charge) on the value of the assets of the trust at that date (to be paid within four months of that date).

There are exemptions to the DTT charge but these are not dealt with here.

Once the Revenue receive a form SA.2 disclosing the existence of a discretionary trust, the form SA.2 will be forwarded to the Revenue DTT section for confirmation that DTT has been paid when due and Revenue will follow up with the solicitor who filed the SA.2.

If the deceased created a discretionary trust either in their lifetime (*inter vivos*) or under their will, full particulars will have to be ascertained. In particular, details of any child, predeceased child, or spouse named as an object of that discretionary trust will have to be obtained. The age of any such child or children of a predeceased child may be important in delaying the liability to discretionary trust tax.

The personal representative may have to seek the assistance of the deceased's successors and his professional advisers (e.g. for tax planning). The Revenue, in asking these questions, determines whether or not discretionary trust tax is payable, and is able to trace dispositions of assets not forming part of the estate which may give rise to capital gains tax.

- **Was the deceased entitled at the date of death to an interest in expectancy in any property?**

If the deceased was entitled to an interest in expectancy in any property, the Revenue Commissioners will want full details, particularly whether that interest in expectancy is taken under the will of the deceased or whether it passes under the terms of the original disposition. An interest in expectancy is a benefit which the deceased is entitled to but will not come into possession of until a future date. It would include an interest in a pension fund.

- **Did any person become entitled on the death of the deceased to an interest in any property by virtue of the deceased person's exercise of, or failure to, exercise a general power of appointment?**

A general power of appointment is a power given by deed or will to a person who may appoint property to whomsoever he wishes, including himself. Should he appoint property, he is deemed to be the disponer.

If a person fails to make an appointment during their lifetime, the property will pass according to the terms of the original deed or will.

In such scenarios the Revenue is addressing the CAT implications of the general power, and two questions arise. First, was CAT paid at the time? Second, what are the CAT implications for the beneficiary of the deceased's exercise or failure to exercise the power?

Example: if the deceased held land under a power of appointment '*To X for life and thereafter to whomsoever X at his absolute discretion may appoint*', full particulars of the beneficiary who receives the land will have to be provided to the Revenue Commissioners: s 36 of the Capital Acquisitions Tax Consolidation Act, 2003 deals with powers of appointment. See CAT Lecture Notes (see Preface).

6.9.7 INDIVIDUAL BENEFICIARY SCREEN AND SUMMARY OF BENEFITS

The following details entered earlier in the form SA.2 will be presented under the heading 'Beneficiary Benefit':

- the total gross Irish estate;
- the total Irish debts;
- the net Irish estate;
- the total net foreign estate if applicable.

Each beneficiary receiving a benefit greater than €12,000 is included in this section. For each beneficiary, the following details will be presented from information provided earlier in the form SA.2:

- beneficiary's name and PPSN;
- relationship to the deceased person;
- applicable threshold applying to the inheritance;
- all prior benefits;
- assigned benefits (benefits passing under nomination or by survivorship).

6.9.7.1 The approximate value of benefits section:

Benefits passing to the named beneficiary are categorised as:

1. **Assigned benefits**

   These are benefits that are passing outside the estate of the deceased i.e.to a joint tenant by survivorship or to a nominated beneficiary under a nomination. The approximate value of assigned benefits will be presented based on information provided in the asset detail screen.

2. **Other benefits**

   These are benefits that are passing from the estate under the terms of the deceased's will or on intestacy. In this section the approximate value of benefits passing to the named beneficiary from the estate of the deceased must be entered. Where there are no benefits passing from the estate of the deceased, enter '0'.

6.9.7.2 Self-assessment CAT return (form IT38)

The Revenue will contact each beneficiary whose current benefit, when aggregated with prior gifts or inheritances within the same threshold exceeds 80 per cent of that person's group threshold, and that beneficiary will have to file a return (known as the IT38) either online or in paper form, whether they have to pay tax or not.

As noted in the CAT Lecture Notes (see Preface), the paper version of the form (known as the IT38S) can be used where the benefit is an absolute interest without restrictions or conditions, no reliefs or exemptions (other than the small gift exemption) are claimed, and no other benefits from the same or any other disponer arise on the same day. In all other cases the online version of the form must be filed using the Revenue On-Line Service (ROS).

When calculating the 80 per cent, the Revenue will not make allowances for reliefs or exemptions. Reliefs and exemptions are dealt with in the CAT Lecture Notes (see Preface).

It is important to remember that where the beneficiary is not resident or ordinarily resident in Ireland, the estate will be secondarily liable for any CAT due by that beneficiary. See CAT Lecture Notes (see Preface).

6.9.8 NOTICE OF ACKNOWLEDGEMENT (PROBATE)

Once the form SA.2 is successfully submitted, the applicant's ROS inbox will receive a notification of receipt of submission. Where the Revenue Commissioners are satisfied that the required information in the form SA.2 has been delivered by the applicant or by another person acting under the applicant's authority the Revenue shall issue, by electronic means, a notice of acknowledgement of such delivery. This notice of acknowledgement (probate) contains a unique ID number. It must be printed and signed by the applicant or their solicitor and presented to the Probate Office or District Probate Registry with all the other documentation necessary to lead to the appropriate grant of representation.

The notice of acknowledgement (probate) contains the following information:

- a summary of the application to include the type of grant, the deceased's domicile at date of death, the name, address, and date and place of death of the deceased;
- the applicant's name, address, and relationship to the deceased;
- the gross foreign assets, the net foreign assets, the gross Irish estate, and the net Irish estate;
- the contact details of the applicant or lodging solicitor;
- the unique document ID number;
- details of Irish assets;
- details of Irish liabilities.

The Probate Office notify the Revenue Commissioners as soon as practicable by electronic means of the date on which the grant of representation was granted. It must also notify the Revenue that a will delivered to the Revenue pursuant to reg 3(1) of the CAT (Electronic Probate) Regulations, 2020 corresponds to the will delivered to the Probate Office.

CHAPTER 7

EXTRACTING A GRANT OF PROBATE

7.1 Probate Practice Background

Probate practice primarily involves the rules of court relating to applications for grants of representation and the information which must be contained in the relevant probate forms and documentation when making such applications. It is a technical and sometimes difficult area of law and overflows into many areas of practice such as conveyancing and family law. When applying for a grant of representation it is not sufficient merely to establish that the person applying is the person entitled to the grant. It is also important to ensure that the information contained in the forms is accurate and sufficient to satisfy Probate Office requirements and indeed that the correct forms are used. Documentation is used extensively in probate practice.

7.1.1 USE OF PRECEDENT FORMS

An understanding of probate law and practice is incomplete without a detailed knowledge of the correct documentation used in applying for grants. The nature of the documentation required will depend on whether the deceased died testate or intestate. Precedent forms for use in probate and administration matters are set out in Appendix Q of the Rules of the Superior Courts, 1986 as amended by SI 590/2020 and may also be accessed on the Probate page of the Courts Service website at http://www.courts.ie. Many of these forms are available from law stationers, either as pre-printed forms or on disk, and in many offices are set up as precedent documents on office PCs. Sample forms used in processing grants are contained in the following chapters dealing with the different types of grants of representation. Of great assistance to practitioners are the marginal notes contained in the sample forms, and these should be read carefully when completing the forms. In addition, every probate practitioner should have a copy of Eamonn G Mongey's wonderful book, *Probate Practice in a Nutshell*, 3rd edn (2006). The Probate Office recently reviewed the probate forms with the purpose of reducing the paperwork and number of copy documents sought when filing applications for grants of representation. It has reintroduced the notice of application to avoid the necessity of providing a copy of the oath. It has also merged the oath and the administration bond form required for grants of administration.

7.1.2 CONTENTIOUS AND NON-CONTENTIOUS PROBATE APPLICATIONS

In addition to applying for a grant of representation, probate practice may involve applications to either the Probate Officer or the court before the grant of representation can in fact be applied for. These applications are known as contentious and non-contentious probate applications. The applications are formal applications to either the High Court or the Probate Officer and strict proofs are required in order to be successful in obtaining the

EXTRACTING A GRANT OF PROBATE

necessary order. These applications will frequently arise for probate practitioners. The Probate Officer is given limited power in both the Succession Act, 1965 and O 79 of the Rules of the Superior Courts to deal with non-contentious applications and is allowed to make orders in relation to procedural matters in certain limited circumstances. The District Probate Registrars have no jurisdiction to make such orders.

Non-contentious applications are dealt with in **Chapter 11**.

Contentious matters may involve any of the following:

- the validity or the construction of a will;
- the manner in which the estate is being administered;
- the entitlement of a spouse or a civil partner to a legal right share;
- a claim pursuant to s 117, 117A, or 67A of the Succession Act, 1965 brought by a child of the deceased; or
- a claim pursuant to the Civil Partnership and Certain Rights and Obligations of Cohabitants Act, 2010 brought by a qualified cohabitant.

These contentious probate applications are probate actions and are commenced either by originating summons in the High Court or by testamentary/Succession Act or Equity Civil Bill in the Circuit Court.

7.1.3 ISSUE OF GRANTS

Grants of representation issue from either the Probate Office or a District Probate Registry. Pursuant to O 79, r 3 of the Rules of the Superior Courts, applications to the Probate Office and District Registries for grants may be made personally, through town agents, by post or document exchange service, or by delivery to a 'drop box'. When making a postal application to the Probate Office Dublin, the Probate page of the Courts Service website (http://www.courts.ie) should be accessed for the procedure relating to this. The Probate Office has jurisdiction for the twenty-six counties. The District Registries are controlled by County Registrars, with authority to issue grants only where the deceased had a fixed place of abode in the counties within the jurisdiction of the particular District Registry. For information on applications to District Registries, the Registry in question should be contacted as there may be regional variations.

7.1.3.1 District probate registries

The location of each District Probate Registry and the areas covered by each registry are as follows:

Castlebar:	County Mayo
Cavan:	Counties of Cavan and Longford
Clonmel:	County of Tipperary
Cork:	County and County Borough of Cork
Letterkenny:	County Donegal
Dundalk:	Counties of Louth and Monaghan
Galway:	Counties of Galway and Roscommon
Kilkenny:	Counties of Carlow, Kilkenny and Laois
Limerick:	Counties of Limerick and Clare; County Borough of Limerick
Mullingar:	Counties of Offaly and Westmeath

Sligo: Counties of Leitrim and Sligo

Tralee: County of Kerry

Waterford: County and County Borough of Waterford

Wexford: County of Wexford

7.1.3.2 Postal applications

Solicitors' applications for grants of representation submitted by post to the Dublin Probate Office must be accompanied by a completed Form S1 and must be clearly addressed to the 'SEAT OFFICE'. All postal applications must be accompanied with a stamped addressed envelope with sufficient value to cover posting back all documents.

A call-in counter service is available in the Dublin Probate Office. However, applications for *de bonis non* grants and all grants involving a foreign dimension (other than UK grants i.e. grants of representation that issue in England and Wales or in Northern Ireland) will not be accepted at the Seat Office public counter. It is preferred that such applications be submitted by post or DX, or deposited in the drop-in box located in the Seat Office.

7.1.4 GRANTS OF REPRESENTATION GENERALLY

As stated at para **6.1.1**, the term 'grant of representation' is a generic term and can in fact refer to any of the following types of grants, namely a grant of probate; a grant of administration with will annexed, a grant of administration intestate, or a *de bonis non* grant among others. The importance of a grant of representation is that it gives confirmation to the appointment of the personal representative and acts as an assurance to financial institutions and to others that they can safely transfer the deceased's assets into the hands of the personal representative for distribution according to the terms of the will or the intestacy, having first discharged any debts of the deceased.

Section 28 of the Succession Act, 1965 confirms that representation to real and personal estate may be granted separately or together. This follows on from the Administration of Estates Act, 1959, which provided in s 10 that real and personal estate both pass to the personal representative.

As referred to at para **6.4.2**, s 29 of the Succession Act, 1965 gives the High Court jurisdiction to make a grant of representation in respect of a deceased's estate notwithstanding that the deceased left no estate in the jurisdiction. It is sometimes necessary to obtain a grant for the purpose of making title where there are no assets, or in the case of a *de bonis non* grant where the estate has not been completely administered. This can arise, for example, in the case where the last surviving trustee of a settlement dies leaving no estate, but the only person entitled to appoint new trustees would be his or her personal representative. Where these grants are applied for, the Probate Office or District Registry will, however, seek the reason for them.

Order 79, r 33 of the Rules of the Superior Courts provides that no grant of representation may issue within fourteen days of the death of a person unless the court or the Probate Officer orders otherwise.

7.1.5 PERSONAL REPRESENTATIVES

The term 'personal representative' can be used for both *executors* (these are the persons nominated by a testator or testatrix in the will to administer the estate of that testator or testatrix), and *administrators*, who are persons appointed by the court to undertake these duties where a person dies intestate, or where someone other than an executor is seeking to prove a will. The rules and methods by which such persons are chosen are dealt with later.

EXTRACTING A GRANT OF PROBATE

Prior to the Administration of Estates Act, 1959, only personal property devolved on the personal representative. Now, when a death occurs on or after 1 June 1959, both real and personal property do so. The function of the legal personal representative is to collect all the assets of the deceased, pay all debts and funeral expenses, and distribute the balance of the estate, either according to the terms of the particular will or according to statute.

7.1.6 TYPES OF GRANTS OF REPRESENTATION

1. *Grant of probate*. This grant is given only to the executor or executors of a will.
2. *Grant of administration with will annexed*. This grant is given where there is a will but where someone other than an executor applies for a grant.
3. *Grant of administration intestate*. This grant is given when a person dies without having made a valid will.
4. *Second or subsequent grants*. This grant is given when a grant, which has already been given in the same estate, ceases, for example by reason of the death of the grantee.
5. *Limited grants*. Grants can be limited as regards duration (e.g. during minority), purpose (e.g. to substantiate proceedings), or subject-matter (e.g. trust property).
6. *Special grants* (e.g. grants given pursuant to s 31(1) or s 27(4) of the Succession Act).

The procedures for applying for the grants just mentioned are outlined in the following chapters.

7.2 Extracting a Grant of Probate

7.2.1 WHEN DOES A GRANT OF PROBATE ARISE?

To review executors, see para **3.1**.

Where an executor has been appointed, he or she has the first right to prove the will. The type of grant which issues when an executor or executrix proves the will is known as a grant of probate. Once appointed, an executor or executrix is not bound to act: he or she may accept, reserve, or renounce office. If an executor does not wish to prove the will, he or she may renounce his or her rights. Furthermore, any one of two or more executors may apply for a grant of probate without notice to the other executors and simply reserve the rights of those other executors. Renunciation and reservation are dealt with at para **3.5**.

While a grant of probate is probably the easiest grant of representation to obtain, nevertheless the Probate Officer rejects a significant number of these applications because of errors in the forms submitted.

It is important to determine from the outset whether the executor will act and do all that is necessary to apply for the grant of probate. The executor must be appraised of the consequences of either agreeing to act, or renouncing or reserving his or her right to act.

7.2.1.1 Acting as executor

When an executor agrees to act and duly applies for the grant of probate, such executor cannot, once the grant issues, seek to renounce office without the consent of the High Court.

7.2.1.2 Reservation of rights to act

As stated earlier, where several executors are appointed by will, all of them may apply for the grant of probate, or one or more only of them may apply, reserving the rights of the other named executors. Reservation of rights only arises where more than one executor is appointed. A sole executor cannot reserve his rights.

220 EXTRACTING A GRANT OF PROBATE

The proving executor(s) need not notify the executor who is not proving the will. It is sufficient to include the following sentence in the oath for executor form:

> *'Reserving the rights of AB the other executor or one of the other executors named in the will.'*

It is preferable, however, to obtain a letter from such executor, confirming his wish to reserve his rights. In the UK such a letter of confirmation from an executor reserving his rights is necessary for production to the court in order to obtain a grant. No such requirement exists as yet in Ireland.

Where an executor is not applying for a grant it is advisable for him to reserve his rights, rather than to renounce. If the executor(s) has/have renounced their right to obtaining the grant of probate, then, if there are no other executors named in the will, it will be necessary to apply for a grant of administration with will annexed, which will require a bond and other additional documentation. Grants of administration with will annexed are dealt with in detail in **Chapter 9**.

An executor whose rights are reserved may apply for a grant of double probate while the acting executor is still alive.

7.2.2 RENUNCIATIONS GENERALLY

Section 27(3) of the Succession Act, 1965 provides that the person to whom administration is to be granted shall be determined in accordance with the Rules of the Superior Courts.

Order 79, r 5 of the Rules of the Superior Courts sets out the order of priority in which persons with a beneficial interest in the deceased's estate shall be entitled to a grant.

Rule 5(1) deals with the order of priority to a grant of administration intestate in cases where the deceased died intestate on or after 1 January 1967, domiciled in Ireland. This is dealt with in **Chapter 8**.

Rule 5(6) deals with the order of priority to apply for a grant of administration with will annexed in cases where the deceased died testate on or after 1 January 1967, domiciled in Ireland. This is dealt with in **Chapter 9**.

Order 79, r 28(1) states:

> *'The oath of an administrator shall be so worded as to clear off all persons having a prior right to the grant. Where there are prior interests the grant shall show on the face of it how they have been cleared off.'*

When applying for any grant of representation, persons with priority over the applicant must in all cases be 'cleared off' in the oath. In intestacy cases, if the person having priority to the grant has since died, they can be 'cleared off' by an averment in the oath of administrator that they are now deceased (live interests are preferred to dead interests: O 79, r 5(9) (b)). This is dealt with in greater detail in **Chapter 8**.

However, where a person having priority to a grant of representation is alive, that person must renounce their rights to apply for the grant before the person having a lesser priority to such grant can apply.

7.2.2.1 Forms of renunciation

Where a person is renouncing their rights to a grant of representation, such renunciation must be in writing and must be signed by the renunciant in the presence of a disinterested witness. The renunciant must be over the age of eighteen years. The applicant must refer to the form of renunciation in the oath and it must be marked as an exhibit by both the applicant and by the commissioner for oaths/practising solicitor before whom the oath is being sworn. The forms of renunciation are prescribed by the Rules of the Superior Courts and are Forms 18 and 19 of Appendix Q in those rules.

These forms do not require the person renouncing to consent to or nominate the person making the application. Once the signed renunciation is available, an applicant with a beneficial interest in the estate under the Succession Act may apply in his own right for the grant exhibiting in the oath the renunciation of the person with priority to the grant.

7.2.2.2 Sample form of renunciation

There follows a sample form of renunciation appropriate where the deceased died testate and the executor in the will wishes to renounce his rights to probate, or where a person entitled to extract a grant of administration will annexed wishes to renounce. A form of renunciation for use where a deceased died intestate is set out in para **8.3.6.1**.

THE HIGH COURT

(PROBATE)

The Probate Office/The District Probate Registry at

Renunciation of Probate or Administration with the will Annexed.

In the Estate of   Whereas

                          Late of

                          In the county of

Deceased

Died on the day of 20   , at

[Where application is made in a District Probate Registry, add, 'having a fixed place of abode at the time of his/her death at   within the district of   ']

And whereas, he/she made and duly executed his/her last will

(or will and codicils)

bearing date the day of [*19 or 20*   ], and thereof appointed AB his sole Executor, (or as the case may be).

Now I, the said AB aged 18 years and upwards, do declare that I have not intermeddled with the) Estate of the said deceased and will not hereafter intermeddle therein, with the intent to defraud creditors; and I do hereby expressly renounce my right to Probate of the said will (or will and codicils) or to Letters of Administration with the said will (or will and codicils) Annexed, of the estate and effects of the said deceased.

Dated the day of 20   .

Signed [AB]

Witness*

[*One disinterested witness sufficient.*]

If the testator died before 1 January 1967, insert the word 'personal' before 'estate'.

7.2.2.3 Consequence of renunciation

Once a grant has issued on foot of a renunciation, the renunciation is final and cannot be withdrawn except by order of the court. It is important to explain to a client that they cannot come back into the administration at any stage in the future once they renounce, without an application to court, when advising them on the question of renunciation. Therefore, to prevent a second grant being required at a later date, one should only consider allowing a person to renounce if their renunciation is required to allow the applicant to apply for the grant.

7.2.2.4 Renunciation with nomination or consent

A renunciation with a nomination or consent can be used in two circumstances only, to allow persons who do not have a beneficial interest in the estate to apply for the grant of representation.

Situation 1

The first instance is where one person is entitled to the whole estate of the deceased, whether under the will or on intestacy. The person so entitled may renounce and nominate a person or persons who would be entitled to share in the renouncing party's estate, should he die intestate, to apply instead.

Order 79, r 5(12) provides that:

> 'where a person is entitled to the beneficial interest in the whole estate of a deceased, administration may on the renunciation and nomination of that person be granted to the person, or jointly to the persons, who would be entitled to the estate or to a share in the estate of the person so renouncing if that person had died intestate.'

The usual form of renunciation referred to earlier should be used, but with an additional sentence:

> 'And I hereby nominate A and B my lawful daughters (as the case may be) to apply for a Grant in the said estate.'

The rule may be used in the following situation:

> Jim Doe, the deceased, *'died intestate a single person who never married or entered into a civil partnership without issue or parent or brother or nephew or niece the issue of a predeceased brother or sister leaving him surviving one lawful and only sister namely Emma Deer who has duly renounced her rights and nominated us her lawful daughters to apply for a Grant.'*

The grant will issue to them in their capacity as *'the lawful daughters and nominees of the said Emma Deer'* and will not be limited in any way.

Situation 2

Order 79, r 5(13) provides that:

> 'where the parents of a deceased are entitled to the entire beneficial interest in the whole of the estate of the said deceased, administration may on the renunciation and consent of those parents be granted to the child or jointly to the children nominated by the parents.'

These grants are sometimes referred to in practice as *spes successionis* grants because they are frequently granted to a child of a renouncing parent who is entitled to all the estate on the basis that such child has a hope of succeeding to his parent's estate.

Once again, the form of renunciation referred to earlier should be used with an additional sentence whereby the parents or surviving parent consent and nominate one or more of their children by name to apply for the grant. The title in the oath in these circumstances will be as follows:

> *'died intestate a single person who never married or entered into a civil partnership without issue leaving him surviving Matthew Cane his lawful father and Liadhan Cane his lawful mother both of whom have duly renounced their rights and consented to us David Cane and Sean Cane their lawful children applying for the grant herein.'*

The grant will issue to them in their capacity as *'the lawful sons of the said Matthew Cane and the said Liadhan Cane'* and will not be limited in any way.

Summary

These rules are very helpful where the parents or the persons entitled to the whole estate of a deceased are elderly and do not wish to take on the administration of the estate themselves. The renunciation and consent must, as before, be referred to in the oath and marked as an exhibit by the applicant(s) and the commissioner for oaths or practising solicitor in the usual way.

7.2.2.5 Renunciation of executors

Section 17 of the Succession Act, 1965 provides that in the event of an executor renouncing his right to act, his right in respect of the executorship shall wholly cease. If a sole executor named in a will renounces his rights to probate, then a grant of administration with will annexed must be applied for, with the added complexities this will entail. Where an executor does not wish to act, it is always advisable for him to reserve his rights.

An executor who has intermeddled in the deceased's estate cannot renounce without an order of the court, as he may be deemed to have accepted office and may be compelled to act. The form of renunciation requires the executor to confirm that he has not intermeddled in the estate (see form at para **7.2.2.2**).

A person who renounces probate of a will or letters of administration with will annexed of the estate of a deceased person in one capacity cannot obtain representation to the same deceased in another capacity without an order of the court (O 79, r 38). This could happen, for example, where an executor renounces his rights as executor and subsequently wishes to apply as the legal personal representative of a residuary legatee or devisee or next of kin.

7.3 Who May Apply for a Grant of Probate?

Only persons who are appointed executors by a testator in his will are entitled to apply for a grant of probate, or persons who are constituted executors according to the tenor by virtue of the functions assigned to them by the will. The executor may, as outlined earlier, act, renounce, or reserve his rights to apply for probate. The title or capacity of the applicant is set out in the oath for executor form when applying for grant of probate and will always refer to the fact of the appointment of an executor. See para **7.4.4.2** for the title of the executor in each case.

Generally, the applicant for a grant of a grant of probate will be any one of the following:

1. The executors;
2. The sole executor named in the will;
3. One of the executors named in the will, reserving the rights of the other executors named in the will;
4. The surviving executor named in the will, or one of the surviving executors;
5. One of the executors named in the will, the other executor having duly renounced;
6. The person nominated by the resolution of a trust corporation named as executor to swear the documents under s 30(4) of the Succession Act, 1965;
7. The substituted executor; or
8. The solicitor/partner executor.

The appropriate title in each of these cases will be provided at para **7.4.4.2**.

7.3.1 NUMBER OF PROVING EXECUTORS

There is no limit to the number of executors that can be appointed in a will. However, O 79, r 5(14) of the Rules of the Superior Courts provides that:

> 'No grant of administration shall be made jointly to more than three persons unless the Probate Officer otherwise directs.'

7.4 Documents/Proofs Required for Grant of Probate

As noted earlier, an application for a grant of probate can be made either to the Probate Office or the District Probate Registry where the deceased was ordinarily resident.

224 EXTRACTING A GRANT OF PROBATE

Applications for grants may be made personally, through town agents, by post, by document exchange, or by delivery into a drop box.

Refer to the probate page of the Courts Service website (http://www.courts.ie) for details regarding procedure in respect of probate applications to the Probate Office. When applying for a grant of probate, the following documents must be lodged in the Probate Office or a District Probate Registry, as the case may be:

1. The *original* will and codicils (if any);

2. A certified copy of the will and codicils (if any) or a probate engrossment of the will and codicils (if any) This will be incorporated into the grant of probate;

    A certified copy is a photocopy of the will and codicils (if any) which is certified by the solicitors instructed in the estate to be a true copy of the original document(s). A probate engrossment is a typed version of a handwritten or otherwise unclear version of the will and codicils (if any), which again is certified by the solicitors instructed in the estate to be a true copy of the original document(s). The certified copy will is marked on the back by the applicant and the commissioner for oaths/ practicing solicitor before whom the oath was sworn;

3. The oath of executor;

4. The Notice of Acknowledgement (Probate) Form for deaths on or after 5 December 2001.

    Once the form SA.2 is successfully processed, the ROS will auto generate the Notice of Acknowledgement (Probate) Form. This form contains a unique number and must be printed and signed by the solicitor for the applicant. The form contains a summary of the Statement of Affairs (Probate) Form SA.2 to include details of the type of grant and the names, addresses, and details of both the deceased and the applicant. It also contains contact details of the solicitor acting for the applicant together with the gross and net estate. These have been dealt with in **Chapter 6**.

    Where the deceased died prior to 5 December 2001 the Inland Revenue affidavit form CA24 must be lodged in duplicate with the Revenue Commissioners before applying for a grant, and a certificate for the High Court must be obtained from them. A form CA6, Schedule of Lands and Building, must also be lodged with the Revenue where the estate comprises immoveable property. The form CA24, as certified by the Revenue, together with the certificate for the High Court and the form CA6 must then be lodged in the Probate Office. The date of death values and tenure must be inserted.

5. Original death certificate of the testator or coroner's interim notice of death where the final death certificate is not yet available. The original death certificate is required and it will be retained by the Probate Office/District Registry.

6. Probate Office fees payable in all cases as per schedule of fees in para **11.9.3**. Current fees are outlined in the Supreme Court and High Court (Fees) (Amendment) Order, 2021 (SI 80/2021) and are payable on the net estate except in the case of a *de bonis non* grant where a fixed fee applies. The fees are endorsed on the back of the notice of application, and since 27 July 2020 fee notes are no longer acceptable.

7. Notice of application. This form was reintroduced on 1 November 2019 to replace the copy oath for executor previously filed. A notice of application form is required when applying for a grant of probate and for all other grants of representation. It enables details of the application to be recorded immediately and it must be printed and not handwritten. The notice requires the following details:

    (i) The grant type;
    (ii) The name, address (including former addresses, occupation, PPS number, and domicile of the deceased;

(iii) The date and place of death of the deceased;

(iv) Details of the applicant(s) to include their name and address occupation and relationship to the deceased;

(v) The gross assets as per the form SA.2 and the net assets as per the form SA.2.

(vi) The name and address of the solicitors filing the application and to whom the grant will be posted in due course.

(vii) Fees (see para **7.4.15**) must be endorsed on the back of the form.

Documents that may be required in certain cases:

8. Form S1 (postal application by solicitor) if applicable. (Please see the relevant page on the Court Service website dealing with postal applications for a grant of representation);

9. Affidavit of due execution of will or codicil;

10. Affidavit of plight and condition (note that an affidavit of attesting witness dealing with both plight and condition and/or due execution may be used instead of two separate forms);

11. Affidavit of testamentary capacity;

12. Renunciation of executor;

13. Resolution of Trust Corporation;

14. Miscellaneous affidavits, for example, dealing with the identity of the executor or of the deceased;

15. Charitable bequest form from the Charities Regulatory Authority.

The most important of these documents will now be considered.

7.4.1 DEATH CERTIFICATE

As noted at para **6.6.3.2**, it is not uncommon for the prospective personal representative to attend at your office with the medical certificate showing cause of death, which may not yet have been registered. This is not a death certificate. Thus, the first job in relation to extracting a grant is usually to ensure that the next of kin or the relevant informant register the death at the earliest possible opportunity. On receipt of the death certificate, check it to make sure the details appearing on it are correct. It is not unknown for the deceased's name and even the date of death to be referred to incorrectly, and this will cause problems at a later stage. (See 'Oath of executor' at para **7.4.4**.) Obviously, if any amendments need to be made, these should be dealt with at once, prior to applying for a grant. The precise date of death must be stated in the oath. However, the date of death appearing in the oath is not prima facie evidence of the death of the deceased. While a duly authenticated death certificate should be produced to provide evidence of death whenever a grant is being applied for, if this is not immediately forthcoming due to the circumstances of the death, the Probate Office and District Probate Registry will accept a coroner's certificate as to the fact of death.

7.4.2 ORIGINAL WILL (AND CODICIL IF APPLICABLE)

The will, codicil, and any other testamentary document must be exhibited in the oath of executor and it must be marked by the executor and by the person before whom the oath is sworn (see O 79, r 37 of the Rules of the Superior Courts). Any such marking is usually made on the back of the will or elsewhere, so as not to interfere with the will or the attestation of it. The actual will must be signed and an exhibit sheet is not acceptable.

Where the will and/or codicil has already been proved in another jurisdiction, a sealed and certified copy of the said will must be obtained from the court where it was proved and it must be similarly marked by the executor and exhibited in the oath, together with a sealed and certified copy of the grant which issued in that jurisdiction. In all cases where the domicile of the deceased is outside Ireland, for example the UK, unless the will is executed in Ireland an affidavit of Law must be furnished confirming the will is executed in accordance with the law of domicile of the testator.

Order 79, r 13 provides that if a will contains a reference to any deed, memorandum, map, or other document of such nature as to raise a question whether it ought or ought not to form a constituent part of the will, such deed, memorandum, map, or other document shall be produced with a view to ascertaining whether it should be admitted to probate and, if not produced, its non-production shall be accounted for. Also, no deed, memorandum, or other document shall be admitted to probate as part of a will unless it was in existence at the time when the will was executed and is referred to specifically in the will.

7.4.3 CERTIFIED COPY WILL/ENGROSSMENT OF WILL (AND CODICIL IF ANY)

This is the copy of the will which will be subsequently included in the original grant of probate. The copy of the will must be written in a legible hand, or printed, typed, or photocopied, provided that it is a clear, legible copy on durable paper. It is subject to the directions of the Probate Officer. The paper should be A4 size and there should preferably be a margin on the left-hand side.

7.4.3.1 Probate engrossments (engrossment of will)

A probate engrossment should be a plain copy (not a photocopy) of the contents of the original will, with no corrections being made in the spelling. It should be written, typed, or printed without a break and it is usually prepared on green judicature paper. It is typically used nowadays where a will is not fully legible. Where interlineations or any other alterations are admitted to proof, they should not be so interlined in the engrossment, but should be inserted in their proper place.

7.4.3.2 Photocopy wills

The Probate Office will accept photocopies of wills for inclusion in the grant of probate and this is what is generally used in practice. All copy wills and engrossments should be certified by the solicitor for the applicant as being a true copy of the original will (and codicil, if any), or of a sealed and certified copy (if the will has already been proved in another jurisdiction). Two certified copies (or engrossments) of the will must be filed where the application for the grant is being made to a District Probate Registry. Please note that if the photocopy will is not legible you must prepare your own typed engrossment of the original will.

7.4.4 OATH OF EXECUTOR

The oath of executor outlines the capacity or title of the applicant to prove the will, i.e. to extract the grant of probate. Any will or copy of a will exhibited in the oath of the executor must be marked by the executor and the person before whom the oath is sworn. The actual will must be marked by the applicant. An exhibit sheet is not acceptable. The Probate Officer may, where he or she deems it necessary, require further proof of the identity of the deceased or of the parties applying for the grant, in addition to the information contained in the oath. See O 79, r 36 of the Rules of the Superior Courts. It is important to ensure that the correct title is used to avoid the application being rejected. A sample oath with different precedent titles is set out later in this chapter and can also be found in Appendix Q of the Rules of the Superior Courts as inserted by SI 590/2020.

7.4.4.1 Completing the oath of executor

The heading on all oaths (not just oaths for executors) should identify the type of oath and should contain the following information:

(a) The name of the deceased and any variations on that.

Where the name and address of either the deceased or the executors as set out in the oath are different from what is in the will, it will be necessary to explain the differences in the oath.

For example, where John Browne is named as the deceased on the death certificate and he is named as 'John Brown' in the will, it will be necessary to recite as follows:

'**John Browne** erroneously described in the will as John Brown'

or

'**John Brown** (otherwise known as John Browne)'.

For purposes of examination of the register of wills at a later time it is imperative that correct spellings of names of deceased persons and any variations used by them of their name be provided in the oath.

(b) The last address of the deceased and any former address (particularly an address given in the deceased's will).

Where the address of the applicant executor or testator has changed since the will was executed, the oath should show both addresses, with the words *'formerly of'* or *'in the will erroneously stated to be of'*, as the case may be. In any case, where the applicant's address differs from that given in the deceased's will, this should be explained in the oath. It is sometimes appropriate to have former addresses of a deceased testator set out in the grant where stocks and shares are registered in the name of the deceased at a former address. If there are more than three different addresses appearing on the oath for either the testator or the applicant, an order of the Probate Officer is necessary.

(c) Occupation of the deceased.

The descriptions of both the deceased testator and the applicant must be included in the oath for executor. 'Description' means the occupation of the person, and if this has changed since the date of the will, this must be referred to in the oath. If a person is retired, he or she may be described as *'retired teacher'*, for example, or *'pensioner'*.

(d) Place of death.

Details of the place and date of death of the testator should be included in the oath, and this information will be in the death certificate.

(e) The relationship (if any) between the executor and the testator.

The relationship between the executor and the deceased testator, if one exists, must appear in the oath. If the relationship is inconsistent with that stated in the will, the correct relationship should appear in the oath. If the applicant is not a blood relation of the deceased testator, this must be covered in the oath and the applicant may be described as a *'stranger in blood'* or *'no relation of the deceased'*.

(f) Several executors: reservation and/or renunciation.

This has been dealt with at para **7.2.2**.

   (a) Where several executors are appointed by will, all may apply for the grant or one or more only, the other executors renouncing their rights, or having them reserved.

   (b) Where an executor has renounced, the form of renunciation must be exhibited in the oath.

(c) Where one or more executors have died, the proving executor should be described as 'the surviving executor' or 'one of the surviving executors named in the will'.

(g) Office holder.

Where the holder of a particular office is appointed as executor, he or she must swear that he or she was the office holder 'for the time being at the date of death and, as such, the executor named in the will'.

(h) Firm of solicitors named as executor(s).

Where a firm of solicitors is appointed executor, it is the members of the firm at the date of the will who may act, unless the will provides otherwise, and they must swear the oath accordingly. This is an exception to the rule that a will speaks from death.

(i) Substituted executors.

An executor may also be substituted. The reason for the substitution, for example, the death of the first named executor, or the happening of some other contingency or fulfilment of a condition must be stated in the oath. An example of this would be where a *commorientes* clause takes effect on the spouse predeceasing the testator. The executor then acting would be the substitute executor.

(j) Trust corporations.

If a trust corporation is named as an executor, the resolution nominating a person to swear all the documents necessary to apply for a grant of probate on its behalf must be exhibited in the oath, and the way in which the trust corporation qualifies as such under s 30 of the Succession Act, 1965 must be clearly stated. As noted at para **3.2.2**, trust corporations under s 30 fall into three categories:

1. A corporation appointed by the High Court in any particular case to be a trustee.
2. A corporation empowered by its constitution to undertake trust business, and having a place of business in the State or in Northern Ireland, and being either an associated bank under the Central Bank Act, 1942 or a company which fulfils certain conditions.
3. A corporation which satisfies the President of the High Court that it undertakes the administration of any charitable, ecclesiastical, or public trust without remuneration, for example, the Representative Church Body, the Maynooth Mission to China, the Irish Cancer Society.

Banks and companies which are entitled to extract grants in other countries, but which do not qualify as trust corporations here, must appoint attorneys to extract grants (of administration) in this jurisdiction.

(k) 'That he/she did not intermarry or enter into a civil partnership with any other person after the making of the will.'

The main reason for including this statement in the oath is that if the testator had married after the execution of the will that subsequent marriage would have revoked the will, unless it was established that the will was made in contemplation of marriage. If such is the case, the date of the marriage must be referred to in the oath. Section 85(1) of the Succession Act, 1965 provides that a will shall be revoked by the subsequent marriage or entry into a civil partnership of the testator except a will made in contemplation of that marriage or entry into a civil partnership, whether so expressed in the will or not. In all cases the oath must now state that the deceased did not enter into a marriage or civil partnership after the execution of the will. A will is also automatically revoked when a civil partnership is registered unless the will was made in contemplation of the registration of that civil partnership. Since the enactment of the Marriage Act, 2015, no civil partnerships can be registered in Ireland.

See para **2.3.1**.

(l) The gross value of the estate.

The oath must contain a statement of the gross value of the estate (both real and personal) of the testator, within this jurisdiction, without any deductions for debts. This figure should be the market value at the date of death.

(m) The Jurat and the filing clause.

The Jurat must comply with SI 95/2009 and cannot be executed before the lodging solicitor. All oaths should contain a full filing clause. This will provide details of the applicant solicitor's name and address to which ultimately the grant is to be posted.

7.4.4.2 Precedent oath of executor

The titles for executors in this precedent sample are titles based on the list of different types of applicants at para **7.3**.

THE HIGH COURT

PROBATE

OATH OF EXECUTOR/ EXECUTRIX

The Probate Office, Phoenix House, Smithfield, Dublin 7 / The District Probate Registry at

PART A

Name of Deceased:. . . . .

Address of Deceased:. . . . .

Date of Death:. . . . .

Place of Death:. . . . .

Name of Applicant:. . . . .

Address of Applicant:. . . . .

Gross value of Estate:. . . . .

PART B

I the above named applicant aged eighteen years and upwards, make Oath and say that I believe the paper writing hereto annexed and marked by me to contain the true and original last will [or last will with . . . codicil/s] of the above named deceased; that same was made by the said deceased after attaining the age of eighteen years and that the said deceased did not intermarry or enter into a civil partnership with any person after the making of same,

That I am the [state relationship] of the said deceased and * [insert title] in the said will [or will and codicils] named.

Sample Titles:

1. We are [the relationship of the executor/s to the deceased is inserted here] of the said deceased and the two Executors in the said will (with codicil(s)) named.

Or

2. I am (relationship of executor to deceased) and the sole Executor in the said will (with codicil(s)) named.

Or

3. I am (relationship of executor to deceased) and one of the Executors in the said will (with codicil(s)) reserving the rights of X the other Executor/Executrix in the said will named.

Or

4. I am (relationship of executor to deceased) and the surviving Executor named in the will (with codicil/s) the other Executor X therein named having predeceased the

deceased, and I beg to refer to a copy of his/her death certificate upon which I have signed my name prior to the swearing hereof.

Or

5. I am (relationship of executor to deceased) and the surviving Executor named in the will (with codicil/s) the other Executor X therein named having duly renounced his/her rights by Renunciation dated the day of 20, upon which renunciation marked with the letter 'A' I have signed my name prior to the swearing hereof.

Or

6. That the Bank is the sole Executor in the said will named; and that I the said XY am the person appointed by Resolution of the Bank dated the day of 20   to swear on behalf of the Bank the documents necessary to lead to a Grant of Probate of the said will and I beg to refer to a sealed copy of the said Resolution marked 'A' upon which I have signed my name prior to the swearing hereof; that the Bank is a Trust Corporation within the meaning of s 30(4)(b)(ii) of the Succession Act, 1965 being a Corporation empowered by its constitution to undertake Trust business and having a place of business in the State, and being an associated Bank under the Central Bank Act, 1942; that the Bank will faithfully administer the estate.

Or

7. That he did therein name as sole instituted executor AB who predeceased the testator/died simultaneously with him on the day of 20   and that I am (relationship of executor to deceased) and the substituted executor in the said will named.

8. I am an Executor in the said will named as the deceased did therein appoint the partners at the date of his/her death in the firm of X in the County of Dublin or the firm which has succeeded to and carries on its practice to be the Executors thereof and whereas there were two partners only in the firm of X at the date of death of the deceased and at the date hereof, namely X and I the Deponent and I refer to a copy of a Resolution of the said X and I this Deponent dated the day of 20   ; upon which marked with the letter 'B' I have signed my name prior to the swearing hereof, nominating, constituting and appointing I the Deponent to extract the Grant of Probate in the estate of the above named deceased.

9. I was a partner in the firm AB at the date of death of the deceased and as such one of the Executors named in the Will reserving the rights of XY the other Executrix in the Will named.

That I will faithfully administer the estate of the said deceased by paying the deceased's just debts and the legacies bequeathed by the deceased said will (or will and codicil(s)), so far as the same shall thereto extend and the law bind me; that I will exhibit a true Inventory of the said estate, and render a true account thereof, whenever required by law so to do; that the deceased died at the above named place of death on the date of death recited above.

(Where application is made in District Probate Registry add) and that the deceased had at the time of death a fixed place of abode at the above named address within the district of ..... and that the whole of the Estate without any deductions for debts, which devolves on and vests in the deceased's legal personal representative amounts in value to the figure cited above as the gross value of the estate and no more to the best of my knowledge, information and belief. (Note the gross Irish assets without any deduction for debts are included here).

SWORN at

in the County of

by the said

this   day of   **20**

before me a Commissioner for Oaths and I know the Deponent

(or–I–know who–certifies to–his/her knowledge of the Deponent)

Commissioner for Oaths/Practising Solicitor

Filing clause

This affidavit is filed on behalf of the Executor/s by Solicitors

Of

This the day of 20

7.4.5 NOTICE OF APPLICATION

As and from 1 November 2019 the Probate Officer requires practitioners to file a notice of application in lieu of providing a copy oath of executor. The notice of application must be printed and cannot be completed by hand to ensure legibility as the Probate Office scans these forms. The fees are endorsed on the back of this form and payment by way of fee note or cheque is no longer acceptable. See para **7.4.9** dealing further with the notice of application.

7.4.6 RENUNCIATION OF EXECUTOR

Where an executor has been appointed in a will and does not wish to act, he may renounce his rights. The forms for renouncing probate and letters of administration with will annexed may be found at para **7.2.2.2**. The renunciation form should be exhibited in the oath of executor. The executor applying for the grant and the commissioner for oaths/practising solicitor should sign the back of the renunciation form. The title of the oath of executor, where one executor is applying for the grant and the other is renouncing, would read as follows:

> 'I am one of the executors named in said will, the other executor named, Niall Murray has duly renounced his rights upon which renunciation dated 16 October 20 I have marked my name prior to the swearing hereof.'

7.4.7 STATEMENT OF AFFAIRS (PROBATE) FORM SA.2

For applications for grants of representation filed on or after 14 September 2020 in respect of deaths on or after 5 December 2001 the Statement of Affairs (Probate) Form SA.2 replaces the Inland Revenue Affidavit Form CA24. The form SA.2 is completed and submitted electronically on ROS as provided for in s 48A CATCA, 2003 (as inserted by s 63 of the Finance Act ,2019) as amended.

Section 48A sets out the information to be provided in the form SA.2, which may include the following:

1. A full account of the deceased's assets valued at the date of death.
2. The nature and situation of the property.
3. All liabilities in the estate to include funeral expenses, tax owing to the Revenue, utilities, amounts owing to financial institutions, mortgages, HSE Nursing Home Support Scheme charge, and nursing home fees.
4. Details about the deceased to include name, address, PPS number, residence, ordinary residence, and domicile at the time of death.
5. The type of grant required.
6. Details of the beneficiaries receiving a benefit from the estate in excess of €12,000, their PPS Numbers, and relationships to the deceased and information of any prior aggregable benefits received. Details of any charitable bequest.

7. Details of the applicant for the grant and the contact details of the solicitor filing the form.

8. Information on, amongst other things, assets passing outside the will by survivorship or nomination.

Once the form SA.2 is processed, the Revenue will generate a notice of acknowledgement (probate) with a unique number that must be printed, signed, and certified by the solicitor for the applicant and submitted to the Probate Office/District Probate Registry with the other papers required to lead to the grant of representation.

Once the application for the grant is approved and the grant of representation issues, the Probate Office will notify the Revenue electronically. The form SA.2 will then be activated on the Revenue systems.

The form SA2 is dealt with in greater detail in **Chapter 6**.

For deaths prior to 5 December 2001 the form CA24 is filed in duplicate with the Revenue Commissioners together with a form CA6 where the estate includes immoveable real or leasehold property. In due course, one copy of both the forms CA24 and CA6 duly certified by the Revenue are returned with a certificate for the High Court attached. This certified Inland Revenue affidavit form CA24, form CA6, and certificate for the High Court are then lodged with the other probate papers in the Probate Office or District Probate Registry. This practice is applicable only in respect of deaths occurring before 5 December 2001.

- The value of properties in the forms SA.2 and CA24 is shown as at the *date of death* of the deceased.

As noted at para **6.9**, the Inland Revenue affidavit is a private document containing sensitive information from a privacy and a data protection viewpoint and access to it is strictly restricted by Practice Direction HC 49 (as amended).

This direction provides that on the issue of the grant of representation certain documents are to be made available for public inspection including the grant of representation itself. However, in the context of the Inland Revenue affidavit certain conditions apply:

'(A) *The inventory of a deceased's person's estate as is contained in the inland revenue affidavit may be inspected by a person who is:*

   (i) *a beneficiary named in the will of the deceased person which has been proved in the Probate Office or a District Probate Registry,*

   (ii) *entitled to share in the estate of a deceased person,*

   (iii) *a creditor of the deceased whose debt has been admitted by the estate or proved by the creditor in question, or is a creditor of the deceased in any other case where the Judge of the High Court exercising probate jurisdiction shall so direct,*

   (iv) *entitled to bring proceedings against the estate pursuant to Section 117 of the Succession Act 1965.*

(B) *All information as is contained in the Inland Revenue affidavit and in which a government department or government agency has a legitimate interest may be inspected by an employee of such department or agency.*

Provided that the person/s seeking to inspect such documentation under (A) or (B) establishes to the satisfaction of the Probate Officer, District Probate Registrar or Judge of the High Court exercising probate jurisdiction, as the case may be, that it is appropriate to authorise such inspection.'

7.4.8 PROBATE TAX CLEARANCE CERTIFICATE

The Finance Act, 1993 introduced probate tax for all deaths from 17 June 1993. The tax was abolished on 6 December 2000. Returns (form PT1) for payment of this tax (where payable) must be prepared and submitted to the Revenue Commissioners at the same time as the Inland Revenue affidavit, and the clearance certificate (form PT2) which is received back from the Revenue Commissioners must be submitted with the papers to the Probate Office. Because it has now been abolished, it is very easy to forget that this tax still applies for deaths occurring between these two dates. For further details, see CAT Lecture Notes (see Preface) for Lecture 27.

7.4.9 NOTICE OF APPLICATION

As and from 1 November 2019 the notice of application is required in both the Principal Probate Registry (the Probate Office) and in the District Probate Registries and has replaced the requirement to lodge two photocopies of the oath of executor. The notice of application is a simple one-page document reciting the name, address, and date and place of death of the deceased; the name, address, and capacity (title) of the applicant; and the name and address of the solicitor lodging the papers to lead to the grant. It also states the type of grant being applied for and the gross and net assets as per the SA.2. See para **7.4.5**.

7.4.10 AFFIDAVIT OF ATTESTING WITNESS OR WITNESSES

The affidavit of attesting witness form reproduced here can be used both when dealing with problems arising from both the due execution of the will and/or for problems concerning the plight and condition of the will itself. A sample may be found in Appendix Q of the Rules of the Superior Courts Form No 2.

7.4.11 AFFIDAVIT OF DUE EXECUTION

It is a prerequisite of s 78 of the Succession Act, 1965 that, in order for a will to be valid, such will must be validly executed. Although, strictly speaking, the fact that one will or may require an affidavit of attesting witness often comes to light when proving the will, it is very important to remember the provisions of s 78 at the will-drafting stage. If these formalities are properly complied with, then such affidavits may not in fact be required. Section 78 deals with the form and execution of a will and its provisions are dealt with at paras **2.13**, **2.14**, and **2.15**.

7.4.11.1 Essential elements of execution

To be valid, a will must be in writing and the testator/rix must sign or acknowledge his or her signature in the presence of two or more witnesses. Those witnesses must each sign the will in the presence of the testator/rix but not necessarily in the presence of each other, although it is good practice to have both witnesses present at the same time.

Unlike the signature of the testator/rix, the signatures of the witnesses may be placed anywhere in the will, provided that they intended to attest the signature of the testator/rix.

There is a vast amount of case law outlining the judicial interpretation of the various terms contained in s 78, and those cases dealing with the duty of care of the solicitor regarding execution of wills are of particular interest. Practitioners are referred to para **5.9**, which outlines some of these cases.

7.4.11.2 Execution of wills and Probate Office concerns

When the will is presented to the Probate Office for proof, the primary concern of the Probate Office is that the will is a validly executed document and complies with the s 78 formalities. The emphasis is on the technical execution of the will and not the manner in which the estate of the deceased is distributed. The fact that the content of the will may appear unusual and inconsistent need not interfere with its validity as a legal document. With this in mind, the official in the Seat Office will read the will and, if it appears that on the face of it the statutory formalities are complied with, the remainder of the probate papers will be processed.

However, if the attestation is defective or there are alterations, deletions, or additions made to the will, an affidavit of attesting witness will be required by the Probate Office. To prevent delays, practitioners should anticipate when such an affidavit would be required and it is advisable to furnish it at the outset when lodging the papers to lead to a grant of probate (or of letters of administration with will annexed), rather than waiting for a request from the Probate Office to furnish it.

7.4.11.3 When will an affidavit of due execution be required?

Nowadays, most wills are prepared and executed in a solicitor's office and are proved without any question arising as to their due execution. However, it is not unusual to be asked to go to the hospital or to the house of a testator/rix to take instructions for a will or to have a will executed. It sometimes happens that because the will is being executed in difficult and stressful circumstances, mistakes can be made regarding its execution. In such circumstances it is prudent to swear an affidavit of attesting witness to be left with the will. It is possible to anticipate in advance when an affidavit will be required. The following are the more usual circumstances where such an affidavit will be required.

7.4.11.4 Where the testator's signature appears below those of the witnesses

Although s 78(1) provides that the will must be signed at the 'foot or end' by the testator, case law has given a broad interpretation to these words. In addition, s 78(4) and (5) should be noted. These subsections provide as follows:

Section 78(4)

'No such will shall be affected by the circumstances:

(a) that the signature does not follow or is not immediately after the foot or end of the will; or

(b) that a blank space intervenes between the concluding words of the will and the signature; or

(c) that the signature is placed among the words of the testimonium clause or of the clause of attestation, or follows or is after or under the clause of attestation, either with or without a blank space intervening, or follows or is after, or under, or beside the names or one of the names of the attesting witness; or

(d) that the signature is on a side or page or other portion of the paper or papers containing the will on which no clause or paragraph or disposing part of the will is written above the signature; or

(e) that there appears to be sufficient space on or at the bottom of the preceding side or page or other portion of the same paper on which the will is written to contain the signature;

and the enumeration of the above circumstances shall not restrict the generality of rule 1.'

Section 78(5)

'A signature shall not be operative to give effect to any disposition or direction inserted after the signature is made.'

Therefore, in a situation where the testator's signature appears below those of the witnesses, an affidavit of attesting witness must be given, confirming that the signature was intended to give effect to the will and that the execution was otherwise regular. This affidavit should be sworn at the time of execution and left with the will.

7.4.11.5 Where the testator signs twice

It happens frequently that the testator inadvertently signs the will twice, perhaps by signing the will in the 'wrong place' first and then signing again in the correct place, or being unhappy with the style of the signature, signs again before being told that the first signature is in order. Where this occurs, it is necessary for an affidavit of attesting witness to be supplied, confirming that both signatures were made in one continuous act of execution.

This affidavit should be sworn and left with the will at the time of its execution.

Sample clause:

'The two signatures appearing in the said will were made by the Testator in error the Testator having first signed below the attestation clause and when the error was pointed out to him he signed his name above the attestation clause, [or, that the Testator signed his name twice because he had difficulty signing his name]. I confirm that both signatures were made in one continuous act of execution.'

7.4.11.6 Where the testator signs with a mark

The testator may sign with a mark if he or she is unable to write because of illiteracy or physical infirmity. In this situation the will must be read over to the testator prior to execution or alternatively the testator must read the will and be satisfied with its contents. The attestation clause in the will should state the reason for signature by mark and should confirm that the will was read to or by the testator prior to execution and that the testator was of sound dis-posing mind.

Sample clause:

'and I further say that the Testator signed his name by affixing his mark at the foot or end thereof as the same now appears thereon he being unable to write due to physical debility or illiteracy, in the presence of me and of AB [name of other witness] both of us being present at the same time and we then in the presence of the Testator signed our names as witnesses.

And I further say that before said Testator executed said will same was read over to him by me [or by X in my presence] and said Testator appeared to fully understand the same and was at the time of execution thereof of sound memory and understanding.'

7.4.11.7 Where the testator's signature is feeble, indecipherable, or poorly formed

If the testator is likely to make an enfeebled, indecipherable, or poorly formed signature, perhaps by reason of suffering from a stroke or some such illness, then the same procedures as for signature by mark should be adopted.

Sample clause:

'The signature of the Testator as appears from the said will is enfeebled and/or poorly formed. This was because the Testator was suffering from a stroke and had lost some of the power of his right hand and was thus unable to make his signature properly.

And I further say that before said Testator executed said will same was read over to him by me [or by X in my presence] and said Testator appeared to fully understand the same and was at the time of execution thereof of sound memory and understanding.'

(Note: this clause can be adapted to fit the circumstances.)

7.4.11.8 Where the testator's signature is made on his behalf by another person

A third party may sign the will on behalf of the testator and this person may sign either the testator's name or his or her own name. The third party must make the signature at the direction of and in the presence of the testator. Both witnesses must witness the fact that the signature was made at the direction of the testator and in his presence.

Sample clause:

'The said will was executed on the day of 20 by Q [this is the person who actually signs the will] signing the name of the Testator [or his or her name] at the foot or end of the will at the direction of the Testator and in his presence in lieu of the Testator signing his name he being unable to write due to physical debility [or whatever the reason is] in the presence of me and Y [name of other witness] both of us being present at the same time and we then in the presence of the Testator signed our names as witnesses.

Prior to the execution of the will as aforesaid the will was read over to the Testator by me or by X [name of the person who read the will over to the Testator] in my presence and the Testator appeared fully to understand same and was at the time of execution of the will of sound mind and understanding.'

7.4.11.9 Where the testator is blind

In the case of a blind testator the law requires that the witnesses sign their names to the will in such a position that had the testator sight he or she would have been able to see them sign; however, the witnesses themselves must not be blind, even if the testator has sight. The requirement of 'presence' of the witnesses means 'visual presence'. The blind testator should sign the will in the normal way, in the presence of two witnesses. An affidavit of attesting witness, averring that the will was read over to the testator and that he appeared to understand it, and that the witnesses signed their names in such a position that he could have seen them so sign if he had eyesight, should be sworn at the date of execution of the will and left with the will, even if the attestation clause in the will contains such a statement.

Order 79, r 63 of the Rules of the Superior Courts requires an affidavit to confirm that the will was read over to a blind testator.

Sample clause:

'I further state that at the time of execution of said will the Testator was blind and that I and the said X, the other subscribing witness, signed our names in such a position that had the Testator been possessed of his eyesight he could have seen us so sign. I further state that before said will was executed by the Testator in the manner aforesaid the same was read over to him by me [or X in my presence] and said Testator appeared fully to understand the same and was at the time of the execution thereof of sound memory and understanding.'

7.4.11.10 Where the will is written on several sheets of paper

Where a will is drawn up on separate sheets of paper it is imperative that all the sheets of paper be in the same room at the time of execution and an affidavit of attesting witness will be required, confirming that all the sheets were in the same room at the time of execution by the testator and that nothing of a testamentary nature was at any time attached to the said will.

It would be prudent to draft and swear the affidavit at the time of the execution of the will. If the sheets of paper are separate sheets and are not joined together at the time of execution, it is better to leave them in this condition, rather than joining them together by clip, pin, or staple, as this may give rise to a query as to whether anything additional of a testamentary nature was attached to the will.

7.4.11.11 Where the problem relates to the date of the will

Where the will is undated, or contains different dates, or if any doubt arises concerning the date of the will, an affidavit will be required from one or both of the witnesses present at the time of execution, or from some other person having information, confirming the date of execution of the will.

7.4.11.12 Amendments, interlineations, alterations, erasures, or obliterations

If there are any alterations to the will prior to its execution, the amendment should be covered in the attestation clause and the attestation clause should state that the particular amendment, by giving details of it, was made prior to the execution of the will. In addition, the testator and both witnesses should initial the amendments in exactly the same manner as for the execution of a will. It is prudent to swear an affidavit of attesting witness, outlining all the amendments, and these amendments must be specifically referred to in the affidavit. It is not sufficient to say 'all the amendments etc.'

Provisions regarding alterations and amendments in a will are contained in s 86 of the Succession Act. This section provides that all alterations, obliterations, and interlineations made in a will after execution shall not be valid or have any effect unless such alteration is executed as is required for the execution of a will. An alteration made before the execution of a will is validated by the proper execution of the will. If no evidence is forthcoming regarding amendments to the will, they are presumed to have taken place after execution.

Sample clause:

> '(1) The words "including my collection of cuneiform clay tablets" were interlineated between the sixth and seventh line on page one of the said will prior to its execution by the Testator, and
>
> (2) the word "sister" at line twenty of said will was altered to read "brother" and
>
> (3) the figure "€6,000" at line ten of said will was amended to read "€6,500", and
>
> (4) the erasure/deletion of the words "my farm at Loughville" over which is written the words "my farm at Kilamley" on the fourteenth line on the second page of the said will, and
>
> I further say that the said recited interlineations, alterations and overwritten erasures were written and made in the said will prior to the execution thereof by the Testator.'

7.4.11.13 Attestation clause

Where a will appears to be properly signed and witnessed, nevertheless without the inclusion of an attestation clause, there is no evidence to satisfy the Probate Officer as to the due execution of the will.

Rule 2 of s 78 of the Succession Act, while setting out the requirement for witnesses to attest to the signature of the testator, does not require any form of attestation. The attestation of a witness will be operative even if only his or her signature appears on the will. Nevertheless, the use of a proper attestation clause is desirable. Order 79, r 6 states that where there is no, or no sufficient, attestation clause, or it is defective, for example by not setting out clearly that the will was executed according to the provisions of the Succession Act, the Probate Officer will require an affidavit from at least one of the attesting witnesses to prove due execution. A note signed by the Probate Officer will be made on the copy of the will to the effect that such an affidavit has been filed.

It is important to ensure that the will has a proper attestation clause. There is no need to have an overly long or complicated clause and the following sample clause is perfectly adequate to satisfy Probate Office requirements:

> *'Signed by the Testator in our presence, both present at the same time, and by us in the presence of the Testator.'*

Where different circumstances arise in relation to the due execution of the will, for example where the testator is blind or feeble, or where the testator signs twice, or where the will is written on a number of separate sheets of paper, these matters should be covered in the attestation clause. The Probate Officer is at liberty to ask for an affidavit of attesting witness and usually does so even where all matters concerning due execution are fully set out in the attestation clause. For this reason it is advisable, even though the attestation clause may contain a full statement of what transpired at the execution of the will, to prepare at the time of said execution an affidavit of attesting witness confirming that all the relevant matters were attended to.

7.4.11.14 Who may make an affidavit of attesting witness dealing with due execution?

1. The attesting witness: when making any affidavit to admit a will to proof, such witness must deal with due execution (O 79, r 41). If the witnesses are dead or if, from other circumstances, no affidavit can be obtained from either of them, then

2. an affidavit from some other person present at the execution who was not a witness may be accepted (O 79, r 8); or from

3. persons who drafted the will or read it over to the testator (as far as the amendments are concerned).

4. If no affidavit of any such person can be obtained, an application must be made to court, giving evidence on affidavit of the handwriting of the deceased and the witnesses and also of the circumstances, which may raise a presumption in favour of due execution (O 79, r 9).

7.4.11.15 Will condemned

Where the will is not duly executed the Probate Officer has power to refuse probate of the purported testamentary document. An affidavit of attesting witness may be submitted, but if it is evident from its contents that the requirements of the Succession Act as to the due execution of a valid will were not complied with, the Probate Officer may make an order refusing probate in the circumstances. He or she may also refuse probate of part of a will. The Probate Officer may then refer the matter to court (O 79, rr 6 and 7).

7.4.12 AFFIDAVIT OF PLIGHT AND CONDITION

When admitting a will to probate, the physical condition of the will is important. As with the affidavit of attesting witness dealing with the due execution of the will, a solicitor will generally realise when an affidavit of plight and condition will be required, simply by looking at the physical condition of the will. An affidavit will be required in any of the following situations:

1. If the will has any paper-clip marks, pin holes, or traces of adhesive.
2. If the will has a tear on any part of it, for example torn edges on the top or bottom corners.

In both of these situations the Probate Officer will seek evidence to show how the marks and tears occurred and evidence stating that nothing of a testamentary nature was at any time attached to the said will or codicil.

3. If there are any tears, burns, obliterations, or attempted cancellations, evidence will be required to show that the testator did not intend to revoke the will or codicil.

7.4.12.1 Who may make such affidavits of plight and condition?

1. The attesting witness.
2. The person responsible for the mark or tear.
3. The person in whose custody the will was retained.
4. The person who found the will.

7.4.12.2 Sample clause on plight and condition

This clause may be added to the sample precedent affidavit of attesting witness form at para **7.4.12.3**. In practice, the one form of affidavit is generally used when dealing with both 'due execution' and 'plight and condition', although in some instances a separate form of affidavit will be used (where different persons are dealing with separate aspects).

> 'And having particularly observed that the said will is torn along the left-hand side and that certain pinholes and paper-clip marks appear at the top left-hand corner, I further say that I tore the page on which the will was written from a jotter [or as the case may be] prior to the execution of the said will and that the said pinholes and paper-clip marks were caused when attendance instructions for the will were inadvertently attached to the said will [or as the case may be]. Nothing of a testamentary nature was at any time attached to the said will which is now, apart from the pin holes and paper-clip marks, in the same plight and condition as when executed by the Testator.'

7.4.12.3 Sample form of affidavit of attesting witness

THE HIGH COURT

PROBATE

The Probate Office/The District Probate Registry at

(a) Address and description of witness	In the Estate of *(b)* Deceased. I Of *(a)* In the County of Aged 18 years and upwards make Oath
(b) Address and description of deceased	That I am one of the subscribing witnesses to the last will (and Codicil(s)) of the said Late of *(b)* In the County of
(c) By signing his/her name or affixing his/her mark, being illiterate or being unable to write from physical debility (as the case may be). *If testator/rix was blind or had defective vision the appropriate clause as to location should be added.*	Deceased; the said will (and Codicil(s)) being now hereunto annexed, bearing date the day of one/ two thousand and that the said Testator/rix executed the said will (and Codicil(s)) on the day of the date thereof by *(c)* at the foot or end thereof, as the same now appears thereon in the presence of me and of [*insert name* of *other witness*] the other subscribed witness thereto, both of us being present at the same time, and we immediately after such execution by the Testator/rix attested and subscribed the said will (and Codicil(s)) in the presence of the Testator/rix and of each other.
(d) If there are alterations, interlineations, erasures or obliterations in the will, the affidavit should state them specifically and say whether they were made prior to execution.	*(d)* And I further say that before the said Testator/rix executed the said will (and Codicil(s)) in manner aforesaid, the same was truly audibly and distinctly read over to him/her by me [or by AB in my presence] and that the said Testator/rix appeared fully to understand the same and was at the time of the execution thereof of sound mind memory and understanding. *(e)*
(e) If the will is on a half or torn sheet of paper, the affidavit should state that at the time of execution there was no other document of a testamentary nature annexed thereto, and should also state whether or not the will was on a torn or half-torn sheet at the time of execution.	SWORN at in the County of by the said **this** day of **20** before me a Commissioner for Taking Affidavits and I know the Deponent (or– who–certifies to–his/her knowledge of the Deponent) .... I Certify that I know the Deponent or the identity of the Deponent has been established by reference to a relevant document containing a photograph Document Type................................. Issue No:...................................... Commissioner for Oaths/Practising Solicitor

7.4.13 AFFIDAVIT OF MENTAL OR TESTAMENTARY CAPACITY

Section 77(1) of the Succession Act, 1965 provides:

'To be valid a will shall be made by a Person who:

(a) has attained the age of eighteen years or is or has been married, and

(b) is of sound disposing mind.'

Soundness of mind is normally presumed, but where a doubt as to the testamentary capacity of a testator is raised, an affidavit confirming that the testator was of sound disposing mind at the time of making the will is required.

This affidavit will always be required where there is a doubt as to the testamentary capacity of the testator when he made the will. Such a doubt is raised in the following circumstances:

1. Where the testator was a ward of court.

2. Where the deceased died in a psychiatric institution.

3. Where the will was made while the testator was a patient in a psychiatric institution.

4. Where the testator's death certificate refers to a mental condition such as Alzheimer's disease, dementia, or cognitive impairment as being either a cause of death or a co-existing condition.

The Probate Office will examine the will to determine if there is any potential for conflict if the will was admitted to proof. If, for example, the testator leaves all his estate to his spouse or, in the event of his spouse predeceasing, to his children in his will, no issue will be raised as to the testamentary capacity of the testator. These are persons who might be expected to benefit under the testator's will and seeking an affidavit of testamentary capacity in this instance should not be necessary. Similarly, if there is only one will in existence and distribution of the estate is the same as it would be on an intestacy basis, no issue will arise. Where, however, a testator leaves his property to a stranger or one member of his family to the exclusion of other members of his immediate family, it is highly probable that an affidavit of testamentary capacity will be sought in the matter. As a guideline, if the will exhibits a potential for conflict, an affidavit will be sought.

The death certificate will very often state the length of time the person has been suffering from the mental illness. If the will was made a reasonable time prior to the period referred to in the death certificate, an affidavit may not be required. However, it does not override the requirement for an affidavit of testamentary capacity where the death certificate indicates any of the conditions referred to earlier. The Probate Officer will take the facts of each case into account. Passage of time in and of itself does not allow the Probate Office to draw an inference that the testator had the requisite capacity to make the will at the time in question. The requirement where the testator, for example, suffered a stroke and as a result became incapacitated suddenly would differ from a case where the testator was, for example, suffering from Alzheimer's disease, which takes effect gradually over a period of time. Each situation will be reviewed within the context of its own set of circumstances.

7.4.13.1 Who should swear the affidavit of testamentary capacity?

Annette O'Connell, the former Probate Officer, in a DSBA Probate & Tax seminar held on 10 May 2011 outlined the persons who should swear an affidavit of testamentary or mental capacity as follows.

The doctor

The preferred evidence is an affidavit sworn by the medical practitioner who was attending the testator at the time of execution of the will. A precedent of this affidavit is shown at para **7.4.13.2**. The medical practitioner confirms the period during which he attended the deceased testator, refers to the date of the will, and confirms that in his opinion the testator was of sound disposing mind on that date and capable of making a will. A more detailed affidavit can be sworn if considered necessary.

If the medical practitioner attending the testator at the date of the will is deceased, an affidavit from the medical practitioner who has taken over his practice is acceptable where:

(i) his more recent doctor has access to the previous medical records of the deceased which cover the time of execution of the will; or

(ii) his more recent doctor has known the testator for a number of years and during this period the testator has displayed good health and issues of mental capacity have only become evident at a later and perhaps more recent point in time. The timeframe of concern regarding capacity should be identified by the said doctor in the affidavit.

Ultimately, if no one is available or prepared to give an opinion of the deceased's testamentary capacity at the time of the execution of the will or if a conflict is evident from the evidence submitted, for example if the doctor and the solicitor hold contrary views as to capacity, the matter will have to be brought before the Probate Judge. This application is made through the Probate Office on foot of motion grounded on affidavit.

If at the time of the execution of the will there is any doubt about the testamentary capacity of a testator, it is advisable to have the testator examined by a doctor to ascertain their capacity to make a will. *The doctor should be asked to swear an affidavit at that time and this affidavit should be kept with the will.*

In addition, one should obtain an affidavit of testamentary capacity immediately on sight of the death certificate where it is stated that the deceased died in a psychiatric hospital.

7.4.13.2 Sample affidavit of mental capacity by doctor

THE HIGH COURT

PROBATE

The Probate Office, Phoenix House Smithfield, Dublin 7

In the estate of

Late of

In the County of

Deceased

Date of Death

I   of

In the County of   Medical Practitioner aged 18 years and upwards make Oath and say as follows;

1.   I attended the above named   in my professional capacity for a period of (specify number) years between 19/20   and 19/20   . I am informed and believe that he/she made his/her last will on the day   of 20   . I am quite satisfied that he/she was of sound disposing mind on that date and fully capable of making his/her will.

SWORN at

in the County of

by the said

this   day of   **20**

before me a Commissioner for taking Affidavits and I know the Deponent (or

who certifies to his/her knowledge of the Deponent)

....

I Certify that I know the Deponent

or the identity of the Deponent has been established by reference to a relevant document containing a photograph

Document Type.................................

Issue No:..

Commissioner for Oaths/Practising Solicitor

The solicitor

If the testator was not attending a doctor at the time of the execution of the will, or if that doctor is deceased, then the affidavit can be sworn by the solicitor who drew up the will. The solicitor should state in the covering affidavit why an affidavit from a doctor is not available. The solicitor should refer to the facts within his knowledge pertinent to the testator's testamentary capacity, for example, how long he knew the testator, if the testator was in employment at the time the will was made, and when the testator started suffering from mental health issues.

7.4.13.3 Affidavit of mental capacity by solicitor

THE HIGH COURT

PROBATE

The Probate Office, Phoenix House, Smithfield, Dublin 7

In the estate of

Late of

In the County of

Deceased

Date of Death

I   of

In the County of   Solicitor aged 18 years and upwards make Oath and say as follows;

1. I knew the above named for a number of years prior to her death on the   day of 20 . During that period she consulted me in relation to her legal affairs.

2. On the day of   20   I called to her house at   , for the purpose of making her Will. I found her lucid and fully capable of discussing all her affairs and giving me instructions for drawing up her Will. I am quite satisfied that she had full testamentary capacity at that time. At the time she made her Will the said deceased   was engaged actively in family life and was living at her home with her husband and her daughter and her daughter's family. She continued to do so up until her death on the day of   20 as aforesaid.

3. As far as I have been able to ascertain and am aware, although the said   was attending her local doctor for normal medical problems there were no problems regarding her mental capacity and she was of sound disposing mind at the time of the execution of her Will. I discussed the contents of her Will thoroughly with her prior to the execution and she understood the implications of making her Will at that time.

SWORN at

in the County of

by the said

this day of **20**

before me a Commissioner for taking Affidavits and I know the Deponent (or

who certifies to his/her knowledge of the Deponent)

I Certify that I know the Deponent

or the identity of the Deponent has been established by reference to a relevant document containing a photograph

Document Type................................

Issue No:..

Commissioner for Oaths/Practising Solicitor

Any other responsible person

If there is no medical evidence available and there was no solicitor involved in the preparation of the will, or if the solicitor is deceased, an affidavit should be obtained from some responsible person. Such person should be someone having no interest in the deceased's estate. The Probate Officer confirmed that in the majority of cases where an affidavit of testamentary capacity is required, it is forthcoming. It is only where the evidence produced is unsatisfactory that the matter is referred to court.

7.4.14 CHARITABLE BEQUEST FORM

When instructed to extract a grant of probate, or indeed a grant of administration with will annexed, read the will carefully to see whether it contains any charitable bequests. Many wills will contain pecuniary legacies or gifts of specific items of personal property and realty to charity.

7.4.14.1 Probate Office requirements

Section 58 of the Charities Act, 1961 provided that the Probate Officer must make returns to the Board of Commissioners for Charitable Donations and Bequests for Ireland ('the Commissioners'). The main provisions of the Charities Act, 2009 (the 2009 Act), which was enacted on 28 February 2009, came into effect on 16 October 2014. The purpose of the 2009 Act is to provide for the better regulation of charitable organisations (charities), to ensure greater accountability, and to protect against abuse of charitable status and fraud. A further aim is to enhance public trust and confidence in charities and to increase transparency in the sector. By virtue of s 81 of the 2009 Act the Commissioners for Charitable Donations and Bequests for Ireland was dissolved. By virtue of s 82 of the same Act, it was replaced by the Charities Regulatory Authority (Charities Regulator) (CRA) which was established on 16 October 2014 to secure compliance by charities with their legal obligations and also to encourage the better administration of charities. The CRA is now the statutory body responsible for regulating charitable organisations in Ireland. It is also responsible for the administration of all charitable devises and bequests contained in any will. It maintains a public register of charities and monitors their compliance with the Charities Act 2009 which sets out a charity's legal obligations for operating in Ireland.

Previously where there was a bequest to a charity in a will, solicitors applying for a grant of probate or a grant of letters of administration with will annexed were obliged to lodge a summary 'charitable bequest form' (form PAS3) setting out details of all such charitable bequests. Such form was then remitted to the CRA by the Probate Officer/District Probate Registrar once the grant of probate or the grant of letters of administration with will annexed issued in compliance with the statutory obligations of the Probate Office under the Charities Acts.

The Probate Office and the Charities Regulator have introduced a revised practice commencing on 1 October 2019 whereby a solicitor applying for either a grant of probate or a grant of administration with will annexed, where the will contains a charitable legacy, must complete a new electronic form entitled the 'Charitable Bequest Form' which replaces the existing PAS3 form previously used.

The new charitable bequest form must be submitted electronically to the Charities Regulator via the Charities Regulator 'My Account' system and, in addition, must be downloaded and printed for signing by the solicitor and finally lodged with all the other papers necessary to lead to a grant of probate or a grant of letters of administration with will annexed in the Probate Office or District Probate Registry.

Before the charitable bequest form may be submitted, a solicitor must either log in or create a new account in the Charities Regulator's 'New Account' system. Information about this system is available by visiting the 'My Account' page at https://www.charities-regulator.ie/en/myaccount.

Further information about the charitable bequest form may be obtained by visiting the Charities Regulator website.

To create the charitable bequest form online the following four sections must be completed:

1. Details of all the personal representatives and their addresses.
2. Details of the beneficiary charity. If a registered charity, details of the nature of the registered charity.
3. Number. All the beneficiaries must be included. Details of the deceased, his/her address, the date of death, and the date of the will must be included.
4. Details of the bequest, to include the type of bequest and, for example, its monetary value. If there is more than one charitable bequest in the will all of these must be included.

The declaration section provides a review of the application.

The original signed signature file (i.e. application form) is then lodged in the Probate Office/District Registry together with all other papers necessary to lead to the appropriate grant.

The charitable bequest form is also available on the probate page of the Court Service Website and a precedent is to be found in the next section. For further information on charitable bequests, see para **2.7.2.6**. Once the grant of representation issues, the CRA will seek evidence that all charitable legacies outlined in the charitable bequest form are discharged and will require a receipt from the relevant charitable organisation.

7.4.14.2 Precedent charitable bequest form

FORM TO BE COMPLETED FOR THE CHARITIES REGULATORY AUTHORITY

Sections 52 and 58 of the Charities Act, 1961, as amended by

Section 16 of the Charities Act, 1973 and Section 82 of the Charities Act, 2009.

Note: this form must be completed in electronic form and must be submitted electronically to the Charities Regulator via the Charities Regulator 'My Account' system. In addition, it must be downloaded and printed for signing by the solicitor and lodged in the Probate Office with the application for grant where a testator or testatrix has made charitable gifts in his or her will.

NAME OF DECEASED:

ADDRESS OF DECEASED:

DATE OF DEATH:

DATE OF WILL:

DATE OF CODICIL(S), IF ANY:

NAMES AND ADDRESSES OF LEGAL REPRESENTATIVES:

CHARITABLE BEQUEST(S):

[*Set out exact wording of bequest(s). Type or print in block capitals.*]

Please annex extra page(s) if required.

Signed..Solicitors

Address.

For official use only:

Date of Grant:

7.4.15 FEES

The appropriate fees (in respect of the net estate) must be submitted to the Seat Office with the application. The appropriate Probate Office fees required are outlined in Supreme Court, Court of Appeal and High Court (Fees) (Amendment) Order, 2021 (SI 80/2021). Since 1 April 2020, the Probate Office will no longer accept fee cards as payment of fees for probate applications lodged either by post, DX, or in person. The fees must be endorsed on the back of the notice of application form. A schedule of all Probate Office fees is contained at the end of **Chapter 11** and may also be accessed on the probate page of the Courts Service website. These are currently under review.

7.5 The Grant Itself

When a grant issues from the Probate Office, it is stated on the face of it that the original will has been duly proved and registered, and that the administration has been granted to the applicant. As noted earlier, at least fourteen days must elapse from the death of the testator before a grant of probate can issue, unless otherwise ordered by the court or the Probate Officer (Rules of the Superior Courts, O 79, r 33).

7.5.1 REVOCATION OF GRANT

If an issue arises as to the executor's right to extract the grant, for example, if a later will is discovered, or if the executor applying dies before the grant issues, then the grant will have to be revoked and a further grant applied for. Revocation of grants is dealt with in **Chapter 11**.

7.6 Office of Executor

The assets of a testator vest on death in his executor(s). The executor, as stated earlier, is the person entitled to take out the grant of probate to the estate of the deceased. The executor's powers and duties arise at the date of death of the deceased. From date of death he can issue proceedings and enter into a contract to sell land. However, he cannot obtain judgment or execute a formal deed of assurance (conveyance, transfer, or assignment) transferring the land until the grant of probate issues.

7.6.1 EXECUTOR ACCORDING TO TENOR

As noted at para **3.3.1**, where the testator omits to appoint an executor but nevertheless gives a person the functions of an executor, for example authorises him to pay his debts, that person is called an executor according to the tenor of the will. This status will also be accorded to persons who are given an executor's authority in foreign wills where they apply for a grant of Irish probate (Rules of the Superior Courts, O 79, r 5(8) (c)).

In the absence of an express or implied appointment of an executor, the order of the individuals entitled to extract a grant (of letters of administration with will annexed) is strictly determined by O 79, r 5 of the Rules of the Superior Courts. In that event, the person entitled to the residue of the estate is usually the person next entitled to extract a grant.

7.6.2 EXECUTOR UNDER DISABILITY: GRANT TO A COMMITTEE OF A WARD OF COURT

As noted at para **3.2.6**, a grant of representation will not be given to a person who has mental health issues and is incapable of managing his affairs. A person must have capacity to act as an executor. Where more than one executor has been appointed in the will, those executors who are capable may prove the will and the rights of the incapable executor may be reserved.

Order 79, r 26 of the Rules of the Superior Courts provides:

> *'A Grant of Administration (which includes administration with will annexed) may be made to the committee of a person of unsound mind for such person's use and benefit.'*

When a person of unsound mind is entitled to a grant of representation, the grant issues to the committee of such person for that person's use and benefit. The grant is limited during the incapacity of the person of unsound mind. Order 79, r 27 goes on to provide:

> *'In the case where a person of unsound mind has not a committee appointed by the Court, a Grant may issue to such person as the Probate Officer may by order assign with the consent of the Registrar of Wards of Court.'*

Where the person entitled to the grant is not a ward of court, a grant can issue to such person as the Probate Officer may by order assign with the consent of the Registrar of the Wards of Court. Again, where the applicant becomes a person of unsound mind before the grant issues, the appropriate procedure is to revoke the grant and reapply either for a grant of probate or for grant of administration with will annexed.

The procedures relating to grants to a committee of a ward of court are set out in **Chapter 11**.

7.7 Other Problems with Wills and Possible Solutions

7.7.1 WILL IN PRE-PRINTED STANDARD WILL FORM

When instructed to extract a grant of probate of a will on a standard will form or a handwritten will, the solicitor should take particular care to ensure that all statutory formalities have been complied with (see earlier). Common problems which may be encountered are:

1. the testator has signed at the top of the will;
2. the testator has continued writing after his or her signature;
3. the testator has failed to dispose of the residue.

Where the solicitor has any doubts whatsoever concerning the validity of the will's execution, the Probate Officer should be contacted. Do not ever take it upon yourself to decide on the validity of a will or its provisions. The Probate Officer has authority to decide on the validity of the will and/or its provisions and the solicitor should never take it upon himself to do so.

7.7.2 ORIGINAL WILL IS MISSING

As noted at para **2.3.2** at point 7, where it is known that a will was executed and was in the possession of the testator but it cannot be found, then there is a presumption that the testator destroyed it *animo revocandi*. However, like most presumptions, this can be rebutted by concrete evidence to the contrary. The person seeking to prove that such a lost will existed must establish the following:

1. That the will was duly executed—this will be done by obtaining an affidavit of attesting witness by somebody who was present at the same time, for example, a doctor or nurse (see *Re Yelland* [1975] 119 SJ 562).

2. The contents of the will—there are numerous ways in which you can prove the contents of the will, for example:

    (a) A person may have read the will and be aware of the contents and could give an affidavit in relation to it, for example the person who typed or printed it.

    (b) The original will could well have been drawn up by a solicitor who may have kept a photocopy of the will on the file, or at the very least will have a comprehensive instruction sheet. See *Re Regan* [1964] IR Jur Rep 56, where the court granted probate to a typed copy of a reconstructed will made from statements of the next of kin of the testator where neither the original will nor a contemporary copy nor instructions were forthcoming.

    (c) If the original will is lost, an order must be sought from the High Court before the original will may be admitted to proof in terms of a copy. This order is obtained from either the Probate Officer or the court (if the Probate Officer so determines). All applications are made to the Probate Officer on foot of motion and affidavit and filed through the Rules Office division of the Probate Office. Counsel's opinion should be obtained if necessary. Where the Probate Officer considers that the order sought may be made in the Office, the order is made and the practitioner is notified to collect the official order in due course. Where the matter must be referred to the court, the solicitor will be contacted to that effect with a court date. Appropriate notice parties (if applicable) should be put on notice by the solicitor making the application. If satisfied as to proofs the court will make an order to prove the will in terms of a copy. Also note that this grant will be limited until the original or a more authentic copy thereof is lodged in the Probate Office.

7.7.3 APPLICATION TO PROVE A WILL IN TERMS OF A COPY

Such an application arises where there is no original will, i.e. it has been lost or mislaid. If the original will is not forthcoming, then the issue that initially arises is as to whether that will has been revoked. If an original will can be traced to the custody of the deceased prior to his or her death but cannot be located thereafter, there is a presumption that it has been revoked by that deceased as dealt with earlier.

7.7.4 DOCUMENT REFERRED TO IN A WILL/INCORPORATION BY REFERENCE

A testator may refer in his will to a document, for example, a deed of transfer or a trust set up during the lifetime of the testator. This reference makes that document part of the will and therefore admissible to probate. However, it is necessary to determine whether that document should be admitted to proof as part of the will. This is not a decision for the solicitor to make, and it should be left to the Probate Officer to do so.

There are three requirements:

1. The document must be in existence at the date of the execution of the will; it cannot be a reference to a future document.
2. It must be clearly identified in the will.
3. It must be referred to in the will as being in existence.

In practice, a copy of such document will need to be submitted to the Probate Office along with the will.

7.8 Precedent Probate Application—John Smyth Deceased—*Obiter* 8 March 2021

(i) Will of John Smyth deceased, dated 10 August 1998.

(ii) Notice of application.

(iii) Notice of acknowledgement (probate).

(iv) Oath of executor.

(v) Grant of probate in estate of John Smyth deceased.

7.8.1 WILL DATED 10 AUGUST 1998

I, John Smyth of 6 Green Cove Place, Cabra, Dublin 7, Retired Porter, declare this to be my last Will and Testament and I hereby revoke all former wills or other testamentary dispositions at any time heretofore made by me.

I appoint my sister Kara Smyth to be the sole Executrix of this my Will and I GIVE DEVISE AND BEQUEATH all of the property both real and personal and whosesoever situate of which I might die seized or possessed of to the said Kara Smyth absolutely.

IN WITNESS whereof I have hereunto signed my name this 10th day of August One thousand nine hundred and ninety-eight.

John Smyth

Signed and acknowledged by the said Testator as and for his last Will and Testament in the presence of us both present at the same time who in his presence at his request in the presence of each other have hereunto signed our names as witnesses.

Emer Murray *Joan Groarke*

24 Plover Street,   24 Plover Street,

Dublin   Dublin

Solicitor   Solicitor

7.8.2 NOTICE OF APPLICATION

The High Court

Probate

Notice of Application

Grant Type:	Probate		
Deceased			
Domicile @death	Ireland		
Name(s)	John Smyth		
Address: (incl. former addresses)	6 Green Cove Place, Cabra, Dublin 7		
Occupation:	Retired Porter	PPS Number:	5186846H
Date of Death:	08 March 2021		
Place of Death	Beaumont Hospital, Dublin 9		
Applicant 1			
Name:	Kara Smyth		
Address:	6 Green Cove Place, Cabra, Dublin 7		
Occupation:	Secretary	Relationship to Deceased	Sister
Applicant 2			
Name:			
Address:			
Occupation:		Relationship to Deceased	
Applicant 3			
Name:			
Address:			
Occupation:		Relationship to Deceased	
Gross Assets (as per SA2):	€358,263	**Net Assets** (as per SA2):	€353,463
No. Of Codicils	None		
Lodging Solicitor (Name and Address)	Barry White, White & Co Solicitors, Flour Place, Dublin 2		

250 **EXTRACTING A GRANT OF PROBATE**

For use of The Probate Office only

Fees:		Case Officer	
		HC Cert	

7.8.3 NOTICE OF ACKNOWLEDGEMENT (PROBATE)

Statement of Affairs (Probate) Form SA.2

Summary

Status of the application: Pending

Document ID   000001596R

Version   1

* Required

Information relating to the deceased person

PPSN:	01033364J
Date of death (dd/mm/yyyy):	08/03/2021
Forename:	John
Surname:	Smyth
Address line 1:	6 Green Cove Place
Address line 2:	Cabra
Eircode:	D07E0R6
County/city:	Dublin
Country:	Ireland
Date of birth (dd/mm/yyyy):	14/08/1936
Place of death (City/Town/County/State):	Ireland
Occupation:	Retired Porter
Domicile at death (Country/State):	Irish
Domicile of origin (Country/State):	Ireland
Resident or ordinarily resident in Ireland at the date of death:	Yes
Individual status:	Single
Surviving relatives:	Remoter relative
Define the remoter relationship:	Sister

Contact details

Forename:	Barry
Surname:	White
Firm:	White & Co. Solicitors
Address line 1:	Flour Place
Address line 2:	Dublin 2
County/city:	Dublin
Country:	Ireland
Phone number:	01 1264876
Email address:	b.white@whitesolicitors.ie
Solicitor reference:	99-5-148-11
TAIN:	

Applicant details

Person #1	
Forename:	Kara
Surname:	Smyth
Occupation:	Secretary
Relationship to the deceased:	Brother/sister
Phone number:	011234567
Email address:	kara@smyth.ie
Address line 1:	6 Green Cove Place
Address line 2:	Cabra
Eircode:	D07 E0R
County/city:	Dublin
Country:	Ireland
Request details	
Grant request:	Probate

Details of beneficiaries

Is the surviving spouse or surviving civil partner the sole beneficiary?:   No

Is every beneficiary expected to receive a benefit of less than €12,000?:   No

Will the whole estate be donated to charity?:   No

Person #1	
Forename:	Kara
Surname:	Smyth

Date of birth:	01/01/1960
PPSN:	1033364J
Address line 1:	6 Green Cove Place
Address line 2:	Cabra
Eircode:	D07 E0R
County/city:	Dublin
Country:	Ireland
Is the beneficiary resident or ordinarily resident in the state:	Yes
Is the beneficiary domiciled in the State?:	Yes
Relationship to the deceased:	Brother/sister
Threshold for this relationship should be B	
Threshold A prior amount:	€0.00
Threshold B prior amount:	€0.00
Threshold C prior amount:	€0.00

Assets cover screen

Irish property (land/buildings)

Irish property (land/buildings): Yes

Show details

Details of assets

        Value

  1   €350,000.00

Irish estate value €350,000.00

Bank/Building Society/An Post account

Bank/Building Society/An Post account: Yes

Show details

Details of assets

        Value

  1   €5,175.00

Irish estate value €5,175.00

Credit Union account

Credit Union account: No

Cash

Cash: Yes

Show details

Details of assets

> **Value**
>
> 1   €2,000.00
>
> **Irish estate value €2,000.00**

Cars/boats

Cars/boats: No

Insurance policy/mortgage protection policy/annuity

Insurance policy/mortgage protection policy/annuity: No

Superannuation/capital sum or ex-gratia payments

Superannuation/capital sum or ex-gratia payments: No

Agricultural/business assets

Agricultural/business assets: No

Stocks/shares/securities

Stocks/shares/securities: Yes

Show details

Details of assets

> **Value**
>
> 1   €1,015.00
>
> **Irish estate value €1,015.00**

Accrued dividends

Accrued dividends: No

Debts owing to the deceased

Debts owing to the deceased: No

Unpaid purchase money of property contracted to be sold in the deceased's lifetime

Unpaid purchase money of property contracted to be sold in the deceased's lifetime: No

Other assets (any asset not covered under the above headings)

Other assets (any asset not covered under the above headings):   Yes

Show details

Details of assets

> **Value**
>
> 1   €13.00
>
> **Irish estate value €13.00**

Foreign assets

Foreign assets: No

Total asset value summary – Asset summary

Total gross estate	Net foreign estate
€358,263.00	€0.00

Liabilities details

Liabilities owing to Revenue:	€0.00
Creditor:	€0.00
Funeral expenses:	€4,800.00
Utilities (total amount):	€0.00
Amounts due to financial institutions #1:	€0.00
Personal loans owing by the deceased #1:	€0.00
Mortgage owing #1:	€0.00
Fair deal/nursing home fee:	€0.00
Other #1:	€0.00
Total of all Irish based debts and liabilities:	€4,800.00

Mandatory questionnaire

Was the deceased in receipt of any DSP (Department of Social Protection) payments?   No

Has the DSP any claim against the estate of the deceased?   No

Was the deceased in receipt of payments under the Nursing Home Support Scheme?   No

Has the HSE (Health Service Executive) any claim against the estate of the deceased?   No

Was the deceased survived by a spouse or civil partner?   No

Was a charitable donation bequeathed under the will of the deceased?   No

Was the deceased at the date of death the owner of a limited interest? (For example, an

annuity, right of residence, interest in a house, lands, securities, and so on.)   No

Did any person on or at any time after 5 December 1991, take under a disposition (for example, a transfer or settlement):

A)   Gift?   No

B)   Any other benefit in possession – for example, the remainder interest on the death of a life tenant?   No

Did the deceased at any time make a disposition

A) That was subject to a power of revocation (can be taken back)?   No

B) By surrendering a limited interest in part or in full?   No

C) That allowed (on or after 5 December 1991) the use of a property free of charge or for reduced rent?   No

Did the deceased create a discretionary trust during their lifetime?   No

Was this under their will?   No

Was the deceased entitled to any interest in expectancy in any property at the date of their death?   No

Did any person become entitled on the death of the deceased to an interest in any property by virtue of the deceased's exercise of or failure to exercise a general power of appointment?   No

Did any person become entitled on the death of the deceased to the proceeds of a Section 72/73 policy?   No

Beneficiary benefit

Total gross Irish estate:	€358,263.00
Total Irish debts:	€4,800.00
Total net Irish estate:	€353,463.00
Beneficiary 1	
Beneficiary name:	Kara Smyth
PPSN:	1033364J
Relationship to the deceased:	Brother/sister
Applicable threshold:	B
Prior aggregable benefit for this threshold:	€0.00
Assigned benefits:	€0.00
Other benefits:	€353,463.00
Total benefits:	€353,463.00

Notice of Acknowledgment (Probate)

Notice of Acknowledgment (Probate) to be given to the Probate Office.

This date of death has been verified by Revenue.

Summary of application

Version	1
Original grant type	Probate
Deceased's domicile at death	Irish
Name of deceased	John Smyth
Address of deceased	6 Green Cove Place, Cabra, , Dublin, D07E0R6, Ireland
Date of death	08/03/2021
Place of death (City/Town/County/State)	Ireland

Applicant #1

Applicant's name	Kara Smyth
Applicant's address	6 Green Cove Place, Cabra, , Dublin, D07 E0R, Ireland
Applicant's relationship to deceased	Brother/sister
Gross foreign assets	€0.00
Net foreign assets	€0.00
Gross Irish estate	€358,263.00
Net Irish estate	€353,463.00

Contact details for lodging solicitor/applicant in person

Contact person's name	Barry White
Contact person's address	White & Co. Solicitors, Flour Place
Contact person's phone number	011264876
Contact person's email	b.white@whitesolicitors.ie

Document ID — 000001596R

It is hereby certified by the Office of the Revenue Commissioners that the requirements of Section 48A (2) of the Capital Acquisitions Tax Consolidation Act 2003 have been satisfied by this applicant for a Grant of Representation.

I hereby confirm that the Will lodged in the Probate Office is the original of the Will provided to the Office of the Revenue Commissioners under Section 9 Capital Acquisitions Tax (Electronic Probate) Regulations 2020 by this applicant for a Grant of Representation associated with the unique reference number in this case (not for intestacy cases).

Submission date: 04/11/2021

Name: _____
Date: _____

Signed and dated by the lodging solicitor or applicant in person

Details of assets

Bank account #1

Value	€5,175.00
Name of institution	Permanent TSB
IBAN	IE63AIBK93101200102493
Address	Permanent TSB, Bank Lane, , Dublin, , Irelan
How was property held	Solely by deceased

Cash

Value	€60.00

Household contents

Household contents details	Household Contents
Value	€2,000.00

Other asset #1

Value	€13.00
Other description	Prize Bonds

Irish property (land/buildings) #1

Property type	Residential
Address	6 Green Cove Place, Cabra, , Dublin, DO7EOR6, Ireland
Property value	€350,000.00
Tenure	Leasehold
Date of lease	18/08/1922
Length of term (years)	999
How was property held	Solely by deceased

Stock/share #1

Description of holding	ANIMEX
Quantity of holding	1105
Price per unit at date of death.	€1.00
Property value	€1,015.00
How was property held	Solely by deceased

Liabilities

Liabilities owing to Revenue	€0.00
Creditor	€0.00
Funeral expenses	€4,800.00
Utilities (total amount)	€0.00
Amounts due to financial institutions #1	€0.00
Personal loans owing by the deceased #1	€0.00
Mortgage owing #1	€0.00
Fair deal/nursing home fee	€0.00
Other #1	€0.00
Other description	
Total of all Irish based debts and liabilities	€4,800.00

7.8.4 OATH OF EXECUTOR

THE HIGH COURT

PROBATE

OATH OF EXECUTOR

The Probate Office, Phoenix House, Smithfield, Dublin 7. ~~The District Probate Registry At~~

PART A

Name of Deceased:	John Smyth
Address of Deceased:	6 Green Cove Place, Cabra, Dublin 7,
Date of Death:	8th March 2021
Place of Death:	Beaumont Hospital, Dublin 9
Name of Applicant:	Kara Smyth
Address of Applicant:	6 Green Cove Place, Cabra, Dublin 7.
Gross value of the Estate:	€358,263. 00

PART B

I, the above named applicant aged eighteen years and upwards, make Oath and say, that I believe the paper writing hereto annexed, and marked by me to contain the true and original last will

of the above named deceased; that same was made by the said deceased after attaining the age of eighteen years, and that the said deceased did not intermarry or enter into a civil partnership with any person after the making of the same;

that I am

the lawful sister of the said deceased and the sole Executrix [1]

~~one of the Executos/rix reserving the rights of the others~~ in the said will ~~(With Codicil(s))~~ named

that I will faithfully administer the estate of the said deceased by paying the deceased's just debts and the Legacies bequeathed by the deceased's said will ~~[or will and Codicil(s)]~~, so far as the same shall thereto extend and the law bind me; that I will exhibit a true Inventory of the said Estate, and render a true account thereof, whenever required by law so to do; that the deceased died at the above named place of death on the date of death cited above [2]

~~and that the Testator/rix had at the time of his/her death a fixed place of abode at the above named address within the District of)~~

and that the whole of the Estate without any deduction for debts which devolves on and vests in the deceased's legal personal representative amounts to the figure cited above as the gross value of the estate and no more,

to the best of my knowledge, information and belief.

1. The relationship of executor to the deceased (if any) and title of the applicant.
2. The following sentence should be omitted where application is made to the Principal Registry

Sworn at Flour Street, In the county of City of Dublin, This the 19th day of April 20 21

Kara Smyth

By the said Kara Smyth

Before me a ~~Commissioner for Oaths~~/Practising Solicitor and I know ~~the deponent~~ (or Barry White who certifies to his/her knowledge of the deponent).

Charles Farrell

~~Commissioner For Oaths~~/Practising Solicitor

I Certify that I know the Deponent *Barry White*

Filing clause:

This Affidavit is filed on behalf of
Kara Smyth the Executrix by
Messrs White & Co, Solicitors, of
Flour Place, Dublin 2,
Solicitors for the Executrix
This the   20th   day of April   20 21

7.8.5 GRANT OF PROBATE INCORPORATING PROBATE ENGROSSMENT

Probate No 6

THE HIGH COURT

PROBATE

BE IT KNOWN, that on the   16th   day of July 2021 the last will a copy of which, signed by me is hereunto annexed, of John Smyth, late of 6 Green Cove Place, Cabra, Dublin 7 deceased, who died on or about the 8th day of March 2021 at Beaumont Hospital, Dublin 9

was proved, and registered in the Probate Office and that the administration of all the estate which devolves on and vests in the personal representative of the said deceased was granted by the Court to Kara Smyth   of 6 Green Cove Place, Dublin, sister of deceased, the sole executrix

named in the said will,

She   having been first sworn faithfully to administer the same.

And it is hereby certified that an Affidavit for Inland Revenue has been delivered wherein it is shown that the gross value of all Estate of the said deceased within this jurisdiction (exclusive of what the deceased may have been possessed of or entitled to as a Trustee and not beneficially) amounts to €358,263 and that the net value thereof amounts to €353,463.

John Glennon

Probate Officer

Extracted by   *White & Co.*   Solicitors
€350.00

I, John Smyth of 6 Green Cove Place, Cabra, Dublin 7, Retired Porter declare this to be my last Will and Testament and I hereby revoke all former wills or other testamentary dispositions at any time heretofore made by me.

I appoint my sister Kara Smyth to be the sole Executrix of this my Will and I GIVE DEVISE AND BEQUEATH all of the property both real and personal and wheresoever situate of which I might die seized or possessed of to the said Kara Smyth absolutely.

IN WITNESS whereof I have hereunto signed my name this 10th day of August One thousand nine hundred and ninety eight.

John Smyth

Signed and acknowledged by the said Testator as and for his last Will and Testament in the presence of us both present at the same time who in his presence at his request in the presence of each other have hereunto signed our names as witnesses.

Emer Murray	*Joan Groarke*
24 Plover Street	24 Plover Street
Dublin	Dublin
SOLICITOR	SOLICITOR

We hereby certify that the above had been compared with and is a true copy of the last will.

Signed *White & Company, Solicitors.*

7.9 Where a Trust Corporation Acts as Executor

Under s 30 of the Succession Act, 1965 (as amended), a 'trust corporation' as defined under the Act can be appointed sole or joint executor (and, indeed, executor and trustee) in a will. Officers of the corporation, as authorised by the directors of the corporation, can extract the grant and administer the estate on behalf of the corporation. However, the grant is in the name of the corporation, not of any officer acting on its behalf. Unlike 'ordinary' executors, a trust corporation is entitled to charge remuneration for its services.

7.9.1 OATH FOR EXECUTOR WHEN EXECUTOR IS A TRUST CORPORATION (IN THIS CASE AIB)

OATH OF EXECUTOR

THE HIGH COURT

PROBATE

THE PROBATE OFFICE

In the Estate of: Anne Byrne   I, TREVOR JAMES WILLIAMS Executor and Trustee

Late of: Bushy   Park Department of ALLIED IRISH BANKS LIMITED

Road, Rathgar   whose registered office is situated at Ballsbridge,

In the County of City of Dublin 6   in the City of Dublin

Widow   Deceased   (hereinafter called 'the Bank')

aged 18 years and upwards make Oath and say that I believe the paper writing hereto annexed and marked by me, to contain the true and original last will of Anne Byrne late of Bushy Park Road, Rathgar, in the County of City of Dublin 6, Widow, deceased; that same was made by the said Anne Byrne after attaining the full age of eighteen years, and that she did not intermarry or enter into a civil partnership with any person after making of the same; that the Bank is the sole Executor in said will named; that I the said Trevor James Williams am the person appointed by Resolution of the Bank dated the 9th day of March 2021 to swear on behalf of the Bank the documents necessary to lead to Grant of Probate of the said will and I beg to refer to a sealed copy of the said Resolution marked 'A' upon which I have signed my name prior to the swearing hereof; that the Bank is a Trust Corporation within the meaning of Section 30(4)(b)(ii) of the Succession Act, 1965 being a Corporation empowered by its constitution to undertake trust business, and having a place of business in the State, and being an Associated Bank under the Central Bank Act, 1942; that the Bank will faithfully administer the estate.

7.9.2 RESOLUTION OF BANK BOARD REFERRED TO IN AFFIDAVIT

THE HIGH COURT

PROBATE

Re: **Deceased**

At a Meeting of a Board of Directors of Allied Irish Banks Limited held on the 9th day of March 2021 it was resolved that each of the following persons, that is to say:–

> Robert Wade Cuppage,
> Catherine Cecilia Donaghy,
> Thomas William Colvin Given,
> Patrick Michael Greany,
> Thomas Noel Kelleher,
> Andrew Alan Macfarlane,
> Edmond Thomas O'Regan,
> David Herbert Taylor,
> Vincent Anthony Teahan,
> Margaret Ann Walsh,
> Trevor James Williams,
> Ronald Ian Terrence Williamson,

Be and he/she is hereby appointed and authorised

1. to apply for Probate of the will of any deceased person who shall have appointed the Bank his or her Executor or co-Executor;

2. to apply for Letters of Administration (intestate) or Letters of Administration with will annexed of the Estate of any deceased person in any case in which the Bank is empowered to apply for such Grant either as Attorney or otherwise;

3. to swear the documents necessary to lead to Grants.

A true copy

Dated this 9th Day of March 2021

7.10 Seat Office Checklist

Please refer to http://www.courts.ie for an updated version of requirements.

Grant of Probate—Application by Executors only

Note: Form S1 must be completed and lodged with the papers when applying through the post or DX. If sending by post the application must be accompanied with a stamped addressed envelope with sufficient value to cover posting back all documents.

Documents to be lodged	Common queries
(1) Notice of application	Contains details of the deceased's name, address, and date and place of death together with name and address of applicant and details of the filing solicitor to whom the grant will be posted once it issues. It also states the type of grant being applied for. It must be printed and not handwritten. It enables details of the application to be recorded immediately. Fees must be endorsed on the rear of the notice of application.
(2) The **original** death certificate	An original coroner's interim death certificate will be accepted if the final death certificate is not yet issued.
(3) Original will and codicil (if applicable)	To be marked on the back by applicant and commissioner/practising solicitor before whom the oath was sworn. Where will already proved in another jurisdiction, copy of the will/codicil sealed and certified by the court where it was proved to be marked. A sealed and certified copy of the grant which issued in that jurisdiction should also be lodged (O 79, r 37).
(4) Engrossment of will/codicil	Photocopy of will/codicil or typed engrossment certified by solicitor to be a true copy.
(5) Oath for executor (Form No 3, Appendix Q of Rules of the Superior Courts as inserted by SI No 590/2020)	Heading to include type of oath, name of deceased, and any variation of same, last address of deceased and any former address referred to in will, full filing clause. Date of death value of Irish gross estate as per CA24/notice of acknowledgment (probate) to be included. Jurat must comply with SI No 95/2009 and cannot be executed before lodging solicitor.
(6) Renunciation of executor (if applicable)	To be exhibited and marked on the back by applicant (if applicable) — and commissioner/practising solicitor before whom the oath was sworn. An exhibit sheet may not be used.
(7) Notice of acknowledgement (probate) or Inland Revenue affidavit form CA24	For deaths on or after 5 December 2001 and applications since 14 September 2020, the CA24 is replaced by the notice of acknowledgement (probate) which form auto generates from the Revenue once the form SA.2 is successfully submitted online. It is required in order to comply with s 48A of the CATCA, 2003. For deaths prior to 5 December 2001, the CA24 must be lodged in duplicate with the Revenue Commissioners and a certificate for the High Court obtained from them prior to applying for the Grant. A form CA6 (Schedule of lands) is required for deaths before 5 December 2001 if there is immoveable property in the estate. The date of death value and tenure must be inserted.

EXTRACTING A GRANT OF PROBATE

Documents to be lodged	Common queries
(8) Affidavit of attesting witness (if required) (Form No 2, Appendix Q of the Rules)	Always required where: i. no or defective attestation clause (O 79, r 6) ii. blind or illiterate testator—affidavit to confirm will read over to Testator (O 79, r 63) iii. will written in loose sheets of paper (affidavit to confirm all sheets present at time of execution) iv. will written on front side only of paper and attestation clause does not confirm number of pages v. Testator's signature is weak or feeble—affidavit should confirm testator was of sound mind, memory, etc. and that the will was read over to the testator, etc. (all affidavits of attesting witness should cover due execution). All affidavits of attesting witness must cover due execution no matter the reason for requesting same.
(9) Affidavit of plight and condition (if required)	Required where pinholes/paper-clip marks, and torn edges etc. appear on the will. The affidavit should be sworn by the person responsible for the marks, tears etc.
(10) Affidavit of Testamentary Capacity	Required where deceased was a ward of court, died in a mental institution, or suffered from a mental illness. To be sworn by doctor attending testator at time of execution of will. If the deceased was not attending a doctor at that time or the doctor is deceased, it may be possible for an affidavit to be sworn by a doctor who was treating them at a later point and can specify when dementia/Alzheimer's was first diagnosed. If this is not possible, the affidavit can be sworn by the solicitor who prepared the will. If the solicitor makes such an affidavit, reference should be made to the whereabouts etc. of the doctor.
(11) Charitable bequest form	Required where there are charitable bequest(s) in the will relating to Irish charities. The electronic application is submitted online to the CRA via the 'My Account' system. Money bequeathed for masses should be inserted. Exact wording as per the will must be inserted. It allows the Charity Regulatory Authority to ensure that charitable bequests are discharged.
(12) Fees	(See Seat Office fees table at end of **Chapter 11**.) Required under SI No 80/2021. These should be endorsed on the back of the notice of application. A fee card is no longer acceptable.

CHAPTER 8

EXTRACTING A GRANT OF ADMINISTRATION INTESTATE

8.1 Introduction

This chapter will deal with the procedures involved in extracting a grant of letters of administration intestate, paying particular reference to the following matters:

1. establishing title to extract the grant; and
2. taking instructions and completing the papers necessary to lead to the grant of administration intestate.

In the previous chapter we have dealt with the situation where the deceased died having made a will and an executor is willing to act. The appropriate grant to extract will be a grant of probate. In **Chapter 9** we will deal with the situation where the deceased died having made a will but there is no executor to prove the will, and the appropriate grant to extract will be a grant of letters of administration with will annexed.

In this chapter, we will be dealing with the situation where a person dies without having made a valid will; where he is deemed to have died *intestate*.

Section 27(1) of the Succession Act, 1965 provides the statutory authority for making grants of letters of administration (both intestate and with will annexed):

> 'The High Court shall have power to grant administration (with or without will annexed) of the estate of a deceased person, and a grant may be limited in any way the Court thinks fit.'

Where a person dies without having made a valid will, they are said to have died intestate and their estate is distributed amongst the next of kin in accordance with Part VI of the Succession Act, 1965. Before the distribution may take place, however, a grant of letters of administration intestate may need to be extracted in the estate. The documents required to extract such a grant are set out in this chapter. The probate page of the Courts Service website at https://www.courts.ie/probate is also a very useful source of information in this regard.

While the Succession Act sets out the persons who are entitled to share in the intestate's estate, the Rules of the Superior Courts, 1986 (O 79, r 5) determine who is entitled to apply for the grant of letters of administration intestate. As a general principle, it follows that an entitlement to apply for a grant of letters of administration intestate follows a right to take a share in the estate on an intestacy basis.

8.2 Notes on Establishing Entitlements to Grants

The two cardinal principles of law to remember when establishing entitlements to grants of administration intestate are:

1. the interest in an estate (ie entitlement to inherit) is determined at date of death; and
2. the grant follows the interest.

8.2.1 THE INTEREST IS DETERMINED AT DATE OF DEATH

The entitlement to extract the grant of administration intestate is conclusively determined at the date of death of the deceased. Section 71 of the Succession Act states that:

'the person or persons who at the date of death of the intestate [emphasis not in Act] stand nearest in blood relationship to him shall be taken to be his next-of-kin.'

Many applications are made to the Probate Office where the applicant claims to be the sole next of kin simply because all the deceased's other relatives are now dead. If a person is not a next of kin of the deceased at the date of death, he can never become a next of kin of the deceased. Many practitioners make the determination as to who is the correct applicant on the basis of the current situation within the family, at the time they are applying for the grant, rather than the prevailing situation as at the date of death, the point in time in fact when the entitlement is actually determined.

8.2.1.1 Blood relations and step-relations

It should be stressed that 'next of kin' means a blood relation. Therefore, step-relations—that is, stepchildren, stepbrothers, and stepsisters—have no right to succeed or to apply for a grant. However, relatives of the half blood, for example half-brothers and half-sisters, have an equal right to succeed and to apply for a grant, as do brothers and sisters of the whole blood. The difference between stepsiblings and half-siblings is that half-siblings have one common parent. This is dealt with further at para **8.6**.

Non-marital blood relations are entitled to apply under the provisions of the Status of Children Act, 1987, where the deceased died after 14 June 1988, and adopted children can apply by virtue of the Adoption Act, 1952.

8.2.1.2 Civil partner

The civil partnership legislation has been in force since 1 January 2011 and, as has been outlined elsewhere in this book, a surviving civil partner has almost exactly the same rights as a surviving spouse. The Rules of the Superior Courts have been amended to allow for a surviving civil partner to extract a grant on intestacy in the same manner as a surviving spouse (SI 348/2011). Since the coming into force on 16 November 2015 of the Marriage Act, 2015 there will be no new civil partnerships; however, existing civil partnerships will continue to be recognised and therefore civil partnerships and the possibility of a civil partnership need to be taken into account when ascertaining entitlement to extract the grant as dealt with below in para **8.2.2**.

8.2.2 THE GRANT FOLLOWS THE INTEREST

For the related titles in most cases, see para **8.3.1.1**. Order 79, r 5(1) of the Rules of the Superior Courts states:

'the persons having a beneficial interest in the estate of the deceased shall be entitled to a grant of administration in the following order of priority, namely:

↓ *Persons entitled to extract grant*

(a) the surviving spouse or, as the case may be, the surviving civil partner;

(b) the surviving spouse or, as the case may be, the surviving civil partner jointly with a child of the deceased nominated by the said spouse/civil partner;

(c) the child or children of the deceased (including any person entitled by virtue of the Status of Children Act, 1987, to succeed to the estate of the deceased);

(d) the issue of any child who has died during the lifetime of the deceased;

(e) the father or mother of the deceased [or where the presumption contained in s 4A(2) of the Succession Act, 1965 (inserted by s 29 of the Status of Children Act, 1987) applies, the mother];

(f) brothers and sisters of the deceased (whether of the whole or half-blood);

(g) where any brother or sister survived the deceased, the children of a predeceased brother or sister;

(h) nephews and nieces of the deceased (whether of the whole or half-blood);

(i) grandparents;

(j) uncles and aunts (whether of the whole or half-blood);

(k) great grandparents;

(l) other next-of-kin of nearest degree (whether of the whole or half-blood) preferring collaterals to direct lineal ancestors [first cousins, great uncles or great aunts, grand-nephews and grand-nieces, great-great grandparents];

(m) the nominee of the State [the State as the ultimate intestate successor where there are no known next of kin or any other person with an interest in the estate: see O 79, rr 65 and 66 and s 73(1) of the Succession Act, 1965. In such a case the Attorney-General usually nominates the Chief State Solicitor to take the grant on his behalf, though he has power to nominate anyone].'

★ Order 79, r 5(2) goes on to provide:

'The personal representative of any of the persons hereinbefore mentioned (other than the nominee of the State) shall have the same right to a grant as the person whom he represents, subject to sub-rule (9)(b) hereof which provides that live interests be preferred to dead interests.' [This would include persons entitled under a *spes successionis*: see O 79, r 5(12) (see para 7.2.2). Another example would be where a person dies intestate leaving a spouse/civil partner and no children: on the death of the spouse/civil partner the legal personal representative of that spouse/civil partner would be the person entitled to extract the grant.]

Any member of a class entitled to share in the estate may apply for the grant of administration intestate without reference to those equally entitled. If there are conflicting claims for a grant among the members of a class equally entitled, the grant shall be made to such of the claimants as the Probate Officer shall select, having first given not less than twenty-one days' notice to the rival claimant or, on an objection made in writing within the twenty-one-day period, to such person as the court shall select. See O 79, r 5(3) and rival applications procedures dealt with in **Chapter 11**.

Under O 79, r 5(4) a creditor may apply for a grant. In practice, an order of the Probate Court is required as the creditor must prove his debt to the court and all next of kin with an interest in the estate must be put on notice.

The chart at para **8.4** sets out, in table form, the provisions of the Succession Act, 1965, Part VI, ss 67–75.

8.2.3 NUMBER OF APPLICANTS

No grant of representation shall be made jointly to more than three persons unless the Probate Officer otherwise directs: see para **7.3.1**. Thus, if a large class of persons are equally entitled to take out the grant, for example four nephews and three nieces, then it is better practice to have them nominate one of the group who will extract the grant and have them confirm this in writing.

8.3 Documents Required when Applying for a Grant of Letters of Administration Intestate

The following documents must be lodged in the Probate Office or in the District Probate Registry as appropriate:

1. Notice of application.
2. Original death certificate or coroner's fact of death certificate. See para **6.6.3.2**.
3. Oath of administrator intestate incorporating administration bond Parts A, B, and C.
4. Notice of acknowledgment (probate). See para **6.9**. → Signed SA2 + Submitted.
5. Where the application for the grant is made more than two years after the date of death, a letter of current market value from an auctioneer may be required. See para **8.3.5**.
6. Renunciation on intestacy (if necessary).

For the purposes of this chapter only, the documents unique to a grant of administration intestate will be dealt with in detail.

8.3.1 NOTICE OF APPLICATION

As set out in paras **7.4.5** and **7.4.9**, notice of application sets out the name, address, and date and place of death of the deceased; the name, address, and capacity (title) of the applicant; and the name and address of the solicitor lodging the papers to lead to the grant; the type of grant being applied for; and the gross and net estate. As we will see, the type of grant has a direct bearing on title to extract the grant.

8.3.2 OATH OF ADMINISTRATOR INTESTATE WITH THE BOND

Since 1 March 2021 the oath of administrator/rix has been combined with the bond at Part C of the form. The combined oath and bond is broken up into three parts, A, B, and C.

8.3.2.1 Part A

Part A is the same as Part A of the new form of oath for executor/executrix and lists details of the deceased, the applicant, and the estate as follows:

PART A

Name of Deceased: (including all variations thereof)

Address of Deceased:

Date of Death:

Place of Death:

Name of Applicant:

Address of Applicant:

Gross value of Estate:

It is very important to note that it is the current value of the immovable (real and leasehold) property that must be used when calculating gross value of the estate, as the applicant, as we shall see, binds him or herself to a penal sum of twice the gross value of the estate in Part C of the combined oath and bond.

Where the applicant is applying for a grant of administration intestate within two years of the date of death then is it appropriate to use the gross estate figure provided in the notice of acknowledgment (probate). However, when applying for a grant of administration (either intestate or with will annexed) significantly after the date of death, then current values for the immoveable assets must be used and a letter of current market value from an auctioneer must be obtained. It is the value of the assets as per that letter of current market value along with the value of the moveable assets listed in the form SA.2 that would be used for the gross estate figure.

8.3.2.2 Part B Oath and Title

Part B of the oath of administrator sets out the correct history of entitlement of the applicant to extract the grant. It refers to the name, address, and occupation of the deceased as set out in Part A. The oath of administrator intestate also proves the right of the applicant to extract the grant by setting out his title to do so. Therefore, the title is so worded as to 'clear off' all persons having a prior right to the grant.

It is important to note that it is the responsibility of the solicitor instructed in the estate to establish the correct title in the oath. Where there is doubt as to same the advice of counsel may be required. The Probate Office will not approve draft titles in advance of lodgement of documents. The title of the applicant in the oath is of paramount importance, and a number of precedent titles for deaths intestate on or after 1 January 1967 are set out below:

8.3.2.3 Specimen titles administration intestate *[note title goes into oath]*

The Probate Office prefers gender neutral designations such as 'spouse' instead of 'widow' or 'widower' and 'child' instead of 'son' or 'daughter'. The term 'single person who never married or entered into a civil partnership' has replaced the words 'bachelor' or 'spinster'.

In the case of civil partners, the term 'civil partner' will replace 'married man/woman' and the term 'surviving civil partner' will replace 'lawful widow/husband'. For surviving civil partners, a copy of their Civil Partnership Registration will have to be lodged with the application.

For surviving widows or widowers the Probate Office is insisting that the phrase 'who did not enter into civil partnership' be inserted after widow or widower despite the fact that widow or widower is a valid civil status.

(a) **Surviving spouse**

'Died intestate a married man/woman and I am the lawful spouse.'

(b) **Surviving civil partner**

'Died intestate in Civil Partnership and I am the surviving Civil Partner'

(c) **Child of a married man/woman still alive** *spes successionis*

'Died intestate a married man/woman and leaving him/her surviving his widow/her lawful husband X who has duly renounced her/his rights [*exhibit renunciation*] and I am the lawful child of the deceased.'

(d) **Child of a married man/woman/civil partner who survived and died**

'Died intestate leaving him/her surviving his/her lawful spouse/civil partner X who has since died and I am the lawful child.'

(e) **Child of widow/widower/surviving civil partner**

'Died intestate a widow/widower who did not enter into civil partnership/surviving civil partner and I am the lawful child.'

EXTRACTING A GRANT OF ADMINISTRATION INTESTATE 269

(f) **Child of single person who never married or entered into a civil partnership**

'Died intestate a single person who never married or entered into a civil partnership and I am the lawful child.'

In this case a long form birth certificate of the applicant will be required.

(g) **Grandchild (no surviving child)**

'Died intestate a widow/widower who did not enter into civil partnership without child him/her surviving and that I am the lawful grandchild.'

8.3.2.4 Specimen titles administration intestate—other family members

Where the surviving family member is not a spouse/civil partner or issue (child, grandchild, etc.) then the possibility of issue have to be cleared off. This will arise in the following cases:

1. Where the deceased was a single person who never married or entered into a civil partnership) without issue, this must be stated in the title unless a child of the single person is actually applying for grant (see specimen title (f)).

2. Where the deceased was a widow/widower/divorced person/surviving civil partner without issue.

    (a) **Father or mother**

    'Died intestate a single person who never married or entered into a civil partnership OR widow/widower who did not enter into civil partnership /divorced person/surviving civil partner without issue and that I am the lawful father/mother.'

    (b) **Brother or sister**

    'Died intestate a single person who never married or entered into a civil partnership with OR widow/widower who did not enter into civil partnership/divorced person/surviving civil partner without issue or parent and that I am the lawful brother/sister.'

    (c) **Nephew or niece**

    'Died intestate a single person who never married or entered into a civil partnership OR widow/widower who did not enter into civil partnership/divorced person/surviving civil partner without issue or parent, brother or sister and that I am the lawful nephew/niece.'

    (d) **Grandparent**

    'Died intestate a single person who never married or entered into a civil partnership OR widow/widower who did not enter into civil partnership/divorced person/surviving civil partner without issue or parent, brother or sister, nephew or niece and that I am the lawful grandfather/grandmother.'

    (e) **Uncle or aunt**

    'Died intestate a single person who never married or entered into a civil partnership OR widow/widower who did not enter into civil partnership/divorced person/surviving civil partner without issue or parent, brother or sister, nephew or niece or grandparent and that I am the lawful aunt or uncle.'

    (f) **First cousin**

    'Died intestate a single person who never married or entered into a civil partnership OR widow/widower who did not enter into civil partnership/divorced person/surviving civil partner without issue or parent, brother or sister, nephew or niece, grandparent, uncle or aunt or great grandparent and that I am the lawful first cousin.'

(g) **First cousin once removed** [Note that a first cousin once removed is the child of a first cousin; second cousin is the relationship between the children of two first cousins.]

'Died intestate a single person who never married or entered into a civil partnership OR widow/widower who did not enter into civil partnership/ divorced person/surviving civil partner without issue or parent or other lineal ancestor, brother or sister, nephew or niece or descendant of such uncle or aunt in any degree or first cousin and that I am the lawful first cousin once removed.'

(h) **Representative of child**

'Died intestate a single person who never married or entered into a civil partnership OR widow/widower who did not enter into civil partnership/ divorced person/surviving civil partner without grandchild or other descendant who would have been the issue of a predeceased child and leaving him/her surviving two lawful and only children, "A" who has since died and "B" who has duly renounced her rights [*exhibit renunciation*] and that I am the legal personal representative of the said "A" under a grant of Probate/Letters of Administration Intestate or with Will Annexed which issued to me on the X day of Y 2021 from the Probate Office/District Probate Registry at …'

(i) **Representative of brother or sister**

'Died intestate a single person who never married or entered into a civil partnership OR widow/widower who did not enter into civil partnership/ divorced person/surviving civil partner without issue or parent or nephew or niece who would have been the child of a predeceased brother or sister leaving him/her surviving one lawful and only brother "A" and two lawful and only sisters "C" and "D", all of whom have since died and that I am the legal personal representative of the said "A" under a grant of Probate/Letters of Administration Intestate or with Will Annexed which issued to me on the X day of Y 2021 from the Probate Office/District Probate Registry.'

(j) **Issue of predeceased child—surviving child renouncing**

'Died intestate a married man leaving him surviving his widow "A" who has since died and one lawful and only child "B" who has duly renounced his rights [*exhibit renunciation*] and that I am the lawful child of "C" who was a lawful child of and who predeceased the deceased.' (*per stirpes* rule)

(k) **Child of predeceased brother or sister**

'Died intestate a single person who never married or entered into a civil partnership OR widow/widower who did not enter into civil partnership/ divorced person/surviving civil partner without issue or parent leaving one lawful and only brother "A" and one lawful and only sister "B" both of whom have since died and that I am the lawful child of "C" who was a lawful brother/sister of and who predeceased the deceased.' (*per stirpes* rule)

Having established title by reference to both the status of the deceased who died intestate and the relationship of the applicant, Part B goes on to deal with the oath of the administrator itself. The applicant swears to administer the estate according to law, and the estate is defined by reference to the gross value of the estate provided at Part A including current values for all immoveable property. The oath used to make a distinction between real and personal property but this has been removed.

Where the applicant is applying for a grant of administration intestate within a year of the date of death then is it appropriate to use the gross estate figure provided in the notice of acknowledgment (probate). However, when applying for a grant of administration (either intestate or with will annexed) significantly after the date of death then current values for the immoveable assets must be used and a letter of current market value from an auctioneer must be obtained. It is the value of the assets as per that letter of current market value along with the value of the moveable assets listed in the form SA.2 that would be used for the gross estate figure.

8.3.3 PART C ADMINISTRATION BOND

This is an important additional requirement, formerly a stand-alone document but now incorporated into Part C of the combined oath and bond, and now sworn by reference to parts A and B. The applicant binds him or herself and is personally liable to a penalty of double the gross value of the estate as set out in Part A if he or she fails to administer the estate according to law. This is known as the penal sum.

This was always required where a grant of administration (whether with will annexed or intestate) is applied for. A bond is never required when applying for a grant of probate, as an executor is never required to execute a bond.

Section 34 of the Succession Act, 1965 provides that every person to whom a grant of letters of administration is made shall give a bond to the President of the High Court to inure for the benefit of the President of the High Court and if the High Court or the Probate Officer, or in the case of a grant from a District Probate Registry, the District Probate Registrar, so requires, with one or more surety or sureties conditioned for duly collecting and administering the estate of the deceased.

The section goes on to provide that the administration bond shall be in the form of a penalty of double the gross assets in the estate, including the current value of any land or immovable property.

An administration bond is therefore needed in all administrations where an executor is not extracting the grant, except where either the Chief State Solicitor or the solicitor for the Attorney-General is the administrator. It is security for beneficiaries or creditors in the event of an estate not being administered properly. Even though it is now included as Part C of the oath and bond it is a document which potentially may stand alone as it may be used to sue the administrator in the event of the administrator failing to administer the estate according to law.

Section 34 goes on to provide that where the Probate Officer or the District Probate Registrar decides that a surety or sureties will be required they should be provided. Since 1 September 2004, these will be required only in special cases. Sureties and justification of sureties are dealt with at para **8.3.4**.

The following administrators, although requiring a bond, do not require a surety, namely:

1. a trust corporation;
2. a bank; and
3. an insurance company.

There are three different administrations with will annexed bond forms available, depending on the date of death of the deceased. Care must be taken to ensure that the correct bond form is used, otherwise the Probate Officer will reject it. In chronological order, these forms are:

1. Administration with will annexed bond (for deaths before 1 June 1959). This bond only deals with the personal estate. 1 June 1959 was the date on which the Administration of Estates Act, 1959 came into force.

2. Administration with will annexed bond (for deaths between 1 June 1959 and 31 December 1966, inclusive). This deals with all the estate, both real and personal. (Administrations prior to 1 January 1967 are not dealt with in this book.)

3. Administration bond (for deaths on or after 1 January 1967). For applications post 1 March 2021, this bond form is incorporated into both the oath for administrator

intestate and the oath for administrator with the will at Part C, as outlined above; see SI 590/2020.

It is important to note that Part C of the oath and bond for administrators on intestacy includes the following paragraph:

> '... [A]nd further do, if so required, render and deliver up the letters of administration in the High Court if it shall hereafter appear that any will was made by the deceased which is exhibited in the said Court with a request that it be allowed and approved accordingly then this obligation shall be void and no effect, but shall otherwise remain in full force and effect.'

This merely confirms that should a will be found and probated that the administration on intestacy ceases and the administrator/rix will surrender the letters of administration and any relevant documentation and assets to the executors/administrators of that will.

An example of the current bond can be found at para **8.6**. For deaths prior to 1 January 1967 or 1 June 1959 see Mongey, *Probate Practice in a Nutshell*, 3rd edn (2006).

The oath and bond for administration intestate cannot be sworn before the solicitor for, or agent of, the party who executes it (see O 79, r 29) and both Parts B and C must be sworn before the same solicitor or commissioner for oaths. It must also be executed under seal.

8.3.4 JUSTIFICATION OF SURETY

From 1 September 2004, it shall not be required of a person applying for either a grant of letters of administration intestate or a grant of letters of administration with will annexed to furnish a surety or sureties in addition to an administration bond, unless required to do so by the High Court, the Probate Officer, or, in the case of a grant from the District Probate Registry, the District Probate Registrar. Note that the administration bond will still be required. However, the only party to the bond will be the principal; that is, the applicant for the grant.

8.3.4.1 Where a justification of surety is required

Where the High Court, the Probate Officer, or, in the case of a grant from a District Probate Registry, the District Probate Registrar specifically requires a surety, as discussed at para **8.3.4**, an additional form called a Justification of Surety must be filed where there is an individual as opposed to an insurance company acting as 'guarantor' or 'surety' to the proper behaviour of the administrator. The surety can be related to the applicant and indeed may even be entitled to a share in the estate. The surety must be a person who is worth at least half the penal sum in the bond, which is in fact the gross estate. If more than one person acts as surety, they are jointly and severally liable on foot of that surety. Solicitors, law clerks, and apprentice solicitors cannot act as surety without the consent of the court or the Probate Officer.

The person who swears the affidavit of market value should not act as surety. It is dangerous for practitioners to consistently use the same people as 'professional sureties'.

8.3.5 AUCTIONEER'S LETTER OF CURRENT MARKET VALUE

This document is never required when a grant of probate is being applied for. A letter of current market value from an auctioneer may be required when applying for a grant of letters of administration intestate or with will annexed or *de bonis non grant* where the estate includes any real or personal immoveable property (e.g. agricultural land or business land or a dwellinghouse). If the papers are lodged within twenty-four months of the date of death no proof of current value will be needed. If the papers are lodged more than twenty-four months after the date of death a detailed description of the property is not required and a single-page letter from the auctioneer (not a solicitor) containing these three lines is sufficient.

EXTRACTING A GRANT OF ADMINISTRATION INTESTATE

1. 'I am an auctioneer with X years' experience valuing property in _____,'
2. 'I have inspected the property at _____,'
3. 'I would value the property at _____ at € (Euros) if offered for sale on the open market subject to title and planning etc . . .'

The letter must show the current market value of the land and, as noted, is not required where the application for the grant is made within twenty-four months of the date of death on the basis that the penal sum in the bond being double the value of the estate is sufficient safeguard for fluctuations in price.

8.3.6 RENUNCIATION ON INTESTACY

Order 79, r 5(1) of the Rules of the Superior Courts sets out the current order of priority to extract a grant of administration intestate, as noted at para **8.2.2**. The nearest next of kin as at date of death are the persons entitled to the grant. However, on occasion not all persons entitled to inherit may extract the grant, and for them to proceed to extract the grant a renunciation may be required from the person with priority to the grant to allow him or her to be 'cleared off'. For example, when a married person dies intestate their spouse and children are entitled to inherit the estate. However, the spouse has priority to the grant, and if the children wish to apply the spouse will need to execute a document called a renunciation to allow the children or any one of them to proceed to extract the grant. This renunciation must be in writing and signed by the person renouncing their rights in the presence of any disinterested witness. It need not be sworn. It must be exhibited in the oath and marked as an exhibit by the applicant for the grant and by the commissioner for oaths/practising solicitor.

8.3.6.1 Sample form of renunciation of letters of administration intestate

THE HIGH COURT

PROBATE

RENUNCIATION OF ADMINISTRATION

THE PROBATE OFFICE/THE DISTRICT REGISTRY AT

(a) insert name of deceased	**IN THE MATTER OF THE ESTATE OF** *(a)*.
(b) address and occupation	**LATE OF** *(b)* **DECEASED**
(c) State whether Bachelor, Widower, etc	**WHEREAS:** **1.** *(a)* late of *(b)* died intestate a *(c)* on the day of at
(d) Insert name (s), Renunciant(s)	**2.** I/We *(d)* are the lawful *(e)* of the said *(a)* deceased.
(e) Relationship to Deceased (f) Insert name of nominee(s)	**NOW I/WE** the said *(d)* both aged 18 years and upwards, do hereby renounce all my/our rights to letters of administration of the estate of the deceased Dated this day of 20 Signed: Witness: Signed: Witnessed:

8.3.7 SPECIMEN RENUNCIATION ON INTESTACY TITLES

Surviving kin	Wording of titles in oath
1. Husband JC (renouncing)	INTESTATE leaving her surviving/her husband JC who has duly renounced his rights by Renunciation dated the day of 20 upon which I have marked my name prior to the swearing here of I am the lawful son.
2. Two children, A (renouncing) and B (survived and died) and one grandchild R issue of predeceased child C	INTESTATE a widow/widower who did not enter into civil partnership leaving her/him surviving two lawful and only children A and B, A having duly renounced his rights by Renunciation dated the day of 20 upon which I have marked my name prior to the swearing hereof and B having since died on the day of 20 I am the lawful son/daughter of C who was a lawful son/daughter of and who predeceased the deceased.
3. Two brothers A (renouncing) and B (survived and died) and one nephew R the child of a predeceased brother/sister C	INTESTATE a single person who never married or entered into a Civil Partnership without issue parent or sister leaving her/him surviving two lawful and only brothers A and B, A who has duly renounced his rights by Renunciation dated the day of 20 upon which I have marked my name prior to the swearing hereof and B who has since died on the day of 20. I am the lawful son/daughter of C who was a lawful brother/sister of and who predeceased the deceased.
4. Two children, A (renouncing) and B (survived and died) and LPR of B applying for grant	INTESTATE a widow/widower who did not enter into civil partnership without grandchild or other descendant the issue of a predeceased child leaving her/him surviving two lawful and only children A and B, A who has duly renounced by Renunciation dated the day of 20 upon which I have marked my name prior to the swearing hereof and B who has since died on the day of 20 . I am the Legal Personal Representative of B under Grant of Letters of Administration dated the day of 20 which issued from the Probate Office/District Probate Registry at
5. Two sisters, A (renouncing) and B (survived and died) and LPR of B applying for grant	INTESTATE a single person who never married or entered into a Civil Partnership without issue, parent or brother or nephew or niece the child of a predeceased brother or sister leaving him/her surviving two lawful and only sisters A and B, A who has duly renounced her rights by Renunciation dated the day of 20 upon which I have marked my name prior to the swearing hereof and B who survived the deceased and has since died on the day of 20 and I am the Legal Personal Representative of B under Grant of Probate/Letters of Administration dated the day of 20 which issued to me from the Probate Office/District Probate Registry at
6. Mother K (renouncing to allow son A to extract a grant *spes successionis* for her benefit)	INTESTATE a single person who never married or entered into a Civil Partnership without issue or father leaving him/her surviving his/her mother K who has duly renounced her rights **and consented hereto by Renunciation (note that consent paragraph should be added to Renunciation in this instance)** dated the day of 20 and I am the lawful son of K.

8.4 Order of Entitlement on Intestacy after 1 January 1967

When a person dies testate, that is, leaving a will, his assets are distributed in accordance with instructions contained in that will. If a person dies intestate, however, that is, without leaving a will, the distribution of his assets is governed by statute. The authoritative law in the Republic of Ireland is the Succession Act, 1965. The rules of distribution on intestacy are set out in Part VI (ss 67–75) of the Succession Act as amended.

Note: for relatives in column C to qualify as next of kin, there must be no relatives in column B alive at the date of death of the deceased.

A	B	C	Relevant section of Succession Act
Deceased	Without relative(s) alive at his/her death	Next of kin entitled	
A married man/woman	Without issue (i.e. child/grandchild/great-grandchild, etc	Spouse takes all	s 67(1)
A civil partner	Without issue	Surviving civil partner takes all	s 67A(1)
A married man/woman		Spouse takes two-thirds	s 67(2)
		Children: remaining one-third divided equally among them	
		(Grandchildren issue of predeceased child (if any) keeping parent's share alive and dividing it equally among them = *per stirpes* rule)	s 67B (2)
A civil partner		Surviving civil partner takes two-thirds	s 67A(2)
		Children: remaining one-third divided equally among them	
		(Grandchildren issue of predeceased child (if any) keeping parent's share alive and dividing it equally among them = *per stirpes* rule)	s 67B(2)
		Subject to s 67A(3): see para **4.6.4.3**	
A married man/woman/civil partner	Without child	Spouse/civil partner: two-thirds	
		Grandchildren: remaining one-third divided equally among them.	s 67(2) and s 67A(2)
		(Great-grandchildren issue of predeceased grandchild (if any) keeping parent's share alive and dividing it equally among them = *per stirpes* rule)	s 67B (2)

A	B	C	Relevant section of Succession Act
A married man/woman/civil partner	Without child or grandchildren	Spouse/civil partner takes two-thirds Great-grandchildren remaining one-third divided equally among them	s 67(2) and s 67A(2)
		(Great-great-grandchildren issue of predeceased great-grand-children (if any) keeping parent's share alive and dividing it equally among them = *per stirpes* rule)	s 67 B (2)

Note: for relatives in Column C to qualify as next of kin, there must be no relatives in column B alive at the date of death of the deceased.

A	B	C	Relevant section of Succession Act
Deceased	Without relative(s) alive at his/her death	Next of kin entitled	
Note: 'Issue represents a man *ad infinitum*' means that as long as a man leaves a child/grandchild, etc and his spouse alive at his date of death, that child/grandchild, etc will inherit (one-third interest, with the spouse inheriting the other two-thirds).			
A widow/widower		Children share all equally	s 67B (1)
		(Grandchildren issue of predeceased child (if any) keeping parent's share alive and dividing it equally among them)	s 67 B (2)
(Note: where the spouse has predeceased the deceased, issue of a man represents him *ad infinitum* to inherit the whole estate.)			
A bachelor/single woman having never married		Both parents share all equally	s 68
A widower/widow	Without issue	(Parents entitled and if only one parent survived deceased he/she takes all)	
A bachelor/single woman having never married	Without parent	Brothers and sisters share all equally (nephews/nieces issue of any predeceased brothers or sisters keeping alive their parent's share and dividing it equally among them = *per stirpes* rule)	s 69(1)
A widower/widow	Without issue or parent		

A	B	C	Relevant section of Succession Act
A bachelor/single woman having never married	Without parent, brother or sister	Nephews and nieces share	s 69(2)
A widower/widow	Without issue, parent, brother or sister	Nephews and nieces take equally	

A	B	C	Relevant section of Succession Act
A bachelor/single woman having never married	Without parent, brother or sister, nephew or niece	Grandparents share equally	
A widower/widow	Without issue, parent, brother or sister, nephew or niece	(If only one survived, he/she takes all)	ss 70 and 71

Note: for relatives in Column C to qualify as next of kin, there must be no relatives in column B alive at the date of death of the deceased.

A	B	C	Relevant section of Succession Act
Deceased	Without relative(s) alive at his/her death	Next of kin entitled	
A bachelor/single woman having never married	Without parent, brother or sister, nephew or niece, or grandparent	Uncles and aunts share all equally	ss 70 and 71
A widower/widow	Without issue, parent, brother or sister, nephew or niece, or grandparent		
A bachelor/single woman having never married	Without parent, brother or sister, nephew or niece or grandparent, uncle or aunt	Great-grandparents share equally	ss 70 and 71
A widower/widow	Without issue, parent, brother or sister, nephew or niece or grandparent, uncle or aunt	(If only one survived deceased, he/she takes all)	

A	B	C	Relevant section of Succession Act
A bachelor/single woman having never married	Without parent, brother or sister, nephew or niece, grand parent, uncle or aunt, great-grandparent	First cousins Great-uncles/aunts Great-nephews/nieces share equally	ss 70 and 71
A widower/widow	Without issue, parent, brother or sister, nephew or niece, grandparent, uncle or aunt, great-grandparent		

8.4.1 REVOCATION OF GRANT OF ADMINISTRATION INTESTATE

Should it arise that a grant issues and a person with a prior title is discovered, for example a non-marital child of a single person coming forward after a grant of administration intestate has been issued to a sibling, then the procedure is to revoke the grant on production of evidence by way of long form birth certificate with father's name on same or declaration of parentage. Revocation of grants is outlined in **Chapter 11.** The correct applicant then applies for a new grant in the estate.

8.5 *Per Stirpes* Rule (i.e. By the Roots)

The *per stirpes* rule is an exception to the general intestate rule that to inherit on intestacy one must be the nearest next of kin entitled at the date of death of the deceased.

The rule allows kin to inherit the share of their parent, which would otherwise have lapsed where their parent predeceased the deceased, while others of their parent's next of kin entitled (e.g. children/brothers of the deceased) survived the deceased.

The next of kin entitled of the deceased at death (e.g. surviving children/brothers) inherit full shares (*per capita*).

The kin inheriting through their parent who predeceased the deceased (e.g. surviving grandchildren/nephews/nieces) inherit the share their parent would have been entitled to had he survived the deceased, dividing the share equally among them (*per stirpes*).

It applies in two situations.

8.5.1 ISSUE OF A DECEASED ARE INHERITING (SECTIONS 67(2) AND 67B(2))

Section 67B(2) of the Succession Act allows distribution *per stirpes* down through all the issue of a deceased person. This means, for example, that if A dies intestate a widower leaving him surviving two children, Y and Z, and two grandchildren/great-grandchildren/great-great-grandchildren, B and Q, the issue of a predeceased child X, then the one-third share that X would have inherited had he survived the deceased will not lapse but will pass to B and Q equally. See **Figure 8.1**.

EXTRACTING A GRANT OF ADMINISTRATION INTESTATE

FIGURE 8.1

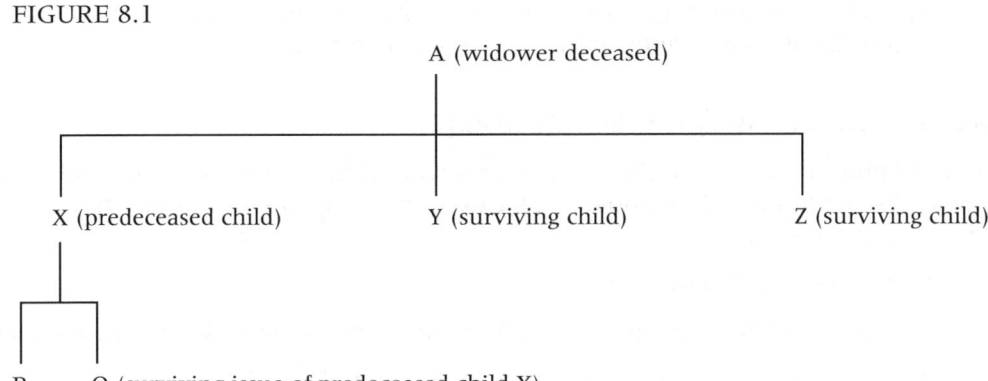

Distribution

- Y and Z, as surviving children, receive one-third each.
- B and Q, as surviving issue of predeceased child Z, share his one-third between them and receive one-sixth each.

Two conditions are necessary for the rule to apply:

1. At least one child must survive. If no child survives the deceased then all grandchildren share the estate equally.
2. At least one child predeceases leaving *issue* (as opposed to 'children') alive at the deceased's death. If the predeceased child does not leave issue alive at the deceased's death, then the surviving children share the estate equally.

8.5.2 WHERE SIBLINGS OF A DECEASED ARE INHERITING (SECTION 69(1))

To explain the operation of the rule, again by way of example:

A dies intestate, a bachelor (widower without issue), without parent or sister, leaving him surviving one lawful and only brother, X, and one lawful and only nephew, Q, the lawful child of a predeceased sister R, then the half-share that R would have inherited had she survived the deceased will not lapse but will pass to Q. See **Figure 8.2**.

FIGURE 8.2

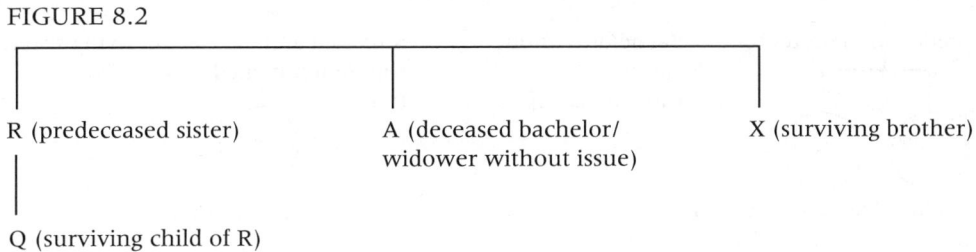

Distribution

X gets half as surviving brother and Q gets half as only surviving child of predeceased sister.

Sections 69(1) and 70(2) restrict the operation of the *per stirpes* rule in the brother/sister circle to allow *children* only (*not issue*) of a brother/sister to inherit *per stirpes*. (Read the sections.)

Grand-nephews/nieces cannot therefore inherit *per stirpes*, unlike grandchildren/great-grand-children/great-great-grandchildren, etc (see para **8.5.2.3**).

8.5.2.1 Two conditions necessary for the rule to apply

These conditions are critical to the *per stirpes* rule applying to nephews and nieces. Practitioners who apply the rule without taking these conditions into account are guilty of professional negligence.

1. At least one sibling must survive.
2. At least one sibling must predecease leaving *children* alive at the deceased's death.

If no sibling survives the deceased, then all nephews and nieces share the estate equally.

If the predeceased sibling does not leave *children* alive at the deceased's death, then the surviving siblings share the estate equally.

8.5.2.2 Establishing entitlement when the per stirpes rule applies

Remember that the entitlement is frozen at date of death of the deceased.

1. Interest is determined at the date of death of the deceased.
2. The grant follows the interest.

Once the next of kin at the date of death of the deceased is clearly ascertained, the person(s) who are entitled to extract the grant are ascertained just as clearly.

If all the next of kin alive at the date of the deceased are now dead, then their personal representatives are entitled. However, O 79, r 5(9)(b) provides that grants are given to a living member of a class entitled, in preference to the personal representative of a surviving *and* subsequently dying member of the class (live interests preferred to dead interests). See **Figures 8.3** to **8.6** for examples where the *per stirpes* rule applies.

8.5.2.3 Examples where the *per stirpes* rule applies

Example 1: Predeceased sibling leaving children

FIGURE 8.3

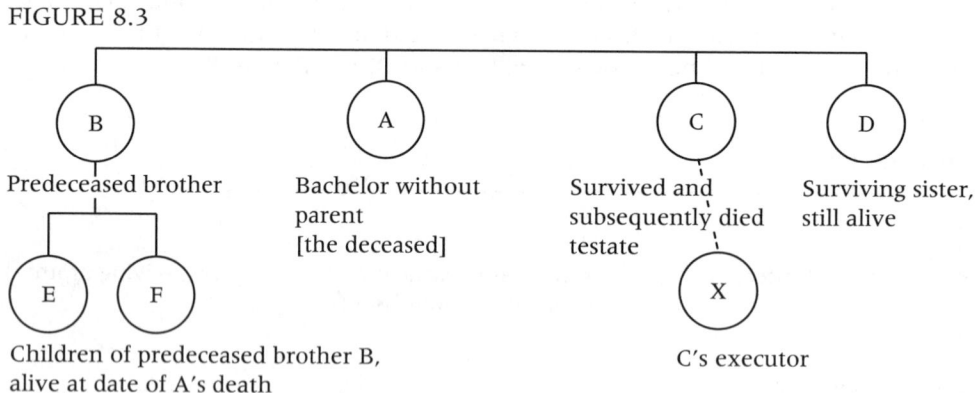

- A: bachelor without parent [the deceased];
- B: a predeceased brother leaving E and F his children;
- C: a brother who survived A and subsequently died testate (X has extracted a grant in his estate);
- D: a surviving sister now.

EXTRACTING A GRANT OF ADMINISTRATION INTESTATE

Distribution

- one-third to C —for distribution under his will by X his executor;
- one-third to D {one-sixth to E
- one-third to E and F {Kept share alive and shared it equally
   {one-sixth to F.

D has priority to take out the grant and her title would be *'Died intestate a Bachelor without parent and I am a lawful sister'*.

Example 2: Predeceased child leaving issue

- A: a widower [the deceased];
- B: a predeceased child leaving his issue E and F: grandchildren of A;
- C: a surviving child, since died (X) his proving executor;
- D: a surviving child now.

FIGURE 8.4

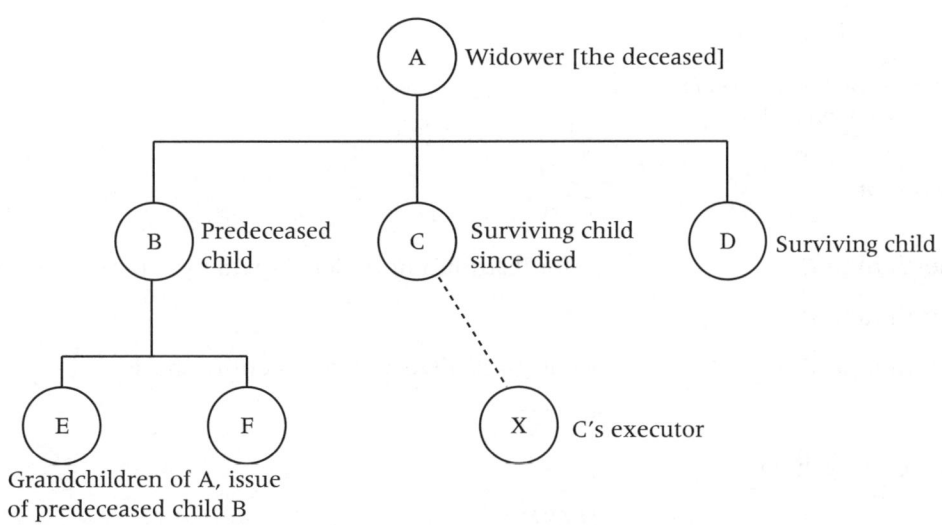

Distribution

- one-third to C —for distribution under the terms of Cs will by X his executor;
- one-third to D {one-sixth to E
- one-third to E and F {Kept share alive and shared it equally
   {one-sixth to F.

D would have priority to take out the grant and his/her title would be *'Died intestate a Widower and I am a lawful son/daughter'*.

Example 3: Siblings with more remote issue surviving

- A: a bachelor without parent [the deceased];
- B: a predeceased brother;

282 EXTRACTING A GRANT OF ADMINISTRATION INTESTATE

- C: a brother who survived A testate and X extracted a grant in his estate;
- D: a surviving brother;
- E: a predeceased nephew, being a son of predeceased brother B;
- F: a surviving nephew, being a son of predeceased brother B;
- G: a grand-nephew, being issue of predeceased nephew E.

FIGURE 8.5

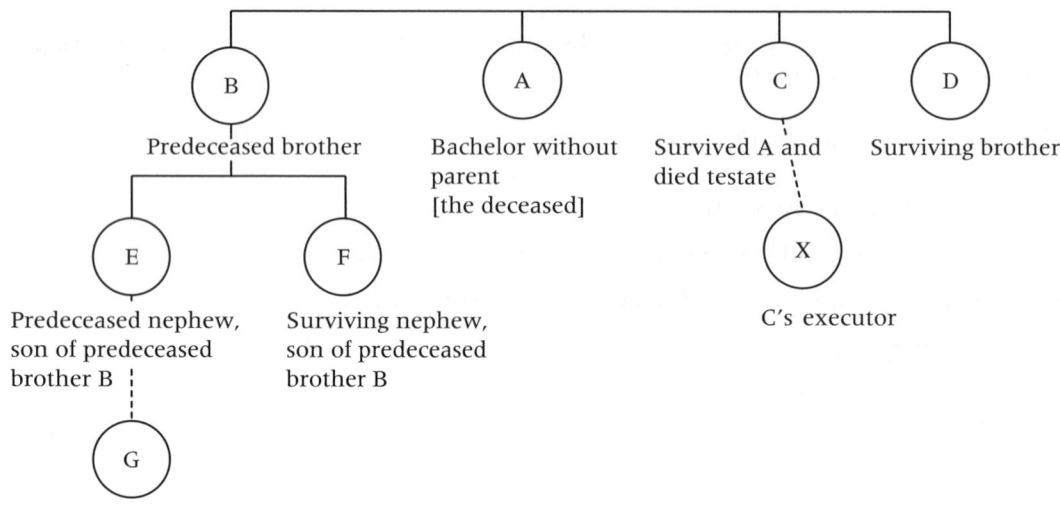

Distribution

- one-third to C   —for distribution under C's will by X his executor;
- one-third to D
- one-third to F   Kept share alive and keeps entire share
                          {s 70(2)
- *(G) Gets nothing   {
                          {s 69(1).

D would have priority to take out the grant and his title would be *'Died intestate a Bachelor without parent and I am a lawful brother'*.

Example 4: Predeceased child with more remote issue surviving

- A: a widower [the deceased];
- B: a predeceased child;
- C: a surviving child since died X his proving executor;
- D: a surviving child;
- E: a predeceased grandchild, being child of predeceased child B;
- F: a surviving grandchild, being child of predeceased child B;
- G: a great-grandchild, being issue of predeceased grandchild E and of predeceased child B.

FIGURE 8.6

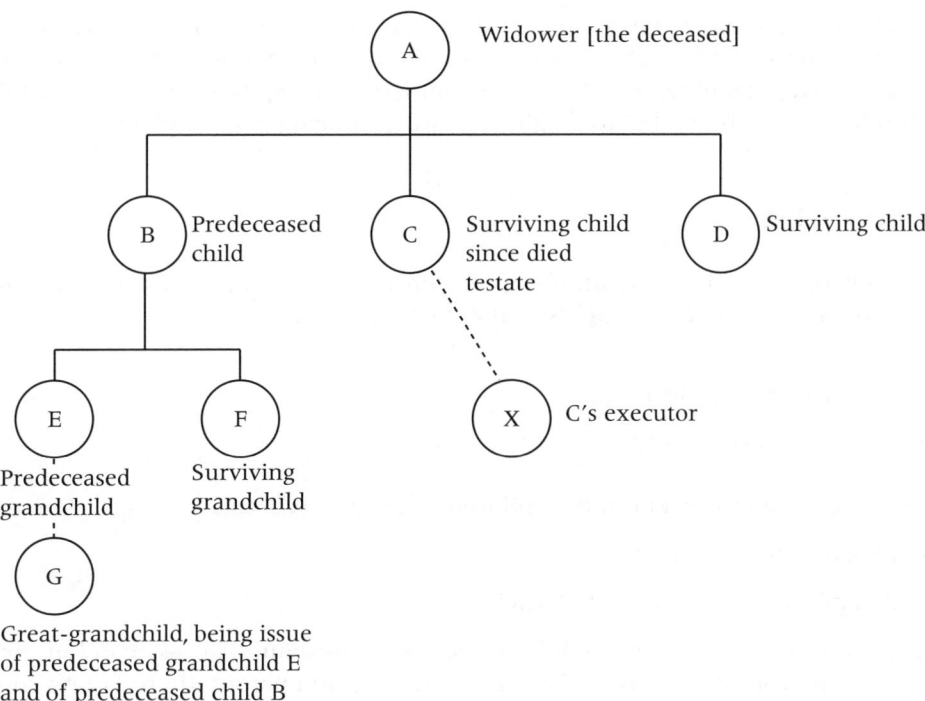

Distribution

- one-third to C—(X) his executor;
- one-third to D;
- one-sixth to F;
- one-sixth to G—s 67 B(2) (which students should read: issue of a man represents him ad infinitum).

D would have priority to take out the grant and his/her title would be *'Died intestate a Widower and I am a lawful son/daughter'*.

8.6 Relatives of Half-Blood and Step-Relatives (No Blood Relationship)

8.6.1 RELATIVES OF HALF-BLOOD

A person is a relative of the half-blood where he has only one parent or other ancestor in common with another relative. Section 72 of the Succession Act states that:

'Relatives of the half-blood shall be treated as, and shall succeed equally with, relatives of the whole blood in the same degree.'

Relatives of the half-blood have equal succession rights to relatives of the whole blood.

Example of half-blood relationship

- Xavier and Yvonne marry and have one child, Zelda.
- Xavier subsequently dies and Yvonne later marries Anthony.
- Yvonne and Anthony have a child, Brendan.

- The relationship Zelda–Brendan is brother–sister of the half-blood.

- Zelda and Brendan have one common parent, Yvonne. They have full succession rights to Yvonne's estate and to each other's estates. If, however, Anthony was to die intestate, Zelda as his step-daughter would have no inheritance rights to his estate, while her half-brother Brendan would have rights by virtue of being Anthony's son.

8.6.2 STEP-RELATIVES

As kinship is based on blood relationship, if you have no common blood with another person, you have no succession rights to that person's estate.

8.6.2.1 Example of a step-relationship

If the example just given is carried further, as follows:

- Yvonne (the common parent of the children of the first two relationships) then dies.
- Anthony later marries Claire.
- Anthony and Claire have a child, Patrick.
- The relationship between Zelda (child of the first union) and Patrick (child of the third union) is step-brother/step-sister. They have no common parent, therefore no common blood; therefore no succession rights *inter se*. Brendan and Patrick, however, are half-brothers.

Note: a step-child is treated as a blood child for CAT purposes only—s 2(1) of the Capital Acquisitions Tax Consolidation Act, 2003.

8.7 Ascertainment of Next of Kin

Section 70(1) of the Act provides that where an intestate is not survived by a spouse/civil partner, issue, parent, brother, sister, niece, or nephew, his estate is to be divided in equal shares among his 'next of kin'.

Section 70(2)

'Representation of next-of-kin shall not be admitted amongst "collaterals" except in the case of children of brothers and sisters of the intestate where any other brother or sister of the intestate survives him.'

This has already been dealt with in s 69(1). 'Collaterals' are not defined in the Act but are defined as 'a person having the same descent as another but by a different line'.

An example of this would be: my first cousin is collateral to me in terms of descent from my grandparents. We both share that common ancestry and can trace back to that common ancestry through different lines of parentage, arriving back at that common ancestry.

8.7.1 EXAMPLES

The basis of ascertainment of next of kin of an intestate is provided in s 71 of the Succession Act, the effect of which can be broken down into four rules which follow on from each other, until the next of kin is finally identified.

Section 71(1) provides the first rule: that the next of kin is the person who is nearest in blood relationship to the deceased. Section 71(2) then provides for calculating the degree of relationship.

Following on from the first rule, the second rule is the most straightforward: the degrees of relationship between the deceased and a direct lineal ancestor are calculated by counting upwards from the deceased to the direct lineal ancestor. See Examples 1, 2, and 3, in **Figures 8.7** to **8.9**, which trace the degrees upwards from the deceased to a great-great-grandparent.

Example 1—Grandparent, two degrees

FIGURE 8.7

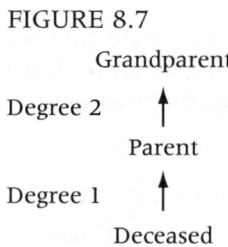

Example 2—Great-grandparent, three degrees

FIGURE 8.8

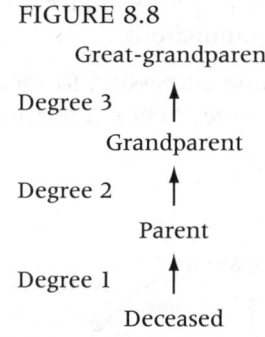

Example 3—Great-great-grandparent, four degrees

FIGURE 8.9

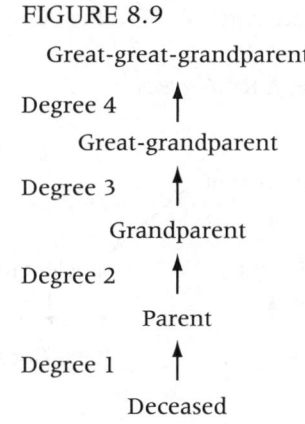

The third rule provides that the degree of relationship between two 'other relatives' (i.e. collaterals) is determined by counting the steps from one relative up to their common ancestor and down to the other relative. See Example 4 in Figure **8.10**.

Example 4—Uncle/aunt, three degrees

FIGURE 8.10

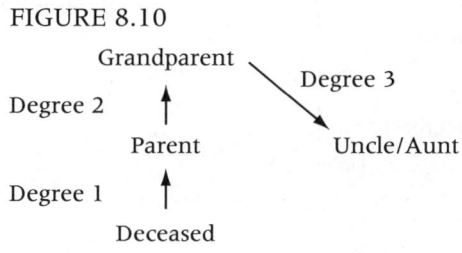

It will be noted that the uncle or aunt at three degrees of 'separation' is an equal number of steps removed from the deceased as the great-grandparent in Example 2. This brings us neatly to the fourth and final rule.

Where a direct lineal ancestor is an equal number of steps removed from the deceased as some 'other relative', the 'other relative' takes precedence over the direct lineal ancestor. In the example given earlier, the uncle or aunt will take the benefit ahead of the great-grandparent.

The common law reasoning behind the fourth rule was 'that the direct lineal ancestor was less likely to need the inheritance being closer to death than the "other relative" and more likely at his age to have been sufficiently provided for'.

This is now specifically provided for in s 71(2).

By way of further illustration of the operation of these rules, consider an estate where a deceased died leaving the following kin: a first cousin, a great-aunt, a grand-niece, and a great-great-grandparent, each four steps removed from him.

The first three, being collaterals, would rank equally as next of kin in priority to the great-great-grandparent, the lineal ancestor (see Examples 5 to 7 in Figures **8.11** to **8.13**), and see Example 3 for the great-great-grandparent.

Figure **8.14** shows a chart of intestate succession for deaths on or after 1 January 1967, and Figure **8.15** shows a chart of degrees of blood relationship.

Example 5—First cousin, four degrees

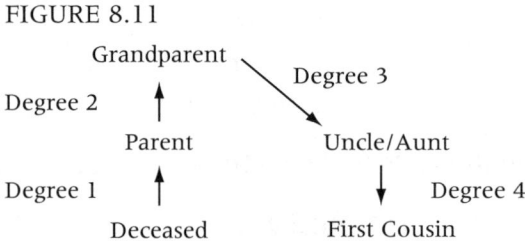

Example 6—Grand-nephew/niece, four degrees

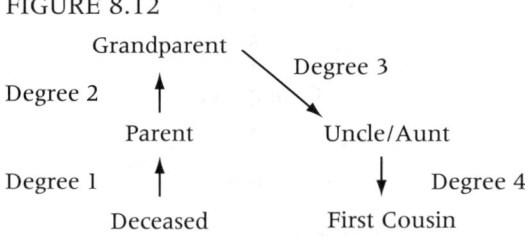

Example 7—Great-aunt, four degrees

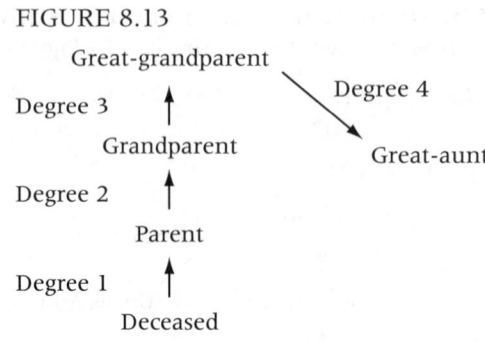

8.7.2 CHART OF INTESTATE SUCCESSION FOR DEATHS ON OR AFTER 1 JANUARY 1967

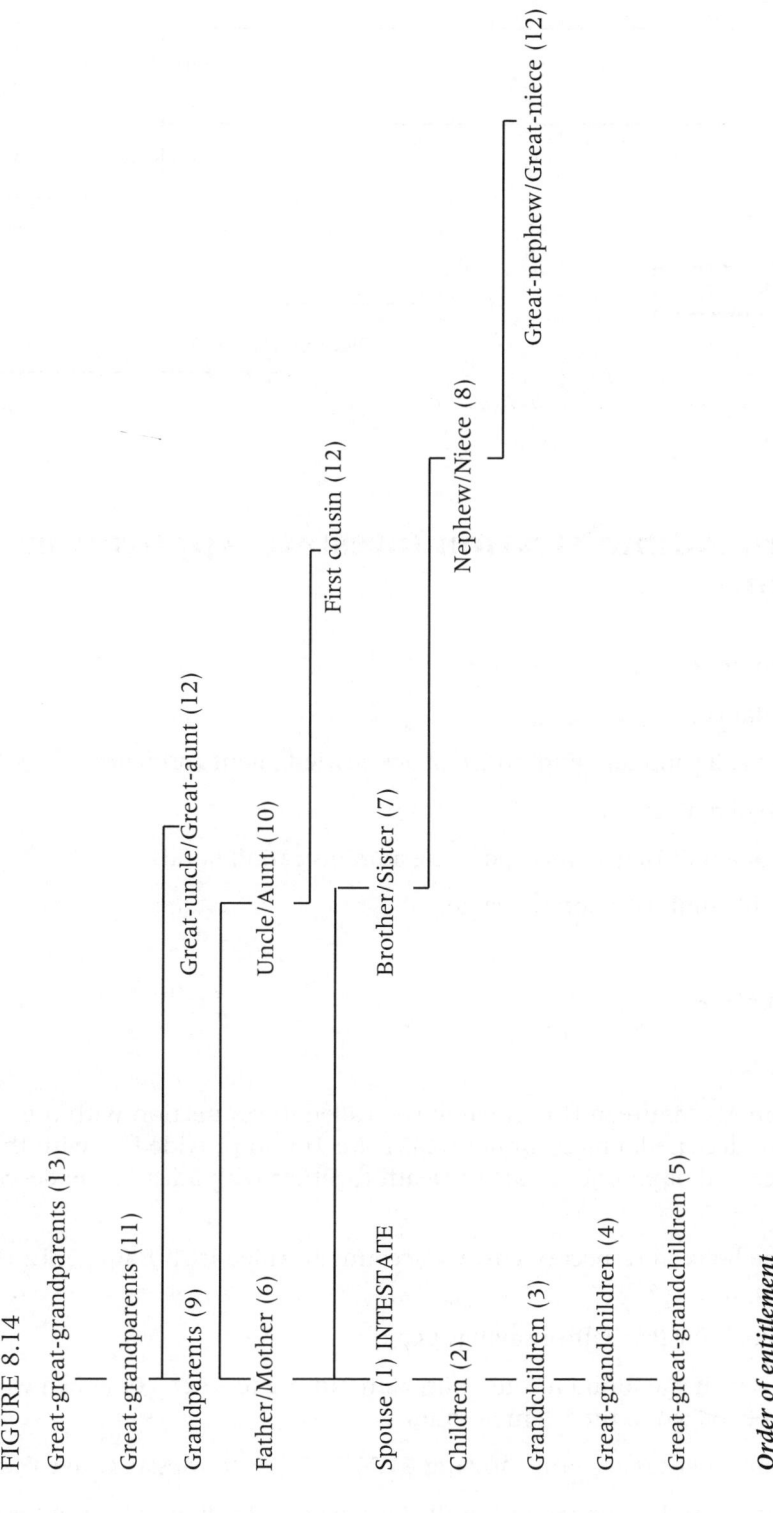

FIGURE 8.14

8.7.3 CHART OF DEGREES OF BLOOD RELATIONSHIP

FIGURE 8.15

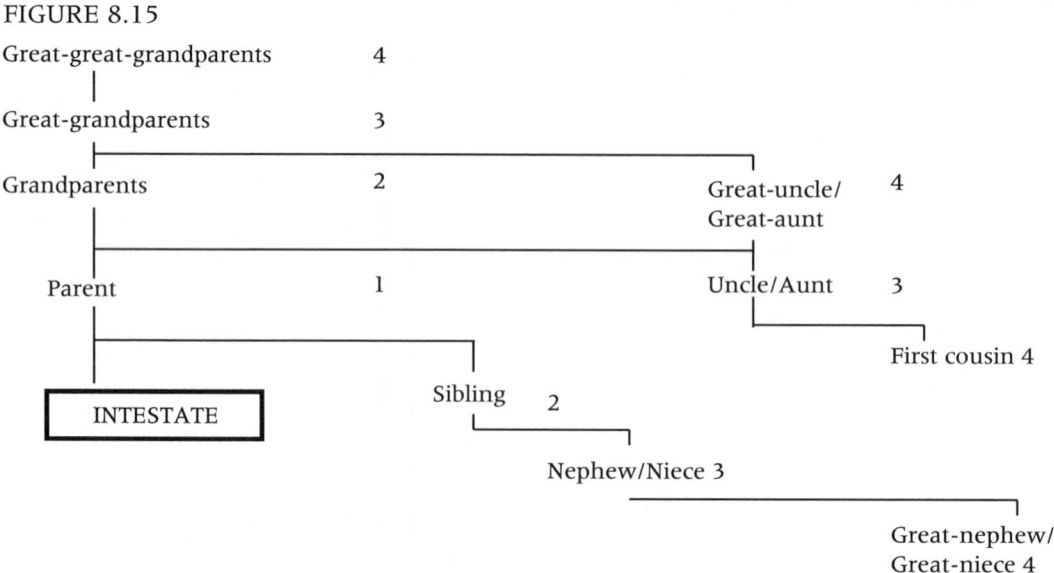

8.8 Precedent Administration Intestate Application Documents

Angela Moran deceased.

(i) Attendance(s).

(ii) Form SA.2 summary and notice of acknowledgment (probate).

(iii) Notice of application.

(iv) Oath of administatrix incorporating administration bond.

(v) Grant of administration intestate.

8.8.1 ATTENDANCE

19 January 2021

Attendance on Ms Maureen Horan when she called in connection with the estate of Mrs Angela Moran deceased, obit 7 January 2021. Ms Horan provided us with the death certificate of deceased or coroner's Fact of Death together with a list of the deceased's assets as follows:

1. cheque book in respect of current account at Allied Irish Bank, 7/12 Dame Street, Dublin 2;

2. pass Book for Post Office savings bank;

3. cash, which she found in the house, amounting to €125.70, which was handed to us to be lodged to the client account;

4. funeral expenses account showing €3,777.47 due to Messrs Grave & Son;

5. account from Doctor James Smith showing €1,015.79 due to him for professional fees.

She advised us that the title deeds to the house were with the bank and the bank manager had said that the solicitor could collect these from him. She showed me a copy bill of costs which had been drawn up in connection with the administration of her late father Joseph Moran's estate, which showed that he died in March 1995 and a grant of probate was extracted in Dublin and that all of the property under the will was devised to his wife, Angela Moran, now deceased.

Ms Horan is the deceased's only daughter and the sole next-of-kin. Ms Horan is married to Thomas Horan and is living at 11 O'Gorman Street, Harold's Cross. She is hoping to have the house transferred into the joint names of herself and her husband when the administration is complete.

She said she would put a value of €2,539.48 on the contents of the house and this included clothes, jewellery, etc. She said that the furniture was not of very high quality as she and her husband had been living in England for the past number of years and had only returned to Ireland last year when her mother became ill. She said that the mother did not take any particular interest in the house due to her illness and that it was their intention to do it up and live in it now.

She asked me to arrange for payment of the funeral expenses as soon as possible in order to get the discount from the undertakers. She also mentioned that she would like the expenses to be paid from the balance standing to credit in the current account and to discharge the doctor's fees from the balance standing to credit in the Post Office savings bank account.

She said, as far as she was aware, her mother never was liable for income tax and made no returns. She said that her mother had been in receipt of a widow's pension but the last cheque had been cashed just prior to her death. I told her I would write to the Department of Social Protection and check that there were no further arrears of pension due to the estate.

She said that there were no fees due to the nursing home as Doctor Smith's bill included all of that. She said that he was in charge of the nursing home and that the bill for €1,015.79 covered all medical expenses. I explained briefly the procedure to her and told her I would arrange for her to call to swear the schedule of assets. She confirmed that she is an only child.

8.8.1.1 Further attendance on Ms Horan dated 4 February 2021

I told Ms Horan that we were proceeding apace with the administration of her late mother's estate and had received the final valuations from the various financial institutions and the estate agents. These are as follows:

Assets	Value in Euro €
House at 11 O'Gorman St: valuation received from O'Connor & Sons Auctioneers and Valuers on 28 January 2015	190,000.00
Contents	2,539.48
AIB current account	2,095.07
Post Office savings bank	3,809.21
Cash in house	125.70
Prize bond	6.35
Gross estate	198,573.81
Liabilities	Value in Euro €
Dr Smith: Professional fees	1,015.79
Messrs Grace & Sons, Undertakers	3,777.47
	4,973.26

I had completed the Statement of Affairs (Probate) on this basis and on her instructions have proceeded to submit same with the Revenue Commissioners.

8.8.2 FORM SA.2 SUMMARY AND NOTICE OF ACKNOWLEDGEMENT (PROBATE)

Summary

Please fill out the declaration and submit the form

Information relating to the deceased person

Information relating to the deceased person

PPSN:	01033364J
Date of death (dd/mm/yyyy):	07/01/2021
Forename:	Angela
Surname:	Moran
Address line 1:	11 O Gorman Street
Address line 2:	Harolds Cross
County/city:	Dublin 6
Country:	Ireland
Date of birth (dd/mm/yyyy):	01/01/1960
Place of death (City/Town/County/State):	St Patricks Baldoyle
Occupation:	Pensioner
Domicile at death (Country/State):	Ireland
Domicile of origin (Country/State):	Ireland
Resident or ordinarily resident in Ireland at the date of death:	Yes
Individual status:	Widowed
Surviving relatives:	Children
No. of children:	1

Contact details

Forename:	Mr
Surname:	Solicitor
Address line 1:	11 Upper O'Connell Street
Address line 2:	Dublin 1
County/city:	Dublin
Country:	Ireland
Phone number:	0871234567
Email address:	Solicitor@lawfirm.ie
Solicitor reference:	

EXTRACTING A GRANT OF ADMINISTRATION INTESTATE

Applicant details

Person #1	
Forename:	Maureen
Surname:	Horan
Occupation:	Married Woman
Relationship to the deceased:	Child
Phone number:	0871234567
Email address:	maureen@horan.com
Address line 1:	11 O'Gorman Street
Address line 2:	Harolds Cross
Eircode:	
County/city:	Dublin 6
Country:	Ireland
Request details	
Grant request:	Administration for intestacy

Details of beneficiaries

Is the surviving spouse or surviving civil partner the sole beneficiary?: No

Is every beneficiary expected to receive a benefit of less than €12,000?: No

Will the whole estate be donated to charity?: No

Person #1	
Forename:	Maureen
Surname:	Horan
Date of birth:	01/01/1960
PPSN:	9865658N
Address line 1:	11 O'Gorman Street
Address line 2:	Harolds Cross
Eircode:County/city:	Dublin 6
Country:	Ireland
Is the beneficiary resident or ordinarily resident in the state:	Yes
Is the beneficiary domiciled in the State?:	Yes
Relationship to the deceased:	Child
Threshold for this relationship should be A	
Threshold A prior amount:	€0.00
Threshold B prior amount:	€0.00

Assets cover screen

Irish property (land/buildings)

Irish property (land/buildings): Yes

Show details

Details of assets

       Value

1   €190,000.00

Irish estate value   **€190,000.00**

Bank/Building Society/An Post account

Bank/Building Society/An Post account: Yes

Show details

Details of assets

       Value

1   €2,095.07

2   €3,808.21

Irish estate value   **€5,903.28**

Credit Union account

Credit Union account: No

Cash

Cash: Yes

Show details

Details of assets

       Value

1   €125.70

Irish estate value   **€125.70**

Household contents

House contents: Yes

Show details

Details of assets

       Value

1   €2,538.48

Irish estate value   **€2,538.48**

Cars/boats

Cars/boats: No

Insurance policy/mortgage protection policy/annuity

Insurance policy/mortgage protection policy/annuity: No

Superannuation/capital sum or exgratia payments

Superannuation/capital sum or exgratia payments: No

Agricultural/business assets

Agricultural/business assets: No

Stocks/shares/securities

Stocks/shares/securities: No

Accrued dividends

Accrued dividends: No

Debts owing to the deceased

Debts owing to the deceased: No

Unpaid purchase money of property contracted to be sold in the deceased's lifetime

Unpaid purchase money of property contracted to be sold in the deceased's lifetime: No

Other assets (any asset not covered under the above headings)

Other assets (any asset not covered under the above headings): Yes

Show details

Details of assets

	Value
1	€6.35
Irish estate value	**€6.35**

Foreign assets

Foreign assets: No

Total asset value summary – Asset summary

Liabilities details

Liabilities owing to Revenue:	€0.00
Creditor:	€1,015.79
Funeral expenses:	€3,777.47
Utilities (total amount):	€0.00
Amounts due to financial institutions #1:	€0.00
Personal loans owing by the deceased #1:	€0.00
Mortgage owing #1:	€0.00
Fair deal/nursing home fee:	€0.00
Other #1:	€0.00
Total of all Irish based debts and liabilities:	€4,793.26

Mandatory questionnaire

Was the deceased in receipt of any DSP (Department of Social Protection) payments? No

Has the DSP any claim against the estate of the deceased? No

Was the deceased in receipt of payments under the Nursing Home Support Scheme? No

Has the HSE (Health Service Executive) any claim against the estate of the deceased? No

Was the deceased survived by a spouse or civil partner?: No

Was a charitable donation bequeathed under the will of the deceased? No

Was the deceased at the date of death the owner of a limited interest? (For example, an annuity, right of residence, interest in a house, lands, securities, and so on.) No

Did any person on or at any time after 5 December 1991, take under a disposition (for example, a transfer or settlement):

A) Gift? No

B) Any other benefit in possession – for example, the remainder interest on the death of a life tenant? No

Did the deceased at any time make a disposition

A) That was subject to a power of revocation (can be taken back)?: No

B) By surrendering a limited interest in part or in full? No

C) That allowed (on or after 5 December 1991) the use of a property free of charge or for reduced rent? No

Did the deceased create a discretionary trust during their lifetime? No

Was this under their will? No

Was the deceased entitled to any interest in expectancy in any property at the date of their death? No

Did any person become entitled on the death of the deceased to an interest in any property by virtue of the deceased's exercise of or failure to exercise a general power of appointment? No

Did any person become entitled on the death of the deceased to the proceeds of a Section 72/73 policy? No

Beneficiary benefit

Beneficiary benefit

Total gross Irish estate:	€198,573.81
Total Irish debts:	€4,793.26
Total net Irish estate:	€193,780.55
Beneficiary 1	
Beneficiary name:	Maureen Horan
PPSN:	9865658N
Relationship to the deceased:	Child
Applicable threshold:	A

Prior aggregable benefit for this threshold:	€0.00
Assigned benefits:	€0.00
Other benefits:	€193,780.55
Total benefits:	€193,780.55

Total gross estate	Net foreign estate
€198,573.81	€0.00

Notice of Acknowledgment (Probate)

Notice of Acknowledgment (Probate) to be given to the Probate Office.

This date of death has been verified by Revenue.

Summary of application

Version	1
Original grant type	Administration for intestacy
Deceased's domicile at death	Ireland
Name of deceased	Angela Moran
Address of deceased	11 O Gorman Street, Harolds Cross, , Dublin 6, , Ireland
Date of death	07/01/2021
Place of death (City/Town/County/State)	St Patricks Baldoyle

Applicant #1

Applicant's name	Maureen Horan
Applicant's address	11 O'Gorman Street, Harolds Cross, , Dublin 6, , Ireland
Applicant's relationship to deceased	Child
Gross foreign assets	€0.00
Net foreign assets	€0.00
Gross Irish estate	€198,573.81
Net Irish estate	€193,870.55

Contact details for lodging solicitor/applicant in person

Contact person's name	Mr Horace Nelson, Nelson & Co Solicitors
Contact person's address	Trafalgar Square, Dublin 2, , Dublin, , Ireland
Contact person's phone number	01 6724803
Contact person's email	h.nelson@nelson&co.ie

Document ID | 000001597T

It is hereby certified by the Office of the Revenue Commissioners that the requirements of Section 48A (2) of the Capital Acquisitions Tax Consolidation Act 2003 have been satisfied by this applicant for a Grant of Representation.

I hereby confirm that the Will lodged in the Probate Office is the original of the Will provided to the Office of the Revenue Commissioners under Section 9 Capital Acquisitions Tax (Electronic Probate) Regulations 2020 by this applicant for a Grant of Representation associated with the unique reference number in this case (not for intestacy cases).

296 EXTRACTING A GRANT OF ADMINISTRATION INTESTATE

Submission date: 06/11/2021

Name: _____
Date: _____

Signed and dated by the lodging solicitor or applicant in person

Details of assets	
Bank account #1	
Value	€2,095.07
Name of institution	AIB
IBAN	IE63AIBK93101200102493
Address	AIB Harolds Cross, Main Street, , Dublin 6, , Ireland
How was property held	Solely by deceased
Bank account #2	
Value	€3,808.21
Name of institution	An Post Savings
IBAN	IE29AIBK93115212345678
Address	An Post , Harolds Cross, , Dublin 6, , Ireland
How was property held	Solely by deceased
Cash	
Value	€125.70
Household contents	
Household contents details	General Assets
Value	€2,538.48
Other asset #1	
Value	€6.35
Other description	Prize bond
Irish property (land/buildings) #1	
Property type	Residential
Address	11 O Gorman Street, Harolds Cross, , Dublin 6, , Ireland
Property value	€190,000.00
Tenure	Freehold
Folio number	FN2020
How was property held	Solely by deceased
Liabilities	
Liabilities owing to Revenue	€0.00
Creditor	€1,015.79
Funeral expenses	€3,777.47
Utilities (total amount)	€0.00
Amounts due to financial institutions #1	€0.00
Personal loans owing by the deceased #1	€0.00
Mortgage owing #1	€0.00
Fair deal/nursing home fee	€0.00
Other #1	€0.00
Other description	
Total of all Irish based debts and liabilities	€4,793.26

8.8.3 **NOTICE OF APPLICATION**

THE HIGH COURT

PROBATE

NOTICE OF APPLICATION

Grant Type:	Administration Intestate				
Deceased					
Domicile @death	Ireland				
Name(s)	Angela Moran				
Address: (incl. former addresses)	11 O'Gorman Street, Harold's Cross, Dublin 6 D6W C602				
Occupation:	Widow		PPS Number:		8742697J
Date of Death:	07 January 2021				
Place of Death	St Patrick's Nursing Home, Dublin Street, Baldoyle, Dublin 13 D13				
Applicant 1					
Name:	Maureen Horan				
Address:	11 O'Gorman Street, Harold's Cross, Dublin 6 D6W C602				
Occupation:	Married Woman		Relationship to Deceased		Lawful Daughter
Applicant 2					
Name:					
Address:					
Occupation:			Relationship to Deceased		
Applicant 3					
Name:					
Address:					
Occupation:			Relationship to Deceased		
Gross Assets (as perSA2):	€198,574		**Net Assets** (as per CA24):		€193,871
No. Of Codicils	None				
Lodging Solicitor (Name and Address)	Horace Nelson, Nelson & Co. Solicitors, Trafalgar Square, Dublin 2				

FOR USE OF THE PROBATE OFFICE ONLY

Fees:		Case Officer	
		HC Cert	

8.8.4 OATH FOR ADMINISTATRIX INCORPORATING ADMINISTRATION BOND

OATH FOR ~~ADMINISTRATOR~~/ADMINISTATRIX

INCORPORATING ADMINISTRATION BOND

THE HIGH COURT

PROBATE

The Probate Office Phoenix House, Smithfield Dublin 7 / ~~The District Probate Registry at~~

† If not a District Probate Registry strike out inappropriate words

PART A

Name of Deceased:	Angela Moran
Address of Deceased:	11 O'Gorman Street, Harold's Cross, Dublin 6
Date of Death:	07 January 2021
Place of Death:	St. Patrick's Nursing Home,
Name of Applicant	Maureen Horan
Address of Applicant:	11 O'Gorman Street, Harold's Cross, Dublin 6 D6W C602
Gross value of Estate:	€198,574

PART B

I, the above named applicant aged 18 years and upwards, make oath and say that the above named deceased, died intestate

A widow who never entered into civil partnership

that I am the *[insert title] . . . Lawful Child

of said deceased

and that I will well and faithfully administer the estate of the said deceased by paying the deceased's] just debts and distributing the residue of said estate according to law, and that I will exhibit a true inventory of the said estate and render a true account thereof, whenever required by law so to do; that the said deceased died at the above named place of death on the date of death cited above

[where application is made in District Probate Registry add] and that the said deceased had at the time of death a fixed place of abode at the above named address within the district of ....]

and that the whole of the estate without any deductions for debts, which devolves on and vests in the deceased's legal personal representative amounts in value to the figure cited above as the gross value of the estate and no more

to the best of my knowledge, information and belief.

Sworn at 11 Lower Baggott Street	Maureen Horan
in the County of	I Certify that I know the Deponent
City of Dublin	This Affidavit is filed by
this 14th day of April 20 21	Nelson & Company
by the said Maureen Horan	Solicitors for The Applicant
before me a Commissioner for taking Affidavits and I know the Deponent (or	this 18th day of April 20 21
who certifies to his/her knowledge of the Deponent)	
or the identity of the Deponent has been established by reference to a relevant document containing a photograph	
Document Type..............................	
Issue No:.......................................	
Joseph Kilkenny	
Commissioner for Oaths/Practising Solicitor	

PART C

I, the above named applicant am liable in full to pay to the President of the High Court the sum of double the gross value of the estate as specified in PART A above, for which payment I bind myself and my executors and administrators

Sealed with my seal this 14th day of April 2021

The condition of this obligation is that if I, the intended *[administatrix] of the estate of the said deceased do fulfil the obligations referred to in PART B above and furthermore

do pay all taxes and duties payable in respect of the estate of the deceased for which the personal representative is accountable and all income tax and surtax payable out of the estate and further do, if so required, render and deliver up the letters of administration in the High Court if it shall hereafter appear that any will was made by the deceased which is exhibited in the said Court with a request that it be allowed and approved accordingly then this obligation shall be void and no effect, but shall otherwise remain in full force and effect.

Signed, Sealed and Delivered by the said

Maureen Horan

in the presence of

Joseph Kilkenny

~~Commissioner for Oaths~~/Practising Solicitor

Filed on the 18th day of April 2021

by ... Nelson & Co ...

Solicitors for the Applicant

8.8.5 LETTERS OF ADMINISTRATION

Admon Int No 7

THE HIGH COURT

PROBATE

BE IT KNOWN, that on the 29th day of June 2021

LETTERS OF ADMINISTRATION of all the estate which devolved to and vests in the personal representative of Angela Moran late of 11 O'Gorman Street, Harold's Cross, Dublin

deceased, who died on or about the 7th day of January 2021 at St Patrick's Nursing Home Dublin INTESTATE a Widow

was granted by the Court to Maureen Horan of 11 0'Gorman Street, Harold's Cross, Dublin, Married Woman, lawful daughter of deceased,

she having been first sworn faithfully to administer the same.

And it is hereby certified that an Affidavit for Inland Revenue has been delivered wherein it is shown that the gross value of all Estate of the said deceased within this jurisdiction (exclusive of what the deceased may have been possessed of or entitled to as a Trustee and not beneficially) amounts to €198,574 and that the net value thereof amounts to €193,781

John Glennon

Probate Officer

Extracted by
€200.00

Nelson & Co.   Solicitors

EXTRACTING A GRANT OF ADMINISTRATION INTESTATE

8.9 Seat Office Checklist—Grant of Administration Intestate

Refer to Probate page of Courts Service website https://www.courts.ie/probate-intestacy-application for checklist where application is being lodged by post or DX.

Documents to be lodged	Common queries
(1) Notice of application	Contains details of the deceased's name, address, and date and place of death together with name and address of applicant and details of the filing solicitor to whom the grant will be posted once it issues. It also states the type of grant being applied for. It must be printed and not handwritten. It enables details of the application to be recorded immediately. Fees must be endorsed on the rear of the notice of application
(2) The **original** death certificate	An original coroner's interim death certificate will be accepted if the final death certificate is not yet issued
(3) Oath for administrator incorporating bond (Form No 5, Appendix Q of Rules of the Superior Court as inserted by SI 590/2020)	Original Only. No copies required Ensure names and addresses of all parties are consistent across all documents Ensure that the deceased in the oath is the same person referred to in the death certificate All differences in names and addresses must be accounted for in the oath Ensure correct Title (see Title for more information) State relationship of applicant to deceased Date and place of death must be as per the death certificate Total gross Irish estate—if date of death within two years of papers being lodged use value as per notice of acknowledgement (probate) form If date of death is more than two years of papers being lodged, use current market value for property. A Statement of (not an affidavit of market value which has been abolished) current market value will also be required. Jurat must comply with SI No 95/2009 and cannot be executed before lodging solicitor Complete the filing clause All exhibits must be signed by deponent and the person who administered the oath The date of the exhibit must be cited in the oath NB: the actual exhibit must be signed. Exhibit sheets are not accepted Ensure that the deceased in the bond is the same person referred to in the death certificate and oath. Penal sum must be double the gross current value of the estate Bond must be signed sealed and delivered—it is not sworn A seal must be affixed to the bond Bond must be executed before the same Commissioner/practising solicitor before whom oath was sworn

Documents to be lodged	Common queries
(4) Notice of Acknowledgement (Probate) or Form CA24. with Certificate for the High Court depending on the date of death of the deceased person	For deaths on or after 5 December 2001 and applications since 14 September 2020, the CA24 is replaced by the notice of acknowledgement (probate) which form auto generates from the Revenue once the form SA.2 is successfully submitted online. It is required in order to comply with s 48A of the CATCA, 2003. This form should have date of death values while the oath and bond will have current market values. For deaths prior to 5 December 2001, the CA24 must be lodged in duplicate with the Revenue Commissioners and a Certificate for the High Court obtained from them prior to lodging Probate Papers A Form CA6 (Schedule of lands) is required for deaths before 5 December 2001 if there is immoveable property in the estate. The date of death value and tenure must be inserted
(5) Letter of current market value of auctioneer	Where there is immovable property in the estate AND papers are being lodged in Probate Office more than twenty-four months from date of death
(6) Justification of surety (if required) (Form No 16, Appendix Q of Rules)	Required where an individual acts as surety to bond (i) person who swears affidavit of market value cannot act as surety (ii) no practising solicitor or clerk or apprentice solicitor can act as surety without leave of the court or Probate Officer (O 79, r 73)
(7) Fees	(See Seat Office fees table of Probate Office at end of **Chapter 11**.)

8.10 Disclaiming on Intestacy

8.10.1 DEEDS OF DISCLAIMER IN GENERAL

Nobody can be compelled to accept an inheritance. A proposed beneficiary can disclaim his inheritance. To qualify as a disclaimer, the refusal of the inheritance must take place before the beneficiary accepts any benefit from it. Further, it is not possible to disclaim in favour of anyone; in other words, one cannot try to redirect to someone else the inheritance one is not taking. In that case it would be an inheritance followed by a gift and it would be treated as a conveyance for value, with stamp duty and gift tax implications. A disclaimer must simply be that and the better practice is that it is done formally by way of deed.

Where an inheritance under intestacy is disclaimed, the property will automatically pass to the person next entitled under the rules of intestacy. Disclaimers can, of course, be for consideration, and then the consideration is an inheritance taken from the deceased and not a benefit taken from the person giving the consideration.

8.10.2 EFFECT OF DISCLAIMERS ON INTESTACY PRIOR TO 5 MAY 1997

Prior to the provisions of s 6 of the Family Law (Miscellaneous Provisions) Act, 1997, there was uncertainty as to the distribution of a disclaimed estate or part of a disclaimed estate on intestacy. The problem essentially can be summed up by saying there are two schools of thought in relation to such disclaimers.

1. They are effective to pass an interest in the property to the persons who are next entitled (or if the persons who are disclaiming are in the same 'class' of next of kin to the remainder of that class).
2. A disclaimer of an intestate share is not so effective because s 67(2) of the Succession Act states that certain portions of the intestate's property shall vest in the spouse and issue.

Those who follow this second school of thought hold that some of the sections of the Succession Act which provide for who is entitled to an intestate's estate use mandatory language and accordingly there is no possibility of effectively disclaiming an intestate's share. It is still quite a common idea among a substantial number of practitioners that the intestate's property vests automatically in the person specified in the Succession Act, and thus it is impossible for a beneficiary to decline to accept it.

They would argue that on a disclaimer by such a person, the interest does not revert back to the estate, since, never having accepted his interest in the first place, he cannot vest it back.

Section 73 of the Succession Act provides:

'In default of any person taking the estate of an intestate, whether under this part or otherwise, the State shall take the estate as ultimate intestate successor.'

The second school of thought therefore holds that it is impossible to disclaim a share on intestacy, since the effect is to bring about a forfeiture to the State.

The adherents of the first school of thought would argue that s 73 can never have any application where an intestate is survived by any of the persons mentioned at ss 67 and 71 of the Succession Act because that would mean that no one could take the estate. In other words, the provisions of Part VI of the Act merely apply to the order in which the surviving next of kin of the intestate are entitled, and the word 'shall' is used in such a sense and not in a mandatory sense.

8.10.3 EFFECT OF DISCLAIMERS ON INTESTACY AFTER 5 MAY 1997

To clarify the issue of whether or not a deed of disclaimer in an intestate estate is effective to pass title, s 6 of the Family Law (Miscellaneous Provisions) Act, 1997 inserted a new s 72A into the Succession Act, 1965. Please read the section.

It provided that where a person disclaims on intestacy after 5 May 1997, that person shall be regarded as having predeceased the intestate when distributing his estate. It further provided that if the person disclaiming is *not the spouse or lineal ancestor of the intestate* he will also be regarded as having died without issue.

However, this only applies to disclaimers on intestacy after 5 May 1997. Therefore, for all disclaimers prior to this date, the previous discussion is still relevant.

It should be pointed out to any client intending to disclaim that, in addition to losing any entitlement to a share of the estate, he or she will also lose any right that he or she has to extract a grant of representation to the estate of the deceased, in accordance with O 79, r 5 of the Rules of the Superior Courts, unless a grant has been extracted before the disclaimer is signed.

In the event of a disclaimer being signed after the person disclaiming has applied for a grant, but before the grant has issued, the application should be withdrawn, as the applicant would no longer be one of the persons 'having a beneficial interest' as provided for in O 79, r 5(1). Note also that if an applicant's right to a grant arises from a disclaimer having been signed by a person who had a prior right, then the original of such a disclaimer must be lodged with the papers in the Probate Office.

An article in the July 1998 edition of the *Law Society Gazette* deals with this topic and will be of interest to practitioners.

8.10.4 SPOUSE DISCLAIMING ON INTESTACY

If a spouse, for example a wife, disclaims her two-thirds share on intestacy in her husband's estate, his issue (who in normal course would also be her issue) would inherit his whole estate. The section does not deem a spouse disclaiming to have died without issue, as that would exclude the issue from inheriting the one-third share of their parent's estate they would otherwise be entitled to inherit. While a specific wording could have been inserted into the section to exclude a disclaiming spouse from passing the two-thirds share to the issue, the legislature, in the wording of the section, obviously wished to permit disclaimers of spouses to operate in such manner.

Example

John dies intestate leaving him surviving his spouse, Mary (who disclaims) and his two children, Colm and Imelda. See Figure **8.16**.

FIGURE 8.16

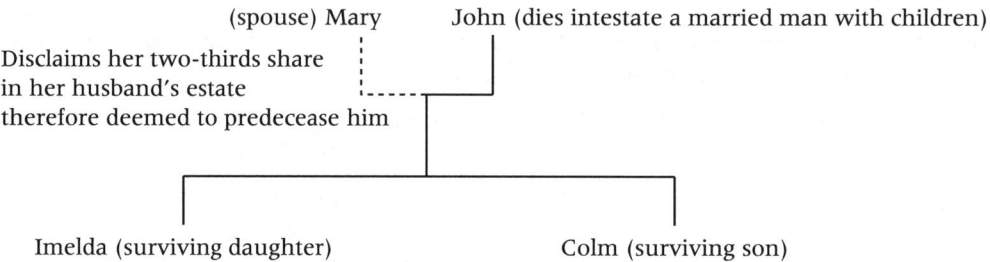

Distribution

- Son Colm will inherit a half-share.
- Daughter Imelda will inherit a half-share.
- Either can extract the grant.

8.10.5 DIRECT LINEAL ANCESTOR (E.G. FATHER, GRANDFATHER) DISCLAIMING ON INTESTACY

Disclaiming direct lineal ancestors, such as spouses, while deemed under s 72A to have predeceased the intestate in the distribution of his estate, are not presumed to have predeceased without issue.

Example

A man dies intestate, a bachelor, without mother, leaving him surviving his father. If his father disclaims his share after 5 May 1997, the father is deemed under the section to have predeceased the intestate. The effect of this is that the intestate's estate will pass to the father's other children, i.e. the brothers and sisters of the intestate. Section 72A does not deem the disclaiming father to have died without issue. See Figure **8.17**.

FIGURE 8.17

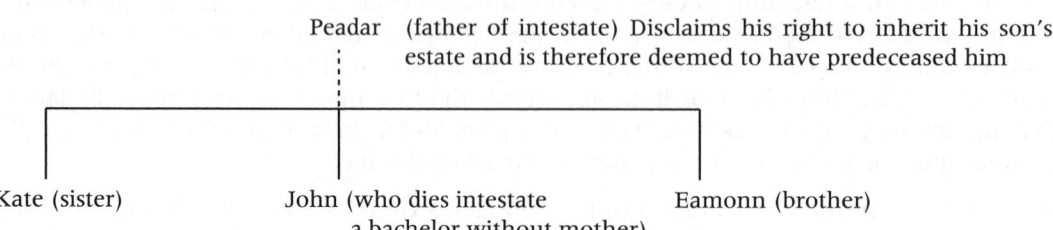

Distribution

- Sister Kate will inherit a half-share.
- Brother Eamonn will inherit a half-share.
- Either can extract a grant.

8.10.6 GENERAL OPERATION OF SECTION 72A (EVERYONE ELSE)

If a person other than a spouse or direct lineal ancestor of the intestate (e.g. issue of the intestate) disclaims after 5 May 1997, that person is presumed to have predeceased the intestate and died without issue. A child therefore who disclaims cannot pass the disclaimed share to his issue, as you might expect. The disclaimed share will pass to his brothers and sisters and to nephews and nieces, the children of a brother or sister who have *actually* and are not simply *presumed to have* predeceased the intestate.

Example

(See specimen titles at para **8.10.8**.) Widower Tom dies intestate, leaving him surviving two lawful and only children, Anthony and Bernard. Anthony disclaimed in 20 and Bernard survived the intestate and has since died. The other surviving issue are: a grandchild, Patrick, issue of disclaiming child Anthony. As Anthony is deemed to have predeceased the intestate without leaving issue, Patrick is deemed, in effect, never to have existed. There are three grandchildren, Joseph, Kieran, and Liam, issue of a predeceased child Michael.

Grandchild Patrick, as noted, is deemed never to have existed.

Distribution

- Richard will inherit half of Tom's estate on behalf of the estate of Bernard.
- Joseph, Kieran, and Liam will inherit the remaining half of Tom's estate in equal shares, one-sixth each.

See Figure **8.18**.

Joseph, Kieran, and Liam have priority to extract the grant. See sample title at **8.10.8**.

FIGURE 8.18

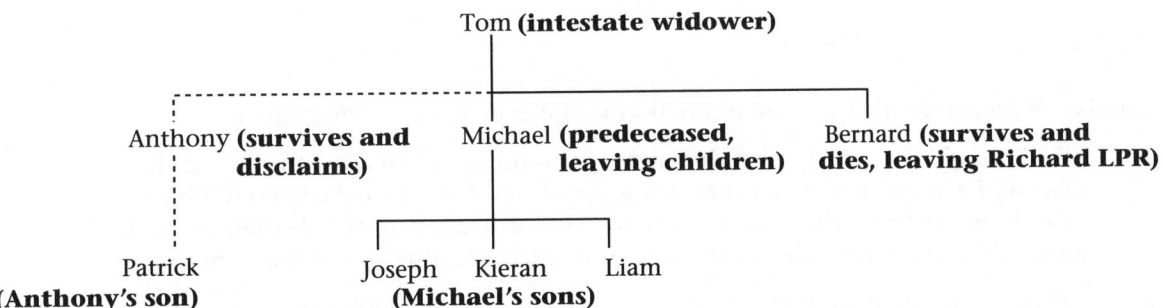

8.10.7 SAMPLE DEED OF DISCLAIMER ON INTESTACY

Disclaimer of AB On Death Intestate of CD

OBIT—DAY OF—20

THIS DEED OF DISCLAIMER is made this   day of   20   by me, AB [occupation] of   in the County of

WHEREAS:

1) CD (late of   ) (hereinafter called 'the deceased') died on the   day of   20 , having died intestate as to the interest hereby disclaimed.

2) The deceased was [marital status] and [occupation] and was survived by [state if survived by, for example, spouse and two children or as the case may be].

3) I am a [relationship] of the deceased and, as such, I am entitled to a [for example, one-sixth or whatever the case may be] share of the deceased's estate, or that part of the deceased's estate as to which he died intestate (hereinafter called 'the said share') under the rules for distribution and intestacy set out in the Succession Act, 1965.

4) I have not accepted the said share from the personal representative of the estate or otherwise, nor have I exercised any degree of beneficial ownership, control or possession in respect of the said share.

5) Now it is hereby witnessed that I irrevocably disclaim absolutely all my right to the said share.

6) [Insert the following paragraph unless the grant has already issued to the person disclaiming or he or she has already signed a renunciation.]

7) And I hereby acknowledge that on the execution by me of this disclaimer I will lose any right I may have (by virtue of my entitlement to the said share) to extract a grant of administration to the estate of the deceased.

8) In witness whereof, I have here and to set my hand and affixed my seal the day and year first above written.

Signed, sealed and delivered by the said AB in the presence of:

A number of points should be noted in relation to the execution of a disclaimer:

1. It is desirable that the person disclaiming should be advised by an independent solicitor, i.e. a solicitor who is not acting for either the personal representative or, indeed, any person who will benefit from the execution of the disclaimer. Such solicitor should, if possible, be the witness to the execution of the disclaimer.

2. Further, such independent solicitor should explain the implications of the disclaimer and ideally should confirm his advice in writing. This will involve enquiries being made with the solicitor as to the assets and next of kin of the deceased. The person disclaiming should be made aware of:

    (a) the share of the estate to which he is entitled;
    (b) the assets owned by the deceased, an estimation of their value, and the approximate value of the share being disclaimed;
    (c) any relevant tax liabilities which might arise if the disclaimer was not signed;
    (d) the tax liabilities on the signing of the disclaimer; and
    (e) the effect of signing the disclaimer (and in particular to whom the disclaimed share will pass, pursuant to s 72A as amended).

8.10.8 SPECIMEN TITLES WHEN DISCLAIMING ON INTESTACY

Surviving kin	Wording of titles in oath
1. Two children surviving, Anthony (disclaiming) and Bernard (survived and died); one grandchild Patrick, issue of disclaiming child Anthony; and three grandchildren, Joseph, Kieran, and Liam, issue of predeceased child Michael See para **8.10.6**.	INTESTATE a widower/widow leaving him/her surviving two lawful and only children Anthony and Bernard, Anthony having duly disclaimed his rights by Deed of Disclaimer dated the day of 20 upon which I have marked my name prior to the swearing hereof and thereby is deemed by Section 72A of the Succession Act (as inserted by Section 6 of the Family Law (Miscellaneous Provisions) Act, 1997) to have predeceased the deceased and Bernard who survived the deceased and has since died on the day of 20 and I am [either] Joseph, Kieran [or] Liam the lawful child of Michael, who was a lawful child of and who predeceased the deceased
2. Two brothers, A (disclaiming) and B (survived and died); one nephew P, child of disclaiming brother A, and three nieces, X, Y, and Z, children of predeceased sister L	INTESTATE a single person who never married or entered into a civil partnership and died without issue without parent or sister leaving him/her surviving two lawful and only brothers A and B, A having duly disclaimed his rights by Deed of Disclaimer dated the day of 20 upon which I have marked my name prior to the swearing hereof and thereby is deemed by Section 72A of the Succession Act (as inserted by Section 6 of the Family Law (Miscellaneous Provisions) Act, 1997) to have predeceased the deceased without issue and B who survived the deceased and has since died on the day of 20 and I am (X/Y/Z) the lawful daughter of L who was a lawful sister of and who predeceased the deceased

8.11 Status of Children Born Outside Marriage and Their Property Rights

8.11.1 HISTORICAL AND LEGAL BACKGROUND

The law governing the succession rights of non-marital persons falls into distinct periods:

1. The common law position (which applies to all deaths prior to 19 May 1931). This was a time when non-marital children had no succession rights.

2. The law between the Legitimacy Act, 1931 and the Status of Children Act, 1987 (operative date for property rights in Part V: 14 June 1988). The Legitimacy Act, 1931, is existing law for all wills (and instruments creating powers of appointment) made before 14 June 1988 and all deaths intestate before that date.

It provides that where both natural parents of a child subsequently marry each other (both of whom must have been in a position to marry each other at birth of child or at some time during the preceding ten months) the child is *legitimated*. Section 9 of the Act conferred succession rights on a child to its mother but only where she leaves no legitimate issue surviving. Likewise, a mother was granted succession right to her child as if he was born legitimate.

3. The law since the Status of Children Act, 1987 (all wills made on or after 14 June 1988 and all deaths intestate on or after 14 June 1988).

The purpose of the Act was to equalise the rights under law of all children whether born within or outside marriage. This is achieved by setting out the general principle that in this and in all future legislation relationships are to be determined without regard to whether the parents of any person have married each other.

8.11.2 STATUS OF CHILDREN ACT, 1987: COMMENCEMENT DATE AND EFFECTS

Part V of the Act deals with property rights and came into operation on 14 June 1988.

Section 3 sets out the general principle central to the Act, that in determining relationships no regard shall be had for the fact that the parents of the child were not married to each other. An adoption order terminates the legal relationship between a child and his natural parents and all rights *inter se* are lost save and except for Group A CAT Threshold. See Part 10 of the Second Schedule to the Capital Acquisitions Tax Consolidation Act, 2003.

8.11.2.1 Wills

Where a will is made on or after 14 June 1988 and it refers to 'child' or 'issue', this will now include non-marital children, for example in the residuary clause *'all my rest residue to my children'*. Unless he particularly specifies his *'legitimate children'* or *'the children of his marriage to X'*, all his children will benefit and be entitled (after the executor) to apply to prove will. Note that it does not matter when the testator dies: it is the date of execution of the will that counts.

Before the coming into force of the Act (it was held in *O'B v S* [1984] IR 316), the words simply referred to legitimate persons. A codicil made after 14 June 1988 does not bring an earlier-dated will under the operation of the Act.

Note: where a testator includes a contrary intention to s 3 in his will, then only legitimate children may benefit. For examples of a contrary intention, see negation of the precedent Status of Children Act clause contained in the precedent will at para **2.17**. Practitioners should also read para **4.6.3.4** and the reference therein to naming children or grandchildren, rather than putting in a specific Status of Children Act reference.

Section 31 of the Act gives s 117 of the Succession Act, 1965 rights to children of testators dying after 14 June 1988, which is wider than s 27, which applies only to testators who have made wills after 14 June 1988.

8.11.2.2 Intestate succession

This is governed by s 29, which amends s 4 of the Succession Act, 1965, stating effectively that all relationships shall be deduced for the purposes of the 1965 Act irrespective of the marital status of a person's parents. With the abolition of the status of illegitimacy, non-marital children now have equal succession rights with the marital children to the estates of all their blood relations, and vice versa.

8.11.2.3 The presumptions

Two presumptions were inserted in the Act to reduce considerably the substantial obligation of enquiry and conduct on personal representatives to ascertain persons entitled under the Act.

Section 29(2) creates a rebuttable presumption that a child whose parents have not married each other and who dies intestate is not survived by his father or by any person related to him through his father.

Section 30 creates a rebuttable presumption for the purposes of determining who is entitled to take out probate or letters of administration. The section states that a deceased person was not survived by any relative whose parents have not married each other or who is related to him through such a person.

The s 29 presumption deals specifically with the father of a non-marital child, where said child dies intestate, and presumes the father and all those claiming through him to have predeceased the child. The s 30 presumption is far more general, covering testacies and intestacies, presuming that where a non-marital child relationship affects the title to a grant, all those persons entitled to apply for a grant on the basis of that non-marital relationship have predeceased the deceased.

8.11.3 DEATHS INTESTATE BEFORE 14 JUNE 1988

In relation to applications under s 29 of the Legitimacy Act, 1931, where a mother or her child died intestate before the coming into effect of the Status of Children Act, 1987, application must be made to the Probate Officer by motion on affidavit. The affidavit should establish the relationship by exhibiting the 'long version' birth certificate and should confirm that the mother was not survived by any legitimate issue.

8.11.4 DEATHS INTESTATE AFTER 14 JUNE 1988

What are the necessary proofs for the following applicants for a grant and what procedures must they follow to obtain this?

1. Non-marital child to mother and mother to non-marital child.
2. Non-marital child to father and father to non-marital child.
3. Where the applicant is applying for a grant on the basis of a relationship which is deduced through a person whose parents have not married each other; for example, non-marital nephew to his uncle.

The most important proof in all these cases is obviously the birth certificate. The 'long form' of birth certificate must be exhibited in the oath for administrator. The standard of proof in all these cases is proof on the balance of probabilities and no corroboration is required. The Law Reform Commission, at p 111 of its report, proposed the dropping of the requirement for corroboration and proposed the standard of proof required being proof on the balance of probabilities, as it felt 'the requirement for corroboration could cause injustice since the court might be perfectly satisfied on the evidence that a person is the parent of a child but would be obliged nonetheless to refuse the application on account of the absence for corroboration'. The Act, at s 10 on guardianship, s 15 on maintenance, and s 35(8) on declarations of probate, adopts this standard of proof.

Non-marital child to mother or mother to non-marital child

The 'long form' of birth certificate must be produced, showing the mother's name and address. Where the mother's name and/or address has changed from that set out in the birth certificate, the applicant must swear a separate affidavit clearly identifying the mother and clarifying the change of name and/or address.

Non-marital child to father or father to non-marital child

Where the father's name and address appear on the birth certificate (long form) and it corresponds to those of the deceased at the time of death, all that is required is that the birth certificate be exhibited in the oath, as noted earlier. Section 46(3) presumes the father registered on the birth certificate to be the father of the child. Where the father's name and/or address in the birth certificate has changed since the date when he was registered as father, a detailed affidavit is required, identifying the father and clarifying the change of name and/or address.

Where the father's name does not appear on the birth certificate, an application must be made to the Circuit Court under the Status of Children Act for a declaration of parentage.

8.11.5 REMOTER RELATIONSHIPS THAN PARENT–CHILD WHERE THE APPLICANT IS CLAIMING THROUGH A PERSON WHOSE PARENTS HAVE NOT MARRIED EACH OTHER, E.G. 'NON-MARITAL NEPHEW' TO UNCLE

Where a title is traced through a person whose parents have not married each other, it will be necessary for the applicant to establish that relationship in the same manner as described earlier, for example a nephew applying for a grant in the estate for his paternal uncle will have to establish his parenthood and swear that his father was the brother of the deceased.

First, the applicant must swear the usual title in the oath for administrator intestate:

'a bachelor without parent brother or sister and I am the lawful nephew'.

He must then go on to state:

'being the lawful son of XX lawful brother of and who predeceased the deceased. I beg to refer to my supplemental affidavit sworn the   day of   establishing my parenthood filed herewith'.

A separate affidavit establishing the parenthood of the nephew in accordance with the requirements set out earlier would also be filed with the oath.

Declarations of paternity (Part VI)

Section 35 confers rights, on the children only, to make such applications for declarations.

Blood tests (Part VIII)

The major innovation in the Act is to allow the court to draw such inference as is reasonable in the circumstances where a party refuses to cooperate in allowing blood tests to be taken.

It widens the definition of 'blood tests' in order to avail of the major technological developments in this field, including DNA profiling.

Registration/re-registration of births

The position for the registration of the birth of a non-marital child is now the same as for marital children.

Warning: While the Act allows personal representatives to rely on the rebuttable presumptions of ss 29 and 30 and effectively ignore the rights of persons entitled under the Act, the dropping from the Act of further securities which had been provided for them in the Bill, relieving them from liability where they administer estates in ignorance of such claimants, now fixes personal representatives with a duty to make reasonable enquiries before administering estates.

8.11.6 PRUDENT GUIDELINES

It is suggested that in circumstances where a claim could arise under the Act, a prudent solicitor would adopt the following guidelines:

1. If the applicant knew that the father or any non-marital next of kin survived the deceased, he or she cannot rely on the presumptions. Once he or she knows that they survived, he or she cannot publish s 49 notices and rely on the fact that those notices have not been replied to (see *Re Beatty* (1888) 29 LRIR 290).

2. By making reasonable enquiries, it could be easily ascertained whether the father or non-marital next of kin survived the deceased. For practical reasons, to avoid a lot of unnecessary trouble later when they would assert their rights, it would not be advisable to rely on the presumptions without first making those enquiries and publishing the appropriate s 49 notices.

3. If reasonable enquiries would not reveal a claimant under the Act because, for example, the identity of the father is unknown and no father's name appears on the birth certificate, then the presumptions can be relied upon to the full, as regards both entitlement to grants and in the distribution of the estates. The onus clearly rests on the non-marital father and non-marital next of kin in such cases to assert their rights. If the marital next of kin extracts a grant and waits six years, any possible claims against them will be statute-barred.

CHAPTER 9

EXTRACTING A GRANT OF ADMINISTRATION WITH WILL ANNEXED

9.1 Notes on Grant of Administration with Will Annexed

This chapter deals with the situation where, although the deceased died testate, the executor is not proving the will. When someone other than the executor is proving the will, the appropriate grant of representation to apply for is called a 'grant of letters of administration with will annexed'. Section 27(1) of the Succession Act, 1965 provides the statutory authority for making grants of letters of administration with will annexed:

> 'The High Court shall have power to grant administration (with or without will annexed) of the estate of a deceased person, and a grant may be limited in any way the Court thinks fit.'

Such grants, like grants of probate dealt with in **Chapter 7**, are based on the existence of a will and share a common feature with a grant of letters of administration intestate dealt with in **Chapter 8** in that the persons entitled to apply for both of these grants are set out in the Rules of the Superior Courts, 1986.

This grant is required where:

(a) No executor is appointed in the deceased's will;

(b) Executors are appointed, but they predecease the deceased or have died without proving the will;

(c) The appointment of the executor(s) is void for uncertainty;

(d) The executor is under a disability, for example, where the executor is a minor or is a person of unsound mind;

(e) The executor is living abroad or is suffering from physical disability and appoints an attorney;

(f) The grant is made pursuant to s 27(4) of the Succession Act and there is a will involved;

(g) The executor refuses to apply for the grant, and refuses to renounce, despite having being served with a citation; and

(h) The executor renounces.

9.2 Entitlement to Extract the Grant

The two points to remember when establishing entitlement to extract a grant are:

1. The grant follows the interest;

2. The interest is determined at the date of death, i.e. the entitlement to inherit under a will is determined at the date of death.

Based on who gets the residue not relationships

EXTRACTING A GRANT OF ADMINISTRATION WITH WILL ANNEXED 313

Regarding the first of these, in the case of an administration with will annexed grant; the grant follows the interest, which is the residue. The appropriate question to ask is: 'Who will inherit the residue?' The order of priority of persons entitled to apply for a grant of letters of administration with will annexed is based on the will. The title of the applicant in the oath is taken from the will and does not necessarily depend on any relationship existing between the deceased and the applicant (except in the case of a partial intestacy). Contrast this with the order of entitlement on intestacy (see para **8.2.1**), which very much depends on a relationship existing between the deceased and the applicant for the grant.

9.2.1 WHO IS ENTITLED TO EXTRACT THE GRANT?

Order 79, r 5(6) of the Rules of the Superior Courts sets out the order of priority of those persons entitled to apply for a grant of letters of administration with will annexed for deaths on or after 1 January 1967.

Order 79, r 5(6) is reproduced as follows:

'Where the deceased died on or after the 1st day of January, 1967, domiciled in Ireland, leaving a Will appointing no executor, or appointing an executor or executors who have been cleared off by death, renunciation, citation or otherwise, the person, or persons entitled to a grant of administration with will annexed shall be determined in accordance with the following order of priority, namely:

(a) *Any residuary legatee or devisee holding in trust for any other person;*

(b) *Any residuary legatee or devisee for life;*

(c) *Any other residuary legatee or devisee or, subject to sub-rule (9) (b) hereof, which provides that* live interests be preferred to dead interests, *the personal representative of any such residuary legatee or devisee;* [see O 79, r 5(9) (b), which provides that grants are given to a living member of a class entitled in preference to the personal representative of a surviving and subsequent dying member of the class—live interests are preferred to dead interests]

(d) *Any residuary legatee or devisee for life jointly with any ultimate residuary legatee or devisee on the renunciation or consent of the remaining residuary legatees or devisees for life;*

(e) *Where the residue is not in terms wholly disposed of, the Probate Officer may, if he is of opinion that the testator has nevertheless disposed of the whole or substantially the whole of the estate as ascertained at the time of the application for a grant, allow a grant to be made to any legatee or devisee entitled to, or to share in, the estate so disposed of, without regard to the person entitled to share in any residue not disposed of by the will;* [i.e. a partial intestacy situation]

(f) *Where the residue is not wholly disposed of by the will, any person (other than a creditor) entitled to a grant in the event of a total intestacy according to the order of priority set out in sub-rules (1) to (5);* [entitlement on intestacy has been dealt with in detail in **Chapter 8**]

(g) *Any legatee or devisee or any creditor or, subject to sub-rule (9) (b), the personal representative of any such person.'* [On renunciation of any person entitled ahead of those at (g)].

Those entitled at (c) and (d) are most common in practice, as in almost all cases the applicant is either the sole *residuary* devisee and legatee or one of the residuary devisees and legatees or the legal personal representative of a residuary devisee and legatee. The point to remember is that the grant follows the interest, which is the residue. The person who inherited the residue of the estate is the first person after the executor to prove the will. A legatee or devisee is only entitled on the renunciation of those entitled to the residue. A creditor may apply but it will be necessary first to obtain an order of the Probate Court as the creditor must be able to prove his debt before proceeding to extract a grant.

To put this simply:

(a) If the residuary legatee and devisee is alive now, he extracts the grant.

(b) If the residuary legatee and devisee predeceased the deceased or if none was in fact appointed, the next of kin extracts the grant. As this is a partial intestacy, the rules of entitlement on intestacy apply—see para **8.4**.

314 EXTRACTING A GRANT OF ADMINISTRATION WITH WILL ANNEXED

(c) If the sole residuary legatee and devisee survived the deceased and subsequently died, his legal personal representative extracts the grant. Section 98 of the Succession Act, which is dealt with at para **8.8**, may be relevant in ascertaining whether the residuary legatee and devisee 'survived' the deceased where the residuary legatee and devisee is a child or other issue of the deceased who left children or issue alive at the date of death of the deceased.

(d) There may be a substitutionary legatee and devisee as outlined at para **2.9.2** where there is a 'gift over'.

9.2.1.1 'Universal legatee and devisee'

As noted at para **2.9.2**, all references to a residuary legatee and devisee apply equally to a universal legatee and devisee.

9.2.1.2 Attorneys

In the case of a person residing out of or about to leave the jurisdiction of the court or who, in the opinion of the court or the Probate Officer, is suffering from a severe continuing physical disability, administration with the will annexed may be granted to his or her attorney acting under a power of attorney. See para **11.1.4.8**.

9.2.1.3 Guardians

A grant of administration may be made to the guardian of a minor for a minor's use. In a case where a minor does not have a testamentary guardian or a guardian appointed by the court, or under the provisions of the Guardianship of Infants Act, 1964, a guardian must be assigned by order of the court. See para **11.1.4.9**.

9.3 What Proofs (Documents) are Required to Apply for the Grant?

The documents/proofs necessary to lodge in the Probate Office or in the District Probate Registry to lead a grant of letters of administration with will annexed are as follows:

(1) Original death certificate or if not available a coroner's interim certificate of the fact of death;

(2) Original will (and codicil if any);

(3) Engrossment of will or certified photocopy (and codicil if any);

(4) Oath for administrator with will annexed incorporating administration bond in Part C;

(5) Notice of application, printed and not handwritten;

(6) For deaths after 5 December 2001, notice of acknowledgement (probate) form received from Revenue duly signed. For deaths pre-5 December 2001, Inland Revenue form CA24 duly certified by the Revenue with certificate for the High Court and form CA6 (Schedule of buildings and lands);

(7) Letter of current market value of immoveable property from auctioneers where the papers are lodged more than two years after the date of death. If the papers are lodged within two years of the date of death, no proof of current market value will be needed. An affidavit of market value will never be required;

(8) Probate Office fees to be endorsed on the back of the notice of application.

The following documents may be necessary, depending on the circumstances:

(a) Form S1 (postal application form) if applicable;

(b) Affidavit of attesting witness;

EXTRACTING A GRANT OF ADMINISTRATION WITH WILL ANNEXED

(c) Affidavit of plight and condition;
(d) Affidavit of mental capacity;
(e) Charitable bequest form;
(f) Renunciation of executor;
(g) Power of attorney.

Practitioners are also referred to the Seat Office checklist at para **9.9** and the Probate page of the Courts Service website at: https://www.courts.ie/probate.

It should be noted that many of the documents which are required to be submitted when applying for this grant are similar to those required when applying for a grant of probate—with some exceptions, for example, oath for administrator with the will incorporating the administration bond, and the auctioneer's letter of current market value of immoveable property, both of which have been dealt with in **Chapter 8**.

The following documents have been dealt with previously in **Chapters 6 and 7**, dealing with the grant of probate, namely:

(a) Original will and codicil—if any;
(b) Engrossment of will or certified photocopy will;
(c) Statement of Affairs (Probate) Form SA.2 and notice of acknowledgement (probate);
(d) Inland Revenue Affidavit Form CA24 and certificate for the High Court for deaths pre-5 December 2001.
(e) Affidavit of attesting witness;
(f) Affidavit of plight and condition;
(g) Affidavit of mental capacity;
(h) Charitable bequest form;
(I) original death certificate or other proof of death.

The queries that arise in relation to these forms are as discussed in **Chapter 7** under the grant of probate applications and will not be dealt with here any further.

The auctioneer's letter of current market value for immoveable property has been dealt with in **Chapter 8** under the grant of letters of administration intestate and will also not be dealt with here any further.

This chapter will deal primarily with the oath for administrator with the will annexed incorporating the bond. While the oath for administrator intestate with the bond has been dealt with previously in **Chapter 8** and the oath for administrator with will annexed with the bond share some features, there are significant differences which will be outlined below.

9.3.1 OATH FOR ADMINISTRATOR WITH THE WILL ANNEXED INCORPORATING ADMINISTRATION BOND

The combined oath for administrator with the will incorporating administration bond is provided for in SI 590/2020 amending Appendix Q of the Rules of the Superior Court and is similar in layout to the oath for administrator intestate as set out in Chapter 8, para **8.3.2**. It replaces the oath for executor as, although there is a will, there is no executor to prove the will. For applications for grants of administration with will annexed lodged on or after 2 February 2021, the oath incorporates the administration bond at Part C of the form. The heading must include the type of oath. Part A of the oath contains details of the name of the deceased and any variations of same; the last address of the deceased; the occupation of both the deceased and the applicant; the date and place of death of the deceased; and the gross value of the estate. Part B of the oath sets out the title of the applicant to apply for the grant and is so worded to ==clear off all persons having a prior right to the grant== (usually the executor). Where there are persons having any prior interest, the oath should show on its face how they were cleared off, for example by exhibiting renunciations, consents, etc. The order of entitlement to extract the grant is set out in O 79, r 5(6) of the Rules of the Superior Courts as referred to at para **9.2.1**.

As with the grant of probate, the original will (and codicil if any) or a sealed and certified copy will (and codicil if any) as appropriate must be exhibited in the oath and marked by the applicant and the person before whom the oath was sworn.

The most common query received from the Probate Office concerning this form is that the title of the applicant is incorrect. The title of the applicant in the oath for administrator with the will annexed is taken from the will and, although details of the relationship to the testator (if any) should be inserted on the form, the relationship is generally immaterial (except in the case of a partial intestacy).

Part C of the ==oath incorporates the administration bond==.

A number of sample titles that may be used when applying for a will-annexed grant are outlined below at para **9.3.1.1**. These should be followed and adapted where necessary. For example, instead of 'I am the Residuary Legatee and Devisee named in said will', the title may be 'I am one of the Residuary Legatees and Devisees in common named in said will' or 'We are the Residuary Legatees and Devisees named in said will'.

9.3.1.1 Sample titles administration with will annexed (deaths on or after 1 January 1967)

1. **Where no executor is appointed**

   —and that he did not therein name any executor and that I am the Residuary Legatee and Devisee named in said will.

2 (a). **Where the executor predeceased the deceased**

   —and that he did therein name as sole executor XY, who predeceased the deceased and that I am the Residuary Legatee and Devisee named in said will.

2 (b). **Where the executor survived the deceased and has since died**

   —and that he did therein name as sole executor XY who survived the deceased and has since died without proving said will and that I am the Residuary Legatee and Devisee named in said will.

3. **Where the executor renounces**

   —and that he did therein name as sole executor XY who has duly renounced his rights upon which renunciation dated the day of 20 marked with the letter 'A' I have endorsed my name prior to the swearing hereof and that I am the Residuary Legatee and Devisee named in said will.

4. **Where no executor is appointed and the residue is not disposed of**

   —and that he did not therein name any executor or Residuary Legatee and Devisee and that I am the lawful widow [*for example*] of the deceased [*See O 79, r 5(1) (Entitlement on Intestacy) and titles for intestacy at para 8.3.1.1.*]

5. **Where no executor is appointed and residuary legatee and devisee renounces**

   —and that he did not therein name any executor but that he did therein name as Residuary Legatee and Devisee XY who has duly renounced his rights [*exhibit renunciation*] and that I am a legatee named in said will.

EXTRACTING A GRANT OF ADMINISTRATION WITH WILL ANNEXED

6. **Where no executor is appointed and residuary legatee and devisee survived and died**

   —and that he did not therein name any executor but did therein name as Residuary Legatee and Devisee XY who survived the deceased and has since died without proving said will and that I am the Personal Representative of the said XY under Grant of **Probate/Administration Intestate/Administration with Will annexed** *For example* which issued to me from the Probate Office on the day of 20.

7 (a). **Where the executor, universal legatee and devisee predeceased and next-of-kin applies (no gift over in will)**

   —and that he did therein name as sole executor, Universal Legatee and Devisee his spouse XY who predeceased the deceased and that I am the lawful child [*for example*] of the said deceased. [*See O 79, r 5(1) (Entitlement on Intestacy) and titles for intestacy at para* 8.3.1.1.]

7 (b). **Where the executor, universal legatee and devisee predeceased and substituted universal legatee and devisee applies (gift over)**

   —and that he did therein name as sole executor and instituted Universal Legatee and Devisee XY who predeceased the deceased and that I am the substituted universal legatee and devisee named in said will.

8. **Where the attorney of executor applies**

   —and did therein name as his sole executor AB who is aged eighteen years and upwards and is now residing at [*give address abroad in full and description of executor*] that I am the attorney lawfully appointed of the said AB under power of attorney dated the day 20, upon which I have signed my name.

These precedents should be amended and even combined to suit the precise circumstances of each individual application.

The will itself is exhibited in the oath and must be marked by the administrator and by the person before whom the oath is sworn.

Where the applicant is the attorney of the executor or is applying on foot of a renunciation by the executor, such power of attorney or form of renunciation(s) must be referred to in the title and marked by both the applicant and the person before whom the oath is sworn.

For deaths prior to 1 June 1967 the oath refers separately to the value of the real and personal assets. Details of the real and personal estate must be included in the oath. Leasehold property is to be shown as personal estate and if there is no freehold property it must be stated, 'There is no real estate', and not merely show a zero or nil value for real estate. The current version of the oath refers merely to the gross value of the estate in Part A and no distinction is made between realty and personalty.

The current market value (not necessarily the date of death value as per the Inland Revenue affidavit) of immovable property as per auctioneer's letter of current market value must be stated in the oath. It is important to remember that the value of the assets in the Inland Revenue affidavit is the date of death value. The market value in the oath and in the bond must be the current market value.

9.3.1.2 Residuary estate

To constitute a gift of the residue there must be a disposition of the whole of the residue of the estate. In no case will a specific gift of property, even though it comprises all the known estate of the deceased, be considered a gift of residue. In such cases the law always presumes a residue, and a grant of letters of administration with will annexed will be given to those entitled on intestacy.

Order 79, r 5(6) (e) of the Rules of the Superior Courts allows the Probate Officer a discretion in this matter. The rule provides as follows:

'Where the residue is not in terms wholly disposed of, the Probate Officer may, if he is of the opinion that the testator has nevertheless disposed of the whole or substantially the whole of the estate as

ascertained at the date of the application for a grant, allow a grant to be made to any legatee or devisee entitled to, or to share in the estate so disposed of without regard to the person entitled to share in any residue not disposed of by the will.'

This is dealt with in further detail at para **11.1.4.3**.

Practitioners should also note that a universal legatee and devisee applies in exactly the same manner as a residuary legatee and devisee.

9.3.1.3 Residuary devisee

A residuary devisee is the person to whom the residue of the *real* estate has been left. A gift of 'the rest of my land' also constitutes the beneficiary as residuary devisee. 'Real estate' is defined in s 4 of the Act as including:

> *'chattels real, and land in possession, remainder, or reversion, and every estate or interest in or over land (including real estate held by way of mortgage or security, but not including money to arise under a trust for sale of land, or money secured or charged on land.'*

As discussed at para **2.7.11**, s 92 of the Act provides that a general devise of land will include leasehold as well as freehold interests, subject to a contrary intention appearing in the will.

9.3.1.4 Residuary legatee

A residuary legatee is the person to whom the residue of the *personal* estate is left. This can include the person to whom insurance policies, furniture, jewellery, money, and all other personal belongings are left. It is important to remember that personal estate also comprises leasehold immovable property, and so will include any lands or buildings held under a lease.

9.3.1.5 Joint residuary legatees and devisees and tenants in common

Where *joint* legatees and devisees are named as such in the will, *all* must apply for the grant of letters of administration with will annexed. If only one of them applies for the grant, the others must consent. Ultimately, only the personal representative of the survivor is entitled to the grant.

If they are appointed residuary legatees and devisees as *tenants in common* in the will, *any one* of them may apply for the grant without reference to the other. On the death of them all, the personal representative of any of them may apply.

9.3.1.6 Lapse of residue (joint tenants or tenants in common)

If a legatee or devisee dies in the lifetime of the testator, the legacy or devise lapses and as a rule falls into the residue under s 91 of the Act, unless the will provides otherwise (under a 'gift over' clause or otherwise). Section 98, which is one of the exceptions to the rule, is dealt with in this context at para **9.8**.

Where the residue or a 'share' in the residue lapses, it goes on intestacy, unless otherwise provided for in the will.

However, where two (or more) legatees and/or devisees are joint tenants and one dies before the testator, the lapsed share goes to the survivor(s).

Where two (or more) legatees and/or devisees are tenants in common (e.g. 'the residue of my estate to X and Y in equal shares') and one dies before the testator, the lapsed share goes on intestacy. In this case, there has been a partial failure of the residuary disposition. The persons entitled on intestacy are equally entitled to extract a grant with the residuary legatees and/or devisees whose shares have not lapsed.

9.3.1.7 Administration Bond at Part C

As discussed at para **8.3.3**, there are three different forms of bonds, depending upon the date of death, and for the purpose of this book we will be focusing on the administration bond form for deaths on or since 1 January 1967 and in particular on the form of combined oath and bond introduced on 1 February 2021.

For applications on or after 1 March 2021, this bond form is incorporated into both the oath for administrator with the will and the oath for administrator intestate at Part C. However, in the case of a will-annexed grant the ultimate paragraph is different to the bond in intestacy cases in that the paragraph dealing with a will being found is excluded.

A precedent set of papers, including oath for administrator with will annexed incorporating administration bond, is included at para **9.6**.

Essentially, the bond is a guarantee. However, it is a penal guarantee as stated, in that it must cover *double the gross Irish assets* (including the current value of any immovable property to include dwellinghouses, land, etc). This is called the *penal sum*.

When dealing with earlier bonds, the applicant's legal entitlement to extract the grant must be set out in the bond. Generally, it is when dealing with the title and with the penal sum that most mistakes are made when completing the administration bond form. With a little bit of attention, these mistakes need not happen. Regarding title, one should check the title in the oath and insert the capacity, for example, 'the residuary devisee named in the will' or 'the attorney lawfully appointed by the executor' in the bond. It is not necessary to clear off persons having prior entitlement to the grant in the bond.

With regard to the penal sum in the bond, this figure will be double the gross estate at the date of the swearing of the bond. As noted when dealing with the oath for executor or administrator, it is the current value of all assets (ignoring liabilities) in the estate that makes up the gross estate. Prior to 1 March 2021, when the oath and bond were two separate forms, many practitioners went to the form CA24 to determine the penal sum in the bond. They simply multiplied by two the gross estate as appearing in the Inland Revenue affidavit, or for deaths on or after 5 December 2001, they looked at the gross figure of the estate as it is represented on the notice of acknowledgement (probate) form or on the certificate for the High Court and they multiplied this by two.

On many occasions this is correct, but in many instances it is incorrect. The form SA.2, the notice of acknowledgement (probate), and the Inland Revenue affidavit represent the values of the deceased's estate as at the date of death, whereas it is the current market values which are relevant when the question of computing the penal sum is concerned. Consequently, the oath, which represents the current-day value of all immovable property in the deceased's estate, is the more accurate source of information for arriving at the penal sum. For applications lodged on or before 1 March 2021 the oath of administrator calls for the values of both the personal property (which includes leasehold property) and the real property to be set out separately on the form. To arrive at the penal sum, these two values should be added together and multiplied by two, and this figure is then indicated in the bond. The current value is secured from the auctioneer's letter of market value in respect of the immovable property of the deceased.

The only figure which is taken from the form SA.2 or the Inland Revenue affidavit is that which represents movable property. Therefore, a sample illustrating the manner in which the penal sum is computed is as follows:

Add Personal estate (other than immovable property, i.e. leasehold property) (this may be established by examining the figures in the notice of acknowledgement (probate) or the Inland Revenue affidavit) to *current market value of all immovable property* of the deceased (see the valuations of property).

Multiply this figure by two and you will have arrived at your *penal sum*.

It is worthwhile to always bear in mind that the form SA.2, the notice of acknowledgement (probate) and the Inland Revenue affidavit form CA24 reflects the position of the deceased's estate as at the date of death, while the oath must reflect the current position (i.e. in respect of immovable property), and it is the current value which determines the correct penal sum. The current version of the bond as incorporated into the oath for administrator with will annexed/administrator simplifies matters in that the applicant recites

320 EXTRACTING A GRANT OF ADMINISTRATION WITH WILL ANNEXED

that they are 'liable to pay to the President of the High Court the sum of double the gross value of the estate as specified in Part A of the Oath' without having to set out the exact calculation or figures.

Remember that the administration bond must be sworn before the *same* commissioner/practising solicitor/court clerk who administers the oath. It cannot be sworn before the solicitor for, or agent of, the party who executes it (see O 79, r 29). It must also be executed under seal.

9.3.2 JUSTIFICATION OF SURETY

Since 1 September 2004 sureties to an administration bond are no longer necessary unless required by the High Court, the Probate Officer, or the relevant District Probate Registry. The proposed administrator is still required to give a bond, as this is necessary pursuant to s 34(1) of the Succession Act, 1965. A proposed administrator may still provide a surety to the administration bond if he so wishes.

This form used to be required when an individual was acting as surety of the applicant for the grant. The surety used to act as the guarantor to the proper behaviour of the administrator.

9.3.3 AUCTIONEER'S LETTER OF CURRENT MARKET VALUE

As noted in para **8.3.5** this document is never required when a grant of probate is being applied for or when the papers are lodged within two years of the date of death. If the papers are lodged more than two years after the date of death a description of the property is not required and a single-page letter from the auctioneer outlining the market value of the property is sufficient.

The letter must show the current market value of the land and will never be required where the application for the grant is made within twelve months of the date of death on the basis that the penal sum in the bond being double the value of the estate is sufficient safeguard for fluctuations in price.

9.4 Letters of Administration with Will Annexed Grants Compared with Other Grants of Representation

9.4.1 GRANT OF PROBATE

Such grants share a common feature with grants of probate in that there is a will. The procedures for obtaining a grant of probate are outlined in **Chapter 7**. To recap, such grants issue solely to persons who are appointed executors by a testator in his will, or to persons who are construed as executors according to the tenor of the will. This grant is regarded generally as being the easiest grant of representation to extract. The applicant's title or capacity in the oath is usually one of the following:

> 'The sole executor named in the will' or 'the surviving executor' or 'one of the executors so named.'

A bond is never required, nor is a letter of current market value.

9.4.2 GRANT OF LETTERS OF ADMINISTRATION INTESTATE

They share a common feature with grants of letters of administration intestate in that the persons entitled to apply for both types of such grants are set out in the Rules of the Superior Courts. As outlined in **Chapter 8**, in both cases, the grant follows the interest.

In the case of intestacy this interest is conclusively established at the date of death. Many applications are made to the Probate Office, where the applicant claims to be the sole next of kin simply because all the deceased's other relatives are now dead. If a person is not a next of kin of the deceased at the date of death, he can never become a next of kin. In the case of intestacy, the order of entitlement for extracting such grant is set out in O 79, r 5(1)–(5).

A bond is always required, and an auctioneer's letter of current market value is required where the papers are lodged more than twelve months after the date of death.

9.5 Conclusion

Having outlined the procedures for obtaining a grant of letters of administration with will annexed, practitioners will appreciate that it is a more complicated grant to extract than a grant of probate. It serves as a reminder of the importance of taking care in will drafting to ensure that appropriate executors are appointed, as noted at para **2.4**. Practitioners should ensure that more than one executor is named in the will and that such executors are able, willing, and prepared to extract the grant in due course, preventing the need for a will-annexed grant.

9.6 Precedent Application for a Grant of Letters of Administration with Will Annexed

In Re: Estate of William Ferry deceased obit 15 March 2021

- (i) Statement of facts.
- (ii) Copy will.
- (iii) Notice of acknowledgement (probate).
- (iv) Notice of application
- (v) Oath for administrator with the will incorporating administration bond.
- (vi) Auctioneers letter of current market value.
- (vii) Charitable bequest form.

9.6.1 STATEMENT OF FACTS

Estate of:	William Ferry deceased
Date of death:	15 March 2021
Address:	41 Holly Park, Donnybrook, Dublin
Place of death:	The Mater Hospital, Dublin.
Domicile:	Ireland
Occupation:	Stockbroker
Marital status:	Legally separated from Lucy Ferry since August 2003
Will:	Dated 8 July 2006

Your client, Toby Alexander Allen, is an old friend of the deceased and is no relation.

He is the residuary devisee and legatee named in the deceased's will. The deceased's will appointed his brother James Ferry sole executor. However, James died on 3 January 2019, prior to the testator, and obviously cannot prove the will.

Assets	€
Mews House at 41 Holly Park, Donnybrook; title is Folio DN 242F	1,240,000
Contents valued by auctioneer	30,000
AIB account, Donnybrook	50,000
Prize bonds	1,000
Liabilities	
Funeral expenses, Graves & Co	5,000

9.6.2 WILL OF WILLIAM FERRY

I, William Ferry, of 41 Holly Park, Donnybrook in the City of Dublin hereby revoke all former wills and testamentary dispositions at any time heretofore made by me and I DECLARE this to be my last will and testament.

1. My wife Lucy Ferry has waived her rights of inheritance under the Succession Act pursuant to a Deed of Separation made the 16th day of August 2003.

2. I appoint my brother James Ferry to be the Executor of this my will and I direct him to pay all my just debts and funeral expenses as soon as may be after my death.

3. I give and bequeath the sum of €20,000 (Twenty Thousand Euro) to The Everton Junior Club for the purpose of training young players in the club and I direct that a receipt by the Chairman of the club shall be a sufficient discharge for my executors.

4. All the rest residue and remainder of my estate both realty and personalty I give devise and bequeath to my good friend, Toby Alexander Allen of 15 Abbey View, Ennis, County Clare for his own use and benefit absolutely.

IN WITNESS whereof I have hereunto signed my name this the 8th day of July 2006

William Ferry

Signed published and declared by the said William Ferry as and for his last will and testament in the presence of us both being present at the same time who at his request in his presence and in the presence of each other have hereunto subscribed our names as witnesses the day and year first above written.

Fionn Casey	*James Thomson*
Solicitor	Secretary
41 Herbert Park	41 Herbert Park
Dublin 4	Dublin 4

EXTRACTING A GRANT OF ADMINISTRATION WITH WILL ANNEXED

9.6.3 NOTICE OF ACKNOWLEDGEMENT (PROBATE)

Summary

Status of the application: Pending

Document ID 000001599A

Version 1

*Required

Please fill out the declaration and submit the form

Information relating to the deceased person

Information relating to the deceased person

PPSN:	01033364J
Date of death (dd/mm/yyyy):	15 March 2021
Forename:	William
Surname:	Ferry
Address line 1:	41 Holly Park
Address line 2:	Donnybrook
County/city:	Dublin
Country:	Ireland
Date of birth (dd/mm/yyyy):	22/01/1954
Place of death (City/Town/County/State):	Dublin
Occupation:	Stockbroker
Domicile at death (Country/State):	Ireland
Domicile of origin (Country/State):	Ireland
Resident or ordinarily resident in Ireland at the date of death:	Yes
Individual status:	Legally separated
Surviving relatives:	None

Contact details

Forename:	Student
Surname:	Student
Address line 1:	Student
Address line 2:	Student
County/city:	Student
Country:	Ireland
Phone number:	1234567
Email address:	student@student.ie
Solicitor reference:	

Applicant details

Person #1	
Forename:	Toby Alexander
Surname:	Allen
Occupation:	Actor
Relationship to the deceased:	Other/stranger in blood
Occupation:	No relation
Phone number:	01234567
Email address:	tobyalexander@allen.com
Address line 1:	5 Abbey View
Address line 2:	Ennis
Eircode:	
County/city:	Clare
Country:	Ireland
Request details	
Grant request:	Administration with will annexed
Are there any codicils to the deceased's will?:	No

Details of beneficiaries

Details of beneficiaries

Is the surviving spouse or surviving civil partner the sole beneficiary?: No

Is every beneficiary expected to receive a benefit of less than €12,000?: No

Will the whole estate be donated to charity?: No

Person #1	
Forename:	Toby Alexander
Surname:	Allen
Date of birth:	01/01/1960
PPSN:	1033364J
Address line 1:	5 Abbey View
Address line 2:	Ennis
Eircode:	
County/city:	Clare
Country:	Ireland
Is the beneficiary resident or ordinarily resident in the state:	Yes

Is the beneficiary domiciled in the State?:	Yes
Relationship to the deceased:	Other/stranger in blood
Threshold for this relationship should be C	
Threshold A prior amount:	€0.00
Threshold B prior amount:	€0.00
Threshold C prior amount:	€0.00

Assets cover screen

Irish property (land/buildings)

Irish property (land/buildings): Yes

Show details

Details of assets

        Value

1   €1,240,000.00

Irish estate value €1,240,000.00

Bank/Building Society/An Post account

Bank/Building Society/An Post account: Yes

Show details

Details of assets

        Value

1   €50,000.00

Irish estate value €50,000.00

Credit Union account

Credit Union account: No

Cash

Cash: No

Household contents

Household contents: Yes

Show details

Details of assets

        Value

1   €30,000.00

Irish estate value €30,000.00

Cars/boats

Cars/boats: No

Insurance policy/mortgage protection policy/annuity

Insurance policy/mortgage protection policy/annuity: No

Superannuation/capital sum or ex-gratia payments

Superannuation/capital sum or ex-gratia payments: No

Agricultural/business assets

Agricultural/business assets: No

Stocks/shares/securities

Stocks/shares/securities: No

Accrued dividends

Accrued dividends: No

Debts owing to the deceased

Debts owing to the deceased: No

Unpaid purchase money of property contracted to be sold in the deceased's lifetime

Unpaid purchase money of property contracted to be sold in the deceased's lifetime: No

Other assets (any asset not covered under the above headings)

Other assets (any asset not covered under the above headings): Yes

Show details

Details of assets

	Value
1	€1,000.00

Irish estate value €1,000.00

Foreign assets

Foreign assets: No

Total asset value summary – Asset summary

Total gross estate	**Net foreign estate**
€1,321,000.00	€0.00

Liabilities details	
Liabilities owing to Revenue:	€0.00
Creditor:	€0.00
Funeral expenses:	€5,000.00
Utilities (total amount):	€0.00
Amounts due to financial institutions #1:	€0.00
Personal loans owing by the deceased #1:	€0.00
Mortgage owing #1:	€0.00

Fair deal/nursing home fee:	€0.00
Other #1:	€0.00
Total of all Irish based debts and liabilities:	€5,000.00

Mandatory questionnaire

Was the deceased in receipt of any DSP (Department of Social Protection) payments? No

Has the DSP any claim against the estate of the deceased? No

Was the deceased in receipt of payments under the Nursing Home Support Scheme? No

Has the HSE (Health Service Executive) any claim against the estate of the deceased? No

Was the deceased survived by a spouse or civil partner?: No

Was a charitable donation bequeathed under the will of the deceased? No

Was the deceased at the date of death the owner of a limited interest? (For example, an annuity, right of residence, interest in a house, lands, securities, and so on.) No

Did any person on or at any time after 5 December 1991, take under a disposition (for example, a transfer or settlement):

A) Gift? No

B) Any other benefit in possession – for example, the remainder interest on the death of a life tenant? No

Did the deceased at any time make a disposition

A) That was subject to a power of revocation (can be taken back)?: No

B) By surrendering a limited interest in part or in full? No

C) That allowed (on or after 5 December 1991) the use of a property free of charge or for reduced rent? No

Did the deceased create a discretionary trust during their lifetime? No

Was this under their will? No

Was the deceased entitled to any interest in expectancy in any property at the date of their death? No

Did any person become entitled on the death of the deceased to an interest in any property by virtue of the deceased's exercise of or failure to exercise a general power of appointment? No

Did any person become entitled on the death of the deceased to the proceeds of a Section 72/73 policy? No

Beneficiary benefit

Beneficiary benefit	
Total gross Irish estate:	€1,321,000.00
Total Irish debts:	€5,000.00

Total net Irish estate:	€1,316,000.00
Beneficiary 1	
Beneficiary name:	Toby Alexander Allen
PPSN:	1033364J
Relationship to the deceased:	Other/stranger in blood
Applicable threshold:	C
Prior aggregable benefit for this threshold:	€0.00
Assigned benefits:	€0.00
Other benefits:	€1,316,000.00
Total benefits:	€1,316,000.00

Attachments

File name	**File type**	**Attachment date**
Joint Assets Will.docx	Copy of will	16/11/2020

Notice of Acknowledgment (Probate)

Notice of Acknowledgment (Probate) to be given to the Probate Office.

This date of death has been verified by Revenue.

Summary of application

Version	1
Original grant type	Administration with will annexed
Deceased's domicile at death	Ireland
Name of deceased	William Ferry
Address of deceased	41 Holly Park, Donnybrook, , Dublin, , Ireland
Date of death	01/01/2020
Place of death (City/Town/County/State)	Dublin

Applicant #1

Applicant's name	Toby Alexander Allen
Applicant's address	5 Abbey View, Ennis, , Clare, , Ireland
Applicant's relationship to deceased	Other/stranger in blood
Gross foreign assets	€0.00
Net foreign assets	€0.00
Gross Irish estate	€1,321,000.00
Net Irish estate	€1,316,000.00

Contact details for lodging solicitor/applicant in person

Contact person's name	Student Student
Contact person's address	Student, Student, , Student, , Ireland
Contact person's phone number	1234567
Contact person's email	student@student.ie

Document ID

000001599A

It is hereby certified by the Office of the Revenue Commissioners that the requirements of Section 48A (2) of the Capital Acquisitions Tax Consolidation Act 2003 have been satisfied by this applicant for a Grant of Representation.

I hereby confirm that the Will lodged in the Probate Office is the original of the Will provided to the Office of the Revenue Commissioners under Section 9 Capital Acquisitions Tax (Electronic Probate) Regulations 2020 by this applicant for a Grant of Representation associated with the unique reference number in this case (not for intestacy cases).

Submission date: 16/11/2020

Name: _____
Date: _____

Signed and dated by the lodging solicitor or applicant in person

Details of assets

Bank account #1
Value	€50,000.00
Name of institution	Allied Irish Bank
IBAN	IE63AIBK93101200102493
Address	1 Bank Street, Bank Street, , Dublin, , Ireland
How was property held	Solely by deceased

Household contents
Household contents details	Furniture
Value	€30,000.00

Other asset #1
Value	€1,000.00
Other description	Prize Bonds

Irish property (land/buildings) #1
Property type	Residential
Address	41 Holly Park, Donnybrook, , Dublin, , Ireland
Property value	€1,240,000.00
Tenure	Freehold
Folio number	DN 242F
How was property held	Solely by deceased

Liabilities
Liabilities owing to Revenue	€0.00
Creditor	€0.00
Funeral expenses	€5,000.00
Utilities (total amount)	€0.00
Amounts due to financial institutions #1	€0.00
Personal loans owing by the deceased #1	€0.00
Mortgage owing #1	€0.00
Fair deal/nursing home fee	€0.00
Other #1	€0.00
Other description	
Total of all Irish based debts and liabilities	€5,000.00

9.6.4 NOTICE OF APPLICATION

The High Court

Probate

Notice of Application

Grant Type:	Administration with Will Annexed		
Deceased			
Domicile @death	Ireland		
Name(s)	William Ferry		
Address: (incl. former addresses)	41 Holly Park, Donnybrook, Dublin 46		
Occupation:	Stockbroker	PPS Number:	4424126H

EXTRACTING A GRANT OF ADMINISTRATION WITH WILL ANNEXED

Date of Death:	15 March 2021		
Place of Death	The Mater Hospital Dublin 7		
Applicant 1			
Name:	Toby Alexander Allen		
Address:	15 Abbey View Ennis, County Clare		
Occupation:	Actor	Relationship to Deceased	Stranger in Blood
Applicant 2			
Name:			
Address:			
Occupation:		Relationship to Deceased	
Applicant 3			
Name:			
Address:			
Occupation:		Relationship to Deceased	
Gross Assets (as per CA24):	€1,321,000	**Net Assets** (as per SA2):	€1,316,000
No. of Codicils	None		
Lodging Solicitor (Name and Address)	John Edwards, Messrs EJD&R Solicitors, 2 Tigris Place, Dublin 2		

For use of The Probate Office only

Fees:		Case Officer	
		HC Cert	

9.6.5 OATH OF ADMINISTRATOR WITH THE WILL ANNEXED INCORPORATING ADMINISTRATION BOND

OATH OF ADMINISTRATOR WITH THE WILL, INCORPORATING ADMINISTRATION BOND

THE HIGH COURT

PROBATE

†The Probate Office, Phoenix House, Smithfield, Dublin 7

PART A

Name of Deceased:	William Ferry
Address of Deceased:	41 Holly Park, Donnybrook in the County of City of Dublin 4
Date of Death:	15th day of March 20 21

Place of Death: Mater Hospital in the County of City of Dublin
Name of Applicant: Toby Alexander Allen
Address of Applicant: 15 Abbey View, Ennis in the County of Clare
Gross value of Estate: €1,321,000

PART B

I, the above named applicant aged 18 years and upwards, make oath and say, that I believe the paper writing hereunto annexed, and marked by me, to contain the true and original last will [or last will with .... codicils] of the above named deceased late of the above named address of deceased;

that same was made by the said deceased after attaining the age of 18 years, and that the said deceased did not intermarry or enter into a civil partnership with any person after the making of same;

and *[insert title]

He did therein name as sole Executor, his brother James Ferry who predeceased the deceased

And that I am a stranger in blood of said testator and the Residuary Legatee and Devisee named in the said Will

that I will well and faithfully administer the estate of the said deceased, by paying the deceased's just debts and the legacies bequeathed by the deceased's said will [or will and codicils] and distributing the residue of the deceased's estate according to law; and that I will exhibit a true and perfect inventory of the said estate, and render a true account thereof whenever required by law so to do; and that the deceased died at the above named place of death on the date of death cited above

[where application is made in District Probate Registry add] and that the deceased had at the time of death a fixed place of abode at the above named address within the district of ....]

and that the whole of the estate, without any deductions for debts, which devolves on and vests in the deceased's legal personal representative amounts in value to the figure cited above as the gross value of the estate and no more

to the best of my knowledge, information and belief.

Sworn at 30 Molesworth Street in the County of City of Dublin

this 20th day of April 2021 by the said Toby Alexander Allen

before me a Commissioner for taking Affidavits and I know the Deponent (or

who certifies to his knowledge of the Deponent)

or the identity of the Deponent has been established by reference to a relevant document containing a photograph

Document Type..............................

Issue No:..

..... *Joan Groarke*............

Commissioner for Oaths/Practising Solicitor

Toby alexander Allen

I Certify that I know the Deponent

....

This Affidavit is filed by

EJD & R

of 2 Tigris Terrace, Dublin 2 Solicitors for Toby Alexander Allen this 21st day of April 2021

EXTRACTING A GRANT OF ADMINISTRATION WITH WILL ANNEXED

PART C

I, the above named applicant am liable in full to pay to the President of the High Court the sum of double the gross value of the estate as specified in PART A above, for which payment I bind myself and my executors and administrators

Sealed with my seal this day of 2021

The condition of this obligation is that if I, the intended *[administrator] *[administratrix] of the estate of the said deceased do fulfil the obligations referred to in PART B above and furthermore do pay all taxes and duties payable in respect of the estate of the deceased for which the personal representative is accountable and all income tax and surtax payable out of the estate then this obligation shall be void and no effect, but shall otherwise remain in full force and effect.

Signed, Sealed and Delivered by the said }

Toby Alexander Allen

in the presence of ....
Joan Groarke

9.6.6 FORM TO BE COMPLETED ONLINE FOR THE CHARITIES REGULATORY AUTHORITY

CHARITABLE BEQUEST FORM.

Section 52 and 58 of the Charities Act, 1961, as amended by Section 16 of the Charities Act, 1973 and Section 82 of the Charities Act, 2009

NOTE: This form must be completed in electronic format and submitted in electronic form to the Charity Regulator via the Charity Regulator's 'My Account' system and in addition must be downloaded and printed for signing by the solicitor and lodged in the Probate Office with application for Grant where a Testator or Testatrix has made charitable gifts in his/her Will.

NAME OF DECEASED: William Ferry

ADDRESS OF DECEASED: 41 Holly Park, Donnybrook, Dublin 4

DATE OF DEATH: 15 March 2021

DATE OF WILL: 8 July 2006

DATE OF CODICIL(S) IF ANY: None such

NAME AND ADDRESS (ES) OF LEGAL PERSONAL REPRESENTATIVES: Toby Alexander Allen

CHARITABLE BEQUEST(S)

[Set out exact wording of bequest(s). Type or print in block capitals.

Please annex extra page(s) if required.]

'I GIVE AND BEQUEATH THE SUM OF €20,000 (Twenty Thousand Euro) to The Everton Junior Club for the purposes of training young players in the club and I direct that a receipt by the Chairman of the club shall be a sufficient discharge for my Executors.'

Signed: *E J D & R*   Solicitor

   2 Tigris Terrace, Dublin 2   Address

For Official use only
Date of grant:

9.7 Simultaneous Deaths (*Commorientes*)—Section 5 of the Succession Act

Section 71 of the Succession Act provides that the next of kin of any intestate are determined at the date of death of the intestate. As discussed at para **2.9.1**, s 91 of the Succession Act provides that a beneficiary under a will must survive the testator to receive a devise or bequest in his will.

When acting in the administration of both testate and intestate estates, the executors/administrators must be able to ascertain whether a potential beneficiary survived the deceased or not. Issues that would potentially arise are spouse's legal right share/share on intestacy, lapse under s 91, survivorship of joint tenancies, shares on intestacy, and applying the terms of a will.

In the normal course of events, dates of death can easily be verified by perusal of the death certificates of the persons concerned. However, there are situations where it may not be possible to ascertain the order of deaths of persons, such as where they die in common disasters such as car/plane/train crashes.

Section 5 of the Succession Act deals with these situations and applies equally to persons who die testate and those who die intestate.

Section 5 of the Succession Act (as amended by s 68 of the Civil Law (Miscellaneous Provisions) Act, 2008) states:

> *(1) Where after the commencement of this Act* [1 January 1967], *two or more persons have died in circumstances rendering it uncertain which of them survived the other or others, then, for the purposes of the distribution of the estate of any of them, they shall be presumed to have died simultaneously.*
>
> *(2) Where immediately prior to the death of two or more persons they held any property as joint tenants and they died, or under subsection (1) were deemed to have died, simultaneously, they shall be deemed to have held the property immediately prior to their deaths as tenants in common in equal shares.*
>
> *(3) Property deemed under subsection (2) to have been held by persons as tenants in common shall form part of their respective estates.*

The section applies in all cases where there is uncertainty as to which person died first, whether testate or intestate. While the most common application of the section is that of a common disaster, for example, car/plane/train crash, this is not the only circumstance in which the section can apply. For example, if a person goes missing while on holiday and in the meantime the other person dies, it is 'uncertain which of them survived the other'.

Section 5 in effect abolishes succession rights among all persons who are deemed to have died simultaneously. The effect is that each is presumed not to have survived the other or others. Where title to the grant is affected by the application of s 5, application has to be made to the Probate Judge. The procedure is set out at para **11.3**, in particular at para **11.3.9**.

Where two persons die simultaneously and own property as joint tenants, prior to the coming into force of the Civil Law (Miscellaneous Provisions) Act, 2008 on 14 July 2008 the common law rule applied which provided that those entitled to a share or interest in the estates would take the share or interest as joint tenants and not as tenants in common. See *Wylie, Irish Land Law*, 3rd edn (1997), para 7.06.

This is now amended as outlined earlier. Where all the joint tenants die simultaneously, the joint tenancy is severed, and each share forms part of the estate of the deceased 'joint' tenant for distribution. One effect of this is that it removes the presumption of resulting trust where joint tenants die simultaneously.

9.7.1 EXAMPLE 1

A husband and wife, Andrew and Brenda, die in a plane crash, without issue, having made wills leaving their respective estates to each other without a 'gift over' clause as referred to at para **2.9.2.2**. In both cases, their respective parents are still alive.

On successful application to the Probate Judge, s 5 deems Andrew and Brenda to have died simultaneously where they died in circumstances rendering it uncertain which of them survived the other. Applying s 5, neither is deemed to have survived the other. Brenda is deemed not to have survived Andrew (when administering Andrew's estate). Andrew is deemed not to have survived Brenda (when administering Brenda's estate).

Therefore, Andrew's universal legatee and devisee and spouse Brenda did not survive Andrew. We have already established that Andrew, who died without issue, so following the rules of intestacy as set out in para 8.4 Andrew's two parents inherit his whole estate. Similarly, Brenda's universal legatee and devisee and spouse Andrew did not survive Brenda, who also died without issue, so Brenda's two parents will inherit her whole estate.

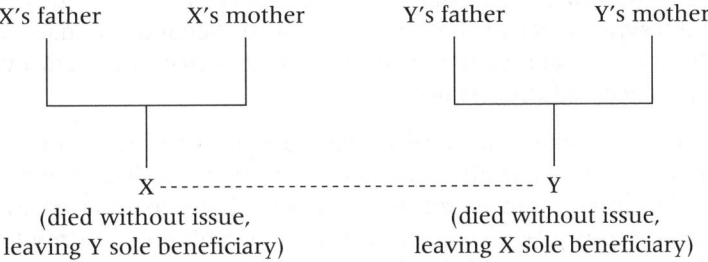

- X's mother and father share X's estate equally.
- Y's mother and father share Y's estate equally.

9.7.2 EXAMPLE 2

Problem

Father Alan, mother Bridget, son Colin (aged fourteen), and daughter Deirdre (aged sixteen) all died together in a car crash. However, son Eamonn survived the crash but died one hour later in hospital. Son Frank survived, as he was not in the car at the time. Alan, Bridget, Colin, and Deirdre all died intestate. Eamonn made a will leaving all his estate to his girlfriend, Sabrina.

Solution

(i) *Distribution of estates of Alan and Bridget*

Both husband and wife will be deemed not to have survived the other, so their surviving issue will inherit their estates. Eamonn and Frank (as the only surviving family members) will share their estates equally. As Eamonn died *subsequently* his estate will receive his inheritances, which will pass under his will to Sabrina.

(ii) *Distribution of estates of Colin and Deirdre*

Neither child will inherit their parents' estates, as they will be deemed not to have survived them. Eamonn and Frank will inherit any estate they may have had. As Eamonn died *subsequently* his inheritances will similarly pass into his estate and under his will to Sabrina.

(iii) *Distribution of estate of Eamonn*

As Eamonn survived his parents and his brother and sister, he will, as stated earlier, inherit a half-share of their estates with Frank. On his subsequent death, any estate he may have had himself, together with his inheritances, will pass under his will to his girlfriend Sabrina.

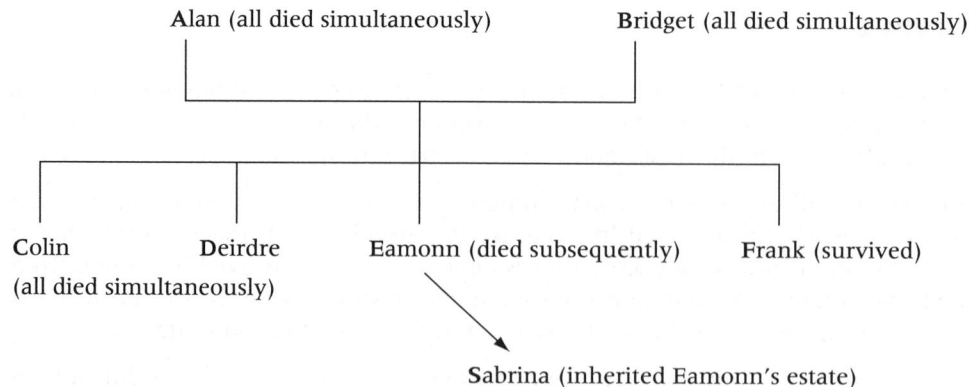

9.8 Exception to Doctrine of Lapse—Section 98 of the Succession Act

The general rule is that for a beneficiary to receive his devise or bequest under a will, he must survive the testator (s 91 of the Succession Act). Section 98 enacts an exception to this general rule in that it allows the estate of a beneficiary to benefit even though that beneficiary has predeceased the testator.

Section 98 provides that where a person, being a child or other issue of the testator to whom any property is given (whether by a devise or bequest or by the exercise by will of any power of appointment, and whether as a gift to that person as an individual or as a member of a class), for any estate or interest not determinable at or before the death of that person, dies in the lifetime of the testator leaving issue, and any such issue of that person is living at the time of the death of the testator, the gift shall not lapse, but shall take effect as if the death of that person had happened immediately after the death of the testator, unless a contrary intention appears from the will.

9.8.1 THREE CONDITIONS MUST BE SATISFIED FOR SECTION 98 TO APPLY

1. The testator must make a gift in his will to issue (i.e. he must die testate).
2. The issue to whom the gift was given must predecease the testator.
3. The issue to whom the gift was given must leave issue alive at the date of death of the testator.

If all three conditions are satisfied, the gift does not lapse, but passes to the estate of the beneficiary. In effect, s 98 presumes the beneficiary to have survived and then died immediately.

9.8.2 ISSUE MAY NOT NECESSARILY BENEFIT UNDER SECTION 98

It may very well arise that the issue who prevent the gift from lapsing do not benefit directly or perhaps at all. If the predeceased beneficiary (for example) made a will leaving his entire estate to his spouse, then the s 98 inheritance would pass as part of his estate under his will to his spouse, and the issue who 'kept the bequest alive' inherit nothing.

9.8.3 DISTINCTION BETWEEN SECTION 98 AND SECTION 67 (*PER STIRPES*)

However, if the predeceased beneficiary died *intestate* then, of course, his issue would inherit the s 98 inheritance as part of the intestate estate of the predeceased beneficiary and would inherit under the operation of Section 67 (as amended) and possibly under the *per stirpes* rule. See para **8.5** for details of the *per stirpes* rule.

A common error is to confuse the *per stirpes* rule with s 98. Section 98 arises only where the deceased died testate. The *per stirpes* rule applies only to intestacy (and only in limited situations then).

9.8.4 DOES NOT APPLY TO BENEFITS CEASING ON THE DEATH OF THE PREDECEASED BENEFICIARY

Section 98 applies only to lineal descendants where the benefit survives the predeceased beneficiary. Where a benefit, for example, a right to reside or a life tenancy would cease on the death of a beneficiary, that benefit would lapse in any event. Similarly, if a child is left a joint tenancy and predeceases the testator, the surviving joint tenants take the benefit.

9.8.5 EXAMPLE OF OPERATION OF SECTION 98

Problem

Ruth gave the residue of her estate to her son, Niall, who predeceased her leaving two children, Matthew and Sean, alive at the date of death of Ruth. Ruth's executor is dead. Niall made his wife, Liadhan, sole executrix and universal legatee and devisee of his will. What happens to the gift of the residue and who will now extract the grant of administration with will annexed in Ruth's estate?

The first question to ask is: are the three conditions met that are necessary for s 98 to apply?

1. Did the testator make a bequest in a will to issue?

2. Did the issue to whom the bequest was made predecease the testator?

3. Did the issue to whom the bequest was given leave issue alive at the date of death of the testator?

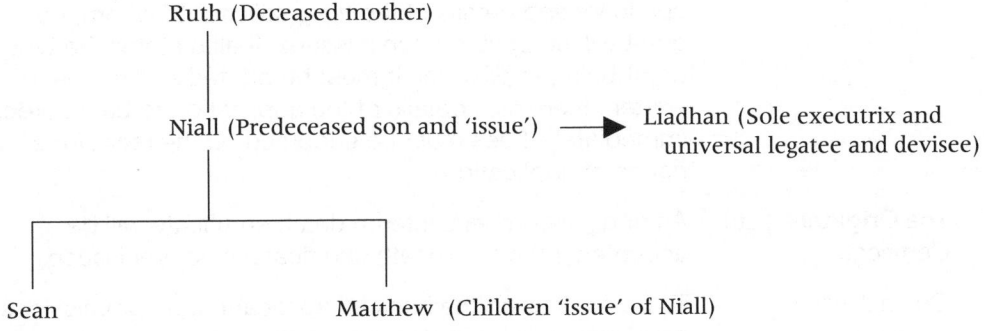

Solution

The conditions for s 98 to apply are satisfied. Ruth made a bequest in her will to Niall, who is issue.

Niall predeceased Ruth, leaving issue (Matthew and Sean) alive on Ruth's death. Niall is deemed to die immediately after Ruth.

Distribution

Under Niall's will, all his property goes to Liadhan. The gift of the residue will go to Liadhan as universal legatee and devisee of his will. Liadhan, as sole executrix of Niall's estate, will extract the grant of administration with will annexed in Ruth's estate.

Title

'*did therein name as Executor AB who* [either] *predeceased her* [or] *survived the deceased and has since died without proving said will and did therein name as residuary legatee and devisee her son Niall who predeceased her leaving issue alive at the date of death of the testatrix and I am the Legal Personal Representative of Niall under Grant of Probate which issued to me from the Probate Office on the day of 20'*

If Niall had died **intestate** the distribution and title would be as follows:

Distribution

Niall died intestate leaving a spouse and two children surviving him. His estate will go via intestacy two-thirds to his spouse Liadhan and the remaining one-third equally between his children Matthew and Sean. The gift of the residue will be divided similarly. Liadhan, as the person entitled to extract the grant of intestacy in Niall's estate, will extract the grant of administration with will annexed in Ruth's estate.

Title

'*did therein name as Executor AB who* [either] *predeceased her* [or] *survived the deceased and has since died without proving said will and did therein name as residuary legatee and devisee her son Niall who predeceased her leaving issue alive at the date of death of the testatrix and I am the Legal Personal Representative of Niall under Grant of Administration Intestate which issued to me from the Probate Office on the day of 20'*

9.9 Seat Office Checklist—Grant of Administration with Will Annexed

	Form S1 (postal application form)	Completed form S1 must be lodged with all applications submitted by post or DX. If posted a stamped addressed envelope with sufficient value to cover posting back all documents must be included
(1)	Notice of application	Contains details of the deceased's name, address and date and place of death together with name and address of applicant and details of the filing solicitor to whom the grant will be posted once it issues. It also states the type of grant being applied for. It must be printed and not handwritten. It enables details of the application to be recorded immediately. Fees must be endorsed on the rear of the notice of application
	The **Original** Death Certificate	An original coroner's interim death certificate will be accepted if the final death certificate is not yet issued
	Original will and codicil (if applicable)	To be marked on the back by applicant and commissioner/ practising solicitor before whom the oath was sworn. Where will already proved in another jurisdiction, copy of the will/codicil sealed and certified by the court where it was proved to be marked. A sealed and certified copy of the grant which issued in that jurisdiction should also be lodged. (O 79, r 37)
(4)	Engrossment of will/codicil	Photocopy of will/codicil or typed engrossment certified by solicitor to be a true copy

EXTRACTING A GRANT OF ADMINISTRATION WITH WILL ANNEXED 339

(5) Oath for administrator with the will incorporating administration bond

(Form No 4, Appendix Q of Rules of the Superior Courts as inserted by SI 590/2020)

Original only, no copies required

Ensure names and addresses of all parties are consistent across all documents

Confirm testator did not enter into civil partnership after making will

Ensure that the deceased and the applicant(s) in the oath are the same persons referred to in the will and the death certificate.

All differences in names and addresses must be accounted for in the oath

Ensure correct title

State relationship of applicant to deceased

Date and place of death must be as per the death certificate

Penal sum must be double the gross current value of the estate

Bond must be signed sealed and delivered—it is not sworn

A seal must be affixed to the bond

Bond must be executed before the same commissioner/practising solicitor before whom oath was sworn

Total gross Irish estate—if date of death within two years of papers being lodged use value as per notice of acknowledgement (probate) form

If date of death is more than two years of papers being lodged, use current market value for property. Statement of current market value will also be required

Jurat must comply with SI No 95/2009 and cannot be executed before lodging solicitor

Complete the filing clause

All exhibits must be signed by deponent and the person who administered the oath. The date of the exhibit must be cited in the oath. NB the actual exhibit must be signed. Exhibit sheets are not accepted

(6) Renunciation of executor (if applicable) (Form No 18, Appendix Q of Rules)

To be exhibited in oath and marked by applicant and commissioner/practising solicitor before whom the oath is sworn

(7) Power of attorney (if applicable)

To be exhibited in oath and marked by applicant and commissioner/practising solicitor before whom the oath is sworn

(8) Letter of current market value

From auctioneer if the papers are lodged more than twenty-four months after the date of death. If the papers are lodged within twenty-four months of the date of death no proof of current market value will be needed

(9)	Notice of Acknow-ledgement (Probate) or CA24 (Inland Revenue affidavit) depending on the date of death.	For deaths on or after 5 December 2001 and applications since 14 September 2020, the CA24 is replaced by the notice of acknowledgement (probate) which form auto generates from the Revenue once the form SA.2 is successfully submitted online. It is required in order to comply with s 48A CATCA, 2003. Date of death values should be used in the notice of acknowledgment/CA 24 For deaths prior to 5 December 2001: The CA24 must be lodged in duplicate with the Revenue Commissioners first and a Certificate for the High Court obtained from them before lodging same in the Probate Office. A form CA6 (Schedule of lands) is required for deaths before 5 December 2001 if there is immoveable property in the estate. The date of death value and tenure must be inserted
(10)	Justification of surety (if required) (Form No 16, Appendix Q of Rules)	[No longer required since 1 September 2004 unless required by the High Court/Probate Office/District Probate Registry] Where an individual acts as surety to bond: (i) person who swears affidavit of market value cannot act as surety (ii) No practising solicitor or clerk or apprentice solicitor can act as surety without leave of the court or Probate Officer (O 79, r 73)
(11)	Affidavit of attesting witness (if required) (Form No 2, Appendix Q)	Always required where: (i) no or defective attestation clause (O 79, r 6) (ii) blind or illiterate testator—affidavit to confirm will be read over to testator (O 79, r 63) (iii) will written on loose sheets of paper (affidavit to confirm all sheets present at time of execution) (iv) where will written on front side only of paper and attestation clause does not confirm number of pages (v) Where testator's signature is weak or feeble— affidavit should confirm testator was of sound mind, memory, etc and that the will was read over to the testator etc (all affidavits of attesting witness should cover due execution).
(13)	Affidavit of plight and condition (if required)	Required where pinholes/paper-clip marks, torn edges, etc.
(14)	Affidavit of testamentary capacity	Required where deceased was ward of court died in a mental institution or suffered from a mental illness. To be sworn by doctor attending testator at time of execution of will. If the deceased was not attending a doctor at the time or the doctor is deceased the affidavit can be sworn by the solicitor who prepared the will. If the solicitor makes such an affidavit, reference should be made to the whereabouts etc of doctor
(15)	Charitable bequest form	Where charitable bequests in will
(16)	Fees	(See Seat Office fees table of Probate Office at end of **Chapter 11**.) These must be endorsed on the rear of the Notice of Application. A fee card is no longer acceptable

CHAPTER 10

SECOND AND SUBSEQUENT GRANTS (*DE BONIS NON* GRANTS)

10.1 Background and Introduction to *De Bonis Non* Grants

This chapter details the procedures and proofs necessary to obtain second and subsequent grants. On occasion, it may be necessary to extract a second grant of representation in an estate. This usually (but not always) arises where the first legal personal representative has died without completing the administration of the estate.

Where a personal representative has extracted a *primary grant* of representation and dies prior to fully completing the administration, a further grant will be required to complete the administration of the deceased's estate.

Where there is another executor available who had reserved his rights when the original grant was extracted, this executor can take out a grant of unadministered probate as outlined at para **10.10.1**. In all other cases, the second grants are called *de bonis non* grants or 'DBN grants' for short.

These DBN grants appear to cause problems for solicitors when in fact they should not do so. They are easier to extract than the primary grant because, when applying for the *de bonis non*, the assets are clearly established and the version of the Inland Revenue affidavit used (the form A3) is a simple, easy-to-complete document requiring details of only the assets remaining unadministered. For deaths on or after 5 December 2001 the form A3(C) is now incorporated in the Statement of Affairs (Probate) Form SA.2 and is submitted electronically to the Revenue on ROS. A Notice of Acknowledgement (Probate) Form with a unique number will auto-generate for the applicant once the form SA.2 is successfully completed and submitted electronically. This must be printed and signed and lodged with the other probate papers in the Probate Office/District Registry.

In practice the only asset remaining unadministered tends to be a house or land remaining in the name of the registered owner, the person to whose estate the first (primary) grant was extracted.

The documents which are required to be lodged in the Probate Office are almost exactly the same as for a primary grant, and it is advisable to use the Seat Office checklists contained in **Chapters 8** and **9** as a guideline and the Probate page of the Courts Service website at http://www.courts.ie. Obviously, certain documents, which are outlined at **10.4**, are never required because these will have been sent to the Probate Office when the primary grant was applied for. When applying for a *de bonis non* grant, the procedure for ascertaining 'title' is based on exactly the same principles as when applying for the primary grant.

If practitioners have any problem in relation to the completion of *de bonis non* probate papers, or indeed any probate papers, particularly concerns as to the correct order of entitlement to the particular grant, or if unsure of the wording of the title in the oath, they should either call down to the Seat Office of the Probate Office or speak to the personnel there, and they will find them of huge assistance in this sometimes complex area of law. The Probate Office will not, however, enter into correspondence on matters of title as it is ultimately the responsibility of the solicitor instructed in the administration of the estate to determine this.

10.1.1 DISTINCTION BETWEEN *DE BONIS NON* GRANTS AND REVOCATION OF GRANT

In the situation where a practitioner has lodged an application for a grant of representation and the applicant dies between the time the application is made and the grant issues, it is imperative to let the Probate Office know of this development without delay. The application by the proposed applicant may then be withdrawn and the next person with legal entitlement to extract the grant may proceed with their application. If the grant issues prior to this information being furnished to the Probate Office, the correct procedure is to apply for a revocation of that grant. This application is made on foot of a grounding affidavit setting out the facts. When the grant is revoked, the person who is next entitled to extract the grant may then proceed with their application. Revocation of grants is dealt with at para **11.2**.

A DBN grant becomes relevant when the person to whom a primary grant issued in an estate has now died without fully completing the administration of the said estate. In this instance the correct procedure is to apply for a DBN grant. Simply put, where a personal representative (X) dies during the course of the administration of the estate of a deceased (Y) a second grant to (Y) will be required to complete the administration of Y's estate This second grant is known as a *de bonis non* grant.

10.1.2 *DE BONIS NON* GRANTS AND DEEDS OF ASSENT

Perhaps *de bonis non* grants are greeted with dismay by the profession because they typically arise in the context of conveyancing transactions, for example the sale of or perfecting title to land or houses. They often arise when dealing with applications for first registration and s 49 applications to the Land Registry. Similarly, the need to extract the grant is often discovered by a solicitor who receives instructions to sell property on behalf of a client and, following a perusal of the title documents or having conducted a search in the appropriate registry of the Property Registration Authority, discovers that the client (the proposed vendor) is not the registered owner of the property. Instead, an ancestor or other relation, usually a parent, grandparent, or indeed a great-uncle, is still named as registered owner of the property.

Deeds of assent are dealt with in more detail at paras **10.11** and **15.2**.

10.1.3 PROBATE FEES

The fee for applying for a *de bonis non* grant is currently €150.00, regardless of the amount or value of the estate. The current fees are outlined in SI No. 80/ 2021). As fees change from time to time it is prudent to check possible changes on the probate page of the Courts Service website.

10.2 How to Determine What Type of *De Bonis Non* Grant to Apply For

The type of DBN grant to be extracted depends on whether the deceased died testate or intestate. There are two possible types of DBN grants:

1. Grant of letters of administration with will annexed *de bonis non*:

    Where the person who took out the first grant has died and all executors have been cleared off and where the estate has not been fully administered, a grant of administration with will annexed *de bonis non* is the appropriate type of second (or subsequent) grant in the circumstances.

If the deceased died *testate*, the primary (or original) grant extracted by the personal representative to his estate was either a grant of probate or a grant of letters of administration with will annexed.

If a primary grant is issued to a sole executor or a residuary legatee and devisee and either dies before the estate is administered, the appropriate DBN (or second) grant in this case will be *a grant of letters of administration with will annexed DBN*. There is no such thing as a grant of probate DBN.

2. Grant of letters of administration intestate *de bonis non*:

If the deceased died *intestate*, the primary grant extracted by the personal representative was a grant of letters of administration intestate. If the administrator/rix subsequently dies without fully administering the estate, the parties entitled on intestacy can apply for a second grant. The appropriate second grant in this case will be a *grant of letters of administration intestate DBN*.

Grant of Unadministered Probate

If one executor extracts a grant of probate, reserving the rights of another executor, the executor whose rights are reserved can apply for a second grant where the first proving executor has died. This is a grant of unadministered probate. When applying for a grant of unadministered probate the oath for executor form is used and adapted as appropriate. Details of the first grant and how it was terminated are recited as for example by the death of the first executor, including reservations of the current applicant's rights as executor. The market value of the gross estate must be included. A letter of current market value from an auctioneer is never required for an unadministered probate, nor is a bond ever required.

10.2.1 WHO IS ENTITLED TO APPLY FOR THE *DE BONIS NON* GRANT?

In all cases the grant follows the interest, and the interest is determined at the date of death. The rules of distribution on intestacy are set out in Part VI (ss 67–71) of the Succession Act and the order of entitlement to the grant is set out in O 79, r 5(1) of the Rules of the Superior Courts, 1986. This has been dealt with at para **9.2**.

If extracting a grant of letters of administration with will annexed DBN (i.e. there is a will), and the acting executor has died, and all other executors have either died or renounced, the grant will be given to the person next entitled in order of priority under O 79, r 5(6) of the Rules of the Superior Courts at the date of death. Such a person will be entitled to apply for a grant of letters of administration with will annexed *de bonis non*, thus allowing that person as the new administrator to continue with the administration of the estate.

10.2.2 WHERE TO APPLY FOR A *DE BONIS NON* GRANT

Section 37 of the Succession Act provides that second and subsequent grants shall be made in the Probate Office or District Probate Registry, as the case may be, from which the primary grant issued.

However if the primary grant was extracted *post*-1 January 1967 in a District Probate Registry, then application must be made to that District Registry for the DBN grant.

Where the primary grant was extracted *prior to* 1 January 1967 in a District Registry, then application must be made to the Probate Office itself for the DBN grant.

Applications to either the Probate Office or to the relevant District Registry may be made personally, through a town agent or by post.

10.3 Documents/Proofs Required to Extract a *De Bonis Non* Grant in Either Case

The forms/documents required when applying for a DBN grant are much the same as those used when applying for the primary grant of representation, together with the additional documents/forms listed in this chapter. *De bonis non* grants deal only with the unadministered estate. When preparing the papers necessary to lead to a DBN grant, one must remember that there are no special DBN forms as such.

The forms that are used when extracting the primary grant, be they the oath or the bond or whatever, must be adapted by inserting the words '*De Bonis Non*' after the heading in the form in each case. For example, oath for administrator with will annexed *de bonis non* when applying for a grant of administration with will annexed *de bonis non* or oath for administrator intestate *de bonis non* when applying *de bonis non* for a grant of administration intestate *de bonis non*. This is to identify for the Probate Registrar that a DBN, rather than a primary grant, is being extracted. It is no longer necessary to put the word 'unadministered' before the word 'estate' in either the oath or bond forms.

Of great assistance to practitioners are the printed probate forms. They contain excellent marginal notes.

10.3.1 ORIGINAL OR PRIMARY GRANT

The primary grant, whatever it was, must be surrendered to the Probate Office in all cases. Frequently the primary grant is lost or mislaid, particularly if the deceased died a number of years ago. If this is the case you must bespeak a certified copy of the primary grant (together with a certified copy of the will where relevant). There is a straightforward bespeak form to be completed in the General Office of the Probate Office. It is wise to check the probate page of the Courts Service website to establish the correct fee which must be paid for same. Normally, if the grant is less than twenty years old, a copy will be available within two to three days. For grants that issued before 1991 where the original grant is lost or mislaid, the Probate Office records only go back as far as 1991 and a certified copy will have to be obtained from the National Archives in Bishop Street Dublin 8 and this may take longer.

If the original primary grant is not available when lodging the papers to lead to the DBN grant, the Probate Office will request a letter from you explaining the circumstances regarding its loss and will seek your undertaking to surrender it to the Probate Office if it is ever found or becomes available.

10.3.2 INLAND REVENUE FORM A3(E) OR A3(C) FOR DEATHS ON OR BEFORE 5 DECEMBER 2001

For *de bonis non* applications where the date of death of the deceased person is pre-5 December 2001, the Revenue form to be used is either the form A3(C) or A3(E). These Revenue forms are a one-leaf sheet and are completed by the proposed administrator in all pre-2001 DBN cases. All of these forms can be completed online at the Revenue website (http://www.revenue.ie/en/tax/cat/forms/index.html) and printed off for execution. The form A3(E) and form A3(C) are used for deaths prior to 5 December 2001 and are sent to the Revenue Commissioners in duplicate with a form D1 or CA6 where there is immoveable property.

The purpose of the form A3 is to provide the Revenue with sufficient information to determine the possible tax liability (if any) and there are three versions of the form A3, depending on the date of death of the deceased:

1. The form A3(E) is used when the deceased died prior to 1 April 1975, and is headed Estate Duty. Estate Duty was replaced by inheritance tax on that date. It is completed with the form D1 (Schedule of land and buildings), as outlined later.

2. The form A3(C) to be used when the deceased died on or after 1 April 1975 and before 5 December 2001 and is headed Capital Acquisitions Tax. This version is also completed with a form CA6 (Schedule of land and buildings).

3. The current version of the form A3(C) is used for deaths on or after 5 December 2001 and is included in the Statement of Affairs (Probate) Form SA.2. The current market value of the property as at the date of swearing and not at the date of death is used in all versions of the form A3.

10.3.2.1 Current version of form A3(C) now part of the Statement of Affairs (Probate) Form SA.2

When applying for a DBN Grant on or after 14 September 2020 where the deceased person died on or after 5 December 2001 the form A3(C) is now incorporated into the form SA.2. The application is made through the online form SA.2 whereby a simplified version of the form A3(C) will be presented to the user on selecting that a secondary or subsequent grant (a DBN) is required. Once the application form SA.2 is successfully submitted electronically on ROS, a notice of acknowledgment (probate) will be automatically generated by the Revenue. The applicant for the DBN grant must present this notice to the Probate Office/District Registry along with the other papers to request a second or subsequent grant. When completing the form SA.2 the applicant completes the applicants details section which asks them to indicate the type of grant required. One of these options is a *de bonis non* Grant. Where a DBN or secondary grant is required the applicant must indicate the type of grant required from the available options:

1. Double probate of the will.
2. Administration with will annexed of the unadministered estate.
3. Administration intestate of the unadministered estate.

The original/primary grant of representation must be attached and submitted electronically with the application.

As with the forms A3(E) and A3(C) dealt with above the applicant must reply to the following queries:

1. Is the personal representative deceased and if so the date of their death?
2. The reason why a fresh grant is required.
3. The date the original grant of representation was extracted.
4. The place of issue of the original grant.

Question 1 often poses a problem. This query relates to the date of death of the personal representative to the primary grant and to the grant of representation to the personal representative's estate and not to the deceased's estate as you would think from a normal reading of the words. Question 3 requires the date of the primary grant of representation which issued to him/her in the deceased's estate.

These are a repeat of the questions posed in the forms A3(E) and A3(C) dealt with above.

Once these four queries are replied to, the applicant proceeds to the asset cover sheet in the form SA.2 to enter details of the unadministered Irish estate.

When completing the forms A3 and SA.2, details of the deceased's name, address, description, and occupation can be obtained from the primary grant. It is only the unadministered assets that are included in the form, and the relevant value of the property to be inserted on the form is the *current market value* of the unadministered property and not the value of the property at the date of death of the deceased. Details of all Irish real and leasehold immoveable property remaining unadministered to include the property type, whether residential, agricultural, development land, commercial property, single site, industrial property, office, leased property, or retail property must be indicated, and the address, tenure, and Folio number supplied where applicable. In due course the Probate Office will require an auctioneer's letter of current market value of the property as at the date of swearing the A3 or submitting the form SA.2 where the date of death was not within the past two years.

346   SECOND AND SUBSEQUENT GRANTS (*DE BONIS NON* GRANTS)

10.3.2.2   Old version of form A3(C) and form CA6

As noted, these forms are used where the deceased died after 1 April 1975 and prior to 5 December 2001. These forms must be lodged in duplicate with the Revenue first and a certificate for the High Court must be obtained. You will note that on the top left hand corner of both this form and the form A3(E) the Revenue requires sight of the primary grant. Under no circumstances should you send them the original grant because you will need to surrender it to the Probate Office and it may not be returned by the Revenue.

Where there is unadministered immovable property in the State, a form CA6 (Schedule of land and buildings) is required. This form is a separate record of the details of the lands and buildings in the State remaining unadministered, and similar details to those provided in the asset cover sheet of the SA.2 are sought.

10.3.2.3   Form A3(E) 'Estate duty' and form D1

As noted earlier, where the deceased died prior to 1 April 1975, the form A3(E) is used and is headed 'Estate duty'. Again, this form is lodged in duplicate with the Revenue and a Certificate for the High Court must be obtained. (This certificate in fact forms part of Form A3(E) and is filled in by the Revenue.)

Where there is unadministered immovable property, a form D1, which is a separate schedule of lands and buildings, remaining unadministered in the State, is also completed and again, similar details to those provided in the asset cover screen of the form SA.2 are sought.

Again, it is the current market value that is sought.

10.4   Proofs Required for Grant of Letters of Administration with Will Annexed *De Bonis Non*

The papers necessary to lead to a grant of administration with will annexed DBN are similar to those listed in the Probate Office checklist for an ordinary will annexed grant and dealt with in **Chapter 8**. They are as follows:

1. Notice of application to be printed and not handwritten.

2. The original primary grant of probate/administration with will annexed.

    If the original grant is unavailable then a sealed and certified copy of the primary grant is required, together with a letter addressed to the Probate Office as outlined at para **10.3.1** undertaking to lodge the original grant if and when it comes to hand.

3. Form A3(C) or A3(E), depending on the date of death of original deceased, as outlined at para **10.3.2** together with forms CA6 or D1 where appropriate for deaths on or before 5 December 2001 if there is immoveable unadministered property in the estate. For deaths on or after 5 December 2001 a Notice of Acknowledgement (Probate) Form duly printed and signed. When the form SA.2 is successfully completed and submitted the ROS inbox will receive a notification of receipt of the submission.

4. Oath for administrator with will annexed *de bonis non* which for applications lodged after 1 March 2021, and for deaths on or after 1 January 1967, incorporates the administration bond.

5. There are three forms of bond:

    (a) Administration bond for deaths on or after 1 January 1967. This is now incorporated in Part C of the oath for administrator with the will annexed for applications lodged on or after 1 March 2021;

(b) Administration with will annexed bond for deaths between 1 June 1959 and 1 January 1967;

(c) Administration with will annexed bond for deaths prior to 1 June 1959.

The appropriate form of bond as per date of death suitably adapted to singular form if appropriate with the words '*de bonis non*' included in the heading.

6. Auctioneer's letter of current market value of property. This is only required if the papers are not lodged within two years of the date of death.

7. Probate engrossment or certified copy will.

8. Probate Office fees: €150.00 to be endorsed on the back of the notice of application.

9. Form S1 duly completed must be lodged with all applications submitted by post.

The following documents are never required for a grant of letters of administration with will annexed *de bonis non* (see para **10.6**):

1. Death certificate;

2. Original will (and codicils if any);

3. Affidavit of plight and condition;

4. Affidavit of due execution;

5. Affidavit of attesting witness;

6. Affidavit of testamentary capacity.

These are never required, as the will has already been admitted to proof.

However, we will now go on to outline certain points to bear in mind when completing these forms.

10.4.1 OATH FOR ADMINISTRATOR WITH THE WILL ANNEXED *DE BONIS NON* INCORPORATING ADMINISTRATION BOND

A sample of this form is contained in Appendix Q of the Rules of the Superior Courts (Form 4) and must be suitably adapted for use for a *de bonis non* grant. The chain of entitlement must be evident on the face of the oath. The applicant must establish his legal entitlement to extract the grant in the oath.

(a) The heading of the form must include the type of oath and must be amended to read 'Oath for Administrator with the Will Annexed *De Bonis Non*'. Part A contains details of the name of the deceased and all variations of same, the last address of the deceased, the date and place of death of the deceased, the name, address, and occupation of the applicant and the gross value of the estate must be included.

(b) Part B refers to the fact that the original will is already proved and remains in the Probate Office and therefore will not be exhibited with this oath. The exhibit will be the original grant of probate or, if it is lost or mislaid, the official sealed and certified copy grant of probate and official sealed and certified copy will. This is exhibited in the usual way (see O 79, r 37 of the Rules of the Superior Courts).

(c) Part B also contains the title of the applicant to the grant. The title of the administrator must be indicated in the oath and the applicant must clear off all persons having a prior entitlement.

The person entitled to extract the grant is the person next entitled in the order of priority at the date of death, as set out in O 79, r 5(6) of the Rules of the Superior Courts.

Two sample titles are reproduced at para **10.4.1.1** and these precedent titles can be adapted to suit the particular circumstances. They should be read in conjunction with the precedent will annexed titles contained at para **9.3.1.1.** It must be stressed again that the grant follows the interest at the date of death, and, where there is a will, the interest is the residue. Whoever is entitled to the residue (or their legal personal representative) is entitled to extract the *de bonis non* grant.

(d) It is no longer necessary to insert the word 'unadministered' before or above the word 'estate' throughout the form. We are however only dealing with the unadministered estate.

(e) The issue of the primary grant and the reason why, and date when it terminated, must be recited in the oath.

(f) For applications lodged in the Probate Office or District Registry on or after 1 March 2021, the gross value of the estate is outlined in Part A of the oath. The estate is no longer split into real and personal estate. The current value of the unadministered immoveable property as per letter of valuation obtained from an auctioneer is to be inserted.

(g) Do not forget to include the filing clause in the oath, as this provides details of the solicitor's name and address to which the grant is to be posted.

Part C of the oath contains the administration bond.

10.4.1.1 Sample titles will annexed *de bonis non* (deaths on or after 1 January 1967)

Sole executor survives, takes out grant and dies:

'And did therein name as his sole executor A who extracted a grant of Probate from the Probate Office on the   day of   and died on the   day of   leaving part of the estate of the said deceased unadministered and that I am the Residuary Legatee and Devisee (or one of them) named in the said will.'

No executor appointed, residuary legatee and devisee takes out grant and dies:

'And did not therein name any executor but did therein name as Residuary Legatee and Devisee A who extracted a grant of Administration with will annexed from the Probate Office on the   day of   and died on the   day of   leaving part of the estate unadministered and that I am the Personal Representative of the said A under a grant of Administration Intestate which issued to me from the Probate Office on the   day of   .'

The precedent titles may be adapted to suit the particular circumstances and should be read in conjunction with the will annexed sample titles at para **9.3.1.1**.

10.4.2 PROBATE ENGROSSMENT OR CERTIFIED COPY WILL

The single most frequent query from the Probate Office regarding will annexed DBN grant application papers concerns the failure to furnish either a certified copy will or probate engrossment of the will. Practitioners simply forget to include a certified copy will, thinking that they need not submit one with the papers because the Probate Office already has a copy. The certified copy will is required for insertion in due course in the DBN grant. The copy of the will must be written in a legible hand, or printed, typewritten, or photocopied, subject to the direction of the Probate Office. It must be certified by the solicitor applying for the grant, and this is something very frequently forgotten by solicitors.

10.4.3 EVIDENCE OF CURRENT MARKET VALUE

Where the deceased died possessed of immoveable property regardless of whether it is a freehold or leasehold title a letter of current market value from an auctioneer is required. If the papers are lodged within two years of the date of death no proof of current market value is required. The letter or report from the Auctioneer must show the current market value of the property. A description of the property or photographs of it are not required—a single page outlining the current market value is sufficient.

10.5 The Administration Bond *De Bonis Non*

Section 34 of the Succession Act, 1965 provides that every person to whom a grant of letters of administration is made shall give a bond to the President of the High Court to ensure for the benefit of the President of the High Court that the estate will be properly administered. It is no longer necessary to provide sureties unless specifically required by the Probate Office.

The section goes on to provide that the administration bond shall be a penalty of *double the current gross assets* in the estate. The bond is security for the beneficiaries or creditors in the event of an estate not being administered properly.

There are three different administration with will annexed bond forms available, depending on the date of death of the deceased. Care must be taken to ensure that the correct bond form is used, otherwise it will be rejected by the Probate Office. The three forms are as follows.

10.5.1 ADMINISTRATION WITH WILL ANNEXED BOND *DE BONIS NON* (FOR DEATHS PRE-1 JUNE 1959)

This bond deals with only the personal estate and is a stand-alone bond.

10.5.2 ADMINISTRATION WITH WILL ANNEXED BOND *DE BONIS NON* (FOR DEATHS BETWEEN 1 JUNE 1959 AND 31 DECEMBER 1966)

This bond deals with all the estate, both real and personal and is a stand-alone bond.

10.5.3 ADMINISTRATION BOND *DE BONIS NON* (FOR DEATHS POST-1 JANUARY 1967)

For deaths on or after 1 January 1967 there is no longer a stand-alone bond. All bonds have been amalgamated into the form of oath. The new forms came into effect on the 1 March 2021 in an amendment to the Rules of the Superior Court by SI 590/2020 entitled The Rules of the Superior Courts (Probate and Administration Oaths and Bonds) 2020. The form of administration bond specified in the forms 4 and 5 in Appendix Q, Part 1 is the form prescribed for use in the case of estates of persons dying on or after 1 January 1967. In the case of persons dying before 1 January 1967, the forms of bond heretofore in use in connection with such estates shall continue to be used.

As stated above, this bond form is incorporated in Part C of the oath and is used in the case of intestacies (Part 5 Appendix Q) and in the case of will annexed grants (part 4 Appendix Q) for all deaths from 1 January 1967. However, in the case of a will annexed grant, the penultimate paragraph is different to that of the administration intestate bond in that the paragraph dealing with a will being found is excluded.

Because the executors will never apply for a *de bonis non* grant, an administration bond is always required when applying for a grant of administration will annexed DBN. The usual exceptions apply where either the Chief State Solicitor or the solicitor for the Attorney-General is the administrator. Obviously, the type of bond form required will depend on the date of death of the deceased, as outlined earlier. The following matters should be considered when completing earlier versions of the Bond:

350 SECOND AND SUBSEQUENT GRANTS (*DE BONIS NON* GRANTS)

1. The heading of the bond form must be amended by adding the words '*de bonis non*'.
2. The title of the applicant is taken from the oath, but it is not necessary to clear off persons having prior entitlement to the grant in the bond.
3. Be careful with the penal figure in the bond and ensure that it is for an amount at least, if not greater than, double the gross assets contained in the oath.
4. It is no longer necessary to insert the word 'unadministered' before all references to 'estate' on the form.
5. The name, address, and occupation of the applicant(s) must be indicated in full on the face of the bond.
6. If it is intended to use an individual surety, for whatever reason, to join in the bond, a justification of surety form will be required.
7. The current version of the bond as incorporated in Part C of the oath for administrator with will annexed simplifies matters in that the applicant recites that they are liable to pay to the President of the High Court the sum of double the gross value of the estate as specified in Part A of the oath without having to set out the exact calculation of figures.

The applicant should swear the bond before the same commissioner/practising solicitor before whom the oath was sworn and the form must be under seal.

10.5.4 RENUNCIATION IF APPROPRIATE

A renunciation of a person with prior entitlement to the applicant duly exhibited and a power of attorney reciting date of same in the oath and marked by the applicant will be required if appropriate.

10.6 Documents Never Required for a Will Annexed *De Bonis Non* Grant

The original will, affidavits of plight and condition, affidavits of due execution, affidavits of attesting witnesses, and affidavits of testamentary capacity are never required when applying for a grant of administration with will annexed *de bonis non* because the will has already been admitted to proof.

A death certificate is never required when applying for a second grant of representation.

10.7 Proofs Required for a Grant of Letters of Administration Intestate *De Bonis Non*

Where the administrator dies during the course of the administration of an intestate estate, a grant of letters of administration intestate *de bonis non* will be required to complete the administration.

The appropriate papers to file when applying for such a grant are:

1. Original primary grant of administration intestate or sealed and certified copy of the primary grant of administration intestate. If lodging an official copy of the primary grant a letter of undertaking to lodge the original if and when it comes to hand is required;

2. Form A3(C) with or without form CA6 or A3(E) with form D1, depending on date of death;

   Notice of Acknowledgment (Probate) Form printed and signed for deaths on or after 5 December 2001.

3. Oath for administrator intestate *de bonis non* incorporating administration bond if the date of death is after 1 January 1967 and papers filed after 1 March 2021.

4. (a) Administration bond for deaths on or after 1 January 1967 (now incorporated into Part C of the oath) as per SI 590/2020, Schedule 5;

   (b) Administration intestate bond for deaths between 1 June 1959 and 1 January 1967;

   (c) Administration intestate bond for deaths prior to 1 June 1959.

5. Auctioneer's letter of current market value of property where the papers are being lodged more than two years after the date of death.

6. Probate Office fees: €150.00 to be endorsed on the notice of application.

7. Notice of application duly printed.

These are similar to the proofs required when applying for the primary grant of letters of administration intestate, as per the Probate Office checklist, however, the form A3(E) or A3(C) and the forms D1 or CA6, where there is unadministered immovable property, will be required where the deceased person died on or before 5 December 2001.

The forms must also be adapted to reflect the nature of the grant applied for, and the words '*de bonis non*' must be added to the headings of the various forms.

10.7.1 SAMPLE TITLES ADMINISTRATION INTESTATE *DE BONIS NON* (DEATHS ON OR AFTER 1 JANUARY 1967)

' Died Intestate a (married man/civil partner) leaving him surviving his widow/civil partner A who extracted a grant of Letters of Administration Intestate from the Probate Office on the day of 19/20 and died on the day of 19/20 leaving part of the estate of said deceased unadministered that I AM the lawful son of the deceased .'

Or

' Died Intestate a single person who never married or entered into civil partnership without issue or parent and that on the day of 19/20 a grant of Letters of Administration Intestate issued forth of the Probate Office to A, her lawful brother who died on the day of 19/20 leaving part of the said estate unadministered that I AM the lawful sister of the said deceased .'

These precedent titles may be adapted to suit the particular circumstances, and should be read in conjunction with specimen titles for deaths intestate at para **8.3.1.1**.

10.8 When is a *De Bonis Non* Grant Not Required?

10.8.1 APPLICATIONS UNDER THE REGISTRATION OF TITLE ACT, 1964

Section 61(7) of the Registration of Title Act, 1964 allows an applicant who claims entitlement under a proven will of a registered owner but without the assent of the executor who has since died, to apply to court for an order dispensing with further representation to the estate of a deceased registered owner and for an order directing the Registrar to register the applicant without a *de bonis non* grant to the registered owner. The court has power under s 61(7) to dispense with the raising of further representation to a deceased registered owner in certain circumstances.

Section 61(7) of the Act reads as follows:

> *'Where, on the application of any person claiming to be registered as owner of registered land in succession to a deceased full owner of such land, the Court is satisfied:*
>
> *(a) that at least six years have elapsed since the death of the deceased full owner, and*
>
> *(b) that the Personal Representative of such owner is dead or out of the jurisdiction, the Court, may, if it thinks fit, notwithstanding anything in the Administration of Estates Act, 1959, or this Act, dispense the applicant from the necessity of raising representation to the deceased full owner or of giving notice to his Personal Representatives and may order that the applicant be registered as owner of the land.'*

However, if the death of the registered owner occurred within six years of the application, the Registrar will call for a *de bonis non* grant. If the death of the registered owner occurred between six and twelve years previously, the Registrar will refer the applicant to s 61(7) and call for either a *de bonis non* grant or an order of the court dispensing with further representation, and directing the Registrar to register the applicant. See Land Registry Practice Directions (1998) No 15 relating to '*Title by Possession to Registered Land*': this should be consulted by practitioners.

An application under this section is made to the court by notice of motion and supporting affidavit with which appropriate fees are lodged with:

- the Property Registration Authority's Court Registrar, in the case of proceedings in the High Court;

Or

- The County Registrar, in the case of proceedings in the Circuit Court.

The applicant seeks an order dispensing with the raising of further representation and for the registration of the applicant as the owner of the particular lands. When the order of the court is obtained, an official copy is then lodged in the Property Registration Authority for registration of the new owner, as in any other dealing.

10.8.2 RELYING ON THE DECISION IN *MOHAN V ROCHE*

The Property Registration Authority's Practice Directions referred to earlier refer to the decision in *Mohan v Roche* [1991] 1 IR 567, and acknowledge that this decision should be noted by its Registrars.

While the Law Society has issued practice notes advising practitioners of the defects in the decision, knowledge of its existence is useful. The decision provided that a *de bonis non* grant was not required where a personal representative and the beneficiary are one and the same person, and the personal representative died without executing an assent. His/her personal representative was then entitled to sell without a *de bonis non* grant. This decision may be applied to registered land in s 49 cases. Although this decision can be helpful, and may obviate the necessity of seeking a *de bonis non* grant in the absence of an assent, it will in the majority of cases be far more satisfactory to have a formal assent completed. It is nevertheless possible to rely on the decision to contract out of the necessity to apply for a *de bonis non* grant.

The decision of *Mohan v Roche* was considered in the recent decision of *Trentdale v Mary O'Shea* [2018] IEHC 47. In a decision of Ms Justice Creedon delivered on 25 January 2018 it was concluded that 'it is unlikely that Mohan v Roche can be read as having any application to registered land. It would seem that, in the case of registered land, an assent is required to be made by a personal representative in order to vest property in the party entitled thereto, even if said party is, in fact, the personal representative herself'.

The Land Registry are currently reviewing their practice direction following this decision.

10.9 Chain of Executorship

Prior to the Succession Act, 1965, the acting executor of a sole or last surviving executor was the executor of the original testator and was entitled to administer the assets of the original testator without extracting a new grant, and this 'chain of executorship' could be carried on ad infinitum.

Section 19 of the Succession Act, 1965 abolished the chain of executors with effect from 1 January 1967 and it does not arise in the case of an executor who died after 1 January 1967.

Section 19(1) provides that:

> 'Where the sole or last surviving executor of a testator dies after the commencement of this Act the executor of such executor shall not be the executor of that testator.'

The basis of the chain is that the executor of a sole or last surviving executor of a testator is the executor of that testator to the extent that the interest vested in the original executor by probate of the will of the testator is continued and kept alive, without requiring a further grant of probate of the original will. It made matters very simple where, for example, the original executor had failed to execute an assent: his executor could do it for him/her when he became acting executor of the original executor's estate. A *de bonis non* grant was not required.

However, the downside of this was that it often imposed an obligation on an executor to administer the estate of someone he never knew or may not have even heard of. Nevertheless, the abolition of the chain of executorship has proved a fruitful area for *de bonis non* grants.

However, the chain of executorship continues to apply in respect of an executor who was such by reason of a chain of executorship arising before the Succession Act came into operation, i.e. where the executor whose death created the chain died before 1 January 1967. In this case, if the acting executor is still alive, he can complete the administration of the estate of the original testator without any new grant to such testator. It is the date of death of the sole or last surviving executor that counts, not the date of death of the testator.

10.10 Other Second or Subsequent Grants

10.10.1 UNADMINISTERED PROBATE

If an executor extracts a grant of probate, reserving the rights of another executor, and subsequently dies, a grant of unadministered probate will be given to the executor whose rights were reserved. This is a grant of unadministered probate. In this situation the oath of executor form is adapted as appropriate, for example, reference is made to the original grant and details of the first grant are recited including reservation of the applicant's rights and stating how the first grant terminated (as in the death of the first executor). It is no longer necessary to place the word 'unadministered' before the word 'estate' throughout. The current market value of the gross estate must be included although the Probate Office will not seek a letter of current market value from an auctioneer. A bond is never required.

10.10.2 DOUBLE PROBATE

If an executor extracts a grant of probate, reserving the rights of another executor, such other executor may extract a grant while the first executor is still alive, and this grant is called a grant of double probate.

10.10.3 SUPPLEMENTAL PROBATE

If a will has been proved by an executor and, subsequently, a codicil is discovered, a supplemental grant of probate will issue to the acting executor.

10.11 Deeds of Assent

The Administration of Estates Act, 1959 gave power to the personal representative to vest any land of a deceased person dying after 1 June 1959 in the person entitled thereto by means of an assent in writing. Thereafter, a deed of assent is the document required to transfer or vest land by the personal representative in a person entitled under the will or intestacy of a deceased. The assent must be in writing to be effectual to pass an estate or interest in land.

10.11.1 PROPERTY REGISTRATION AUTHORITY TITLES

These provisions were re-enacted by s 61 of the Registration of Title Act, 1964, as amended by s 54 of the Succession Act, 1965, which provided in addition that, in the case of an application accompanied by an assent in the prescribed form:

> *'it shall not be the duty of the Registrar, nor shall he be entitled, to call for any information as to why any assent or transfer is or was made and he shall be bound to assume that the Personal Representative is or was acting ... correctly and within his powers.'*

The correct Property Registration Authority forms relating to transmissions on death must be used when dealing with its titles, and these are found in the Land Registration Rules, 2012. They can be adapted. The forms most familiar to practitioners are as follows:

1. Form 35—where the legal personal representative assents to the registration of a beneficiary under a will where a registered owner dies testate on or after 1 June 1959;

2. Form 36—application for registration by a beneficiary under a will who claims to be entitled as full owner on the assent of the legal personal representative where a registered owner dies testate on or after 1 June 1959;

3. Form 38—where the legal personal representative applies for and assents to his/her own registration as full owner as beneficiary under a will where a registered owner dies testate on or after 1 June 1959;

4. Form 41—assent by the legal personal representative to the registration of a person entitled as full owner where a registered owner dies *intestate* on or after 1 June 1959;

5. Form 42—application for registration by a person entitled on intestacy where a registered owner dies intestate on or after 1 June 1959;

6. Form 44—where the legal personal representative assents to the registration of him/herself as full owner on the death intestate of a registered full owner on or after 1 June 1959.

The Property Registration Authority fees on an assent are €130.

10.11.2 REGISTRY OF DEEDS TITLES

Section 53 of the Succession Act, 1965 contains special provisions in relation to assents when dealing with unregistered land. It provides that the assent must be in writing and be signed by the personal representatives. This is then lodged together with a form 1 (if completed by the solicitor) or form 1A (if completed by a personal applicant) in the property registration authority registry of deeds section, together with fees of €50.

The forms can be completed online at http://www.landregistry.ie, and they replace the memorial of assent.

10.11.3 PERSONAL PROPERTY

In relation to personal property, the assent to property vesting in the person(s) entitled may be oral, and the transfer effected by delivery or handing over the property in question.

10.11.4 PROBLEMS REGARDING ASSENTS

In the case of land, if a personal representative dies before he or she has executed the requisite assent, a further grant (a *de bonis non* grant, usually) will be necessary in order to pass an estate or interest in the land and to complete the administration commenced when the primary grant was extracted.

Unfortunately, it is easy to overlook the preparation and execution of a deed of assent when acting in the administration of an estate. Quite often, the personal representative is the appropriate person in whose favour an assent should be executed, and this assent vesting the property in him/herself is never done. The decision in *Mohan v Roche* is relevant and was referred at para **10.8.2**.

As solicitors acting in the administration of an estate, *always ensure* that a deed of assent is prepared and signed where appropriate and stress to the client the importance of calling to the office to sign the deed.

10.12 Precedent Application Documents for Grant of Letters of Administration Intestate *De Bonis Non*

In the estate of Sean Kelly, deceased obit 12 July 1989:

(i) Statement of facts.

(ii) Completed estate form A3(C).

(iii) Schedule of lands and buildings (CA6).

(iv) Original grant of letters of administration intestate in the estate of Sean Kelly, deceased.

(v) Oath of administrator incorporating administration bond *de bonis non* (form No 5)

(vi) Auctioneer's letter of current market value.

(vii) Grant of letters of administration *de bonis non*.

(ix) Notice of application.

10.12.1 STATEMENT OF FACTS

In the Estate of Sean Kelly, deceased

Date of death:	12 July 1989
Address:	Liscannor, Co Clare
Occupation:	Farmer
Place of death:	At same place
Domicile/Residence:	The State
Testate/Intestate:	Intestate
Previous grant:	Ex Probate Office—grant of letter of administration intestate on 2 March 1990.
	Granted to widow, Robyn Kelly
Marital status:	Married man. He is survived by his widow, Robyn, and three children, namely Robert, Jane and John.
Note:	Robyn Kelly died on 4 July 2021

10.12.2 INSTRUCTION SHEET

You are consulted by Robert Kelly of Cusack Road, Ennis, County Clare, regarding the sale of family lands at Liscannor, County Clare. He has agreed to sell the lands by public auction next week. He believes that the lands are in the name of his mother, Robyn, who would have inherited them from his father, Sean Kelly, over thirty years ago.

You inspect the Land Registry Folio and Folio 8123F (County Clare) containing 22 acres 1 rood 2 perches or thereabouts statute measure which shows Sean Kelly as the registered owner of the Folio. Robyn Kelly's name does not appear on the folio.

You are advised by your client that Sean Kelly, his father, died on 12 July 1989, and, having searched through your old files, you find a grant of letters of administration intestate which issued to his widow, the said Robyn Kelly, forth of the Probate Office on 2 March 1990.

From reading the file, it appears that Robyn used the grant to release monies from the various financial institutions but she did not deal with the land. In any event, her three children were too young to sign a release of their distributive one-ninth share each in the estate to her, even if they so wished. The grant was left on the file and nothing further was done in relation to it.

The said Robyn Kelly died on 4 July 2021. No grant has been extracted to her estate as yet. She died without having executed an assent in relation to the estate of her late husband, Sean Kelly, although all her children are now over eighteen years.

You explain to the client that because the lands in Folio 8123F (County Clare) are still in his late father's name, he will have to apply for a grant of letters of administration intestate *de bonis non* to the estate of Sean Kelly in order to provide title to any purchaser.

Market value of the lands as per auctioneer's valuation: €180,000

SECOND AND SUBSEQUENT GRANTS (*DE BONIS NON* GRANTS)

10.12.3 REVENUE FORM A3(C) AND CA6

PPS No. | 4 7 8 2 4 6 7 J

CAPITAL ACQUISITONS TAX

Insert here the Name and Address of the person to whom this affidavit is to be returned:

CAROLAN WALSH & BROOKS
SOLICITORS
BINDON STREET
ENNIS
COUNTY CLARE

Note: The Original Grant must be delivered with this Affidavit to —
The Revenue Commissioners, Capital Acquisitions Tax Unit.

Affidavit or Affirmation for Revenue, where an application is made for a second or subsequent grant of representation except where the Estate was within the operation of the previous grant in which case the appropriate form of affidavit as for an original grant should be used.

Agent's Reference: NC/EA

The High Court
(PROBATE)

(^{1}) Delete as appropriate.

(^{2}) Insert here the address and occupation of Deceased and his or her personal description as "Bachelor", "Spinster", "Widower" or "Widow".

(^{3}) Insert here the name, postal address, and description of each person who joins in the Affidavit or Affirmation.

(^{4}) If affirmed substitute "do solemnly and sincerely affirm".

(^{5}) Insert here "Double Probate of the Will", or "Administration (with Will) (or Administration) of the unadministered estate", or as the case may be.

(^{6}) State the name of the place where the Deceased died.

THE (^{1}) PROBATE OFFICE (^{1}) _____

In the ESTATE of SEAN KELLY

who died on 12TH JULY 1989   late of (^{2}) LISCANNOR, COUNTY CLARE

FARMER AND MARRIED MAN

I (^{3}) ROBERT KELLY, CUSACK ROAD, ENNIS, COUNTY CLARE, PILOT

(^{4}) make oath and say as follows:—

1. I desire to obtain a grant of (^{5}) LETTERS OF ADMINISTRATION INTESTATE DE BONIS NON

of the above-named who died at (^{6}) LISCANNOR, COUNTY CLARE

domiciled in IRELAND

2. The replies to the following questions are correct, viz.:

QUESTIONS	ANSWERS
(i) What further assets, if any, have been discovered since the original grant was sworn?	NONE
(ii) Why is a fresh grant required?	TO DEAL WITH UNADMINISTERED ESTATE OUTLINED OVERLEAF
(iii) Is the original personal representative dead? If so, state the date of death, and date and place of grant of representation	YES, ROBYN KELLY, OBIT 4 JULY 2021. NO GRANT EXTRACTED TO APPLICANTS KNOWLEDGE

3. The account on page 2 is a true account of the particulars and value, *at the date of this Affidavit,* so far as I _____ have been able to ascertain the same, of all the UNADMINISTERED property of the Deceased within the operation of the previous grant, whether in possession or reversion, within the State, exclusive of what the Deceased may have been possessed of or entitled to as a trustee and not beneficially, but including property over which the Deceased had and exercised a general power of appointment. The gross value thereof is € 180,000 _____ of which € NIL _____ is personal property.

All of which is true to the best of my _____ knowledge and belief.

(^{7}) Insert the names of the deponents and if affirmed substitute "Affirmed" for "Sworn".

(^{7}) Sworn by the above-named ROBERT KELLY _____

at BINDON STREET ENNIS _____ in the County of CLARE

_____ this 10th _____ day of September 20 21

Before me, a Commissioner for Oaths/Practising Solicitor

Form A3(C)

358 SECOND AND SUBSEQUENT GRANTS (*DE BONIS NON* GRANTS)

ACCOUNT — Unadministered Estate

The property herein to be valued at the date of this Affidavit.

	€	
Leasehold Property and Tenancies from year to year, *as per Schedule - Form CA6 annexed.* Other personal property, viz.: **NONE**	NIL	
Freehold Registered Land - as per Schedule - Form CA6 - annexed.	180,000	
Other Real Estate - as per Schedule - Form CA6 - annexed.		
GROSS VALUE OF THE PROPERTY IN THIS AFFIDAVIT	180,000	
Debts due and unpaid, viz.: €	NIL	
NET VALUE OF THE PROPERTY IN THIS AFFIDAVIT	180,000	

CERTIFICATE FOR THE HIGH COURT
For Official Use Only

THE { PROBATE OFFICE / DISTRICT PROBATE REGISTRY AT _____ } *delete where not applicable*

In the goods of _____, deceased

I certify that an Affidavit has been delivered to the Revenue Commissioners showing that the property of the said Deceased within the jurisdiction of this Court (exclusive of what the Deceased may have been possessed of or entitled to as a trustee and not beneficially) amounts to the Gross Value of € _____ and to the Net Value of € _____, and I also certify that

delete where not applicable {
- an adequate payment on account of inheritance tax in respect of the property passing under the Deceased person's will or intestacy or Part IX or section 56 of the Succession Act, 1965, has been made.
- payment of inheritance tax in respect of the property passing under the Deceased person's will or intestacy or Part IX or section 56 of the Succession Act, 1965, has been deferred.

Capital Acquisitions Tax Unit

_____
For Revenue Commissioners

Date_____

SECOND AND SUBSEQUENT GRANTS (*DE BONIS NON* GRANTS)

CAPITAL ACQUISITIONS TAX
SCHEDULE OF LANDS AND BUILDINGS

Disponer's PPS No. 4782467

Disponer's name: SEAN KELLY

Disponer's address: LISCANNOR, COUNTY CLARE

Disponer's date of death (if applicable): 12 03 89

The date on which the property is to be valued: 18 09 21

Agent's name: CAROLAN WALSH BROOKS SOLICITORS

Agent's address: BINDON STREET, ENNIS, COUNTY CLARE

Agent's reference: NC/EA

Agent's code:

Agent's phone no.: 065-123456

Agent's signature:

PTO

For official use only

1. File Number
2. Tax involved (☒ the box)   Gift ☐   Inheritance ☐   Discretionary Trust ☐
3. (i) Group threshold (☒ the box)   A ☐   B ☐   C ☐
   or
   (ii) Threshold amount
4. Aggregate of taxable values of gifts/inheritance to date
5. Donee/Successor is a farmer (☒ the box)   Yes ☐   No ☐
6. Adjudication File No.   and the parties to the relevant deed are:

7. Auctioneer's valuation enclosed (☒ the box)   Yes ☐   No ☐
8. Other relevant reference/observations:

Signed   Date DD MM YY

Form C.A.6
Edition 2012

Revenue
Cáin agus Custaim na hÉireann
Irish Tax and Customs

360 SECOND AND SUBSEQUENT GRANTS (*DE BONIS NON* GRANTS)

Disponer's PPS No. | 4 | 7 | 8 | 2 | 4 | 6 | 7 |

Milk Quota
Is there a super levy milk quota attached to any of the property described below?
If so, identify the property and the number of litres involved.
Item no.
Litres

Is the estimated value supported by a professional valuation? Insert ☒ in the box Yes ☒ No ☐

Timber
Is any of the property described below agricultural property which consists of trees or underwood? If so, identify clearly the lands involved.
The value of the lands should include the value of the trees and underwood.
Item no.

Consecutive Number	SITUATION OF PROPERTY			NATURE OF PROPERTY		AREA (Hectares)	TENURE		Estimated Market Value of property	For Valuation Office use only
	County / City / Town	Townland or Street and Number	Electoral Division or Ward	Lands ☒	Buildings ☒		If leasehold, date of lease and length of term	If registered, folio number		Official Opinion of Market Value €
1.	CLARE	LISCANNOR	DOOLIN	☒ Agricultural ☐ Development ☐ Residential ○ ☐ Commercial ○ ☐ Mix ☐ Single Site	☒ Residential ☐ Commercial ☐ Retail ○ ☐ Industrial ○ ☐ Office ○ ☒ Agricultural ☐ Mix	22A 0R 2P		8123F CLARE	180,000 €	
2.				☐ Agricultural ☐ Development ☐ Residential ○ ☐ Commercial ○ ☐ Mix ☐ Single Site	☐ Residential ☐ Commercial ☐ Retail ○ ☐ Industrial ○ ☐ Office ○ ☐ Agricultural ☐ Mix					
3.				☐ Agricultural ☐ Development ☐ Residential ○ ☐ Commercial ○ ☐ Mix ☐ Single Site	☐ Residential ☐ Commercial ☐ Retail ○ ☐ Industrial ○ ☐ Office ○ ☐ Agricultural ☐ Mix					

For Commissioner of Valuation

10.12.4 PRIMARY GRANT OF ADMINISTRATION INTESTATE

Admon Int No 7

THE HIGH COURT

PROBATE

BE IT KNOWN, that on the 2nd day of March 1990

LETTERS OF ADMINISTRATION of all the estate which devolved to and vests in the personal representative of Sean Kelly late of Liscannor in the county of Clare Farmer/Married Man

deceased, who died on or about the 12th day of July 1989

at   Same Place

INTESTATE

was granted by the Court to Robyn Kelly of Liscannor in the county of Clare Nurse and lawful widow of deceased.

she   having been first sworn faithfully to administer the same.

And it is hereby certified that an Affidavit for Inland Revenue has been delivered wherein it is shown that the gross value of all Estate of the said deceased within this jurisdiction (exclusive of what the deceased may have been possessed of or entitled to as a Trustee and not beneficially) amounts to

£31,000.00 and that the net value thereof amounts to £28,500.00 and that it appears by a Certificate issued by the Revenue Commissioners that the payment of inheritance tax has been deferred.

Cornelius Costello

Assistant Probate Officer

Extracted by   *Carolan Walsh Brooks*   Solicitors
£36.00

10.12.5 OATH OF ADMINISTRATOR INCORPORATING ADMINISTRATION BOND *DE BONIS NON*

For deaths on or after 1 January 1967

THE HIGH COURT

PROBATE

The Probate Office

***The District Probate Registry At**

* If not a District Registry, please strike out inappropriate words.

362 SECOND AND SUBSEQUENT GRANTS (*DE BONIS NON* GRANTS)

PART A

Name of deceased	Sean Kelly
Address of deceased	Liscannor in the County of Clare, Farmer/Married Man Deceased.
Date of death	12th July 1989
Place of death	Liscannor, County Clare.
Name of Applicant	Robert Kelly.
Address of Applicant	Cusack Road, Ennis in the County of Clare Pilot.
Gross value of the estate	€180,000.00

PART B

I, the above named applicant aged eighteen years and upwards, Make Oath and say, that the above named deceased Sean Kelly

died Intestate a married man leaving him surviving his widow Robyn who extracted a grant of Letters of Administration Intestate from the Probate Office on the Second day of March 1990 and died on the fourth day of July 2021 leaving part of the estate of said deceased unadministered

that I am the lawful son of said Deceased and that I will well and faithfully administer the Estate of the said Deceased by paying the

deceased's just debts, and distributing the Residue of said Estate

according to law, and that I will exhibit a true Inventory of the said

Estate and render a true account thereof, whenever required by law so to do; that the said Deceased died at the above named place of death on the date of death cited above. (Where application is made in District Probate Registry add 'and had at the time of his death a fixed place of abode at the above named address within the said district of...........') and that there whole of the estate without any deductions for debts, which devolves on and vests in the deceased's legal personal

representative amounts in value to the figure cited above as the gross value of the estate and no more to the best of my knowledge, information and belief.

Robert Kelly

SWORN at Bindon Street, Ennis

in the County of Clare

by the said Robert Kelly

this 21st day of September 2021

before me a Commissioner for Oaths/Practising Solicitor and I know the Deponent

(or I know who certifies to his/her

knowledge of the Deponent)

Niall Casey

Commissioner for Oaths/Practising Solicitor

This Affidavit is filed on behalf of
Robert Kelly by Carolan Walsh Brooks
Solicitors 24-26 Upper Ormond Quay, Dublin 7
This 27th Day of September 2021

PART C

I *the above named applicant am l*iable in full to pay to the President of the High Court the sum of *double the gross value of the estate as specified in* **PART A** above for which payment I/~~we~~ bind myself/~~ourselves~~ and ~~each of us~~, my/~~our~~

Executors and Administrators

Sealed with my/~~our~~ seal~~(s)~~ and dated the 21st day of September 2021

The condition of this obligation is such that if I the intended administrator of the estate of the said deceased do fulfil he obligations referred to in **PART B** above and furthermore do pay all taxes and duties payable in respect of the estate of the deceased for which the personal representative is accountable and all income tax and surtax payable out of the estate

And further do, if so required, render and deliver up the letters of administration in the High Court if it shall hereafter appear that any will was made by the deceased which is exhibited in the said Court with a request that it be allowed and approved accordingly then this obligation shall be void and of no effect, but shall otherwise remain in full force and effect.

SIGNED SEALED AND DELIVERED

by the within named

Robert Kelly *Robert Kelly*   Seal

in the presence   of

Niall Casey

Bindon Street, Ennis

~~Commissioner for Oaths~~/Practising Solicitor

Filed on the   day of   20

10.12.6 LETTER OF CURRENT MARKET VALUE

I, Niamh O'Keeffe of Abbey Street, Ennis in the County of Clare, Auctioneer

1. I am acquainted with the value of the lands in the vicinity of Doolin, Liscannor in the County of Clare where lands belonging to the said Sean Kelly deceased are situate.

2. I have inspected the holding of the deceased at Doolin, Liscannor and in my opinion the said holding on the date hereof is of the current market value of about €180,000 (One Hundred and Eighty Thousand Euro).

Signed this 18th day of August 2021   *Niamh O'Keeffe*

10.12.7 PRECEDENT *DE BONIS NON* GRANT

Admon Intestate (dbn). No 12

THE HIGH COURT

PROBATE

BE IT KNOWN, that Sean Kelly late of Liscannor, County Clare, Farmer

Deceased who died on or about the 12th day of July 1989, at Liscannor, in the County of Clare

INTESTATE and that since his death, on the 2nd Day of March 1990, LETTERS OF ADMINISTRATION of the estate which devolves on and vests in the personal representative of the said deceased were granted at the Probate Office to ROBYN KELLY the widow

(Which Letters of Administration Now remain on Record) which Said ROBYN KELLY after taking such administration upon herself intermeddled in the estate of said deceased; and

364 SECOND AND SUBSEQUENT GRANTS (*DE BONIS NON* GRANTS)

afterwards on or about the 4th day of July 2021 died leaving part of the estate unadministered

And that on the 1st day of November 2021

LETTERS OF ADMINISTRATION of the said estate which devolves in and vests in the personal representative of the said deceased and which was so left unadministered were granted to ROBERT KELLY of Cusack Road Ennis, in the County of Clare, Pilot, Lawful son of deceased

he having been first sworn faithfully to administer the same.

And it is hereby certified that an Affidavit for Inland Revenue has been delivered wherein it is shown that the gross value of all Estate of the said deceased within this jurisdiction (exclusive of what the deceased may have been possessed of or entitled to as a Trustee and not beneficially) amounts to €180,000.00 and that the net value thereof amounts to €180,000.00.

John Glennon

Probate Officer

Extracted by €150.00

Carolan Walsh Brooks   Solicitors

CHAPTER 11

NON-CONTENTIOUS APPLICATIONS (EITHER TO THE PROBATE OFFICER OR TO THE COURT)

11.1 Practice and Procedure in Respect of Non-Contentious Matters Coming before the Probate Officer

11.1.1 INTRODUCTION

In certain circumstances, applications have to be made to the Probate Officer before an application for a grant may be lodged. This section will go through the legal context and background in which such applications are made, the circumstances in which an application has to be made, and the procedure and proofs necessary in each case.

11.1.2 POWERS OF THE PROBATE OFFICER

The Probate Officer's powers derive from the Court of Probate (Ireland) Act, 1859 and the Court Officers Act, 1926, while s 25 of the Administration of Estates Act, 1959 and s 128 of the Succession Act, 1965 confer the same powers on the Assistant Probate Officer.

These powers are:

(i) to prove and condemn wills;

(ii) to issue grants of probate and administration;

(iii) to issue citations and subpoenas; and

(iv) to make orders and rulings pursuant to O 79 of the Rules of the Superior Courts, 1986.

When proving wills and issuing grants of administration, the primary consideration of the Probate Office is whether or not the person applying for the grant of representation is the person with legal entitlement to the grant. To this end, the central piece of legislation employed by the Probate Office is the Succession Act, 1965, which sets out the law of succession in this jurisdiction for deaths on or after 1 January 1967. For deaths prior to this date, the law of succession is governed by the Administration of Estates Act, 1959 and the Intestates' Estates Act, 1954.

Under s 27(3) of the Succession Act:

> 'the person or persons to whom administration is to be granted shall be determined in accordance with rules of the High Court.'

The rules referred to are those set out under O 79 and O 80 of the Rules of the Superior Courts. Some of these rules require an order of the Probate Officer before an application can be made to proceed to extract a grant of representation.

11.1.3 ORDERS OF THE PROBATE OFFICER PURSUANT TO ORDER 79 OF THE RULES OF THE SUPERIOR COURTS

1.	O 79, r (5)(1)(e)	Natural child
2.	O 79, r 5(3)	Rival applicants
3.	O 79, r 5(6)(e)	Residue not in terms wholly disposed of
4.	O 79, r 5(8)	Grants in situations of foreign domicile
5.	O 79, r 5(10)	Will in foreign language
6.	O 79, rr 6 and 7	Execution of will
7.	O 79, r 13	Documents referred to in a will
8.	O 79, r 23	Grant to attorney in case of physical disability
9.	O 79, r 25	Grant to guardian
10.	O 79, r 27	Where person entitled to grant is of unsound mind and has no committee.

11.1.4 REQUIREMENTS OF PROBATE OFFICE IN RESPECT OF APPLICATIONS UNDER ORDER 79 OF THE RULES OF THE SUPERIOR COURTS

11.1.4.1 Natural child

Order 79, r 5(1)(c)

'In determining to whom letters of administration of the estate of a person who died on or after the 1st of January 1967, wholly intestate and domiciled in Ireland shall be granted, the persons having a beneficial interest in the estate of the deceased shall be entitled to a grant of administration in the following order of priority, namely:

...

(c) The child or children of the deceased (including any person entitled by virtue of the Status of Children Act, 1987, to succeed to the estate of the deceased).'

The Status of Children Act, 1987 equalised the rights under law of all children, whether born within or outside of marriage. Section 3 sets out:

'(i) In deducing any relationships for the purposes of the Act or any Act of the Oireachtas passed after the commencement of this section the relationship between every person and his father and mother (or either of them) shall unless the contrary intention appears, be determined irrespective of whether his father and mother are or have been married to each other and all other relationships shall be determined accordingly.'

From a probate perspective, this now means that in respect of deaths as and from 14 June 1988, a non-marital child has an equal entitlement to a marital child when applying for a grant of administration.

When a natural child makes application for a grant of administration in his parent's estate he must first establish to the satisfaction of the Probate Officer that he is in fact the child of the deceased. An acceptable proof is the birth certificate (long form) of the child, which generally contains the names of the parents of the child. In situations where the deceased in question is the father of the child applying for the grant and the father's name does not appear on the birth certificate, a declaration of parentage must be obtained from the Circuit Court and produced to the Probate Office as proof of parentage.

In the event of a case prior to 14 June 1988, an order of the Probate Officer is required before a natural child or mother of a natural child can proceed with an application for administration. The application is made under s 9(1) and (2) of the Legitimacy Act, 1931, which conferred an interest on a natural child in the estate of his mother (provided that she had no lawful issue) and an interest on the mother in the estate of her natural child.

The Probate Officer will require an affidavit wherein it is established that either the child in question is the natural child of the deceased mother or the mother is the mother of the deceased natural child, whichever is appropriate in the circumstances. The Probate Officer must also be satisfied that the mother left no lawful issue. In the event of there being lawful issue, the natural child has no interest in his mother's estate and has no entitlement to extract a grant of administration.

Prior to 19 May 1931, the common law position prevailed and this in essence deemed that the only next of kin a natural child could have was his own lawful issue. He had no succession rights to either of his parents' estates, or they to his, or to any relation of his.

11.1.4.2 Rival applicants

Order 79, r 5(3)

> 'Where there are conflicting claims for a grant among the members of a class entitled to administration, the grant shall be made to such of the claimants as the Probate Officer shall select having given not less than 21 days' notice to the rival claimants, or on objection made in writing within the said period, to such person as the Court shall select.'

Members of a class constitute a group of persons who have equal entitlement to extract a grant of representation. For example, in a situation where a bachelor dies without parent, leaving brothers and sisters, the brothers and sisters together constitute 'members of a class'.

If in this situation there were differences between the brothers and sisters as to who should extract the grant and if it resulted in two of the siblings making individual applications in the estate, this Rule of Court comes into play. In effect, there are now rival applicants for the grant of representation in question.

In practice, what tends to occur is that a solicitor applies for the grant of administration on behalf of one of the siblings. The Probate Office notifies the solicitor that a rival application exists. The solicitor then files an affidavit in the Probate Office, setting out:

(a) his client's entitlement to the grant;

(b) the details of the rival application which should include:

  (i) name and address of rival;

  (ii) relationship to deceased;

  (iii) date of application; and

  (iv) details of solicitor (if any) acting on his behalf.

A request is made in affidavit to the Probate Officer to issue the statutory twenty-one-day notice to the rival applicant.

The notice is prepared in the Probate Office and the solicitor who requested it arranges to have the notice served on the rival applicant.

In the event of the rival applicant lodging no objection in the Probate Office within the twenty-one days, an affidavit of service is lodged in the Probate Office, indicating that the statutory notice was served on the rival applicant and that twenty-one days have now elapsed and that an order of the Probate Officer is now being sought to allow the client to proceed with his application. If the Probate Officer is satisfied that the rules have been complied with, she makes an order allowing the applicant moving the application to proceed with his application.

If objections are raised, the matter must be set down for the Probate Judge by the solicitor who initiated the procedure under this Rule of Court. See also para **11.3.6**.

Sample 21-day notice

THE HIGH COURT

**The Probate Office,
Courts Service,
Phoenix House,
Smithfield,
Dublin 7.**

NOTICE

In the Estate of

                    Marie Mullaney   Deceased

An application has been made to me on behalf of Anne Mullaney of 70 Grange Road, Tubbercurry in the County of Sligo for an Order pursuant to Order 79 Rule 5(3) of the Rules of the Superior Courts giving her liberty to extract a Grant of Letters of Administration Intestate in the estate of the above named deceased.

Any objections which you might have to the granting of such an Order to the said Applicant should be made in writing to me within twenty-one days of the date of service on you of this notice.

TAKE NOTICE that in default of the submission of such objections within the aforesaid period the Order will be given to the said Applicant as sought.

DATED the   day of   20

                Signed: *Annette O'Connell*

                                    Probate Officer

To Patrick Mullaney,

Cloghane,

Tralee,

County Kerry.

Sample grounding affidavit

THE HIGH COURT

PROBATE

In the estate of

                    Marie Mullaney   Deceased

I, Anne Mullaney of 70 Grange Road, Tubbercurry in the County of Sligo, Pharmacist, aged 18 years and upwards make Oath and say:

1. Marie Mullaney in the title hereof named died intestate on the 4th day of January 20 and I beg to refer to her Death Certificate upon which marked with the letter 'A' I have endorsed my name prior to the swearing hereof.

2. The deceased died a single person never having married without parent leaving her surviving this deponent her lawful and only sister and Patrick Mullaney of Cloghane, Tralee in the County of Kerry her lawful and only brother. She left no nephew or niece the issue of a predeceased brother or sister.

3. On 4th November 20 Gallagher & Co, Solicitors of Ballina in the County of Mayo lodged on my behalf in the Principal Probate Registry in Dublin an Application for a Grant of Letters of Administration of the estate of said deceased.

4. On 21st November 20 my Solicitors were informed by the Probate Office that a rival application had been lodged in the Probate Office by O'Connell Moriarty & Co., Solicitors of Rock Street, Tralee in the County of Kerry on behalf of the aforesaid Patrick Mullaney.

5. On 4th December 20 my Solicitors wrote to Messrs O'Connell Moriarty & Co, informing them of my application and requesting them to withdraw the application on behalf of the said Patrick Mullaney. I beg to refer to a copy of the said letter marked 'B' upon which I have endorsed my name.

6. I am informed that up to the date of swearing hereof the application has not been withdrawn.

7. I say that Patrick Mullaney will not administer the estate of the said Marie Mullaney because [state reason]

8. I therefore request the Probate Officer to issue the 21-day Notice pursuant to Order 79 Rule 5(3) of the Rules of the Superior Courts and direct same to the said Patrick Mullaney.

Signed

Sworn by the said
This day of   20
Before me a Commissioner for
Oaths/Practising Solicitor and I know the deponent

Filed by   Solrs

11.1.4.3 Residue not in terms wholly disposed of

Order 79, r 5(6)(e)

'where the residue is not in terms wholly disposed of, the Probate Officer may, if he is of opinion that the testator has nevertheless disposed of the whole or substantially the whole of the estate as ascertained at the time of application for the grant, allow a grant to be made to any legatee or devisee entitled to, or a share in, the estate so disposed of, without regard to the person entitled to share in any residue not disposed of by the will.'

When a testator makes a will and makes no disposition of the residue, the general rule is that the next of kin are the persons legally entitled to extract the grant of administration with will annexed. However, in situations where it is apparent that the testator has disposed of the whole (or substantially the whole) of his estate and that there is in actual fact no residue, this rule may be accessed to allow either a legatee or devisee to apply for a grant of administration with will annexed.

The oath for administrator with will annexed should contain the following averments:

1. that there is no residuary legatee or devisee named in the will;
2. that the testator had nonetheless disposed of all his estate (or substantially all);
3. that the applicant is either a legatee or devisee named in the will.

On being satisfied of the foregoing facts, the Probate Officer makes an order giving the legatee/devisee liberty to proceed with the application.

11.1.4.4 Grants in situations of foreign domicile

Order 79, r 5(8)

'Where the deceased died on or after the 1st day of January, 1967, domiciled outside Ireland,

    (a) a grant of administration intestate or with will annexed of the moveable estate may be made by the Probate Officer as follows, namely:

        (i) to the person entrusted with the administration of the moveable estate by the Court having jurisdiction at the place where the deceased died domiciled; or

(ii) to the person entitled to administer the moveable estate by the law of the place where the deceased died domiciled;

(b) a grant of administration intestate or with will annexed of the immoveable estate may be made by the Probate Officer in accordance with the law which would have been applicable if the deceased had died domiciled in Ireland.'

Movable estate is administered in accordance with the law of domicile, while immovable estate is administered in accordance with the law where it is situate, i.e. the *lex situs*. If a person applies to the Probate Office for a grant in the Irish estate of a deceased with foreign domicile, the Probate Officer will issue a full grant in respect of both movable and immovable assets of the deceased, provided that she is satisfied that the person applying is the person entitled under the law of domicile and the person entitled under Irish law.

Where the applicant is unable to show title under both systems of law, the foregoing rule allows the Probate Officer to grant limited grants of representation in the circumstances.

When a person with a foreign domicile dies leaving estate in Ireland which comprises movable estate only (i.e. stocks and shares or money on deposit in Ireland), the law of his domicile will apply in determining who should extract the grant of administration in Ireland. If his country of domicile has issued a grant in his estate, the Probate Office will request a sealed and certified copy of that grant (and will, if applicable), as this grant will determine to the satisfaction of the Probate Office who has been *entrusted* with the administration of the deceased's estate in his country of domicile. The Probate Officer will then make an order allowing this person to proceed to extract a grant within this jurisdiction, but limited to the movable estate.

If a grant has not issued from the country of domicile, the Probate Officer will seek an affidavit of law from a legal practitioner who is conversant with the succession laws within the country of domicile and consequently is in a position to advise as to who is the person *entitled* to administer the estate according to the law of the domicile. The Probate Officer will then make the appropriate order.

Where the deceased is possessed of only immovable property within this jurisdiction, the Probate Officer will apply the law of this jurisdiction (i.e. *lex situs*) when issuing a grant of representation and this grant will be limited to immoveable estate.

When a person with a foreign domicile dies leaving estate in Ireland which comprises both moveable and immoveable estate and different persons are entitled under the law of domicile and the *lex situs*, rather than extracting two grants in this jurisdiction with two different administrators it may be more efficient to apply to the Probate Court pursuant to s 27(4) of the Succession Act, 1965 to have the same persons take one grant in the estate.

11.1.4.5 Will in foreign language

Order 79, r 5(10)

'Where a will is in any language other than the Irish or English language the Probate Officer may admit it to proof in terms of a translation thereof in the Irish or English language.'

Background

Two elements are of concern to the Probate Office in these applications:

1. Is the will valid?
2. Does the person applying for the grant have legal entitlement to extract it?

When proving foreign wills the Probate Officer must have regard to s 102 of the Succession Act, 1965, which requires that the will is valid under any one of seven alternative systems of law.

The seven alternative systems of law listed in s 102(a)–(d) are the internal laws of:

1. the place where the testator made the will;
2. the testator's nationality when he made the will;

3. the testator's nationality at death;
4. the testator's domicile when he made the will;
5. the testator's domicile at death;
6. the testator's habitual residence when he made the will;
7. the testator's habitual residence at death.

As part of the process of proving a will in terms of a translation, proof of its validity under one of foregoing systems is required. The context in each case is relevant in terms of the proofs necessary in these applications, and in light of this it is good practice to contact the Probate Officer in advance of making such an application to make an appointment to discuss the estate in question. Please note, however, that the Probate Officer will not enter into correspondence with you on these matters as resources do not allow for this.

While proving the validity of the will under any of the foregoing systems is acceptable, because wills are normally first proved in the country of domicile at death, proof of the validity of the will under the law of that jurisdiction is generally the proof furnished in these situations. A sealed and certified copy of the will and grant which issued from the country of domicile constitutes such proof and the probate authorities in that country must provide such sealed and certified documentation. This is then furnished to the Probate Office as part of the conventional documentation for a grant of representation and the sealed and certified copy of the will is the will which is exhibited in the oath submitted as part of the application. However, when wills are in a foreign language there is a further dimension to be addressed prior to lodgement of the substantive application for a grant. An order must be obtained from the Probate Officer.

Proofs required by the Probate Office when applying to have will proved in terms of a translation

1. Grounding affidavit from applicant setting out all the facts of the estate, exhibiting all relevant documentation and identifying that an order to prove the will in terms of a translation is being sought in the matter.

2. Affidavit of translator, which must be made by an official translator of legal documents, and the credentials of the translator must be indicated in affidavit.

   The specific translator who translated the documents must exhibit:

   (i) either the original will; or
   (ii) a sealed and certified copy of the original will from the notary before which it was made; or
   (iii) if the will has been proved in the country of domicile a sealed and certified copy from the court/office in which it was proved; and
   (iv) he or she must then exhibit the translation of this and the translation of the grant if applicable; and
   (v) any other relevant documents.

   He or she must swear that the translations in question are true and accurate copies of the documents in the foreign language.

3. Affidavit of law from lawyer with expertise in succession law in country of domicile of deceased:

   (a) setting out facts of case, including the domicile at death of the deceased and, where the system of administration of estates in the country of death is different to that in Ireland, it is helpful if the lawyer gives a comprehensive explanation as to the legal process for the administration of an estate in the country in question from the date of death to the completion of the administration;
   (b) exhibiting all relevant documents, i.e. death certificate, original will, or if will made in notary's office a sealed and certified copy by notary of the said will,

or a sealed and certified grant of representation and will if one has issued in country of domicile (please note that where grant has issued, the authority/court from which grant issued must seal and certify the documents);

(c) quoting the piece of legislation which determines the validity of the will;

(d) quoting the legislation which determines the entitlement of the person who is proposing to apply for the grant;

(e) containing an apostille (where applicable).

All of these affidavits and exhibits must first be submitted to the Probate Officer for consideration before any further documents are completed for an application for a grant. If satisfied with the proofs, an order will be made by the Probate Officer allowing the will to be proved in terms of a translation and the substantive application for the grant may be submitted to the Probate Office.

11.1.4.6 Execution of will

Order 79, rr 6 and 7

> '6. If there be no attestation clause to a will or if the attestation clause thereto be insufficient, the Probate Officer shall require an affidavit from at least one of the subscribing witnesses . . .
>
> 7. If on perusing such affidavits as are filed it appears to the Probate Officer, that the statutory provisions applicable were not complied with, the Probate Officer shall refuse probate of the purported will.'

Where the will is not duly executed, the Probate Officer has power to refuse probate of the purported testamentary document. Affidavits of attesting witnesses are submitted and if it is evident from their contents that the formalities pertaining to execution of the will have not been complied with, the Probate Officer will make the order refusing probate in the circumstances.

If evidence is not forthcoming, the matter must be referred to court.

11.1.4.7 Documents referred to in the will

Order 79, rr 13 and 14

> '13. If a will contains a reference to any deed, paper, memorandum, or other document, of such a nature as to raise a question whether it ought, or ought not, to form a constituent part of the will, such deed, paper, memorandum, or other document shall be produced, with a view to ascertaining whether it be entitled to probate; and if not produced, its non-production shall be accounted for.
>
> 14. No deed, paper, memorandum, or other document shall be admitted to probate as part of a will, unless it was in existence at the time when the will was executed, and is therein referred to.'

The question as to whether or not a document etc should be incorporated with and proved as part of the will depends on three proofs:

1. it must be in existence at the time of execution of the will;
2. it must be referred to as being in existence;
3. it must be clearly identified.

An affidavit from a witness covering these aspects should be furnished to the Probate Officer, and if the Probate Officer is satisfied that the requirements are met, he will make an order incorporating the document in question.

11.1.4.8 Grant to attorney in case of physical disability

Order 79, r 23

> '*In the case of a person . . . who in the opinion of the Court or the Probate Officer, is suffering from a severe continuing physical disability, administration, or administration with the will annexed, may be granted to his attorney, acting under a power of attorney.*'

To employ this Rule of Court, an affidavit from the applicant's medical adviser will be required by the Probate Officer, who, on being satisfied that the applicant is of sound mind but is labouring under a physical disability, will then give liberty to the applicant's attorney to proceed with the application for the grant of representation.

When furnishing the medical affidavit, the solicitor should also submit a grounding letter setting out the situation and requesting that the attorney of the applicant be allowed to proceed in the circumstances.

Sample medical affidavit

THE HIGH COURT

PROBATE

In the Estate of

Megan Murtagh   Deceased

I, Anne O'Brien of 10 Drumcondra Road, Dublin, Medical Practitioner aged 18 years and upwards make Oath and say

1. I have been attending Annette Murtagh of 123 Griffith Avenue, Dublin in my professional capacity for upwards of 10 years.

2. The said Annette Murtagh is mentally competent but is suffering from Rheumatoid Arthritis and as a result is severely and permanently physically disabled.

    or alternatively

The said Annette Murtagh is mentally competent but suffers from severe continuing physical disability by reason of old age.

Sworn etc . . .

11.1.4.9 Grant to guardian

Order 79, r 25

> 'In a case where any infant has not a testamentary guardian or a guardian appointed by the Court, or by or under the provisions of the Guardianship of Infants Act, 1964, a guardian shall be assigned by Order of the Court or the Probate Officer. The application for such order shall be grounded on an affidavit showing as nearly as possible the amount of the assets, the age of the infant, and with whom he resides, that the proposed guardian is either the nearest relation of the infant, or that the nearest relation has renounced his right to the guardianship, or is consenting to the assignment of the proposed guardian, and that such proposed guardian is ready to undertake the guardianship. On such application the Court or Probate Officer shall have regard to the expressed wishes of any infant over the age of twelve years.'

This rule is quite comprehensive regarding the requirements to be satisfied before an order can be made. In practice, the applicant prepares a document called a petition, wherein he swears to the facts of the situation as directed under the rule and he then petitions the Probate Officer to assign a proposed individual (the nearest relation of the infant or on his renunciation and consent another person) as guardian of the infant in question.

In situations where there is a guardian in place, such guardian must still apply to the Probate Officer on foot of petition for liberty to proceed with the application. Their assignment as guardian is already in place but their liberty to proceed to extract the grant must be passed by the Probate Officer.

Sample petition to be appointed as guardian of a minor

THE HIGH COURT

PROBATE

In the Estate of

Alan Kelly; Deceased late of
Templeogue Road, Dublin

Petition to be appointed as Guardian of a Minor

The Petition of Maria Murphy, the natural and lawful grandmother of Adam Murphy, a minor, the natural and lawful child and only next of kin of Alan Kelly deceased late of Templeogue Road, Dublin

SHOWETH

1. That the said Alan Kelly died on or about the 27th March 20   intestate a bachelor leaving him surviving the said minor Adam Murphy, his natural and lawful child and only next of kin.

2. That the said minor is aged 7 years having been born on the 2nd day of June 20 and by reason thereof is incapable in law of taking upon himself Letters of Administration of the estate of the said deceased.

3. That there is no testamentary or other lawfully appointed guardian of the said minor.

4. That the said minor lives and resides at 3 Ballyroan Road, Rathfarnham, Dublin with your petitioner who is the natural and lawful grandmother of the said minor.

5. That the lawful mother X of the said minor is not in a position to proceed as guardian herein or that she has renounced her rights to extract the Grant of Administration Intestate upon which renunciation I have marked my name at the time of swearing hereof.

6. That the Petitioner made an Application to the Circuit Court on the 14th June 20 for a Declaration of Parentage under the Status of Children Act, 1987 and on said day an Order was made by said Court declaring that Alan Kelly Deceased late of Templeogue Dublin was the lawful father of Adam Murphy, the said minor. A Copy of said Order is annexed hereto.

7. That the entire estate of the deceased is comprised of both real and personal estate (the details of which are more particularly set out in the inventory annexed hereto) and is valued at in or around €470,000 and for the due administration thereof the petitioner is willing to offer sufficient surety.

8. That the Petitioner has no interest antagonistic to the interest of the said minor.

May it therefore please the Probate Officer to appoint your Petitioner guardian of the said minor and grant her Letters of Administration of the estate of the said deceased for the use and benefit of the said minor and during his minority.

The said Maria Murphy MAKES OATH AND SAYS that the contents of the foregoing Petition are true as therein set forth to the best of her knowledge, information and belief.

Sworn etc

On receipt of this petition, the Probate Officer makes the requisite order under the Rules of the Superior Courts. On collection of said order, the solicitor having carriage of the administration in question is then in a position to lodge his administration papers (which should include a copy of the order) in the Seat Office section of the Probate Office.

Sample title in oath for administrator where guardian appointed of three children for the purpose of extracting grant in the father's estate

> 'INTESTATE a widower and I am the guardian lawfully appointed of his lawful and only children Peter aged 7 Paul aged 5 and Mary aged 3 by order of the Probate Officer dated the   day of   20   limited for the use and benefit of said minors and until they shall attain the age of 18 years or until Peter or Paul having attained said age shall apply for and obtain Administration of his estate.'

Election of guardian

Where the children of a deceased have reached the age of twelve years they must sign a form of election expressing the wish that the petitioner be appointed their guardian for the purpose of extracting the grant of representation for their benefit. Order 79, r 25 provides that the Court or Probate Officer will have '*regard to the expressed wish of any infant over the age of 12 years*'.

This form of election is lodged, together with the petition, with the Probate Officer who will, if satisfied, make an order giving liberty to the proposed guardian to extract the grant, limited for the use and benefit of the minors and during their incapacity.

Sample form of election

In the following sample, the minors, Niall, aged fifteen, and Darragh, aged fourteen years, must elect the petitioner to be their guardian. Kate, aged eight years, will not elect.

THE HIGH COURT

PROBATE

ELECTION BY MINORS OF A GUARDIAN.

In the estate of AB   Whereas AB
                                                 late of Blackhall Place, Dublin 7

late of Blackhall Place, Dublin 7
                                                 deceased, died a widower and intestate,
deceased.   on or about the day
                                                 of   20 , at

leaving his lawful and only children, the said Niall B being a minor of the age of 15 years only, the said Darragh B being also a minor of the age of 14 years only and the said Kate B being of the age of 7 years only.

Now we the said Niall B and Darragh B do hereby make choice of and elect our lawful maternal uncle [as the case may be] and one of our next-of-kin to be our guardian for the purpose of his obtaining letters of administration of the estate of the said deceased, to be granted to him for our use and until one of us shall attain the age of 18 years, and shall apply for and obtain letters of administration of the said estate, or until all of us shall attain the age of 18 years [or for the purpose of renouncing for us, and on our behalf all our right, title, and interest to and in the letters of administration etc, [as the case may be], [add in cases where a solicitor appears for the minors]] and we hereby appoint CD of CD & Co. Solicitors our solicitor to file or cause to be filed this our election for us in the Probate Office [or District Probate Registry at].

Dated

(Signed)

Witness

11.1.4.10 Where next of kin of unsound mind and has no committee

Order 79, r 27

> *'In a case where a person of unsound mind has not a committee appointed by the Court, a grant may issue to such person as the Probate Officer may assign with the consent of the Registrar of Wards of Court. The application for such order shall be grounded on an affidavit of the applicant showing the amount of the assets, the age and residence of the person of unsound mind and his relationship to the applicant together with an affidavit of a medical practitioner relating to the incapacity of such person.'*

When a person entitled to a grant is under a disability rendering him incapable of managing his affairs, it is open to this person's committee to apply for a grant of administration for the use and benefit of said next of kin as referred to at para **3.2.6**. However, there are instances where no committee has been appointed and in these situations it is often possible to avail of this rule without having to make a court application. When the affidavit as required under the rule is prepared, together with the affidavit from his medical practitioner, an application is made by way of letter to the Registrar of Wards of Court for his consent in the matter.

The Wards of Court Office has an interest in the affairs of a person of unsound mind, as one of its functions is to manage the financial affairs of such persons. If no committee has been appointed, the Registrar would have a real concern as to who is being assigned to manage the individual's financial affairs. Hence the reason for his consent. When this consent is furnished to the solicitor having carriage of the matter, an application is then made to the Probate Officer for the requisite order. The Probate Officer will only consider a next of kin of the person of unsound mind as a committee in these circumstances.

Sample title in oath for administrator with will annexed where sole executrix and universal legatee and devisee a person of unsound mind not so found, i.e. not a ward of court

> 'did therein name as sole executrix and universal legatee and devisee Joanne Collins and I am the committee lawfully appointed of the said JC by order of the Probate Officer dated the   day of   20   limited for the use and benefit of the said JC and during her incapacity'.

In situations where a person entitled to the grant is already a ward of court and a committee is already in place, a letter of consent is required from the Registrar of Wards of Court to allow the applicant to proceed. No formal Order of Probate Officer is required in this situation.

11.2 Revocation and Amendment of Grants

Sections 26 and 27 of the Succession Act provide that the High Court has the power to amend or revoke grants of probate (s 26(2)) or administration (s 27(2)). Section 35(1) provides that an application for such a revocation may be made to the Probate Officer or District Probate Registry.

11.2.1 REVOKING AND CANCELLING A GRANT

It is worth noting the difference between 'revoking' a grant and 'revoking and cancelling' a grant. A grant is revoked where a grant issues in an estate and at the time of issue the grant was regular in all respects but subsequent events justify its revocation. A grant is revoked and cancelled because it was fundamentally flawed from the outset (i.e. incorrect pertinent information is submitted to the Probate Office and a grant issues in an estate on foot of this information).

11.2.2 AMENDING A GRANT

A grant can be amended without the need for revocation in cases where a minor alteration to the name of the deceased or the date of death or some other such slight alteration which does not affect title or otherwise go to the root of the grant is necessary. A fuller list of circumstances where the grant can be amended is set out in detail in Mongey, *Probate Practice in a Nutshell*, 3rd edn (2006), Chapter 8.

The procedure is to apply to the Probate Officer (or to the District Probate Registrar if the original grant issued from the District Probate Registry) to amend the grant. The application is supported by affidavit by the grantee, setting out the facts and outlining the reason for the amendment. The original grant is lodged with the application. A precedent affidavit to amend a grant can also be found in Mongey.

11.2.3 REVOKING A GRANT

Where the error is fundamental and affects title to take out the grant, then an application must be made to the Probate Officer to revoke the grant. Circumstances where such revocation prove necessary are set out in detail in Mongey, *Probate Practice in a Nutshell*, 3rd edn (2006), Chapter 8 and include the following:

1. where a grant of administration intestate issues while a valid will of the deceased is in existence;
2. where a later will than that proved has been discovered;
3. where a codicil has been discovered which alters the appointment of the executors in the will;
4. where one of two or more acting executors has become a person of unsound mind;
5. where a grant issues after the death of the grantee.

Where any of these circumstances arises, then an application has to be made to the Probate Officer supported by affidavit.

The affidavit must be made by or with the consent of the original grantee, where possible, and the original grant must be lodged with the application.

However, where a grant has been obtained by fraud, the procedure set out earlier cannot be used; if the validity of the will proved is challenged, the grant can only be revoked by a court order made in an action or on consent, on motion before the Probate Judge.

11.2.4 PRECEDENT APPLICATION TO LEAD TO REVOCATION OF A GRANT

An application for a grant of letters of administration intestate in the estate of Albert Barry, late of 3 Main Street, Adare, County Limerick, who died on 21 January 20   , a bachelor, was made by Ciaran Dolan, solicitor, on behalf of Elaine Farrell, of 154 Ballymore Gardens, Limerick, the lawful sister of the deceased, to the Probate Office on 24 of March, 20   . Tragically, Elaine Farrell died on 4 April, 20   and the grant issued on 11 April, 20   .

THE HIGH COURT

PROBATE

The estate of Albert Barry late of 3 Main Street, Adare, in the County of Limerick deceased.

I, Ciaran Dolan, solicitor, of 115 O'Connell Street, Limerick in the County of Limerick make Oath and say as follows:

1. The above named Albert Barry late of 3 Main Street, Adare, in the County of Limerick died a bachelor without parent on the 21st day of January 20   and Grant of Letters of Administration Intestate issued to Elaine Farrell, lawful sister of the said Albert Barry from

the Probate Office on the 11th day of April 20   . I acted as solicitor in the extraction of the said Grant.

2.   Subsequent to the issue of the said grant it came to my attention that the said Elaine Farrell had died on the 4th day of April 20   and I beg to refer to a certificate of her death attached hereto on which I have signed my name.

3.   I am therefore desirous that the said Grant of Letters of Administration Intestate of the said estate of the said deceased granted to the said Elaine Farrell as aforesaid should be revoked and cancelled.

Ciaran Dolan

Sworn at 115 O'Connell Street, Limerick in the County of Limerick this   day of   20

by the said Ciaran Dolan before me a Commissioner for taking Affidavits/~~Practicing Solicitor~~ and I know the Deponent ~~(or who certifies to his knowledge of the Deponent)~~

...Michael McDonald...
Commissioner for Oaths/~~Practising Solicitor~~

11.3   Practice and Procedure in Respect of Non-Contentious Probate Matters Coming before the High Court

11.3.1   INTRODUCTION

Non-contentious applications heard before the Probate Officer (who is an officer of the court) who would deal with the vast majority of all non-contentious applications have been dealt with in the preceding section.

This section will deal solely with applications before the High Court exercising its non-contentious probate jurisdiction. This jurisdiction is limited to the High Court. There is no equivalent jurisdiction in the Circuit Court or the District Court. The non-contentious probate jurisdiction is heard in the High Court Probate Motion List upon application before a judge of the High Court assigned for that purpose, presently Miss Justice Butler. It is usually heard on a Monday at 10.30 am. Where it is proposed to seek an adjournment at the Monday hearing, the applicant must inform the Assistant Probate Officer in the Probate Office by close of business on the Thursday preceding the court sitting.

The jurisdiction is an originating one. The application brought before the Probate Motion List stands alone; that is, it is not necessary to institute or to have instituted prior proceedings (although one is not precluded from doing so) and the documentation required is either a notice of motion or motion paper grounded upon affidavit or affidavits.

This aspect of probate practice and procedure is described as the non-contentious probate jurisdiction. In one sense it is the court 'arm' of the Probate Office, where matters that would usually be dealt with by the Probate Office, because of some impediment regarding the will itself, require that the High Court adjudicate upon it.

11.3.2   WHERE SUCH APPLICATIONS ARE NECESSARY

There are a number of instances where it is necessary to apply to court in non-contentious cases. The principal instances include the following:

(a)   application for a grant pursuant to s 27(4) of the Succession Act, 1965;

(b) where the original will is lost but a copy of it is available and the proofs are inadequate to allow the Probate Officer to make an order allowing the will to proof in terms of a copy;

(c) where there are rival applications for a grant and neither party has withdrawn their application;

(d) where leave is sought to presume death on information and belief for the purposes of extracting a grant of probate;

(e) to admit a will to proof by presumption as to due execution;

(f) simultaneous deaths invoking the concept of *commorientes* as set out in s 5 of the Succession Act, 1965;

(g) to set aside a caveat (see notes on caveats at Part 3);

(h) applications for a grant for a particular purpose or for a specific portion of an estate;

(i) to prove a will in common form where there are issues regarding capacity.

11.3.3 PRACTICE AND PROCEDURE

Where there are notice parties to the application, then it is made by way of notice of motion. If there are no notice parties and it is an *ex parte* application, then it is made by way of motion paper. In any notice of motion or motion paper in non-contentious probate proceedings it always begins with a series of recitals which essentially contain a short outline of the facts giving rise to the application and will conclude with the terms in which the motion is brought.

Both types of motion require to be grounded upon affidavit or affidavits, and the normal rules applying to affidavits should be complied with.

It is now proposed to highlight a number of these court applications and to examine the practice and procedure relating to each of them in greater detail.

The most common applications before the Probate Judge are undoubtedly applications pursuant to s 27(4) and applications seeking to prove a lost will in terms of a copy. These will be dealt with initially.

11.3.4 SECTION 27(4) OF THE SUCCESSION ACT, 1965

This is an extremely broadly drafted section of the 1965 Act and sets out that a grant of administration may be made:

*'Where by reason of any **special** circumstances it appears to the High Court (or, in a case within the jurisdiction of the Circuit Court, that court) to be necessary or **expedient** to do so, the court may order that administration be granted to such person as it thinks fit.'* [emphasis added]

Accordingly, this subsection gives the court a general discretion to depart from the usual priorities for the extraction of any grant of probate, whether the deceased died testate or intestate.

There may be any number of circumstances that arise in practice whereby the person next entitled to extract a grant may be unable, unwilling, or incapable of extracting such a grant or, in the alternative, the death of the relevant deceased person may have taken place so many years ago that it is now impossible either to trace or to obtain instructions from that relevant person.

Where, as in the words of this Act, it is deemed 'just and expedient', then an application may be made by the person wishing to extract such a grant of probate. Clearly, in such cases the court would require a cogent reason or reasons in order to grant such an order, for example extracting a grant for the purposes of furnishing title to land which is currently registered in the name of a person long since deceased. The Probate Judge requires

380 NON-CONTENTIOUS APPLICATIONS

these reasons to be set out in detail in the affidavits before them. It is therefore necessary, in any of the affidavits before the court, to show reasons for:

(a) the necessity for the grant (why is it expedient to make the Order);

(b) the reason why it is not possible or appropriate for the person legally entitled to the grant to extract same; the special circumstances; and

(c) the proposed applicant being the appropriate person in all the circumstances to extract a grant to the estate of the deceased.

The grounding affidavit of the applicant must set out the necessity for the application before the court. The affidavit evidence before the court must deal with the background facts and circumstances which provide the reason for the court granting liberty to that applicant to extract a grant of administration in the estate of that deceased person. Clearly, much depends on the facts and circumstances of each case, but certainly there must be stated the reason for those entitled to extract a grant being unable, unwilling, or incapable of doing so.

Where there are notice parties there must, of course, be an affidavit of service in respect of those notice parties. That affidavit of service must, in all cases in which it is required, aver to the service of both the notice of motion and affidavit(s) and exhibit the certificate of posting.

If the court is satisfied that the application is necessary, then costs will usually be awarded from the estate.

Where the court makes an order under s 27 of the Succession Act, 1965 it is imperative that practitioners be aware that the person in whose favour the court order is made has no entitlement to administer the estate until a grant is applied for and extracted in the estate in question (s 27(5)).

11.3.5 APPLICATION TO PROVE A WILL IN TERMS OF A COPY

Such an application arises where the original will is lost or mislaid. Until recently, all of these applications had to be made to the court. This practice has now changed and the Probate Officer has authority to make orders allowing such wills to proceed provided she is satisfied as to the proofs produced. Where she is not satisfied, the solicitor will be directed to bring the matter before the court. Please note that the Probate Officer does not advise on draft applications herein.

If the original will is not forthcoming, then the issue that initially arises is as to whether that will has been revoked. If an original will can be traced to the custody of the deceased prior to his death but cannot be located thereafter, there is a presumption that it has been revoked by that deceased by destruction with the intention of destroying it.

Accordingly, the basic proofs required in such an application, which again must be dealt with in the affidavit(s) grounding the application, are as follows:

(a) That the will was duly executed. This is best dealt with by providing affidavits from the attesting witnesses. If they are dead, then their death certificates should be exhibited in an affidavit. If the witnesses are untraceable, then all efforts to trace them should also be set out in an affidavit. Even if the will appears, on its face, to have been properly executed, then such evidence is required with regard to the copy will. Not having an affidavit from the attesting witnesses is not necessarily fatal. The court may well rely upon the presumption *omnia praesumuntur rite esse acta*; that is, that everything necessary is presumed to have been done that ought to have been done.

There should be secondary evidence by someone who recognises the signature(s) of the attesting witnesses and the testator as the names of the person set out on the face of the copy will.

(b) The court must be satisfied that at the time of death the will of the deceased was unrevoked. The rebuttal of the presumption of revocation by destruction necessitates an averment in an affidavit to the effect that someone saw the will, or was aware of its existence, after the testator's death or that the original was held in the office of solicitors who drafted it but that it now cannot be located by that office. If the original will was destroyed *per incuriam*, the full facts and circumstances should also be fully established.

This difficulty arose in the case of *Re Coster* (unreported) 19 January 1978, Supreme Court. Mrs Coster made a will in a solicitor's office. Some two years later, she called into the solicitor's office and took the original will. The firm of solicitors continued to retain a copy. After her death the original will could not be located. What was found among her papers was a pre-printed will form which had not been completed. Because the original will was traceable to Mrs Coster's custody but could not be located thereafter, there was a prima facie presumption that the will had been revoked and could not therefore be proved.

In that case the argument was whether the doctrine of dependent relevant revocation might be applied; that is, on the facts of this case, Mrs Coster had only revoked the will based upon her understanding that her revocation would only take effect and was conditional upon her execution of a new will upon the pre-printed will form found in her papers. Given the fact that condition was not fulfilled, then the argument is that the will was not truly revoked because of the failure of Mrs Coster to comply with the condition precedent, that is, to execute the pre-printed will form.

On the facts of the case, the court held that the doctrine of dependent relevant revocation did not apply (reversing the decision of Gannon J in the High Court), as there was no evidence to connect the taking of the will from the solicitor's office with the purchase of the pre-printed will form. As there was no evidence that the original will was in existence after Mrs Coster's death, the court operated on the presumption that she was deemed to have revoked it. Accordingly, she died intestate.

(c) The next proof is that the copy before the court is an authentic copy of the original will which is now lost. Some judges focus very strongly upon this aspect of the proofs. This would require affidavit evidence from the person who prepared the copy, of the manner of its preparation, or alternatively affidavit evidence from someone who was aware of the contents of the original will and can confirm that it accords in all respects with the copy. If there is no copy of the will on paper but it is retained on disk or word processor, then someone would have to give evidence as to the office practice or the means by which the 'copy' appeared on the disk or in the word processor to enable the court to infer, on the balance of probabilities, that this is a true copy of the original lost will.

(d) As part of the formal proofs, the court may require evidence that the applicant or their solicitors have advertised for the original will in the *Law Society Gazette* or, if the circumstances demand it, the national press. This requirement depends on the context of the case.

(e) Each case depends on its own context but sometimes the court may require that all persons entitled to inherit upon intestacy should be put on notice of the application. If all are in agreement, then the written consent of all such persons should be exhibited to one of the affidavits and it would not, in those circumstances, be necessary to serve those persons with notice of the application. The consents should indicate an awareness of the facts of the application, the implications for the person concerned, and a statement to the effect that they have had an opportunity or been advised to obtain independent legal advice.

(f) The grounding affidavit must, of course, establish the more formal proofs, being the death of the deceased, by exhibiting the death certificate; exhibiting a copy of the will that is sought to be proved; and giving the general facts and circumstances giving rise to the application. The court usually also wishes to be appraised of the approximate size of the deceased's estate and the nature of its assets.

(g) If there are notice parties to the particular application, then an affidavit of service is also required in respect of those persons if they do not appear. This motion is normally a motion for the sitting of the court. If it cannot be served on the notice party's solicitors as they are not on record, then it is as well to have an affidavit of service drafted prior to the hearing of the motion.

(h) The issue of costs is, as always, at the discretion of the court. If it is perceived by the court that the original will has been lost because of an error at the solicitor's office, then the court usually considers it unfair that the estate should be asked to bear the costs of the application. In those circumstances it is likely that the court will make no order as to costs. However, if the court takes the view that the solicitor was blameless, for example if the original will is now lost as a result of a theft from a solicitor's office, then it may well exercise its discretion in awarding costs out of the estate.

The set text of the oath should be amended as follows:

'Marked by me to contain the true copy of the Will marked with the letter "B" referred to in the order of Court dated the   day of   20   .'

The title in the oath for executor will read as follows:

'the sole executor named [amend as appropriate] in said Will proved in terms of the copy Will marked with the letter "B" referred to in the order of Court dated the   day of   2. If the original will is subsequently found it must be lodged in the Probate Office.'

11.3.6 RIVAL APPLICATIONS FOR A GRANT OF ADMINISTRATION

This has already been referred to at para **11.1.4.2**, which outlined the procedure before the Probate Officer. The Succession Act, 1965 and the Rules of the Superior Courts (O 79(6) and O 80(6)) lay down the order of priority of entitlements to administer any estate.

Among those entitled to extract a grant of administration there may be a number of persons who have an equal entitlement. Rival applications are between two persons equally entitled to extract a grant but where neither applicant is willing or, for some reason, able to allow the other to proceed to extract the grant.

While there is jurisdiction within the Probate Office to adjudicate between rival applications, unless both sides agree to be bound by the Probate Office's decision, the matter is usually referred straight to the High Court.

Essentially, such an application usually arises where there is a serious family division and neither applicant is willing to withdraw its application for whatever reason. Accordingly, one of the rival applicants must issue a motion on notice, the notice party being the other applicant. It will be a motion for the sitting of the court.

The grounding affidavit will set out all the facts, matters, and circumstances relevant to the application and why that applicant should be preferred to the other. It is usual that the rival applicant will then put in a replying affidavit countering the allegations made in the grounding affidavit and seeking to assert a separate and independent reason why that applicant should be preferred. Even though this application is within the non-contentious probate jurisdiction, clearly the application is in itself contentious, but nevertheless there is no substantive issue involved. Any substantive issue requires a contentious probate application.

The court would have a discretion as to the award of costs but might, in the interests of attempting to achieve some degree of family harmony, award both sets of costs from the estate, thereby depleting its assets.

11.3.7 LEAVE TO PRESUME DEATH ON INFORMATION AND BELIEF FOR THE PURPOSE OF EXTRACTING A GRANT

This application is entirely different from a *Benjamin* order (from the case of *Re Benjamin* [1902] 1 Ch 723) which is generally made to the Circuit Court. With a *Benjamin* order it is sought to distribute the assets of the estate in the absence of a particular beneficiary to an estate whose whereabouts cannot be located, and accordingly the order is sought to distribute in the absence of that person.

An application for leave to presume death on information and belief is made to the Probate Judge in the High Court and it is utilised in circumstances where the deceased person cannot be located and no positive averment can be made in an affidavit as to the death of that person. Accordingly, no death certificate has issued. In such circumstances, a grant of probate cannot be issued to the estate of that person.

We have all read of unfortunate incidents where persons disappear but surrounding tragic facts and circumstances render it probable that the person has in fact died, although no body has ever been located. In such circumstances the executor cannot extract a grant, as there is no body, no death certificate, and, accordingly therefore, no entitlement to extract such a grant. It is therefore necessary to apply to court that the executor or person entitled on intestacy is entitled to depose and aver to the death of the deceased person upon information and belief for the purposes of obtaining a grant of representation in the estate.

In such circumstances it is not necessary to wait seven years (after seven years there is a presumption at law that the person is dead). The affidavit must contain full and comprehensive details of the circumstances surrounding the disappearance of the deceased person and the reasons, if reasons can be given, why no body has ever been located. Often in such circumstances, it is necessary to include affidavit evidence from the Gardaí or other search and rescue bodies who were involved in searching for the person now presumed to be dead as to the searches that were made and that may be ongoing. The court will also require a reason as to why the grant of representation is now required, for example in order that the pension fund or other life assurance policies might now take effect. If this is the case, then the relevant insurance company should be given notice of the application.

Again, the procedure is by way of motion paper with affidavit or affidavits in support of it. The order will be such that the applicant will be allowed to swear not as of certainty but to the best of their knowledge or belief that the deceased died 'on or around . . .'.

11.3.8 TO ADMIT A WILL TO PROOF BY PRESUMPTION AS TO DUE EXECUTION

In this instance there is some defect in the attestation clause on the face of the will. Indeed, the attestation clause may be missing entirely. While there is the presumption *omnia praesumuntur rite esse acta*, nevertheless without the inclusion of an attestation clause there is no evidence to satisfy the Probate Office as to due execution of the will. There may be other reasons why the Probate Office is reluctant to admit the will for probate on the basis of due execution and accordingly again an application to court is required by way of motion paper and grounding affidavit.

In such an instance it is necessary to put all available evidence before the court in order that it might establish, on the balance of probabilities, whether the will has been duly executed.

It is a prerequisite of s 78 of the Succession Act, 1965 that, in order to be valid, a will must be validly executed. That requires the following:

> '*To be valid a will shall be in writing and be executed in accordance with the following rules:*
>
> *(1) It shall be signed at the foot or end thereof by the Testator or by some person in his presence and by his direction.*
>
> *(2) Such signature shall be made or acknowledged by the Testator in the presence of each of two or more witnesses, present at the same time, and each witness shall attest by his signature the signature of the Testator in the presence of the Testator, but no form of attestation shall be necessary nor shall it be necessary for the witnesses to sign in the presence of each other.*'

Section 78 then goes on to explore these two paragraphs in greater detail but, again, if the Probate Office has sufficient doubt that the requirements just noted have not been complied with, it will refer the matter to court.

In the absence of an attestation clause, the court will require evidence of due execution. Accordingly, the best evidence available, preferably from the attesting witnesses, should be put forward. The absence of an attestation clause may, in certain circumstances, prove fatal to the validity of a will. In the case of *Clarke v Earley* [1980] IR 223, both attesting witnesses were dead. However, the wife of one of the attesting witnesses was able to verify the signature of the late husband as one of the attesting witnesses and that of the other attesting witness as a near neighbour who had known the deceased all his life. Yet the Supreme Court held that in the absence of any evidence to support or verify that the signature of the testator was in fact genuine, there was insufficient evidence to justify a grant of administration with the will annexed.

While this case has been the subject of some criticism subsequently, it is nevertheless a reminder of the consequences that can occur where an attestation clause is omitted from a will.

11.3.9 SIMULTANEOUS DEATHS—SECTION 5 OF THE SUCCESSION ACT, 1965

Students should read the notes on s 5 at para **9.7**.

If the title to the grant is affected, then apply by motion granted on affidavit to the Probate Judge, setting out all the circumstances of the deaths of the persons concerned. If the judge is satisfied that the order of deaths cannot be established, he will declare the persons concerned to have died simultaneously, pursuant to s 5 of the Succession Act.

In a case before the non-contentious probate list, *Re Kennedy* (unreported) 31 January 2000, High Court, the court was, in very unfortunate circumstances, called upon to determine whether one of the persons in fact survived the other or whether the doctrine of *commorientes*—that is, the presumption of simultaneous deaths in cases of uncertainty— applied on the facts of the case.

The facts of the case were that the two deceased persons, a husband and wife, had both been dining at a restaurant and had, when leaving the restaurant and driving home, unfortunately taken a wrong turn; their car drove over a pier and plunged into the water below. The medical evidence was that the wife had died from drowning but that the husband had in fact sustained a heart attack. It was suggested in the medical report that the husband's death from a heart attack may well have been swifter and faster than the wife's death from drowning. In the absence of any agreement between the various beneficiaries, an application was brought before the court to determine whether s 5 applied or whether the husband had in fact predeceased his wife.

Clearly, if one predeceases the other, then this has implications with regard to legal right share and the rights accruing to various beneficiaries, rather than a simultaneous death in which each is deemed to have died together and accordingly neither husband nor wife will take from the estate of the other.

On the facts of the case, Kearns J stated that he would require cogent evidence in applying or seeking to apply who had predeceased the other. While there was a suggestion in the medical reports that one death may have been faster than another, on the basis of the facts before him, the learned judge held that as an element of uncertainty remained, this was an instance of *commorientes*, and accordingly declared that both died simultaneously and that their estates would therefore be distributed accordingly.

11.3.10 APPLICATIONS FOR A GRANT LIMITED FOR A PARTICULAR PURPOSE OR TO A PARTICULAR PART OF THE ESTATE

Examples of such applications are as follows:

(a) On occasion it may not be possible to extract what is termed a full grant in an estate but the estate needs to be safeguarded and protected in the interim. In such circumstances it is appropriate for an application to be made to the Probate Court for a grant *ad colligenda bona*. The person who extracts the *ad colligenda bona* grant has power to preserve and safekeep the estate pending further directions of the court.

Again, the procedure is by way of motion and affidavit, with the relevant facts and circumstances being clearly set out in the grounding affidavit or affidavits.

Sample title in oath for administrator where next of kin cannot be found and a grant is required urgently, to protect the assets of the estate

'The person appointed by order of the Court dated the   day of   20   pursuant to Section 27(4) of the Succession Act to be the Administrator of the estate limited for the purpose of collecting and preserving but not distributing the estate of the deceased.'

(b) Application for an *ad litem* grant to substantiate proceedings in some other court.

Sample title in oath for administrator where grant is being applied for by a nominated practitioner for the purpose of defending proceedings which your client intends instituting against the estate, arising out of a road accident in which the deceased was killed and your client was injured; as a result of the negligence of the deceased

'The person appointed by order of the Court dated the day of   20 pursuant to Section 27(4) of the Succession Act, 1965 to be the Administrator of the estate limited for the purpose of defending proceedings to be instituted against the estate by John Taylor of   arising out of a road accident which occurred on the   day of   20   at Church Street, Sligo, County Sligo.'

Applications for *ad litem* grants are made pursuant to s 27(4) and (1) of the Succession Act. Once the order is made by the court, it is still necessary to apply to the Probate Office for a grant as the proposed legal personal representative is not constituted as personal representative until such time as the grant issues.

Section 27(5) clarifies this point:

'(5) On administration being granted, no person shall be or become entitled without a grant to administer any estate to which that administration relates.'

Applications for such grants no longer require the filing of an Inland Revenue affidavit. As the legal personal representative in these situations has limited powers which do not include meeting tax obligations on behalf of the estate, the requirement has been dispensed with in the circumstances.

11.4 Caveats

11.4.1 WHAT IS A CAVEAT?

Section 38 of the Succession Act provides:

'*A Caveat against a grant may be entered in the Probate Office or in any district probate registry.*'

A caveat is a formal warning that nothing is to be done in relation to a grant of representation without prior notice being given to the person lodging the caveat, enabling him to appear and object to the grant.

The Probate Officer in recent years will only accept a caveat where the person lodging the caveat can prove a beneficial interest in the estate. Caveats are no longer accepted from creditors.

11.4.2 WHO MAY LODGE A CAVEAT AND WHAT IS ITS EFFECT?

Any person who wants to prevent the issuing of a grant can enter a caveat in the Probate Office. A caveat must be entered as a preliminary to the issue of a non-contentious citation. A plaintiff must enter a caveat as a preliminary step before issuing a writ or commencing proceedings, but commencement of an appropriate action, whether or not a caveat has been entered, operates to prevent the issuing of a grant just like a caveat.

The effect of entering a caveat is to place a notice on the records of the court that nothing is to be done in the estate without reference to the caveator. No grant will issue if the Registrar has knowledge of a live caveat (see para **11.4.5**).

11.4.3 WHY LODGE A CAVEAT?

There are many reasons for a person wishing to lodge a caveat. However, the following are the primary reasons for doing so:

1. to give the caveator time to make enquiries and to obtain information to determine whether there are grounds for opposing a grant—in essence it is a holding action;
2. to give the caveator an opportunity to raise any questions arising in respect of the grant on motion before the court;
3. it is a preliminary step to the commencement of an action between the caveator and the person warning the caveat (see para **11.5**)—the warning and the appearance disclosing the respective interests of the parties.

11.4.4 HOW MAY A CAVEAT BE LODGED?

A caveat may be entered by any person having an interest in the estate or by his solicitor, by attending and completing the relevant form in the caveat book in the Probate Office.

11.4.5 HOW LONG DOES A CAVEAT LAST?

A caveat ceases to be effective at the end of six months from the date of entry provided it has not been warned. The caveat in force at the commencement of proceedings remains in force until the person shown to be entitled by the decision of the court applies for a grant. See also s 38 of the Succession Act.

Once a caveat has been lodged in respect of any particular estate, then a grant of probate cannot be extracted to that estate unless the caveat expires, which happens automatically after six months (unless it is renewed within this period), is withdrawn by the caveator, or is set aside by the Probate Judge. (Once a court order proves a will in solemn form of law, no caveat can be entered against it.)

However, where a caveat is lodged, there is no procedure or rule obliging the practitioner to advise his opposite number of such lodgement. Notwithstanding the absence of such a rule, the Probate and Taxation Committee recommends that, subject to the consent of the client, the solicitor lodging the caveat should, as a matter of good practice and professional courtesy, inform his colleague of that fact.

Let us assume that at some point a person entitled to prove a will learns that a caveat has been lodged. If the view is taken that the caveator has serious grounds to challenge the will, then the person entitled to prove that will may consider instituting proceedings immediately to prove the will in solemn form of law. Alternatively, that person can either:

(i) warn the caveator (see para **11.5**); or
(ii) wait until the caveat expires.

11.5 Warnings

11.5.1 WHAT IS A WARNING AND WHEN IS IT APPROPRIATE TO USE IT?

Where a doubt exists as to the *locus standi* of the caveator and/or his grounds for disputing the will's validity, then a warning to that caveator may be issued (from the Probate Office). This warning calls upon the caveator to enter an appearance in the Probate Office within fourteen days.

The warning is issued from the Probate Office and the signature of the Probate Officer added. The warning in the prescribed form must state the interest of the person at whose instance it is to issue, and, if he claims under the will, the date of the will.

It would also give the address of the caveator for service. The address for service must be within this jurisdiction.

It must be served on the caveator by leaving the original and true copy thereof at the address given in the caveat as an address for service or by sending it to the caveator at that address by prepaid registered post.

One would adopt this course where the caveator's interest is known, and it is clear that no agreement can be reached between the parties. If there is a possibility that an agreement may be reached, the obvious thing to do is to attempt to arrange a meeting, rather than proceed down the road of caveats and warnings.

A caveat may be warned only in the Probate Office in Dublin: O 79, r 47 of the Superior Courts Rules.

11.5.2 WHAT IS THE EFFECT OF THE WARNING?

It calls upon the caveator within fourteen days of service by him to enter an appearance setting forth his interest in the estate.

If a period of fourteen days allowed after the service of warning has expired, and no appearance has been entered, and no contentious proceedings have been issued, the caveat can be removed at the instance of the person warning. The warning party files an affidavit of service of the warning to caveat on the caveator in the Probate Office and obtains a certificate of no appearance to warning (side-bar order) from the Probate Officer setting aside the caveat. Then the application to extract a grant to the estate of the deceased can proceed in the normal way.

11.5.3 APPEARANCE TO WARNING

If the caveator after the service of the warning wishes to proceed, then he or his solicitor must enter an appearance to the warning in the Probate Office within fourteen days of service of the warning upon him.

An appearance will not be accepted unless the caveator can show a good cause of action. Obviously, this is not something to be undertaken lightly. The appearance must give the address for notice for service and a copy must be delivered or sent by the caveator to the person warning.

Given the cost of proceedings, which generally come out of the estate, it is in everyone's best interests to attempt to settle the issues before this occurs.

If there is no movement to settle the dispute, the next step would be the issue, by either side, of a writ to commence an action in the High Court. The caveator then has a further choice. He can either withdraw by executing a consent form with the warning parties (see Mongey, *Probate Practice in a Nutshell*, 3rd edn (2006), p 112) or proceed.

However, if an appearance is entered to the caveat then the person entitled to extract a grant to the will has two choices. Again, as set out earlier, he can institute proceedings seeking to prove the will in solemn form of law or, alternatively, if the view was taken that the caveator lacked sufficient *locus standi* and/or was simply being vexatious or malicious, or that the caveat has been incorrectly applied for, then application should be made to have that caveat set aside.

The caveator should be initially requested to remove the caveat by letter. It is often the case that prior to instituting proceedings pursuant to the provisions of s 117 of the Succession Act, 1965, the applicant issues a caveat. This is procedurally incorrect as it precludes a grant being issued, which is a prerequisite to any proceedings being issued pursuant to the provisions of s 117. However, some people do perhaps use it to give them 'breathing space' while they seek advice or determine what steps they should take, where there may be a potential difficulty with the will or potential grounds for challenging its validity.

If the caveator refuses, for whatever reason, to remove the caveat, then an application is brought by way of motion on notice, grounded on affidavit, in the non-contentious probate list.

An example of this is the case of *Re Nevin* (unreported) 13 March 1997, High Court.

In that case the mother of the deceased, Thomas Nevin, wished to prevent his widow, Catherine Nevin, from extracting a grant to the estate of her late husband (whom Catherine Nevin was suspected of murdering) and had lodged a caveat for that purpose. The caveat had not been withdrawn (no warning to caveat was issued in this case).

The deceased's widow applied to the court by notice of motion, before the then Probate Judge, the late Shanley J, to have the caveat set aside. The widow's grounding affidavit alleged that to allow the caveat to remain in force would be an abuse of the process of the court. The responding affidavit for the caveator alleged that the widow was under investigation by the police authorities, as a suspect for the murder. The court held that it had:

> 'No function in adjudicating in any allegation of a criminal kind, and it will only assume the jurisdiction to preclude a person from a share in a deceased's estate where the matters set out in Section 120(1) are established in evidence. It is therefore worthwhile re-emphasising that the decision of this Court should not be seen as one which is grounded upon a preference for one account of fact over the other; rather it is a decision based solely on the Caveator's interest (as mother of the deceased) in absence of want of bona fides.'

In his judgment, the judge confirmed the inherent jurisdiction of the court to set aside any caveat that it determines has been lodged vexatiously or where the caveator has insufficient *locus standi*. In this instance, the judge confirmed the *locus standi* of the deceased's mother. The court in that instance did not set aside the caveat, but directed that if the applicant applied to the court a grant of administration would issue to her provided it was limited to the collecting in and preserving of assets, but not their distribution (essentially a grant *ad colligenda bona*).

11.6 Citations

11.6.1 WHAT IS A CITATION?

A citation is a document issued at the instance of a person with an interest in the estate, calling upon another person with priority to extract the grant.

A person who has a beneficial interest in the estate or a creditor may cite all persons having a prior right to take the grant if those persons are unwilling to renounce their right in his favour.

11.6.2 WHAT IS THE VALUE OF A CITATION?

If there was no procedure for issuing citations, the administration of estates would be suspended for inordinate lengths of time, or indeed would remain for years unadministered. In essence, an executor or administrator is under no compulsion in law to apply for a grant, as there is no legal obligation to apply for a grant or liability for a failure or refusal to do so. See *Re Stevens* [1897] 1 Ch 422.

11.6.3 WHY ISSUE A CITATION?

An application for a grant may have to be preceded by an issue of a citation. All citations issue from the Probate Office.

This would be applicable in the following types of cases:

1. when the persons who have a right to take out the grant delay or simply decline to apply for a grant and refuse to renounce their rights; or
2. where such a person has knowledge of the existence of the purported testamentary document but wishes to proceed in reliance on an earlier will or on intestacy.

11.6.4 PROCEDURAL STEPS

The procedural steps to be taken when issuing a citation are listed in Mongey, *Probate Practice in a Nutshell*, 3rd edn (2006), Chapter 9, pp 53 and 54. In essence, in order to obtain the citation to call upon the executor to prove the will, the applicant must swear an affidavit setting out the necessary matters. See O 79, rr 52–57 of the Rules of the Superior Courts for the exact procedure to follow in such an instance, and see also Brady, *Succession Law in Ireland*, 2nd edn (1995), pp 278 and 279.

11.6.5 EXAMPLE OF A CITATION IN OPERATION

Facts: your client Patrick Moroney attends your office one day and informs you that his father died on 12 August 2004, intestate. He tells you that his father was married twice and that his first wife (Patrick Moroney's mother) died on 17 August 1984. He tells you that his father subsequently remarried and that the second wife (your client's stepmother) has not extracted a grant of representation. He further tells you that there were no children of the second marriage. He asks your advice on how to obtain his share of his father's estate.

11.6.5.1 What is the problem?

Your client is not the person entitled to take out the grant. His father's second wife is first entitled and has priority. She is declining to do so. Therefore, your client cannot obtain his share of the estate.

11.6.5.2 Procedure

Obviously, you first try to negotiate with the widow, either directly or through her solicitors. If she fails to extract a grant, then this would be the perfect situation in which to issue a citation. There follows an example of the affidavit to be sworn in an intestate situation.

This example is easily adapted to any situation. The concept is as follows:

1. Establish the facts.
2. Give the client's interests.
3. List all and every effort to contact the person entitled, to get him to act.
4. Show failure of same.
5. Ask for the issue of the citation.

11.6.5.3 Sample affidavit

THE HIGH COURT

PROBATE

In the estate of James Moroney late of Elfin in the County of Roscommon deceased.

I, Patrick Moroney of Dublin Road, Elfin, in the County of Roscommon, Auctioneer make oath and say as follows:

1. The above named James Moroney late of Elfin in the County of Roscommon died on the 12th day of August 2004 intestate, a married man, leaving him surviving his wife Mary Moroney of Elfin of aforesaid. The said James Moroney was married twice. I am his only child by his first marriage. My mother died on the 17th day of August 1984 and my father married the said Mary Moroney on the 1st day of June 2002. There is no issue of the said second marriage.
2. By virtue of the provisions of Section 67 Subsection 2 of the Succession Act, 1965 I believe that I am entitled to one-third of the estate of the said James Moroney, the said Mary Moroney being entitled to other two-thirds.
3. The said Mary Moroney has neglected or refused to extract a grant of Letters of Administration (Intestate) to the estate of the said James Moroney, as a result of which I have been unable to obtain my said share.

4. By letters dated the 28th day of August 20 , the 13th day of September 20 and the 10th day of October 20 my solicitors Messrs O'Connor & Co have requested the said Mary Moroney to extract a grant of Representation to the estate of the said James Moroney. I beg to refer to copies of the said letters when produced. No reply has been received to any of the said letters.

5. I am desired therefore that a Citation should be issued against the said Mary Moroney to accept or refuse letters of administration of the estate of the said James Moroney.

Sworn etc Patrick Moroney

11.7 Rival Applications

Paradoxically, an application to decide between two rival applicants equally entitled to a grant of representation is made under the Non-Contentious High Court Probate procedure, even though there may be quite a degree of contention in the application. This is because there is no issue in relation to the validity of the will or the entitlement to extract the grant.

11.7.1 PROCEDURE FOR OBTAINING TWENTY-ONE-DAY ORDER FROM PROBATE OFFICER—ORDER 79, RULE 5(3)

11.7.1.1 General

The rule only applies to rival applicants 'entitled to administration'. It does not apply where one or both parties are attempting to prove wills. If one applicant applies for probate of a will and the other is disputing the validity of same and files an application for a grant of administration, O 79, r 3 does *not* apply and the rival applicants must apply to court to resolve the dispute. In certain instances the dispute may be resolved by application or motion to the Probate Judge. Where the matter cannot be resolved by the Probate Judge, probate actions may be commenced by plenary summons in the High Court and Testamentary Civil Bill in the Circuit Court.

11.7.1.2 Procedure

1. One rival applicant (e.g. a brother) files an affidavit setting out the facts and petitions the Probate Officer to make a twenty-one-day order.

2. The Probate Officer no longer hears the application for a twenty-one-day order but makes the order which is then given to the solicitor who applied for the Order for the purpose of service on the rival applicants solicitor.

3. The solicitor waits twenty-one days from the service of the order and enquires in the Rules Office as to whether an objection in writing to his order has been filed.

5. If no objection in writing has been filed within the twenty-one days from the service of the order, the Probate Officer will, on production of an affidavit of service of the order, make a second order setting aside the prior application.

6. If an objection in writing, stating even simply 'I object', is filed within the twenty-one days, the Probate Officer will refuse to make the second order. The Rules of Court do not require the Probate Officer to consider the merits or demerits of the grounds of objection, simply the fact of the objection.

7. Where an objection is filed, an application should be made to the court. If a solicitor believes that the rival applicant is determined to dispute the matter

in issue, he should apply to court directly at the outset, bypassing the procedure described.

11.8 Precedent Testamentary Pleadings

(i) Caveat.

(ii) Warning to caveat.

(iii) Appearance to warning.

(iv) Citation.

(v) Plenary summons.

(vi) Statement of claim.

(vii) Defence.

(viii) Reply.

(ix) Notice of motion at sitting of court.

11.8.1 CAVEAT

THE HIGH COURT

PROBATE

The Principal Probate Office, Phoenix House, Dublin 7

In the Estate of Karen Woodwright
late of 4 Clare Drive, Glasnevin **in the County of** City of Dublin **(occupation) Widow Deceased.**

Let nothing be done in the Estate of Karen Woodwright

Late of 4 Clare Drive, Glasnevin in the County of City of Dublin (occupation) Widow

who died on the 14th day of January 20

at 4 Clare Drive, Glasnevin

Unknown to me   Kevin Heffernan & Co.

Solicitors for Richard Woodwright

Of 6 Beech Avenue, Ranelagh in the County of City of Dublin having interest as a brother of the deceased

Dated this 12th day of June 20

Signed *Kevin Heffernan & Co*
Solicitors
8 Quinns Road
Bray, County Wicklow

To: The Probate Office, Phoenix House, Dublin 7

Sir,

I send you above as Notice of Caveat, entered on the said date here, which please enter accordingly in your books.

11.8.2 WARNING TO CAVEAT

THE HIGH COURT

PROBATE

The Principal Probate Office, Phoenix House, Dublin 7

In the Estate of Karen Woodwright
late of 4 Clare Drive, Glasnevin **in the County of** City of Dublin **(occupation)** Widow **Deceased.**

To Mr Kevin Heffernan of 8 Quinns Road, Bray in the County of Wicklow Solicitor for Richard Woodwright Of 6 Beech Avenue, Ranelagh in the County of City of Dublin

You are hereby WARNED, within Fourteen Days after the Service of this Warning upon you, inclusive of the day of such Service to enter an appearance for Richard Woodwright

in the Probate Office, the Caveat entered by you in the Estate of Karen Woodwright late of 4 Clare Drive, Glasnevin in the County of City of Dublin (occupation) Widow Deceased,

who died at 4 Clare Drive, Glasnevin in the County of City of Dublin on the 14th day of January 20
and set forth your (or your said Client's) interest; and take Notice that in default of you so doing the said Caveat will cease to have any effect.

Signed..
Probate Officer

Dated this 20th day of August 20

Issued at the instance of * Messrs Carty & Co. Solicitors

Address 4 Parnell Road in the County of City of Dublin

Solicitor for Francis Ryan (Otherwise Referred in Will of Deceased as Francis Mary Ryan)

* Client's interest, and if he claims under a Will, or codicil or otherwise, give date and description of Document, if any and give an address for service.

Fee on issuing this Warning is, €6.00

Indorsement of Service:
This warning was served by Ruairi Murphy Solicitor of 24 Quinns Road, Bray, County Wicklow, by attending at the said office of Kevin Heffernan and handing a true copy of the within Caveat to him on the 28th day of August 20 .

11.8.3 APPEARANCE TO A WARNING

THE HIGH COURT

PROBATE

The Principal Probate Office, Phoenix House, Dublin 7

In the Estate of Karen Woodwright
late of 4 Clare Drive, Glasnevin **in the County of** City of Dublin **(occupation)** Widow **Deceased.**

I Kevin Heffernan appear for Richard Woodwright being the brother, and one of the next-of-kin of the said Karen Woodwright deceased

Dated this 2nd Day of September 20

(Signed) *Kevin Heffernan*

Solicitor for Richard Woodwright

8 Quinns Road, Bray, in the County of Wicklow

TO:
The Probate Office
Phoenix House,
Phoenix Street,
Smithfield, Dublin 7

11.8.4 CITATION TO INTRODUCE AND DEPOSIT A WILL, AND TO ACCEPT OR REFUSE PROBATE THEREOF

THE HIGH COURT
PROBATE
The Principal Probate Office, Phoenix House, Dublin 7

To Richard O'Brien
of 14 Shrewsbury Mews, Blackrock, in the County of Dublin

Whereas, it appears by an affidavit of Jonathan Greenwood of 28 Blackhall Villas, in the County of City of Dublin filed in the Probate Office on the 3rd day of January 20 , that you are the executor named in the last will of Colin Greenwood late of Jobsworthtown, County Tipperary who died on or about the 13th day of May 20 , and that the said Jonathan Greenwood the residuary legatee of said deceased desires to have said will proved.

NOW THIS IS TO COMMAND YOU, that within fourteen days after service hereof on you, inclusive of the day of such service, you appear in the Probate Office personally, or by your solicitor, and introduce and deposit in the Probate Office said will, and accept the execution thereof, and in case you refuse same, show cause, if any, why letters of administration of the estate of said deceased with said will annexed, should not be granted to the said Jonathan Greenwood

Dated 2nd March 20
(Signed)

Probate Officer
Solicitor for said Jonathan Greenwood
44 Oxford Road
Dublin 4

11.8.5 PLENARY SUMMONS

20   Record No **345 P**

THE HIGH COURT

PLENARY SUMMONS

In The Estate of Stephen Morrissey Deceased

BETWEEN/

Jonathan Maher

PLAINTIFF

and

Michelle Joyce

DEFENDANT

To the defendant Michelle Joyce

of Bohola
in the County of Mayo

This Plenary Summons is to require that within eight days after the service thereof upon you (exclusive of the day of such service) you in person or by Solicitor do enter an Appearance in the Central Office, Four Courts, Dublin 7, in the above action; and TAKE NOTICE that in default of your so doing, the Plaintiff may proceed therein and Judgment may be given in your absence.

By Order—The Hon Frank Clarke,

Chief Justice of Ireland, theday of

Two Thousand and

N.B.—This Summons is to be served within **TWELVE** calendar months from the date hereof, and if renewed within **SIX** calendar months from the date of the last renewal, including the day of such date and not afterwards.

The defendant may appear hereto by entering an appearance either personally or by solicitor at the Central Office, Four Courts, Dublin 7.

GENERAL ENDORSEMENT OF CLAIM

The Plaintiff's claim is

The Plaintiff is a sole executor named in the last Will of Stephen Morrissey late of Ballyduff in the County of Cork, who died on the third Day of March 20 , the said Will being dated the second day of September 20 .

The Plaintiff claims that the Court shall pronounce for the force and validity if the said Will in solemn form of law.

The defendant is sued as the lawful sister of the deceased and because she has entered a caveat.

Andrew Joyce Barrister at Law

This Summons was issued by Murphy & Co. Solicitors

whose registered place of business is at 24/26 Upper Ormond Quay, Dublin 7

Solicitor for the plaintiff who resides at Ballyduff, County Cork

and is

This summons was served by me at

on the defendant

on the   day of   20

Indorsed the   day of   20

Signed ....
Address ....

THE HIGH COURT

In The Estate of Stephen Morrissey Deceased

BETWEEN\

Jonathan Maher

PLAINTIFF

and

Michelle Joyce

DEFENDANT

PLENARY SUMMONS

11.8.6 STATEMENT OF CLAIM

20   Record No **345 P**

THE HIGH COURT

In The Estate of Stephen Morrissey Deceased

BETWEEN/

Jonathan Maher

PLAINTIFF

and

Michelle Joyce

DEFENDANT

STATEMENT OF CLAIM

Delivered the 10th Day of January 20 by Murphy & Company

Solicitors for the Plaintiff or 24/26 Upper Ormond Quay, Dublin.

1. Stephen Morrissey late of Ballyduff, Co. Cork made his last Will on the second day of September 20 in which he appointed the Plaintiff as his sole executor.
2. The deceased died on the third day of March 20 without having revoked his said Will.
3. The deceased died a bachelor without parent or brother or child of any predeceased brother or sister and left him surviving as his lawful only sister, Michelle Joyce, the defendant.
4. The defendant has entered a caveat in the estate of the deceased.
5. The plaintiff claims that the courts shall pronounce for the force of validity of the said Will in solemn form of law.

Andrew Joyce BL

11.8.7 DEFENCE

20   Record No **345 P**

THE HIGH COURT

In The Estate of Stephen Morrissey Deceased

BETWEEN/

Jonathan Maher

PLAINTIFF

and

Michelle Joyce

DEFENDANT

DEFENCE

Delivered the 20th Day of February 20 by Bushe & Company of 3 Park Street Dublin, Solicitors for the defendant.

1. The alleged Will dated the second day of September 20 of the deceased was not executed in accordance with the provisions of the Succession Act.
2. The deceased at the time the alleged Will purports to have been executed was not of sound disposing mind.

   At the time the deceased executed the said Will he was eighty-seven years of age and was suffering from senile dementia. He had been confined to the Happy Home,

Glasnevin, Dublin, which is a home for geriatrics. At the time he executed the alleged Will he was in such a condition of mind and memory as to be unable to understand the nature of the Act and its effects, the extent of the property which he was disposing, or to comprehend and appreciate the claims to which he ought to give effect.

3. The deceased at the time of execution of the alleged Will did not know and approve the contents thereof.

    The deceased never gave any instructions for the alleged Will, and the said alleged Will was not read over or properly explained to him, nor did he read it himself before it was executed, nor was he capable of comprehending or appreciating its provisions and effect for the causes pleaded in paragraph two of this defence.

4. The execution of the said alleged Will was procured by the undue influence of the plaintiff.

    The plaintiff called from time to time to the said Happy Home and brought him to his own home. The said alleged Will was executed in the home of the plaintiff on one of those occasions. The plaintiff so took advantage of the extreme old age of the deceased and of his weak state of mind that he persuaded the deceased that he was the only person to whom the deceased owed a duty, and the plaintiff himself drafted the said alleged Will.

5. The defendant claims that the court shall pronounce against the said alleged Will.

    Jonathan Rogan, Barrister at Law

11.8.8 REPLY

20   Record No **345 P**

THE HIGH COURT

In The Estate of Stephen Morrissey Deceased

BETWEEN/

Jonathan Maher

PLAINTIFF

and

Michelle Joyce

DEFENDANT

REPLY

Delivered the 14th Day of March 20   by Murphy & Company
Solicitors for the Plaintiff, 24/26 Upper Ormond Quay, Dublin.

1. The plaintiff joins issue with the defendant upon his defence save in so far as it contains, or implies, admission.
2. The said Will of the deceased dated the second day of September 20 was duly executed according to the provisions of the Succession Act.
3. The deceased at the time of the execution of the said Will was of sound disposing mind and the plaintiff denies each and every allegation contained in paragraph two of the said defence.
4. The deceased at the time of the execution of the said Will knew and approved of the contents thereof and he denies each and every allegation contained in paragraph three of the said defence.
5. The plaintiff says that the execution of the said Will was not procured by the undue influence of the plaintiff or by anyone acting on his behalf, as alleged or at all.
6. The plaintiff denies each and every allegation contained in the said defence as if the same were herein expressly set out and traversed seriatim.

Andrew Joyce, Barrister at Law

11.8.9 NOTICE OF MOTION

THE HIGH COURT

PROBATE

In the matter of the estate of Mary McCarthy deceased and in the matter of an application by Patrick O'Shea

NOTICE OF MOTION

WHEREAS Mary McCarthy late of Moate in the county of Westmeath died on the eighteenth day of June 20   having made her last Will on the eighth day of September 20   in which she named the applicant, Patrick O'Shea as her sole executor.

AND WHEREAS the said Will is lost or mislaid and is not now forthcoming.

TAKE NOTICE that Counsel on behalf of the applicant will apply to the Honourable Court sitting at the Four Courts in Dublin on Monday the thirtieth day of July 20   at 11.00 in the fore noon at the sitting of the court for an order admitting the said Will to proof in terms of a copy thereof or such further or other order as to the Honourable Court seems proper and for an order for costs.

WHICH APPLICATION will be grounded on the affidavit of Patrick Nugent and Eileen O'Sullivan, the exhibits, and other documents they will refer to, the nature of the case and the reasons to be offered.

Dated the first day of June 20   .

Signed Peter Moran & Company Solicitors for Patrick O'Shea.

To: Terence McCarthy
McCormack Street,
Athlone,
CO WESTMEATH

11.9 Appendices

- **A** Probate Officer's Guidelines for preparation of Wills on Word Processors.
- **B** Notes on Time Limits in both the Succession Act, 1965, as amended, and O 79 of the Rules of the Superior Courts.
- **C** Probate Office fees:
    - (i) Probate Fees on Grant—Seat Office;
    - (ii) General and Rules Office fees;
    - (iii) Probate Officer's fees.
- **D** Structure of the Probate Office.

11.9.1 APPENDIX A: PREPARATION OF WILLS ON WORD PROCESSORS

The following guidelines are suggested for the preparation of wills by word processors, IBM personal computers, laser printers, and so forth. These guidelines have been agreed with the Law Society's Technology Committee.

Wills prepared on single sheets, with writing on one side only, should be bound in the traditional methods. These include:

- (a) ribbon or tape;
- (b) staples covered over by heavy adhesive material;
- (c) brass eyelets.

Each page containing written material should be numbered in the following manner. In the case of a will consisting of ten separate sheets with writing on one side of each sheet, each written page should be numbered 'page 1 of 10', 'page 2 of 10', and so forth.

The suggested attestation clause would read as follows:

> *'Signed and acknowledged by the above-named testator as and for his last will and testament in the presence of us both present at the same time who in his presence at his request and in the presence of each other have hereunto subscribed our names as witnesses, this will having been printed on the front side only of the foregoing ten sheets of A4 paper.'*

The shortened form of attestation clause may, of course, be used:

> *'Signed by the testator in the presence of us and signed by us in the presence of the testator.'*

The statement regarding the content of the will must, of course, be added.

11.9.2 APPENDIX B: TIME LIMITS

The Succession Act, 1965

1. **Special grants—s 31—grants** durante absentia

   Twelve months after the death of the deceased

   Where twelve months have elapsed since the death of the deceased and the sole acting legal personal representative (LPR) is residing outside the jurisdiction, application may be made to the court under s 31 to appoint a special administrator to administer the estate during his absence. The grant will determine automatically on the return of the original LPR only if it is so limited. Otherwise, it does not determine either on his return or on his death. In practice, the estates in such cases are fully administered under these special grants, as obviously applications are not made for such grants if the LPR's absence is likely to be a short one.

2. **Notice to creditors—s 49**

   One month after service of last notice

   Where the LPRs have served s 49 notices seeking creditors and a minimum of one month has elapsed since the serving of the last of such notices, the LPRs are entitled to administer the estates having regard only to those claims of which they then have notice. LPRs may allow a longer period than this if they so wish. The usual practice is to place two advertisements in one national and one local paper with one week's interval between them. The period of notice given runs from the date of the last notice. They are still liable to the extent of unadministered assets in their possession at the time they receive notice of any debt outside the notice period.

3. **Court order for LPRs to execute assent—s 52(4)**

   Twelve months after the death of the deceased

   Under s 52(4) the court has power on application to it, twelve months after the death of the deceased, to order the LPRs to execute an assent vesting the property in the beneficiary and in default of compliance with that order to make a further order vesting the land in the person entitled, as fully and effectually as might have been done by a transfer thereof by the LPRs.

4. **Notice of intention of appropriate assets—s 55**

   Within six weeks after service by LPRs an application to court to prohibit appropriation may be made

   Where LPRs have served s 55 notices of intention to appropriate assets on all parties entitled to a share in an estate, such persons have six weeks from the service of such notices to apply to court to prohibit the appropriation—s 55(3).

5. Spouse's right of election to appropriate family home and chattels—s 56

Six months from receipt of notice or one year from extraction of grant, whichever is the later

It is the duty of the LPR to notify a spouse of his rights under s 56 to appropriate the family home and chattels. The spouse must elect to claim his rights within six months from the receipt of such notice or one year after the extraction of the grant, whichever is the later. The right to elect does not automatically cease one year after the extraction of the grant unless notice has been served and six months have elapsed since the service thereof. Until notice is served on the spouse, his rights survive and cannot be lost.

6. Executor's year—s 62(1)

One year after the death of the deceased

Proceedings cannot be brought by a beneficiary against an LPR for his failure to distribute an estate before the expiration of one year from the date of death of the deceased. A creditor may bring proceedings against an estate at any time—s 62(2).

7. Spouse's legal right share—s 111

Six months from receipt of notice or one year from extraction of grant, whichever is the later.

Six years where no benefit given to the spouse in will—see s 126 Succession Act, 1965.

The LPR has no statutory obligation to inform a spouse of his legal right share unless he has been given a benefit under the will. While the spouse is entitled to such share, it will become statute barred under s 45(1) of the Statute of Limitations, 1957 as amended by s 126 of the Succession Act, 1965—six years from the date when the right to receive the share accrued.

Where a benefit has been given to the spouse in the will, it is the duty of the LPR to notify a spouse of his rights to claim his legal right share under s 111. Under s 115(4) the spouse must elect to claim the rights within six months from the receipt of such notice or one year after the extraction of the grant, whichever is the later.

As under s 56, the rights of the spouse cannot be lost unless notice has been served and the six months' notice period thereafter, at least, has expired.

7(a) Separated and divorced spouses—s 15A of the Family Law Act, 1995 as inserted by s 52(g) of the Family Law (Divorce) Act, 1996

Where an order has been made under s 14 of the Family Law Act, 1995, under s 17 of the Judicial Separation and Family Law Reform Act, 1989 extinguishing succession rights on or after *judicial separation,* and one spouse dies, the other spouse can apply within six months of the grant issuing for provision out of the estate of the deceased spouse as the court deems appropriate, up to that spouse's legal right share, taking into account any provisions made by the deceased spouse for the other spouse during his or her lifetime and any bequests made.

No such order will be made if the other spouse has since remarried. The personal representative of the deceased spouse is obliged to 'make a reasonable effort' to notify the other spouse of the death of the deceased spouse.

If the personal representative so notifies the other spouse, the other spouse has one month to notify the personal representative of any intention to apply, of any application, or of any order granted.

Similar provisions apply in the case of a divorced spouse under s 18 of the Family Law Divorce Act, 1996.

8. **Child's legal right share—s 117 as amended by s 46 of the Family Law (Divorce) Act, 1996**

    Within six months of the extraction of the grant

    An application to court under this section must be made within six months of the extraction of the grant in the estate. In *MPD v MD* [1981] ILRM 179, Carroll J held that *'Section 117(6) laid down a strict timetable which goes to the Jurisdiction of the court and cannot be ignored, even where a defendant does not rely on it as a defence.'*

9. **Unworthiness to succeed—s 120**

    Continuous desertion from deceased for two years prior to his death

    Under s 120(2) where a spouse has been in desertion, which has continued up to the death for two years or more, said spouse is precluded from taking any share as legal right or an intestacy. Under s 120(3) a spouse who was guilty of conduct which justified the deceased in separating and living apart from him is deemed to be guilty of desertion within the meaning of s 120(2).

    Please note that s 14 of the Family Law Act, 1995 and s 18 of the Family Law (Divorce) Act, 1996 amend s 120 of the Succession Act, 1965.

10. **Dispositions for the purpose of disinheriting spouse and children—s 121**

    Within one year of the extraction of the grant

    Where a person has, within three years of his death, made a disposition of property for the purposes of defeating or substantially diminishing the shares of the spouse or children, application may be made pursuant to s 121 to have the court deem the purported disposition to be a devise or bequest made by the deceased by will and to form part of his estate at death. If the donee has disposed of the property to a purchaser, the section applies to the consideration given by the purchaser. The application must be made by the spouse or children within one year of the extraction of the grant. The court must be satisfied that the disposition was intended to disinherit the shares of the spouse or children. The effect of a determination is to increase the estate of the deceased at death for the purposes of claims by the surviving spouse and/or children under ss 56, 111, and 117.

11. **Limitation of actions**

    Within two years of death—s 9(2) of the Civil Liability Act, 1961

    Any claim which survives the death of a deceased must be brought within two years of his death: s 9(2) of the Civil Liability Act, 1961.

12. **Limitation of actions**

    Beneficiaries must sue within six years from the date when the right of action accrued—s 126.

    The period of limitation in respect of any claim to the estate of a deceased person or to any share or interest in such estate was contained in s 45(1) of the Statute of Limitations, 1957, which provided that such claim must be brought within twelve years of the accrual of the right to receive the share or interest. Section 45(2) provided that no action to recover arrears of interest in respect of any legacy or damages in respect of such arrears could be brought after the expiration of six years from the date at which the interest became due. Section 46 of said Act provided that no period of limitation applied if any claim against an LPR was founded on fraud.

    Section 126 of the Succession Act amended s 45, by reducing the period of limitation from twelve years to six years in respect of claims for shares in an estate whether under a will, or intestacy, or under s 111 of the Act. It reduced the period of limitation from six years to three years in respect of claims for interest on such shares.

While the entitlement of a person to share in an estate is normally determined at the date of death of the deceased, his right to receive and therefore to claim may not accrue on that date. The dates upon which beneficiaries in estates become entitled to receive their shares and therefore the dates upon which the limitation periods begin to run against them, are as follows:

Legacies generally—in the case of an immediate legacy where there are sufficient assets in the estate to meet it, time begins to run from the death of the testator.

Contingent legacies—where the legacy is contingent and vests at a future date, time will ordinarily run from the date the contingency is satisfied:

Rudd v Rudd [1895] 1 IR 15.

Legacies and reversionary interests of testator—in respect of reversionary interests belonging to the testator, time does not run until they have come into the possession of the LPR:

Adams v Barry (1845) 2 Coll 285.

Succession rights on intestacy and rights of residuary legatees and devisees—in respect of intestacy rights and rights under residuary clauses in wills, time runs normally from the date the asset claimed came into the possession of the LPR:

Adams v Barry (1845) 2 Coll 285.

Devisee's rights—s 14(2) of the Statute of Limitations, 1957 states that rights of action in relation to land accrue at the date of death of a deceased.

Legal right share of a spouse under s 111 of the Succession Act, 1965—where a spouse has been given a benefit under a will, he cannot enforce payment of a share under this section until such time as he has made an election under s 115 of the Act, and the period of limitation, therefore, runs from that date:

JH v WJH (unreported) 20 December 1979, High Court.

Finally, it should be remembered that s 62(1) of the Act prevents beneficiaries from suing to claim their shares for one year after the death of the deceased, even though the period of limitation may be running against them from his date of death.

13. Limitation of actions

LPRs may sue up to twelve years from the date of accrual of the action to recover assets of the deceased from a person, whether a beneficiary or stranger holding adversely to the estate.

In *Drohan v Drohan* [1981] ILRM 473 McMahon J held that s 45 of the Statute of Limitations, 1957 as amended by s 126 of the Succession Act, 1965 (which section provides for a limitation period of six years) only applied to actions by beneficiaries against LPRs and not to actions taken by LPRs to recover assets from persons holding assets of the deceased. Both sections clearly refer only to actions against an estate, and not to actions taken by LPRs of estates to recover assets. The Supreme Court upheld this decision in the case of *Gleeson and Feehan and O'Meara* [1991] ILRM 738. In this case it was held that the said limitation period of six years did not apply to an action for recovery of the land in succession to the owner. The relevant limitation period in such case was held to be a period of twelve years, as set out by s 13(2) of the Statute of Limitations, 1957 in relation to claims for the recovery of land.

14. Limitation of actions

LPRs may plead the Statute of Limitations against beneficiaries—s 123.

Section 10 of the Succession Act, 1965 states that LPRs hold the estate as trustees for the persons by law entitled thereto. Section 123, however, states that LPRs shall not, by reason only of s 10 of the Act, be a trustee for the purpose of the Statute of Limitations, 1957.

15. Limitation of actions

Spouse of deceased, bailiff of shares of minor children, may plead Statute of Limitations against children who have left the family home or reached maturity—s 124.

A bailiff could not before the Act plead the benefit of the Statute of Limitations against a person beneficially entitled to a share in the estate of a deceased person. A common example of such a situation would arise where the deceased died leaving a widow and minor children. The widow would usually hold the shares of the minor children as bailiff. Section 124 provides that notwithstanding any rule of law to the contrary, 'trustee' in the Statute of Limitations, 1957 shall not include a person whose fiduciary relationship arises merely because he is in possession of property comprised in the estate of a deceased person in the capacity of bailiff for another person.

16. Limitation of actions

Next of kin in possession of land hold not only as joint tenants their own shares but also as joint tenants any shares acquired through adverse possession—s 125.

Section 125(1) states that where each of two or more persons is entitled to any share in land comprised in the estate of an deceased person, whether such shares are equal or unequal and any or all of them enter into possession of the land, then, notwithstanding any rule of law to the contrary, those who enter shall, as between themselves and as between others who do not enter, be deemed, for the purposes of the Statute of Limitations, 1957, to acquire title by possession as joint tenants and not as tenants in common as regards the respective shares of those who do not enter. Section 125(2) provides that s 125(1) applies even if the person had extracted a grant before he took possession or extracted a grant having taken possession.

17. Limitation of actions

Acknowledgement or part-payment by an LPR or by a person accountable for property to an LPR causes the limitation period to run from the date of acknowledgement or part-payment.

An acknowledgement by any of several LPRs of a claim against an estate of a deceased causes the limitation period to run from the date of the acknowledgement—s 59(5) of the Statute of Limitations, 1957. Similarly, if the LPR makes a part-payment of a claim against, or a share in, an estate, the period of limitation will run from that date—s 68(5) of the Statute of Limitations, 1957. Similar provisions are contained in said Act in relation to acknowledgement and part-payments made by debtors of estates to LPRs, where the latter are pursuing claims of the estate against the former.

18. Limitations of actions

The Statute of Limitations does not run against beneficiaries suffering under a disability—s 127.

Where a beneficiary is suffering under a disability, time does not run until the disability ends or the person in question dies. The disability must have been present when the right of action accrued and be in some form continuous. The period of limitation which applies is three years from the ending of the disability or until the normal limitation period expires, whichever is the later.

The Rules of the Superior Courts

1. Caveat

Expires after six months unless renewed or warned.

2. Warning

Where a caveat is preventing the issue of a grant, a warning to caveat may be filed. The warning gives the caveator fourteen days within which to file an appearance thereto or otherwise his caveat may be set aside. The warning must be served within fourteen days of its filing in the Probate Office. Where no appearance has been filed the warning party, on filing an affidavit of service of the warning, obtains a certificate of no appearance to warning, setting aside the caveat.

3. **Citation**

   A citation must be personally served on the relevant person within fourteen days of it being filed in the Probate Office, unless the court or Probate Officer extends the time for service. If no appearance has been filed within fourteen days of the service thereof or such further period as the court or Probate Officer has allowed, the citing party on filing an affidavit of service thereof may obtain a certificate of no appearance to citation. This certificate states that the non-appearance of the citee to the citation has been taken as and for a renunciation of his rights to a grant. If the citee simply files an appearance and does not extract a grant, a further side-bar order may be obtained requiring him to extract a grant within fourteen days or otherwise his rights to a grant will be set aside. If he does not apply for a grant within these further fourteen days a side-bar order will issue, setting aside his rights.

4. **Subpoena**

   A subpoena must likewise be personally served, and requires the party served to deliver to the Probate Office, within fourteen days of the service thereof, the original will of the deceased in his possession.

5. **Probate motions—O 79, rr 87 and 88**

   (A) *Ex parte* **probate motions**

   A motion paper must be filed in the Probate Office at least two clear days before the motion day.

   (B) **Motions on notice**

   Where a motion is being served solely on a firm of solicitors, the notice party must be served and the motion filed in the Probate Office at least two clear days before the motion day.

   (C) **Motions at the sitting of the court**

   Where a motion is being served on a lay party, the lay party must be served four clear days before the motion day and the application filed in the Probate Office at least two clear days before the motion day.

11.9.3 APPENDIX C: PROBATE OFFICE FEES

Probate fees on grant

Seat Office fees payable on or after 01 March on a primary grant of representation, Supreme Court, Court of Appeal and High Court (Fees) (Amendment) Order, 2021 (SI 80/2021):

Where the net value of the estate does not exceed	*Fee payable*
€100,000	€100
€250,000	€200
€500,000	€350
€750,000	€500
€1,000,000	€650

Where the net value of the estate exceeds €1,000,000 in addition to the €650 now chargeable, for every €500,000 increase in the value of the estate, a further €400 will be charged, for example:

€1,500,000	€1,050315
€2,000,000	€1,450
€393,750	€339
€425,000	€351

€456,250	€363
€487,500	€375
€518,750	€387
€550,000	€399
€581,250	€411
€612,500	€423
€643,750	€435
€675,000	€447
€706,250	€459
€737,500	€471
€768,750	€483
€800,000	€495

The fee for lodging a corrective affidavit (i.e. if you discover that the value of the estate is greater than initially believed) is the total fee for the estate, including the extra value less the fee initially charged subject to a minimum fee of €30.

On every occasion on which an application for a grant of representation is resubmitted to the Probate Office/District Probate Registry a fee of €40 is charged. This is a new fee, applying for the first time from 10 July 2013, and further stresses the importance of ensuring that the application is correct on the first application.

General office fees

Description	*Fee applicable*
Official copy grant	€10
Official copy will	€10
Sealed and certified copy grant	€15
Sealed and certified copy will	€15
Sealed and certified copy will and grant bespoken at the same time	€20
Attested copy of Inland Revenue affidavit	€15
Official copy renunciation form, oath, unproved wills, etc	€10
Search fee for *each* search made	€10
Search fee for each search made through the post	€15
To lodge	
Notice of application	€20
Notice of motion	€40
Affidavit	€20
Caveat	€50
Warning to caveat	€25
Citation	€25
Grounding affidavit to citation	€20
Subpoena	€25
Appearance to warning, citation, subpoena	€25
Consent	€25
Notice of change of solicitor	€25
To withdraw	
Caveat	€20
Application	€20

Description | *Fee applicable*
To collect
Court order (first copy) — €20
Side-bar order (first copy) — €20
Consent order — €25
Certificate of no appearance — €20
Order of probate officer — €25
Judge's certificate — €25

Probate Officer's fees

Probate Officer's orders		**Appointment of guardian for minor**	
Re different commissioners	€25	Petition	€20
Re defective jurats	€25	Each grounding affidavit	€20
Grant be limited to movable property	€25	Probate Officer's order	€25
Grant be limited to immovable property	€25	**Total**	€65
Follow will for order of executors	No fee	**Admission of will to proof**	
Revocation of grant		Probate Officer's order	€25
Probate Officer's order	€25	Each grounding affidavit	€20
Each grounding affidavit	€20	**Total**	€45
Total	€45	**Judges' certificates**	
Amendment of grant		S and C copies fee be paid, judge's certificate	€25
Probate Officer's order	€25	**Probate Officer's list motions (Applications lodged with Rules Office)**	
Each grounding affidavit	€20		
Total	€45	Motion paper	€40
Impoundment of grant		Each grounding affidavit	€20
Probate Officer's order	€25	**Total**	€60
Each grounding affidavit	€20	Fee for all affidavits grounding applications to Probate Officer and court	€20
Total	€45		
Appointment of committee of person of unsound mind			
Petition	€20		
Each grounding affidavit	€20		
Probate Officer's order	€25		
Total	€65		

11.9.4 APPENDIX D: STRUCTURE OF THE PROBATE OFFICE

1. *Seat Office section*

    (i) Lodge papers of application for grant (i.e. oath, schedule, etc).

    (ii) Attend to reply to queries raised by the section.

    This section takes in all papers and handles all title queries relating to applications for grants.

2. *General Office section*

    (i) Records of all grants issued from Probate Office or District Registries may be inspected in this section where the grant has issued in the past twenty years. After thirty years, all records are transferred to the National Archives Office, Bishop Street, Dublin 8.

(ii) Copies of any documents relating to grants issued from Probate Office in the past thirty years may be bespoken in this section. Data protection legislation govern the availability of the Inland Revenue Affidavit.

(iii) All queries relating to the dates of issue of grants on foot of current applications are made in this section.

Any documents required to be inspected will be available the day following the request for inspection. It takes two days to obtain a copy of any document bespoken. Documents are paid for in advance and posted out when ready.

3. *Rules Office section*

(i) Lodge caveats, warnings, appearances, citations and subpoenas, etc.

(ii) Motion papers to Probate Judge and Probate Officer's list lodged.

(iii) Check to see if application stopped by caveat.

CHAPTER 12

ADMINISTRATION AFTER THE GRANT HAS ISSUED

12.1 Introduction and Overview

For the purposes of this and succeeding chapters, the generic phrase 'grant of representation' or simply 'grant' will be used instead of 'grant of probate/grant of administration either intestate or with will annexed'. It is assumed that the necessary grant has been obtained and that the personal representative has sufficient title (including any necessary foreign grant or grants) to collect the relevant assets. Where specific issues arise that solely affect grants of probate or grants of administration either intestate or with will annexed, the individual type of grant and the resulting issue raised will be highlighted. Similarly, the generic phrase 'legal personal representative' sometimes shortened to 'LPR' will be used instead of 'executor' and 'administrator' and, again, where specific issues arise that solely affect executors or administrators, the individual type of personal representative and the resulting issue raised will be highlighted.

From the time probate papers including the Inland Revenue affidavit have been lodged and the grant issues from the Probate Office, a period of time will have elapsed in which not much will have been happening on the file. During this period of relative inactivity, it is advisable to keep the file under review pending the issue of the grant, and any changes in circumstances should be noted and taken into consideration during this period.

On the issue of the grant, the collection of the assets can commence. It is the next very active stage in the administration and is similar to the period after the date of death when there is a flurry of activity in seeking to value and identify all the assets in the estate. The forthcoming chapters will deal first with the collection of assets, concentrating on assets which may be problematic, and then with the vesting of assets in the persons entitled. Re-reading **Chapter 6** of this book is advised.

The personal representative is faced with myriad issues to resolve before distribution. Many of these issues must be dealt with concurrently, rather than successively. Prior to any distribution of assets, the debts of the estate, especially any outstanding taxation or social welfare issues, must be identified and cleared. This is to ensure that all matters which can be dealt with at this stage, in particular the submission of inheritance tax returns, valuation, dates, finalisation of income tax affairs, and other related matters, are resolved.

Also, the issues surrounding spouses', civil partners', cohabitees', and children's rights must be resolved before distribution takes place. Areas that may cause difficulty include the exercise of the power of appropriation, and the problems surrounding the collection and distribution of certain assets, such as stocks and shares and joint property. Prior to the payment of legacies, the forms of receipts and indemnities that should be sought from the beneficiaries should be clarified.

12.1.1 RE-READ THE FILE (ESPECIALLY THE WILL)

It is essential for the practitioner to familiarise himself once again with the content of the will (if any), the names of the various beneficiaries, and their entitlements. The file, and in particular the checklist, should be reviewed as well. The status of each beneficiary should be checked, as this may have altered in the interim. Perhaps some may have died or changed address. The location and approximate value of assets should be clear from the Inland Revenue affidavit, but some may have increased or decreased in value since the date of death. Any chattels that have been passed to beneficiaries should be accounted for.

Note in particular any undertakings which may have been given at the commencement of the administration to any financial institution to pay the proceeds of a beneficiary's share of the estate to that financial institution. It is essential, prior to giving an undertaking, to obtain an appropriate irrevocable authority in writing from the beneficiary, as well as the consent of the personal representative. See also para **14.1**. If also acting for a beneficiary in the calculation, payment, and filing of any return in relation to any CAT payable by that beneficiary, the proceeds, net of any CAT, would be paid to the financial institution.

Undertakings are dealt with in **Chapter 14**. Suffice it to say at this stage that the giving of undertakings is generally not advisable.

12.1.2 READ THE RESIDUARY CLAUSE CAREFULLY—PARTIAL INTESTACY

As noted earlier, where a bequest lapses, the subject-matter of the bequest 'falls' into residue. Where a gift of residue fails, depending on how the residuary gift was phrased, all or part of the residue may lapse. Where this occurs, there is a partial intestacy, and that portion of the residue that lapses will be distributed on intestacy. This is one of the most complex issues to be dealt with during the administration of an estate, and the practitioner should proceed extremely cautiously.

First, one must be absolutely sure that a partial intestacy has in fact occurred. This will depend on the precise phrasing of the residuary clause (assuming, of course, that there is a residuary clause). See para **2.9**.

The situations that can occur are as follows:

- There is no residuary clause in the will: automatically, there is a partial intestacy.
- The residuary clause fails entirely because the sole residuary beneficiary has predeceased the testator without there being a gift over or a s 98 situation: there is a partial intestacy.
- The residuary clause is to a number of people as tenants in common, i.e. words of severance have been used: should one of those residuary beneficiaries predecease the testator, his or her 'share' of the residue falls into intestacy assuming no gift over or s 98 situation. This circumstance should not be confused with a residuary bequest to a group of people jointly, where no words of severance have been used. In that case, the surviving joint residuary legatees and devisees share the residue between them.

12.1.3 DEALING WITH A PARTIAL INTESTACY

12.1.3.1 Only one grant needed

A common misconception is that where there is a partial intestacy, the practitioner needs two grants—a grant of probate/administration with will annexed to deal with the testate estate and a grant of administration intestate to deal with the intestate estate. This is *not* the case! The grant of probate/administration with will annexed gives the personal representative the authority to administer the entire estate, testate *and* intestate. See *RG v PSG and JRG* (unreported) 20 November 1980, High Court, Carroll J.

12.1.3.2 Identifying the intestate portion of the estate

When calculating the value of the partial intestacy, one must first deduct all liabilities from the value of the intestate part of the estate. If this is not done, there is an incorrect calculation and this error has the effect of falsely raising the value of the partial intestacy. See para **12.4.2**, which deals with the order of payment of debts in a solvent estate.

Once this has been done, the next step is to identify the persons entitled on intestacy.

12.1.3.3 Entitlement on partial intestacy

Section 74 of the Act provides that:

'Where the will of a testator effectively disposes of part only of his estate, the remainder shall be distributed as if he had died intestate and left no other estate.'

Entitlement on intestacy has been covered in detail in **Chapter 9** and does not need repetition. However, practitioners should note that if there is a failure of residue, it is extremely likely that such failure occurred because a close family member predeceased the testator. This should be borne in mind when establishing entitlement on intestacy.

12.1.4 EXECUTOR'S ACCOUNT

Should an executor's/administrator's account have been opened, check with the bank as to the balance currently standing to credit or overdrawn.

As the liquid assets are collected, they should be placed in a deposit account. One should advise the personal representative on receipt of funds that these will be lodged to a deposit account. Should the personal representative request that the monies are placed in a current account, this instruction should be obtained in writing. See Solicitors Accounts Regulations 2014 (SI 516/2014) and paras 6.5 and 14.2 of the *Guide to Good Professional Conduct for Solicitors*, 3rd edn. See also Stephenson Solicitors' 22nd Seminar, *Who Pays the Ferryman?*, 16 November 2012, pp 51–69.

12.2 Further Meeting with the Personal Representative

The practitioner should advise the personal representative in writing that the grant has issued and that assets of the estate are being collected. Should there be any outstanding queries arising from the file review, arrange for the personal representative to call to discuss these various matters. When the personal representative does call, make sure the checklist is ready and obtain specific answers to the queries. Issues that may need to be discussed with the personal representative include:

1. collection of assets, noting of grant;
2. spouses', civil partners', cohabitees', and children's rights (including appropriation of the family home under s 56);
3. 'ordinary' appropriation of assets under s 55;
4. obtaining Social Welfare and/or HSE 'Fair Deal' clearance;
5. joint property;
6. dealing with transfer and sale of stocks and shares;
7. management of dividends and interest;
8. taxation issues;
9. payment of liabilities;
10. vesting of personal property and payment of legacies;
11. vesting of real property.

12.2.1 COLLECTION OF ASSETS OF THE ESTATE INCLUDING NOTING OF THE GRANT

As outlined at para **6.8.4.1**, when originally writing to financial institutions the solicitor would have requested the necessary withdrawal forms for completion and any further requirements.

When applying for a grant of representation from the Probate Office, it is of considerable assistance, where there are a number of assets, to requisition several certified copies of the grant at the time of lodgement of papers.

These will be available shortly after the grant, and will facilitate efficient collection of the assets.

If sealed and certified copy will and grant is required for a Northern Irish, Scottish, or England and Wales grant, application for this should be made at time of applying for the grant.

Collection of assets will be dealt with in detail at para **12.3**.

Quite often, in order to pay debts and legacies, a sale of some or all of the assets may have to take place. Having regard to any such sale, the following should be considered:

1. Who is to handle the sale of the assets, investments, or real property?

2. (a) Is there an increase in value now from the date of death valuation, and, if so, does a liability to capital gains tax arise?

    (b) Will a sale of the assets give rise to an additional probate (if applicable)/inheritance tax liability?

    (c) Will it be necessary to sell assets for the purpose of paying existing inheritance tax?

3. Is there a beneficiary in the estate who is anxious to purchase the property? If so, what procedure is to be adopted to deal with, for example, appropriation/valuation/sale/disclaimer for value or deed of family arrangement?

4. Are there government stocks in the estate? If so, is it the intention of the personal representative that these be retained for the payment of tax or appropriated to a non-resident beneficiary for the purpose of reducing the tax liability?

5. Is there a power of appropriation in the will, and, if so, how broad is this? (See paras **3.8.1.3** and **13.7**.)

6. What are the specific instructions under the will with regard to contents of the house and personal effects of the deceased? Is there a discretion granted to the personal representative to divide these among the main beneficiaries? If this is the case, has the personal representative reached a conclusion, or is your assistance or advice required with the matter?

7. If there are no specific instructions with regard to the contents of the house, what is to happen?

8. Before a sale of any asset, it is important to remember that the personal representative does not have any capital gains tax allowance, but a beneficiary does have. Similarly, a personal representative cannot claim CAT exemptions or reliefs so the taxation implications of a sale in the course of administration as opposed to a vesting and subsequent sale should be considered. See CAT Lecture Notes (see Preface).

12.2.2 SURVIVING SPOUSE/CIVIL PARTNER/QUALIFYING COHABITEE—PART IX OF THE SUCCESSION ACT, 1965

This topic has already been discussed at length in **Chapter 4**. It is now necessary to consider it from the aspect of the administration of the estate. The matter should be discussed with the personal representative so that he is fully aware of the implications of Part IX of

ADMINISTRATION AFTER THE GRANT HAS ISSUED

the Succession Act and the Civil Partnership and Certain Rights and Obligations of Cohabitants Act, 2010 (hereinafter called the 'civil partnership legislation') and how it impinges on the particular administration.

The personal representative should now be reminded that the estate cannot be distributed until such time as the spouse's/civil partner's legal right share has been resolved. In particular, and where applicable, the right of election of the surviving spouse/civil partner must be considered. It is imperative that the appropriate notice in relation to legal right share and right of election (if appropriate) is served immediately. See para **4.5.7.1** and **Chapter 13**.

Where no bequest was left to the surviving spouse/civil partner in the will, the surviving spouse/civil partner is automatically entitled to their legal right share and should be informed of this. See para **13.6.4.2**.

12.2.2.1 Intestacy: spouse and minor children

In an intestacy situation where the personal representative is also the spouse or civil partner of the deceased, there is an onus on the practitioner to explain the following fully:

1. the precise shares to which the spouse and children are entitled and an approximate valuation of these; take care to consider if there is a predeceased child or children who left a child or children;
2. that he is trustee under s 57 of the Succession Act of the share of his infant/minor children;
3. that for the purpose of appropriating the family home under s 56 of the Succession Act, he is entitled to take into account the shares of any minor children, which are then held in trust for those minor children;
4. that he is accountable to his children when they reach the age of eighteen years for their share. It is necessary to advise him of the various procedures to enable this to be done.

12.2.2.2 Intestacy: civil partner and minor children

Where the personal representative on intestacy is also the civil partner of the deceased and there is a minor child or children of the deceased, the solicitor has to explain in similar but different terms the role of the civil partner on administration. This will be dealt with in more detail in **Chapter 13**.

12.2.2.3 Intestacy: cohabitant and minor children

Where a cohabitant dies intestate, the surviving cohabitant is not necessarily the personal representative, unless he is the surviving parent of a minor child or children of the deceased cohabitant, who would be the person(s) entitled to the entire estate. In such circumstances, he would extract the grant on their behalf limited to their minority, as parent and next friend, but not as surviving cohabitee. If the cohabitee is considering seeking redress against the estate under s 194 of the Civil Partnership Act (see para **4.7**), there will be a conflict of interest between this and acting as LPR as next friend of minor beneficiaries. See **Chapter 13**.

12.3 Collection of Assets of the Estate

12.3.1 CASH IN HOUSE

Any cash in the house should have been collected immediately on death and lodged to credit of the executor's deposit account or the client account. If there is a substantial sum, this may assist with payment of funeral expenses, or other immediate liabilities.

Where the deceased leaves a spouse/civil partner or family, this sum may immediately be required by them for payment of expenses. Use discretion in relation to this. Remember also that the amount of cash in the house should have been inserted in the Inland Revenue affidavit.

12.3.2 BANK ACCOUNTS

Monies will be released to the personal representative (or preferably to the solicitor acting for the personal representative) on completion of an ordinary withdrawal form and production of the grant. The form should be on hand if applied for when information regarding the account was requested. See para **6.6.5.1**. If the amount is small, the bank may dispense with the necessity for a grant and accept a death certificate and certificate of clearance from CAT as referred to at para **6.3.3**. The bank may also require a certified copy of the documentation furnished to the solicitor for anti-money laundering purposes.

Joint accounts are dealt with at para **12.6**.

With a single-name account over a particular sum a grant of representation is necessary, as discussed.

When the grant issues, a copy of it should be sent to the bank, requesting it to transfer the balance either to the credit of the solicitor's client account or to the executor's deposit account. A certificate in respect of interest earned on any accounts between the date of death and the date of closing the account should be requested, as it is required for income tax purposes.

Should the executor's current account be overdrawn, the overdraft should be cleared as soon as possible. If the executor's account is not held with that particular bank, a withdrawal form will have to be completed by the executor and sent to the bank, who should forward a draft directly to the solicitor, which should then be lodged to the executor's account. Ensure that this is noted on the instruction sheet.

As previously indicated, certificates for any interest paid on loans or overdraft should also be obtained.

12.3.3 BUILDING SOCIETY/CREDIT UNION

These follow the same procedure as banks. A withdrawal form must be completed and the grant of representation produced. Where the amount does not exceed a certain figure, the building society may dispense with the grant and accept a death certificate and a letter of clearance from CAT. Similar to cash received from banks, any sum received from financial institutions should be lodged in the executor's account. Nominated accounts with the credit union have already been dealt with at para **6.9.6.2**. To recap, a member of a credit union aged 16 or over can nominate up to €23,000, which will pass outside the estate i.e. not under the will or distributed according to intestacy. Any sum in excess of this will go under the terms of the will or intestacy. Separately from this, the directors of a credit union can pay out up to €15,000 to the person entitled under the terms of a will or intestacy without requiring a grant of representation.

12.3.4 POST OFFICE SAVINGS ACCOUNT, SAVINGS CERTIFICATES, AND BONDS

Similar to the procedure for other financial institutions, a withdrawal form/encashment form will have been requested when applying for a valuation. The form, completed by the personal representative, is sent to An Post, together with the grant and the savings certificates/bonds. The monies will then be released. If a grant is not necessary, a special form of application for payment must be completed. The names and addresses of the next of kin and details of the beneficiary, together with the death certificate, must be furnished in this case.

When encashing savings bonds/savings certificates, the original bonds/certificates must be sent to An Post, who will then issue a warrant for the value of the entire holding to include any interest as at the date of payment. It is essential prior to the encashment of savings bonds to consider the date of encashment in order to maximise the interest payable.

If any of the foregoing has been validly nominated by the deceased in his lifetime, the proceeds should not form part of the estate. See para **6.9.6.2** dealing with nominations. Bear in mind, however, that in certain circumstances a nomination asset may form part of the estate under s 121. See para **4.5.11**.

As noted earlier, it is important that any interest earned post-death on any of the accounts mentioned here should be noted separately, as it will be necessary to account for the said interest in dealing with the income of the estate.

12.3.4.1 Precedent letter to financial institution

To: The Manager

Re: Deceased

   Late of

   Account No(s):

Dear Sirs,

We enclose certified copy Grant of Probate/Administration [as appropriate] in the estate of the above named deceased for notation and return. We also enclose the relevant passbook [if applicable] together with the withdrawal form/payment authorisation form duly completed by the Executor/Administrator [as appropriate].

We look forward to receiving:

1. (a) a cheque made payable to this firm in respect of the balance of the account together with interest to date;

[OR]

1. (b) confirmation that an electronic funds transfer has been made to the designated account provided as per the payment authorisation form attached.

[DELETE WHERE APPLICABLE]

2. a certificate of interest from the date of death to date of closure of the account for each tax year;

3. a statement on the account from the date of death to the date of closure of the account;

4. confirmation that your institution does not hold any other accounts in the name of the deceased whether in his sole name or jointly with any other person and that you do not hold any items in safekeeping on behalf of the deceased.

Please return the certified copy Grant of Probate/Administration to us as soon as possible as we require it urgently for the purposes of administration, and let us know your further requirements if any to close off the account.

Yours faithfully,

Solicitors

12.3.5 STOCKS AND SHARES (TRANSFER AND/OR SALE)

The Registrar of the company will already be aware of the death of the deceased and should have advised the solicitor of the precise shareholding held in the name of the deceased, of any dividends outstanding, and should have been requested to withhold future dividends pending the issue of the grant. The grant of representation together with the share certificate(s) and any dividends held on file should be sent to the Registrar for noting. See para **6.6.5.9** and precedent letter to Company Registrar at para **6.8.4.1** and see also para **12.3.5.1** for further notes on dividends and/or interest.

Shares are transferred by means of a share transfer form. For Irish shares it is recommended that an Irish stock transfer form is used, and for UK shares the UK equivalent should be used. The form is required in duplicate for each separate shareholding. The name of the transferor is always *'X as Executor of Y deceased late of'*. There is no stamp duty on the transfer of shares if it is to a beneficiary entitled to a legacy of shares or as part of the residue of the estate under a will or to a beneficiary who is entitled on intestacy. To obtain the exemption from stamp duty it is necessary to complete a certificate on the back of the transfer form, and this needs to be attended to carefully. On the front of the transfer form, the signature of the personal representative and the stamp of the person lodging the form are both necessary.

Any transfer of shares should be of the exact number of shares to which a beneficiary is entitled and should conform with the number on the register of the company.

Where shares are being transferred to any person other than the person entitled under the will or on intestacy, this is an appropriation of the shares and the transfer could be liable to stamp duty (if a power to appropriate under s 55 without notice or consent has not been included in the will: see para **2.10**).

Any variation of the legal position on death will have legal and taxation consequences and should not be entertained without considering those consequences.

Caution should be exercised when dealing with stocks and shares. The value of these may have increased or decreased since the date of death, and the tax consequences of any action taken should always be considered carefully prior to any dealings. Any proposed transactions should be fully discussed with the personal representative and their firm instructions in writing should be obtained and, if appropriate, the instructions of the beneficiary.

Should the personal representative wish to sell some or all of the shares, a CREST form is required in duplicate for each individual shareholding, then those shares which he intends to sell should be put in the name of the personal representative. Otherwise the shares may be transferred *in specie* to the beneficiaries as noted earlier. Prior to selling any shares, it is important to consider the potential capital gains tax consequences.

The personal representative selling in his capacity as personal representative is not entitled to the annual €1,270 small gains exemption for capital gains tax purposes. A beneficiary is entitled to this exemption even if he sells the shares immediately they are vested in him.

12.3.5.1 Precedent letter to Registrar

Re: Estate of:

Late of:

Date of death:

Holding:

Account no:

Dear Sirs,

A Grant of Probate/Administration [*as appropriate*] in the estate of the above named deceased has now issued. We enclose certified copy of same for noting in your records and return.

At the date of death of the deceased s/he [*as appropriate*] was entitled to the following shareholding, namely:

[*insert details of shares held*]

We enclose the following certificates in the name of the deceased [*list the share certificates enclosed and if possible retain copies on the file*].

We should be obliged if you would note the interest of the Executor/Administrator [*as appropriate*] on the enclosed certificates and return the Certified Copy Grant to us as soon as possible as we require same in the administration of the estate.

[*Include the following paragraph if transferring shares now.*]

We enclose [*recite number of*] stock transfer forms signed by the Executor/Administrator [*as appropriate*] transferring shares into the name(s) of   . Please issue us with fresh certificates in the names of the transferee(s) at your earliest convenience.

We enclose dividend warrants which have been retained by us pending receipt of the Grant of Administration/Probate [*as appropriate*]. Please amend same into the name of the Executor/Administrator [*as appropriate*] and re-date any dividends, which are more than six months from the date of issue.

OR

We would be obliged if you would forward to us all dividend warrants retained by yourselves since the date of death with the interest of the Executor/Administrator [*as appropriate*] noted thereon in order that we may apply same.

Yours faithfully,

Solicitors

12.3.5.2 Irish small estates

The limits under which one may deal with an estate without a grant of probate are very small, and set out here are the limits within which the small estates procedure is operated.

- *Capita Corporate Registrars*

    Registrars for Independent News and Media, CRH, Grafton Group, and Ryanair, for example.

    Their small estates procedure can be used provided the estate does not exceed €20,000 at date of death and the assets being transferred do not exceed €20,000 at date of death.

    If the holding falls within these limits, write to the Registrar requesting to use their small estates procedure for the holding and they will send out the following documents:

    — small estates indemnity; and

    — stock transfer form.

    They will then require that the next of kin of the deceased shareholder fill in the paperwork and return it along with the death certificate, a certified copy of the will if available, and a cheque for their fees. For current fees and requirements see their website at http://www.capitaassetservices.com/.

    This will then result in the share being transferred from the deceased shareholder into the names of the next of kin. When doing this, the practitioner can also arrange for any uncashed dividends to be reissued.

- *Computershare Investor Service, Dublin*

    Computershare in Dublin are Registrars for Bank of Ireland, FBD Holdings, and Paddy Power, for example.

    Their small estates procedure requires that the value of the shares at date of death does not exceed €23,500 and that inheritance tax is not payable on the estate. Where the holding falls within these limits, a similar procedure is followed with different fees applying depending on the value of the shareholding.

- *Diageo Plc*

    Despite this now being a dual listed UK company, the company maintains its own register here in Dublin and so this company is an Irish company for CAT, which means that although its primary quote is in London, it is an Irish asset.

Irish shareholders should write to the company at the Edinburgh address to note death; if they write to the company at the St James Gate address, it will be forwarded to Edinburgh. Their small estates threshold is €30,000 or Stg£20,000 at date of death, and when using this facility they will issue the following documents:

— small estates indemnity—if holding is more than 1,000 shares this needs to be guaranteed by an insurance company, otherwise it needs to be stamped by a solicitor, bank, or commissioner for oaths;

— statutory declaration—signed before a commission of oaths; and

— letter of assent—if there are children as well as a spouse.

The solicitor will, in addition to these documents, need to provide a death certificate, the original share certificates, and a certified copy of the will if available.

- *Kerry Group Plc*

    The company itself maintains its own register, and the solicitor will need to write to its offices in Tralee to request the small estates documents.

    Its small estates threshold is €12,500; it requires much the same documentation as the other registrars, those being: the death certificate, original share certificates, and a certified copy of the will or an indemnity signed by the next of kin if no will exists.

12.3.5.3 ShareGift

Where the amount of shares held is so low as to make their sale or transfer uneconomical (e.g. a number of people who bought small amounts of Eircom shares held even smaller amounts of Vodafone shares as part of the purchase of Eircell and now hold even smaller amounts of Verizon shares as a result of the purchase of Vodafone), it is possible to donate those shares, using ShareGift (http://www.sharegift.org), at minimal cost to the estate. Some Irish stockbrokers provide this service in favour of particular charities in Ireland.

12.3.5.4 Small UK estates

The situation may arise where the shareholding is the only UK asset in an Irish estate and, to save time and money, the solicitor does not want or need to take out a grant of probate in the jurisdiction. There is a facility subject to certain limits that facilitates the administration of these securities.

UK inheritance tax (IHT) allowance is currently Stg£325,000 with provision for a family home allowance when passed on to children or grandchildren from April 2017. The rate of tax is presently 40 per cent on the amount over the threshold. There are tax avoidance measures but specialist advice should be taken and these will not be discussed in this manual.

If the deceased's spouse/civil partner predeceases and has not utilised all his or her IHT on the death of the deceased (being the surviving spouse of the predeceased spouse), then both the outstanding IHT allowance of the first deceased spouse/civil partner and the current IHT allowance of the second deceased spouse/civil partner can be utilised by the estate of the second deceased spouse/civil partner.

However, Registrars have different thresholds for dealing with small estates; here are the limits for the three largest Registrars at the moment.

- *Computershare*—the value of the entire UK estate must not exceed the IHT allowance and the value of the shareholdings must not exceed Stg£20,000. Computershare are Registrars for Vodafone, Standard Life, and Tullow Oil.

- *Equiniti*—the value of the entire UK estate must not exceed the IHT allowance and the value of the shareholdings must not exceed Stg£10,000. Equiniti are Registrars for Aviva, who comprise Church & General, Norwich Union and Hibernian Insurance; they also act as Registrars for GlaxoSmithKline, Marks & Spencer, Smiths Group, Royal Dutch Shell, BP, and Tesco, among others.

- *Capita Registrars UK*—the value of the entire UK estate must not exceed Stg£20,000 and the value of the shareholdings must not exceed Stg£10,000. Capita UK are Registrars for Compass Group and Home Retail for example.

All three Registrars have a 'small estates package' which comprises: a formal declaration of indemnity to be completed by either a bank or an insurance company, the Irish grant, an administration fee, and the stock transfer form completed by the LPR.

The second factor in dealing with shares in UK estates is that some other Registrars do not recognise the right of Irish grant-appointed executors to deal with the paperwork and insist on having next of kin deal with the paperwork, but care needs to be exercised that they are either entitled to or will deal with the shares in accordance with the will.

Computershare are the easiest to deal with, as they will recognise the Irish grant accompanying a specific small estates declaration/affidavit, and as they are Registrars of Vodafone this is very helpful.

Please note that UK Registrars do not recognise unsealed court-attested copies of the grant of probate, so it is usually easier to send the original.

Where a UK grant is required, be careful to have the same executors as the Irish grant and not a personal representative, say a UK solicitor, for the Irish personal representatives, as this confuses the issue and will require another set of signatures, which can be time-consuming and slow down the process from the point of view of administering shares.

12.3.5.5 Management of dividends and interest

Dividends and interest must be held until the grant issues. They cannot be encashed, as they are in the name of the deceased. They should be forwarded to the Registrar of the company with the grant and share certificate to be amended into the name of the executor/administrator and re-dated, if necessary. The proceeds are lodged in the executor's account or the solicitor's client account as appropriate. Any pre-death income goes into the residue of the estate and any post-death income goes to the person who inherited the shares. This may give rise to income tax issues for the beneficiary.

This can be problematic, but the essential point to note with shares is what dividends have been declared and/or paid during the course of the administration. When a Registrar is notified of a death, it will automatically stop the payment of any further dividends until the grant is noted. Once the grant is noted, it will reissue the dividends in the name of the personal representative. As noted earlier, dividends on file that the personal representative has not been able to lodge should have been returned with the share certificates and the grant for noting and reissuing of the dividends.

It is essential to keep the counterfoils for income tax purposes. Difficulties can arise in keeping track of dividends, particularly where there is a large estate with a diverse amount of shares. If in difficulties, it is possible to write to the Registrar and ask for details of all dividends paid during a certain period. If the Registrar is being asked to merely repeat information that would have been available from the dividend counterfoils it will normally charge for this. Alternatively, the Registrar will answer queries on the shareholding by phone. It will be necessary to group the payment of the dividends into the appropriate tax years for income tax purposes.

12.3.5.6 Government stock

Certain government stocks can be tendered at par in the payment of probate tax (if applicable)/inheritance tax. These stocks should be identified as soon as possible. These stocks must be transferred to the Minister for Finance in payment of the tax. The benefit of tendering these at par value is lost if sold and the proceeds of sale are used to pay tax.

(At present, July 2021, the main government stocks are trading above par value at time of printing and so would not be suited for this purpose. Always ensure that the trading value is lower than par value if tendering government stocks.)

418 ADMINISTRATION AFTER THE GRANT HAS ISSUED

Also, similar government stock, if held by the deceased for the requisite period, can be bequeathed to non-domiciled residents or ordinarily resident beneficiaries free from inheritance tax. Students should review the CAT Lecture Notes (see Preface) for more details.

See https://www.ntma.ie/business-areas/funding-and-debt-management/government-securities for the most up-to-date listing of current government stocks available for payment of CAT at par and for Exemption of Government Securities for non-resident beneficiaries.

12.3.6 INSURANCE POLICIES

We are only dealing with insurance policies in favour of the estate which are the responsibility of the estate. Insurance policies may have been nominated in favour of an individual and as such would not be considered part of the estate and thus not the responsibility of our client, the personal representative.

The date-of-death value of the policy will already have been obtained from the appropriate insurance company. The value of this policy may have increased between the date of death and the date of encashment. If the sum assured is small, it may be collected on production of a death certificate and production of the policy, and the amount is paid on completion of a claim form by the personal representative.

This may prove useful, as it will provide funds to discharge expenses. In other cases a grant will be required.

In all cases, when obtaining the date-of-death value of the policy, the solicitor should ask the insurance company for its requirements to release the funds, together with the appropriate form for completion so that it will be available as soon as the grant issues.

12.3.7 PRIZE BONDS

As mentioned at para **6.6.5.3**, prize bonds registered in the name of the deceased's person continue to participate in all draws for up to twelve years following the end of the month in which the death occurred.

Prize bonds are payable/transferable to executors of the estate or next of kin, following notation of the death and written application declaring entitlement. Proof of death of the deceased, i.e. grant, death certificate, memorial card, newspaper obituary notice, or a photocopy of any of these will suffice. See p 4 of the Prize Bonds FAQs for further details:

http://www.statesavings.ie/Downloads/PrizeBondsFAQs.pdf.

Prize bonds registered in the joint names of a deceased's person with another person automatically become the sole property of that other person as survivor with absolute ownership. The Prize Bond Company corresponds directly with the survivor under separate cover.

Any specific requirements regarding prize bonds will need to be noted in a will and the relevant extract sent to the Prize Bond Company where appropriate. When written application is made by the personal representative, enquiries should be made as to whether the deceased had any other prize bonds registered in his name or in the joint name of him/herself and other(s) giving all known variations of names and addresses used by the deceased at any time since March 1957, when prize bonds began.

The forms are available at http://www.statesavings.ie or telephone 1850 30 50 60.

12.3.8 SOCIAL WELFARE OLD-AGE PENSIONS

Shortly after the date of death, it is necessary to ascertain from the Department of Social Protection if there is any outstanding pension due to the estate of the deceased as at the date of death. The pension book is returned to the Department of Social Protection and the necessary claim form can be downloaded for completion by the executor/administrator from the website: http://www.welfare.ie.

If the pension received is a non-contributory one, or indeed if the deceased was ever in receipt of a non-contributory payment during his or her lifetime, para **14.3** sets out in detail the potential obligations of the personal representative to the Department, which are quite onerous.

A statutory notice to creditors (s 49 notice) does not protect the personal representative from a claim by the Minister for Social Protection.

12.3.9 CIVIL SERVICE GRATUITIES

Death gratuities together with salary due and unpaid at death of serving civil servants and arrears of pensions of retired civil servants are payable from the Pay-Master General's office on production of a grant of probate/administration. As noted at para **6.6.5.11**, if the amount payable is under a certain figure and extraction of a grant is not otherwise necessary, the amount will be paid on completion of a statutory declaration giving particulars of death, next of kin, etc. Payment is made by way of warrant to be signed on the face by the payee.

12.3.10 MISCELLANEOUS

There may be additional assets for collection, i.e. directors' fees, debts due to the deceased, rental income, etc, all of which must be paid into the estate, and which if not included in the original Inland Revenue affidavit, may be the subject of a corrective affidavit, depending on the amount involved.

12.4 Payment of Liabilities (First Schedule, Parts I and II, Succession Act, 1965)

It is very important that prior to any payments being made from an estate, it should be clear whether the estate is solvent or insolvent and whether there it is fully testate, partially testate, or fully intestate.

12.4.1 INSOLVENT ESTATES

An insolvent estate is when the assets of the deceased are insufficient to pay the funeral, testamentary, and administration expenses, debts, and liabilities of the estate. Section 46 of the Act provides that where the estate of a deceased person is insolvent, it shall be administered in accordance with the rules set out in Part I of the First Schedule. Part I of the First Schedule is reproduced here:

'PART I

Rules as to payment of debts where the estate is insolvent

1. The funeral, testamentary and administration expenses have priority.

2. Subject as aforesaid, the same rules shall prevail and be observed as to the respective rights of secured and unsecured creditors and as to debts and liabilities provable and as to the valuation of annuities and future and contingent liabilities, respectively, and as to the priorities of debts and liabilities as may be in force for the time being under the law of bankruptcy with respect to the assets of persons adjudged bankrupt.

3. In the application of the said rules the date of death shall be substituted for the date of - adjudication in bankruptcy.'

Current bankruptcy legislation is contained largely in the Bankruptcy Act, 1988, operative from 1 January 1989, which should be consulted by solicitors acting in the administration of an insolvent estate. It is extremely rare for anyone but a creditor to administer an insolvent estate. This is provided for in s 81, which outlines the order of payment of debts, and at Part VI (ss 115–122) of the Bankruptcy Act, 1988 and O 79, r 5(4), which provides for a creditor extracting the necessary grant. Practitioners are referred to Sanfey and Holohan, *Bankruptcy Law and Practice in Ireland*, 2nd edn (2010), Chapter 17. Practitioners are also referred to articles in the *Law Society Gazette*: Patrick Shee (solicitor), 'At Debt's Door', October 2010 and Cian O'Sullivan (solicitor), 'Night of the Living Debt', January/February 2010. The Personal Insolvency Act, 2012 does not affect the administration of the estate of a bankrupt significantly and if the deceased was subject to a debt relief notice, debt settlement arrangement, or personal insolvency arrangement the effect of these is unchanged by their death.

Section 115 of the Bankruptcy Act allows a petition for the administration of the estate of a deceased person to be presented to the court by any creditor whose debt would have been sufficient to support a bankruptcy petition against the deceased if he had been alive or by the personal representative. The result of this (see s 116(1)) is that the payment by the personal representative who has received such a notice shall operate as a discharge to him as between himself and the official assignee.

Under the provisions of the Bankruptcy Act, 1988, there is a restriction on the personal representative's right of retainer (see para **12.4.2.1**). In essence, where an order is made for administration under Part VI of the Act, the right of the personal representative shall not be exercisable, but he may prove any debt due to him, which would otherwise be provable.

Under s 116(2) of the Bankruptcy Act, 1988, nothing in the Act shall invalidate any payment made or any act or thing done in good faith by the personal representative before the date of the order for the administration.

Section 117 of the Bankruptcy Act, 1988 allows the court, on presentation of a petition, providing that there is reasonable probability that the estate can pay the deceased's debts, to make an order for the administration of the deceased's estate and the property of the deceased will vest in the official assignee for realisation and distribution.

Where a creditor takes out a grant of administration (whether with will annexed or intestate) funeral expenses have long had first priority in the administration of the deceased's estate: *McCausland v O'Callaghan* [1904] 1 IR 376. This is also provided for in s 119 of the Bankruptcy Act, 1988 which states:

> '*In the administration under this Part of the deceased's estate, the proper funeral and testamentary expenses incurred shall, notwithstanding anything to the contrary in this or any other enactment, be payable in full in priority to all other payments.*'

However, the funeral expenses incurred must be reasonable and determined in the light of any particular case, and in insolvent cases only those funeral expenses which are absolutely necessary will be paid: see *Re Wester Wemyss* [1940] Ch 1. If such expenses are paid by someone other than the personal representative, they may be recovered from the deceased's estate.

When the funeral, testamentary, and administration expenses have been discharged, the personal representative must apply the assets of the deceased in payment of his debts according to the rules laid down in bankruptcy legislation: see para **12.4.1.1** and s 81 of the Bankruptcy Act, 1988. A creditor who has security for his loan is adequately covered if the value of his security equals or exceeds the amount of the debt; conversely, if the value of the security is less than the debt, he can realise his security and prove for the balance of his debt: *Re McEntee* [1960] IR Jur Rep 55.

As stated, caution should be exercised in any case where it is likely that there could be insufficient assets to discharge all liabilities. The personal representative has a duty to minimise the liabilities insofar as is reasonable; thus where funds are available to discharge liabilities, particularly where interest is accruing on same, then this should be attended to as soon as possible, always ensuring, however, that preferential payments, as outlined in s 81 of the Act, are paid first. See also Stephenson Solicitors' 22nd Seminar, *Who Pays the Ferryman?*, 16 November 2012, pp 102–14.

12.4.1.1 Priority and preferential payments

Once the funeral, testamentary, and administration expenses have been discharged, the personal representative must apply the assets of the deceased according to the rules laid down in the legislation. As already pointed out, secured creditors who have security by way of mortgage or charge are in a more favourable position. However, in the class of unsecured creditors there are certain preferential debts, as laid down in the bankruptcy legislation.

Preference is a right whereby the personal representative may prefer one creditor against another in respect of debts of equal degree (s 46(2)). These debts are:

1. Rates and taxes due at the testator's death, including the Universal Social Charge—see Spierin, *The Succession Act 1965 and Related Legislation: A Commentary*, 5th edn (2017), paras 258–67; Holohan and Sanfey, *Bankruptcy Law and Practice in Ireland*, 2nd edn (2010), paras 17-01–17-03 and 13-28; and ss 960P and 982 of the Taxes Consolidation Act, 1997;

2. Wages or salary for labour of workmen, clerks, or servants in respect of services rendered within four months of the deceased's death;

3. Sums due in respect of contributions payable by the deceased in the twelve-month period prior to death upon social welfare national insurance legislation—see Social Welfare Consolidation Act, 2005.

Once these preferential debts have been discharged, ordinary debts can then be paid. While there is a right to prefer creditors of equal priority under s 46(2)(b), it would be advisable to abate all debts proportionately where insufficient funds are available to pay all the ordinary debts in full.

12.4.2 SOLVENT ESTATES

As the name suggests, a solvent estate is one where there are sufficient assets to pay the debts and the funeral and testamentary expenses. In most cases, there are sufficient assets to pay all the debts, funeral, and testamentary expenses and pay all of the legatees and devisees in full. In all cases, where there are more assets than liabilities the estate is solvent, even if there are not sufficient funds to pay all pecuniary bequests after payment of all debts, funeral, and testamentary expenses.

When this arises, s 46 directs that the assets of a solvent estate are to be distributed in accordance with the rules set out in Part II of the First Schedule as set out at para **12.4.2.2**. This sets out the order in which the legatees and devisees are to be paid. If an asset is not administered in the correct order, any legatee and/or devisee who is adversely affected by this is entitled to have the assets *marshalled* (applied in correct order, which may result in the burden of any deficiency falling on some other legatee before it falls on his share).

In calculating the value of a claim by a spouse or civil partner to a legal right share, this is to be calculated as if it were a claim against the assets of the estate to a sum equal to the value of that share—see s 46(6). Section 112 of the Act provides that the right of a spouse/civil partner has priority over devises, bequests, and shares on intestacy.

Where there are sufficient assets to discharge all liabilities, but the balance remaining will not cover the bequests to beneficiaries, the legacies and possibly devises will have to be reduced proportionally to ensure a proper distribution, i.e. abatement. See para **12.4.2.3**.

12.4.2.1 Personal representative's right of retainer

Section 46(2) of the Succession Act gives the personal representative the right of retainer. This allows a personal representative, who is himself a creditor of the estate, to pay his own debts before paying other creditors *of equal degree*. However, the right of retainer only applies to debts owing to the representative in his own right, whether solely or jointly with another person (not in his capacity as trustee) (see Spierin, 5th edn (2017), para 262), and the right of retainer is not exercisable where the estate is insolvent (see Spierin, 5th edn (2017), p 264).

12.4.2.2 Order of payment of funeral, testamentary and administration expenses, debts, and legal right share

In the case of a solvent estate, the assets must be applied to pay the funeral, testamentary, and administration expenses, together with the debts and liabilities of the estate. The personal representatives must then satisfy the legal right share of any surviving spouse/civil partner. In making the relevant payments, the personal representatives will have to resort to the assets of the deceased in the order provided for in Part II of the First Schedule as outlined here:

> 'PART II
>
> *Order of application of assets where the estate is solvent.*
>
> 1. *Property of the deceased undisposed of by will, subject to the retention thereout of a fund sufficient to meet any pecuniary legacies.*
>
> 2. *Property of the deceased not specifically devised or bequeathed but included (either by a specific or general description) in a residuary gift, subject to the retention out of such property of a fund sufficient to meet any pecuniary legacies, so far as not provided for as aforesaid.*
>
> 3. *Property of the deceased specifically appropriated or devised or bequeathed (either by a specific or general description) for the payment of debts.*
>
> 4. *Property of the deceased charged with, or devised or bequeathed (either by a specific or general description) subject to a charge for, the payment of debts.*
>
> 5. *The fund, if any, retained to meet pecuniary legacies.*
>
> 6. *Property specifically devised or bequeathed, rateably according to value.*
>
> 7. *Property appointed by will under a general power, rateably according to value.*
>
> 8. *The following provisions shall also apply—*
>
>   (a) *The order of application may be varied by the will of the deceased.*
>
>   (b) *This Part of this Schedule does not affect the liability of land to answer the death duty imposed thereon in exoneration of other assets.'*

To deal with each in order:

1. Property 'undisposed of by will' refers to a partial intestacy. See para **12.1.2**.

2. '*Residue*' refers to 'net residue' which is normally calculated as follows:

    Gross estate (see paras **4.5.1** and **4.5.2**)

    Less **legacies and devises** (see para **2.7**)

    Leaves the **gross residue**

    Less **debts and funeral and testamentary expenses payable out of residue**

    Leaves the **net residue.**

    Practitioners should always start with the gross estate and not the net estate, as some debts etc are not payable out of residue.

3. It is unusual but possible to have a specific fund set aside under the terms of the will to be applied for the payment of debts and funeral and testamentary expenses.

4. It is again unusual but possible that a particular bequest in a will could be charged with or conditional upon the payment of debts and funeral and testamentary expenses.

5. Any debts and funeral and testamentary expenses and then legal right share outstanding will be paid out of any monies available to pay pecuniary (cash) legacies. As these are normally paid out of residue, this issue tends to be moot.

6. Any debts and funeral and testamentary expenses and then legal right share still outstanding will be paid 'rateably according to value' out of the specific devises or bequests. The effect of this in practice would be that any specific devises or bequests would be 'charged' proportionally with any outstanding debts and funeral and testamentary expenses and legal right share, i.e. they would be paid as follows:

$$\frac{Individual\ specific\ bequest}{Total\ amount\ of\ specific\ bequests} \times Outstanding\ debts\ etc$$

7. Finally, if there are still debts and funeral and testamentary expenses outstanding, any property over which the deceased exercised a power of appointment in the will, again rateably according to value.

In a typical case, where there is no partial intestacy, no property over which the testator had a power of appointment, and no provisions in the will (apart from the usual instruction to executors to pay debts and funeral and testamentary expenses) for the payment of debts from a particular asset or fund, the order of application of assets to pay debts will be as follows:

1. any assets falling into residue, residue in this case being the sum of money 'leftover' having already taken pecuniary legacies into account;

2. any sum of money set aside to pay pecuniary legacies (rateably according to value if the legacies are greater than the outstanding debt);

3. any property specifically bequeathed (personalty) or devised (realty) rateably according to value. There is no distinction made between personalty and realty when apportioning the remaining debts.

Where any doubt as to the solvency of the estate arises, it is more prudent for personal representatives to distribute the assets among creditors on the basis that the estate is insolvent until it is clear that there are sufficient assets to discharge all debts and liabilities of the deceased and that there is in fact a surplus.

It is emphasised that the deceased has the power to specify in the will the order in which the assets are to be used for the payment of debts, but he cannot adversely affect the priority of a surviving spouse/civil partner's legal share.

It is also emphasised that any variation in the order of the application of assets must be specifically specified in the will, not just the usual general instruction to pay debts as provided for in the precedent will at para **2.17**. It should also be noted that a specific instruction in relation to the payment of debts does not, of course, apply to the legal right share.

12.4.2.3 Abatement

Abatement was referred to with some examples at para **2.7.5**. To the extent that legacies of a particular class must be resorted to for the payment of debts or of the spouse/civil partner's legal right share, the rule is that legacies within the same class will abate proportionately: *Samson v Devereaux* [1996] 1 ICLMD 75; [1996] 3 ICLMD 75. Thus, for example, if the personal representatives must resort to the fund reserved for pecuniary legacies, they may need to only partly utilise that fund (so that the pecuniary legatees will receive part of their share). The funds will abate in accordance with the following formula:

$$\frac{Funds\ available}{Total\ amount\ of\ pecuniary\ legacies} \times Legacy\ bequeathed$$

Example

Personal representatives must resort to the fund of €20,000.00 set aside for payment of pecuniary legacies. They require €5,000.00 to pay off the surviving spouse's legal right share, leaving them with a net pecuniary legacy fund of €15,000.00. The testator had directed that legatee A was to receive €1,000.00. His legacy will in fact abate to €750.00 as follows:

$$\frac{€15,000.00}{€20,000.00} \times €1,000.00 = €750.00$$

A similar procedure is applied to specific legacies or devises where it is necessary to pay debts or the surviving spouse's/civil partner's legal right share. In that case, in order to receive the specific legacy or devise, the legatee or devisee would need to pay the proportionate amount prior to vesting of the asset.

Example—the 'illiquid' estate

The total of the specific devises of real property amount to €1 million; there is €100,000 outstanding to be paid to creditors after the residue of the estate was spent on this purpose. One specific devisee is entitled to land valued at €100,000. Another specific devisee is entitled to land valued at €200,000 and the final specific devisee is entitled to land valued at €700,000.

Each devisee must pay their share of the outstanding €100,000 rateably in proportion to the value of the specific legacy or devise to be received by him or her.

The first devisee is entitled to 10 per cent of the specific devises and thus must pay 10 per cent of the outstanding debt/legal right share, i.e. €10,000, prior to the land being vested in him. This gives him a 'net' asset of €90,000, which will be the value of the bequest for CAT purposes.

The next devisee is entitled to 20 per cent of the specific legacies and devises and thus must pay 10 per cent of the outstanding debt/legal right share, i.e. €20,000, prior to the land being vested in him. This gives him a 'net' asset of €180,000, which will be the value of the bequest for CAT purposes.

The final devisee is entitled to 70 per cent of the specific legacies and devises and thus must pay 70 per cent of the outstanding debt/legal right share, i.e. €70,000 prior to the land being vested in him. This gives him a 'net' asset of €630,000, which will be the value of the devise for CAT purposes.

If (as in this example) land (often referred to in this context as immovable property) is to be vested, it is important that the relevant portion of the outstanding debt is paid by the beneficiary to the estate prior to the immoveable asset being vested in the beneficiary.

As stated earlier, there is no distinction between legacies and devises for this purpose. If one of the beneficiaries outlined in this chapter was receiving movable assets instead of immovable, the same procedure would apply.

12.5 Steps to Take Prior to Distribution of Assets

As noted earlier in **Chapter 6**, it may not be necessary in all cases for somebody acting as the representative of the deceased to extract a grant of representation. In so far as an executor is concerned, he has authority to act from the date of death of the testator by virtue of having been appointed in the deceased's will. In contrast, the administrator has no authority to act until he has been granted letters of administration. It would, therefore, be possible in some cases for an executor to perform his duties without formally extracting a grant of probate, depending on the nature of the assets.

The personal representative will normally extract a grant of representation for two reasons. The first is that until he obtains the grant, he has no *official proof of title*. He may not require proof of title in dealing with certain assets of the deceased (such as land which had been held by the deceased as a joint owner), which thus passes to the surviving joint tenant by way of survivorship; joint bank accounts, where the balance passes automatically to a co-owner; the ability to withdraw small sums of money from accounts under s 58 of the Friendly Societies Act, 1896, nominated insurance policies, Credit Union accounts, etc.

However, where other assets are involved (such as land registered in the deceased's own name, shares in public limited companies, and large sums and deposits in financial institutions), the personal representative will find it impossible to deal with these assets, as they will not be released to him unless he can prove his title by producing his grant of representation.

12.5.1 PROTECTION OF REPRESENTATIVES

Extracting the grant also acts to protect anybody who transfers or deals with the assets at the personal representative's request and also protects the personal representative himself.

This protection is afforded by s 22, which provides that any person making a payment or disposition of property of the deceased in good faith under a grant of representation is indemnified and protected in doing so. This is the case notwithstanding the fact that it transpires the grant may not have been valid. Equally, any person who pays over property of the deceased to such a personal representative is regarded as having received a valid discharge in respect of such payment.

12.5.2 SECTION 49 NOTICE TO CREDITORS

There is a common law rule that the personal representative of the deceased will be liable for his (the deceased's) debts to the extent of the deceased's assets, notwithstanding that he may have distributed them to legatees because he was not aware of the debts in question.

Section 49 of the Succession Act confers a protection on a personal representative, which provides that if the personal representative has issued suitable notices (usually referred to as 's 49 notices') to creditors and anyone else with a claim against the estate, and he has not received notification of any such claims, then he may proceed to distribute the estate and cannot afterwards be made responsible for any claim which was not made known to him.

No specific rules are laid down as to what the court would regard as appropriate notices, but normal practice is to place an advertisement in a newspaper with a national circulation for two consecutive weeks and normally, in addition, an advertisement in a regional newspaper in the area where the deceased lived. This notice would clearly specify the deceased and notify the public that the personal representative is about to distribute the estate. It would call on anyone with a claim against the estate to contact the personal representatives (or normally their solicitors) within the period specified in the notice. The period specified is usually one calendar month after the date of the second or last notice. The personal representative is still liable to the extent of unadministered assets in his possession at the time he receives notice of any debt outside the notice period. A precedent statutory notice to creditors is provided at para **14.5.1**.

It should be noted that while the personal representative is protected where any distribution is made following this procedure, this does not prejudice the right of any creditor to subsequently trace the assets into the hands of the legatees to whom they have been distributed. Section 59 makes clear that the legatee or any person to whom he has passed the property (other than a purchaser) will remain accountable to a creditor in respect of the property which he has received.

The implication of s 49 is that if the personal representative is to be protected against creditors in respect of any distribution of assets which he makes, he should postpone distribution until he has placed relevant notices to creditors in an effort to ascertain all claims against the deceased's estate. See Stephenson Solicitors' 22nd Seminar, *Who Pays the Ferryman?*, 16 November 2012, pp 34–8.

12.5.2.1 Exceptions to section 49

Section 49 notices do not protect the personal representative against claims by the Minister for Social Protection under s 339 of the Social Welfare Consolidation Act, 2005 (see para **14.3**), the 'Fair Deal' Scheme under the Nursing Homes Support Scheme Act, 2009 (see para **14.4**), or any outstanding taxation liabilities.

12.5.3 EXECUTOR'S YEAR

It is a general rule of law that the personal representative has a period of one year from the date of the testator's death in which to complete administration of the estate. Section 62 requires the personal representative to complete administration *as soon as is reasonably practicable,* having regard to the nature of the estate and all relevant circumstances. It confirms, however, that the personal representative cannot be sued for their failure to distribute within the period of one year from the deceased's death, unless this is done with the consent of the court.

This does not prejudice the rights of any creditor to sue the personal representative before the expiration of the executor's year. The personal representative should promptly discharge all debts which are due and it appears that failure to do so, necessitating court action against the deceased's estate and therefore additional costs and loss to the beneficiaries, would result in the personal representatives being held personally liable and negligent: *Re Tankard* [1942] Ch 69.

12.5.4 PROTECTION OF PURCHASERS AND CREDITORS

12.5.4.1 Purchasers: sections 51 and 61 of the Succession Act

Sections 51 and 61 of the Succession Act provide that a purchaser of property from a personal representative is entitled to assume that the personal representative is acting correctly and within his powers. So long, therefore, as the purchaser provides valuable consideration, he will obtain a good title to the property he has acquired from a personal representative. Section 67 of the Civil Law (Miscellaneous Provisions) Act, 2008 amended the definition of 'Purchaser' found in s 3 of the Succession Act, 1965 by deleting the words 'in good faith' from 20 July 2008.

12.5.4.2 Creditors

Brief mention has already been made of s 49 of the Succession Act. We have seen that so long as the personal representative has advertised for creditors, he may proceed to distribute the deceased's assets to the beneficiaries under the will or intestacy. If, however, it transpires that a creditor then makes a claim within the relevant period set down by the Statute of Limitations (e.g. a legatee who has been presumed dead, and whose share was distributed), that person has the right to follow the property of a deceased to the beneficiary to whom it was given, and he may ultimately trace the property to any person to whom that beneficiary passed it, so long as it is not a bona fide purchaser for value.

12.5.5 PARTIAL DISTRIBUTION

As a general rule, distribution of the estate takes place when the final accounts are ready. However, in some estates, advances/payments on account may be made to the residuary legatees/successors pending completion of the administration, and accordingly there may be several valuation dates.

Where there are different valuation dates, the beneficiary should be advised to pay and file on the appropriate date after each individual valuation date. Where the solicitor is also acting for the beneficiary in the filing and payment of tax, the sum net of any tax due should be sent to the beneficiary and the tax paid and return filed prior to the appropriate date.

Before making any payment on account to a beneficiary, it is imperative that:

1. all debts of the estate are known; and
2. there are sufficient funds to discharge them.

Payments to beneficiaries and receipts and indemnities will be covered later in this chapter and in **Chapter 14**, but suffice to say that the beneficiary's CAT history should have been disclosed to the personal representative and all necessary receipts and indemnities should be provided prior to payment. Where all the beneficiaries are Irish residents, CAT is not an issue for the personal representative and is entirely the responsibility of the beneficiary. Where there is a non-resident beneficiary, the estate is secondarily liable for the payment of CAT. Students should review the CAT Lecture Notes (see Preface) for more detail. Where the solicitor for the estate is paying CAT on behalf of the beneficiary (whether resident or non-resident), any payment of a bequest to a beneficiary should be net of this amount.

Before making any partial distribution, personal representatives should also ensure that any liability to CGT is quantified and paid.

12.6 Joint Property

Practitioners should be aware of the issues surrounding joint property. This section will concentrate on some of the practical issues surrounding the collection of joint property and the clearances that will be required. Practitioners should re-read para **6.6.7**, and students should refer to the CAT Lecture Notes (see Preface) for more detail before proceeding. It is also strongly recommended that practitioners read the Practice Note in relation to joint property and elderly clients issued by the Guidance and Ethics Committee of the Law Society, published in the December 2008 issue of the *Law Society Gazette*.

Where assets are held in joint names it is important to establish at the outset whether such interest is a joint tenancy or a tenancy in common. Title documents should always be examined to establish the nature of the deceased's interest in the premises and to determine what property is affected by the terms of the will.

Where true joint accounts, other than current accounts, are concerned, a death certificate is usually the only requirement but, as mentioned previously, if it exceeds €50,000 (formerly €31,750) the bank will require evidence that no CAT is payable. A certificate of clearance should then be obtained from the Revenue Commissioners; however, this is not necessary where the surviving joint tenant is the surviving spouse or civil partner.

12.6.1 PRESUMPTION OF ADVANCEMENT/RESULTING TRUST

At this stage of the administration the beneficial ownership of the funds should have been clearly identified. The solicitor should now be fully aware of the status of the survivor, as surviving joint owner, and whether the presumption of advancement applies. The solicitor should also by now have fully investigated any possibility of a resulting trust in favour of the estate.

An example of where this may arise is where a testator left a bank account to two persons jointly, both of whom survive the testator. Should one of the joint legatees die before the administration of the estate is complete, it is strongly arguable that his or her half of the account does not go to the surviving joint tenant by survivorship but would form part of the deceased joint tenant's estate by resulting trust.

The legal position of a co-owner holding by way of a joint tenancy is that there is a right of survivorship, and their undivided share passes automatically to the survivor on death.

In a case where the survivor has not provided any consideration for the property, equity presumes that the individual holds the property upon a resulting trust for the estate.

It may be possible to rebut this presumption, and the following are examples of situations where the presumption can be rebutted:

1. Where the deceased held the joint property in his capacity as a trustee;

2. Where there is a presumption of advancement. This applies where the transferee is the wife or child of the transferor or is otherwise a person to whom the transferor stands *in loco parentis*;

3. Where there is evidence that the transferor intended to benefit the transferee. This is the situation covered by *Lynch v Burke and Allied Irish Banks Plc* [1991] IR 1 (HC); [1996] 1 ILRM 114 (SC), and this is probably the situation that will be the most difficult to prove;

4. Where the trust is created for a fraudulent or illegal purpose. If a donor puts property in the name of another in order to achieve an unlawful or illegal purpose, the transferor can still claim title, as long as he can rely on some ground other than the illegal or unlawful purpose.

12.6.1.1 Presumption of advancement

The presumption of advancement is an area of law where a distinction between the sexes is deemed still to apply.

Historically, the presumption of advancement has always applied in the case of a husband to wife and a father to child and to anyone else in relation to whom a father stands *in loco parentis*. There is a limited furtherance of the presumption where a widow places property in the joint names of herself and her children. This was on the basis that the wife (widow) had taken on the moral obligation of the husband/father once slight circumstantial evidence supported this. This presumption is not traditionally applied to any other set of relationships.

It is difficult to imagine that such a narrow interpretation of the presumption would be entertained in today's society. However, should a solicitor be instructed to claim the presumption outside the traditional interpretation, as the High Court can only look to the Constitution if pleaded, the constitutional significance of any such application should be pleaded.

To rebut the presumption of advancement, sufficient evidence must be brought by the person challenging it. It is more difficult to rebut the presumption of advancement than to rebut the presumption of resulting trust.

The doctrine of advancement is not rebutted by the retention of title deeds by the disponer.

12.6.2 DISTINCTION BETWEEN REAL/LEASEHOLD PROPERTY AND JOINT DEPOSITS

The question of joint real/leasehold property must be distinguished from the position pertaining to monies held on joint deposit. There are three separate accepted reasons for two or more persons holding monies on joint deposit, and the succession and tax treatment of all three differ.

12.6.2.1 Monies placed on joint account for the convenience of the beneficial owner

This often arises where the beneficial owner of the money, who provided all the money in the account, places the account in the joint names of himself and another solely to enable the joint tenant to utilise the account, but only for the beneficial owner's benefit. Examples of this would be where the beneficial owner is elderly or incapacitated and the joint holder pays bills etc out of the joint account on his behalf. Similarly, a business account of a sole trader may be in the joint names of the sole trader and a manager, to enable the manager to sign cheques to pay creditors, etc.

The contents of this account will remain the assets of the provider, and the presumption of advancement will not arise. No beneficial interest passes to the surviving joint tenants.

12.6.2.2 Monies provided by both (or all)

Where the funds were provided in equal shares by the joint tenants and each has the power to withdraw without limit, no difficulty arises. The account passes by survivorship and outside the estate.

12.6.2.3 Monies provided by one party with the intention that surviving joint holder benefit on death

There is a presumption of benefit, but only on the death of the beneficial owner of the account. This is the most usual type of joint account. Such joint deposits were traditionally seen as a method of passing property while evading estate duties (particularly in rural Ireland). The history of such joint deposits has been contentious. For such a joint deposit to pass by survivorship, evidence is required that the beneficial owner intended that the survivor should benefit (as outlined at para **12.6.1**, Example 3). Where there is evidence showing that the transferor intended to benefit the donee or the person in whose name the legal title is taken, then no resulting trust will arise. The donee will be allowed to keep the property absolutely. As noted earlier, the Supreme Court decision in *Lynch v Burke and Allied Irish Banks Plc* [1991] IR 1 (HC); [1996] 1 ILRM 114 (SC) radically changed the law in dealing with such joint accounts. In the UK case of *Aroso v Coutts & Co* [2002] 1 All ER (Comm) 241 at 248–9, it was held that the fact that one of the holders of the joint account did not contribute to or draw upon the account did not prevent that person from having a beneficial interest. Moreover, the fact that the person was not aware of the existence of the account and it was never intended that that person use the account while the other was alive did not prevent that person from succeeding to the whole of the account by survivorship.

Full instructions should be taken, and it will be necessary that provable evidence of such intention exist. *Lynch and Burke* does not automatically provide that all joint accounts go to the survivor, but merely allows joint accounts to pass to the survivor when it can be clearly shown that this was the intention of the disponer. In the case of *Lynch and Burke*, the intention of the disponer was so clear that the Chief Justice found that he could not possibly have made any other finding regarding the disponer's intention than the one that he did make.

This may not always necessarily be the case, and each time a particular intention of the disponer is claimed, it must be provable. Practitioners are advised to read both the High Court and Supreme Court judgments in this very important case.

12.6.3 BEST PRACTICE

In all cases, where joint property, whether real property, a leasehold interest, or a joint account, is disclosed, the solicitor should check all the surrounding circumstances and consider whether the property is passing by survivorship or forms part of the deceased's free estate. In particular, a copy of the account mandate should be sought from the bank where there is any doubt.

Once this has been clarified, having made the fullest enquiries (particularly in the case of joint accounts), only where the solicitor is fully satisfied as to which presumptions, if any, apply, should he proceed to deal with the joint account.

12.6.3.1 Section 121(9) of the Succession Act

The subject of joint property must also be looked at in the light of s 121(9) of the Succession Act. This deals with the disposition of property under which the beneficial ownership of property vests in possession in the donee within three years before the death of the donor or on his death or later i.e. where the deceased gave assets away within three years of his or her death.

Under this section, accrual by survivorship on the death of a joint tenant of property will, for the purposes of the section, be deemed to be a vesting of the beneficial ownership of the entire property in the survivor(s). Obviously, the transfer of property into joint names could have been carried out with the intention of defeating the provisions of s 121. This brings such a disposition within the reach of s 121, and it would accordingly be voidable.

This would only be applicable if the joint tenancy was created in the first instance for the purpose of defeating or substantially diminishing the shares of a surviving spouse or children.

12.6.4 TAXATION CONSEQUENCES OF JOINT PROPERTY

As noted in the CAT Lecture Notes (see Preface), s 13(1) of the Capital Acquisitions Tax Consolidation Act, 2003 deals with the position where persons are joint tenants and one of them dies. That subsection states that the survivor or survivors are deemed to take the deceased's share as an inheritance derived from him.

Section 13(2) of the Act follows s 7 (gift tax) by stating that the liability to inheritance tax in respect of an inheritance taken by persons as joint tenants shall be the same in all respects as if they took the inheritance as tenants in common in equal shares.

Should two persons (for example) inherit property absolutely from a disponer as joint tenants, they are deemed to inherit half the property each from him as tenants in common. Should one of the joint tenants then die, the surviving joint tenant inherits half the property from the deceased joint tenant and not the original disponer.

As noted in the CAT Lecture Notes (see Preface), s 109 of the Capital Acquisitions Tax Consolidation Act, 2003 states that sums of money held in joint deposit accounts in excess of €50,000 can be transferred to the surviving joint tenant on production of a letter of clearance (form IT8) from the Revenue Commissioners. It is the practice to file a form CA4 with the Revenue Commissioners in order to obtain the letter of clearance before such assets are released. The form CA4 is a four-page form, similar in format to the Inland Revenue affidavit, but does not have to be sworn.

Where the surviving joint account holder is the surviving spouse or civil partner, no certificate or form is necessary.

As far as the paying bank is concerned, it appears to operate on the following lines: *see Paget's Law of Banking*, 14th edn (2007), which states at p 219:

> 'When an account is a joint account and one party dies, the survivor [or survivors] is [or are] in ordinary cases entitled to the whole amount, either under the Law of Devolution between joint owners or by custom of bankers or by express or implied agreement. The banker obtains a good discharge by paying the survivor.'

12.6.4.1 Potential charge to gift tax

In addition to inheritance tax being payable on the death of a deceased joint holder, there may also be gift tax due, backdated from the date on which the property was put into joint names.

This underlines the need to obtain full details to ascertain the extent of the tax liability. Even if the deceased joint holder enjoyed the income solely, it is possible that the surviving beneficiary will take an inheritance of the entire property.

Regard must also be had to the inheritance tax implications of creating a joint tenancy. The essential questions raised by the Revenue Commissioners are:

1. Who provided the joint property? and
2. Who gets the entire property?

To answer these questions, the following points must be clarified:

1. the source of the joint property;
2. the relationship of the parties;
3. evidence to rebut or support advancement or resulting trust;
4. in relation to personalty, how the income was dealt with.

As far as a joint tenancy is concerned for tax purposes, it can be argued that a beneficiary takes a moiety by survivorship. If this is argued, there is a possible claim for gift tax in relation to the original creation of the joint tenancy. However, if the property was put into joint names prior to 5 December 1991 (assuming an inheritance after 5 December 2001) there will be no aggregation between the previous gift and subsequent inheritance. If a gift is argued, evidence supporting this argument will be required by the Revenue Commissioners.

At the outset of any administration, the practitioner should obtain all the information as set out earlier and be satisfied as to the status of ownership.

12.7 Nominations

Nominations, which are also dealt with at para **6.9.6.2**, are dealt with under two headings: statutory and non-statutory. Successfully nominated assets fall outside the estate but are still liable to CAT.

12.7.1 STATUTORY NOMINATIONS

The following are the statutory nominations that persons may avail themselves of.

12.7.1.1 Industrial and provident societies

The Industrial and Provident Societies Act, 1893, as amended, and the Trustee Savings Bank Acts permit persons to dispose of property by nomination, during their lifetime, to take effect on death. The value of property that can be nominated was restricted; for example, under the Industrial and Provident Societies Act, 1893 it is restricted to approximately €7,618. This applies to accounts in Trustees Savings Bank, which are now held in Irish Life and Permanent Plc.

12.7.1.2 Credit unions

The Credit Union Act, 1997, as amended, provides for the power of nomination of property in a credit union, which will pass outside the terms of a deceased's will or on intestacy. As noted earlier, a member of a credit union, over the age of 16, can nominate, by written statement, a person to become entitled to his assets (whether by way of savings, loans, insurances, or otherwise) in the credit union up to a limit of €23,000.

It is extremely important to remember that any credit union assets in excess of this amount will form part of the estate of the deceased. This nomination is variable and revocable by the nominator; it is revoked by subsequent marriage/entrance into civil partnership but is not revoked by subsequent will.

12.7.2 NON-STATUTORY NOMINATIONS

These topics have been covered at paras **6.6.5.10** and **6.6.5.11**.

12.7.2.1 Pension schemes

Most modern pension schemes give the employee a power of nomination under which the employee can name the person he wishes to take the benefit payable under the scheme on death. This is because most pension funds are set up in the form of a trust. The trustees of the pension scheme will normally exercise their discretion in favour of the person nominated, provided that they are within the definition of 'beneficiaries' within the terms of the scheme.

The nomination takes effect on request to the trustees of the scheme and is usually not binding on them and the property, therefore, is not regarded as property which is owned beneficially by the deceased or property which the deceased had power to give. It is arguable, therefore, that property nominated under a pension scheme is not to be taken into account in ascertaining the legal right share of a spouse or civil partner. Following the same line of argument, such a nomination of pension scheme is not a disposition under s 121 of the Succession Act.

Property under a pension scheme may be liable to capital acquisitions tax, except in the case of a spouse or civil partner benefiting, where there is complete exemption from CAT.

When dealing with monies paid under pension schemes, it is essential to obtain correct details of the class of beneficiaries entitled under the scheme. It is also important to note that property under the scheme may be liable to CAT. If the scheme comes within the terms of s 80 of the Capital Acquisitions Tax Consolidation Act, 2003 then the disponer would be the deceased for the purpose of determining the tax liability.

12.7.2.2 Insurance policies

A deceased may have insured his life for the benefit of himself or his estate and on his death the proceeds of the policy will form part of his estate. If, on the other hand, the deceased created a trust of the property (policy) for the benefit of, say, a person with whom he is living but who is not his spouse or civil partner, the proceeds will not form part of his estate.

Dealing with an insurance policy in such a way may be considered a disposition for the purpose of s 121 of the Succession Act, 1965, i.e.:

1. a disposition made for the purpose of defeating or substantially diminishing the share of the disponer's spouse;

2. a disposition of property other than a testamentary disposition; or

3. a disposition to a purchaser under which the beneficial ownership of the property vests in possession in the donee within three years before the death of the person who made it, or on his death, or later.

In dealing with insurance policies it is also necessary to establish who owns the proceeds, whether they are taxable, and whether some person other than the deceased gave consideration. Did the donee pay the premiums?

Normally, if the deceased paid the premiums, the proceeds of the policy would be taxable for CAT purposes in the hands of the donee, but if the donee paid the premiums, then no CAT would arise.

12.7.3 NOMINATIONS AND THE LEGAL RIGHT SHARE

Questions have arisen as to whether property passing under a form of nomination should be taken into the calculation for the purpose of ascertaining the 'legal right share' of a spouse or civil partner, as it is not passing under the will of the deceased.

One should be mindful of s 109(2) of the Succession Act, which states that:

'References to the estate of the testator are to all estate to which he was beneficially entitled.'

Therefore, nominations need to be looked at carefully to ensure whether or not they come within the section.

It is necessary to consider:

1. Did the insured (deceased) pay all the premiums? He may have done so, but nominated a particular beneficiary.

2. Did the insured (deceased) pay some of the premiums and the donee pay some? If so, it may be necessary to apportion the benefit for CAT purposes.

3. Did the beneficiary pay all the premiums? If so, it is not an asset of the estate, as the beneficiary of the proceeds of the policy gave full consideration.

4. Section 121 as outlined at para **12.6.3.1**.

12.8 Section 72 Policies (Formerly Known as 'Section 60 Policies')

See also the CAT Lecture Notes (see Preface), which deal with s 72 policies in detail.

To summarise, the provisions of s 72 of the Capital Acquisitions Tax Consolidation Act, 2003 provide that if the deceased took out a life insurance policy to pay inheritance tax which was termed a 'qualifying insurance policy' and:

1. it is in a form approved by the Revenue Commissioners;

2. in respect of which annual premiums are paid by the insured during his life; and

3. which is expressly effected for the purpose of paying 'relevant tax', then the proceeds of that policy so used, to pay inheritance tax, are not taxable.

'Relevant tax' refers to inheritance tax arising in respect of a disposition made by the insured. Relief is restricted to paying inheritance tax in respect of an inheritance 'taken on or after the death of the insured and not later than one year after that death'.

The proceeds of s 72 policies can also be utilised to pay probate tax (if applicable) and if so used to pay either probate/capital acquisitions tax are themselves exempt from the taxes. Any excess proceeds after payment of said taxes are taxable as an inheritance in the normal fashion.

When drafting a will where there is a s 72 policy, it is wise to give the personal representative power to use the proceeds to pay 'all relevant tax'.

12.9 Appropriation

This has already been discussed at para **3.8.1.2**.

As discussed, s 55 confers on the personal representative power to appropriate any part of the estate of the deceased in its actual condition or state of investment at the time of appropriation, in or towards satisfaction of any share in the estate, subject to notification and consent, as provided for in the section. A power to appropriate without notice or consent can be provided for in the will, as illustrated at para **2.17** (precedent will). For taxation reasons, as outlined at para **4.9.1.2**, it is recommended that this power be included in the will.

Surprisingly, this section has given rise to very little litigation, perhaps because the power is exercised relatively rarely. Prior to the case of *Strong v Holmes* [2010] IEHC 70, the only reported case on the question of appropriation is the decision of the Supreme Court in *H v O* [1978] IR 194.

The plaintiff originally sought an order under s 56, which was refused by the High Court in *H v H* [1978] IR 138. She then commenced an action in the High Court, claiming the same division under s 55. McWilliam J upheld the plaintiff's claim.

On appeal to the Supreme Court, the decision of McWilliam J was reversed.

Henchy J stated, *inter alia*, that the right of appropriation given by s 55 is an enabling right, which may be exercised only by the personal representative. A person entitled to a share is given no right to compel the personal representative to propose an appropriation under s 55. Henchy J went on to say that the court only acquires jurisdiction in the matter when a party on being served with notice of an intended appropriation applies within six weeks to the court to prohibit the appropriation.

In this case, the Supreme Court set down principles which would be adopted by a court on an application to prohibit an appropriation under subsection (3). Henchy J, at p 206 of the report in *H v O* [1978] IR 194, stated:

'It must be assumed, having regard to the tenor, the scope and the purpose of the section, that the Court should prohibit an intended appropriation only:

(a) When the conditions in the section have not been complied with; or

(b) When, notwithstanding such compliance it would not be just or equitable to allow the appropriation to take place, having regard to the rights of all persons who are or will become entitled to an interest in the estate; or

(c) When, apart from the section, the appropriation would not be legally permissible.'

The section was considered by Finnegan J in the High Court in the case of *Messitt v Henry* [2001] 3 IR 313. This case has been referred to at para **3.8.1.2**.

This highlights the importance of very precise valuations, in so far as this is possible, and valuations are dealt with at para **12.9.1**.

The share may be that of a beneficiary who was entitled to a legacy outright, or the appropriation may be made towards a separate share, or held subject to a trust. It is a useful and flexible power, but must be used strictly in accordance with the Act. In particular, an appropriation (save for an appropriation of the family home by the surviving spouse under s 56) cannot prejudicially affect any specific devise or bequest.

A personal representative can appropriate without obtaining the necessary consents and serving the required notices, if there is a direction in the will to this effect. Where there is such direction in the will, the personal representative is entitled to appropriate any part of the estate in or towards satisfaction of any beneficiary's share without obtaining any consents or serving any notices. It is imperative to check the will to ensure the exact powers of appropriation given by it.

The court has jurisdiction under s 55 to prohibit an appropriation on the application of an interested party. This gives the court an element of control, but only where the personal representative has already sought consent to appropriate from those interested.

12.9.1 VALUATION FOR APPROPRIATION PURPOSES

This may cause some difficulty. The correct view appears to be that the asset should be valued at the date of appropriation and the case of *Strong v Holmes* mentioned above is instructive in this regard. This underlines the necessity to treat the question of appropriation, once it arises, as a matter of urgency. As the consent of beneficiaries affected by the appropriation has to be obtained, in order to further protect the personal representative, such written consent should refer to the value of the asset for appropriation purposes.

The value of the asset may substantially increase or decrease from the date of death, and the payment of equality money may arise. In relation to this, the question of capital gains tax, stamp duty, and/or gift tax may arise.

Especially where there is a portfolio of shares, do not enter into the question of appropriation lightly. The easiest and safest way of dealing with a portfolio of shares which has to be divided between a number of beneficiaries is either to divide each shareholding equally among those entitled *in specie* or to sell them (with consent) and distribute on a cash basis. If a legatee instructs you to sell his share of the shareholdings, you must ensure that comprehensive instructions in writing as to the price have been received from the personal representative and also from the beneficiary concerned.

Take care to sell only that share of each individual shareholding to which that beneficiary is entitled in order to create a cash asset, on the basis that there is another holding or holdings of equal value which can be transferred to or sold on behalf of other beneficiaries.

In order to minimise disputes and to protect the personal representative, it is advisable that, where possible, any increase or decrease in the value of assets from the date of death be borne equally by those entitled to those assets. For a discussion on this, see Brady's *Succession Law in Ireland*, 2nd edn (1995) and Wylie's *Casebook on Irish Land Law* (1984).

12.9.2 APPROPRIATION *IN SPECIE*

Appropriation *in specie* means that the executor or personal representative appropriates certain specified assets of the deceased in or towards satisfaction of a particular share to which a beneficiary is entitled. The assets in respect of which an appropriation is made are valued as at the date of appropriation.

Personal representatives have power to have valuations prepared for the purpose of appropriation and should be extremely careful about using qualified valuers to value the assets as at the time of appropriation. An appropriation, once properly made, is binding, regardless of any change in the value of the asset either appropriated or retained.

Where an executor appropriates specific assets of the estate in satisfaction of a bequest to a beneficiary, this appropriation should be noted in the final account. A proper receipt and discharge should be obtained by the personal representative when affecting such appropriation.

Remember that where appropriating *in specie*, the beneficiary who is in receipt of the asset concerned is responsible for any CAT payable on the inheritance.

All the following matters need to be carefully considered:

1. valuation;
2. capital gains tax;
3. capital acquisitions tax;
4. stamp duty;
5. consent;
6. timing of the appropriation.

The statutory powers of appropriation apply whether the deceased died testate or intestate.

CHAPTER 13

BENEFICIARIES INCLUDING: SPOUSES/CIVIL PARTNERS, COHABITANTS, AND CHILDREN OF THE DECEASED

13.1 Introduction

This chapter deals with issues that may arise with beneficiaries in general before going on to deal with 'family' beneficiaries in particular.

The rights of spouses, civil partners, cohabitants, and children have been discussed at length in **Chapter 4** in the context of will drafting. Prior to reading this chapter, it is advised to re-read **Chapter 4** in its entirety. In the latter part of this chapter, the focus will be on the duties imposed on the personal representative by the Succession Act and the civil partnership legislation in regard to the surviving spouse, civil partner, cohabitant, and children of the deceased (if any).

13.2 Dealing with Beneficiaries in General

A rule of thumb in every administration is: the client is the personal representative. A conflict of interest may well arise if the solicitor also acts for a beneficiary in the estate. Practitioners should exercise care in this regard to ensure that such a conflict does not occur. Dealing with beneficiaries can be problematic. Difficulties may arise where the beneficiary cannot give a receipt for various reasons, or where the beneficiary is contentious or elderly.

13.2.1 A BENEFICIARY UNDER AGE

A beneficiary who is under age cannot give a valid receipt and discharge to the personal representative. In the case of a small pecuniary bequest, it is accepted practice for the personal representative and guardian/parent of the beneficiary to hold the entitlement of a beneficiary in their joint names pending the beneficiary attaining the age of majority.

In practice, where this arises, it is vital that a birth certificate should be obtained for the beneficiary, which should be kept on file, to ascertain the date upon which the property should be released, and the personal representative obtains a full discharge. Where the will gives the executors the power to accept the receipt of the parent or guardian, as outlined in the precedent will at para **2.17**, this can be availed of and it will not be necessary to keep the minor beneficiary's birth certificate on file. This type of clause is only recommended for small pecuniary bequests and certainly not for devises of real property where a trust would be the more appropriate way of holding the property.

If no specific trust has been established under the will for a minor beneficiary and there are no trustees of such beneficiary who are able and willing to act, trustees may be appointed either under the provisions of s 57 of the Succession Act, as noted at para **3.8.1.4**, or possibly under s 19 of the Land and Conveyancing Law Reform Act, 2009 if a trust of land arises.

One should further note the provisions of s 58, which give such trustees powers to deal with the property of minor beneficiaries during their minority, as noted in Chapter 1 of the Trusts Lecture Notes (see Preface). It should also be noted that trustees of property vested under s 57 are deemed to be trustees for the purpose of ss 42 and 43 of the Conveyancing Act, 1881, which confer wide powers on the trustees.

As noted in Chapter 1 of the Trusts Lecture Notes (see Preface), s 58(2), which deemed a settlement to exist where the person entitled in possession to an estate or interest in land is an infant (minor), has been repealed by the Land and Conveyancing Law Reform Act, 2009, which provides that a trust for land under Part 4 of that Act comes into existence in those circumstances.

Note: any investment during the minority of a beneficiary has to be strictly in accordance with the provisions set out in the Trustee Act, 1893, as amended, unless the trust is a trust for land under Part IV of the Land and Conveyancing Law Reform Act, 2009. The powers of investment are extremely limited unless the will gives additional powers of investment. The current list of authorised investments is contained in the Trustee (Authorised Investments) Order, 1998 (SI 28/1998), as amended by the Trustee (Authorised Investments) Order, 1998 (Amendment) Order, 2002 (SI 595/2002).

13.2.2 BENEFICIARY UNDER DISABILITY

If a beneficiary is mentally incapacitated, and therefore not capable of giving a valid receipt, and the will does not appoint trustees for such a bequest to an incapacitated beneficiary it may be necessary to apply to make the beneficiary a ward of court. While the Succession Act makes no provision for the appointment of trustees in circumstances other than minority, the recently passed, but not enacted, Assisted Decision-Making (Capacity) Act, 2015 will.

If it is necessary to make the beneficiary a ward of court, evidence of two medical practitioners confirming the state of health of the beneficiary must be obtained. Notice of the intended application has to be served on the beneficiary, so as to allow the beneficiary sufficient time to oppose the application. If there is no opposition, the court will normally appoint a committee of the ward, who, from that day on, will be responsible for giving a valid receipt to the personal representative in respect of the benefit.

Normally, the court will allow the appointment of a person as a committee who would not be prejudiced in their handling of the affairs of the ward and who could be relied upon to act impartially. The duties and responsibilities of a committee are extremely onerous and should not be taken on lightly. Accounts have to be passed annually by the court and costs must be taxed before payment. Refer to the Rules of the Superior Courts, 1986 for further elaboration.

On the coming into force of the Assisted Decision-Making (Capacity) Act, 2015 the Wards of Court Office will be replaced by the Decision Support Service, which will be tasked with supervising and registering the decision-making agreements provided for in the Act. A person in relation to whom capacity is an issue (referred to as a 'relevant person') will have a range of options up to and including wardship, depending on the circumstances.

The significant change will be that the approach to capacity will be a 'functional' one and will be issue-specific and time-specific in relation to each and every decision to be made by a relevant person. The Act provides for a range of representatives to assist the relevant individual, including a 'decision-making assistant', a 'co-decision-maker', and a 'decision-making representative' (appointed by the court).

In each case, full details should be sought and it should be clear who is in a position to provide a valid receipt and indemnity to the estate.

438 BENEFICIARIES

13.2.3 MISSING BENEFICIARY

It is important in any administration to ascertain the whereabouts of each beneficiary. The solicitor should consider all or any of the following:

- Write by registered post, at least once if not twice, to the last known address of the beneficiary.

- Gather as much information as possible from known family members and keep a detailed record of such enquiries. Contact should immediately be made with those persons most likely to have been in contact with a particular beneficiary.

- It may be necessary to place advertisements in local papers in endeavouring to trace any missing beneficiary.

- Depending upon the value of the funds held on behalf of the missing beneficiaries, it may be worth considering appointing a professional firm of searchers.

If, after making all reasonable enquiries, it is impossible to locate a beneficiary, then a decision will have to be made as to whether the funds should be lodged in court or elsewhere. Where there is a large amount of money involved the funds can be placed in the Central Office of the High Court with an affidavit under the Trustee Act 1893 (Rules of the Superior Courts, O 73 and O 77).

Alternatively, funds can be held for a period of seven years on joint deposit with a bank in the names of the legal personal representative and the solicitor's firm. Of course the account should only be operable on both signatures. Ensure all funds are held on deposit. If a beneficiary cannot be traced within that period of time, there is a presumption that the beneficiary is dead.

Where necessary for the administration of the estate, a *Benjamin order* (from the case of *Re Benjamin* [1902] 1 Ch 723) can be sought from the court to distribute the assets of the estate in the absence of a particular beneficiary to an estate whose whereabouts cannot be located. However, the proofs necessary are demanding and could prove expensive, as they may involve advertisements in national newspaper(s) in the country (or countries) where the beneficiary was last known to be.

The Civil Law (Presumption of Death) Act, 2019 may be of assistance. On application, a court can make a 'presumption of death order' if it is satisfied that the circumstances suggest that the missing person's death is either virtually certain or highly probable or where the length of disappearance indicates it is highly probable the person has died.

If the value of the funds held is low, whether this is a worthwhile application is a matter for discussion between the solicitor and the legal personal representative, who may wish to proceed on the basis of indemnities from the beneficiaries. This would be a cheaper and quicker option. It depends on how many beneficiaries are missing, the value of the funds, and the likelihood of the beneficiaries being found. Either way, this step cannot be taken until full searches have been initiated and failed to yield up the beneficiaries.

This decision should not be made lightly, and a practitioner may well be advised to obtain counsel's advice on the matter.

13.2.4 CONTENTIOUS BENEFICIARY

Any practitioner dealing with administration is bound to come across the problem of a contentious beneficiary. The task of dealing with such a beneficiary is made much easier by remembering that the practitioner's client is the personal representative. In the event of a beneficiary proving contentious about any matter whatsoever, it is preferable to deal with that beneficiary's solicitor.

Practitioners should never get involved in disputes between beneficiaries, which would affect one's position in advising the personal representative. In practice, one should not accept confidences from individual beneficiaries and should never engage in any arrangement with a beneficiary that would result in a fraud on the Revenue. If contacted by an Inspector of Taxes on behalf of a beneficiary, the solicitor is not entitled to disclose any information regarding that beneficiary unless prior written instructions from that beneficiary to divulge information have been obtained and are on file.

13.2.5 ELDERLY BENEFICIARY

The treatment of elderly beneficiaries is also an area of concern. Great care must be taken by the solicitor when advising the personal representative (and indeed the testator) when providing for elderly beneficiaries. Practitioners are advised to read the Practice Note in relation to administering an estate where there is an elderly beneficiary, personal representative, or surviving spouse, issued in the March 2009 issue of the *Law Society Gazette*. Obviously, similar procedures apply to civil partners.

In the past, the concepts of rights of residence and maintenance were very popular when drafting wills attempting to provide for elderly beneficiaries. These concepts of rights of residence and maintenance had been losing favour, as they rarely confer any comfort, and, in the view of many leading practitioners, can cause difficult conveyancing issues in the future. However, where a client is in a second or subsequent relationship outside marriage, quite often a right to reside or a right of residence, support, and maintenance has been provided for the current 'life' partner or cohabitant with a remainder interest to the testator's children.

The concept of a life interest in dealing with elderly spouses tended in the past to be utilised in almost every circumstance, regardless of the provisions of the Succession Act.

Notwithstanding the legal right of spouses, it can be useful in certain circumstances, where there is an element of vulnerability and the question of protection and management is a necessary consideration. It is possible to come across situations where a surviving spouse has had no wish to be proactive in making all financial decisions and is delighted with the concept of this type of trust.

Where the use of the life interest falls into difficulties is where it is simply not set up properly. In the past some solicitors have overlooked the fact that where a limited interest is created in land, a settlement, formerly under the Settled Land Acts, 1882–90 and now under the Land and Conveyancing Law Reform Act, 2009, is in fact created. It is crucial that trustees are appointed who are willing and able to administer the property in the best interests of both the elderly life tenant and those entitled to the remainder interest in the property. In the absence of appointment of trustees, the personal representative or personal representatives are the trustees. See the Trusts Lecture Notes (see Preface) for further details. A further issue that can arise is the provision of funds to maintain the property during the period of the residency or life interest. The elderly spouse may not have the funds or the motivation to properly or even adequately maintain the property and thought should be given to providing a sum of money with the property for this purpose.

Assistance may be found in the future when the Assisted Decision-Making (Capacity) Act, 2015 is fully in force.

13.2.6 DECEASED BENEFICIARY

It is crucial to establish when exactly the beneficiary died; whether the beneficiary predeceased the deceased or whether the beneficiary survived the deceased and subsequently died.

When a beneficiary predeceases a testator, generally the inheritance lapses and falls into residue under the terms of s 91 of the Succession Act unless otherwise provided for in the will. However, s 98 of the Succession Act applies to save the bequest where the predeceased beneficiary is the child of the testator leaving issue alive at the date of the testator's death. Again, the implication of s 98 may be overruled by the will, by using a substitutionary clause as per the precedent will at para **2.17**. Where the deceased dies intestate, practitioners are aware of the provisions and effect of s 67 B (2).

440 BENEFICIARIES

Where a bequest to a beneficiary is expressed to be in recognition of an obligation or a debt, then and in that event, the bequest may survive as the estate of the beneficiary may have a legitimate expectation and the personal representative will hold the bequest in trust for the estate of the predeceased beneficiary. In such circumstances, the facts must be examined closely to establish whether such an obligation or debt arises.

If a beneficiary survives the testator but dies before receiving their inheritance, then it is transferred to the deceased beneficiary's legal personal representative for distribution according to the deceased beneficiary's will or intestacy. A signed receipt and indemnity from the deceased beneficiary's legal personal representative is the only absolute protection for your client, the legal personal representative.

13.2.7 CHARITABLE BENEFICIARY

Many wills will contain pecuniary legacies, specific bequests, or residuary bequests to charity. Charitable bequests and the register of charities overseen by the Charities Regulatory Authority (CRA) have been discussed at para **2.7.2.6**.

At para **7.4.14**, practitioners are made aware of the importance of completing the online charitable bequest form. Sections 52 and 58 of the Charities Act, 1961 as amended by s 16 of the Charities Act, 1973 and s 82 of the Charities Act, 2009 provide that the CRA may at their discretion require the personal representative to notify them that the property has been transferred to the charity specified in the will or that the trustees of the charity are aware of the devise or bequest or to publish a notice of the particulars of such bequest. Under the section as amended, general exemption from publication is given unless the CRA requires publication to be made in any particular case.

The CRA's requirements (if any) issue when the charitable bequest in wills summary form has been received from the Probate Office and examined by them. The CRA may ask for evidence of payment by way of receipt of a charitable bequest from the appropriate officer or a letter of awareness from the charity concerned. Under s 16, a personal representative is required to comply with such requirements as the CRA may specify, within six months of the date of probate or within two months of the date of their requirement, whichever is the later.

13.2.7.1 Letter of awareness

It is best practice when informing a charity of the terms of the bequest to obtain from it a letter of awareness, i.e. a letter from it stating that it has been informed of the bequest. When writing initially to the charitable beneficiary, request evidence of its charitable status on its headed paper to include its charity registration number, its Revenue CHY number, and its certificate of incorporation (CRO number) if any.

13.2.7.2 Receipts

It is necessary to ensure that the personal representative is protected when dealing with charities and that proper receipts are obtained. If the will does not stipulate what officer of the charity should give a receipt, it is appropriate to obtain a receipt from one of the following:

- in the case of a lay organisation or group, one of the officers, i.e. Chairman, Secretary Treasurer;
- in the case of a religious community, from the Superior or Bursar of the community;
- in the case of a trust corporation, from the Secretary of the company. Such a receipt is a sufficient discharge for the personal representative.

Problems can be experienced where a charitable bequest is inadequate in amount for the purpose for which it is given or where the validity of the bequest is contested.

For appropriate solutions for these problems, one should refer to Spierin, *The Succession Act 1965 and Related Legislation: A Commentary*, 5th edn (2017), appendix L, which sets out some problems frequently encountered by practitioners in dealing with charitable bequests.

In any court proceedings which are to be taken in the estate of a deceased where a charity has an interest, it is necessary to join the Attorney-General as a party. The Attorney-General's role is to protect the interests of the charity.

13.2.7.3 Tax and charities

Where the charity is registered as such with the Revenue Commissioners, i.e. it has a CHY number quoted on its headed paper, any bequest to that charity is free of tax by virtue of s 76 of the Capital Acquisitions Tax Consolidation Act, 2003. Since 9 June 1987, that total exemption applies whether the benefit is to be applied in Ireland or not, provided the benefit could be regarded as charitable within the general law of the State.

Where the charity is not registered, then tax is payable by the charity at the Group C rate, and it is a matter for the charity, not the personal representative, to prove its charitable status to the Revenue Commissioners. Charitable trusts are referred to in the Trusts Lecture Notes (see Preface) and it is not proposed to deal with the law relating to charities in any detail in this book.

13.3 Communication with Beneficiaries

As was highlighted at para **6.7.1**, potential beneficiaries should be contacted shortly after the date of death, to inform them of the terms of their bequest in the will. A precedent letter to potential beneficiaries is shown at para **6.8.4.2**.

This letter should advise the beneficiary of the terms of the bequest in the will. In all cases this should be qualified by a statement that the personal representative is currently collecting details of the assets and liabilities and that payment will be made provided that there are sufficient net assets in the estate. It is usual to recite the terms of the legacy contained in the will in the initial letter to the beneficiary.

The will does not become a document of public record until such time as it is proved in the Probate Office of the High Court. The only person entitled to authorise the release of a copy of the will is the personal representative. Exercise the utmost discretion in giving out a complete copy of the will to any beneficiary.

The letter will also request from the beneficiary their PPS number and their tax history. Where a beneficiary has received a prior gift or inheritance, it is safer to obtain details of all benefits received from any source for the relevant period. The solicitor is better placed to decide on their relevance for aggregation purposes, rather than the beneficiary. The letter should make it clear to the beneficiary that this information will be provided to the Revenue Commissioners as part of the Statement of Affairs (Probate).

13.4 Summary of Guidelines for Dealing with Beneficiaries in Any Estate

The following are guidelines for dealing with beneficiaries in any estate:

1. Identify each individual beneficiary clearly and where they are resident, ordinarily resident, and domiciled.
2. Identify any minor beneficiaries and the issue of any predeceased children who may receive a benefit, whether under the rules of intestacy or under s 98 of the Succession Act.

442 BENEFICIARIES

3. Identify all specific/general/demonstrative legacies and identify the funds out of which such legacies are to be paid.

4. Notify each beneficiary of the legacy or bequest as soon as possible after the will of the testator has been established as being valid.

5. Notify each beneficiary of their share under the rules of intestacy as soon as the fact of intestacy or partial intestacy has been established and next of kin have been properly ascertained.

6. Ensure that, in any correspondence with the beneficiaries, you clarify that payment of the legacy/share in the estate will be made subject to there being sufficient assets in the estate to meet all liabilities both ascertained and as yet unascertained. Should there be insufficient funds to discharge payment of a legacy, it may be abated.

7. Inform each beneficiary that it may be necessary for them to file a tax return and pay the necessary CAT themselves. The estate and/or the solicitor are only responsible when the beneficiary/personal representative is non-resident. See the CAT Lecture Notes (see Preface). The solicitor can offer to calculate, file, and pay CAT on behalf of the beneficiary. This is an additional service and one that would be charged to the beneficiary and not to the estate.

8. In dealing with residuary beneficiaries, ensure that all necessary clearances are obtained from (if applicable) CAT, capital gains tax, income tax, stamp duty, and the Department of Social Protection (where the deceased was in receipt of a non-contributory pension/assistance), and the HSE where the deceased availed of the 'Fair Deal' Scheme.

13.5 Spouses, Civil partners, Cohabitants, and Children

Recent legislative changes have made the provision of advice to the personal representative in relation to the surviving spouse, civil partner, cohabitant, and children quite complex. Practitioners should re-read **Chapter 4** and the relevant sections of **Chapter 8** and should take great care in identifying the precise nature of the relationship in all cases whether the deceased died testate or intestate.

13.5.1 INTESTACY

Where the deceased died intestate, matters are slightly more straightforward. The rules of intestacy outlined in **Chapter 8** provide that where only the spouse or civil partner survives the intestate deceased, he or she is entitled to the entire estate.

Where a spouse or civil partner and issue (children and/or children of a predeceased child) survive the intestate deceased, the surviving spouse or civil partner is entitled to two-thirds of the estate and the children divide the remaining one-third per capita. Children of a predeceased child take the share out of that one-third that their parent would have taken and divide it among themselves *per stirpes*. However, children of a deceased civil partner have a right to sue the estate for provision from the share left to the surviving civil partner up to the amount they would receive on intestacy had their parent died without a civil partner.

As noted in **Chapter 4**, where a cohabitant dies intestate, the surviving cohabitant has no right to the estate. The surviving cohabitant is not the personal representative, unless he or she is the surviving parent of minor children of the deceased cohabitant, who would be the persons entitled to the entire estate. In such circumstances, he or she would extract the grant on their behalf limited to their minority, as parent and next friend, but not as surviving cohabitee. Again, he or she has a right of redress against the estate in certain circumstances, as outlined in **Chapter 4**. If the cohabitee intends exercising his or her right of redress under s 194 of the Civil Partnership and Certain Rights and Obligations of Cohabitants Act, 2010 there will be a conflict of interest between this and acting as personal representative to extract a limited grant as next friend for the minority of a beneficiary. Where such a conflict of interest arises, someone else should extract the grant of administration intestate for the minority of the beneficiary.

These rules apply to a partial intestacy, as will be dealt with at para **13.6.3**.

13.6 Testate Estates and the Spouse/Civil Partner's Legal Right Share

This has already been outlined in **Chapter 4**, which should have been re-read prior to reading this chapter. In any administration where there is a will and a surviving spouse or civil partner, the personal representative has certain duties imposed on him. It is vital to recap on the matter with the personal representative. As noted earlier, the legal right share does not arise where the deceased died wholly intestate, but will arise on a partial intestacy. When dealing with the legal right share for these purposes, it is assumed that the surviving spouse or civil partner still retains the legal right share and has not 'ceased' to be a spouse or civil partner for Succession Act purposes, as outlined at para **4.5.8**.

It is also assumed for this chapter that any bequest to the surviving spouse or civil partner in the will is *not* in addition to the legal right share, but is in fact deemed to have been intended to be in satisfaction of the share as outlined in s 114 and at para **4.5.4**. It is extremely rare, if ever, that a bequest is declared to be in addition to the legal right share.

As outlined, s 111 of the Succession Act as amended confers on a surviving spouse or civil partner a legal right to a share in the deceased's estate. The share depends on whether a testator has left surviving children. If he has, then the surviving spouse or civil partner is entitled to a one-third share of the estate. If there are no children, then the legal right share is increased to one-half. The children have to be children of the testator. (Children can include marital and non-marital children as well as legally adopted children.) They do not have to be children of the spouse or civil partner. See para **4.6** for details on the calculation of same.

The Children and Family Relationships Act, 2015 at Part 11 provides for civil partners to apply to adopt children. At present the relevant Part of the Act is not in force but practitioners should ascertain when the commencement order for the relevant provisions comes into force.

It is important to advise the personal representative that children are not automatically entitled to any share of the deceased parent's estate where the deceased parent died fully testate (having made a will with a fully functioning residuary clause).

13.6.1 PRIORITY OF LEGAL RIGHT OF SPOUSE/CIVIL PARTNER

Section 112 of the Succession Act (as amended) directs that the spouse or a civil partner's legal right is to have priority over devises, bequests, and shares on intestacy. The result is that the only persons who have priority over the surviving spouse are creditors of the deceased. As noted, children of a deceased civil partner, on application to the court, may have priority over the surviving civil partner. After all relevant debts and expenses, including funeral and testamentary expenses, have been discharged, the spouse's legal right share must be paid next.

Section 45(1) of the Succession Act states that the entire estate of the deceased forms assets for the payment of funeral, testamentary and administration expenses, debts, liabilities, and any legal right. The section goes on to say that any disposition in the will that is inconsistent with this section is void as against creditors and any person with a legal right, and that if necessary the court will administer the property for the purpose of paying expenses, debts, and the legal right. It follows from this that any personal representative who administers an estate without taking the legal right into account will almost certainly face a challenge in the court.

Section 46(6) of the Succession Act gives an instruction on the payment of the legal right share. It states that the legal right share is treated as if it were a claim against the estate, equivalent to the value of the share. Payment of the legal right share as a claim against the estate will follow the payment of all such actual claims against the estate, following Part II of the First Schedule as outlined in **Chapter 12**.

It is important to note that it is a 'claim' against the estate in priority to all other claims and not a 'debt' of the estate, and a clause in the will stating that (for example) a beneficiary inherits a bequest subject to their paying the 'just debts, funeral and testamentary expenses' does not mean that the beneficiary has to pay the legal right share.

Sections 112, 45(1), and 46(6) clarify the priority of the legal right share and deal to a limited extent with the effect of the legal right share on the other beneficiaries. Only after the legal right share has been satisfied are other beneficiaries paid their entitlements under the will. Where the assets of the estate, after satisfaction of the spouse's legal right share, are insufficient to pay the remaining legacies and devises in full, they will abate according to the terms of Part II of the First Schedule.

Where the spouse or civil partner elects to appropriate the family home under s 56 will be dealt with at para **13.7.1**.

When dealing with the surviving spouse's/civil partner's right to elect, the right to elect under the will where the deceased died fully testate will be dealt with first, and then the right to elect under a partial intestacy will follow. Again, this has been outlined at para **4.5.5**, where s 115 of the Succession Act has been set out.

13.6.1.1 Example of Legal Right Share on Estate

Students should re-read para **12.4**, Payment of Liabilities, and in particular para **12.4.2**, Solvent Estates, before continuing.

Take for example a situation where the deceased left a surviving spouse and children. The 'family home' is in joint names and falls outside the will, and the net estate is €450,000 of which €50,000 is the net residue, and there are specific bequests totalling €400,000 to the children. There is no bequest to the surviving spouse in the will.

The legal right share of one-third, in this case €150,000, will vest automatically in the surviving spouse, and assuming that the surviving spouse does not disclaim, the effect on the estate is as follows:

We are told in *H v O* [1978] IR 194 that the legal right share 'is to be discharged in the same manner as if the one half or one third of the estate had been expressly given in the will in priority over all devises and bequests'.

The order of application of assets for the payment of the legal right share will be the same as for a debt of the estate, even though the legal right share is not a debt as such. It would follow Part II of the First Schedule as set out in para **12.4.4.2**.

In this case, the net residue of €50,000 will be used up in its entirety and the residuary legatee(s) and devisee(s) get nothing. However, there is still an outstanding balance of the legal right share of €100,000 to be paid. This will be paid proportionally by the specific legatees and devisees.

The formula to be applied will be similar to the formula applied for the payment of outstanding debts from the specific bequests:

$$\frac{\text{Individual Specific Bequest}}{\text{Total Amount of Specific Bequests}} \times \text{Outstanding LRS} = \text{Share of LRS Payable}$$

For example, if one child had been left a specific bequest valued at €200,000, his share of the outstanding legal right share would be calculated as follows:

$$\frac{€200,000}{€400,000} \times €100,000 = €50,000$$

That child would have to pay €50,000 to the surviving spouse before they could receive the specific bequest.

13.6.1.2 Priority of legal right of civil partner

As noted earlier, unlike a spouse, the children of a deceased civil partner who are not considered the child of the surviving civil partner can challenge the legal right share of a surviving civil partner. See para **4.6.4.1**. Apart from that, the legal right share of a civil partner is treated exactly the same as the legal right share of a spouse. Practitioners should review the Children and Family Relationships Act, 2015 to ensure they have identified the correct relationship between children and civil partners.

13.6.2 RIGHT TO ELECT BETWEEN LEGAL RIGHT SHARE AND BEQUEST UNDER WILL WHERE THE TESTATOR DIED WHOLLY TESTATE

Where the deceased has died wholly testate, leaving a bequest to a spouse or civil partner in the will (and such bequest is not stated to be in addition to the legal right share), the surviving spouse or civil partner has a right of election between the bequest under the will or the legal right share together with any share on intestacy.

Furthermore, should the surviving spouse or civil partner elect to take the legal right share, such spouse or civil partner may further elect to take any benefit to him in the will less in value than the legal right share in partial satisfaction of the legal right share.

The personal representative is obliged by s 115 to give the surviving spouse or civil partner notice in writing of his right of election under s 115 (see para **4.5.5.1**).

In addition, the personal representative should advise the spouse or civil partner to seek independent legal advice. The solicitor advising the personal representative should never advise the surviving spouse or civil partner as to his legal rights.

In default of election after receipt of notice of election, the surviving spouse or civil partner is deemed to take the bequest under the will and not the legal right share.

Failure to act promptly will delay the date on which the administration of the estate can be completed. The surviving spouse or civil partner's right to make an election only expires either:

1. six months after he has received the notification from the personal representative of his right of election; or
2. one year from the date of taking out representation to the estate;

either whichever is the latter.

Obviously, time does not begin to run until notice is served, and the minimum amount of time is one year after the grant issues. Failure to notify ensures delay. However, as can be seen when dealing with potential s 117 applications, it may be in the surviving spouse or civil partner's interest not to elect until the six-month period for applications under s 117 has expired. This will be elucidated upon at para **13.8.4.1**.

To recap briefly, where the deceased died wholly testate, the surviving spouse or civil partner has three choices:

1. to take the bequest under the will; or
2. to take the legal right share as a pecuniary bequest ranking in priority over all other bequests; or

446 BENEFICIARIES

    3. to take the legal right share, taking some or all of the bequests under the will less in value than the legal right share in partial satisfaction thereof and taking the remaining part of the legal right share as a pecuniary bequest ranking in priority over all other bequests.

Failure to choose (or elect) within six months of notification of these rights means that the right to elect is lost and the spouse or civil partner takes the bequest under the will by default.

Where the spouse or civil partner elects to take the legal right share, whether as a pecuniary bequest or with bequests under the will in partial satisfaction, this will, of course, have a profound effect on the distribution of the estate. The solicitor advising the surviving spouse or civil partner (who should never be the solicitor advising the personal representative) should outline the nature of the effect on the other beneficiaries, particularly family members, to the surviving spouse or civil partner.

13.6.3 RIGHT TO ELECT BETWEEN LEGAL RIGHT SHARE AND BEQUEST UNDER WILL WHERE THE TESTATOR DIED PARTIALLY INTESTATE

This possibility is covered by s 115(2)(a) (see para **4.5.5.4** and **4.5.5.5**) but, to recap briefly:

Where the deceased dies partly testate and partly intestate, the surviving spouse or civil partner's choice is between:

1. the spouse or civil partner's bequest under the will, together with the share on partial intestacy (which will be all of or two-thirds of the intestate portion of the estate, depending on whether or not the deceased left children); or

2. the legal right share of the entire estate (testate and intestate) (which will be one-half or one-third, depending on whether or not the deceased left children).

Again, the spouse or civil partner can further elect to take some or all of his bequests under the will less in value than the legal right share in partial satisfaction thereof.

The personal representative is under a similar duty to notify the surviving spouse or civil partner in writing, and the right to elect will expire either one year after the grant has issued or six months after notification, whichever is the latter. In default of election after receipt of notice of election, the spouse or civil partner will be deemed to have taken the share under intestacy plus the bequest, and not the legal right share. See precedent notice of election at para **4.5.6.2**.

Again, where the spouse or civil partner elects to take the legal right share, whether as a pecuniary bequest or with bequests under the will in partial satisfaction, this will, of course, have a profound effect on the distribution of the estate. The solicitor advising the surviving spouse or civil partner should outline the nature of the effect on the other beneficiaries, particularly family members, to the surviving spouse or civil partner. This may or may not affect their choice but any client should be informed of the consequences of their choice.

13.6.4 DISTINCTION BETWEEN THE LEGAL RIGHT SHARE AND THE RIGHT TO ELECT

There is a critical distinction to be made between the right to elect under s 115 and the legal right share under s 111. The right to elect only arises where there is a bequest to a spouse or civil partner in the will. In that case, the spouse or civil partner must choose (or 'elect') between the bequest and the legal right share.

As highlighted on numerous occasions, there is a six-month notice period after notice is served, or one year after the grant issues, whichever is the latter. In default of election, after notice is provided, the spouse or civil partner is deemed to take the bequest under the will.

The benefit passing to the spouse or civil partner has to be a bequest under the will, not merely a benefit arising on death. For example, the surviving spouse or civil partner may also be a surviving joint tenant, they may be the nominee of a nominated insurance policy, or they may be entitled to a pension under a pension scheme. All of these arise outside the will and are not bequests for the purpose of s 115.

If there is no bequest to the spouse or civil partner in the will, the right to elect does not arise as there is no 'election' or choice to be made. In that case, the legal right share passes to, or vests in, the spouse or civil partner automatically at the date of death, and the spouse or civil partner has an entitlement to the legal right share and should be notified of this by the personal representative in a similar fashion to a spouse or civil partner being notified of their share on intestacy.

The spouse or civil partner may choose to disclaim their legal right share on being notified of it, but this is not the same as election under s 115. Unless they disclaim, the personal representative must provide them (or their estate) with their legal right share. The time limits that apply to election do not arise. As with all beneficiaries, the spouse or civil partner has a six-year time limit to claim against the estate.

A look at the relevant case law may illuminate the point.

13.6.4.1 Case law

Two cases are of particular significance when discussing this issue; first, the case of *Re Urquhart* [1974] IR 197. In this case, a testatrix died leaving a legacy to her husband conditional on his surviving her by one month. In fact the husband, who was unconscious at the time of his wife's death and remained so, died within twenty-four hours.

The Revenue Commissioners brought a case that tax should be levied on the husband's estate, as if it included 50 per cent of his late wife's estate. The court ruled that the husband could not be treated as being 'competent to dispose' of the 50 per cent of his wife's estate; since he had never exercised his right of election to take a legal right share, he had not been capable of 'taking', as he only survived her by twenty-four hours.

In default of election, he was treated as taking the legacy which she had left to him but, as that was conditional on his surviving her for one month, the legacy failed. However, the existence of the legacy prevented the legal right share from automatically vesting in his estate.

In short, where there was a bequest to the spouse in the will (albeit a conditional bequest), the legal right share did not automatically vest in the surviving spouse and did not form part of her estate.

Consider and contrast this case with *Re Cummins; O'Dwyer v Keegan* [1997] 2 IR 585; [1997] 2 ILRM 401 as outlined at para **4.5.6**. In this case, neither the husband nor the wife was aware of the death of the other.

The husband died childless leaving a net estate of £2.4 million. His widow, who was in a coma at the date of her husband's death, died twelve hours later, leaving an estate worth approximately £400,000. In this case, the husband made no provision for his wife in his will. The wife's relatives claimed that the wife was entitled to 50 per cent of his estate, under s 111 of the Succession Act, and that therefore those assets should pass to them on her death.

The High Court ruled that the right conferred by s 111 was a purely personal right, which died with the spouse. If she had survived, she could have decided to exercise the right to a 50 per cent share of her husband's estate.

However, the Supreme Court held that the widow had an entitlement to 50 per cent of her husband's assets as a legal right share on his death, since she had not renounced her rights or been disinherited. That right vested in the wife on her husband's death, under s 111.

In short, where there was no bequest to the spouse in the will, the legal right share automatically vested in the spouse and formed part of her estate.

448 BENEFICIARIES

13.6.4.2 Notifying the spouse/civil partner

As noted earlier, where a spouse or civil partner is given a legacy, there is a specific procedure in s 115(4) to notify the spouse or civil partner of the right to elect. There is no similar procedure set out in the Succession Act for notifying a surviving spouse or civil partner of his or her legal right share where there is no bequest to that spouse or civil partner in the will.

However, the personal representative is under a general duty to notify beneficiaries of their entitlements under the will or otherwise. The surviving spouse or civil partner has six years from the date of death to claim such share under s 126 of the Succession Act.

The important distinction is that where a spouse or civil partner is left a bequest in a will, they have a right to elect between the bequest and the legal right share. This right of election is personal to them and dies with them. On their death, the bequest to them would form part of their estate, assuming that it is a bequest that does not die with them, such as a life interest or a right to reside or a conditional bequest where the condition was not met, as in *Urquhart*.

Where a spouse or civil partner is left nothing in a will, the legal right share vests in them on the death of the other spouse or civil partner, and should they die prior to claiming the legal right share, it (the entire legal right share) forms part of their estate on death. In the case of civil partners, this may be subject to any application made by children of the deceased civil partner as outlined at para **4.6.4.1**.

13.7 Right of Spouse/Civil Partner to Appropriate Dwellinghouse and Contents

Section 56, as outlined at para **4.5.7**, confers on the surviving spouse or civil partner the right to appropriate the dwellinghouse in which he or she was ordinarily resident at the time of the deceased's death, together with any household chattels in or towards satisfaction of any share to which he or she was entitled under the estate of the deceased. This would include the legal right share, as well as any interest due to him or her under a will or intestacy. If the dwellinghouse or chattels are worth more than his or her share, he or she may have to make a contribution to obtain the property, although in cases of hardship s 56(10)(b) states that the court may release him or her from the necessity of having to so do. Section 56(10)(c) states that the court can make such further order in relation to the administration of the estate as the court deems just, having regard to all the circumstances.

The surviving spouse or civil partner may also exercise the rights of any minor child(ren), in relation to whom he or she would be a trustee under s 57 who are entitled to a share of the deceased's property, to assist in acquiring the dwellinghouse and chattels. The surviving spouse or civil partner will hold the infant/minor's share of the property in trust for them until they become 18, at which time the share will have to be accounted for. This means that the family home will be subject to a Land Act trust for the purposes of the Land and Conveyancing Law Reform Act, 2009 and that two trustees will need to be appointed if a sale of the property is contemplated in order to provide any purchaser with a valid receipt.

Section 56(6) sets out certain cases where the family home forms part of a greater interest in land, where appropriation of the family home may be made only with the consent of the court, if the court is satisfied that the appropriation is unlikely to diminish the value of the other assets of the deceased, other than the dwelling, or to make it more difficult to dispose of them.

The personal representatives are under a duty to notify the surviving spouse or civil partner of his or her right to exercise an appropriation of the dwellinghouse and chattels under s 56. As the time limits under this section are exactly the same as for election under s 115, it is usual for the spouse or civil partner to be notified by one notice to include both rights where there has been a bequest to the spouse or civil partner in the will. The appropriate notices to be issued both in respect of right of election (s 115) testate and intestate and s 56 (appropriation) are set out respectively at paras **4.5.6.2**, **4.5.6.3**, and **4.5.7.2**.

13.7.1 EFFECT OF SECTION 56 ON BENEFICIARY OF FAMILY HOME

Where the family home has been left to the spouse or civil partner under the will, there is no difficulty. A difficulty will arise, however, where the family home has been left to someone else and the surviving spouse or civil partner successfully exercises the right to appropriate under s 56.

This raises the question: does the disappointed beneficiary receive any compensation? It is not clear from the Act whether the disappointed beneficiary should receive such compensation. However, s 45(1) does state that the estate of the deceased forms assets for the payment of 'any legal right' and that any disposition in the will inconsistent with this is void. The right of the surviving spouse or civil partner to appropriate the family home is a 'legal right'.

It has been stated earlier that in the case of such an appropriation, the court can make such further order as it deems just and equitable in the circumstances. This is to avoid the possibility of an administration suit. It is also worth noting that a child of the deceased who is also a child of the deceased's spouse cannot interfere with either a bequest to the spouse or the legal right share. However, such a child could take an action against a civil partner, particularly if the child was left the house in the will.

Also, such a child could take a s 117 action, and the court would take into account any benefit lost to the child because the surviving spouse or civil partner had taken his or her legal right share to the detriment of the child.

This would lead one to believe that each individual case will be taken on its own merits and that it would be difficult to advise either the surviving spouse or civil partner or the estate as to how the remainder of the estate should be distributed in the event of the surviving spouse or civil partner exercising his or her rights under s 56, particularly if the child of a deceased civil partner was left that house in the will of the deceased civil partner.

The appropriate notices to be issued both in respect of right of election (s 115) testate and intestate and s 56 are set out at paras **4.5.6.2**, **4.5.6.3**, and **4.5.7.2**.

13.8 Children

13.8.1 INTRODUCTION

The rights of children are also discussed at length in **Chapter 4**, and as noted therein the personal representative is not under a duty to notify any of the children of the deceased of their right to take an action against the estate under s 117, s 63, or otherwise. In fact, the personal representative would be deemed to be negligent in his duty to protect the estate from litigation, should he so inform a child. The case of *Rojack v Taylor and Buchalter* [2005] IEHC 28 is instructive in this regard.

Where the deceased died intestate, no right of action under s 117 exists (there is however a right analogous to s 117 under s 67A available to the child of a deceased civil partner against the surviving civil partner: see later) and each child receives a fixed share in the estate under the rules of intestacy. However, a practitioner should be aware of any pending claim under s 63.

13.8.2 SECTION 63: ADVANCEMENTS TO CHILDREN TO BE BROUGHT INTO ACCOUNT

It is important in the context of the rights of children to make reference to the doctrine of advancement as embodied in s 63 of the Succession Act. Practitioners are referred to para **4.6.4.4** in its entirety.

Section 63 applies when siblings 'share' in the estate of a deceased parent. This may arise on intestacy, partial intestacy, where siblings share the residue, or where siblings share a legacy (usually a pecuniary legacy). While it applies to the share a predeceased child would take if still living, it does not apply between grandchildren, who take the share of a predeceased child between them *per stirpes* as provided for in s 67(4).

It does not arise when one child, for example, is left a specific bequest and another child is left a separate specific bequest of lesser value. It also does not arise where a clause is inserted in the will specifically negating the provisions of s 63, as per the precedent will provided at para **2.17**.

While the section may be applicable, it does not arise automatically. A child must apply under the section, asserting that an advancement (as defined) was made under the section. The onus of proof is on the child making the assertion, unless the deceased has expressly described any payment to the child as an advancement. The value of the advancement is fixed at the time of the advancement. It should also be noted that 'child' includes an individual in relation to whom the deceased acted *in loco parentis* (s 63(10)).

Section 63 represents an enlargement of a common law rule which applied in cases of intestacy, requiring children to account for any advancement they had received during the testator's lifetime. This was known as bringing such property into 'hotch-pot' (i.e. into consideration in considering the appropriate distribution of the estate).

If the advancement paid to the child is equal to or greater than the share due to the child under the deceased's estate, the child will be precluded from taking any benefit from the estate. If the advancement amounts to less than the child's share under the will or intestacy, then the child is entitled to the difference between the two, to bring his share up to the requisite level.

Examples of the operation of s 63 can be found at para **4.6.4.4**.

Section 63 expressly provides that the doctrine of advancement is only to apply as between the testator's children (except in the case where a child has predeceased the testator leaving surviving issue who represent him, in which case advancements to the deceased's child will be taken into account in establishing the shares of his children).

As noted earlier, it is not the duty of the personal representative to advise children of their right to apply under s 63, but when notified of such an application, the personal representative must apply the section precisely.

13.8.3 NON-MARITAL CHILDREN AND THE STATUS OF CHILDREN ACT, 1987

Since the Status of Children Act, 1987, 'children' are defined as children of the testator, whether born in or out of wedlock or adopted by him or her. The concept of illegitimacy as regards children has been abolished. The Succession Act has been amended to take account of this interpretation of 'children' and practitioners are referred to para **4.6.3.4**.

It is also worth noting that once a child has been legally adopted, that child cannot claim any right to the estate of his deceased natural parents, despite having a Group A CAT threshold.

The Status of Children Act, 1987 has also amended the interpretation of the word 'issue' (whether in the context of the intestacy rules or interpreting the words of *inter vivos* deeds) and now includes all children, whether born within a marriage, of a non-marital relationship, or children by adoption. Accordingly, children of non-marital parents may be entitled on intestacy to share in the estate of the deceased. Similarly, non-marital nephews and nieces, the non-marital children of brothers and sisters, may be entitled on intestacy.

It is extremely important where the possibility of there being non-marital children is raised that the personal representative establishes whether there are any non-marital children of the testator in existence. It is worth noting that a clause in the will, negating the provisions of the Act, will not prevent a non-marital child from pursuing either a s 63 or (more likely) a s 117 application.

13.8.4 SECTION 117 APPLICATIONS

Where the deceased died testate, all his or her children are entitled to take an action against his estate under s 117. Practitioners are referred to para **4.6.4.1**.

The Succession Act does not give children a fixed right to any share of the deceased's estate; instead, they may make an application under s 117. If the court concludes that the testator has *'failed in his moral duty to make proper provision for the child in accordance with his means, whether by his will or otherwise'* the court can order such provision for the child out of the testator's estate as it thinks just.

Where the deceased died intestate, s 117 does not apply. However, s 67A (as inserted in the Succession Act by the civil partnership legislation) gives the child of a deceased civil partner the right to apply against a surviving civil partner. Even then, the maximum a child can claim is that share of the estate he would be entitled to if the deceased parent died without a civil partner. For example, if the testator died leaving four children and a civil partner, the most a child could claim under s 67A would be one quarter of the net estate.

As noted above, on the commencement of Part 11 of the Children and Family Relationships Act, 2015 it will be possible for civil partners to apply to adopt as civil partners. Where the child of a civil partner is successfully adopted by both civil partners that child will not be able to apply under s 117(3A) or s 67A(3).

Similarly, the Marriage Act, 2015 allows for the dissolution of a civil partnership and its replacement by marriage. In those circumstances the child of the predeceased spouse will be in the same position in relation to a surviving spouse as the child of a predeceased parent who is not the child of the surviving spouse.

However, s 117 will apply where the testator left a valid will, no matter whether any or all of the estate devolves on intestacy. There is a strict time limit of six months from the date of the grant of probate (or administration with the will annexed), after which a child is precluded from taking such an action. The Act does not provide for minority or disability.

Children of both the testator and of the spouse of the testator are precluded from affecting any bequest to that spouse and nothing can affect the spouse's legal right share (which presumably will be one-third of the entire estate) from any child of the testator who is not also a child of the spouse. As noted earlier, the legal right share of a civil partner can currently be affected by a s 117 application taken by a child of the deceased civil partner.

13.8.4.1 'Other' children, the surviving spouse, and section 117

However, where there are non-marital children of the testator or any children of a previous marriage where such children have not been adopted by the spouse, any application by them under s 117 can affect a bequest to the surviving spouse. To date, the courts have not reduced the value of any bequest to a surviving spouse to less than the legal right share but, on a strict reading of the legislation, it is open to them to do so.

For this reason, it is advisable that the surviving spouse is not notified of his or her right to elect until some time after the grant of representation has issued, where there is a possibility of a non-marital child taking a s 117 application. When six months after the grant of representation have elapsed, the surviving spouse will know whether any application(s) have been made under s 117, and this may inform his or her decision to elect.

CHAPTER 14

OBLIGATIONS, DUTIES, AND CLAIMS ON THE ESTATE

14.1 Undertakings

From time to time, a practitioner may be called upon to give undertakings to banks or other financial institutions in respect of benefits due to various beneficiaries. This area is highly contentious and highly dangerous. The rule is that, wherever possible, the practitioner should avoid giving an undertaking in relation to the administration of an estate or any aspect thereof.

Once the grant of representation issues to a named personal representative, it is that personal representative who is in control and not the solicitor. Without reference to the solicitor, the personal representative is entitled to obtain an official copy of the grant and note it himself and collect in the assets.

Further, if the personal representative dies, another person can obtain a grant without reference to the original solicitor who is on record. (The Probate Office will accept a certified copy of the previous grant where the original is not forthcoming.)

While one can never be forced to give an undertaking, solicitors can be forced to complete such an undertaking once given. For this reason, the undertaking should always cover only matters entirely within the control of the solicitor.

Practitioners should always refer to the Law Society guidelines in relation to professional undertakings as set out in para 6.5 of *A Guide to Good Professional Conduct for Solicitors* (3rd edn).

An undertaking should never be given without the irrevocable written authority of the personal representative and the appropriate beneficiary.

Undertakings should be signed only by a principal or partner of the firm, who will be personally liable on foot of them.

The Law Society Practice Note in relation to undertakings and probate practice is reproduced.

> **'Undertakings, non-resident personal representative and probate practice**
>
> *Practitioners are reminded that as soon as a Grant of Representation issues, the personal representative is absolutely entitled to receive the proceeds of any funds in any bank or other financial institution.*
>
> *A solicitor acting for such personal representative(s) should therefore, be extremely cautious in giving any undertaking concerning such funds and should avoid doing so wherever possible.*
>
> *Prior to giving any such undertaking the solicitor should obtain from each of the personal representatives the usual irrevocable authority to act and an irrevocable instruction to the financial institution concerned that the funds can only be paid through the solicitor's office.*

This instruction should be then forwarded to the financial institution concerned and confirmation should be obtained from them that they will only release the proceeds through the solicitor's office.

This should also be done where the solicitor is acting as agent for a non-resident personal representative. In such cases under s. 48(10) of the CAT Consolidation Act, 2003 (as inserted by section 147(1) (l) of the Finance Act, 2010 and further clarified by Section 115 of the Finance Act, 2012) the solicitor shall be assessable and chargeable for the tax to the same extent as the beneficiary.

In all such cases, this should be done as soon as early as possible after the issue arises.'

14.1.1 'CONDITIONAL' UNDERTAKINGS OR LETTERS ON WHICH A THIRD PARTY MIGHT RELY

Apart altogether from undertakings, the solicitor must be extremely careful about giving letters upon which it might reasonably be expected that any third party, including a beneficiary, might rely, to his detriment. The manner in which the information is handled in the administration of an estate is as important as the manner in which assets and liabilities are dealt with.

In giving a conditional undertaking, a solicitor may be misleading the institution receiving the undertaking. The institution would be entitled to assume that a competent solicitor would not give an undertaking about money coming into their hands if they were not certain it was going to come in. Before giving a conditional undertaking in relation (for example) to a life assurance cheque or other form of payment, the solicitor would need to have the following:

(i) the irrevocable authority in writing of the personal representative;

(ii) the irrevocable authority in writing of the beneficiary irrespective of who is the personal representative;

(iii) confirmation from the financial institution that they would only pay the money to the solicitor;

(iv) the further irrevocable authority in writing of the personal representative and/or the beneficiary to negotiate the cheque without further reference to the personal representative;

(v) the grant of representation, which should have issued before any undertaking is given;

(vi) the implication on the proceeds of the policy of any inheritance tax/CGT payable by the beneficiary, especially if that beneficiary resides overseas.

The solicitor should be aware that he would have to make every effort to comply with the undertaking. In the event of the death of the personal representative he would have to secure the cooperation of the new personal representative. If the new personal representative was not prepared to cooperate, he will have to be prepared to take the necessary proceedings to ensure that the funds end up in the right place.

Prior to issuing any definitive statements with regard to entitlements or time limits within which these entitlements might be paid to any party whatsoever, the solicitor should check with the client that he has an irrevocable authority to do this and, in the case of an undertaking, that this irrevocable authority is in writing.

Undertakings may not be simply in a written form: a solicitor can also give undertakings and assurances on the telephone. If ever in doubt as to the manner in which information might be processed by some third party and you or your client are being prejudiced as a result, always take the precaution of following up your telephone conversation with a letter to the relevant party, recording accurately what actually has taken place on the telephone, and your or your client's intentions in this regard.

The solicitor should be particularly careful about being precipitous with information to beneficiaries or banks. You should process all information through your client, the personal representative.

14.1.2 DISCHARGE FROM UNDERTAKING

In the event of any undertaking being given, the solicitor must ensure that a discharge from such undertaking has been received, prior to completion of any administration file. If any matter remains outstanding after distribution, such as the lodgement of title documents with a bank or the handing over of a certificate of discharge, this should be highlighted on the inside cover of the file and a record placed in the solicitor's PC or desk diary and/or on the office file management system.

In practice, these matters should be diarised forward until the undertaking is fully discharged. There are reminder facilities on computers with regard to undertakings and, in many cases, a solicitor's firm will have an annual review of undertakings prior to reviewing their professional indemnity insurance. The problem that arises is that once the administration, particularly a lengthy one, is complete, all parties are generally so relieved at final distribution that matters such as undertakings can be forgotten. Prior to closing any file, one should specifically check that all undertakings have been fully discharged.

14.2 Interest and 'Negative Interest'/Bank Charges

Common law rules have evolved directing that interest is payable on legacies in certain situations with effect from certain dates. A testator may, however, set out specific directions in the will, governing if and how interest is to be dealt with. The general rule is that in so far as specific legacies, residuary legacies, and demonstrative legacies, which are specific in nature, are concerned, the legatees do not have any right to interest as such.

However, they are entitled to any income which arises from the subject-matter of the devise or legacy, from the date of the testator's death. The personal representatives will carry out an apportionment where necessary so that the correct proportion of income in respect of the period to the testator's death belongs to his estate and the proportion attributable to the period after his death will be allocated to the beneficiary.

Note that any expenditure necessary for the upkeep of the assets in question and any losses in respect of it will also be allocated to the beneficiary.

Note too that if the specific legacy consisted of livestock, then any progeny born after the testator's death would be regarded as income and would belong to the specific beneficiary.

At the time of going to press, various financial institutors are introducing 'negative interest' or a percentage charge for accounts in excess of one million euro. These would include solicitor's client accounts, office accounts, etc, and in those circumstances, it should be made clear to the client that this will have to be accounted for from any funds held for the client. This emphasises the importance of dealing with client funds as expeditiously as possible.

14.2.1 THE 'EXECUTOR'S YEAR'

Section 62 of the Succession Act, 1965 provides that the personal representatives have a year from the date of death of the deceased, during which they cannot be compelled to distribute the estate. This period, often referred to as the 'executor's year', was in force prior to the Act.

The personal representatives must pay interest on general legacies (including any demonstrative legacies which are not specific in character) from the end of the executor's year. Interest will be payable from that date and executors are responsible for its payment, even if the assets are unproductive.

The scale applicable is as set out in the Rules of the Superior Courts, 1986. The current rate is 2 per cent since 1 January 2017. (See O 55, rr 41, 42, and 43; s 26 of the Debtors (Ireland) Act, 1840; s 20 of the Courts Act, 1981 and the Courts Act, 1981 (Interest on Judgment Debts) Order 2016, SI 624/2016.)

14.2.2 EXCEPTIONS TO THE 'EXECUTOR'S YEAR'

While the majority of legacies are dealt with in this way, there are exceptions, as follows:

- If the testator has left a legacy to a creditor in satisfaction of a debt, interest will run on that legacy in favour of the creditor from the date of death of the testator to date of payment.
- If a vested legacy is charged on real property, that legacy carries interest from the date of death of the testator.
- Legacies paid to minor children and intended to provide for their maintenance, with no other provision for their maintenance having been made in the will, carry interest from the date of the testator's death.

This situation also arises where:

(a) the legatee is a minor child of the testator or a minor to whom the testator stood *in loco parentis*;

(b) a legacy is given to a minor child from a testator who is not related to the child, where the legacy is clearly intended for the child's support.

14.3 Section 339 of the Social Welfare (Consolidation) Act, 2005 (Liability of Personal Representative)

14.3.1 OUTLINE AND HISTORY

There is an obligation on personal representatives to furnish a schedule of assets of the deceased to the Department of Social Protection (formerly the Department of Social and Family Affairs ('the Department')) where the deceased was in receipt of social welfare assistance (now referred to as social assistance).

There is a misconception that this obligation only applies to the non-contributory old-age pension or blind pension (which was the case originally under s 174 of the Social Welfare (Consolidation) Act, 1981), but s 33 of the Social Welfare Act, 1991 extended the duties and obligations of the personal representative where the deceased was in receipt of social assistance at any time. These duties and obligations are now contained in s 339 of the Social Welfare (Consolidation) Act, 2005 ('the Act' for this purpose).

14.3.2 OBLIGATION ON PERSONAL REPRESENTATIVE TO INFORM MINISTER

The section imposes certain obligations on the personal representatives of a deceased person, where the deceased was in receipt of social assistance at any time, to notify the Minister for Social Protection ('the Minister') of their intention to distribute the deceased's assets, not less than three months before commencing the distribution. The obligation exists if the deceased was in receipt of social assistance at any time. It is important to stress 'at any time' because the initial legislation only referred to the non-contributory old-age pension (now known as the State Pension (non-contributory)) and the blind pension, but has been extended to all forms of 'assistance' received at any time during the lifetime of the deceased.

Under s 139 of the Act, 'assistance' means: unemployment assistance; pre-retirement allowance; State pension (non-contributory); blind pension; widows', widowers', and orphans' (non-contributory) pensions; widowed parent grant; the following allowances which were discontinued in 1997 and replaced by one-parent family payment [deserted wives' allowance, prisoners wives' allowance, lone parents' allowance]; the one-parent family payment; carers' allowance; supplementary welfare allowance; disability allowance; and farm assistance: in other words, most non-contributory social welfare payments.

These are means-tested payments, and where the person receiving the assistance has more than €20,000 in capital, a refund may be due. Details of the means test and the calculation of payment under the various forms of assistance are available on the Department of Social Protection website at http://www.welfare.ie.

The personal representatives must therefore determine whether the deceased was in receipt of any form of social assistance at any time during his life. If so, then not less than three months before commencing to distribute the assets of the estate, the personal representatives must deliver a notice in writing to the Minister, stating their intention to distribute the assets and providing the Minister with a schedule of the assets comprised in the deceased's estate. In practice, as soon as the Notice of Acknowledgment (Probate) Form SA.2, has been submitted, notice should be sent to the Minister, together with a copy of the relevant parts of the notice of acknowledgment (probate). This will save time when the grant issues and the personal representatives intend to distribute the estate.

It should be noted that the legislation refers to 'a schedule of the assets' which is significantly less information than the contents of the entire notice of acknowledgment (probate). Practitioners are referred to Issue 64 of the *Law Society eZine* (August 2015) which refers to a previous article from Issue 55 of the *Law Society eZine* (September 2014).

Deceased details, applicant details, and details of assets in the assets cover screen notice of acknowledgment (probate), including those assets ceasing on death, should be provided.

The Minister has a period of three months from the date of receipt of the schedule of assets/relevant parts of the notice of acknowledgment (probate) to notify the personal representatives that a sum of money is due to the Department in respect of the payment of assistance to the deceased at a time when he was not entitled to it, or which exceeded the amount to which he was entitled. The personal representatives are obliged to retain sufficient assets to discharge that debt.

Section 339(2) entitles the Minister, in determining the amount of the debt due to the Department, to assume that the deceased's assets at the time of death also belonged to him during the period in which he was in receipt of social assistance, in the absence of evidence to the contrary being produced by the personal representatives.

14.3.3 PERSONAL LIABILITY OF PERSONAL REPRESENTATIVE

Any personal representative who contravenes s 339 (e.g. by not notifying the Minister or by not retaining funds when so required by the Minister) is made personally liable by s 339(3) for the amount of any debt due to the Department. In addition, the debt may be recovered against the estate of the deceased by an action brought within six years from the date on which notice or the schedule of assets/relevant parts of the notice of acknowledgment (probate) is delivered to the Minister, whichever is the later.

The extension of the personal representative's liability will, in most cases, extend in turn to practitioners. This is because in the majority of cases the personal representative will have relied on the advice of the practitioner. The practitioner will more than likely find himself the defendant in a professional negligence suit if he ignores the provisions of the social welfare code in this area.

In practice, the Department of Social Protection can request an electronic copy of the notice of acknowledgment (probate), which contains the deceased's PPS number. The Department, in turn, checks this PPS number against its records of claimants.

It is important to note that a statutory notice to creditors (s 49) will not protect the personal representative from a claim by the Minister.

14.3.4 NOTIFICATION

Section 339(1)(b) provides that the Minister must, within three months of notification by the personal representative (probably through his solicitor), request in writing that sufficient assets be retained from the estate to repay any overpayments due. The practice of the Department is to issue such a request only where it appears from the schedule of assets/relevant parts of the notice of acknowledgment (probate) that a real probability of a claim due from the estate to the Department exists. If the Minister does not issue such a request within the three months, then it should be safe for a solicitor to distribute. However, to protect your client (and yourself), you should not distribute until you obtain the necessary letter of clearance, confirming that there are no claims against the estate from the Department.

14.3.5 BEST PRACTICE

It follows from the foregoing that practitioners acting for personal representatives will have to ascertain whether a deceased was, at any time, in receipt of any social assistance. This is already provided for in the mandatory questionnaire contained within the notice of acknowledgment (probate), as referred to at para **6.9.6.4**.

It would be a foolish solicitor who would assume that no such assistance had ever been received at any time in the past and who would accordingly ignore the obligations imposed by s 339.

Therefore, it is essential to obtain, prior to distribution of any estate, clearance from the Minister with regard to any assistance. It is good practice to seek clearance from the Minister at the same time as applying for the grant of representation if the information is available or as soon as practicable thereafter. It is not necessary to wait for the grant to issue to apply for clearance.

14.4 Nursing Home Support Scheme 'Fair Deal'

The Nursing Home Support Scheme Act, 2009 was referred to at para **2.7.6** and should be reviewed before reading this paragraph. It is possible that the testator drafted the will with this in mind and a specific instruction was included in the will for the payment of same overriding the provisions of s 47 of the Succession Act. It is also possible that such an arrangement was entered into after the will was drafted and the will is silent on the matter. Bear in mind that the deceased may never have entered into the arrangement themselves: the attorney of a person who has executed an Enduring Power of Attorney ('the donor') which has been registered can do so on behalf of the donor. Similarly, the committee of a ward of court can do so. Finally, the Nursing Home Support Scheme Act, 2009 in Part 4 brought into being the 'care representative', a completely new category of person enabled with the power to register the charge for ancillary state support against the property of the person needing nursing home care, where that person is unable to look after their own affairs but has not been made a ward of court or appointed an attorney under an EPA.

The Revenue Commissioners have been appointed collection agents for the HSE in respect of monies due in relation to Ancillary State Support. The 'relevant accountable person' can include the personal representatives or the person entitled to the property if it falls outside the estate. This paragraph will deal with the role of the personal representative. As noted at para **6.9.6.4**, the question 'Was the deceased in receipt of payments under the Nursing Home Support Scheme?' is asked by the Revenue Commissioners in the mandatory questionnaire included in the notice of acknowledgment (probate).

Section 27 of the Nursing Home Support Scheme Act, 2009 provides that the personal representatives of a deceased person who is in receipt of ancillary state support are obliged to give the HSE not less than three months' notice in writing of any intended distribution of the assets of the estate and to furnish a copy of the relevant parts of notice of acknowledgment (probate) if requested by the HSE and to ensure that sufficient assets of the estates are retained to repay the amount charged. This is a similar regime to the Social Welfare regime outlined at para **14.3**, and similar provisions apply in the case of failure to comply. Similarly, clearance should be sought as soon as the relevant information has been ascertained and it is not necessary to wait for the grant to issue.

14.5 Statutory Notice to Creditors (Section 49 Notice)

This was referred to at para **12.5.2**. Where the notice is published (see precedent at para **14.5.1**) and if no claims are received within the time specified in the notice, the personal representative may distribute the estate with regard only to claims of which he has notice. They are not liable for debts out of assets they have distributed without notice of a claim. However, they remain liable out of assets they retain or out of assets they distributed before the expiry of the period stated in the notice. Creditors who did not respond to the notice in time and have no claim against the personal representatives are still entitled to trace the assets distributed, i.e. the creditor can proceed against known beneficiaries, provided that the Statute of Limitations has not run against him. (See Spierin, *The Succession Act, 1965 and Related Legislation: A Commentary*, 5th edn (2017).)

This is an expensive procedure and should only be used where there is a distinct possibility that there may be outstanding liabilities not known to the personal representative (e.g. where the deceased was in business and ordered goods and/or services on credit and did not keep accurate records). While it is expensive, it is a protection for the personal representative in these circumstances.

In cases where the appropriate statutory notice to creditors should be published, it must be published in a national newspaper on the same day on two occasions in succeeding weeks.

It should also be noted that a s 49 publication does not protect the personal representative where there is a claim for Social Welfare (see para **14.3**) or the Nursing Home Support Scheme (see para **14.4**).

14.5.1 PRECEDENT STATUTORY NOTICE TO CREDITORS

STATUTORY NOTICE TO CREDITORS

In the estate of   late of   in the County of

NOTICE

Notice is hereby given pursuant to Section 49 of the Succession Act, 1965 that particulars in writing of all claims against the estate of the above named deceased who died on the   day of   20 , Probate of whose will was granted to the Executors on the   day of   20 , should be furnished to the undersigned solicitors for the Executors on or before the   day of   20 , after which date the assets will be distributed having regard only to the claims furnished, if any.

Dated this   day of   20   .

Solicitors

14.6 Payment of Legacies

When assets have been collected and debts paid, the time has come to pay pecuniary legacies. In practice, the appropriate form of receipt and indemnity with a covering letter is sent to each of the beneficiaries. When the receipt is signed and returned, the appropriate cheque is issued.

While an executor gets his power from the will and has authority to deal with the assets of the deceased from date of death, an administrator has no right to deal with any assets until the grant has issued but, once the grant is available, the authority relates back to the date of death.

Where specific legacies have been given, i.e. chattels, one should ensure that these objects have been handed over to the persons concerned. In many cases you will find that the personal representative may have handed over these objects immediately on, or shortly after, the death of the testator.

One should be wary of making any distribution where the estate may be insolvent.

Where the beneficiary is non-resident, the chattels should not be handed over until the CAT has been calculated, paid, and confirmation of payment provided. There is a procedure outlined in the CAT Lecture Notes (see Preface) to protect the personal representative in such circumstances.

14.6.1 PRECEDENT LETTER TO RESIDUARY LEGATEE/INTESTATE SUCCESSOR

This letter to a residuary legatee and devisee/intestate successor details their benefit, and should be accompanied by a form of receipt and indemnity. This letter is based on a set of estate accounts having been made available for review by the residuary beneficiary/intestate successor should they choose to review same.

Re: Deceased

Dear

A Grant of Probate/Administration Intestate/with Will Annexed has now issued in the estate of   and the Executor/Administrator is now in a position to distribute the estate.

In accordance with the terms of the residuary clause in the will/in accordance with your share of the residue of the estate/on intestacy [delete as applicable] we are now in a position to forward a cheque in your favour in the amount of €   made up as follows:

Gross benefit	€....................
Less share of costs	€....................
Less CAT (if paid by solicitor)	€....................
Net amount payable	€....................

This payment is the final payment/a payment on your account to you in respect of your share in the estate of the above named deceased.

We would be obliged if you would kindly sign the enclosed form of receipt and indemnity and return it to us for the purposes of our records and we will then forward the cheque to you immediately on receipt of same.

Yours faithfully,

SOLICITORS

- Note 1: as the benefit is a share on intestacy/residue, a proportionate share of the overall costs will be paid out of the benefit.

- Note 2: costs would also be payable by the beneficiary if you acted for the beneficiary in calculating and paying CAT and filing a CAT return on their behalf.

14.6.2 PRECEDENT RECEIPT AND INDEMNITY

This clearance form of receipt and indemnity should be signed by a beneficiary before payment of legacy, devise, share of residue/intestacy. While the beneficiary is obliged to sign a receipt, they are not strictly speaking obliged to sign an indemnity, save where CAT had been paid on their behalf. In this case, the estate needs to be indemnified against any further claim to CAT based on false or incomplete information provided by the beneficiary. The full receipt and indemnity is normally sought to protect the personal representative and usually this should not be problematic, unless the relationship with the beneficiary was contentious.

FORM OF RECEIPT [AND INDEMNITY]

In the Estate of   Deceased

I   of

hereby acknowledge receipt of a cheque in the amount of

from   as Executor of the will/Personal Representative of the above

named deceased per Messrs   Solicitors, in full

payment of:

a legacy/share of the residue to me under the terms of the will/share in the intestacy of [delete as applicable] the above named   deceased in the following terms

[Quote terms of legacy in the will if applicable].

[I hereby release and indemnify the said executor/administrator against all claims, actions, costs, demands, expenses or tax howsoever arising or which may be due on account of the said payment to me.]

Dated the   day of   20   .

SIGNED _____

ADDRESS _____

14.7 Taxation Obligations

The CAT Lecture Notes (see Preface) contains comprehensive notes on taxation obligations and when secondary liability of the estate for CAT arises. This paragraph is a brief extrapolation of some of the issues raised therein.

14.7.1 INTRODUCTION

A solicitor acting for a personal representative in the administration of an estate has a duty to that personal representative to obtain all necessary evidence that the various taxes and obligations both pre-death and post death have been discharged.

During the course of an administration, a personal representative has in many cases a primary responsibility for the tax which arises, and in some limited other cases is secondarily liable for taxes which arise during the course of administration. Accordingly, the solicitor acting should ensure that all necessary evidence is obtained that the said taxes for which the estate has a primary or secondary liability have been discharged.

The Revenue Commissioners website (https://www.revenue.ie/en/life-events-and-personal-circumstances/death-and-bereavement/information-on-tax-after-a-bereavement/index.aspx) is a very useful source of information in relation to the duty of the legal personal representative in this regard. It deals with all the major taxes arising and with both the post-death and the pre-death liabilities.

14.7.2 CAPITAL ACQUISITIONS TAX

Since 14 June 2010, the estate no longer has secondary liability in relation to CAT and certificates of discharge are no longer required or issued with some exceptions for joint property and where an application is made to the land registry for long possession. However, where either a beneficiary and/or the personal representative are non-resident in the jurisdiction for the tax year in which the date of death arises, the estate and/or the solicitor acting for the estate can be secondarily liable for any CAT due.

Revenue states that an Irish resident personal representative taking out probate or letters of administration will be appointed as an 'Agent' (s 45AA of the CAT Consolidation Act, 2003, as inserted) of a non-resident beneficiary entitled to a benefit exceeding €20,000. This personal representative agent will be responsible for the pay and file requirements of the non-resident beneficiary. In this regard, the personal representative agent will be entitled to retain funds adequate to meet the CAT liability from any amounts due to the beneficiary under the control of the personal representative agent. The liability of the personal representative agent will be restricted to the extent of the funds under their control which are available for distribution to the beneficiary.

Where there is no Irish resident personal representative, the personal representatives must appoint a solicitor holding a practising certificate in the State as agent (s 48(10) of the CAT Consolidation Act, 2003, as inserted) of the personal representative prior to seeking probate or letters of administration.

The Law Society sought and received a number of concessions to protect the personal representative agent and the solicitor agent. These concessions, while limited, are of some use. They include non-disclosure by the non-resident beneficiary either of aggregable prior benefits or assets outside the State.

They also provide for a procedure by which the resident personal representative or solicitor may write by registered post to Revenue at Dublin City Centre District, Revenue Commissioners, 9/14 Upper O'Connell Street, Dublin 2 indicating that he or she is intending to distribute the assets taken by a non-resident beneficiary from the estate of the deceased within one calendar month, where that personal representative or solicitor is satisfied that any relevant pay and file obligations have been met.

If Revenue indicates within the time frame of one calendar month that it is considering auditing the return or lack of return by that beneficiary, the resident personal representative or the solicitor should retain control of the assets relating to that beneficiary's benefit (in so far as he or she has control) until such time as either Revenue confirms in writing that there will be no audit or the audit, including any appeal process, is completed and any taxes are paid to the satisfaction of Revenue.

If Revenue fails to respond within the time frame of one calendar month advising that the file may be audited, then the resident personal representative or the solicitor under s 48(10) are free to distribute the assets concerned to the non-resident beneficiary. They will only be liable where they did not act 'honestly and in good faith' and did not 'deliberately fail to comply' with their obligations.

While this ad hoc arrangement is of some comfort to the resident personal representative and/or the solicitor under s 48 (10), it does not have a statutory basis and there is still a relatively high level of exposure that some resident personal representatives or solicitors may not be comfortable with. For example, where the only asset in the State is immoveable property, it is extremely difficult to sell same without the cooperation of the non-resident beneficiary. It is difficult to claim that the resident personal representative or the solicitor under s 48(10) has actual 'control' over that asset, particularly where it is registered property and there are no title deeds to retain.

The practice note relating to probate undertakings referred to in para 14.1 should be reviewed in this regard.

462 OBLIGATIONS, DUTIES, AND CLAIMS ON THE ESTATE

14.7.3 INCOME TAX CLEARANCE

This will usually be by way of letter from the Inspector of Taxes who has been dealing with the deceased's tax affairs during the course of his life. Ensure that the letter is clear and unambiguous in respect of both pre-death and post-death income tax liabilities.

14.7.4 CAPITAL GAINS TAX

This will be by way of receipt for the capital gains tax, together with a copy of the computation on which the tax paid was based. Ensure that the computation is acceptable to the Inspector of Taxes. In the case of non-resident beneficiaries, it is advisable to obtain a letter of no audit from the Revenue Commissioners.

14.7.5 STAMP DUTY

Stamp duty will arise where stampable assets are distributed not in accordance with the will or intestacy. For example, appropriation where the power to appropriate without notice or consent has not been granted in the will, or where a deed of family arrangement is entered into. Stamp duty will also arise where a beneficiary has to pay to discharge debts arising from the estate before they can take their immovable asset. Stamp Duty is a matter for the purchaser in such cases.

14.7.6 LOCAL PROPERTY TAX

The local property tax (LPT) came into effect on 1 July 2013 following the passing of the Finance (Local Property Tax) Act, 2012 ('the Act'), as amended by the Finance (Local Property Tax) Amendment Act, 2013. The Revenue Commissioners have a consolidated version of the LPT Acts on their website at: https://www.revenue.ie/en/tax-professionals/documents/acts/consolidation-lpt-acts.pdf, and useful details for the legal personal representative at: https://www.revenue.ie/en/property/local-property-tax/deferral-of-payment/personal-representatives.aspx.

For 2013, as the tax did not come into effect until July of that year, the LPT was payable for the last six months of the year and not the full twelve months as is the case for 2014 and all subsequent years.

Although the LPT is a tax on residential property, unlike the non principal private residence charge (NPPR) and the Household Charge (see later), the LPT is administered and collected by the Revenue Commissioners rather than the Local Authorities. In addition, the LPT, again unlike the NPPR and household charge, is not a fixed charge and is based on a self-assessment of the value of the property. The owner of the property is responsible for valuing the property, filing the return, and paying the tax. The liability and valuation date for the LPT for each year is 1 November in the preceding year.

A return must be made in respect of the LPT; paper returns had to be filed by 7 May 2013 and online returns by 28 May 2013. If paying in full by a single payment then this was due by 1 July 2013. Phased payments also began on this date and if the taxpayer selected to authorise the Revenue Commissioners to deduct the funds from their bank then the first payment was deducted on 21 July 2013. For 2014 and subsequent years the single payment due date was 1 January and phased payments also commenced on that date.

Failure to file a return can result in a penalty of up to €3,000 and late payment attracts interest at a rate of 0.0219 per cent in line with other taxes.

The LPT is, as stated, a self-assessed tax based on the value of the property. For properties valued at €1,000,000 or less the charge is 0.18 per cent of the value of the property. The Revenue has introduced a banded system details of which can be downloaded from its website.

14.7.6.1 Who is liable for payment of the LPT?

Section 11 provides that the liability to pay the LPT falls upon any person who

'holds any estate, interest or right in a relevant residential property entitling the person to—

(a) the immediate possession of such property for a period that may equal or exceed 20 years, or

(b) the receipt of rents or profits of such property for a period that may equal or exceed 20 years.'

The owner of a residential property on the liability date (which is 1 January for each tax year) is liable to pay the LPT. Joint owners are jointly and severally liable. In the case of properties leased for more than twenty years the tenant of the property is liable for the tax but in the case of properties leased for twenty years or less, the landlord is liable.

If a person has no legal title to the property but has acquired (or is acquiring) title by adverse possession he will be liable to LPT. Revenue has indicated that a person who has occupied a property on a rent-free basis without challenge, and has a prima facie right to register title under the adverse possession legislation (which normally occurs after twelve years' unchallenged occupation), will be the liable person.

While Revenue is conscious that difficulties can arise in terms of establishing the ownership of property, the LPT deals with this by placing the onus of proof on the taxpayer. Section 11 of the Act provides that the absence of documentary evidence of title to property shall not preclude an assessment and it will be presumed that a person who is in occupation of a relevant residential property, or in receipt of the rents or profits, is a liable person.

Section 11(3) is reproduced in full here to give an idea of the wide reaching implications of who is liable to pay the LPT.

'Without prejudice to subsections (1) and (2) the following persons shall for the purposes of this Act be liable persons in relation to a relevant residential property (the "property")—

(a) a person having an equitable or beneficial estate, interest or right in the property that entitles the person to the possession or receipt referred to in subsection (1)(a) or (b),

(b) a trustee that holds the property by an estate, interest or right in the property that entitles the Trustee or a beneficiary to the possession or receipt referred to in subsection (1)(a) or (b),

(c) a trustee or other person having a power to appoint in the property, an estate, interest or right that entitles a person to the possession or receipt referred to in subsection (1)(a) or (b),

(d) a person having an exclusive right of residence in the property for—

(i) his or her life or the life or lives of one or more others, or

(ii) a period that may equal or exceed 20 years,

(e) the personal representative of the estate of a person who was a liable person by virtue of any of the preceding provisions of this section,

(f) a person occupying the property with the right to be registered, pursuant to the Registration of Title Act 1964, in respect of any estate, interest or right that would entitle the person to the possession or receipt referred to in subsection (1)(a) or (b).'

Section 11(4) provides:

'For the avoidance of doubt—(a) in a case where a person is trustee as referred to in subsection (3)(b), that person shall, for the purposes of this Act, be a liable person in relation to the relevant residential property concerned notwithstanding that the one or more beneficiaries under the trust is or are, for the purposes for this Act, also a liable person or persons in relation to that property.'

What is clear from this is that there may, at any time, be several liable persons all of whom are responsible to discharge the LPT and all of whom may be targeted by Revenue. It is clear that the provisions of the Act have implications for those involved in the administration of trusts and estates.

14.7.6.2 Local property tax and the personal representative and trustees

There is no doubt that the personal representative of a person who was subject to the charge is a liable person under s 11 of the Act.

Unfortunately, however, the Act does not specify that the liability does not arise until after a grant of representation has been extracted and so it is possible that an executor of an estate, who has power from the date of death of a deceased, may be liable for the charge from the date of death, while the personal representative under a grant of administration either on intestacy or with will annexed (i.e. somebody other than the executor) would not be liable from that date.

However, s 4 of the Finance (Local Property Tax) Amendment Act, 2013 amends the primary Act in relation to who is a liable person and creates a period of grace for the estate of an intestate deceased (or an estate where the executor has predeceased the deceased) for twelve months if no grant has been extracted in that time. Once the twelve months are up, then any person in occupation or in receipt of rent from the property is liable. The same provision is not available for the executor of an estate.

A deferral of the LPT is available to the personal representative of an estate in circumstances where there is no grant of representation in the first twelve months after death, where the deceased himself had deferred the LPT, or where there was an outstanding liability to the charge as at the deceased's date of death.

In any event the LPT will be due for payment when the personal representative is in a position to transfer the property to a beneficiary, or distribute the proceeds from the sale of the property, or, at the very latest, three years from the date of death of the deceased. In addition a trustee is liable for the payment as is a beneficiary entitled to possession.

Revenue has suggested that where multiple parties are liable, they should all agree as to who should file the return and pay the tax. However, where relations between the parties are contentious this is easier said than done!

14.7.6.3 Local property tax and solicitors' obligations

The LPT is a charge on property; however, unlike most charges, which have a twelve-year life span, there is no time limit for the LPT. It is important therefore when dealing with a sale or transfer of a property to receive confirmation from Revenue that this has been discharged. There is also a 'snitch clause' in the legislation in that a purchaser will be bound to inform Revenue of vendors who have placed a much lower value on their property than the sale price. Offending vendors will be fined €500 if they refuse to reveal to the purchaser the band in which they valued the property for the purposes of the LPT. In turn the purchaser must file a revised return and valuation where it appears to him or her that the valuation declared by the vendor was too low given the circumstances as at the valuation date. It will usually be the solicitor who will deal with all issues relating to LPT.

It is important to be mindful of these points when acting in the administration of an estate and more particularly when acting for a vendor/purchaser in a conveyancing transaction.

Exempt property

An LPT exemption will be available for the following properties:

1. Commercial property.

2. A property vacated by the occupier due to their long-term physical or mental infirmity.

3. Residential property owned by a charity or similar body that is used solely or primarily to accommodate people with special needs.

4. A residential property purchased or adapted for use as the main or sole residence of a permanently incapacitated individual who has received an award from the

OBLIGATIONS, DUTIES, AND CLAIMS ON THE ESTATE

Personal Injuries Assessment Board or the court, or who is a beneficiary under a trust established for that purpose.

5. Mobile homes, vehicles, and vessels.

6. Houses in certain 'ghost estates' and other unfinished developments as listed in SI 91/2013.

7. Residential properties having pyrite damage.

8. Registered nursing homes.

14.7.7 HOUSEHOLD CHARGE

The annual Household Charge was introduced by the Local Government (Household Charge) Act, 2011 on 19 December 2011, as a temporary measure pending the introduction of the local property tax. It was a €100 flat tax chargeable on 1 January 2012 and to be paid by 31 March 2012. There was a procedure for payment by four equal instalments every two months ending on 10 September 2012.

If the owner of a residential property failed to pay the household charge (or an instalment) when due, a 'late payment fee' was applied. This was 10 per cent if the payment was less than six months late, 20 per cent if it was between six and twelve months late, and 30 per cent for later payments, together with interest at 1 per cent per month or part thereof (a total of 12 per cent per annum). The rate of interest was higher than the standard 'late tax' rate of 0.0219 per cent per day (*c.* 8 per cent per annum).

From 1 July 2013 unpaid household charge was increased to €200 and added to the LPT due on a property. The effect of this was that the outstanding household charge would be 'converted' to LPT and would be chargeable and payable under the LPT system.

14.7.8 THE NON PRINCIPAL PRIVATE RESIDENCE (NPPR) CHARGE

The Local Government (Charges) Act, 2009 was passed on 10 July 2009 and it introduced a local authority charge of €200 on residential properties from 2009 (excluding principal residences). Unlike the household charge, this tax has not been abolished and is still due on an annual basis. The liability date is 31 March and payment is due by 31 May. If payment is not made by the due date there is a late payment penalty of €20 for each month or part of a month that the charge remains unpaid. There is no provision for payment by instalments.

All residential properties (other than principal private residences) in the State are subject to the charge, including apartments, bedsits, 'granny' flats, holiday homes, vacant properties, and residential properties held by companies. The charge does not apply to foreign property, vehicles, or vessels. Where a property is divided into a number of different units the charge will apply separately to each unit, so if a dwelling is divided into four bedsits, four separate NPPR charges are payable (€200 × 4 = €800). A house let as a single unit to a number of separate tenants is only subject to one NPPR charge while a room let under the Revenue 'rent-a-room' scheme is not regarded as a separate residence.

The Act was amended by the Local Government (Household Charge) Act, 2011, which introduced changes to the way penalties are charged for late payment and provided for the secondary liability of agents and legislation for estates. Where the property is being sold or transferred by way of a gift, any individual who receives the sales proceeds or gives advice in relation to the transfer of the property is secondarily liable for any outstanding charges and late payment fees on the property. This secondary liability came into effect on 1 January 2012. If payment is not made by the due date (31 May in 2013) there is a late payment penalty of €20 for each month or part of a month that the charge remains unpaid.

The NPPR exemption may be extended where a person moves house and temporarily owns two properties. A refund can be applied for in relation to the second residential property, provided that it is acquired within one year of the relevant liability date and the first property is sold within six months of the liability date.

14.7.8.1 Estates and NPPR

The 2011 Act introduced measures for property held in estates. If the owner of the property is deceased and there are pre-death NPPR charges and/or late payment fees outstanding, the personal representative of the estate will not be liable until the first grant of representation issues. No further late fees will arise between the period from the date of death to the date of the grant. The personal representative must pay the liability within three months of the grant or else additional late fees will accrue to the estate from the date of the grant. The Act provides that the personal representative will not have a liability to pay the NPPR charge in a relevant year if the grant has not issued by the liability date (i.e. 31 March).

14.7.8.2 Legal charge on property for unpaid NPPR

Any unpaid house charge is charged on the property to which it relates and the charge remains live for twelve years from the due date after which a bona fide purchaser takes free of the charge. The Local Authority is obliged to give a receipt for the payment under the Act and, on application in writing, to give a certificate to the owner of the amount of charge paid by the owner.

CHAPTER 15

DISTRIBUTING THE ESTATE, VESTING OF PROPERTY, AND FINALISING MATTERS

15.1 Introduction

This chapter deals primarily with immovable property and transferring same into the names of those beneficiaries entitled. Practitioners should review para 8.4 of the Law Society of Ireland's *Conveyancing* OUP manual (all references to the *Conveyancing* OUP manual are to the 9th edn, 2019) in relation to registering in the Registry of Deeds, and para 14.7 of the same in relation to change of ownership on death for registered land. The chapter goes on to deal with deeds of family arrangement and disclaimers.

15.2 Assents

Section 10 of the Succession Act directs that all property to which the deceased was entitled (including property over which he exercised a general power of appointment by will) becomes vested in his personal representatives on his death. It further provides that they hold the estate as trustees for the persons entitled by law to it.

Most commentators conclude that this does not mean that the legatees have any beneficial interest in the deceased's property while it is being administered. They are regarded as being entitled to only a chose in action (a legal right to sue if necessary for the due administration of the estate by the personal representatives). The personal representatives carry out such due administration by first of all applying the deceased's assets and paying off any debts or liabilities which he may have had.

Only if there are sufficient assets after that has been done can the rights of the beneficiaries be ascertained. In order to conclude the administration of the estate, the personal representatives must vest the property in the beneficiaries entitled thereto. Where the property is personal property, no formal documentation is required.

However, as a matter of good practice, a personal representative should always obtain an acknowledgement, receipt, and indemnity indemnifying the personal representative against all costs, damages, claims, or taxes that might arise in the future in respect of the personal property being transferred. See para **14.6.2**.

Section 52 of the Succession Act, 1965 deals with the general provisions as to assent or transfer by personal representatives of land owned by the deceased in the course of administration. The references in the section to 'land' include both real (i.e. freehold) and leasehold land. The phrase 'immovable property' is used by the Probate Office to deal with 'land'.

15.2.1 DEFINITION OF 'ASSENT'

An assent is the means by which a disposition of a deceased's property to the person entitled is completed. At common law, it was not necessary for an assent to be in writing, and this continues to be the case in relation to pure personalty, but not for real or leasehold interests in land. Section 52(5) states that an assent not in writing shall not be effective to pass any estate or interest in land. An assent of personalty may be oral or implied.

An assent may be both in favour of a person beneficially entitled and in favour of trustees or personal representatives of such a person. This, no doubt, is intended to include the personal representatives of a beneficiary who predeceased the testator whose gift did not lapse, i.e. where s 98 applies, or of a beneficiary who died after the testator but before distribution of the testator's estate.

15.2.2 WHERE THE PERSONAL REPRESENTATIVE IS ALSO THE BENEFICIARY

The question as to whether a personal representative who is himself entitled as beneficiary or trustee has to complete an assent in his own favour is one that was addressed by Judge Ronan Keane in the case of *Mohan v Roche* [1991] 1 IR 560. In that case, the Judge felt that it was not necessary for an assent to be completed by a personal representative where the property was going to vest in himself.

However, from a practical point of view and a conveyancing point of view, when investigating title it would be difficult to complete the conveyancing transaction where there is no written assent.

The recent High Court case of *Trentdale Ltd v O'Shea* [2018] IEHC 47 confirmed that a written assent is required in all cases where registered land is passing, and long before this decision the Law Society Conveyancing Committee had issued a recommendation (Practice Note, *Law Society Gazette*, December 1997) that even where the personal representative is vesting property in himself there should be a written assent.

15.2.2.1 Registered land and the personal representative assenting to self

Land Registry forms 38 and 44 specifically deal with the situation where the legal personal representative is also the beneficiary. The forms (form 38 in the case of a testate registered owner and form 44 in the case of an intestate registered owner) allow the personal representative to apply for an assent to his or her registration as owner of the property comprised in the folio of which the deceased is the registered owner.

15.2.3 ASSENT SUBJECT TO A CHARGE

Section 52(2) allows a personal representative to make an assent of land subject to a charge, for the payment of any money which the personal representative is liable to pay. Where an assent is made subject to such charge, the liability of the personal representative in respect of the land ceases, except as to acts done, or contracts entered into by him, before the assent or transfer.

In practice, however, a personal representative would be more prudent to discharge all the liabilities before assenting, save for exceptional circumstances. Section 52(4) provides that where the personal representative has failed after more than one year from the deceased's death to make a transfer to the person so entitled, the High Court may make an order to the personal representative directing him to transfer the land to the person entitled. Should the personal representative fail to comply with the court order, the court is empowered to make an order vesting the land in the person entitled.

15.2.4 EXECUTION

It would seem that a purchaser to whom the personal representative has contracted to sell as beneficial owner can insist on the execution of an assent by the personal representative in his own favour. Where there is more than one personal representative, they must all join in the written assent. However, there is an exception where probate has been granted to one or some of the executors: in such a case only the proving executors need execute the assent.

It is also necessary for the personal representative to complete a family law declaration.

In all cases where the title to the deceased's property is registered in the Registry of Deeds, the assent and Form 1 are sent to the Property Registration Authority with a registration fee of €50 to effect registration, as outlined in para **15.2.7**. A precedent assent and PRA Form 1 are included, and further forms of assent are contained in the schedule in Spierin, *The Succession Act 1965 and Related Legislation: A Commentary*, 5th edn (2017), at appendix H, p 553. These assents are all in relation to unregistered land.

The Land Registration Rules, 2012 provide numerous precedents for the various types of assent which are required in respect of registered land. These forms of assent can be found in the Land Registration Rules, 2012 under the heading 'Transmission on Death'; they can be adapted to suit the facts, and examples of these are to be found in para 14.7 of the *Conveyancing* OUP manual.

A personal representative completes the relevant assent in accordance with the Land Registry rules in the format of an affidavit, setting out the particulars, the date of death, the date of the grant of representation, and a request to the Land Registry to register the beneficiary as registered owner. When lodging a deed of assent in the Land Registry, it is also necessary to lodge the original grant of representation and the usual Form 17; a sealed and certified copy of the grant will also be accepted.

At the time of making such lodgement, a request is made to the Land Registry to return the original grant of representation to the person entitled, who will usually be the solicitor for the executor or personal representative. The Land Registry fee payable on such transmission/assent is currently €130.00 but practitioners should apply for a new copy folio as well showing the change of ownership; the current fee for a copy folio is €40.

15.2.5 STAMP DUTY ON ASSENTS

As discussed in the CAT Lecture Notes (see Preface), deeds of assent do not require stamp duty for registration purposes where the property is vested in the persons entitled under the deceased's will or an intestacy or after disclaimer by such persons; see para **8.10**.

However, where the beneficiary 'pays' for the property, then the assent becomes a conveyance on sale and is stampable as such. See under Deeds of Family Arrangement at para **15.3**.

15.2.6 PRECEDENT DEED OF ASSENT

Peter Collins, late of 24 Sandy Road, Stillorgan, Co Dublin, died on the   day of 20   . By his will dated March 2012 he left all his property to his son Francis and appointed Thomas O'Donnell his executor. The property is registered in the Registry of Deeds and is described in the title documents as follows:

ALL THAT AND THOSE the hereditaments and premises together with the dwellinghouse situate thereon known as No 24 Sandy Road, Stillorgan in the Barony of Rathdown in the County of Dublin.

HELD under Lease dated 1st of January 1954 made between Navan Builders Ltd of the one part and the deceased of the other part for a term of nine hundred and ninety-nine years subject to an annual rent of ten pounds and to the covenants and conditions therein contained.

THIS ASSENT made the   day of   20   .

WHEREAS PETER COLLINS (hereinafter called 'the deceased') late of 24 Sandy Road, Stillorgan, Co Dublin, was entitled prior to his death to the premises set out in the Schedule hereto for the interest and term specified therein.

1. The deceased made his last will and testament dated the 14th day of March 2012 and did therein appoint Thomas O'Donnell as sole executor. The deceased died on the   day of   20   without having revoked or altered his will, probate whereof issued from the Principal Probate Registry, Phoenix House, Smithfield, Dublin 7 on the   day of   20   to me, Thomas O'Donnell, the executor.

2. Under the terms of his will the hereditaments and premises described in the Schedule hereto were bequeathed to Francis Collins.

3. Now I as legal personal representative of the deceased do **HEREBY ASSENT** to the vesting in Francis Collins of **ALL THAT AND THOSE** the hereditaments and premises more particularly described in the schedule hereto for all the estate interest and title held by the deceased in the premises prior to his death.

SCHEDULE

[Description of property as per title documents including tenure]

'ALL THAT AND THOSE the hereditaments and premises together with the dwellinghouse situate thereon known as No 24 Sandy Road, Stillorgan in the Barony of Rathdown in the County of Dublin'

HELD under Lease dated 1st of January 1954 made between Navan Builders Ltd of the one part and the deceased of the other part for a term of nine hundred and ninety-nine years subject to an annual rent of ten pounds and to the covenants and conditions therein contained.

SIGNED

By the said Thomas O'Donnell

In the presence of

15.2.7 MEMORIALS OF ASSENT/APPLICATION FORM 1

Under the Registration of Deeds Rules 2008, SI 52/2008, which came into force on 1 May 2008, memorials were abolished and replaced with an application form.

An application for registration of a deed of assent with the Registry of Deeds must consist of the prescribed application Form 1 (see **Form 15.1**) duly completed and signed by the individual solicitor acting for the applicant. In the case of a personal application for registration (i.e. an application by a private individual), the application must be made by way of the prescribed affidavit in Form 1A and must be sworn by the personal applicant.

On lodgement, each application is allocated a priority number. Fixed priority in order of lodgement is maintained. In addition, the application form must contain the following:

- name of the deed (i.e. assent);
- date of the deed;
- all parties to the deed; and
- a description of property to include the townland, barony and county, and/or the city or town and parish. The details given must be in the deed.

The registration fee is currently €50; if any query is raised, a further €20 becomes payable.

When completing the form in relation to an assent, the grantor(s) will be the legal personal representative(s) and the grantee will be the assignee(s). They can of course be one and the same person or persons. Where the assent is of leasehold property, the section 'For assignments only', which details the lease, should be completed, as this will provide a record of the lease should the original assent be mislaid.

Form 1: Registry of Deeds

Application by solicitor for registration of a Deed of Conveyance/Assignment/Grant/Assent/Judgment Mortgage or other document other than those referred to in Forms 2-8 (Rule 6).
See also Forms 13-15 for the registration of Property Adjustment Orders and Forms 16-16B for Judgment Mortgages

I, Named Solicitor   *Solicitor for* Francis Collins

apply for registration of a deed the particulars of which are set out hereunder.
I certify that the particulars are in accordance with the Deed.

For Office Use Only
Fees-Validation

Signed (by Solicitor): _____

Name of Lodging Party: Named Solicitor's Firm

Address of Lodging Party: Address of Named Solicitor's Firm

Solicitor's Reference: Named Solicitor's Reference No.

Name of Deed (Select one, as appropriate):
○ Conveyance   ○ Assignment   ○ Grant   ● Assent   ○ Judgment Mortgage   ○ Other

If 'Other', please give details: [ ]   Date of Deed: [ ][ ][ ][ ][2][0]
DDMMYYYY

Revenue Stamp Issued?   If Yes, please enter Stamp Certificate ID:
○ Yes
● No
Example: 12-0123456-A12B-DDMMYY-A

Name of all Grantors:
	Forename/s	Surname/Company Name
1:	Thomas	O'Donnell
2:		
3:		
4:		

Use additional sheet for further GRANTORS if necessary

Name of all Grantees:
	Forename/s	Surname/Company Name
1:	Francis	Collins
2:		
3:		
4:		

Use additional sheet for further GRANTEES if necessary

Description of the Property
Note - Property Details not included in the Deed should not be provided hereunder.

Address (as in deed): ALL THAT AND THOSE the hereditaments and premises together with the dwellinghouse situate thereon known as No. 24 Sandy Road, Stillorgan in the Barony of Rathdown in the County of Dublin

Situate in TOWN: Stillorgan
TOWNLAND:
PARISH:
BARONY: Rathdown
CITY:
COUNTY: DUBLIN
Area (if in deed):

Map Co-ordinates (if included in deed):
GeoDirectory (if included in the deed):

*use additional sheet for further PROPERTIES if necessary

For Assignments Only
Note - Lease details to be provided where application is made for registration of an Assignment.

Lease Date (DDMMYYYY): 0 1 0 1 1 9 5 4

	Forename/s	Surname/Company Name
Lessor:		Navan Builders Ltd.
Lessee:	Peter	Collins

Term: 999 Years
Commencement Date: 0 1 0 1 1 9 5 4
Rent: £10-00 Per Annum
ROD Reference:

Please print and sign form, and return with the relevant documentation to this address:

Registry of Deeds
Henrietta Street
Dublin 1
DX199

Print Form

Print Blank Copy

Note - clicking Print Blank Copy button clears any inputted data from the form.

FOR OFFICIAL USE ONLY

Application Code:
Official Code:
Date:
Serial No.:

Registration Made by _____

15.3 Deeds of Family Arrangement

15.3.1 INTRODUCTION AND OVERVIEW

The expression 'family arrangements' is not used in the restricted sense of a transaction between members of the same family for the benefit of the family generally, but is used to describe all types of property transactions between persons who are related to each other by blood or marriage, irrespective of the motive for the transaction. The 'family arrangement' may indeed include beneficiaries who are not related to the deceased or each other. Transactions between members of a family may be by way of sale, voluntary disposition, or gift; combination of a sale and a voluntary disposition; or a deed of family arrangement. This chapter will be looking at deeds of family arrangement from the point of view of the personal representative transferring property outside of the terms of the will by way of agreement amongst family members.

15.3.1.1 Sale

Where the family member conveying the property, or an interest in property, receives full value from the party to whom the property or interest is conveyed.

15.3.1.2 Voluntary disposition or gift

Where the family member who is conveying property, or an interest in property, to another family member does so gratuitously.

15.3.1.3 Combination of a sale and a voluntary disposition

For instance, where, on a break-up of a marriage, the husband transfers the property, which is mortgaged, to the wife, in consideration of the wife's assuming liability for the mortgage debt but without requiring any payment to the husband for his equity of redemption.

15.3.2 A DEED OF FAMILY ARRANGEMENT

In the example that follows, the parties to the deed of family arrangement are five siblings. Both parents of the parties to the deed died intestate, and one of the children has taken out a grant of administration intestate to both their estates and has had the property vested in him as personal representative. The four other siblings have agreed to sell the property to him for €200,000, to be divided equally among them.

As discussed in the CAT Lecture Notes (see Preface), an alternative means of carrying out the family's wishes would be that instead of joining the personal representative in the deed, the transaction could be effected by two separate deeds:

1. a deed of family arrangement between the five beneficiaries;
2. an assent by the personal representative in writing in favour of the beneficiary who, by virtue of the combined operation of the will of the testator and the deed of family arrangement, becomes entitled to the entire beneficial interest in the premises.

Students are referred to para 16.7.2 of the *Conveyancing* OUP manual, which deals with this comprehensively.

15.3.3 PRECEDENT DEED OF FAMILY ARRANGEMENT

THIS ASSIGNMENT made the   day of   two thousand and   BETWEEN

KEVIN COSTNER of 15 St Stephens Green in the City of Dublin (hereinafter called 'THE PERSONAL REPRESENTATIVE') of the first part, GRACE KELLY (née Costner) of Shandon View in the City of Cork (hereinafter called 'the First Grantor'), MICHELINA CHEUNG (née

Costner) of Bayview House, Howth in the County of Dublin (hereinafter called 'the Second Grantor'), EILEEN DILLON (née Costner) of Beau Island, Co Cork (hereinafter called 'the Third Grantor'), LINDA COSTNER of Cultra House, Bandon in the County of Cork (hereinafter called 'the Fourth Grantor'), KEVIN COSTNER the aforesaid Personal Representative (hereinafter called 'the Fifth Grantor') (hereinafter collectively called 'THE GRANTORS') of the second part and the aforesaid KEVIN COSTNER of 15 St Stephens Green in the City of Dublin (hereinafter called 'the Grantee') of the Third Part.

RECITALS:

(a) By Indenture of Lease (hereinafter called 'the Lease') specified in the First Schedule hereto the premises (hereinafter called 'the Premises') herein comprised and in the Second Schedule more particularly described and intended to be hereby assigned were demised unto John Costner and Barbara Costner as tenants in common in equal shares for the term of years created by the Lease subject to the payment of the yearly rent thereby reserved and to the performance and observance of the covenants on the part of the said John Costner and Barbara Costner and conditions therein contained.

(b) The said John Costner died on the   day of   20   intestate leaving Barbara Costner his widow, and Grace Kelly (née Costner), Michelina Cheung (née Costner), Eileen Dillon (née Costner) and Linda Costner and the Personal Representative his children him surviving.

(c) The said Barbara Costner died on the   day of   20   intestate without having applied for Grant of Administration Intestate in the estate of the said John Costner and without having intermeddled in the said estate leaving the aforesaid Grace Kelly (née Costner) Michelina Cheung (née Costner), Eileen Dillon (née Costner), Linda Costner and Kevin Costner her children her surviving.

(d) Letters of Administration Intestate in the estate of the said John Costner were on the   day of   20   issued forth of the Principal Probate Registry, The High Court to the Personal Representative.

(e) Letters of Administration Intestate in the estate of the said Barbara Costner were on the   day of   20   issued forth of the Principal Probate Registry, The High Court to the Personal Representative.

(f) By Deed of Assent dated the   day of   20   the premises were vested in the said Personal Representative as personal representative of the said John Costner deceased and the said Barbara Costner deceased for all the estate and interest of the said John Costner and the said Barbara Costner TO HOLD the same as trustee on behalf of the estates of the said John Costner deceased and the said Barbara Costner deceased.

(g) The following persons are the only persons entitled to participate in the distribution of the estate of the said John Costner deceased and the said Barbara Costner deceased under the provisions of the Succession Act, 1965 that is to say:

1. (i) Grace Kelly (née Costner) the first Grantor, (ii) Michelina Cheung (née Costner) the second Grantor, (iii) Eileen Dillon (née Costner) the third Grantor, (iv) Linda Costner the fourth Grantor, (v) Kevin Costner the Personal Representative.

2. The premises are now vested in the Personal Representative upon trust for the parties hereto in the shares following that is to say:

   a) As to one undivided fifth share thereof for the first Grantor;

   b) As to one undivided fifth share thereof for the second Grantor;

   c) As to one undivided fifth share thereof for the third Grantor;

   d) As to one undivided fifth share thereof for the fourth Grantor;

   e) As to one undivided fifth share thereof for the Personal Representative.

(h) The Grantors have attained their respective majorities.

(i) The Grantors are desirous of assigning their respective distributive shares in the premises to the Grantee for the consideration and in the manner hereinafter appearing.

(j) The Personal Representative at the request of the Grantors and the Grantee has agreed to join in these presents for the purpose of giving effect to this Deed.

NOW THIS ASSIGNMENT WITNESSETH as follows:

1. In pursuance of the said agreement and in consideration of the sum of Two Hundred Thousand Euro (€200,000) now paid by the Grantee to the Grantors (the receipt whereof the Grantors do and each of them do hereby respectively acknowledge) the Grantors and each of them as to each of their one undivided fifth share thereof HEREBY ASSIGN to the Grantee ALL AND SINGULAR the said undivided shares of the Grantors and all other (if any) estate right title and interest of the Grantors in ALL THAT AND THOSE the premises TO THE GRANTEE his executors administrators and assigns for the unexpired residue of the term of years created by the Lease subject to the exceptions and reservations as in the Lease and subject also to the payment of the rent thereby reserved and to the performance and observance of the covenants on the Lessee's part and conditions therein contained.

2. The PERSONAL REPRESENTATIVE as personal representative of the said John Costner and Barbara Costner at the request of the GRANTORS and the GRANTEE and in consideration of the release hereinafter contained hereby further assigns to the GRANTEE all the legal estate right title and interest in the premises his executors administrators and assigns for the unexpired residue of the term of years created by the Lease subject to the exceptions and reservations as in the Lease set forth and subject also to the payment of the rent thereby reserved and to the performance and observance of the covenants on the Lessee's part and conditions therein contained.

3. The GRANTEE hereby covenants with the GRANTORS and the PERSONAL REPRESENTATIVE that he, the GRANTEE his executors, administrators and assigns will henceforth pay the yearly rent reserved by the Lease and perform and observe the covenants on the Lessee's part and conditions therein contained and will keep the GRANTORS and the PERSONAL REPRESENTATIVE their executors and administrators their estate and effects fully and effectually indemnified from and against all claims by reason of the non-payment of the said rent or the breach non-performance or non-observance of the said covenants and conditions or any of them.

[*While certification is no longer required by Revenue it remains good conveyancing practice to include certificates.*]

4. IT IS HEREBY CERTIFIED as follows:–

   (a) That section 29 (conveyance on sale combined with building agreement for dwellinghouse/apartment) of the Stamp Duties Consolidation Act, 1999, does not apply to this instrument;

   (b) That the consideration (other than rent) for the sale is wholly attributable to residential property and that the transaction effected by this instrument does not form part of a larger transaction or of a series of transactions in respect of which, had there been a larger transaction or a series of transactions, the amount or value, or the aggregate amount or value, of the consideration (other than the consideration for the sale/lease concerned which is wholly or partly attributable to residential property and other than rent) would have been wholly or partly attributable to residential property.

IN WITNESS whereof the parties hereto have hereunto set their respective hands the day and year first above written.

FIRST SCHEDULE

THE LEASE

Indenture of Lease dated the 22nd day of December 1950 and made between Cyril Reginald Gardiner and Ruth Young of the one part and John Costner and Barbara Costner of the other part whereby the premises herein comprised were demised to the Lessee therein for the term of 900 years from the 1st day of December 1950 subject to the yearly rent of £8.00 (€10.15) and to the covenants and conditions therein contained.

SECOND SCHEDULE

THE PREMISES

The premises comprised in the schedule to the Lease and therein described as 'ALL THAT piece or parcel of ground situate on the north side of Gray's Lane in the Townland of Killiney, Parish of St George, Barony of Rathdown and County of Dublin, together with the dwellinghouse erected thereon known as 2 Dawn View, Killiney, Co Dublin, which said premises are more particularly delineated and described on the map or ground plan thereof hereon endorsed and therein edged red'.

SIGNED AND DELIVERED
by the PERSONAL REPRESENTATIVE
in the presence of:

SIGNED AND DELIVERED
by the FIRST GRANTOR
in the presence of:

SIGNED AND DELIVERED
by the SECOND GRANTOR
in the presence of:

SIGNED AND DELIVERED
by the THIRD GRANTOR
in the presence of:

SIGNED AND DELIVERED
by the FOURTH GRANTOR
in the presence of:

SIGNED AND DELIVERED
by the FIFTH GRANTOR
in the presence of:

SIGNED AND DELIVERED
by the GRANTEE
in the presence of:

Dated this   day of   20

KEVIN COSTNER   1st Part
GRACE KELLY
MICHELINA CHEUNG
EILEEN DILLON
LINDA COSTNER
KEVIN COSTNER   2nd Part

KEVIN COSTNER   3rd Part

ASSIGNMENT AND DEED OF FAMILY ARRANGEMENT

Premises: 2 Dawn View,
            Killiney
            Co Dublin.
            Fraud & Co.
            Solicitors
            Crooked Lane
            Inns Quay
            Dublin 7.

15.3.4 TAX IMPLICATIONS

While the tax implications for a similar type of deed have been reviewed in the CAT Lecture Notes (see Preface), it is opportune to review this deed in a similar fashion.

15.3.4.1 Stamp duty

The deed will attract stamp duty on the consideration for the four undivided one-fifth shares conveyed by the grantor beneficiaries, assuming that €200,000 represents the full value of those shares. Since 10 December 2010, consanguinity relief has been abolished for residential property, and for non-residential property for transfers since 1 January 2015. Stamp duty of 1 per cent of the €200,000 will be payable by the grantee and the stamp duty return must be lodged within forty-four days of the date of execution.

The stamp duty position and rate of charge should always be checked with Revenue, as it is constantly changing. While adjudication is no longer required, the full disclosure must be made to the Revenue Commissioners, as outlined in the CAT Lecture Notes (see Preface).

15.3.4.2 Capital acquisitions tax

In this case, as it is a disposition for value, CAT should not be payable. Given the value of each individual inheritance from parents (Group A), it should not be necessary to file a CAT return. This should be checked by each individual beneficiary depending on prior benefits, but is a matter for each individual beneficiary as in this case all beneficiaries are resident in Ireland based on the addresses provided. It is unlikely that dwellinghouse relief would apply here, as the grantors did not own the property for the requisite period, but it should not be necessary given the value of the house and the relationship of the beneficiaries to the disponers.

15.3.4.3 Capital gains tax

In this case, the deed of family arrangement was made later than two years since the date of death of the first deceased parent. A concession beyond this two-year period would have to be sought by the beneficiaries from the Revenue Commissioners, seeking exemption from their liability to CGT on their one-fifth share of the property on the death of their father. This is, of course, only applicable if the value of the property increased since the date of death of their father. The value of the property on each of the relevant dates should be ascertained. While this extension is usually given, solicitors should never assume that it will apply. The concession is sought on all occasions, not just when the two-year period has passed.

15.3.5 TRANSACTIONS BETWEEN SPOUSES/CIVIL PARTNERS

Assurances between spouses/civil partners where there is no other person involved are exempt from stamp duty (s 96 of the SDCA, 1999, as amended by the Finance (No 3) Act, 2012). Gifts and inheritances between spouses/civil partners are exempt from CAT (ss 71 and 72 of the Capital Acquisitions Tax Consolidation Act 2003, as amended by the Finance (No 3) Act 2012). In all such dispositions, the Family Home Protection Act, 1976 also arises; in particular, the prior written consent to the disposition given by the spouse/civil partner will be required (Family Home Protection Act, 1976, s 3 and the Civil Partnership and Certain Rights and Obligations of Cohabitants Act, 2010, s 28 respectively).

15.3.6 ALL VOLUNTARY DISPOSITIONS

In all voluntary transactions one has to consider the questions of fraud, duress, and undue influence. Therefore, it is advisable to have each party independently advised.

Note: a voluntary disposition may be set aside or voided under various statutory provisions.

1. Section 74 of the Land and Conveyancing Law Reform Act, 2009 repeals and replaces ss 10 and 14 of the Conveyancing Act (Ireland), 1634 and provides that:

    (a) any conveyance of property with intent to defraud creditors is void, but one should take cognisance of subsection (4) of this section;

    (b) any conveyance of property with intent to defraud subsequent purchasers is void.

2. Section 59 of the Bankruptcy Act, 1988 provides that any settlement of property, i.e. a settlement other than one in contemplation of marriage or entrance into a civil partnership, shall:

    (a) if the settlor is adjudicated a bankrupt within three (formerly two) years after the date of the settlement, be void as against the official assignee; and

    (b) if the settlor is adjudicated a bankrupt at any subsequent time within five years after the date of the settlement, be void, as against the official assignee, unless the parties claiming under the settlement prove that the settlor was, at the time of making the settlement, able to pay all his debts without the aid of the property comprised in the settlement, and the interest of the settlor in such property passed on the execution of the settlement.

If there is a voluntary disposition on title, as practitioners are aware from para 15.4.15 of the *Conveyancing* OUP manual, a purchaser will require a statutory declaration of solvency made by the disponer, containing averments that the disposition was not fraudulent and was made bona fide for the benefit of the donee.

Similarly, if there is a voluntary disposition on title within the past five years, a purchaser will normally requisition a statutory declaration made by the disponer, containing averments that at the date of the disposition he was solvent and able to meet all his debts without the aid of the property, the subject of the disposition, with a view to proving that the voluntary disposition could not be voided under s 59 of the 1988 Act. This statutory declaration is known as a declaration of solvency. It is a matter for the purchaser's solicitor whether they carry out bankruptcy searches.

It is recommended that when a voluntary assurance is being drafted, the practitioner should also draft statutory declarations on these lines to be made by the disponer and to be kept with the donee's title in case they are required at any time in the future.

15.4 Disclaimers

Practitioners will be familiar with the concept that no beneficiary can be compelled to accept an inheritance (*Townson v Tickell*, 106 Eng Rep. 575, 576–7 (KB 1819): 'The law certainly is not so absurd as to force a man to take an estate against his will').

There is therefore an opportunity to disclaim, which can result in the desired effect. To qualify as a disclaimer, the refusal of the inheritance must take place before the beneficiary accepts any benefit from it, and so it is a question that should be considered as soon as possible in any administration.

While people speak in terms of disclaiming 'in favour of' a particular person, in such instance it would be an inheritance by the person 'disclaiming' followed by a gift to the particular person he or she wished to benefit.

There would be an assurance with stamp duty and gift tax implications, and in effect it would be a deed of family arrangement.

Although a beneficiary is free to disclaim one or more benefits, he may not disclaim part of a benefit (i.e. a beneficiary may disclaim a specific bequest while taking the benefit of a share in the residue, but he cannot disclaim part only of the specific bequest or part of the residue or his share on intestacy). However, if the will provides that the beneficiary is free to disclaim part only of a single inheritance, then he can do so. However, in the absence of such a direction in the will, a partial disclaimer as set out earlier cannot be affected.

15.4.1 WHAT IS THE EFFECT OF A DISCLAIMER?

Where an inheritance under a will or intestacy is disclaimed, the property will automatically pass to the person next entitled under the will or under the rules of intestacy.

Disclaimers on intestacy and the effect of s 72A of the Succession Act have been discussed at para **8.10**.

In short, this provides that where a person disclaims on intestacy after 5 May 1997, that person shall be regarded as having predeceased the intestate on distribution of his estate. It further provides that if the person disclaiming is not the spouse or lineal ancestor of the intestate, he will also be regarded as having died without issue. However, this only applies to disclaimers after 5 May 1997. Therefore, in regard to all deaths prior to this date, the previous discussion is still relevant. There is no controversy in relation to disclaimers in a testate estate because the disclaimer of a prior interest under a will will accelerate subsequent interests (subject to any contrary intention appearing in the will).

The July 1998 *Law Society Gazette* contains an article in relation to disclaimers and intestacy, which also, in particular, gives a precedent disclaimer drafted by the Conveyancing Committee of the Law Society.

Practitioners are also referred to Anne Stephenson's seminar paper dealing with disclaimers, presented at the September 2015 Law Society Skillnet Essential General Practice Update. As a person disclaiming is usually doing so to benefit another person (quite often their own child), it is important to read s 72A carefully to make sure that it gives and achieves the desired effect.

In particular, note that if on the death of a surviving spouse all the children of the surviving spouse disclaim, the estate will not pass to the grandchildren, but rather to the deceased's brothers and sisters.

15.4.2 WHAT IS THE EFFECT OF DISCLAIMERS ON THE RIGHT TO EXTRACT A GRANT?

Where entitlement to extract a grant of administration depends on entitlement to a share or a specific bequest, it should be pointed out to any client intending to disclaim that, in addition to losing any entitlement to a share of the estate, a person disclaiming will also lose any right they have to extract a grant of representation to the estate of the deceased, in accordance with O 79, r 5 of the Rules of the Superior Courts, 1986, unless a grant has been extracted before the disclaimer is signed.

In the event of a disclaimer being signed after the person disclaiming has applied for a grant, but before the grant has issued, the application should be withdrawn, as the applicant would no longer be one of the persons 'having a beneficial interest' as provided for in O 79, r 5.

Note that if an applicant's right to a grant arises from a disclaimer having been signed by a person who had a prior right, then the original of such a disclaimer must be lodged with the oath for administrator in the Probate Office. The oath for administrator would of course have referred to the disclaimer, see para **8.10.8**.

15.4.3 CAPITAL ACQUISITIONS TAX AND DISCLAIMERS

Practitioners are referred to the CAT Lecture Notes (see Preface). Under s 12 of the Capital Acquisitions Tax Consolidation Act, 2003, if the benefit under a will or intestacy or an entitlement to settled property is disclaimed or a claim under a purported will or alleged intestacy is waived or a right under the Succession Act is renounced, disclaimed, elected against, or lapses, then no liability to tax will arise and no disposition will be regarded as having been made for CAT purposes as a result. However, where a person receives money or money's worth for a disclaimer, renunciation, election, or waiver of a claim, he is to be regarded as receiving a gift or inheritance of the amount paid to him as if he had received the gift or inheritance from the original disponer.

15.5 Finalising Matters

This chapter will now move on to deal with those final outstanding matters that have to be dealt with prior to closing the file. At this stage, all debts of the estate have been ascertained and paid and all relevant assets handed over to the appropriate beneficiaries, having received all appropriate tax clearances, receipts, and indemnities.

Matters remaining to be dealt with include the issue of the solicitor's costs and providing the personal representative and those residuary beneficiaries or those entitled on intestacy who request a copy with an accurate set of accounts showing the distribution of the estate. This chapter also contains an overview of the relevant limitation periods pertaining to the administration of an estate.

15.5.1 SECTION 47 (CHARGES ON PROPERTY)

Section 47 of the Succession Act, 1965 deals with the situation where property of a deceased person is charged with payment of money (mortgage/charge). It provides that the beneficiary inheriting that property is primarily liable for the charge, and that this debt is not paid out of the residue of the estate. Students are referred to para **2.7.6**. The types of charge to which this section applies include legal and equitable mortgages, equitable charges, and liens. Also included, for example, would be a car, the subject of a car loan, i.e. the section does not just refer to immovable assets.

As noted at para **14.4**, sums due under the Nursing Home Support Scheme Act and any other equity release scheme are also covered by s 47.

Charges for tax outstanding on the death of the deceased also fall within s 47. As noted at para **2.7.6**, a general direction to an executor or executors to pay debts or even to pay debts out of the residue will not negate the provisions of s 47.

However, s 47 may be negatived by a specific contrary intention in a will or other document. It is important to check, for example, that there is no provision in the will for the payment of the debt or charge on a particular piece of property to be paid out of the residuary estate or some other part of the estate, for example from a named bank account.

Where no such specific contrary intention appears, the beneficiary who inherits property, either real or personal, subject to a charge, inherits the deceased's equitable interest in the property subject to the charge.

As noted at para **2.7.6**, the overwhelming majority of home loans provide for a mortgage protection policy to be taken out with an insurance company and the proceeds of the policy to be assigned to the financial institution that provided the home loan. Again, practical difficulties may arise if neither the home loan nor the mortgage protection policy were paid up to date.

15.6 Doctrine of Lapse

In dealing with legacies, the doctrine of lapse applies, as provided for in s 91 of the Act and as discussed at paras **2.7.3** and **9.3.1.6**. Generally, if a legatee dies in the lifetime of the testator, the legacy lapses and, as a rule, if otherwise undisposed of, falls into residue.

15.6.1 EXCEPTIONS TO THE DOCTRINE OF LAPSE

However, if the legatee who predeceased is a lawful child or other issue of the testator and leaves lawful issue living when the testator dies, the legacy takes effect as if the legatee had died immediately after the death of the testator, unless a contrary intention is shown (s 98—see paras **2.9.2.1**, **4.6.3.3**, and **9.8**).

Further exceptions arise where the will shows a contrary intention, for example, the gift over or substitutionary clause as provided for at para **2.9.2.3** or where there is a gift to a class, e.g. 'to my grandchildren'.

Exceptions that one comes across less often are where the bequest is in fulfilment of a moral or legal obligation and, in this case, the bequest goes to the estate of the predeceased beneficiary. Usually, in this case, the bequest is stated in the will to be in fulfilment of such a moral or legal obligation.

Charitable bequests have been dealt with at paras **2.7.2.6** and **13.2.7**. As noted there, where the charity no longer exists, the property can be applied *cy près* by application to the Charities Regulation Authority.

15.7 Costs

15.7.1 SECTION 150 NOTICE

After the initial meeting with the personal representative, the practitioner should have advised on the issue of costs payable in writing. This, as practitioners are aware, is a statutory obligation under the terms of s 150 of the Legal Services Regulation Act, 2015 ('the LSRA, 2015') which repealed and replaced s 68 of the Solicitors (Amendment) Act, 1994 on 7 October 2019, as noted at para **6.8.1**.

15.7.2 BASIS OF CHARGING COSTS

The Law Society has no guidelines on fees in relation to any category of legal service, as agreed scale fees are prohibited by the Competition Act, 1991. A number of solicitors use a percentage scheme for charging costs in normal probate and administration cases. Alternatively, solicitors can agree an hourly rate or a fixed 'all in' fee.

A solicitor applying a percentage scheme such as this would normally charge separately for outlay, litigation, or conveyancing work arising on a sale. Similarly, a fee agreed with the personal representative and administrator does not normally include tax advice to beneficiaries.

Such a fee would normally include the following:

(a) all work under the Finance Acts leading to the grant of probate or administration (i.e. the SA.2);

(b) the scale fee in the Rules of the Superior Courts, 1986 for extracting grants etc;

(c) all other work not included in (a) and (b), in the distribution of the assets and completion of the administration.

It is also possible for the solicitor to agree a final figure for costs with the client from the date of instructions. The pitfalls in agreeing a 'final figure' were outlined earlier. It is a matter for solicitors in individual practices to determine the basis on which they charge fees.

Alternatively, if the costs so calculated will not reflect the required amount of time, effort, urgency, or the complexity of the administration, the personal representative should be advised of this as soon as possible and a further fee or new fee agreed. Section 150 provides that the notice should be updated 'whenever required to do so'.

It is recommended that in cases where the gross value of the estate is less than €25,000 and a grant of representation is necessary, practitioners should agree costs directly with the client. Alternatively, in the case of a small estate such as this, it might be worthwhile advising the client of the service available for making personal application to the Probate Office, already referred to at para **6.3.4**. It should be noted that at the time of writing the personal application service is unavailable due to Covid-19 restrictions.

Should one agree to charge a client on a time basis by quoting an hourly charge, one should advise the client in writing of this hourly charge and periodically of the amount that has been charged.

In practice, a percentage fee would appear to be widely used in quantifying costs for an administration. In all instances, however, it must be borne in mind that the personal representative has a right to know what costs are going to be involved, and the solicitor charging for the work of the firm has to be fully accountable to the personal representative for these. Copies of fee notes should also be made available to those indirectly paying the bill, i.e. residuary beneficiaries or those entitled to a share in the estate on intestacy.

15.7.3 BILL OF COSTS

Section 152 provides that a bill of costs be provided as soon as is practicable after the provision of services. In most probate files this would be on the conclusion of the administration. The bill of costs should include:

(i) A summary of the services provided;

(ii) An itemised statement of the amounts charged;

(iii) Your VAT number and amount;

(iv) The time spent where time is a factor in determining the costs;

(v) The amount of money recovered/payable to the client (if any);

(vi) The amount of legal costs recovered (if any);

(vii) The procedures available to your client should they dispute any aspect of your bill.

Where there is a significant difference between that final s 150 notice and the s 152 bill of costs a dispute may arise and both you and your client may have to engage with the procedures for resolving these disputes under the LSRA, 2015.

It is best practice to ensure at each stage of the administration that the client understands the nature of all work done in order to minimise the risk of a bill being disputed. In the event of a dispute, either party may refer the question of costs to the Legal Services Regulatory Authority.

Where there is a significant difference between that final s 150 notice and the s 152 Bill of Costs, this is where a dispute may arise and both you and your client may have to engage with the procedures for resolving these disputes under the LSRA, 2015.

Section 150(4)(c) sets out the basis on which costs can be calculated by reference to paragraph 2 of Schedule 1 of the LSRA, 2015:

'(a) *the complexity and novelty of the issues involved in the legal work;*

(b) *the skill or specialised knowledge relevant to the matter which the legal practitioner has applied to the matter;*

(c) the time and labour that the legal practitioner has reasonably expended on the matter;

(d) the urgency attached to the matter by the client and whether this requires or required the legal practitioner to give priority to that matter over other matters;

(e) the place and circumstances in which the matter was transacted;

(f) the number, importance and complexity of the documents that the legal practitioner was required to draft, prepare or examine;

(g) where money, property, or an interest in property is involved, the amount of the money, or the value of the property or the interest in the property concerned;

(h) whether or not there is an agreement to limit the liability of the legal practitioner pursuant to section 48;

(i) whether or not the legal practitioner necessarily undertook research or investigative work and, if so, the timescale within which such work was required to be completed;

(j) the use and costs of expert witnesses or other expertise engaged by the legal practitioner and whether such costs were necessary and reasonable.'

These are an extended version of the circumstances of the case referred to in the Solicitors' Remuneration General Order 1986.

15.8 Administration Accounts

15.8.1 NECESSITY FOR ACCOUNTS

The most essential element that one should bear in mind throughout the administration of the estate is that the client has taken an oath in which he swears that he will render a true account of his administration whenever required by law so to do.

Further, s 64 of the Succession Act, 1965 imposes a duty as follows:

> 'The personal representatives of a deceased person shall, when lawfully required to do so, exhibit on oath in the court a true and perfect inventory and account of the estate of the deceased, and the court shall have power to require personal representatives to bring in inventories.'

In effect, of course, this means that the solicitor, as legal adviser, will prepare, at the end of the administration, a full account and present it to the legal personal representative. Further, with the consent and the authority of the legal personal representative, it is usual to present this to the residuary legatees or the beneficiaries who are entitled to share in the estate on intestacy. Also, under the terms of the Solicitors Accounts Regulations, 2001, and the Solicitors (Amendment) Act, 1994, in particular s 66(1)(f), a solicitor is under an obligation in relation to client funds to keep:

> 'accounting records containing particulars of and information as to monies received, held, controlled or paid by him.'

The personal representative is entitled to see at the end of the administration a full statement of the conduct of the administration of the estate. Since the introduction of the Solicitors (Amendment) Act, 1994 (s 68)—now found in s 150 of the LSRA, 2015, this statement must be made available to all residuary beneficiaries and/or those entitled on intestacy (see later in this chapter). Care should be taken to see that the accounts reflect accurately what has taken place, and are in the correct format.

A precedent set of accounts is available in the *Law Society Gazette*, March 2014.

As noted at para **6.2.1.1**, practitioners should keep accurate accounts from the commencement of the administration. The more detailed the records taken from the outset, the easier it is at the end of the administration to compile accurate, informative accounts. It is recommended that an Excel spreadsheet or similar package be used to record the detail and the amount of all sums received and paid out as they are received and paid out.

484 DISTRIBUTING THE ESTATE

It is well worthwhile devoting additional time to the preparation of the accounts, as these documents may form the basis of essential information in the future, for individual beneficiaries from a taxation point of view, or from a historical point of view as far as defending the personal representative in the administration of the estate is concerned.

In particular the completed accounts should:

- accurately list the assets and liabilities as at the date of death (the one exception to this is the funeral expenses, which are obviously post-death);
- list all income received during the administration period, broken down into dividend income, rental income, deposit interest (if any), etc;
- list all capital received during the administration period;
- list all outgoings during the administration including, but not limited to, the payment of all pre-death debts outstanding including CAT, VAT, income tax, etc and all testamentary expenses;
- list all payments to beneficiaries during the administration period;
- be comprehensive and include all details and ultimately balance;
- be very clear and easy to understand for those without accounting experience.

When the accounts are prepared, it is essential to have them approved by the executor/ administrator as a true and accurate record of the administration and, once they are so approved, at least one has the recorded endorsement of the client with regard to the entire work done on the case. This may prove invaluable in the event of any dispute arising at a later date with any beneficiary or third party.

Accounts are normally prepared at least in triplicate, a copy to be retained on the file and the original to go to the personal representative. If the Inspector of Taxes is treating the personal representative as liable for income tax up to the date of distribution, then in that case the accounts will be prepared so that a copy is available for the Inspector of Taxes.

A further copy is normally sent to the residuary beneficiaries under a will and/or those entitled to share in the estate of the intestacy when they are signing a final receipt, as obviously they are entitled to know how their benefit was arrived at. It is good practice to include in that final receipt a clause stating that the accounts have been read, understood, and agreed with by the beneficiary.

This also applies to beneficiaries of a discretionary trust. See *Chaine Nickson v Bank of Ireland* [1976] IR 393. This case involved a discretionary trust in which the beneficiaries only held a potential interest. The trustees (Bank of Ireland) maintained that as the beneficiaries were all only 'potential' beneficiaries and did not have a fixed interest in the trust assets, they were not entitled to any information relating to the management of the trust.

Kenny J disagreed and ruled in favour of the potential beneficiaries. He ruled that while their interest in the trust assets was not fixed, they did have a right to the information despite their status on the basis that, otherwise, the result would be that the trustees were not accountable to anyone for the management of the trust.

The accounts are not normally sent to any other category of beneficiaries. The information in the accounts is confidential to the persons affected by it, and as with the will, copies should not be handed out on request.

15.8.2 PURPOSE AND TYPE OF ACCOUNTS

The purpose of administration accounts is to show all assets and liabilities and any alteration in the nature of these between the date of death and the date of distribution. All income and payments need to be identified. As a minimum, three accounts need to be prepared, namely the estate account, the cash account, and the distribution account. It should be noted that the client ledger is *not* the accounts.

Where there is a CAT liability and the solicitor is acting for the beneficiaries in relation to CAT or is a solicitor/agent in relation to this (see CAT Lecture Notes (see Preface)), an additional account will have to be prepared for the Revenue called a capital acquisitions tax residue account. Further, where it is a complex administration, and there is a lot of income during the administration, it is wise to subdivide the cash account into a cash capital account and a cash income account. This is not strictly necessary but can be very useful when calculating the income tax due on the income earned during the administration period (which will be needed whether or not the Revenue has agreed that this income may be taxed in the hands of the beneficiaries). However, if it is a very simple estate, the solicitor should not overcomplicate the accounts unnecessarily.

15.8.2.1 Administration accounts

The administration accounts comprise:

1. estate account;
2. cash account;
3. distribution account.

These accounts should clearly show full details of the entire estate as at the date of death, and also show how each asset and liability was dealt with and, in addition, clearly set out particulars of all receipts and payments made during the course of the entire administration.

The need for proper and accurate accounts of an administration is obvious, and the following is a short explanation of each of the three accounts required.

15.8.3 ESTATE ACCOUNT

This account reflects the situation at the date of death (but including the funeral expenses) and assets are valued as at the date of death. Everything the statement of affairs (probate) and any amendments to same must be included. It is the normal practice for the liabilities to appear on the left of the page and assets on the right, but practitioners can follow any format that they are comfortable with, provided the information is clear. It is good practice to prepare the account as soon as the statement of affairs (probate) is uploaded and accepted. This account will not change once the statement of affairs (probate) is uploaded and accepted unless of course the form is amended. At all times the estate account should match the most recent version of the statement of affairs (probate).

All income accrued on the assets to date of death should also appear.

15.8.4 CASH ACCOUNT

This account reflects, on the receipts side, collection of the cash assets as detailed in the estate account, and also shows details of the sale of any of the assets during the course of the administration. The payment side reflects the discharge of the debts and funeral expenses, details of which are set out in the estate account. It also details other payments, such as testamentary expenses and liabilities incurred through dealing in the assets. Examples here would be solicitors' costs, auctioneers' fees, capital gains tax, and probate fees. Other main items to be included in the cash account are the payment of pecuniary and charitable legacies. These figures should be readily obtained from the solicitor's own records, providing that the solicitor had control over all the cash assets of the estate.

486 DISTRIBUTING THE ESTATE

In some estates, it may be necessary to take up rights on securities, and payment for these should be detailed on the payments side.

Inheritance tax liabilities, which are paid during the course of the administration, should be debited to the individual beneficiaries' residuary accounts.

15.8.4.1 Cash income account

The date-of-death value of the estate is recorded in the statement of affairs (probate). This value includes any interest accrued to date of death. It does not include any interest earned after the date of death. If one is maintaining both a cash capital account and a cash income account, it is vital that both capital and income are accounted for separately.

Any interest which arises after the date of death must be recorded in the cash income account as income of the estate. It is important to keep this separate from the capital of the estate, as it may have to be distributed separately from the capital in the estate; for example, under a will trust, the income and capital may be bequeathed to two separate beneficiaries. It is also important to realise that liabilities relating to income accruing to the estate should be recorded in the cash income account and deducted therefrom. These liabilities would then not affect the cash capital and vice versa. In using the two separate accounts, one can be certain that all outgoings and liabilities will be paid out of the correct funds.

Keeping separate cash capital and cash income accounts also allows the solicitor to apportion the outgoings between capital and income. The rule in *Allhusen v Whittle* (1867) LR 4 Eq 295 apportions outgoings, and while it is generally excluded from a will, if it does apply, the distinction between the capital and income accounts should be clear.

When calculating the income tax due on the income earned during the administration period, it can be far less complicated if a separate income account has been used. This account can then be used when the executor or beneficiaries are calculating the income tax due from the date of death.

15.8.5 DISTRIBUTION ACCOUNT

This account is the one which shows details of all the distributions, whether such distributions were made in cash or *in specie*, i.e. it gives full details of all assets transferred to the beneficiaries and where cash payments were made to them by way of partial distribution. It is also the account which interests the residuary beneficiaries most!

The account gives full details of all assets transferred to the beneficiaries and cash payments made to them.

The left-hand side shows the net balance from the cash account which is available for distribution to the residuary beneficiaries.

The right-hand side details the distribution to the individual residuary beneficiaries.

15.8.6 PRECEDENT SET OF ADMINISTRATION ACCOUNTS

Relevant facts

Annette Stephens died testate a single woman who never married or entered into civil partnership leaving her surviving three nieces and two nephews; namely Danielle Stephens, Mary Stephens, Amy Stephens, Patrick Stephens, Jamie Stephens.

They are all beneficiaries under her will (pecuniary legacies). Danielle, Mary, and Patrick were left €5,000 each while Amy and Jamie were left €10,000 each. In addition there was a €15,000 pecuniary legacy to Mary Jackson, her housekeeper, and €500 to the Parish Priest for masses.

The residue of the estate was left to Patrick, Mary, and Amy in equal shares. At the date of her death Annette owned a house and a car, and had several bank accounts and shareholdings.

The house was sold as per a direction in her will. The shares and contents were transferred to the three residuary beneficiaries *in specie*.

15.8.6.1 Estate account: Annette Stephens deceased

Assets:	Liabilities	Assets
55 Cary Avenue		€ 300,000.00
Household Contents		€ 1,000.00
2008 Volvo		€ 1,500.00
AIB		€ 20,717.46
An Post Savings Certs		€ 129,792.56
EBS		€ 19,244.13
Ulster Bank Investment Bond		€ 13,919.00
Irish Life Investment Bond		€ 23,577.56
1,800 CRH Shares		€ 109,200.00
Shares 900 Marks and Spencer £15,858.90		€ 25,690.75
Prize Bonds		€ 241.30
Liabilities:		
Funeral Expenses	€ 4,049.00	
VHI	€ 605.00	
Total Irish Liabilities/Assets	€ 4,654.00	€ 644,882.76
To Balance (Irish net estate)	€ 640,228.76	
TOTAL (Irish gross estate)	€ 644,882.76	€ 644,882.76
Foreign Assets (rate of conversion)	NIL	
Foreign Liabilities (rate of conversion)	NIL	
Total Foreign Liabilities/Assets	NIL	NIL
To Balance (net worldwide estate)	€ 640,228.76	€640,228.76
TOTAL (gross worldwide estate)	€ 644,882.76	€644,882.76
Notes re Estate Account:		
1 Joint Assets Passing by Survivorship	NIL	
2 Nominations	NIL	

This precedent estate account can be very easily adapted to deal with extensive assets and liabilities. The principle remains the same and the rule is to keep it simple and easy to read.

The values reflected in the estate account, as can be seen from the sample above, are the date of death values only. Only the liabilities outstanding as of the date of death with one exception, the funeral expenses, should be listed here. Any other liabilities, costs, or expenses arising post-death should be included in the cash account.

488 DISTRIBUTING THE ESTATE

The figures for the gross/net Irish estate should be the same as those listed in the Statement of Affairs (Probate) Form SA.2. It is the gross Irish estate as listed there which is inserted in the oath of executor.

If there is a delay exceeding two years from the date of death to the lodging of the probate papers then the current value of the real estate will have to be obtained and that is the figure which will be inserted in the oath for real estate. Remember such a value will have to be vouched by a letter stating the market value which should be submitted with the probate papers.

In addition, for completeness, the estate account should also show any jointly held assets, albeit that same are not part of the estate, any assets passing by survivorship, including any liabilities attaching to same (e.g. charges or mortgages attaching to joint properties and/or guarantees given by the deceased which are a liability of the estate); admittedly in the example above there are no such jointly held assets. Indeed, once again these will have been included in the statement of affairs (probate).

15.8.6.2 Cash account: Annette Stephens deceased

Payments		Receipts	
Computershare Services	€ 42.40	Net Proceeds of Sale of House	€304,110.76
Commissioners Fees	€ 5.00	Sale of car	€ 1,500.00
Smith and Williamson Valuation Fees on Shares	€ 121.00	AIB	€ 20,717.46
Probate Office Fees	€ 370.00	Interest on AIB	€ 20.00
Commissioners Fees	€ 15.00	An Post Savings Certs	€129,792.56
Solicitors Fees including outlay and VAT		Interest on an Post	€ 20.00
Administration	€ 25,817.33	**EBS**	€ 19,244.13
Tax returns,	€ 1,694.00	Interest on EBS	€ 20.00
Sale of House	€ 3,630.00	Prize Bonds	€ 241.30
ESB	€ 31.08	Ulster Bank Bond	€ 13,919.00
Eircom	€ 129.55	Irish Life Bond	€ 23,577.56
Sherry Fitzgerald Fees outlay and VAT re Sale of property	€ 7,259.54	**Dividends** Dividends on Marks & Spencer shares 31/07/12	€ 290.32
Household Charge	€ 100.00	Dividends on CRH shares 31/07/12	€ 1,500.00
Commissioners Fees	€ 9.00	Interest on Insurance policies	
Funeral Expenses	€ 4,049.00	Interest on Irish Life Bond	€ 139.73
VHI	€ 605.00	Interest on First Active account	€ 100.00
By payment of legacies			
Danielle Stephens	€ 5,000.00		
Mary Stephens	€ 5,000.00		
Patrick Stephens	€ 5,000.00		
Amy Stephens	€ 10,000.00		

Payments		Receipts	
Jamie Stephens	€ 10,000.00		
Mary Jackson	€ 15,000.00		
Parish Priest	€ 500.00		
Total Payments	€ 94,377.90	**Total receipts**	€609,570.72
To Balance (to distribution account)	€515,192.82		
TOTAL	€609,570.72	**TOTAL**	€609,570.72

Notes to Cash Account:

1.1.
1. The shares and contents passed *in specie* (see distribution account).
2. No income tax was paid on income arising during the administration as the Collector General agreed to treat same in the income of the beneficiaries.
3. Gain on sale of 55 Cary Avenue €15,000.00.

In this case, the cash account sets out, at its simplest, the receipts and payments during the administration of the estate. The net balance is brought forward to the distribution account.

Listed with, but not part of, the cash account should be any capital gains made on the sale of assets. The advantage of doing this is that the figure on which any capital gains tax might be payable can be easily identified. If you have made a loss on the sale of any asset from the date of death value, you would include the loss not least as same may be utilised to offset a gain.

Dividends arising post-death, irrespective of when same are paid, should be illustrated clearly giving the date of payment and the foreign value where applicable. The interest shown should be the net interest earned on any bank account.

Where the estate is more complex and there are numerous assets and extensive income or there is a strict settlement as referred to in the cash income account at para **15.8.4.1**, a cash capital and a cash income account is needed. Indeed, in such a case, remember also to relate the correct liabilities to the correct income.

15.8.6.3 Distribution account: Annette Stephens deceased

Balance from Cash Account		**Residuary Payments**	
Balance c/f from cash account	€515,192.82	**Patrick Stephens**	€171,730.94
		Mary Stephens	€171,730.94
		Amy Stephens	€171,730.94
Total	**€515,192.82**		**€515,192.82**

Notes to distribution account:

1. The contents passed in specie to the residuary beneficiaries.
2. Shares passed in specie to residuary beneficiaries, each receiving 300 Marks and Spencer's shares and 600 CRH shares. Value at valuation date while not relevant for this account would be taken into account when ascertaining the taxable value of their inheritance for CAT purposes.

This is a very simple distribution account showing the distribution of the balance of the funds available from the cash account to the residuary beneficiaries.

It also shows the transfer, *in specie*, of the two shareholdings and contents.

In some cases, if acting for the beneficiaries as well, an individual CAT account could be prepared, showing the amount due to the beneficiary, the payment of the tax, and the net bequest after tax to the beneficiary. The amount of any CAT paid on their behalf is a private matter between them and the Revenue Commissioners and would not be shown on the distribution account, which is, of course, available to the other residuary beneficiaries. Those details would be sent privately to the individual residuary legatees in the letter sent to them, an example of which is at para **14.6.1**.

In this case, as the three residuary beneficiaries are nephews and nieces and thus Group B beneficiaries, there will be a significant CAT liability, the extent of which would depend on whether there were prior benefits or not. While arguably they are not our clients and assuming they are all Irish resident, their tax liabilities are not a concern of the estate, it would be good practice to advise them that they have a liability to CAT and that they need to obtain appropriate tax and legal advice and should file and pay before the appropriate date.

Practitioners would be aware from the earliest stages of the prior benefits received by beneficiaries. See paras **6.8.4.2**, which deals with the precedent letter to a beneficiary, and **6.9.7**, which deals with the information required to complete the form SA 2 in relation to a beneficiary.

To repeat, details of any CAT paid on their behalf and any prior benefits received by them are a private matter between them and the Revenue Commissioners and would not be shown on the distribution account, which is, of course, available to the other residuary legatees.

Also, in this case it should be noted that there was a 'capital gain' on the sale of the house of €15,000 but costs of at least €14,500 were incurred so that any potential liability to CGT would be minimal. CGT is not taught on the Probate and Tax Module. It should be noted that not all costs are necessarily deductible and professional advice should be sought if required.

15.9 Limitation Periods

15.9.1 INTRODUCTION

The Statutes of Limitations, 1957–91 (as amended) deal with various limitation periods, including the right of a beneficiary to claim against the personal representatives, for actions in existence against the deceased prior to death and for actions against any person holding adversely against the estate or beneficiaries.

15.9.2 CLAIMS BY BENEFICIARIES AGAINST THE ESTATE

This area is covered by s 45(1) of the Statute of Limitations, 1957, as amended by s 126 of the Succession Act, 1965, which reads:

> *'Subject to Section 71, no action in respect of any claim to the estate of a deceased person or to any share or interest in such estate whether under a will or on intestacy or under Section 111 of the Succession Act, 1965 shall be brought after the expiration of six years from the date when the right to receive the share or interest accrued.'*

Originally, the Statute of Limitations provided that such claims must be brought within a period of twelve years, but s 126 of the Succession Act reduced the period to six years from the date when the right to receive the share or interest accrued.

Section 126(2) of the Act further provides:

> 'No action to recover arrears of interest in respect of any legacy or damages in respect of such arrears shall be brought after the expiration of three years from the date on which the interest became due.'

It should be noted that this period also applies to surviving spouses and civil partners where no election takes place.

15.9.3 ACTIONS BY THE ESTATE TO RECOVER LAND BELONGING TO THE DECEASED

In the case of *Drohan v Drohan* [1984] IR 311, McMahon J (*obiter dicta*) pointed out that s 45(1) in neither its original nor its amended form had any application to an action by a personal representative to recover assets of the deceased from a person (whether a beneficiary or a stranger) holding adversely to the estate, but applied only to actions against the personal representatives by those entitled to shares in the estate.

The period of limitation in respect of an action by personal representatives to recover land belonging to the deceased was that in s 13(2) of the Statute of Limitations, 1957, i.e. twelve years from the date of accrual of the action. Professor Brady points out in *Succession Law in Ireland*, 2nd edn (1995) that McMahon J's observations in *Drohan v Drohan* on s 45(1) rank as *obiter dicta* but are perfectly consistent with the language of s 45(1), which refers to claims against the estate of a deceased person whether under a will or on an intestacy.

The logical implication would be that if a personal representative could seek to obtain land for the estate of a deceased person, the question would arise as to who he would hold such lands for, i.e. would it be for individuals who would be statute-barred under s 126?

This question arose in the case of *Gleeson v Feehan and Purcell* (No 1) [1991] ILRM 783.

15.9.3.1 *Gleeson v Feehan and Purcell*

The facts in this case were that the plaintiff was the personal representative of James Dwyer, who was the registered owner of registered land.

James Dwyer died intestate in 1937, leaving a widow and six children, including Edmund Dwyer and Josephine Dwyer (the non-marital mother of one Jimmy Dwyer). At that stage, under the rules of intestacy which then applied, the widow would have been entitled to one-third of the registered land (which devolved as personalty) and the six children entitled to the other two-thirds.

Only Edmund and Jimmy remained on the land when the widow and the other children of James Dwyer left the land or died shortly afterwards. Edmund subsequently died in October 1971, intestate, a bachelor without parent, and after his death Jimmy remained on in possession of the land, enjoying the rents and profits. In 1978 Jimmy Dwyer sold certain of the lands to the first-named defendant and certain of the lands to the second-named defendant.

The plaintiff, who was acting under a power of attorney for the next of kin of Edmund Dwyer, who were living in the United States, obtained a grant of administration intestate to the estate of James Dwyer and to the estate of Edmund Dwyer and issued proceedings against the defendants. The defendants responded that the plaintiff was statute-barred and had been since six years from Edmund Dwyer's death, which date being the crucial one, since James Dwyer had died in 1937 and his title to the lands would have been affected by s 24 of the Statute of Limitations, which extinguishes title to land after twelve years.

Judge Sheridan in the Circuit Court found for the defendants, holding that the rights of Edmund Dwyer's next of kin to share in his estate accrued on his death and were barred after six years from that date. Judge Sheridan concluded that it would appear to defeat the purpose of s 45 as amended if personal representatives of Edmund Dwyer could acquire Edmund Dwyer's assets and vest them in his next of kin outside the six-year limitation period. The defendant's plea that the plaintiff's claim was statute-barred was tried as a preliminary issue. In a judgment delivered on 20 June 1991 ([1993] 2 IR 113; [1991] ILRM 783) it was held by the Supreme Court that the plaintiff's claim was not statute-barred.

The case was remitted to the Circuit Court, and the plaintiff was granted a decree for possession. The defendant then appealed to the High Court (*Gleeson v Feehan* (No 2) [1997] 1 ILRM 522).

At the hearing of the appeal before Morris J, it was accepted that the only issue to be determined was whether Jimmy Dwyer was entitled to be registered as owner of the lands in folios 11057, 3371, and 28973, to the exclusion of Edmund Dwyer's next of kin.

Morris J posed the following questions for the Supreme Court:

1.
   (a) Where, prior to the Succession Act, 1965, several next-of-kin in actual occupation of the lands of a deceased person acquired title to those lands by adverse possession against the personal representative, was the title so acquired the title to which they would have been beneficially entitled on due administration? This was answered in the negative.

   (b) Where such next of kin acquired either by adverse possession against other next of kin, not in occupation, was such title acquired as joint tenants? It was deemed that such title was acquired as joint tenants.

2. Where such next of kin in actual occupation shared such occupation with persons other than the next of kin, was the possession of such other persons adverse possession against:

   (a) the personal representative; or

   (b) the next of kin not in occupation? It was found that such possession was adverse possession against the personal representative, but not against the next of kin not in occupation.

3. If the answer to 1(a) or (b) is 'yes', was such title acquired jointly with the next of kin in occupation as (a) joint tenants, or (b) tenants in common? It was held that such title was acquired jointly with the next of kin in occupation as joint tenants.

Keane J stated as follows:

1. The next of kin have a right in the nature of a chose in action to payment to them of the balance of the estate after the debts have been discharged. This right can be enforced against the personal representative. Regardless of the legal nature of the estate vested in an executor or administrator, he does not hold the property for his own benefit. To that extent he is properly regarded as a trustee who must perform the duties of his office in the interest of those who are ultimately entitled to the deceased's property either as beneficiaries or creditors, and not in his own interest.

2. Until such time as the extent of the residuary estate of a deceased person has been ascertained and the executor is in a position to either vest the proceeds of sale of the property comprised in the residue, or in the residuary legatees, or where appropriate to vest individual items of property *in specie* in an individual residuary legatee, it would be contrary to elementary legal principles to treat the persons entitled to the residuary estate of a deceased person as being the owners in equity of specific items forming part of that residue. The same considerations apply to the rights of the next of kin in relation to the estate of a person who dies intestate. In both situations it is unnecessary and inappropriate to analyse the ownership of the deceased's estate in terms of who is entitled to the legal estate and who is entitled to the equitable estate, as the court will control the personal representative's exercise of his rights in respect of the assets comprised in the estate.

Keane J further stated that even if the next of kin of an intestate owner of land had an equitable interest in the land from the time of the owner's death, it would not follow that they would also have a right to possession which they could enforce against the personal representative.

Furthermore, such a right to possession, even if it existed, could not depend on the purely fortuitous circumstance that a person who was one of the next of kin happened to be in possession of the land at the time of the intestate's death. If the administrator were to institute ejectment proceedings against any other person in possession, it would be no defence for that person to say that he was entitled to remain in possession of the land until such time as the administrator put up the property for sale with a view to paying the debts of the deceased. Keane J stated that there was no reason in principle why different considerations should apply to one of the next of kin who happened to be in possession of the land at the time of the intestate's death.

As from the death of James and Mary Dwyer, the possession of the lands by Edmund Dwyer and Jimmy Dwyer was at all times adverse to the title of the true owner, the President of the High Court, in whom the entire interest in the lands was vested pending the raising of representation.

By virtue of their adverse possession during the relevant period, Edmund Dwyer and Jimmy Dwyer acquired title to the lands as joint tenants. Accordingly, on the death of Edmund Dwyer, Jimmy Dwyer became the sole owner of the lands by virtue of survivorship.

As s 24 of the Statute of Limitations, 1957 extinguished the title of the President of the High Court to the lands and his right to bring an action to recover the lands, no estate or interest could thereafter be vested by anyone in the next of kin, regardless of whether the next of kin were in or out of possession. The grant of letters of administration to the estate of James Dwyer could not revive the title to the land, which had been extinguished by s 24. It was unnecessary to decide in this instance whether a person entitled to a specific bequest or devise could be regarded as the owner in equity of the item of property in question prior to the administration of the testator's estate. See *Gleeson v Feehan*.

15.9.3.2 In the case of disability

In the event of a person having a claim against the estate who is under a disability, s 127 amends s 49 of the Statute of Limitations in respect of a claim by persons to whom a right of action accrued who are under a disability, against the estate of a deceased person to a period of three years from the date when the person ceased to be under a disability or died. Section 49, as amended by this section, prevents time from running where the person entitled is under a disability, provided that the disability was present when the right of action accrued, and the disability in some form is continuous.

Time does not begin to run until disability ends or the person labouring under it dies.

However, time does begin to run on the death of the person under a disability, even if his successor is also under a disability. Note s 49(2)(d) of the Statute of Limitations, which provides for an absolute limitation period of thirty years where the disability does not cease, for example in the case of a person suffering from a mental handicap. Note too that this section does not apply to claims by a child for proper provision under s 117 (see the case of *MPD v MD* [1981] ILRM 179 per Carroll J).

15.9.3.3 Section 125/next of kin

Section 125 amended the previous common law position relating to the acquisition of title to land by adverse possession by two or more of the next of kin or others or those entitled to the land under the will or intestacy of the owner. Prior to the Succession Act, the position that prevailed in relation to those who remained in possession of a deceased's estate without taking out a grant was that they acquired a joint tenancy with regard to the shares of others who remained out, but in respect of their own distributive share they held as tenants-in-common. Section 125(1) amended the position by providing:

> 'Where each of two or more persons is entitled to any share in land comprised in the estate of a deceased person, whether such shares are equal or unequal, and any or all of them enter into possession of the land, then, notwithstanding any rule of law to the contrary, those who enter shall (as between themselves and as between themselves and those (if any) who do not enter) be deemed, for

the purposes of the Statute of Limitations, 1957 to have entered and to acquire title by possession as joint tenants (and not as tenants-in-common) as regards their own respective shares and also as regards the respective shares of those (if any) who do not enter.'

The net effect of subsection (1) is that where two or more persons are entitled jointly or in common to a share in the land of a deceased person and they enter upon the land, they do so for the purpose of the Statute of Limitations as joint tenants. Note also subsection (2), which provides:

'Subsection (1) shall apply whether or not any such person entered into possession as personal representative of the deceased, or having entered, was subsequently granted representation to the estate of the deceased.'

Where a grant of representation has been granted and the title has been vested in those entitled, the rule in s 125 will not apply, since the land has ceased to be comprised in the estate of a deceased person.

It follows that where land has been conveyed to a number of persons as tenants-in-common but only some of them take possession for the limitation period, the old rule applies, since those in possession will acquire the rights of the absent co-owners as joint tenants but they will still retain their own shares as tenants-in-common.

It is important, from a conveyancing point of view, to be fully aware of the pre-Succession Act and post-Succession Act rules.

15.10 Time Limits and Periods of Notice

There are several time limits and periods of notice which apply in the administration of an estate and which it is essential to observe. Some refer to taxation and some to distribution. The list hereunder is not exhaustive.

1. The 'executor's year'—twelve months from the date of death of the deceased.

2. Right of election for a surviving spouse/civil partner—one year from the grant or six months from the notice (s 115 of the Succession Act), whichever one is the latter. See also item 6 in this list.

3. Right of appropriation of surviving spouse/civil partner of the 'family home'—six months from receipt of notification (or one year on from first taking out of representation of the deceased's estate), whichever is the latter (s 56(5)(a) of the Succession Act).

4. Right of child to make s 117 or s 67A(5) application—six months from date of first full grant of representation. See judgment of Laffoy J in *Re F Deceased: S1 v PR1 and PR2* [2013] IEHC 407.

5. Right of a beneficiary to claim assets from the estate of a deceased—six years from the grant (s 126 of the Succession Act).

6. Surviving spouse's/civil partner's legal right share—s 111—six months from receipt of notice or one year from extraction of grant, whichever is the latter. Six years where no benefit given to the spouse/civil partner in the will (s 126).

7. Qualified cohabitant—post-1 January 2010, six months from the date of first taking out grant of representation to apply for provision (s 194 of the Civil Partnership and Certain Rights of Cohabitants Act, 2010).

8. CAT returns must be lodged in accordance with the Capital Acquisitions Tax Consolidation Act, 2003, as amended. Where the valuation date arises *before* 31 August in any tax year, the beneficiary must file and pay by 31 October of that year. Where the valuation date arises *on or after* 31 August in any tax year, the beneficiary must file and pay by 31 October of the following tax year—see notes on valuation dates.

When both paying and filing online using the Revenue ROS system, a further two-week period may be allowed at the discretion of Revenue on an annual basis. Check the Revenue website to ensure you have the correct filing and pay deadline each year.

9. Appeals to Valuation Office against increase in value—twenty-eight days from date of issue of notification of value.

10. Appeals against assessment for income tax—three months from date of assessment.

11. Civil Liability Act, 1961, s 9—actions filed against the estate of the deceased person must be brought within two years or a relevant period applicable under Statute of Limitations, whichever is shorter.

Following the judgments in *Prendergast v McLaughlin* [2009] IEHC 250 and more recently *Cavey v Cavey* (originally [2012] IEHC 537, and now the Supreme Court judgment *Cavey v Cavey* [2014] IESC 16), *all* actions against the estate, including equitable actions such as proprietory estoppel, must be taken within two years of death.

12. Probate tax—nine months from the date of death. Now only applicable where the deceased died between 18 June 1993 and 5 December 2000 leaving a surviving spouse as life tenant who has subsequently died. In that case, it would be nine months from the date of the spouse's death.

13. Stamp duty—forty-four days from the date of execution of the deed.

14. Notice to creditors—s 49—one month after service of the last notice.

15. Court order for personal representatives to execute assent—s 52(4)—twelve months after the death of the deceased.

16. Notice of intention to appropriate assets—s 55—six weeks after service of notice.

17. Unworthiness to succeed, continuous desertion from deceased for two years prior to his death—s 120 of the Succession Act.

18. Where there are dispositions for the purpose of disinheriting spouse/civil partner and/or children (where disposition has been made within three years of the death of the disponer)—one year from the extraction of the grant (s 121).

19. Limitation of actions by beneficiaries—must sue within six years of the date when the right of action accrued (s 126).

    (a) Legacies generally. In the case of an immediate legacy where there are sufficient assets in the estate to meet it—time begins to run from the death of the testator.

    (b) Contingent legacies. Where the legacy is contingent and vested for future date, time will ordinarily run from the date when the contingency is satisfied.

    (c) Legacies and reversionary interests of the testator. In respect of reversionary interests belonging to the testator, time does not run until the interest comes into the possession of the personal representative.

    (d) Succession rights on intestacy and rights of residuary legatees and devisees. In respect of intestacy rights and rights under residuary clauses in wills, time runs from the date that the assets claimed are retainable by the personal representative.

    (e) Beneficiary's rights—s 14(2) of the Statute of Limitations, 1957 states that rights of action in relation to land accrue at the date of death of a deceased.

Note: s 62(1) of the Succession Act prevents beneficiaries from suing to claim their shares for one year after the death of the deceased, but the period of limitation may be running against them from the date of death of the testator.

20. (a) Limitation of actions—personal representatives may sue up to twelve years from the date of accrual of the action to recover assets of the deceased from a person, whether a beneficiary or a stranger holding adversely to the estate. Note *Drohan v Drohan* [1984] IR 311. As a result of this decision, personal representatives are entitled to recover assets for the benefit of those entitled under a will or intestacy, even though under s 126 such beneficiaries are themselves statute-barred from suing for such property.

    (b) Limitation of actions—personal representatives may plead the Statute of Limitations against beneficiaries (s 123). Note also s 10 of the Succession Act, 1965, which states that the personal representatives hold the estate as trustees for the persons entitled by law thereto. Because of s 123, a personal representative, despite having sworn faithfully to administer the estate, is not precluded from claiming adverse possession of property against the beneficiaries of the estate, once he has enjoyed twelve years' unchallenged possession thereof.

    (c) Limitation of actions—spouse of deceased, bailiff of shares of infant children may plead the Statute of Limitations against children who have left the family home or reached maturity—s 124.

    (d) Limitation of actions—next of kin in possession of lands not only hold as joint tenants their own shares but also hold as joint tenants any shares acquired through adverse possession (s 125).

    (e) Limitation of actions—acknowledgement or part-payment by a personal representative, or by a person accountable for property to a personal representative, causes the limitation period to run from the date of acknowledgement or part-payment. See ss 59(5) and 68(5) of the Statute of Limitations, 1957.

    (f) Limitation of actions—Statute of Limitations does not run against beneficiaries suffering under a disability (s 127 of the Succession Act). This does not apply to ss 117 and 67A of the Succession Act.

21. Caveat—expires after six months except where renewed or waived. See **Chapter 11**.

22. Warning to caveat—caveator has fourteen days to file an appearance. See **Chapter 11**.

23. Citation—must be personally served on the relevant persons within fourteen days of being filed in the Probate Office (s 17 of the Succession Act). See **Chapter 11**.

BIBLIOGRAPHY

Textbooks and articles

Assessment of Mental Capacity: Guidance for Doctors and Lawyers, 3rd edn (British Medical Association and Law Society of England and Wales, 2010)

Bielanska, C General Editor, *Elderly Client Handbook*, 6th edn (Law Society of England and Wales, 2019)

—— *Elderly Clients: A Precedent Manual*, 5th edn (Jordans, 2016)

Biehler, H (formerly Delany), *Equity and the Law of Trusts in Ireland*, 7th edn (Round Hall 2020)

Bohan, B, *Capital Acquisitions Tax*, 4th edn (Bloomsbury Professional, 2013)

Bracken, T and Campbell, M, *The Probate Handbook* (Clarus Press, 2011)

—— and —— The Probate Handbook Companion (Clarus Press, 2012)

Brady, JC, *Succession Law in Ireland*, 2nd edn (Butterworths, 1995)

Casey, P, Brady, P, Craven, K, and Dillon, A, *Psychiatry and the Law*, 2nd edn (Blackhall Publishing, 2010)

Corrigan, A and Williams, A, *Trusts and Succession Law: A Guide for Tax Practitioners*, 4th edn (Irish Tax Institute, 2007)

Costello, J, *Law and Finance in Retirement*, 2nd edn (Blackhall Publishing, 2002)

Dowling, K, *Equity & Trusts (Nutshell)* (Thomson Round Hall 2007)

Dowling, K and Grimes, R, *Irish Probate Practitioners Handbook* (Round Hall, 2013)

—— and —— *Succession Law Nutshell* (Round Hall, 2013)

Dowling, K and Martin, S *Practical Probate* (Thomson Reuters 2020)

Hapgood, M, QC, *Paget's Law of Banking*, 14th edn (LexisNexis Butterworths, 2014)

Hayton, D, Matthews, P, and Mitchell, C, *Underhill and Hayton: Law of Trusts and Trustees*, 18th edn (LexisNexis, 2010)

Holohon, W and Sanfey, M, *Bankruptcy Law and Practice in Ireland*, 2nd edn (Round Hall, 2010)

Keane, R, *Equity and the Law of Trusts in the Republic of Ireland*, 2nd edn (Bloomsbury Professional, 2011)

Keating, A, *Probate Law and Practice Case Book* (Round Hall Sweet & Maxwell, 1999)

—— *Probate Causes and Related Matters* (Round Hall Sweet & Maxwell, 2000)

—— *The Construction of Wills*, 2nd edn (Clarus Press, 2017)

—— *The Law of Wills*, 2nd edn (Clarus Press, 2018)

—— 'A Proprietary Estoppel or in the Alternative a "New Model" Constructive Trust' (2003) 8:1 *Conveyancing and Property Law Journal* 9

—— *The Law and Practice of Personal Representatives* Second Edition (Round Hall, 2017)

—— *Equitable Succession Rights* (Thomson Round Hall, 2005)

—— *Keating on Probate*, 5th edn including 1st supplement (Round Hall Sweet & Maxwell, 2015)

—— Probate Motions and Actions Relating to Wills and Intestacies (Round Hall, 2017)

—— *Succession Law in Ireland* (Clarus Press, 2015)

—— *Succession Law in Ireland*: Principles, Cases and Commentary (Clarus Press, 2015)

—— *Will Trusts and Equitable Property Rights* (Clarus Press, 2019)

—— *Probate Precedents Service* (Round Hall, 2009, looseleaf, regularly updated)

Keogan, A and Scully, E, *Law of Capital Acquisitions Tax, Stamp Duty and Local Property Tax, Finance Act 2020* (Irish Tax Institute, 2020)

King, L (general editor), *Probate Practitioner's Handbook*, 6th edn (Law Society of England and Wales, 2009)

Laffoy, M, *Irish Conveyancing Precedents* (Tottel Publishing, online, regularly updated)

Law Society of Ireland, *A Guide to Professional Conduct of Solicitors in Ireland*, 3rd edn (October 2013)

Mee, J, 'Succession and the Civil Partnership Bill 2009' (2009) 14:4 *Conveyancing and Property Law Journal* 86

Mongey, E, *Probate Practice in a Nutshell*, 3rd edn (Fort Publications, 2006)

National Council on Ageing and Older People, *The Law and Older People: A Handbook for Service Providers* (Report No 51, 1998)

O' Sullivan, C, 'Night of the Living Debt', *Law Society Gazette*, January/February 2010

Pettit, PH, *Equity and the Law of Trusts*, 11th edn (Oxford University Press, 2009)

Shannon, G, *Child and Family Law*, 3rd edn (Round Hall, 2020)

Shee, P, 'At Debt's Door', *Law Society Gazette*, October 2010

Spierin, BE, *The Succession Act 1965 and Related Legislation: A Commentary*, 5th edn (Bloomsbury Professional, 2017)

—— *Wills—Irish Precedents and Drafting*, 2nd edn (Bloomsbury Professional, 2012)

Whelan, D, *Mental Health Law and Practice* (Round Hall, 2010)

Whelan, J and Williams, A, *The Taxation of Gifts and Inheritances: Finance Act 2019* (Irish Tax Institute, 2019)

Wylie, JCW, *The Land and Conveyancing Law Reform Act 2009: Annotations and Commentary* (Bloomsbury Professional, 2009)

—— *Irish Land Law*, 5th edn (Bloomsbury Professional, 2013)

Wylie, J, Keogan, A, and Mee, J, *The Law and Taxation of Trusts* (Tottel Publishing, 2007)

Law Reform Commission Reports

Consultation Paper on Law and the Elderly (June 2003, LRC CP 23-2003)

Report: Vulnerable Adults and the Law (December 2006, LRC 83-2006)

Report on Trust Law: General Proposals (December 2008, LRC 92-2008)

Report on Prevention of Benefit from Homicide (July 2015, LRC 114-2015)

Report on Section 117 of the Succession Act, 1965 (May 2017; LRC 118-2017)

Selected Continuing Professional Development/ Continuing Legal Education lectures

- 'Law Society Skillnet—Probate Litigation', 13 May 2010
- 'The Civil Partnership and Certain Rights and Obligations of Cohabitants Act, 2010', Booklet, 22 September 2010
- 'New Probate and Trust Essentials—Legislation and Practice Update 2010', 30 September 2010
- 'Enduring Powers of Attorney', 1 May 2011
- 'How the Civil Partnership Act, 2010 Affects Probate Practitioners', 2011
- 'Nursing Home Support Scheme Act', 2011
- Law Society Skillnet in Association with the Society of Trust and Estate Practitioners 'Legislation and Practice Update', September 2011
- Law Society Professional Training in partnership with the Solicitors for the Elderly Ireland, 'Enduring Powers of Attorney', November 2011
- Law Society Skillnet in Collaboration with Solicitors for the Elderly, 'Managing your Third Age Client—Updates, Guidelines and Precedents', October 2012
- Solicitors for the Elderly in Collaboration with Law Society Professional Training, 'The Assisted Decision Making (Capacity) Bill 2013, Learning from the UK experience and Best Practice Skills', September 2013
- Wills, Probate, Estates and Tax Masterclass, June 2018
- Probate Masterclass 2019
- Wills Drafting Masterclass 2019
- EPA Masterclass 2020

Stephenson Lecture Series

- 'World Wide Wills Seminar', 28 May 2004
- 'Tax Made Simple in the Administration of Estates and Trusts', 5 November 2004
- 'Good Wills, Bad Wills and Other Family Dramas', 8 April 2005
- 'Something Old, Something New, Something Borrowed, Something Blue', 7 October 2005
- 'Post Grant Administration of Estates and Trusts', 2 June 2006
- '3rd Age Exit Strategies', 10 November 2006

BIBLIOGRAPHY

- 'Second Time Around—Spouses Partners and Property', 4 May 2007
- 'Benefits and Beneficiaries', 30 November 2007
- 'The Young Ones', 18 April 2008
- 'Finishing the Job!', 7 November 2008
- 'The Effect of the Economic Downturn on the Administration of Estates', 27 March 2009
- 'Will Drafting for the New Decade: Applying New Legislation and Updating Old Skills', 23 April 2010
- 'Administering Estates in the New Decade: New Forms, Case Law and Legislation', 19 November 2010
- 'Legal Personal Representatives: "The Good, the Bad and the Indifferent!"', 15 April 2011
- '"Who's Your Daddy?" Family Issues arising in the Administration of Estates', 18 November 2011
- 'I'm Still Standing—Advising the Survivor', 20 April 2012
- '"Who Pays the Ferryman?" Financial Issues Arising in Administration of Estates', 16 November 2012
- '"Time's-a-Ticking and it's Later than You Think", Time Limits in Administration of -Estates', 19 April 2013
- '"What's It All About, Alfie?" Definitions in Probate Practice', 15 November 2013
- '"M.I.A.—Missing In Administration", Dealing with Missing Wills, Assets, Beneficiaries, LPRs etc', 4 April 2014
- '"We are Family": Family Issues in Probate Practice', 14 November 2014
- 'Straight from the Horse's Mouth! Updates from the Probate Judge, Probate Officer Probate Administration and Trusts Committee, Senior Counsel and Tax Consultant Action', 24 April 2015
- 'Quis Custodiet Ipsos Custodes Et Al? Supervision of the Various Parties in a Probate Matter', 13 November 2015
- '"Do Ask—Do Tell": Questions the Solicitor Should Ask and Who Should Answer Them', 22 April 2016
- 'Probate Delays; Stop Waiting, Start Working', 18 November 2016
- 'The Probate Dance, In and Out and All About', 12 May 2017
- 'Stranger in a Strange Land', 17 November 2017
- 'All Kinds of Everything', 20 April 2018
- 'It's a Matter of Trust', 9 November 2018
- 'Home is Where the Heart Is', 5 April 2019
- 'Opps! Stop Digging', 22 November 2019
- 'The End is Nigh', 24 April 2020
- 'When to Say No', 6 November 2020
- 'Modern Families', 16 April 2021
- 'Things, We Think We Know', 12 November 2021

These seminar papers are available in the Law Society Library or can be purchased from the authors by contacting stephensonsolicitors@eircom.net.

Websites

- The Revenue Commissioners Website at http://www.welfare.ie has useful information, primarily in the Capital Acquisitions Tax section.

- The Law Society of Ireland website at http://www.lawsociety.ie has useful information, including practice directions from the Probate, Administration and Trusts, and Conveyancing Committees.

- The Charities Regulatory Authority website is at https://www.charitiesregulatoryauthority.ie/

- There are also a number of papers and briefings available from STEP (Society of Trust and Estate Practitioners). Details are available at http://www.step.ie.

- The Courts Service website at http://www.courts.ie has useful information in the Probate Offices Section.

- The Department of Social Protection website at http://www.welfare.ie has useful information on bereavement grants, PPS numbers, and estate cases.

Journals

- *Conveyancing and Property Law Journal*
- *Law Society Gazette*
- *The Parchment (DSBA)*
- *STEP Journal*
- *Trust Quarterly Review*
- *Journal of Elder Law and Capacity*

Legislation

- Conveyancing Act, 1881
- Settled Land Acts, 1882–90
- Trustee Acts, 1893, 1931
- Trustee (Authorised Investments) Act, 1958
- Trustee (Authorised Investments) Order, 1998 (SI 28/1998), as amended by the Trustee (Authorised Investments) Order 1998 (Amendment) Order, 2002 (SI 595/2002)
- Charities Act, 1961–2009
- Civil Liability Act, 1961
- Guardianship of Infants Act, 1964
- Registration of Title Act, 1964
- Succession Act, 1965 (as amended)
- See also http://www.step.ie/wp-content/uploads/2011/04/Restatement-of-the-Succession-Act-1965.pdf for a restatement of the Act up to 22 November 2010
- Age of Majority Act, 1985

- Status of Children Act, 1987
- Judicial Separation and Family Law Reform Act, 1989
- Family Law Act, 1995
- Family Law (Amendment) Act, 1996
- Family Law (Divorce) Act, 1996
- Credit Union Act, 1997
- Taxes Consolidation Act, 1997
- Family Law (Miscellaneous Provisions) Act, 1997
- Social Welfare (Miscellaneous Provisions) Act, 2002
- Capital Acquisitions Consolidation Tax Act, 2003
- Civil Law (Miscellaneous Provisions) Act, 2008
- Charities Act, 2009
- Land and Conveyancing Law Reform Act, 2009
- Nursing Home Support Scheme Act, 2009
- Civil Partnership and Certain Rights and Obligations of Cohabitants Act, 2010
- Criminal Justice (Money Laundering and Terrorist Financing) Act, 2010
- Children and Family Relationships Act, 2015
- Marriage Act, 2015
- Assisted Decision-Making (Capacity) Act, 2015

TAX LEGISLATION

- Taxes Consolidation Act, 2003 (Income Tax and Capital Gains Tax)
- Stamp Duty Consolidation Act, 1999
- Capital Acquisitions Tax Consolidation Act, 2003

See also the amending Finance Acts, particularly Finance (No 3) Act, 2011 which deals with the taxation consequences of the Civil Partnership and Certain Rights and Obligations of Cohabitants Act, 2010.

INDEX

abatement
  application of assets 27
  bequests 20
  devises 27
  general legacies 26–7
  generally 20, 26–7
  pecuniary legacies 26–7
  purpose 20
  rules 26–7
  specific legacies 26–7
accounts *see* **administration accounts; bank accounts; building society accounts; executor's account**
actions against estate
  beneficiaries, by 490–1, 495
  children, by
    advancement 108–11
    application for provision 100–13
    dispositions for disinheriting 106–7
    intestate civil partner with issue 106–8
  claimants under a disability 493
ad colligenda bona
  non-contentious probate applications 384
ad litem **grants**
  non-contentious probate applications 384
addresses
  wills
    beneficiaries 28
    charitable legacies 23
    testators 8
    witnesses 7
ademption
  equitable doctrine 26
  generally 26
  shares 26
  specific bequests generally generally 21
administration accounts
  accurate record keeping 161–2
  administrators
    authority to open 198
    precedent 198
  cash account
    cash income account 486
    composition 485–6
    precedent 488–9
  distribution account
    composition 486
    precedent 489–90
  estate accounts
    accurate record keeping, requirement 161–2
    composition 485
    precedent 486–90
  necessity, for 483–4
  precedent 486–90
  purpose 485
  types 485
administration bond
  de bonis non grants
    deaths 1 June 1959–31 December 1966 349
    deaths post-1 January 1967 349–50
    deaths pre-1 June 1959 349
    generally 318–20, 349
  forms 264
  generally 318–20
  precedent 331–3
  will annexed (DBN) 1 June 1959–31 December 1966 349
  will annexed (DBN) post-1 January 1967 349–50
  will annexed (DBN) pre-1 June 1959 349
administration of estates
see also **administration accounts; instruction and progress sheet**
  appointment, powers of 192
  authority to act 193
  beneficiaries
    information of nature of benefit 191
    potential beneficiaries 191–2
  burial directions 163
  children's rights
    effect of application for provision 105
  civil status 173–4
  costs 193–4
  death certificate 176–7
  debts 185
  distribution
    assents 467–72
    deeds of family arrangement 473–8
    disclaimers 478–80
  domicile at death 177
  family provision, effect on 105
  finalising matters
    administration accounts 483–5
    charges of property 480
    costs 481–2
    generally 480
    lapse, doctrine of 481
  first meeting with personal representatives
    generally 191
    potential beneficiaries 191–2
    protection of assets 192–3
  flow chart 157–8
  foreign assets 184
  generally 159

grant procedure, following
  abatement 423–4
  appropriation 433–5
  assets collection 409
  assets distribution 424–7
  bank accounts 412
  building society
    accounts 412
  cash in house 411–12
  civil partners 410–11
  civil service gratuities 412
  cohabitants 410–11
  credit union accounts 412
  dividends and
    interest 417
  executor's account 409
  executor's year 426
  government stock 417–18
  insolvent estates 419–21
  insurance policies 418,
    432
  intestacy 411
  introduction 407
  Irish small estates 415–16
  joint property 426–9
  minor children 411
  nominations 431–3
  notice to creditors 425
  overview 407
  partial distribution 426–7
  payment of
    liabilities 419–24
  personal representatives
    meeting 409
  Post Office
    savings 412–13
  prize bonds 418
  protection of purchasers
    and creditors 426
  protection of
    representatives 425
  re-read file 408
  residuary clause 408
  savings
    certificates 412–13
  ShareGift 416
  shares 413–14
  small UK estates 416–17
  social welfare old-age
    pensions 418–19
  solvent estates 421–4
  stocks and shares 413–14
  surviving spouse 410–11
grant of representation
  freehold land 165
  joint tenancies 163
  necessity 163, 165
  nominated gratuities 164
  personal application 164
  small estates 164
  summary 164
  wards of court 165
initial interview with
    personal representatives

instruction and progress
  sheet 167–74
introduction 166
preparation, for 166–7
instruction and progress
  sheet
  administrators 178
  beneficiaries details 189
  date of grant 178
  death certificate 176–7
  debts 185
  divorce 190
  domicile at death 177
  executors 178
  foreign assets 184
  general notes on
    completion 174–5
  generally 167
  Irish assets 178–84
  IT8 clearance for joint
    accounts, request
    for 188–9
  joint property 185–9
  joint tenancies 187
  joints accounts 187–8
  PPS numbers 175–6
  relatives surviving 177
  sample sheet 167–74
  separation 190
  social welfare claim
    number 177
  State of Affairs (Probate)
    Form SA.2 175
  tax clearances 190
  trusts 189–90
introduction 157–8
Irish assets
  bank accounts 178–9
  bereavement grant 184
  building society
    accounts 178–9
  car 180
  cash assets 180
  cash in house 180
  credit unions 179–80
  health insurance or
    medical
    entitlements 184
  household contents 180
  index linked bonds 179
  insurance policies 183
  leasehold property 180–1
  pensions 183–4
  Post Office NTMA savings
    accounts 179
  prize bonds 179
  real property 180–1
  savings certificates 179
  stocks and shares 181
joint property 178–81
notice periods 494–6
notification
  immediate task,
    following 161–3

overview 157–8
personal representatives
  first meeting 191–3
  initial interview,
    preparation 166–7
potential beneficiaries
  information
    requirements 191–2
PPS numbers 175–6
precedents
  authority to open
    executor's account 198
  letter for completion and
    return by
    beneficiary 202–3
  letter giving authority to
    act 197
  letter giving estimate of
    charges 195–7
  letter to An Post 200
  letter to
    beneficiary 201–3
  letter to financial
    institution 413
  letter to registrar 414–15
questionnaire, (Statement of
  Affairs (Probate) Form
  SA.2)
  appointment, power
    of 213
  benefits taken from the
    deceased 212
  charitable donations 212
  Department of Social
    Protection, claims
    by 211
  discretionary
    trusts 212–13
  dispositions subject to
    revocation 212
  elections 211–12
  houses 212
  HSE, claims by 211
  insurance policies 210–11
  interest for life 212
  interests in expectancy in
    any property 213
  joint property 209
  land 212
  limited interests 212
  nominations 209–10
  nursing home
    payments 211
  property free of
    charge 212
  residence, right of 212
  securities 212
  social welfare
    payments 211
  spouse/civil partner,
    survival by 211–12
  superannuation
    schemes 210–11
  tenancies in common 209

INDEX

records
   accurate record
      keeping 161–2
relatives surviving 177
social welfare claim
   number 177
stages 161–3
steps
   first meeting, after 193–5
   post-grant 159
   pre-grant 158–9
taxation issues 160
time limits 494–6
trustees
   personal representatives,
      distinguished 165
valuation
   establishment, of 199–203
will 171
   check purported will 162
administration, grant of *see de bonis* **non grants; grant of administration intestate;**
grant of administration with will annexed
administrators
see also **administration accounts; executors; personal representatives**
administration of estates
   ascertainment, of 178
administrator's accounts *see* **administration accounts**
administrator's oaths
de bonis non 361–3
non-contentious
   applications
      de bonis non 361–3
      sample title for defence proceedings 385
      sample title where executrix of unsound mind 376
      sample title where guardian appointed 375
      sample title where next-of-kin not found 385
will annexed 282–3
adoption
children's rights 99
advancement
actions against an estate
   administration of estates, effect on 111
   burden of proof 110–11
   definition 109
   doctrine 109
   effect on inheritance 109
   examples 110–11
   identification 109
   valuation 109
applicable legislation 35–6
best practice 36
burden of proof 110
common errors 36
definition 109
'hotch-pot' 109
inheritance, effect on 109
instruction and progress sheet 186
joint property 426–7
precedent clause 36
presumption 427–8
valuation 109
affidavits
see also **Inland Revenue affidavit**
attesting witnesses 237–8
de bonis grants
   letter of current market value 363
due execution 234–7
grant of administration with will annexed
   current market value 320
grant of probate
   attesting witnesses 237–8
   due execution 234–7
   mental or testamentary capacity 240–3
   plight and condition 238–9
market value
   de bonis grants, letter of market value 363
   grant of administration with will annexed 320
medical affidavit, sample 373
mental or testamentary capacity 240–3
non-contentious
   applications grounding affidavit, sample 368–9
   medical affidavit, sample 373
plight and condition 239
precedents
   affidavit of mental capacity by doctor 241–2
   affidavit of mental capacity by solicitor 242–3
   grounding affidavit 368–9
   medical affidavit 373
sample clauses
   plight and condition 238
age
see also **majority, age of**
marriage 115
underage children 113–15
will drafting 5
agricultural property
see also **farmland**
affidavit of market value 320
Direct Payment Scheme 30
leasehold property 319
Single Farm Payment
   Scheme 29
amendment of grant
non-contentious probate applications 376–7
An Post
administration of estates
   savings accounts 179
   savings certificates 179
   small estates 164
precedents
   letter to An Post regarding savings certificates or savings bonds 200
ancestors
disclaimers on intestacy
   direct lineal ancestors 304–5
ancillary state support
bequest of property subject to charge 27–8
appointment, power of
administration of estates 192
appointments
executors
   method 51
   trustee, distinguished 12
   unnamed persons 50
   will clauses 12–16
guardians
   will clauses 17–18
trustees
   minor beneficiaries 64
   will clauses 13
will clauses
   executors 12–16
   guardians 17–18
apportionment
best practice 37
common errors 37
generally 37
precedent clauses 37
appropriation
applicable legislation 36
beneficiaries
   effect 449
best practice 36–7
common errors 36–7
executors' powers 64
family home
   personal representative's duty 82–3
   restrictions 82–3
   surviving civil partner's entitlement 81–2
   surviving spouse's entitlement 81–2
generally 433–5, 448–9
grant, following 433–5
notification
   precedent 83
   time limits 398

precedents
  clause 37, 41
  notice 83
in specie 435
time limits 398
trustees' powers 39
valuation 426–34

assents
application for registration (Form 1) 470–2
charge, subject to 468
deeds of assent
  generally 341–2, 354
  personal property 355
  precedent 469–70
  problems, regarding 355
  property registration authority titles 354
  registry of deeds titles 355
definition 468
execution 469
generally 467
memorials
  abolition 470–1
  application Form 1 470–2
  sample Form 1 471
personal representative as beneficiary 468
precedent
  deed of assent 469–70
  registered land 468
  stamp duty 469
  time limits 495

assets
asset cover screen
  business assets 206–7
  debts 208
  funeral expenses 208
  liabilities 208
  other assets 208
  partnerships 206–7
  Statement of Affairs (Probate) Form SA.2 205–6
  stocks, shares, and securities 208
  total asset value summary 208
  unquoted (private company) shares 207–8
bank accounts 178–9
bequests
  ancillary assets 29–30
bereavement grant 184
building society accounts 178–9
car 180
cash assets 180
cash in house 180
collection of assets
  bank accounts 412
  building society accounts 412
  cash in house 411–12
  civil service gratuities 419
  credit unions 412
  dividends and interest 417
  government stock 417
  insurance policies 418
  Irish small estates 415–16
  miscellaneous assets 419
  Post Office savings 412
  prize bonds 418
  savings certificates 412–13
  ShareGift 416
  small UK estates 416–17
  social welfare old-age pensions 418–19
  stocks and shares 413–14
credit unions 179–80
currency
  valuation at exchange rate at date of death 180
disposal by will 1
distribution
  partial distribution 426–7
  steps to take prior to 424–7
estate assets
  precedent clause 41
  trustees' powers 39
foreign assets 184
health insurance or medical entitlements 184
household contents 180
index linked bonds 179
instruction and progress sheet 178–84
instructions, taking 132
insurance policies 183
joint property 185–9
leasehold property 180–1
legal right share
  application in a solvent estate 93
meaning 1
partial distribution 426–7
pensions 183–4
personal representatives
  appreciation of value 192
  duty to safeguard 192
Post Office NTMA savings accounts 179
precedents
  letter to financial institution 413
  letter to registrar 414–15
prize bonds 179
protection, of
  business assets 192
  insurance, of 192
  specific legacies 192–3
real property 180–1
savings certificates 179
Statement of Affairs (Probate) Form SA.2
  questionnaire 211–13
stocks and shares 181
valuation
  appreciation, of 192

attendances
drafting
  taking instructions, distinguished 120–3
duty of care 141–2
execution
  precedent 148
execution, regarding 148
grant of administration intestate
  precedent 288–9
instructions
  distinguished 120–3
  regarding 147–8
  precedent 148
solicitors' duty of care 150–1

attestation
see also **execution**
applicable law 40
clauses 5, 40, 144
generally 40
grant of probate 237

attorneys
grant of administration with will annexed 314
grant to in case of physical disability 372–3

awareness, letters of
charitable beneficiaries
  best practice 440

bank accounts
see also **building society accounts; joint deposits**
demonstrative legacy, as 21
grant following collection of assets 412
instruction and progress sheet 178–9, 188–9
IT8 clearance for joint accounts, request for 188–9
joint accounts 188–9

bankruptcy *see* **insolvent estates**

banks
executors, appointment as 13

beneficiaries
actions
  limitations 495
charitable beneficiaries 440
children 449–51
claims against estate 490–1, 495
communication with 441
contentious beneficiaries 438–9
deceased beneficiaries 439–40

elderly beneficiaries 147, 439
generally 436
guidelines for dealing
    with 441–2
identification 28
information
    nature of benefit 191
instruction and progress
    sheet 189
introduction 436
minor beneficiaries
    appointment of trustees,
        for 64
missing beneficiaries 438
potential beneficiaries
    identification, of 191–2
precedents
    letter for completion and
        return 202–3
    letter informing of
        benefit 201–3
residuary beneficiaries
    distinctions, among 31–2
Statement of Affairs
    (Probate) Form SA.2
    approximate value of
        benefits 214
    assigned benefits 214
    beneficiary
        screen 213–14
    benefits, summary
        of 213–14
    other benefits 214
    self-assessment CAT
        return (form IT38) 214
testators
    predeceasing 25
under age 436–7
under a disability 437
universal beneficiary 32
Benjamin orders
    missing beneficiaries 438
    presumption of death,
        distinguished 382–3
bequests
    abatement
        application of assets 27
        generally 20, 26–7
        pecuniary legacies 27
    ademption
        equitable doctrine 26
        generally 26
        shares 26
    ancillary assets 29–30
    applicable legislation 19
    beneficiaries
        identification, of 28
    best practice 19–24
    bloodstock 30
    cash 29
    charged property 27
        common errors 19–24
        conditions
            precedent 21–2

charitable legacies 23
conditional bequests 20
conditional legacies 21–3
conditions subsequent 21–3
cy près doctrine 24
demonstrative legacies
    generally 21, 32
    meaning 20
devises
    general devises 20–1
    meaning 20
    specific devises 20–1
Direct Payment Scheme 30
exceptions 24
farmland 29–31
framing bequests to a
    number of people 24–5
freehold interests in land 32
general legacies
    generally 20, 31, 401
    meaning 20–1
    substantial and
        numerous 20
generally 20
joint accounts 31
lapse 24–6
leasehold interest in land 32
legacies
    demonstrative
        legacies 21, 32
    general legacies 20, 32
    meaning 20–1
    pecuniary legacies 20–1,
        32
    specific legacies 20, 32
lists 31–2
meaning 24
numbers of people, to 24–5
partial intestacy 19
pecuniary legacies
    A to Z list 20, 26
    abatement 27
    common problems 20
    generally 20, 31
property
    ancillary assets 29–30
    bloodstock 30
    Direct Payment
        Scheme 30
    farmland 29–31
    identification, of 28–9
    livestock 30
    plant and machinery 30
    subject to charge 27–8
public policy 22
specific bequests 19–20
specific devises 20–1
specific legacies 20–1
types 19–20
void 21
bereavement grant
    abolition 184
    instruction and progress
        sheet 184

birth certificate
    testators
        name 8
        taking instructions 131
blindness
    blind pension 456
    testator's execution of
        will 236
blood relationships
    chart 288
    meaning 265
bloodstock
    bequests 30
bonds
    see also **administration
        bonds**
    administration of estates
        index linked bonds 179
        Post Office savings
            bonds 200
    collection of assets
        administration of
            estates
        prize bonds 418
        nominations 209–10
        Post Office bonds 412–13
    precedent
        letter to An Post regarding
            savings bonds 200
building society accounts
    grant following
        collection of assets 412
    instruction and progress
        sheet 178–9
burden of proof
    see also **proof**
    moral duty
        parent's failure 102–3
    testamentary
        capacity 139–40
burials *see* **funerals**
business assets

capacity
    applicable law 137–8
    assessment in context 138
    best evidence 142
    burden of proof 139–40
    extent 143
    fluctuating testamentary
        capacity 143–4
    functional approach 138–9
    grant of probate
        affidavit of mental or
            testamentary
            capacity 240–3
    instruction sheet 136
    instructions, taking 136,
        139–44
    medical practitioners,
        working with 141–2
    nursing home residents 144
    outcome approach 138
    presumption 139–40

psychiatric patients 144
revocation 9–10
status approach 138
test 140, 143
wards of court 144
when needed 143
will drafting 5

capital acquisitions tax
see also **taxation**
audit 461
beneficiaries, payable by 72
charities' exemption 24
children 115
deeds of family
  arrangement 477
disclaimers 477
instructions, taking 134
non-marital children 98
personal representatives
  agents, as 461
  obligations 461
returns time limits 461
stepchildren 99

capital gains tax
see also **taxation**
computation 462
deeds of family
  arrangement 477, 480
non-resident
  beneficiaries 462

cars
instruction and progress
  sheet 180

cash
bequest 29
currency
  valuation at exchange rate
    at date of death 180
grant following
  collection of assets 411–12
instruction and progress
  sheet 180

cash account *see*
  administration
  accounts

caveats
non-contentious
  applications
    caveators 385
    duration 386
    effect 385
    expiry 402
    lodgement procedure 386
    meaning 385
    precedent 391
    reasons, for 386
    time limits 496

certified copy of will
grant of probate 226

chain of executorship
de bonis non grants 353

charges
ancillary state support 27–8
beneficiaries' liability 480

bequests of property subject,
  to 27–8, 481
outstanding tax on
  death 480

charging clauses
abatement 38
applicable legislation 37
best practice 38
common errors 38
necessity, for 38
precedent clause 39
solicitor as beneficiary 38
witnessing 38

charities
capital exemption tax
  exemption 23–4
charitable beneficiaries
  capital exemption tax
  charitable bequests
    taxation form 243–5
  exemption generally 440
  letter of awareness 440
  receipts 440–1
  taxation 441
charitable legacies
  cy près doctrine 24
  examples 23–4
  lay charities 23
  religious charities 23
  tax and charities 24
cy près doctrine 24
executors
  capacity to act 49
identification of
  charities 23–4
precedent
  charitable bequest
    form 244–5
  Probate Office
    requirements 243–4
  Statement of Affairs
    (Probate) Form SA.2
    charitable donations 212

Charities Regulation
Authority
register of charities 22

Charities Regulatory
Authority
grant of probate
  charitable bequest
    form 243–4

children
actions against an estate
  advancement 108–11,
    449–50
  application for
    provision 100–13, 451
  dispositions for
    disinheriting 106–7
  intestate civil partner with
    issue 106–8
  'other' children 451
  proprietary estoppel
    actions 112–13

adopted children 99
advancement
  administration of estates,
    effect on 111
  burden of proof 110
  definition 109
  doctrine 109, 449–50
  effect on inheritance 109
  examples 110–11
  identification 109
  valuation 109
age
  majority 115–16
  underage
    children 113–15
applicable legislation 308–9
appointment of
  guardians 17–18
beneficiaries
  generally 449
  under age 436–7
child
  advancements 449–50
  meaning 95
children's rights 73, 97–9
  deaths intestate post-14
    June 1988 309–10
  deaths intestate pre-14
    June 1988 309–10
  guidelines 310–11
  historical
    background 307–8
  legal background 307–8
civil partners
  child of deceased
    partner 100
  child of surviving
    partner 100
  intestate with issue,
    action against 106–8
deceased children
  parent's entitlement to
    body 56–7
dispositions for
  disinheriting, actions
    for 106–7
entitlement
  intestacy, on 95
  testacy, on 95
family provision, application
  for administration of
    estates, effect on 104–5
applicable legislation 100
burden of proof 102–3
costs 106
criteria applied by
  court 101–2, 103
failure of parent's moral
  duty 102–3
legal principles 103–4
notification of
  rights 105–6
procedure 105–6
statutory test 104–5

INDEX 509

foster children 99
infants 115
instructions, taking 133–4
intestacy 411
  meaning 115
  natural child 366–7
  non-marital children 97–9, 450–1
issue 95, 450–1
legal right share
  identification of children of testator 73
  presumption 96
marital children 96
no duty to inform of rights 105–6
tax status 98
non-marital children 97–9
per stirpes rule 97
personal representatives' duties 450–1
predeceased children 97
  example 97
  leaving issue 96–7
  proprietary estoppel actions 112–13
  stepchildren 99
  unborn children 96
  underage children 113–15
remoter relationship claims 310
rights
  actions child may take 95
  entitlement 94
  legislation relating to 95
  tax status 95
  types of children 95
  underage children 95
stepchildren 99
surviving civil partner 100–1
surviving spouse 100
tax status 95, 115
testamentary guardians 115
time limits 101–2
types
  adopted children 99
  child of deceased civil partner 100
  child of surviving civil partner 100
  foster children 99–100

citations
non-contentious applications
  affidavit, sample 389–90
  example of operation 389–90
  nature, of 388
  procedure 388–9
  reasons, for 388
  time limits 402–3
  value 388
time limits 403

Civil Partnership Registration Scheme
application 69
civil partnerships
see also **legal right share**
applicable legislation 67
cessation for succession purposes
  generally 70–1, 84
  renunciation 71, 84
children's rights 71
civil partner 69–70
  definition, generally 70
  rights 71
civil status
  establishment, of 68, 133
  instructions 133
dispositions for disinheriting 94
dissolution
  revocation of will 9–10, 71
foreign civil partnerships, recognition 70
instructions, taking 68
legal right share 71–7, 91–3
nullity 69–71
renunciation
  generally 84
  post-registration of civil partnership 84
  pre-registration of civil partnership 84
revocation 69–71
spouses' rights 71
surviving civil partner status
  post-registration 84
  pre-registration 84
termination 70–1
unworthiness to succeed 71, 89–91
'wholly or partly testate' 71
wills, revocation of 9–10, 70–1
civil servants
death gratuities
  collection of assets 419
  instruction and progress sheet 184
civil status
establishment 68
grant of administration intestate 265
instructions investigation, of 133
clauses in wills *see* **wills**
clients
definition 193
elderly clients
instructions, taking 136, 147
  outside influences 136, 145–7
codicils
certified copy 225–6
definition 1

grant of probate 225–6
revocation clause 12
wills, revocation of 9–10, 10
cohabitation
cohabitants
  civil status, establishment of 133
  definition 117
  instructions 133
definition 117
following grant 410–11
instruction and progress sheet 186
instructions, taking 68
qualified cohabitants redress scheme agreements prior to 1 January 2011
  applicable legislation 118
  contracting out 118
  definition of qualified cohabitant 117
  entitlement 118
  factors considered by court 118
  legal right share of surviving civil partner 118
  legal right share of surviving spouse 118
  notification requirement 118
renunciation 119
rights 115
time limits 118, 494–6
Cohabitation Redress Scheme
application 69
High Court non-contentious applications 384
commorientes
grant of administration with will annexed
  examples 335–6
  generally 334–6
lapse and spouses 34
companies
company registrar precedent letter 200, 414–15
compromise
executors' powers 64–5
conditional legacies
will clauses
  conditions precedent 21–3
  conditions subsequent 21–2
  meaning 21
confidentiality
solicitor's duty of care
  generally 151
  post-death 151–2
  pre-death 151

constructive trusts
  mutual wills 44, 46
contents of house
  personal representatives'
    duties valuation
    and protection of
    assets 57
copies
  de bonis non grants
    certified copy of
      grant 344
    copy oath for
      administrator with will
      annexed *de bonis
      non* 346–7
    grant of administration
      intestate
      de bonis non grants
    grant of administration with
      will annexed
      certified copy
        codicil 314–15
      certified copy Inland
        Revenue 314–15
      certified copy oath of
        administrator 314–15
      certified copy will 314–15
    grant of probate
      certified copy codicil 217,
        226
      certified copy oath of
        executor 226, 258–9
      certified copy will 225–6
    wills
      certified copies 225–6
      photocopy wills 226
      proof in terms of
        copy 247, 380–2
coroners
  rights to a deceased's
    body 56–7
costs
  application by children for
    provision 106
  basis 481–2
  bill of costs 482–3
  client
    definition 193–4
  estimate
    obligation to provide 481
    precedent letter
      (section 150) 195–7
  section 150 notice 481
credit unions
  instruction and progress
    sheet 179–80
  statutory nominations 210
creditors
  protection, of 426
  statutory notice, to
    personal representatives'
    duty to provide 425–6,
    458
  precedent 458

currency
  valuation at exchange rate
    at date of death 180
cy près **doctrine**
  general principle 24

data
  instructions, taking 134
dates
  advancement 109
  death
    role of executor 55–7
  legal rights of spouses and
    civil partners 71
  wills 39
de bonis non **grants (DBN
  grants)**
  administration bond
    deaths post-1 January
      1967 349–50
    generally 349
    precedent 363–4
    renunciation 350
    will annexed deaths 1
      June 1959–31
      December 1966 349
    will annexed deaths pre-1
      June 1959 349
  affidavits
    letter of market value 363
  background 341–2
  death certificate 350
  deeds of assent
    generally 341–2, 354
    personal property 355
    problems, regarding 355
    property registration
      authority titles 354
    registry of deeds titles 355
  determination of type
    needed 342–3
  documents to extract grant
    generally 344–6
    Inland Revenue form
      A3(E) of A3(C) 344–6
    never required, for 350
    original or primary
      grant 344
  entitlement
    persons entitled to
      apply 343
  executorship
    chain, of 353
  grant not required 351–3
  grant of unadministered
    probate 343
  Inland Revenue Form A3(E)
    of A3(C)
    precedent 357–60
    versions 345–6
  instruction sheet
    precedent 356
  introduction 341–2
  location of application 343

market value
  evidence, of 348–9
  oath for administrator
    documentary proof 347–8
    precedent 361–3
precedent
  administration bond
    DBN 363–4
  application for grants of
    letters of administration
    intestate DBN 355–64
  de bonis non grant 363–4
  Inland Revenue Form
    A3(C) and
    CA6 357–60
  instruction sheet 356
  letter of market value 363
  oath for administrator
    DBN 361–3
  primary grant of
    administration
    intestate 361
  statement of facts 356
probate engrossment 348
probate fees 342
proofs required, for
  administration intestate
  (DBN)
  generally 350–1
  sample titles 351
proofs required, for will
  annexed (DBN)
  certified copy will 348
  evidence of current
    market value 348–9
  generally 344–5
  grant of administration
    with will annexed
    (DBN) 346–7
  oath for administrator
    with will annexed
    (DBN) 347–8
  probate engrossment 348
  sample titles for deaths on
    or after 1 January
    1967 349–50
renunciation 350
revocation of grant,
  distinguished 342
sample titles
  administration intestate
    DBN 1 January
    1967 351
  will annexed DBN 1
    January 1967 348
second or subsequent grants
  double probate 354
  supplemental probate 354
  unadministered
    probate 353–4
types 342–3
wills
  certified copy 348
  probate engrossment 348

death
death notification
form 176–7
presumption, of 382–3
registration 176–7
simultaneous deaths 34
time limits 177
death certificates
administration of
estates 176–7
cause of death 177
contents 177
copies 176
grant of probate 225
names 177
place of death 177
debts
executors' duties 57–8
instruction and progress
sheet 185
legal right share 93
deceased beneficiaries *see*
beneficiaries
deeds of assent
see also **assents**
application for
registration 470–2
de bonis non grants
generally 341–2, 354
personal property 355
problems, regarding 355
property registration
authority titles 354
registry of deeds titles 355
execution 469
precedent 469–70
stamp duty 469
**deeds of family
arrangement**
'family arrangements' 473
introduction 473
overview 473
precedent 473–7
sale 473
sale and voluntary
disposition 473
taxation
capital acquisitions tax 477
capital gains tax 477
stamp duty 477
transactions between spouses/
civil partners 477
voluntary disposition or
gift 473, 478–80
defences
testamentary
pleadings 395–6
demonstrative legacies
abatement 21, 27
generally 21, 32
meaning 21
destruction
rebuttal of
presumption 380–2

revocation of will, by 8, 11,
380
devisees
meaning 20
rights 401
devises
ademption 26
applicable legislation 19
best practice 19–24
common errors 19–24
general devises 20–1
legacy, and 20–1
meaning 20
specific devises 20–1
direct linear ancestors
disclaimers 304–5
Direct Payment Scheme
bequests 30
disabled persons \
see also **capacity**
application for provision
special needs 104
attorneys, grant to 312,
372–3
beneficiaries
generally 437
limitations 402
claims against estate 493
executors
acting, as 47–8, 50, 246,
312
disclaimers
capital acquisitions tax 480
effect 479
generally 478–9
intestacy
direct lineal ancestor
disclaiming 304–5
effect post-5 May
1997 303
effect pre-5 May
1997 302–3
execution 306
generally 273
presumption of
predecease 305
sample deed 306
specimen titles 307
spouses disclaiming 304
right to extract grant 479
discretionary trusts
Statement of Affairs
(Probate) Form
SA.2 212–13
disinheritance
actions by children
applicable
legislation 107–8
examples 107–8
time limits 108–9
dispositions within three
years of death 94
instructions, taking 134
time limits 495

distribution account *see*
**administration
accounts**
distribution of assets
steps prior to distribution
executor's year 426
generally 424
notice to creditors 425
partial distribution 426–7
protection of
creditors 426
protection of
purchasers 426
protection of
representatives 425
distribution of estate *see*
**assents; deeds of
family arrangement;
disclaimers**
dividends
grant, following
collection of assets 417
divorce
'blocking orders' 89
foreign divorce
succession rights 89
instruction and progress
sheet 174, 190
succession rights, cessation
of
applicable
legislation 87–8
foreign divorces 89
notice of death of former
spouse 88
wills
revocation 10
doctors *see* **medical
practitioners**
documents
grant of administration
intestate
administration
bond 271–2
certified copy of oath 268
generally 267
justification of surety 272
oath of administrator
intestate 267
renunciation on
intestacy 273
grant of administration with
will annexed
affidavit of due
execution 234–7
affidavit of market
value 320
affidavit of mental or
testamentary
capacity 240–3
affidavit of plight and
condition 238–9
certificate of market
value 320

certified copy codicil 226
certified copy oath 258–9
certified copy will 226
charitable bequest
  form 243–5
codicil 225–6
death certificate 225
generally 225–6, 314–15
justification of surety 320
non-contentious
  applications
    Probate Office
      requirements 372
notice of application 231
oath of executor 227–9
photocopy wills 226
probate clearance
  certificate 231
probate engrossments 226
renunciation of
  executor 222–3
will 225
domicile
foreign domicile
  non-contentious
    applications 369–70
testators
  death, at 177
double probate
de bonis non grants 354
duress *see* **undue influence**
duties *see* **executors;**
  personal
  representatives
duty of care
solicitors
  act expeditiously 152–3
  confidentiality 151–2
  copies of will 155
  execution and return 154
  extent 149–50
  inspection of will 155
  instructions from
    testator's family 152
  liability 149–50
  receipt of a benefit 151
  retainer and
    instructions 150
  risk management 148–56
  storage of will 155
  tax advice 153
  wills safe 155–6
vulnerable clients 4

elderly beneficiaries *see*
  beneficiaries
elderly clients *see* **clients**
election, right of
generally 75–6, 445–6
legal right,
  distinguished 446–8
partial intestacy 76, 446
personal right, as 77
property situate abroad 77

surviving spouse/civil
  partner of unsound
  mind 77
time limits 494–6
enabling clauses
will clauses
  advancement 35–6
  apportionment 36–7
  appropriation 36–7
  charging clause 37–9
enduring powers of
  attorney *see* **powers**
  of attorney
enforcement
mutual wills 44
engrossment *see* **probate**
  engrossment
equities
grant, following
  collection of assets 417–18
estate account *see*
  administration
  accounts
estoppel
promissory estoppel
  bequests of
    farmland 30–1
evidence
best evidence
  testamentary capacity 142
execution
assents 469
disclaimers 306
due execution of will
  affidavit 234
  amendments and
    alterations 236–7
  attestation clause 237
  date, problem with 236
  elements 233
  presumption 383–4
  Probate Office
    concerns 233–4
  requirements 234
  testator is blind 236
  testator signs with a
    mark 235
  testator signs twice 234–5
  testator's signature feeble,
    indecipherable, or
    poorly formed 235
  testator's signature made
    by another 235–6
  will condemned 238
  will written on several
    pages 236
  witnesses, attesting 237–8
duty of care 154
formalities 5–6
non-contentious applications
  High Court
    procedure 383–4
  Probate Office
    requirements 372

precedent
  instructions for execution
    by post 144
executors
see also **administrators;**
  executors' powers;
  personal
  representative
acceptance of
  appointment 47, 51–2
according to 'tenor' 51
account
  authority to open 198
  grant procedure,
    following 410
  precedent 198
administration of estates
  identification, of 178
alternative executors 13
appointment
  according to tenor 51
  alternative executors 13
  applicable legislation 12–13
  banks 13
  best practice 13–14
  certainty of identity 13
  cessation 13
  common errors 13–14
  conflict of interest 13
  fees 14
  foreign executors 14
  jurisdiction 14
  method 51
  number 13
  powers 13
  precedent clauses 15–16
  request 14, 47
  solicitors 14, 15
  substitute executors 13
  suitability 13
  trust corporations 14
  trustees, distinguished 13
capacity
  charitable bodies 49–50
  disabled persons 47–8
  family members 48
  generally 47
  minors 49
  persons under a
    disability 50
  professional executors 50
  residence within
    jurisdiction 47
  trust corporations 48–9
consent 47
de bonis non grants 353
duties
  administration accounts,
    preparation of 58
  assets, collection in 57–8
  assets, protection and
    valuation of 57
  beneficiaries,
    ascertainment of 57–8

INDEX 513

body, disposal of 56–7
debts, payment of 58
expenses, payment of 58
generally 55–6, 59
grant, extract relevant 58
liabilities, ascertainment
 of 57–8
lifelong duration 59
personal nature 59
Statement of Affairs
 (Probate) Form
 SA.2 58
tax clearances, obtain 58
executor under
 disability 246
executor's year 426, 454–5
family members 48
foreign executors 14
generally 47
gratuitous office 59
guardians, distinguished 66
instructions 132
instructions and progress
 sheet 178
intermeddling 52
number of executors 51
number, of 48
number, proving 223
oaths
 certified copy 258–9
 completion 227–9
 generally 226
 precedent 229–31
removal
 court, by 53–5
 generally 53
renunciation 52–5, 220–3,
 222–3
reservation 52
role 55–9
solicitors
 appointment 14
 liability for inheritance
  tax 47
substitute executors 13
trust corporations
 appointment 14
 capacity to act 48–9
 grant of probate 260–1
 oath 260–1
 resolution of bank
  board 261
trustee, distinguished 66
wards of court
 advice, on 59–60
executor's accounts
 authority to open 198
 grant procedure,
  following 410
 precedent 198
executor's powers
 generally 13, 60
 joint and several 65–6
 statute, conferred by

appointment of trustees
 for a minor
 beneficiary 64
appropriation 61–4
compromises 64–5
generally 60
leases 64
mortgages 64
sale 60–1
will, conferred by
 examples 65–6
 exercise, of 65–6
executor's year
 exceptions 455
 grant, following 426
 personal representatives'
  obligations 454–5
expenses
 executors' duties 58
extensions of time
 family provision
  application 101–2

'Fair Deal' legislation *see*
 **Nursing Home
 Support Scheme**
family home
 appropriation 82–3
family members
 executors, acting as 48
family provision
 administration of estates
 administration of estates,
  effect on 105
 applicable legislation 100
 burden of proof 102–3
 costs 106
 criteria applied by
  court 101–2, 103
 effect, on 104–5
 extension of time
  limits 101–2
 failure of parent's moral
  duty 102–3
 initiation of
  application 105–6
 legal principles 103–4
 notification of rights 105–6
 procedure 105–6
 statutory test 105
 surviving civil
  partner 100–1
 surviving spouse 100
 time limits 101–2
 notification of
  children 105–6
 personal representatives'
  duties 105–6
farmland
 bequests 30–1
 promissory estoppel 30–1
fees
 estimate precedent
  letter 195–7

executors 14
grant of probate 244–5
financial institutions
 precedent letter, to
  199–201, 413
foreign domicile
 non-contentious
  applications
 Probate Office
  requirements 369–70
 Probate Officer
  orders 366
foreign language
 non-contentious
  applications
 Probate Office
  requirements 370–2
foreign property
 instruction and progress
  sheet 184
 instructions, taking 11,
  134
formalities
 will drafting
  capacity 4, 5
  execution 5–6
  statutory formalities 5–6
  writing 6
former wills
 revocation 8–9, 11
forms
 assent
  application for registration
   (Form 1) 470–2
 land registry 468
foster children
 see also **children**
 children's rights 99–100
freehold interests in land
 bequests 32
 grant of representation 165
 leasehold interests
  distinguished 32
funeral arrangements
 instructions 132
funerals
 expenses 208

government stock
 grant, following
  collection of
  assets 417–18
grant of administration
 meaning of term 217
**grant of administration
 intestate**
 see also **de bonis non grants;
 grant of
 administration with
 will annexed;
 Statement of Affairs
 (Probate) Form SA.2**
 administration bond
  generally 271–2

514 INDEX

application for grant
  precedent 288–300
auctioneer's letter of current
  market value 272–3
blood relationship chart 288
charts
  degrees of blood
    relationship 288
  intestate succession for
    deaths after 1 January
    1967 287
disclaiming
  deeds of disclaimer 302
  direct lineal ancestor
    disclaiming 304–5
  effect post-5 May
    1997 303
  effect pre-5 May
    1997 302–3
  execution 306
  general operation of
    section 72A (others)
    305
  presumption of
    predecease 305
  sample deed 304, 306
  specimen titles 307
  spouse disclaiming 304
documents required,
  for 267–74
  notice of application 267
entitlement 265–7, 275–8
  blood relations and
    step-relations 265
  civil partner 265
  grant follows
    interest 265–6
  interest at date of
    death 265
  number of
    applicants 266–7
  order (after 1 January
    1967) 275–8
  principles 265
grant of administration with
  will annexed,
  compared 320–1
grant, following 407–8
half-blood
  relationships 283–4
  examples 283–4
  relatives of 283–4
introduction 264
natural child 366–7
next-of-kin
  ascertainment 284–8
  examples 284–8
non-contentious
  applications
    natural child 366–7
non-marital children
  applicable
    legislation 308–9
  blood tests 310

deaths intestate post-14
  June 1988 309–10
deaths intestate pre-14
  June 1988 309
guidelines 310–11
historical
  background 307–8
intestate succession 308
legal background 307–8
maternal
  relationships 309
paternal relationships 309
paternity, declarations
  of 310
presumptions 308–9
reasonable enquiries 311
registration and re-
  registration of
  births 310
remoter relationship
  claims 310
wills 308
oath of administrator
  intestate with the
  bond 267–71
administration
  bond 298–300
certified copy 268
generally 267
Part A 267–8
Part B oath and title 268
precedent 309–10
sample titles 267–71
specimen titles
  administration
  intestate 268–71
per stirpes rule
  entitlement,
    establishing 280
  examples of
    application 280–3
  generally 278
  issue of deceased
    inheriting 278–9
  necessary conditions 280
  siblings of deceased
    inheriting 279–83
precedent
  application for grant of
    administration
    intestate 288–300
  attendance 288–9
  letters of
    administration 300
  notice of
    application 297–8
  oath for administratrix
    incorporating
    administration
    bond 298–300
  Statement of Affairs
    (Probate) Form
    SA.2 290–6
renunciation

generally 273
intestacy 273
sample form 273
specimen
  renunciations 274
revocation 278
Seat Office checklist 301–2
  common queries 301–2
  documents to be
    lodged 301–2
specimen titles
  administration
    intestate 268–71
  aunt 269
  brother, representative
    of 270
  brother, child of
    predeceased 270
  child of married man/
    woman still alive 268
  child of man/woman/civil
    partner who survived
    and died 268
  child, predeceased 270
  child, representative
    of 270
  child of single person 269
  child of widow/widower/
    surviving civil
    partner 268
  cousins, first 269–71
  cousins, first once
    removed 270
  father 269
  grandchild (no surviving
    child) 269
  grandparent 269
  mother 269
  nephew 269
  niece 269
  sister, child of
    predeceased 270
  sister, representative
    of 270
  surviving civil
    partner 268
  surviving spouse 268
  uncle 269
step-relatives
  example 284
  succession rights 284
sureties
  justification of 272
  requirements 272
**grant of administration
  with will annexed**
  see also **de bonis non grants;
  grant of
  administration
  intestate; Statement
  of Affairs (Probate)
  Form SA.2**
administration bond
  forms 318–19

generally 318–20
  precedent 331–3
affidavits
  market value 320
application for grant
  precedent 320–33
auctioneer's letter of current
    market value 320
certificates
  market value 320
commorientes 334–6
documents required,
  for 314–15
entitlement
  attorneys 314
  generally 312–13
  guardians 314
  persons entitled 313–14
  universal legatee and
    devisee 314
grant of administration
    intestate,
    compared 320–1
introduction 312
joint residuary devisees 318
joint residuary legatees 318
lapse
  conditions 336
  example 337–8
  exception 337
  generally 336
  per stirpes,
    distinguished 336–7
letters of administration
    compared
  grant intestate 320–1
  grant of probate 320
market value, affidavit
  agricultural property 320
  leasehold property 319
  real estate 320
  sample 320–1
  validity 320
market value, certificate
  non-agricultural
    property 320
  real estate 320
oath for administrator
  Administration Bond at
    Part C 318–20
  generally 315–16
  joint residuary
    legatees 318
  residuary devisee 318
  residuary estate 317–18
  residuary legatee 318
  sample titles 316–17
  with will annexed
    incorporating
    administration
    bond 331–3
precedent
  administration
    bond 331–3

application for
  grant 321–33
charitable bequest
  form 333
form of authority for the
  Charities Regulatory
  Authority 333
notice of
  acknowledgement
  (probate) 323–30
notice of
  application 330–1
oath for
  administrator 331–3
Statement of Affairs
  (Probate) Form
  SA.2 323–30
statement of facts 321–2
will 322
proof required 314–15
requirements 312
residuary devisee 318
residuary estate 318
residuary legatee 318
residue, lapse of 318
sample titles
  oath for
    administrator 331–3
Seat Office checklist 338–40
simultaneous deaths 334–6
  distribution of estates 335
  examples 335–6
  generally 334
surety
  justification of 320
tenants in common 318
**grant of administration
  with will annexed *de
  bonis non* see *de bonis
  non* grants**
grant of probate
  see also **probate practice**
affidavit of attesting
  witness 233
affidavits
  attesting witnesses 233
  due execution 233
  plight and
    condition 238–9
applicants 223
application to probe in
  terms of copy 247
bank board referred to in
  affidavit
  resolution of 261
charitable bequest
  form 243–5
Charities Regulatory
  Authority
  requirements 243–4
  precedent 244–5
Probate Office
  requirements 243–4
codicils 225–6

committee of a ward of
  court 246
death certificate 225
district probate registries, by
  county 217–18
documents, required
  for 223–5
due execution of will
  affidavit 234
  amendments and
    alterations 236–7
  attestation clause 237
  date, problem with 236
  elements 233
  Probate Office
    concerns 233–4
  requirements 233–4
  testator is blind 236
  testator signs with a
    mark 235
  testator signs twice 234–5
  testator's signature
    appears below those of
    witnesses 234
  testator's signature feeble,
    indecipherable, or
    poorly formed 235
  testator's signature made
    by another 235–6
  will condemned 238
  will written on several
    pages 236
  witnesses, attesting 237–8
eligible applicants 223
executors
  acting, as 219
  disability 246
  executor according to
    tenor 246
  executor under
    disability 246
  grant to a committee 246
  number proving 223
  oaths 226–31
  office, of 245
  renunciation 222–3, 231
  reservation of rights to
    act 219–20
  right to prove will 219
  tenor, according to 246
  trust corporations 260–1
  ward of court 246
extracting 219–20
fees 245
grant of administration with
  will annexed,
  compared 320–1
grant itself 245
issue of grants 217–18
  district probate
    registries 217–18
  postal applications 218
letters of administration,
  compared 320–1

meaning of term 217
mental capacity,
  affidavit 240–3
  medical
    practitioners 240–1
  sample affidavit by
    doctor 241–2
  sample affidavit by
    solicitor 242–3
notice of acknowledgement
    (probate) 250–7
notice of application 231,
    233
  precedent probate
    application 249–50
oath of executors
  certified copy 258–9
  completion 227–9
  generally 226
  precedent 229–31
  trust corporations 260–1
occurrence 219
plight and condition,
  affidavit 238–9
  eligibility requirements 238
  sample clause 238
  sample form of affidavit of
    attesting witnesses 239
precedent
  charitable bequest
    form 244–5
  mental capacity by
    doctor 241–2
  mental capacity by
    solicitor 242–3
  oath of executor 229–31
  oath for trust corporation
    executor 260–1
  probate
    application 248–60
probate engrossment 259–60
probate tax clearance
    certificate 232–3
renunciation
  consequences 221
  executors, of 222–3
  forms 220–1
  generally 220–3
  nomination or consent,
    with 221–2
  sample form 221
revocation 245
sample clauses
  alterations to a will 236–7
  plight and condition 238
  testator is blind 236
  testator signs with
    mark 235
  testator signs twice 234–5
  testator's signature feeble,
    indecipherable, or
    poorly formed 235
  testator's signature made
    by another 235–6

sample forms
  plight and condition 239
  renunciation 221
  Seat Office checklist 261–3
  Statement of Affairs (Probate)
    Form SA.2 231–2
  notice of
    acknowledgement
    (probate) 250–7
  questionnaire,
    mandatory 254–5
  sample form 256–7
testamentary capacity,
  affidavit 240–3
trust corporations
  executor, as 260–1
  oath for 260–1
wills
  application to prove in
    terms of copy 247
  certified copies 226
  codicil (if applicable) 225–6
  documents
    incorporated 247–8
  missing will 247
  original will 225
  photocopy wills 226
  pre-printed standard will
    form 246–7
  probate engrossments 226
  witnesses' affidavit 234
grants of representation
  assets in jurisdiction,
    no 165
  freehold land 165
  generally 218
  issue, of 217
  joint tenancies 163
  meaning of term 217
  necessity 163
  nominated gratuities 164
  personal application 164
  personal representatives
    218–19
  postal applications 218
  rival applicants 367
  small estates 164
  summary 164
  types 219
  wards of court 165
gratuities
  civil service
    collection of assets 419
    instruction and progress
      sheet 184
    grant, following
      collection of assets 419
    nominated gratuities
      grant of
      representation 164
guardians
  appointment
    applicable legislation 17–18
    best practice 18

  certainty of identity 18
  common errors 18
  non-marital
    children 16–17
  precedent clause 18
  suitability of candidate 18
  testamentary
    guardians 18
executors, distinguished 66
grant of administration with
  will annexed 314
non-contentious
  applications
  grant to guardian 373
  sample petition to be
    appointed as guardian
    of a minor 374–5
non-marital children 16–17
petition to be appointed as
  guardian of a
  minor 374–5
Probate Office
  requirements 373–5
testamentary guardians 18
trustees, distinguished 66
will drafting 5

half-blood relatives
  rights on intestacy 283–4
health insurance *see*
    insurance
High Court
non-contentious
  applications
  applicable
    legislation 379–80
  application to prove will
    in terms of copy 380–2
  introduction 378
  necessary
    applications 378–9
  particular purposes or
    parts of estate 384–5
  practice and
    procedure 379
  presumption of
    death 382–3
  proof by presumption as
    to due execution 383–4
  rival applications 382
  simultaneous deaths 384
household charge
  introduction, of 59–60
  local property tax 465
household contents
  instruction and progress
    sheet 180

illegitimacy *see* **non-marital
    children**
imminent danger of death
  instructions, taking 144
impartiality
  executors' duties 48

improvements
  mortgages
    executors' duties 64
income tax
  appeals, time limits 495
indemnities
  precedent clause 42
index-linked bonds
  instruction and progress
    sheet 179
infants
  terminology 115
Inheritance Enquiry Unit
  personal representatives
    provision of assistance,
      to 29
Inland Revenue affidavit
  precedent
    grant of administration
      with will
        annexed 320–33
  property outside the
    state 209
  property in the state
    business assets 206–7
    debts owed to
      deceased 208
    funeral expenses 208
    generally 205–6
    Irish debts 208
    partnerships 206–7
    stocks, shares, and
      securities 208
    unquoted shares 207–8
  summary of
    benefits 213–14
Inland Revenue forms
  de bonis non grants 344–6
  Form A3 344–6
  Form A3(C)
    current version 345–6
  Form A3(E) 346
  form CA6 346
  form D1 346
insolvent estates
  legal right share 93
  payment of liabilities
    generally 419–20
    priority and preferential
      payments 421
**instruction and progress
  sheet**
  administrators 178
  beneficiaries details 189
  date of grant 178
  death certificate 176–7
  debts 185
  divorce 190
  domicile at death 177
  executors 178
  foreign assets 184
  general notes on
    completion 174–5
  generally 167

Irish assets
  bank and building society
    accounts 178–9
  bereavement grant 184
  car 180
  cash 180
  credit unions 179–80
  health insurance 184
  household contents 180
  index-linked bonds 179
  insurance policies 183
  leasehold property 180–1
  medical entitlements 184
  pensions 183–4
  Post Office NYMA savings
    accounts 179
  prize bonds 179
  real property 180–1
  savings certificates 179
  stocks and shares 181–3
joint property
  advancement,
    presumption of 186
  cohabitees 186
  generally 185–6
joint tenancies
  disputes 187
  taxation 187
joint accounts 187–8
  IT8 clearance, request
    for 188–9
PPS numbers 175–6
precedent 167–74
relatives surviving 177
sample sheet 167–74
separation 190
social welfare claim
  number 177
Statement of Affairs (Probate)
  Form SA.2 175
tax clearances 190
trusts
  deceased life tenant of a
    trust 189–90
  offshore trusts 190
  trust created by will 190
will
  existence of 178
instructions, taking
  assets 134
  attendance, drafting
  distinguished 120–3
  best practice 120–3, 145
  capacity
    applicable law 137–8
    assessment in context 138
    best evidence 142
    best practice 145
    burden of proof 139–40
    extent 143
    fluctuating testamentary
      capacity 143–4
    functional
      approach 138–9

    instruction sheet 136
    medical practitioners,
      working with 141
    outcome approach 138
    presumption 139–40
    status approach 138
    test 140, 143
    when needed 143
  data 134
  death
    clients imminent danger,
      of 144
  definition 120–3
  elderly beneficiaries 147
  elderly clients 136–7
  hospital patients 144
  ill clients 144
    imminent danger, of 144
  informed instruction 120–3
  instruction sheet guidance
    appointment, power
      of 135–6
    assets 134
    capacity 136
    capital acquisitions tax 134
    charities 135
    children 133–4
    civil status 133
    disinheritance 134
    executors 132
    funeral arrangements 132
    previous wills 132
    professional executors 132
    residue 135
    retainer 136
    terms of the will 135
    testator, birth
      certificate 131
    testator, name and
      address 131
    testator, PPS number 131
    title deeds 131
  instruction sheet for a will,
    precedent 123–31
  mental capacity 139–44
  nursing home residents 144
  outside influences 145–7
  precedent instruction sheet
    for a will 123–31
  psychiatric patients 144
  social media 134
  special cases 136–8
  testator's family, from duty
    of care 152
  undue influence
    presumption 146–7
  vulnerable clients 136–7
  wards of court 144
insurance policies
  grant, following
    collection of assets 418
  health insurance
    instruction and progress
      sheet 184

instruction and progress sheet
   health insurance 184
   insurance policies 183
   section 72/73 policies 183
policies
   collection of assets 418
   instruction and progress sheet 183
protection of assets 193

interest
common law rule 454
'executor's year'
   exceptions 455
   generally 454–5
grant procedure, following collection of assets 417

interest in expectancy
Statement of Affairs (Probate) Form SA.2 213

intestacy
see also **disclaimers; grant of administration intestate; partial intestacy**
administration of estates
   civil partner and minor children 411
   cohabitant and minor children 411
   spouse and minor children 411
beneficiaries 442–3
civil partners
   action by children 106–8
grant, following 410–11
succession rights 401

intestate succession
separated spouses 87–8

investments
precedent clause 39

Irish assets
administration of estates
   bank accounts 178–9
   bereavement grant 184
   building society accounts 178–9
   car 180
   cash assets 180
   cash in house 180
   credit unions 179–80
   health insurance or medical entitlements 184
   household contents 180
   index linked bonds 179
   insurance policies 183
   leasehold property 180–1
   pensions 183–4
   Post Office NTMA savings accounts 179
   prize bonds 179
   real property 180–1
   savings certificates 179
   stocks and shares 181
effect of taking 91–3
grant following
   collection of assets 415–16
   small estates 415–16

issue
meaning 95
per stirpes rule 278–83

joint accounts
see also **bank accounts**
bequests 30–1
instruction and progress sheet 187–8

joint deposits
joint real/leasehold property distinguished 428–9
monies placed on joint account for convenience 428
monies provided by both 429
monies provided by one party to benefit survivor 429

joint property
advancement presumption 186, 427–8
asset detail screen 209
best practice 429–30
generally 427–8
instruction and progress sheet
   advancement, presumption of 186
   cohabitees 186
   disputes over joint tenancies 187
   joint accounts 187–8
   taxation of joint tenancies 187
joint deposits, distinguished 428–9
property, as 1
taxation
   generally 430
   potential charge to gift tax 430–1

joint tenancies
bequests 25
grant of administration with will annexed 318
grant of representation 164
instruction and progress sheet
   disputes 187
   taxation 187
joint tenants 318
simultaneous deaths of joint tenants 34

land
Statement of Affairs (Probate) Form SA.2 212

Land registry titles
assents 354

lapse
bequests to several beneficiaries 25–6
conditions 336
doctrine 24–6, 481
example 337–8
exceptions 24–5, 481
generally 24, 336
meaning 24
per stirpes, distinguished 336–7
residue, and 33
spouses, and 34

leasehold interests in land
affidavit of market value 320
freehold interests distinguished 32
instruction and progress sheet 180–1

leasing
executors' powers 64

legacies
see also **bequests**
applicable legislation 19
best practice 19–24
charitable legacies
   cy près doctrine 24
   examples 23–4
   identification of charities 23
   lay charities 23
   religious charities 23
   tax and charities 24
common errors 19–24
conditional legacies
   conditions precedent 21–3
   conditions subsequent 21–3
   meaning 21
conditions 20
contingent legacies 401
demonstrative legacies 21
general legacies 20, 401
meaning 22
payment
   generally 459
   precedent letter to residuary legatee/ intestate successor 459
   precedent receipt and indemnity 460
reversionary interests of testator 401
substantial and numerous 20
types of 32

legal personal representatives *see* **administrators; executors; personal representatives**

INDEX 519

legal right share
appropriation
family home 82–3, 449
precedent notification 84
restrictions 82–3
bequests
addition, to 74
election, between 75–6
calculation 72–3
children
identification 73
civil partners 71–7, 445
conflict of laws 94
debt against estate, as 93
debts properly payable from the residue 73
definition 72
effect of taking share
administration of the estate 91–3
application of assets in a solvent estate 93
surviving civil partners 91–2
surviving spouses 91–2
will 91–2
election
generally 75, 445–6
legal right, distinguished 446–8
notification 80–1
partial intestacy 76, 446
personal right, as 77
property situate abroad 77
right of 75–6
surviving spouse/civil partner of unsound mind 77
wholly testate 445–6
enforceability 77–81
expenses 72
foreign property 77
generally 71, 443
gross estate 72
gross residue 72
liabilities 72
limitation periods 77–81
net estate 72
net residue 72
nominations 431–3
notification of right of election 448
example where partly testate 80–1
example where wholly testate 80
partial intestacy 76, 80–1
payment
insolvent estates 93
solvent estates 93
priority 74, 93, 442–3
property 93–4
qualified cohabitants redress scheme 116
residue distinguished 72
surviving civil partner
cessation of status 84–91
entitlement 71
unsound mind 77
surviving spouse
cessation of status 84–91
entitlement 71
unsound mind 77
time limits 494
unworthiness to succeed 89–90
valuation 79–80
legatees
meaning 20
residuary legatee 32
lending
letters of administration
administration intestate
administration with will annexed, compared 320–1
generally 264
administration with will annexed
grant of administration intestate, compared 320–1
grant of probate, compared 320–1
precedent application 321
de bonis non grant
generally 341–2
precedent 355, 363–4
letters of awareness
charitable beneficiaries 440
liabilities
payment following grant
abatement 423–4
generally 419
insolvent estates 419–21
order of payment 422–3
personal representatives' right of retainer 421–2
priority and preferential payments 421
solvent estates 421–4
limitation periods
acknowledgment or part payment by representative 402
actions to recover assets of deceased 401
actions to recover land of deceased 491–3
applications by children 101–2, 109
beneficiaries' actions 400–1, 490–1
beneficiaries suffering under a disability 402, 493
civil liability claims 400
generally 494
legal right share 77–81, 494
next-of-kin in possession of land 402, 493–4
pleas against beneficiaries 401
pleas against children 401
qualified cohabitants redress scheme 116
recovery of assets by personal representatives 496
lists
bequests 31–2
livestock
bequests 30
local property tax
exempt property 464–5
generally 462
liability for payment 463
personal representatives' obligations 464
solicitors' obligations 464–5
trustees' obligations 464

maintenance
precedent clause 39
majority, age of
malum prohibitum
conditional legacies 21–2
malum in se
conditional legacies 21–2
minor 116
marital children
see also **children**
children's rights 96
marital status *see* **civil status**
marriage
contemplation, of 10
subsequent marriage revocation 9
wills
contemplation of marriage 9
revocation 9–10
married persons
will drafting 5
medical entitlements
instruction and progress sheet 184
medical practitioners
affidavits of testamentary capacity 240–3
legal profession, working with 141–2
precedent for affidavit of mental capacity by doctor 241–2
memorials of assent
abolition 355, 470
mental capacity *see* **capacity**
minors
beneficiaries 449–51

executors, capacity to act 49
grant, following 411
terminology 115–16
trustees
appointment, for 64
missing beneficiaries
see also **beneficiaries**
treatment, of 438
mortgages
executors' powers 64
precedent clause 40
mutual wills
see also **wills**
application 46
characteristics 46
contractual element 46
doctrine, of 46
generally 44–5
intention 45
'matching' wills,
distinguished 44
'mirror' wills
distinguished 44
precedent clause 46
requirements 46
revocation 46

name
death certificate 177
testators 8, 131
natural children
see also **children**
non-contentious
applications
Probate Office
requirements 366–7
next-of-kin natural children
ascertainment
applicable law 284–8
examples 284–8
intestacy 284–8
chart 287
limitations
claims against the
estate 494
meaning 265
non-contentious
applications
Probate Office
requirements 367
nominated gratuities
see also **gratuities**
necessity 164
nominations
asset detail screen 209–10
generally 431
legal right share 432–3
non-statutory nominations
insurance policies 432
pension schemes
431–2
statutory nominations
credit unions 431

industrial and provident
societies 431
Post Office assets 431
non principal private residence (NPPR) charge
estates, and 60–1
exemption 464–5
introduction 465–6
legal charge for
non-payment 466
non principal private residence (NPPR) charge (cont.)
penalties 465
property subject to
charge 465–6
non-contentious probate applications
21–day notice, sample 368
ad colligenda bona 384
affidavits
citation, to obtain,
sample 389–90
grounding affidavit,
sample 368–9
medical affidavit,
sample 373
amendment of grant 376–7
appendices
generally 397
preparation of wills on
word processors 397–8
Probate Office fees 403–5
Probate Office
structure 405–6
time limits 398
caveats
caveators 385
duration 386
effect 385
lodgement procedure 386
meaning 385
precedent 391
reasons, for 386
citations
affidavit, sample 389–90
example of
operation 389–90
nature, of 388
precedent 393
procedure 388–9
reasons, for 388
value 388
High Court
applicable
legislation 379–80
application to prove will
in terms of copy 380–2
introduction 378
necessary
applications 378–9
particular purposes or
parts of estate 384–5

practice and
procedure 379
presumption of
death 382–3
proof by presumption as
to due execution 383–4
rival applications 382
simultaneous deaths 384
introduction 365, 378
precedent testamentary
pleadings
appearance to a
warning 392–3
caveat 391
citation to introduce and
deposit will 393
defence 395
general endorsement of
claim 394
notice of motion 397
plenary summons 393
reply 396
statement of claim 395
testamentary
pleadings 389–90
warning to caveat 392
Probate Office fees 403–5
general office fees 404–5
probate fees on
grant 403–4
Probate Officer's fees 405
Probate Office requirements
documents referred to in
will 372
execution of will 372
grant to attorney in case
of physical
disability 372–3
grant to guardian 373
grants in situations of
foreign
domicile 369–70
natural child 366–7
next-of-kin of unsound
mind 376
residue not in terms
wholly disposed of 369
rival applicants 367
wills in foreign
language 370–2
Probate Office
structure 403–5
probate officer
orders 366
powers 365
revocation of grant
generally 376, 377
precedent 377–8
revoking and
cancelling 376
rival applications
21–day notice,
sample 368
generally 367, 390

grounding affidavit 368–9
procedure 382, 390–1
sample documents
21–day notice 368
affidavit to obtain citation 389–90
form of election of guardian 375
grounding affidavit 368–9
medical affidavit 373
petition to be appointed a guardian of a minor 374–5
title in oath for administrator 375, 376, 385
time limits 398
warnings
appearance 387–8, 392–3
appropriate usage 386–7
effect 387
nature, of 386–7
precedent 391–2
non-marital children
see also **children**
appointment of guardians 17–18
children's rights 71
children's rights 97–9
grant of administration intestate
applicable legislation 308–9
deaths intestate post-14 June 1988 309–10
deaths intestate pre-14 June 1988 309
guidelines 310–11
historical background 307–8
legal background 307–8
remoter relationship claims 310
tax status 98
notice periods
administration of estates 494–6
notice to creditors
exceptions 425
grant, following 425
personal representatives protection, of 456–7
precedent 244–5
time limits 398, 495
Nursing Home Support Scheme
bequests of property subject charge 27
Statement of Affairs (Probate) Form SA.2 211
personal representatives' duties 456–7

oaths
administrators
certified copy 258–9
completion 227–9
de bonis non 361–3
generally 226
precedent 229–31, 260–1, 361–3
trust corporations 260–1
sample titles
defence proceedings arising from road traffic accident 385
next-of-kin cannot be found 385
offshore trusts
instruction and progress sheet 190
order of entitlement
intestacy post-1 January 1967 275–8

parents
failure of moral duty 102–3
partial intestacy
dealing with
entitlement, on 409
intestate portion, identification 409
one grant necessary 408
residuary clause 408
partnerships
protection of assets 192
payment of legacies see **legacies**
payment of liabilities see **liabilities**
pensions
Approved Minimum Retirement Fund (AMRF) Inland Revenue affidavit
Approved Retirement Fund (ARF) 211
grant of administration with will annexed
lapse, distinguished 336–7
grant, following collection of assets 418–19
instruction and progress sheet
civil gratuities 184
generally 183–4
public gratuities 184
non-statutory nominations 431–2
pension adjustment orders 85
per stirpes **rule**
grant of administration intestate
generally 278
issue of deceased inheriting 280

siblings of deceased inheriting 280–3
personal application
Probate Office, to 164
personal property
bequest 19
de bonis non grants 355
Personal Public Service numbers see **PPS numbers**
personal representatives
see also **administrators**; **executors**
assets, duty to safeguard 193
authority to act, for 193
Customer Book Title Stage Supplier Date
duty to notify
children 105–6
separated spouses 87–8
first meeting with personal representatives
generally 191
potential beneficiaries 191–2
protection of assets 192–3
further meeting with personal representatives 409
initial interview with personal representatives
instruction and progress sheet 167–74
introduction 166
preparation, for 166–7
intestacy
civil partner and minor children 411
cohabitant and minor children 411
spouse and minor children 411
notification
duty to notify separated spouses 87
personal application 164
protection, of 425
retainer 421–2
role 47
social assistance
best practice 457
obligation to inform Minister 455–6
personal liability 456–7
schedule of assets 455
trustees
compared, 165
distinguished 165
use of term 218–19
plant and machinery
bequests 30
plenary summons
precedent 393–4

plight and condition, affidavit
  generally 238
  persons who may make 238
  sample clause 238
  sample form 239

Post Office accounts
  grant following collection of assets 412–13
  precedent letter to financial institution 413
  instruction and progress sheet 179
  statutory nominations 210, 431

power of appointment *see* **appointment, power of**

powers of attorney
  see also **attorneys**
  enduring powers of attorney mental capacity 138

PPS numbers
  administration of estates 175–6
  beneficiaries
    non-resident 176
    overseas 176
  deceased overseas 176
  introduction 175
  non-working wives 175–6

pre-printed wills *see* **wills**

precedents
  administration accounts 486–90
  administration bond (administration with will annexed) 331–3
  administration bond DBN 363–4
  advancement 36
  affidavit of market value 320–1
  affidavit of mental capacity by doctor 241–2
  affidavit of mental capacity by solicitor 242–3
  appearance to a warning 392–3
  application for grant of letters of administration intestate DBN 355–64
  application for grant of letters of administration with will annexed 320–33
  application to lead to revocation of a grant 377–8
  appointment of executors 14–15
  appointment of guardians 18

apportionment 37
appropriation 37
attendance administration intestate 288–9
attendance on the execution of will 148
authority to act (Solicitors' Regulation compliant) 197
authority to open administrator's account 198
authority to open executor's account 198
cash account 488–9
  caveat 391
  caveat, warning to 392
charging clause 39
charitable bequest form 244–5
citation to introduce and deposit a will and accept or refuse probate 393
de bonis non grant 363–4
deed of assent 469–70
deed of family arrangement 473–7
defence 395–6
disclaimer on intestacy 307
distribution account 489–90
estate account 486–8
estimate of charges (section 150) 195–7
form of authority for the Charities Regulatory Authority 333
form of receipt and indemnity 460
general endorsement of claim 394
grant of administration intestate 288–300
grant of administration intestate (DBN) 355–64
grant of administration with will annexed 321–33
instruction and progress sheet 167–74
instruction sheet for administration intestate DBN 356
instruction sheet for a will 123–31
instructions for execution of will by post 154
letter for completion and return by beneficiary 202–3
letter giving estimate of charges 195–7
letter for return and completion by beneficiary 202–3

letter to An Post regarding savings certificates or savings bonds 200
letter to beneficiary 201–3
letter to company registrar 200, 414–15
letter to financial institution 199–201, 413
letter of market value 363
letter to registrar 414–15
letter to residuary legatee/intestate successor 459
maintenance clause 39
mutual will 46
notice of motion 397
notification of right of appropriation 84
notification of right of election 80–1
oath for administratix intestate 309–10
oath for administrator *de bonis non* 361–3
oath for administrator with will annexed 282–3
oath of executor 229–31
oath for trust corporation executor 260–1
plenary summons 393
primary grant of administration intestate 361
reply 396
residuary clauses 35
resolution of bank board 261
revocation of a grant 377–8
revocation of previous wills 12
sample form of renunciation 221
scheduling clause 39
section 150 letter 195–7
signature of witnesses 41
statement of claim 395
statutory notice to creditors 458
testamentary pleadings 391–7
warning to caveat 392
will illustrating basic components 41–4

predeceased children leaving issue
  see also **children**
  children's rights 96–7

preferential debts *see* **debts**

presumptions
  advancement 186
  children 308–9
  due execution 383–4
  resulting trusts 427–8
  revocation of will 380–1

priorities
  payment of liabilities 421
prize bonds
  grant, following collection of assets 418
  instruction and progress sheet 179
probate applications *see* **non-contentious probate applications**
Probate Office
  fees 403–5
    general office fees 404–5
    probate fees on grant 403–4
    Probate Officer's fees 405
  General Office section 406
  non-contentious application requirements 366–76
  Rules Office section 406
  Seat Office section 405
  Statement of Affairs (Probate) Form SA.2
    notice of acknowledgement (probate) 214–15
  structure 405–6
probate officer
  orders 366
  powers 365
probate practice
  see also **grant of probate**
  background 216–19
  contentious applications 216–17
  grants of representation
    generally 217–18
    issue, of 218
    postal applications 218
    types 219
  non-contentious applications 216–17
  personal representatives 218–19
  precedent forms 216
professional executors *see* **executors**
promissory estoppel
  children
    actions taken, by 112–13
  farmland 30–1
  instructions, taking 134
property
  bequests, identification of 28–31
  will drafting 1
Property Registration Authority titles
  de bonis non grants 354
proprietary estoppel
  actions against
    children 113–14
  farmland and 30–1

public policy
  conditional legacies 21–3
purchasers
  definition 61

questionnaire
  Statement of Affairs (Probate) Form SA.2
    appointment, power of 213
    benefits taken from the deceased 212
    charitable donations 212
    Department of Social Protection, claims by 211
    discretionary trusts 212–13
    dispositions subject to revocation 212
    elections 211–12
    houses 212
    HSE, claims by 211
    insurance policies 210–11
    interest for life 212
    interests in expectancy in any property 213
    joint property 209
    land 212
    limited interests 212
    nominations 209–10
    nursing home payments 211
    property free of charge 212
    residence, right of 212
    securities 212
    social welfare payments 211
    spouse/civil partner, survival by 211–12
    superannuation schemes 210–11
    tenancies in common 209

real property
  affidavit of market value 320
  certificate of market value 320
  grant of representation 165
  instruction and progress sheet 180–1
  meaning 20
relatives
  see also **next-of-kin**
  chart of degrees of blood relationship 288
  half-blood 283–4
  step-relatives 265
removal from office
  executors 53–5
renunciations
  consequences 221

  executors 222–3, 258–9
  forms 221
  generally 220–3
  grant of administration intestate
    generally 273
    sample form 273
    specimen renunciations 274
  grant of probate 220–3
  nomination or consent, with 221–2
  qualified cohabitants redress scheme 119
  sample forms
    intestate estate 273
    testacy 221
  surviving civil partner status
    post-registration 84
    pre-registration 84
  surviving spouse status
    post-registration 84
    pre-registration 84
repairs
  power to mortgage 64
reservation
  personal representatives 52
residuary beneficiaries
  meaning 32
residuary clauses
  generally 32
  instructions, taking 135
  precedent clauses 35
  words of severance 34
residuary devisees
  grant of administration with will annexed 318
  meaning 32
residuary estate
  grant of administration with will annexed 318
  lapse 33
residuary legatees
  grant of administration with will annexed 318
  joint residuary legatees 318
  meaning 318
  rights of 401
residue
  applicable legislation 33
  best practice 33
  common errors 33
  instructions, taking 135
  lapse 33
  non-contentious applications 369
  simultaneous deaths 34
resulting trusts
  presumption 427–8
retainers
  instructions, taking 136
  solicitors
    duty of care 150

retirement
  personal
    representatives 166
  trustees 166
Revenue On-Line Service (ROS)
  self-assessment CAT return (form IT38) 214
  Statement of Affairs (Probate) Form SA.2 214
revocation
  animus revocandi 11
  applicable legislation 8–9
  de bonis non grants, distinguished 342
  dependent relative revocation 12
  grant of administration intestate 278
  wills
    best practice 10–12
    civil partnership 9
    codicils 9
    common errors 10–12
    destruction with intention to revoke 9
    foreign wills 10–11
    intention to revoke 9
    marriage 9
    methods of revocation 9
    mutual wills 46
    precedent clauses 12
    subsequent wills 9
right of election *see* **election, right of; election, right of risk management**
risk management
  solicitor's duty of care 148–56
rival applications
  non-contentious applications
    21-day notice, sample 368
    generally 367, 390
    grounding affidavit 368–9
    procedure 390–1

sale
  executors' powers 60–1
  purchaser 60–1
sample clauses
  see also **precedents**
  alterations to a will 236–7
sample deeds
  see also **precedent**
  disclaimer on intestacy 306
sample forms
  see also **precedent**
  plight and condition 239
  renunciation of letters of administration

    intestate 273
  renunciation (testate) 221
savings
  grant following collection of assets 412–13
  precedent letter to financial institution 413
  instruction and progress sheet
    index linked bonds 179
    Post Office NTMA savings accounts 179
    savings certificates 179
Seat Office checklist
  grant of administration intestate 301–2
  grant of administration with will annexed 338–40
  grant of probate 261–3
second grants *see* **de bonis non grants**
separation
  applicable legislation 84
  blocking orders 87
  financial compensation orders 85
  intestacy, and 87
  pension adjustment orders 85
  personal representatives, duty to notify 87
  separated spouses 85–7, 87
  succession rights
    cessation, of 84–91
    extinction 86–7
severance
  residuary clauses 34
ShareGift
  grant, following collection of assets 416
shares
  ademption 26
  grant, following collection of assets 413–14
  precedent letter to registrar 414–15
  instruction and progress sheet
    government stock 183
    securities, interest on 182
    share dealing 182
    small UK estates 182
    stockbrokers, engagement of 181–2
    UK grant 182
  stockbrokers, engagement of 181–2
  UK shares 182
signature
  testators
    applicable law 39

    best practice 39–40
    common errors 39–40
    sending out for execution 39–40
    weak signature 40
  witnesses
    applicable law 40–1
    generally 40
    precedent clauses 41
simultaneous deaths
  see also ***commorientes***
  grant of administration with will annexed
    examples 335–6
    generally 334
    non-contentious applications 384
  residue 34
Single Farm Payment Scheme *see* **Direct Payment Scheme**
small estates
  grant of representation 164
social assistance
  administration of estates
    claim number 177
    best practice 457
    notification 457
    payments 211
    personal representatives obligation to inform Minister 455–6
    personal liability 456–7
    schedule of assets obligation to provide 455–6
social media
  instructions, taking 134
social welfare *see* **social assistance**
solicitors
  authority to act
    personal representatives, for 193
    precedent (Solicitors' Regulation compliant) 197
  charging clauses 38
  confidentiality
    generally 151
    post-death 151–2
    pre-death 151
  costs
    basis 481–2
    bill of costs 482–3
    statutory obligation 481
  duty of care
    act expeditiously 152–3
    confidentiality 151–2
    copies of will 155
    execution and return 154
    inspection of will 155
    instructions from testator's family 152

liability 149–50
receipt of a benefit 151
retainer and
  instructions 150
risk management 148–56
storage of will 155
tax advice 153
wills safe 155–6
executors
  appointment, as 14
  charging clauses 14
retainer 136
will drafting 3–4
solvent estates
legal right share 93
payment of liabilities
  abatement 423–4
  example of illiquid
    estate 424
  generally 421
  order of payment 422–3
  personal representative's
    right of retainer 421–2
spouses
see also **appropriation;
legal right share**
beneficiaries
  intestacy 442–3
  testate estates 443–8
civil partnership rights 71
civil status 68
definition 67
disclaimer on intestacy 304
divorce
  applicable
    legislation 88–9
  foreign divorces 89
  notice of death of former
    spouse 88
instructions, taking 68
lapse and 34
legal right share (s 111
    Succession Act,
    1965) 401
renunciation
  post-registration 84
  pre-registration 84
separation
  applicable legislation 85
  financial compensation
    orders 85
  intestate succession
    87–8
  pension adjustment
    orders 85
  personal representative's
    duty to notify 87
  residual rights 85
  separated spouse 85–7
  succession rights,
    extinction of 86–7
surviving spouses
  administration of
    estates 410–11

cessation of succession
    rights 84–91
status 67
unworthiness to
    succeed 89–90
'wholly or partly testate' 71
stamp duty
appropriation 462
assents 469
deeds of family
    arrangement 462, 477
distribution of assets 462
time limits 495
**Statement of Affairs
    (Probate) Form SA.2**
asset cover screen 205–6
beneficiary screen 213–14
  approximate value of
    benefits 214
  assigned benefits 214
  benefits, summary
    of 213–14
  other benefits 214
  self-assessment CAT
    return (form IT38) 214
declaration 205
details of the applicants 205
duties 58
general information 205
general provisions 203–4
grant of administration
    intestate 290–6
  applicant details 291
  assets cover screen 292–3
  banks 292
  beneficiary
    benefits 294–5
  beneficiary details 291
  boats 292
  building societies 292
  capital sum payments 293
  cars 292
  charitable donations 294
  contact details 290
  credit union accounts 292
  debts 293
  discretionary trusts 293
  dispositions 294
  dividends 293
  DSP claims 294
  ex gratia payments 293
  foreign assets 293
  household contents 292
  HSE claims 294
  insurance policies 292
  Irish property 292
  liabilities details 293
  mortgage protection 292
  notice of
    acknowledgement 290,
    295–6
  nursing home support 294
  questionnaire,
    mandatory 293–4

summary 290
superannuation 293
grant of administration with
    will annexed 323–8
  applicant details 324
  assets cover screen 325–7
  banks 325
  beneficiary
    benefits 327–8
  beneficiary details 324–5
  boats 325
  building societies 325
  cars 325
  charitable donations 327
  contact details 323
  credit union accounts 325
  debts 326
  discretionary trusts 327
  dispositions 327
  dividends 326
  DSP claims 327
  foreign assets 326
  household contents 325
  HSE claims 327
  information relating to
    deceased person 323
  insurance policies 326
  Irish property 325
  mortgage protection 326
  notice of
    acknowledgement
    329–30
  nursing home
    support 327
  questionnaire,
    mandatory 327–8
  superannuation 326
grant of probate 231–2
  notice of
    acknowledgement
    (probate) 250–7
  questionnaire,
    mandatory 254–5
  sample form 256–7
instruction and progress
  sheet 175
notice of acknowledgement
    (probate)
  grant of administration
    intestate 214–15
  grant of administration
    with will
    annexed 329–30
property in the state
    forming part of the
    estate 205–6
questionnaire,
    mandatory 211–13
  annuities 212
  appointment, powers
    of 213
  benefits taken from the
    deceased 212
  charitable donations 212

Department of Social
Protection, claims
by 211
discretionary
trusts 212–13
disposition subject to
power of
revocation 212
election 211–12
houses 212
HSE, claims by 211
interest in expectancy in
any property 213
interest for life 212
land 212
limited interests 212
Nursing Home Support
(Fair Deal) Scheme 211
property free of
charge 212
right of residence 212
securities 212
social welfare
payments 211
spouse/civil partner,
survival by 211–12
statement of claim
testamentary pleadings 395
statement of facts
grant of administration
intestate (DBN) 356
grant of administration with
will annexed 321–2
step-relatives
see also **relatives**
example 265
succession rights 265
stepchildren see also
children
children's rights 99
meaning 99
tax status 99
storage of wills see **wills**
substitution
executors 13, 15, 51, 222–3
**superannuation
schemes** 210–11
supplemental probate
de bonis non grants 354
surety
justification, of
grant of administration
intestate 272
grant of administration
with will annexed 320

taking instructions see
instructions, taking
taxation
see also **stamp duty**
charities
bequests 24
capital acquisitions tax 24
exemption 441

grant of probate
probate tax clearance
certificate 231
instruction and progress
sheet
tax clearances 190
joint property
generally 430
potential charge to gift
tax 430–1
obligations
capital acquisitions
tax 461
capital gains tax 462
household charge 465
income tax clearance 462
introduction 460–1
local property tax 462–5
non principal private
residence (NPPR)
charge 465–6
stamp duty 462
self-assessment CAT return
(form IT38) 214
tax advice
solicitor's duty to
give 153
tax clearances
instruction and progress
sheet 190
tax status of children 115
tenants in common
grant of administration with
will annexed 318
testamentary guardians
appointment 18
testators
see also **capacity; wills**
address 8, 131
birth certificates 131
civil status 68
instructions
informed
instructions 120–3
instruction sheet 131
name 8, 131
PPS number 131
signature 39–40
applicable law 39
best practice 39–40
common errors 39–40
sending out for
execution 39–40
weak signature 40
third parties
instructions, taking 152
time limits
caveats 402, 496
child's rights 400, 495–6
citations 403, 496
court order for LPRs to
execute assent 398
dispositions for
disinheritance 400, 495

executor's year 399, 426,
494
generally 494–6
grants durante absentia 398
limitation of actions 400–2,
490–4, 494
notice of intention to
appropriate assets 398,
495
notice to creditors 398, 495
probate motions 403
separated and divorced
spouses 399
spouse's legal right
share 399
spouse's right of election to
appropriate 399, 490
subpoena 403
tax payments 494–5
tax returns 495
unworthiness to
succeed 400, 495
warnings 402–3, 496
trade
precedent clause 40
trustees' powers 40
trust corporations
executor's trustees' powers
appointment, as 14, 48–9
oaths 260–1
precedent 260–1
trustees
appointment for minor
beneficiaries 64
executors, distinguished 13,
66
guardians, distinguished 66
local property tax 464
minor beneficiaries 64
personal representatives
compared 165
distinguished 165
trusts
see also **trustees**
establishment of 32
instruction and progress sheet
deceased life tenant of
trust 189–90
offshore trusts 190
trusts created by will 190

unadministered probate see
de bonis non **grants**
unborn children
see also **children**
underage beneficiaries see
beneficiaries
undertakings
conditional
undertakings 453–4
discharge 454
generally 452–3
undue influence
presumption 146–7

unquoted shares *see* **shares**
unsound mind
  non-contentious
    applications 376
unworthiness to succeed
  civil partners' rights 71,
    89–90
  non-contentious
    applications 400
  spouses' rights 89–90
  time limits 495

valuation
  advancement 109
  appropriations 433–5
  currency 180
  precedents letters to
    establish value of
    estate 199–203
voluntary dispositions
  deeds of family
    arrangement 478
vulnerable clients *see* **clients**

wards of court
  capacity 144
  executors, of 59–60
  grant of probate 246
  grant of representation 165
  instructions, taking 144
  non-contentious
    applications
      Probate Office
        requirements 376
warnings to caveat
  non-contentious
    applications
      appearance 387–8
      appropriate usage 386–7
      effect 387
      nature, of 386–7
      time limits 402–3
    precedent 391–2
wholly or partly testate
  will drafting 71
wills *see also* **instructions,
  taking; residuary
  clauses**
  attestation clause 40
  best practice 10–12
  date, of 39
  definition 1
  destruction with intention
    to revoke 9, 11
  documents referred
    to 371–2

drafting 1–7
due execution of will
  affidavit 234
  amendments and
    alterations 236–7
  attestation clause 237
  date, problem with 236
  elements 233
  presumption 383–4
  Probate Office
    concerns 233–4
  requirements 234
  testator is blind 236
  testator signs with a
    mark 235
  testator signs twice 234–5
  testator's signature feeble,
    indecipherable, or
    poorly formed 235
  testator's signature made
    by another 235–6
  will condemned 238
  will written on several
    pages 236
  witnesses, attesting 237–8
effective date 2
elements
  generally 7, 8
  name and address of
    testator 8
  revocation of previous
    wills 9–12
execution
  inspection after
    execution 155
  precedent instructions for
    execution of will by
    post 154
  Probate Office
    requirements 372
  requirements 5–6
  solicitor's duty of
    care 154–5
foreign language
  affidavits required 374–2
  proof 370–2
formalities
  capacity 5
  execution 5–6
  statutory 5–6
  writing 6
grant of probate
  certified copies 226
  original 225
  photocopy wills 226
  probate engrossment 226

'holographic' wills 3
'home-made' wills 3
'in writing' 6
making
  reasons, for 2–3
  solicitor's role 2
mutual wills 44–6
physical condition 41–2
powers conferred on
  executors 65–6
precedent 42–4
precedent instructions for
  execution of will by
  post 154
preparation on word
  processors
    guidelines 397–8
  presumption of due
    execution 383–4
previous wills
  taking instructions 132
printing 44–5
Probate Office requirements
  documents referred
    to 371–2
  execution 372
  foreign will 370–2
property, disposal of 1–2
reasons to make 2–3
residuary clauses 33
sample clauses
  alterations to a will 236–7
solicitors
  duty of care 148–56
  role 3–4
storage 155
testators
  address 8
  name 8
  signature 39–40
wills safe
  solicitor's duty to
    review 155–6
witnesses
  signature 40–1
word processors 397–8
witnesses
  affidavits 234
  signature
    applicable law 40–1
    generally 40
    precedent clauses 41
word processors
  guidelines for use 397–8
writing
  'in writing' 6